Unix® for Programmers and Users

Third Edition

Graham Glass and King Ables

Pearson Education, Inc.
Upper Saddle River, New Jersey 07458

Library of Congress Cataloging-in-Publication Data

CIP data on file

Vice President and Editorial Director, ECS: *Marcia Horton*
Executive Editor: *Petra Recter*
Editorial Assistant: *Renee Makras*
Vice President and Director of Production and Manufacturing, ESM: *David W. Riccardi*
Executive Managing Editor: *Vince O'Brien*
Assistant Managing Editor: *Camille Trentacoste*
Production Editor: *Lakshmi Balasubramanian*
Director of Creative Services: *Paul Belfanti*
Creative Director: *Carole Anson*
Art Director: *Jayne Conte*
Cover Designer: *Bruce Kenselaar*
Art Editor: *Gregory Dulles*
Manufacturing Manager: *Trudy Pisciotti*
Manufacturing Buyer: *Lisa McDowell*
Marketing Manager: *Pamela Shaffer*
Marketing Assistant: *Barrie Reinhold*

© 2003 Pearson Education, Inc.
Pearson Prentice Hall
Upper Saddle River, NJ 07458

The author and publisher of this book have used their best efforts in preparing this book. These efforts
include the development, research, and testing of the theories and programs to determine their effectiveness. The author and publisher make no warranty of any kind, expressed or implied, with regard to these
programs or the documentation contained in this book. The author and publisher shall not be liable in
any event for incidental or consequential damages in connection with, or arising out of, the furnishing,
performance, or use of these programs.

Printed in the United States of America

10 9 8 7 6 5 4 3 2 1

ISBN 0-13-046553-4

Pearson Education Ltd., *London*
Pearson Education Australia Pty. Ltd., *Sydney*
Pearson Education Singapore, Pte. Ltd.
Pearson Education North Asia Ltd., *Hong Kong*
Pearson Education Canada, Inc., *Toronto*
Pearson Educación de Mexico, S.A. de C.V.
Pearson Education—Japan, *Tokyo*
Pearson Education Malaysia, Pte. Ltd.
Pearson Education, Inc., *Upper Saddle River, New Jersey*

to Truth and Beauty,
wherever they are found
and to Freedom, and all
who have sacrificed for it

Trademark Information

AIX is a trademark of International Business Machines Corporation.

Ethernet is a registered trademark of Xerox Corporation.

FreeBSD is a trademark of Berkeley Software Design, Inc.

GNU is a trademark of the Free Software Foundation.

HP-UX is a registered trademark of the Hewlett-Packard Company.

Itanium is a registered trademark of Intel Corporation.

IRIX is a registered trademark of Silicon Graphics, Inc.

Java is a trademark of Sun Microsystems, Inc.

KDE and K Desktop Environment are trademarks of KDE e.V.

Linux is a trademark of Linus Torvalds.

MacOS is a registered trademark of Apple Computer.

Microsoft Windows, Windows NT, and Windows 2000 are registered trademarks of Microsoft Corporation.

Netscape is a registered trademark of Netscape Communications Corporation.

SCO and Unixware are trademarks of Caldera.

Solaris, Sparc, and Open Windows are trademarks of Sun Microsystems, Inc.

Tru64 is a trademark of the Hewlett-Packard Company.

UNIX is a registered trademark of The Open Group.

VMS and Open VMS are registered trademarks of the Hewlett-Packard Company.

X Window System is a trademark of The Open Group.

Preface

ABOUT THE AUTHORS

Graham Glass graduated from the University of Southampton, England, with a bachelor's degree in computer science and mathematics in 1983. He emigrated to the United States and obtained his master's degree in computer science from the University of Texas at Dallas in 1985. He then worked as a UNIX/C systems analyst and became heavily involved with research in neural networks and parallel distributed processing. He later taught at the University of Texas at Dallas, covering a wide variety of courses, including UNIX, C, assembly language, programming languages, C++, and Smalltalk. He cofounded a corporation called ObjectSpace and currently trains and consults for such companies as DSC Corporation, Texas Instruments, Northern Telecom, J.C. Penney, and Bell Northern Research, using his OOP and parallel systems knowledge to design and build a parallel object-oriented computer system and language based on the Inmos T9000 transputer chip. In his spare time, he writes music, scuba dives, skis, and occasionally sleeps.

King Ables earned his bachelor's degree in computer science from the University of Texas at Austin in 1982. He has been a UNIX user, developer, systems administrator, or consultant since 1979, working at both small start-up companies and large corporations. He has provided support and training, developed UNIX product software and systems tools, and written product documentation and training materials. In the 1990s, he was the sole proprietor of a UNIX consulting concern in Austin before deciding to move to the mountains of Colorado. Prior to this project, he published a book on UNIX systems administration. He has written many magazine articles on various UNIX topics and holds a software patent on an e-commerce privacy mechanism. His professional interests include networking security and Internet privacy, but he likes hiking and skiing a bit more.

ABOUT THE BOOK

One of my jobs before writing this book was to teach UNIX to a variety of individuals, including university students, industry C hackers, and, occasionally, friends and colleagues. During that time, I acquired a large amount of knowledge, both in my head as well as in the form of a substantial library, that I often thought would be good to put into book form. When I began preparing my university lecture series about UNIX, I found that none of the available UNIX textbooks suited my purpose—they were either too unstructured, too specialized, or lacking in suitable exercises and projects for my students. In response to this situation, I wrote the very first version of the current book. After a couple of years of using it, I completely rewrote it, giving careful thought to the organization of the new material. I decided to group the information on the basis of various typical kinds of UNIX users, allowing the book to be utilized by a good range of people without completely going over the top (or underneath) anyone's head. One tricky decision concerned the level of detail to include about things like utilities and system calls. Most of these have a large number of specialized options and features that are rarely used, and to document them all and still cover the range of topics that I had targeted would result in a book about two feet thick. Because of this, I've included information only about the most common and useful features of utilities, shells, and system calls. I include references to other commercially available books for more detail. This hybrid-book approach seemed like a good compromise; I hope that you agree.

This edition adds a chapter on the Bourne Again Shell (also called "bash"), which has become more important because of its integral position in Linux. We have also updated the UNIX/Linux version information and X desktop and window manager details, expanded the existing coverage of **vi, perl**, and IPv6, and added and improved some command descriptions, quizzes, and exercises. Many organizational improvements, including new figure numbering, should make the book easier to use, as well.

LAYOUT OF THE BOOK

UNIX is a big thing. To describe it fully requires an explanation of many different topics from several different angles, which is exactly what I've tried to do. The book is split into the following sections, each designed for a particular kind of user:

1. What is UNIX?
2. UNIX Utilities for Nonprogrammers
3. UNIX Utilities for Power Users
4. The UNIX Shells
5. The Bourne Shell
6. The Korn Shell
7. The C Shell
8. The Bourne Again Shell
9. Networking
10. The Internet
11. Windowing Systems
12. C Programming Tools
13. Systems Programming
14. UNIX Internals
15. System Administration
16. The Future
    Appendix
    Bibliography

I recommend that the various categories of user read the chapters as follows:

Category of user	Chapters
Day-to-day casual users	1, 2
Advanced users	1, 2, 3, 4, 9, 10, 11
Programmers	1 thru 13, 16
System analysts	1 thru 14, 16
Wizards	Everything (of course!)

LAYOUT OF THE CHAPTERS

Every chapter in this book has the following standard prologue:

Motivation

Why it's useful to learn the material that follows.

Prerequisites

What the reader should know in order to negotiate the chapter successfully.

Objectives

A list of the topics presented.

Presentation

A description of the method by which the topics are presented.

Utilities

A list of the utilities covered in the chapter (when appropriate).

System calls

A list of the system calls covered in the chapter (when appropriate).

Shell commands

A list of the shell commands covered in the chapter (when appropriate).

In addition, every chapter ends with a review section, which contains the following items:

Checklist

A recap of the topics.

Quiz

A quick self-test.

Exercises

A list of exercises, rated *easy, medium*, or *hard*.

Projects

One or more related projects, rated *easy, medium*, or *hard*.

A GUIDE FOR TEACHERS

As I mentioned earlier, this book was originally written for an audience of undergraduate and graduate students. I suggest that a lecture series based on the book could be designed as follows:

- If the students don't know the C language, then a medium-paced course could begin with Chapters 1, 2, 4, and 12. The lecturer could then introduce the students to C and use the contents of Chapter 13 for class exercises and projects.
- If the students already know the C language, then a medium-paced course could include Chapters 1, 2, 4, 7, 12, 13, and 14. Projects focusing on parallel processing and interprocess communication will ensure that the students end up with a good knowledge of UNIX fundamentals.
- If the students know the C language and are enthusiastic, I suggest that all of the chapters with the exception of Chapters 3, 5, and 6 be covered in one semester. I know this is possible, as I've taught the class that way!

NOMENCLATURE

Throughout this book, there are references to UNIX utilities, shell commands (i.e., commands that are part of a command shell itself), and system calls (UNIX library functions). It's quite easy to confuse these three things, so I adopted a consistent way to differentiate them:

- UNIX utilities are always written in boldface, like this: "The **mkdir** utility makes a directory."
- Shell commands are always written in italics, like this: "The *history* command lists your previous commands."

- System calls are always followed by parentheses, like this: "The fork () system call duplicates a process."

Formal descriptions of utilities, shell commands, and system calls are supplied in a box, using a modified-for-UNIX Backus–Naur notation. The conventions of this notation are fairly simple and are described fully in the appendix. As an example, here's a description of the UNIX **man** utility:

Utility: **man** [*chapter*] *word*
  man -k *keyword*

The first usage of **man** displays the manual entry associated with *word*. A value for *chapter* is optional. If no chapter number is specified, the first entry found is displayed. The second usage of **man** displays a list of all the manual entries that contain *keyword*.

All utilities, shell commands, and system calls, including the page numbers of the scripts and programs that use them, are fully cross-referenced in the appendix.

Sample UNIX sessions are presented in a Courier font. Keyboard input from the user is always displayed in italics, and annotations are always preceded by ellipses (...). Here's an example:

```
$ ls                      ... generate a directory listing.
myfile.txt   yourfile.txt
$ whoami
glass
$ _                       ... a new prompt is displayed.
```

REFERENCES TO OTHER BOOKS

For the same reason that it's good to reuse existing code, it's also good to use other people's reference material when it doesn't interfere with the natural flow of the presentation. Information that we consider to be too specialized for this book is noted with a reference to a publication listed in the bibliography at the end of the book. For example,

"For information concerning a port of UNIX to a 68030 processor, see p. 426 of Wait 1987."

The information is usually the name of the primary author and the year of publication; in the preceding quote, the book is entitled "UNIX papers." Where we reference specific pages, it is, of course, possible that future editions of these books will have different page numbers. In these cases, the reference will hopefully still remain reasonably close to the quoted page number.

SOURCE CODE AVAILABILITY ON-LINE

Examples of source code used in this edition are available on-line. Short examples are not included, but examples of any "significant" length can be found on the Web at

```
ftp://ftp.prenhall.com/pub/esm/the_apt_series.s-042/glass_ables_unix-3e/
```

(You can type this string into a Web browser, or see Chapter 9, "Networking," for more information on FTP.)

ACKNOWLEDGMENTS

The following people were instrumental in bringing forth previous editions of this book: James F. Peters, III, Fadi Deek, Dr. William Burns, Richard Newman-Wolfe, David Carver, Bill Tepfenhart, Stephen Rago, and Mark Ellis.

This edition had valuable technical input from Lori Murphy, Lawrence B. Wells, and Michael D. Breck. As always, the folks at Prentice Hall—especially Petra Recter, Camille Trentacoste, and Lakshmi Balasubramanian—have been nothing but encouraging and supportive.

Table of Contents

Go to Chapt's 13, 14 + 15 for more system Admin + programming info

— use either bash or Korn   *Chapt8   Chapt6*

— Author's home-made shell example

# CHAPTER 1

What is UNIX?

MOTIVATION

UNIX is a popular operating system in the engineering world and has been growing in popularity lately in the business world. Knowledge of its functions and purpose will help you to understand why so many people choose to use UNIX and will make your own use of it more effective.

PREREQUISITES

To fully understand this chapter, you should have a little experience with a computer and a familiarity with basic computer terms such as *program, file*, and *CPU*.

OBJECTIVES

In this chapter, I describe the basic components of a computer system, define the term *operating system*, and explain why UNIX is so successful. I also present UNIX from several different perspectives, ranging from that of a nonprogrammer to that of an advanced systems programmer.

PRESENTATION

To begin with, I describe the main bits and pieces that make up a typical computer system. I then show how a special program called an *operating system* is needed to control these pieces effectively and present a short list of operating system facilities. Following this discussion is a description of the basic UNIX philosophy, which acts as a framework for the information presented in the rest of the book. Finally, I present a short history of UNIX and a glimpse of where I believe it is heading.

COMPUTER SYSTEMS

A typical single-user computer system is built out of many parts, including a central processing unit (CPU), memory, disks, a monitor, and a keyboard. Small systems like this may be connected together to form larger computer networks, enabling tasks to be distributed among individual computers. Figure 1.1 is an illustration of such a network.

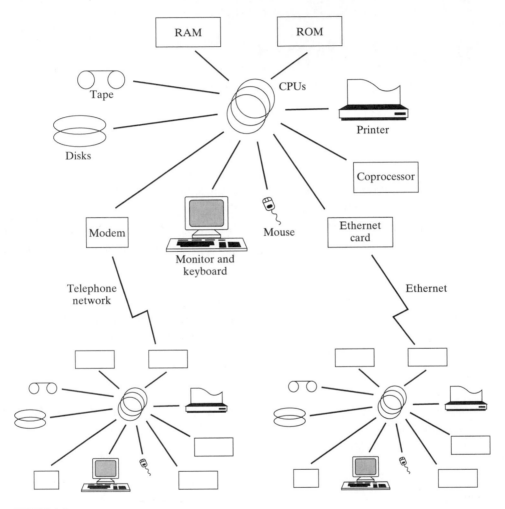

FIGURE 1.1

A typical computer network.

The hardware that goes to make up a computer network is only half the story; the software that runs on the computers is equally important. Let's take a closer look at the various hardware and software components of a computer system.

THE HARDWARE

Computer systems, whether large or small, multiuser or singleuser, or expensive or cheap, include many pieces of hardware.

Central Processing Unit (CPU)

The CPU reads machine code (instructions in a form that a computer can understand) from memory and executes the code. A CPU is often said to be the "brain" of a computer.

Random-Access Memory (RAM)

RAM holds the machine code and data that are accessed by the CPU. RAM normally "forgets" everything it holds when the power is turned off.

Read-Only Memory (ROM)

ROM holds both machine code and data. Its contents may not be changed and are "remembered" even when the power is turned off.

Disk

Disks hold large amounts of data and code on a magnetic or optical medium and "remember" it all even when the power is turned off. Floppy disks are generally removable, whereas hard disks are not. Hard disks can hold a lot more information than floppy disks can.

CD-ROM Drive

CD-ROM drives allow digitally published information on a compact disc to be read by the computer. The information may be in a data stream or may constitute a file system the operating system can read as if it were on a hard disk drive.

Monitor

Monitors display information and come in two flavors: monochrome and color. Monochrome monitors are rare in newer computer systems.

Graphics Card

Graphic cards allow the CPU to display information on a monitor. Some graphics cards can display characters only, whereas others support graphics.

Keyboard

A keyboard allows a user to enter alphanumeric information. Several different kinds of keyboards are available, depending partly on the language of the user. For example, Japanese keyboards are much larger than Western keyboards, as their alphabet is much larger. The Western keyboards are often referred to as QWERTY keyboards, as these are the first six letters on the upper left-hand side of the keyboard.

Mouse

A mouse allows a user to position things easily on the screen by short movements of the hand. Most mice have "tails" that connect them to the computer, but some have radio or infrared connections that make the tail unnecessary. I recommend some form of cordless mouse to anyone who has a cat (I kid you not!), as cats tend to get tangled up with a mouse cord very easily.

Printer

A printer allows a user to obtain hard copies of information. Some printers print characters only, whereas others print graphics.

Tape

Tapes are generally used for making backup copies of information stored on disks. They are slower than disks, but store large amounts of data in a fairly cheap way.

Modem

A modem allows you to communicate with other computers across a telephone line. Different modems allow different rates of communication. Most modems even correct for errors that occur due to a poor telephone connection.

Ethernet Interface

An Ethernet is a medium (typically some wires) that allows computers to communicate at high speeds. Computers attach to an Ethernet by a special piece of hardware called an *Ethernet interface*.

Other Peripherals

There are many other kinds of peripherals that computer systems can support, including graphics tablets, optical scanners, array processors, sound cards, voice recognition cards, and synthesizers (to name a few).

You cannot just connect these pieces of hardware together and have a working computer system: You must also have some software that controls and coordinates all the pieces. The ability to share peripherals, to share memory, to communicate between machines, and to run more than one program at a time is made possible by a special kind of program called an *operating system*. You may think of an operating system as a "superprogram" that allows all of the other programs to operate. Let's take a closer look at operating systems.

OPERATING SYSTEMS

As you've already seen, a computer system can't function without an operating system. There are many different operating systems available for PCs, minicomputers, and mainframes, the most common ones being Windows NT and 2000, VMS, MacOS, and variations of UNIX. UNIX is available for many different hardware platforms, whereas most other operating systems are tied to a specific hardware family. This is one of the first good things about UNIX: It's available for just about any machine. Of the forego-ing operating systems, only UNIX and VMS allow more than one user to use the computer system at a time, which is an obvious requirement for business systems. Many businesses buy a powerful minicomputer with 20 or more terminals and then use UNIX as the operating system that shares the CPUs, memory, and disks among the users. If we assume that we pick UNIX as the operating system for our computer system, what can we do with it? Let's take a look now at the software side of things.

THE SOFTWARE

One way to describe the hardware of a computer system is to say that it provides a framework for executing programs and storing files. The kinds of programs that run on UNIX platforms vary widely in size and complexity, but tend to share certain common characteristics. Here is a list of useful facts concerning UNIX programs and files:

- A *file* is a collection of data that is usually stored on disk, although some files are stored on tape. UNIX treats peripherals as special files, so that terminals, printers, and other devices are accessible in the same way as disk-based files.
- A *program* is a collection of bytes representing code and data that are stored in a file.
- When a program is started, it is loaded from disk into RAM. (Actually, only parts of it are loaded, but we'll come to that later.) When a program is running, it is called a *process.*
- Most processes read and write data from files.
- Processes and files have an *owner* and may be protected against unauthorized access.
- UNIX supports a hierarchical directory structure.
- Files and processes have a "location" within the directory hierarchy. A process may change its own location or the location of a file.
- UNIX provides services for the creation, modification, and destruction of programs, processes, and files.

Figure 1.2 is an illustration of a tiny UNIX directory hierarchy that contains four files and a process running the "sort" utility.

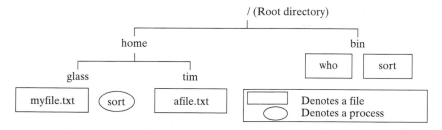

FIGURE 1.2

Directory hierarchy.

SHARING RESOURCES

Another operating system function that UNIX provides is the sharing of limited resources among competing processes. Limited resources in a typical computer system include CPUs, memory, disk space, and peripherals such as printers. Here is a brief outline of how these resources are shared:

- UNIX shares *CPUs* among processes by dividing each second of CPU time into equal-sized "slices" (typically 1/10 second) and then allocating them to processes on the basis of a priority scheme. Important processes are allocated more slices than others.
- UNIX shares *memory* among processes by dividing RAM up into thousands of equal-sized "pages" of memory and then allocating them to processes on the basis of a priority scheme. Only those portions of a process that actually need to be in RAM are ever loaded from disk. Pages of RAM that are not accessed for a while are saved back to disk so that the memory may be reallocated to other processes.
- UNIX shares *disk space* among users by dividing the disks into thousands of equal-sized "blocks" and then allocating them to users according to a quota system. A single file is built out of one or more blocks.

Chapter 14, "UNIX Internals," contains more details on how these sharing mechanisms are implemented. We've now looked at every major role that UNIX plays as an operating system except one—as a medium for communication.

COMMUNICATION

The components of a computer system cannot achieve very much when they work in isolation, as illustrated by the following examples:

- A process may need to talk to a graphics card to display output.
- A process may need to talk to a keyboard to get input.
- A network mail system needs to talk to other computers to send and receive mail.
- Two processes need to talk to each other in order to collaborate on a single problem.

UNIX provides several different ways for processes and peripherals to talk to each other, depending on the type and the speed of the communication. For example, one way that a process can talk to another process is via an interprocess communication mechanism called a "pipe"—a one-way medium-speed data channel that allows two processes on the same machine to talk. If the processes are on different machines connected by a network, then a mechanism called a "socket" may be used instead. A socket is a two-way high-speed data channel.

It is becoming quite common nowadays for different pieces of a problem to be tackled by different processes on different machines. For example, there is a graphics system called the X Window System that works by using something termed a "client–server" model. One computer (the X "server") is used to control a graphics terminal and to draw the various lines, circles, and windows, while another computer (the X "client") generates the data that are to be displayed. Arrangements like this are examples of distributed processing, in which the burden of computation is spread among many computers. In fact, a single X server may service many X clients. Figure 1.3 is an illustration of an X-based system.

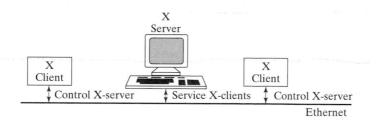

FIGURE 1.3

An X server with X clients.

We will discuss the X Window System further in Chapter 11.

UTILITIES

Even the most powerful operating system isn't worth too much to the average user, unless there is a good chunk of useful software that is available for it. Due to the relatively old age of UNIX and its perceived market value, there is no shortage of good utilities. Standard UNIX comes complete with at least 200 small utility programs, usually including a couple of editors, a C compiler, a sorting utility, a graphical user interface, some shells, and some text-processing tools. Popular packages like spreadsheets, compilers, and desktop publishing tools are also commercially available. In addition, plenty of free software is available from computer sites all over the world via the Internet, which we examine in Chapter 10.

PROGRAMMER SUPPORT

UNIX caters very well to programmers. It is an example of an "open" system, which means that the internal software architecture is well documented and available in source code form, either free of charge or for a relatively small fee. The features of UNIX, such as parallel processing, interprocess communication, and file handling, are all easily accessible from a programming language such as C via a set of library routines known as "system calls." Many facilities that were difficult to use on older operating systems are now within the reach of every systems programmer.

STANDARDS

UNIX is a fairly standard operating system, with a historical lineage consisting of two main paths. As you'll see shortly, UNIX was created in AT&T's Bell Laboratories and subsequently evolved into what is currently known as "System V" UNIX. The University of California at Berkeley obtained a copy of UNIX early on in its development and spawned another major version, known as Berkeley Standard Distribution (BSD)

UNIX. Both System V and BSD UNIX have their own strengths and weaknesses, as well as a large amount of commonality. Two consortiums of leading computer manufacturers gathered behind these two versions of UNIX, each believing its own version to be the best. UNIX International, headed by AT&T and Sun, backed the latest version of System V UNIX, called System V Release 4. The Open Software Foundation (OSF), headed by IBM, Digital Equipment Corporation, and Hewlett-Packard, attempted to create a successor to BSD UNIX called OSF/1. Both groups tried to comply with a set of standards set by the Portable Operating System Interface (POSIX) Committee and other such organizations. The OSF project has fallen by the wayside in recent years, leaving System V as the apparent "winner" of the "UNIX wars," although most of the best features of BSD UNIX have been rolled into most System V-based versions of UNIX. Hence, Solaris (from Sun Microsystems), HP-UX (from Hewlett-Packard), AIX (from IBM), and IRIX (from Silicon Graphics, Inc.), while all System V-based, also include most of the different features of BSD UNIX at varying levels of completeness.

UNIX is written mostly in the C language, which makes it relatively easy to port to different hardware platforms. This portability is an important benefit and has contributed a great deal to the proliferation and success of UNIX. *the rest is in assembler*

LIST OF UNIX FEATURES (A RECAP)

Here is a recap of the features that UNIX provides:

- It allows many users to access a computer system at the same time.
- It supports the creation, modification, and destruction of programs, processes, and files.
- It provides a directory hierarchy that gives a location to processes and files.
- It shares CPUs, memory, and disk space in a fair and efficient manner among competing processes.
- It allows processes and peripherals to talk to each other, even if they're on different machines.
- It comes complete with a large number of standard utilities.
- There are plenty of high-quality, commercially available software packages for most versions of UNIX.
- It allows programmers to access operating features easily via a well-defined set of system calls that are analogous to library routines.
- It is a portable operating system and thus is available on a wide variety of platforms.

Now that we've covered the main features of UNIX, it's time to examine some of the philosophies behind it and explore both its past and its future.

UNIX PHILOSOPHIES

The original UNIX system was lean and mean. It had a very small number of utilities and virtually no network or security functionality. The original designers of UNIX had some pretty strong notions about how utilities should be written: A program should do one thing, it should do it well, and complex tasks should be performed by using these utilities together. To this end, the designers built a special mechanism called a "pipe" into the heart of UNIX to support their vision. A pipe allows a user to specify that the output of one process is to be used as the input to another process. Two or more processes may be connected in this fashion, resulting in a "pipeline" of data flowing from the first process through to the last as shown in Figures 1.4 and 1.5.

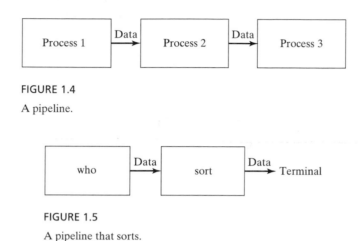

FIGURE 1.4

A pipeline.

FIGURE 1.5

A pipeline that sorts.

The nice thing about pipelines is that many problems can be solved by such an arrangement of processes. Each process in the pipeline performs a set of operations upon the data and then passes the results on to the next process for further processing. For example, imagine that you wish to obtain a sorted list of all the users on the UNIX system. There is a utility called **who** that outputs an unsorted list of the users and another utility called **sort** that outputs a sorted version of its input. These two utilities may be connected together with a pipe so that the output from **who** passes directly into **sort**, resulting in a sorted list of users. This is a more powerful approach to solving problems than writing a fresh program from scratch every time or using two programs, but having to store the intermediate data in a temporary file in order for the next program to have access to the data.

The UNIX philosophy for solving problems can be stated thus:

- If you can solve the problem by using pipes to combine multiple existing utilities, do it; *otherwise*
- Ask people on the network if they know how to solve the problem. If they do, great; *otherwise*
- If you could solve the problem with the aid of some other handwritten utilities, write the utilities yourself and add them into the UNIX repertoire. Design each utility to do one thing well and one thing only, so that each may be reused to solve other problems. If more utilities won't do the trick,
- Write a program to solve the problem (typically in C, C++, or Java).

Inside UNIX is hidden another more subtle philosophy that is slowly eroding. The original system was designed by programmers who liked to have the power to access data or code anywhere in the system, regardless of who the owner was. To support this capability, they built the concept of a "superuser" into UNIX, which meant that certain privileged individuals could have special access rights. For example, the administrator of a UNIX system always has the capability of becoming a superuser so that he or she may perform cleanup tasks such as terminating rogue processes or removing unwanted users from the system. The concept of a superuser has security implications that are a little frightening: Anyone with the right password could wipe out an entire system or extract top-security data with relative ease. Some of the research versions of UNIX do away entirely with the superuser concept and instead subdivide privileged tasks among several different "slightly super" users.

UNIX YESTERDAY

A computer scientist named Ken Thompson at Bell Laboratories built the first version of UNIX. Ken was interested in building a video game called "Space Wars," which required a fairly fast response time. The operating system that he was using, MULTICS, didn't give him the performance that he needed, so he decided to build his own operating system. He called it UNIX because the "UNI" part of the name implied that it would do one thing well, as opposed to the "MULTI" part of the "MULTICS" name, which he felt tried to do many things without much success. He wrote the system in assembly language, and the first version was very primitive: It was only a single-user system, it had no network capability, and it had a poor management system for sharing memory among processes. However, it was efficient, compact, and fast, which was exactly what Ken wanted.

A few years later, a colleague of Ken's, Dennis Ritchie, suggested that they rewrite UNIX using the C language, which Dennis had recently developed from a language called B. The idea that an operating system could be written in a high-level language was an unusual approach at that time. Most people felt that compiled code would not run fast enough[1] and that only the direct use of machine language was sufficient for such an important component of a computer system. Fortunately, C was slick enough that the conversion was successful, and the UNIX system suddenly had a huge advantage over other operating systems: Its source code was understandable. Only a small percentage of the original source code remained in assembly language, which meant that porting the operating system to a different machine was possible. As long as the target machine had a C compiler, most of the operating system would work with no changes; only the assembly language sections had to be rewritten.

Bell Laboratories started using this prototype version of UNIX in its patent department, primarily for text processing, and a number of UNIX utilities that are found in modern UNIX systems—for example, **nroff** and **troff**—were originally designed during this period. But because at that time AT&T was prohibited from selling software by

---

[1]Compiler technology has also improved greatly since then, so the code most compilers produce is much more efficient.

antitrust regulations, Bell Laboratories licensed UNIX source code to universities free of charge, hoping that enterprising students would enhance the system and further its progress into the marketplace. Indeed, graduate students at the University of California at Berkeley took the task to heart and made some huge improvements over the years, including creating the first good memory management system and the first real networking capability. The university started to market its own version of UNIX, called Berkeley Standard Distribution (BSD) UNIX, to the general public. The differences between these versions of UNIX can be seen in many of today's versions.

UNIX TODAY

Many companies produce and market their own versions of UNIX, usually to run on their own hardware platforms. A more recent entry into the UNIX world is Linux, an operating system that behaves[2] very much like UNIX. LINUX was written by many programmers around the world and is now marketed and supported by several different companies. Older versions of UNIX are derived from either System V or BSD, whereas the newer versions tend to contain features from both. Figure 1.6 shows an abbreviated genealogy.

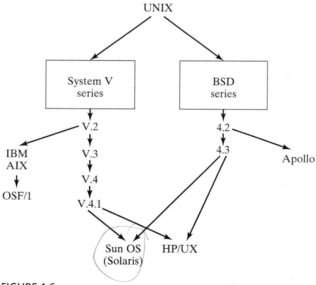

FIGURE 1.6

An abbreviated UNIX genealogy.

As Linux is a complete reimplementation, it shares no common code with any version of UNIX and therefore does not connect to the "family tree." Still, very strong philosophical connections and influences in Linux are derived from all versions of UNIX.

---

[2]Technically, Linux is not UNIX, since it shares no common code (and therefore no licensing restrictions), but to even the experienced UNIX user, it looks and acts the same.

We'll see what versions of UNIX are available for various hardware platforms in Chapter 16.

UNIX TOMORROW

It is likely that future versions of UNIX will follow a philosophy similar to that of contemporary versions of UNIX—for example, incorporating the idea that you can build an application from a collection of interconnected utilities. In addition, UNIX will need to embrace some of the newer trends in computing, such as parallel processing and object-oriented programming. We'll take a look at some of these future-related issues in Chapter 16.

THE REST OF THIS BOOK

As you can probably tell by now, UNIX is a fairly substantial topic and can be properly digested only in small portions. In order to aid this process and to allow individual readers to focus on the subjects that they find most applicable, I decided to write the book's chapters with reference to the different kinds of UNIX user there are. These users tend to fall into one of several categories:

- *Nonprogrammers*, who occasionally want to perform simple tasks like sending and receiving electronic mail, use a spreadsheet, or do some word processing.
- *Shell users*, who use background processing and write small scripts from within a convenient interface.
- *Advanced Nonprogrammers*, who use more complex facilities like file encryption, stream editors, and file processing.
- *Advanced-shell users*, who write programs in a high-level shell language (a little like job control language, or JCL) to perform useful tasks such as backing up files automatically, monitoring disk usage, and performing software installation.
- *Programmers*, who write programs in a general-purpose language such as C for speed and efficiency.
- *System programmers*, who require a good knowledge of the underlying computer system in order to write programs such as network communication programs and advanced file access programs.
- *System architects*, who invent better computer systems. These people provide a vision and a framework for the future.
- *System administrators*, who make sure that the computer system runs smoothly and that users are generally satisfied.

To begin with, read the chapters that interest you the most. Then go back and fill in the gaps when you have the time. If you're unsure about which chapters are most appropriate for your skill level, read the introductory section, "About This Book," for some hints.

CHAPTER REVIEW

Checklist

In this chapter, I mentioned

- the main hardware components of a computer system
- the purpose of an operating system
- the meaning of the terms *program, process*, and *file*
- the layout of a hierarchical directory structure
- that UNIX shares CPUs, memory, and disk space among competing processes
- that UNIX supports communication between processes and peripherals
- that UNIX comes complete with a multitude of standard utilities
- that most major software packages are available on UNIX systems
- that UNIX is an "open" system
- that UNIX has a rosy future

Quiz

1. What are the two main versions of UNIX, and how did each begin?
2. Write down five main functions of an operating system.
3. What is the difference between a *process* and a *program*?
4. What is the UNIX philosophy?
5. Who created UNIX?
6. What makes UNIX an "open" system?

Exercise

1.1 Obtain a list of currently popular operating systems other than UNIX, and determine whether any of them could be serious contenders to UNIX. [level: *medium*]

Project

Investigate the MULTICS system, and find the similarities and differences between it and the UNIX system. [level: *medium*]

UNIX Utilities for Nonprogrammers

MOTIVATION

This section contains the absolute basics that you really need to know in order to be able to do anything useful with UNIX.

PREREQUISITES

In order to understand this chapter, you must have already read Chapter 1. It also helps if you have access to a UNIX system so that you can try out the various UNIX features that I discuss.

OBJECTIVES

In this chapter, I'll show you how to log on and off a UNIX system, how to change your password, how to get on-line help when you're stuck, how to stop a program, and how to use the file system. I'll also introduce you to the mail system so that you can enter the world of computer networking.

PRESENTATION

The information in this section is presented in the form of a couple of sample UNIX sessions. If you don't have access to a UNIX account, march through the sessions anyway and try them out later.

UTILITIES

This section introduces the following utilities, listed in alphabetical order:

cancel	head	mv	wc
cat	lp	newgrp	
chgrp	lpr	page	
chmod	lprm	passwd	
chown	lpq	pwd	
clear	lpstat	rm	
cp	ls	rmdir	
date	mail	stty	
emacs	man	tail	
file	mkdir	tset	
groups	more	vi	

SHELL COMMAND

This section introduces the following shell command:

cd

OBTAINING AN ACCOUNT

If you can't just go buy your own UNIX computer, then you'll need to get an account on someone else's. If you're a student, the best way to get access to a UNIX account is to enroll in a UNIX course or an account from a professor. If you're a professional, it's likely that your company already has some UNIX facilities, in which case it's a matter of contacting either the training staff or a suitable manager. If you have a little cash and a PC, you can download one of several distributions of Linux or buy it at many computer stores. If you have more cash, you could buy a commercial version of UNIX. We'll check out the versions of UNIX that are currently available, both free and commercial, in Chapter 16. The good thing about having your own UNIX system is that you can be a superuser, since you're the one who owns the system. Most companies won't let a nonguru *near* the superuser password.

LOGGING IN

In order to use a UNIX system, you must first log in with a suitable username—a unique name that distinguishes you from the other users of the system. For example, my own username is "glass." Your username and initial password are assigned to you by the system administrator or are set to something standard if you bought your own UNIX system. It's sometimes necessary to press the *Enter* key (also known as the *Return* key) a couple of times to make the system give you a login prompt. Doing this effectively tells UNIX that "somebody's waiting to log in." UNIX first asks you for your username by prompting you with the line "login:" and then asks for your password. When you enter your password, the letters that you type are not displayed on your terminal, for security reasons. UNIX is case sensitive, so make sure that the case of the letters is matched exactly. Depending on how your system is set up, you should then see either a $ or a % prompt. Here's sample login:

```
UNIX(r) System V Release 4.0
login: glass
Password:    ...what I typed here is secret and doesn't show.
Last login:  Sun Feb 15 18:33:26 from dialin
$ _
```

It's quite common for the system to immediately ask you which kind of terminal you're using, so that it can set special characters like the backspace and cursor movement keys to their correct values. You are usually allowed to press the *Enter* key for the default terminal setting, and I suggest that you do this when you log in for the first time. I'll show you later how to change the terminal type if necessary. Other events that might occur when you log in are as follows:

- A help system recognizes that you're a first-time user and asks you whether you'd like a guided tour of UNIX.
- The "news of the day" messages are displayed to your screen, informing you of scheduled maintenance times and other useful information.

Here's an example of a slightly more complex login sequence that asked me what my terminal type was. I pressed the *Enter* key to select the default terminal type, a "vt100":

```
UNIX(r) System V Release 4.0
login: glass
Password:                   ...secret.
Last login: Sun Feb 15 21:26:13 from dialin
You have mail             ....the system tells me I have mail.
TERM = (vt100)            ...I pressed Enter.
$ _
```

SHELLS

The $ or % prompt that you see when you first log into UNIX is displayed by a special kind of program called a *shell*—a program that acts as a middleman between you and the raw UNIX operating system. A shell lets you run programs, build pipelines of processes, save output to files, and run more than one program at the same time. A shell executes all of the commands that you enter. The following are the four most popular shells:

- the Bourne shell
- the Korn shell
- the C shell
- the Bourne Again shell (a.k.a. Bash)

All of these shells share a similar set of core functionality, together with some specialized properties. The Korn shell is a superset of the Bourne shell, and thus users typically no longer use the Bourne shell as their login shell. I personally favor the Korn shell, as it's easy to program and has the best command line interface. This book contains information on how to use all four shells, each discussed in a separate chapter. Chapter 4 describes the core functionality found in all UNIX command shells, and Chapters 5 through 8 describe the specialized features of each shell.

Each shell has its own programming language. One reasonable question to ask is, Why would you write a program in a shell language rather than a language like C or Java? The answer is that shell languages are tailored to manipulating files and processes in the UNIX system, which makes them more convenient in many situations. In this chapter, the only shell facilities that I use are the abilities to run utilities and to save the output of a process to a file. Let's go ahead and run a few simple UNIX utilities.

RUNNING A UTILITY

To run a utility, simply enter its name and press the *Enter* key. From now on, when I say that you should enter a particular bit of text, I also implicitly mean that you should press the *Enter* key after the text. This tells UNIX that you've entered the command and that you wish it to be executed.

Not all systems have exactly the same utilities, so if a particular example doesn't work, don't be flustered. I'll try to point out the utilities that vary a lot from system to system. One utility that every system has is called **date**, which displays the current date and time:

```
$ date                          ... run the date utility.
Thu Mar 12 10:41:50 MST 1998
$ _
```

Whenever I introduce a new utility, I'll write a small synopsis of its typical operation in the format shown in Figure 2.1. It's self-explanatory, as you can see. I use a modified-for-UNIX (Backus–Naur form (BNF)) notation to describe the syntax. This notation is fully documented in the appendix.

Note that I do not list every different kind of option or present a particularly detailed description. Those are best left to the pages of the manual for your particular version of UNIX and to books that focus almost entirely on UNIX utilities.

Utility: **date** [*yymmddhhmm* [*.ss*]]

Without any arguments, **date** displays the current date and time. If arguments are provided, **date** sets the date to the setting supplied, where *yy* is the last two digits of the year, the first *mm* is the number of the month, *dd* is the number of the day, *hh* is the number of hours (use the 24-hour clock), and the last *mm* is the number of minutes. The optional *ss* is the number of seconds. Only a superuser may set the date.

FIGURE 2.1

Description of the **date** command.

Another useful utility, shown in Figure 2.2, is **clear**, which clears your screen.

Utility: **clear**

This utility clears your screen.

FIGURE 2.2

The **clear** command.

INPUT, OUTPUT, AND ERROR CHANNELS

In the example of the **date** command in the previous section, the output was written to the terminal. UNIX can write to files, but there are three default I/O channels that are always assumed to be active for every command or program:

- Standard input, known as "stdin," whereby a program expects to find input
- Standard output, known as "stdout," whereby a program writes its output by default
- Standard error, known as "stderr," whereby a program writes error messages

By default, all three I/O channels are the terminal running the command or program. This arrangement enables commands to interact with the terminal easily and still use input from other places and write output to other places when necessary. The default I/O channels can be easily changed on the command line by using "redirection." We'll see examples of I/O redirection later in this chapter. For details on how the UNIX I/O channels work, see Chapter 13.

OBTAINING ON-LINE HELP: man

There are bound to be many times when you're at your terminal and you can't quite remember how to use a particular utility. Alternatively, you may know what a utility does but not remember what it's called. You may also want to look up an argument not described in this text or one that differs slightly among different versions of UNIX. All UNIX systems have a utility called **man** (short for "manual page") that puts this information at your fingertips. **man** works as described in Figure 2.3.

Utility: **man** [[-s] *section*] *word*

man -k *keyword*
The manual pages are on-line copies of the original UNIX documentation, which is usually divided into eight sections. The pages contain information about utilities, system calls, file formats, and shells. When **man** displays help about a given utility, it indicates in which section the entry appears.

The first usage of **man** displays the manual entry associated with *word*. A few versions of UNIX use the **–s** argument to indicate the section number. If no section number is specified, the first entry that **man** finds is displayed. The second usage of **man** displays a list of all the manual entries that contain *keyword*.

FIGURE 2.3

The **man** command.

The typical division of topics in manual page sections is as follows:

1. Commands and application programs
2. System calls
3. Library functions
4. Special files
5. File formats
6. Games
7. Miscellaneous
8. System administration utilities

Sometimes, there is more than one manual entry for a particular word. For example, there is a utility called **chmod** and a system call called chmod (), and there are manual pages for both (in Sections 1 and 2). By default, **man** displays the manual pages for the first entry that it finds, so it will display the manual page for the **chmod** utility. In case other entries exist, the manual page of the first entry will state "SEE ALSO...," with the other entries listed, followed by their section numbers.

Here's an example of **man** in action:

```
$ man -k mode            ...search for keyword "mode".
chmod (1V)                    - change the permissions mode of a file
chmod, fchmod (2V)            - change mode of file
getty (8)                     - set terminal mode
ieeeflags (3M)                - mode and status function
umask (2V)                    - set file creation mode mask
$ man chmod              ...select the first manual entry.
CHMOD(1V)                      USER COMMANDSCHMOD (1V)
NAME
        chmod - change the permissions mode of a file
SYNOPSIS
        chmod C -fR V mode filename ...
...the description of chmod goes here.
SEE ALSO
        csh(1), ls(1V), sh(1), chmod(2V), chown(8)
$ man 2 chmod            ...select the manual entry from section 2.
CHMOD(2V)      SYSTEM CALLS          CHMOD(2V)
NAME
        chmod, fchmod - change mode of file
SYNOPSIS
        #include <sys/stat.h>
        int chmod(path, mode)
        char *path;
        mode_t mode;
...the description of chmod () goes here.
SEE ALSO
        chown(2V), open(2V), stat(2V), sticky(8)
$ _
```

SPECIAL CHARACTERS

see pg 56, 53 (toct)

Some characters are interpreted specially when typed at a UNIX terminal. These characters are sometimes called *metacharacters* and may be listed by using the **stty** utility with the **-a** (all) option. The **stty** utility is discussed fully at the end of this chapter. Here's an example:

```
$ stty -a                    ...obtain a list of terminal metacharacters
speed 38400 baud;  -parity hupcl
rows = 24; columns = 80; ypixels = 0; xpixels = 0;
-inpck -istrip ixoff imaxbel
crt tostop iexten
erase  kill   werase rprnt  flush  lnext  susp   intr   quit   stop
eof
H     ^U    ^W    ^R    ^O    ^V    ^Z/^Y ^C    ^\    ^S/^Q ^D
$ _
```

The ^ in front of each letter means that the *Control* key must be pressed at the same time as the letter. The default meaning of each option is shown in Figure 2.4.

Some of the characters just listed won't mean much to you until you read some more chapters of the book, but a few are worth mentioning now.

Option	Meaning
erase	Backspace one character.
kill	Erase all of the current line.
werase	Erase the last word.
rprnt	Reprint the line.
flush	Ignore any pending input and reprint the line.
lnext	Don't treat the next character specially.
susp	Suspend the process for a future awakening.
intr	Terminate (interrupt) the foreground job with no core dump.
quit	Terminate the foreground job and generate a core dump.
stop	Stop/restart terminal output.
eof	End of input. *Log-out*

Left margin annotations: ^H ^U ^W ^R ^O ^V ^Z/^Y ^C ^\ ^S/^Q ^D

FIGURE 2.4

stty options. — see pg 56

Terminating a Process: Control-C

Sometimes you run a program and then wish to stop it before it's finished. The standard way to do this in UNIX is to press the keyboard sequence *Control*-C. Although there are a few programs that are immune to this form of termination of a process, most processes are immediately killed, and your shell prompt is returned. Here's an example:

```
$ man chmod
CHMOD(1V)        USER COMMANDS        CHMOD(1V)
NAME
         chmod - change the permissions mode of a file
SYNOPSIS
^C         ...terminate the job and go back to the shell.
$ _
```

Pausing Output: Control-S/Control-Q

If the output of a process starts to scroll rapidly up the screen, you may pause it by typing *Control*-S. To resume generating the output, you may either type *Control*-S again or type *Control*-Q. This sequence of control characters is sometimes called XON/XOFF protocol. Here's an example:

```
$ man chmod
CHMOD(1V)        USER COMMANDS        CHMOD(1V)
NAME
              chmod - change the permissions mode of a file
^S               ...suspend terminal output.
^Q               ...resume terminal output.
SYNOPSIS
              chmod C -fR V mode filename ...
...the rest of the manual page is displayed here.
SEE ALSO
         csh(1), ls(1V), sh(1), chmod(2V), chown(8)
$ _
```

End of Input: Control-D

Many UNIX utilities take their input from either a file or the keyboard. If you instruct a utility to do the latter, you must tell the utility when the input from the keyboard is finished. To do this, type *Control*-D on a line of its own after the last line of input. *Control*-D means "end of input." For example, the **mail** utility allows you to send mail from the keyboard to a named user:

```
$ mail tim    ...send mail to my friend Tim.
Hi Tim,         ...input is entered from the keyboard.
 I hope you get this piece of mail. How about building a country
one of these days?
- with best wishes from Graham
^D                ...tell the terminal that there's no more input.
$ _
```

The **mail** utility is described fully later in the chapter.

SETTING YOUR PASSWORD: PASSWD

After you first log into a UNIX system, it's a good idea to change your initial password. (Someone set it, so you know that at least one other person knows it.) Passwords should generally be at least six letters long and *should not* be a word from a dictionary or a proper noun. This is because it's quite easy for someone to set up a computer program that runs through all the words in a standard dictionary and tries them as your password. I know this firsthand, as I've had someone break into my account using the very same technique. My password is now something like "GWK145W." Get the idea?

To set your password, use the **passwd** utility, which works as shown in Figure 2.5. Here's an example, with the passwords shown. Note that you wouldn't normally be able to see the passwords, as UNIX turns off the keyboard echo when you enter them.

Utility: **passwd**

passwd allows you to change your password. You are prompted for your old password and then twice for the new one. (Since what you type isn't shown on the screen, you would not know if you made a typo.) The new password may be stored in an encrypted form in the password file "/etc/passwd" or in a "shadow" file (for more security), depending on your version of UNIX. Your particular version may store the password in a remote database as well.

FIGURE 2.5

Description of the **passwd** command.

```
$ passwd
Current password: penguin
New password (? For help): GWK145W
New password (again): GWK145W
Password changed for glass
$ _
```

If you forget your password, the only thing to do is contact your system administrator and ask for a new password.

LOGGING OUT

To leave the UNIX system, type the keyboard sequence *Control*-D at your shell prompt.[1] This tells your login shell that there is no more input for it to process, causing it to disconnect you from the UNIX system. Most systems then display a "login:" prompt and wait for another user to log in. Here's an example:

---

[1]The C-shell can be set to ignore ^D for logout, since you might type it by accident. In this case, you must type the "logout" command instead.

```
$ ^D          ...I'm done!
UNIX(r) System V Release 4.0
login:        ...wait for another user to log in.
```

Congratulations! You've now seen how you can log into a UNIX system, execute a few simple utilities, change your password, and then log out. In the next few sections, I'll describe some more utilities that allow you to explore the directory hierarchy and manipulate files.

POETRY IN MOTION: EXPLORING THE FILE SYSTEM

I decided that the best way to illustrate some common UNIX utilities was to describe a session that used them in a natural fashion. One of my hobbies is to compose music, and I often use the UNIX system to write lyrics for my songs. The next few sections of this chapter are a running commentary on the UNIX utilities that I used to create a final version of one of my song's lyrics, called "Heart To Heart." Figure 2.6 shows the approximate series of events that took place, together with the utility that I used at each stage.

Action	Utility
I displayed my current working directory.	pwd
I wrote the first draft and stored it in a file called "heart."	cat
I listed the directory contents to see the size of the file.	ls
I displayed the "heart" file, using several utilities.	cat, more, page, head, tail
I renamed the first draft "heart.ver1."	mv
I made a directory called "lyrics" to store the first draft.	mkdir
I moved "heart.ver1" into the "lyrics" directory.	mv
I made a copy of "heart.ver1" called "heart.ver2."	cp
I edited the "heart.ver2" file.	vi
I moved back to my home directory.	cd
I made a directory called "lyrics.final."	mkdir
I renamed the "lyrics" directory to "lyrics.draft."	mv
I copied the "heart.ver5" file from "lyrics.draft" to "lyrics.final," renaming it "heart.final."	cp
I removed all the files from the "lyrics.draft" directory.	rm
I removed the "lyrics.draft" directory.	rmdir

FIGURE 2.6

Script of upcoming examples.

Action	Utility
I moved into the "lyrics.final" directory.	cd
I printed the "heart.final" file.	lpr
I counted the words in "heart.final."	wc
I listed the file attributes of "heart.final."	ls
I looked at the file type of "heart.final."	file
I obtained a list of my groups.	groups
I changed the group of "heart.final."	chgrp
I changed the permissions of "heart.final."	chmod

FIGURE 2.6   *(Continued)*

PRINTING YOUR SHELL'S CURRENT WORKING DIRECTORY: PWD

Every UNIX process has a location in the directory hierarchy, termed its *current working directory*. When you log into a UNIX system, your shell starts off in a particular directory called your "home directory." In general, every user has a different home directory, which often begins with the prefix "/home." For example, my own home directory is called "/home/glass." The system administrator assigns home directory values. To display your shell's current working directory, use the **pwd** utility, which works as shown in Figure 2.7. To illustrate this utility, here's what happened when I logged into UNIX to start work on my song's lyrics:

Utility: **pwd**

Prints the current working directory.

FIGURE 2.7

Description of the **pwd** command.

```
UNIX(r) System V Release 4.0
login: glass
Password:          ...secret.
$ pwd
/home/glass
$ _
```

Figure 2.8 is a diagram that indicates the location of my login Korn shell in the directory hierarchy.

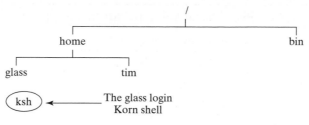

FIGURE 2.8

The login shell starts at the user's home directory.

ABSOLUTE AND RELATIVE PATHNAMES

Before I continue with the sample UNIX session, it's important to introduce you to the idea of *pathnames*.

Two files in the same directory may not have the same name, although it's perfectly OK for several files in *different* directories to have the same name. For example, Figure 2.9 shows a small hierarchy that contains a "ksh" process and three files called "myFile".

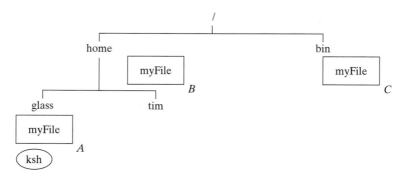

FIGURE 2.9

Different files may have the same name.

Although these files have the same name, they may be unambiguously specified by their *pathname* relative to "/", the root of the directory hierarchy. A pathname is a sequence of directory names that leads you through the hierarchy from a starting directory to a target file. A pathname relative to the root directory is often termed an *absolute* or *full* pathname. Figure 2.10 shows the absolute pathnames of the "A," "B," and "C" instances of "myFile".

File	Absolute PathName
A	/home/glass/myFile
B	/usr/myFile
C	/bin/myFile

FIGURE 2.10

Absolute pathnames.

A process may also unambiguously specify a file by using a pathname *relative* to its current working directory. The UNIX file system supports the special fields shown in Figure 2.11 that may be used when supplying a relative pathname. For example, Figure 2.12 shows the pathnames of the three instances of "myFile" relative to the "ksh" process located in the "/home/glass" directory. Note that the pathname "myFile" is equivalent to "./myFile," although the second form is rarely used because the leading "." is redundant.

Field	Meaning
.	current directory
..	parent directory

FIGURE 2.11

Current and parent directories.

File	Relative PathName
A	myFile
B	../myFile
C	../../bin/myFile

FIGURE 2.12

Relative pathnames.

CREATING A FILE

I already had an idea of what the first draft of my song's lyrics would look like, so I decided to store them in a file called "heart." Ordinarily, I would use a UNIX editor such as **vi** or **emacs** to create the file, but this is a beginner's chapter, so I used a simpler utility called **cat** to achieve the same result. Figure 2.13 shows how **cat** works.

Utility: **cat** -n { *fileName* }*

The **cat** utility takes its input from standard input or from a list of files and displays them to standard output. The **-n** option adds line numbers to the output. **cat** is short for "concatenate" which means "to connect in a series of links."

FIGURE 2.13

Description of the **cat** command.

By default, the *standard input* of a process is the keyboard and the *standard output* is the screen. We can send the standard output of a process to a file instead of the screen by making use of a shell facility called *output redirection.* If you follow a command by a > character and the name of a file, the output from the command is saved to the file. If the file doesn't already exist, it is created; otherwise, its previous contents are overwritten. Right now, use this feature without worrying about how it works; Chapter 4 explains it all in detail. To create the first draft of my lyrics, I entered the following text at the shell prompt:

```
$ cat > heart        ...store keyboard input a the file "heart".
I hear her breathing,
I'm surrounded by the sound.
Floating in this secret place,
I never shall be found.
^D       ...tell cat that the end-of-input has been reached.
$ _
```

LISTING THE CONTENTS OF A DIRECTORY: ls

Once the "heart" file was created, I wanted to confirm its existence in my home directory and see how many bytes of storage it used. To do this, I used the **ls** utility, which lists information about a file or a directory. **ls** works as shown in Figure 2.14.

Utility: **ls** -adglsFR { *fileName* }* { *directoryName* }*

With no arguments at all, **ls** lists all of the files in the current working directory in alphabetical order, excluding files whose name starts with a period. The **-a** option causes such files to be included in the listing. Files that begin with a period are sometimes known as "hidden" files. To obtain a listing of directories other than the current directory, place their names after the options. To obtain listings of specific files, place their names after the options. The **-d** option causes the details, rather than the

---

FIGURE 2.14

Description of the **ls** command.

contents, of the directories to be listed. The **-g** option lists a file's group. The **-l** option generates a long listing, including permission flags, the file's owner, and the last time the file was modified. The **-s** option causes the number of disk blocks that the file occupies to be included in the listing. (A block is typically between 512 and 4K bytes.) The **-F** option causes a character to be placed after the file's name, to indicate the type of the file: * means an executable file, / means a directory file, @ means a symbolic link, and = means a socket. The **-R** option recursively lists the contents of a directory and its subdirectories.

FIGURE 2.14 (*Continued*)

Some of the **ls** options just described won't mean a lot right now, but will become increasingly relevant as this book progresses.

Here's an example of ls:

```
$ ls              ...list all files in current directory.
heart
$ ls -l heart     ...long listing of "heart."
-rw-r--r--   1   glass      106   Jan 30 19:46     heart
$ _
```

I'll describe the exact meaning of each field in the long directory listing later in this chapter, but for now Figure 2.15 will give you a brief overview. You may obtain even more information by using the following additional options:

Field #	Field value	Meaning
1	-rw-r--r--	the type and permission mode of the file, which indicates who can read, write, and execute the file
2	1	the hard link count (discussed much later in the book)
3	glass	the username of the owner of the file
4	106	the size of the file, in bytes
5	Jan 30 19:46	the last time the file was modified
6	heart	the name of the file

FIGURE 2.15

Description of output from the **ls** command.

```
$ ls -algFs          ...extra-long listing of current dir.
total 3              ...total number of blocks of storage.
1 drwxr-xr-x  3    glass    cs    512   Jan 30 22:52 ./
1 drwxr-xr-x 12    root     cs   1024   Jan 30 19:45 ../
1 -rw-r--r--  1    glass    cs    106   Jan 30 19:46 heart
$ _
```

The **-s** option generates an extra first field that tells you how many disk blocks the file occupies. On my UNIX system, each disk block is 1024 bytes long, which implies that my 106-byte file actually takes up 1024 bytes of physical storage. This is a result of the physical implementation of the file system, which is described in Chapter 14. The **-a** option causes **ls** to include a listing of all *hidden* files, which are files whose names begin with a period. For example, "." and ".." are hidden files that correspond to the current directory and its parent directory, respectively. The **-F** option appends a / to all files that are directories, and the **-g** option displays the file's group.

LISTING A FILE: cat/more/page/head/tail /less

To check the contents of the "heart" file that I had created in my home directory, "/home/glass," I directed its contents to the screen using the **cat** utility. Notice that I supplied **cat** with the name of the file that I wanted to display:

```
$ cat heart       ...list the contents of the "heart" file.
I hear her breathing,
I'm surrounded by the sound.
Floating in this secret place,
I never shall be found.
$ _
```

cat can actually take any number of files as arguments, in which case they are listed together, one following the other. **cat** is good for listing small files, but doesn't pause between full screens of output. The **more** and **page** utilities are better suited for larger files and contain advanced facilities such as the ability to scroll backward through a file. Figures 2.16 and 2.17 provide some notes on each utility.

Utility: **more** -f [+*lineNumber*] { *fileName* }*

The **more** utility allows you to scroll through a list of files, one page at a time. By default, each file is displayed starting at line 1, although the + option may be used to specify the starting line number. The **-f** option tells **more** not to fold long lines. After each page is displayed, **more** displays the message "--More--" to indicate that it's waiting for a command. To list the next page, press the space bar. To list the next line, press the *Enter* key. To quit **more**, press the **q** key. To obtain help on the multitude of other commands, press the **h** key.

FIGURE 2.16

Description of the **more** command.

> *Utility*: **page** -f [+*lineNumber*] { *fileName* }*
>
> The **page** utility works just like **more**, except that it clears the screen before displaying each page. This sometimes makes the listing display a little more quickly.

FIGURE 2.17

Description of the **page** command.

While we're on the topic of listing files, there are a couple of handy utilities called **head** and **tail** that allow you to peek at the start and end of a file, respectively. Figures 2.18 and 2.19 show how they work.

> *Utility*: **head** -n { *fileName* }*
>
> The **head** utility displays the first *n* lines of a file. If *n* is not specified, **head** defaults to 10. If more than one file is specified, a small header identifying each file is displayed before its contents are.

FIGURE 2.18

Description of the **head** command.

> *Utility*: **tail** -n { *fileName* }*
>
> The **tail** utility displays the last *n* lines of a file. If *n* is not specified, **tail** defaults to 10. If more than one file is specified, a small header identifying each file is displayed before its contents are.

FIGURE 2.19

Description of the **tail** command.

In the following example, I displayed the first two lines and last two lines of my "heart" file:

```
$ head -2 heart            ...list the first two lines
I hear her breathing,
I'm surrounded by the sound.
$ tail -2 heart            ...list the last two lines
Floating in this secret place,
I never shall be found.
$ _
```

RENAMING A FILE: mv

Now that I'd created the first draft of my lyrics, I wanted to create a few more experimental versions. To indicate that the file "heart" was really the first generation of many versions to come, I decided to rename it "heart.ver1" by using the **mv** utility, which works as shown in Figure 2.20. Here's how I renamed the file using the first form of the **mv** utility:

Utility: **mv** -i *oldFileName newFileName*

     mv -i {*fileName*}* *directoryName*

     mv -i *oldDirectoryName newDirectoryName*

The first form of **mv** renames *oldFileName* as *newFileName*. If the label *newFileName* already exists, it is replaced. The second form allows you to move a collection of files to a directory, and the third allows you to move an entire directory. None of these options actually moves the physical contents of a file if the destination location is within the same file system as the original; instead, they just move labels around the hierarchy. **mv** is therefore a very fast utility. The **-i** option prompts you for confirmation if *newFileName* already exists.

FIGURE 2.20

Description of the **mv** command.

```
$ mv heart heart.ver1         ...rename to "heart.ver1".
$ ls
heart.ver1
$ _
```

The second and third forms of the **mv** utility are illustrated later in the chapter.

MAKING A DIRECTORY: mkdir

Rather than clog up my home directory with the many versions of "heart," I decided to create a subdirectory called "lyrics" in which to keep them all. To do this, I used the **mkdir** utility, which works as shown in Figure 2.21. Here's how I did it:

Utility: **mkdir** [-p] *newDirectoryName*

The **mkdir** utility creates a directory. The **-p** option creates any parent directories in the *newDirectoryName* pathname that do not already exist. If *newDirectoryName* already exists, an error message is displayed and the existing file is not altered in any way.

FIGURE 2.21

Description of the **mkdir** command.

```
$ mkdir lyrics            ...create a directory called "lyrics".
$ ls -lF                  ...confirm.
-rw-r--r--   1   glass   106   Jan 30  23:28   heart.ver1
drwxr-xr-x   2   glass   512   Jan 30  19:49   lyrics/
$ _
```

The letter "d" at the start of the permission flags of "lyrics" indicates that it's a directory file.

In general, you should keep related files in their own separate directory. If you name your directories sensibly, it'll make it easy to track down files weeks, or even years, after you create them.

Once the "lyrics" directory was created, the next step was to move the "heart.ver1" into its new location. To do this, I used **mv** and confirmed the operation by using **ls**:

```
$ mv heart.ver1 lyrics    ...move into "lyrics"
$ ls                      ...list the current directory.
lyrics/                   ..."heart.ver1" has gone.
$ ls lyrics               ...list the "lyrics" directory.
heart.ver1                ..."heart.ver1" has moved.
$ _
```

MOVING TO A DIRECTORY: cd

Although I could remain in my home directory and access the various versions of my lyric files by preceding them with the prefix "lyrics/", doing this would be rather inconvenient. For example, to edit the file "heart.ver1" with the UNIX **vi** editor, I'd have to do the following:

```
$ vi lyrics/heart.ver1    ...invoke the vi editor.
```

In general, it's a good idea to move your shell into a directory if you intend to do a lot of work there. To do this, use the *cd* command. *cd* isn't actually a UNIX utility, but instead is an example of a shell built-in command. Your shell recognizes *cd* as a special keyword and executes it directly. Notice that I write shell commands using italics, in adherence to the nomenclature that I described at the start of the book. Figure 2.22 shows how *cd* works.

Shell Command: **cd** [*directoryName*]

The *cd* (change directory) shell command changes a shell's current working directory to *directoryName*. If the *directoryName* argument is omitted, the shell is moved to its owner's home directory.

FIGURE 2.22

Description of the *cd* shell command.

The following example shows how I moved into the "lyrics" directory and confirmed my new location by using **pwd**:

```
$ pwd                    ...display where I am.
/home/glass
$ cd lyrics              ...move into the "lyrics" directory.
$ pwd                    ...display where I am now.
/home/glass/lyrics
$ _
```

Figure 2.23 is an illustration of the shell movement caused by the previous *cd* command.

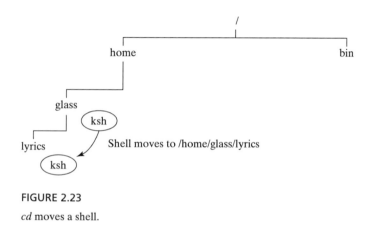

FIGURE 2.23

cd moves a shell.

Since "." and ".." refer to your shell's current working directory and parent directory, respectively, you may move up one directory level by typing "cd ..". Here's an example:

```
$ pwd                    ...display current position.
/home/glass/lyrics
$ cd ..                  ...move up one level.
$ pwd                    ...display new current position.
/home/glass
$ _
```

COPYING A FILE: cp

After moving into the "lyrics" directory, I decided to work on a second version of my lyrics. I wanted to keep the first version for posterity, so I copied "heart.ver1" into a new file called "heart.ver2" and then edited the new file. To copy the file, I used the **cp** utility, which works as shown in Figure 2.24.

Utility: **cp** -i *oldFileName newFileName*

    cp -ir { *fileName* }* *directoryName*

The first form of **cp** copies *oldFileName* to *newFileName*. If the label *newFileName* already exists, it is replaced. The **-i** option prompts you for confirmation if *newFileName* already exists. The second form of **cp** copies a list of files into *directoryName*. The **-r** option causes any source files that are directories to be recursively copied, thus copying the entire directory structure.

FIGURE 2.24

Description of the **cp** command.

cp actually does two things:

- It makes a physical copy of the original file's contents.
- In the directory hierarchy, it creates a new label that points to the copied file.

The new copy of the original file can therefore be edited, removed, and otherwise manipulated without having any effect on the original file. Here's how I copied the "heart.ver1" file:

```
$ cp heart.ver1 heart.ver2        ...copy to "heart.ver2".
$ ls -l heart.ver1 heart.ver2     ...confirm.
-rw-r--r--  1      glass    106   Jan 30  23:28 heart.ver1
-rw-r--r--  1      glass    106   Jan 31  00:12 heart.ver2
$ _
```

EDITING A FILE: vi

At this point, I edited the "heart.ver2" file, using a UNIX editor called **vi**. The way that the **vi** editor works is described later in the chapter, together with information about another editor called **emacs**. For the time being, assume that I edited "heart.ver2" to look like this:

```
$ vi heart.ver2                    ...edit the file.
... editing session takes place here.
$ cat heart.ver2                   ...list the file.
I hear her breathing,
I'm surrounded by the sound.
Floating in this secret place,
I never shall be found.
She pushed me into the daylight,
I had to leave my home.
But I am a survivor,
And I'll make it on my own.
$ _
```

After creating five versions of my song's lyrics, my work was done. I moved back to my home directory and created a subdirectory called "lyrics.final" in which to store the final version of the lyrics. I also renamed the original "lyrics" directory to "lyrics.draft," which I felt was a better name. The commands to do all this is as follows:

```
$ cd                        ...move back to my home directory.
$ mkdir lyrics.final        ...make the final lyrics directory.
$ mv lyrics lyrics.draft    ...rename the old lyrics dir.
$ _
```

The final version of my lyrics was stored in a file called "heart.ver5" in the "lyrics.draft" directory, which I then copied into a file called "heart.final" in the "lyrics.final" directory:

```
$ cp lyrics.draft/heart.ver5 lyrics.final/heart.final
$ _
```

DELETING A DIRECTORY: rmdir

Although posterity is a good reason for keeping old things around, it can interfere with your disk usage in a multiuser system. I therefore decided to remove the "lyrics.draft" directory, to avoid exceeding my modest disk quota. Before I removed it, though, I archived its contents using the **cpio** utility, which is described in Chapter 3. To remove the directory, I used the **rmdir** utility, which works as shown in Figure 2.25.

Utility: **rmdir** { *directoryName* }+

The **rmdir** utility removes all of the directories from the list of directory names. A directory must be empty before it can be removed. To remove a directory and all of its contents recursively, use the **rm** utility with the **-r** option (described shortly).

FIGURE 2.25

Description of the **rmdir** command.

I tried to remove the "lyrics.draft" directory while it still contained the draft versions, and I received the following error message:

```
$ rmdir lyrics.draft
rmdir: lyrics.draft: Directory not empty
$ _
```

To remove the files from the "lyrics.draft" directory, I made use of the **rm** utility, described next.

DELETING A FILE: rm

The **rm** utility allows you to remove a file's label from the hierarchy. When no more labels reference a file, UNIX removes the file itself. In most cases, every file has only one label, so the act of removing the label causes the file's physical contents to be deallocated. However, in Chapter 3, I'll show you some occasions wherein a single file has more than one label. In these cases, a label may be removed without affecting the file that it refers to. Figure 2.26 provides a description of **rm**.

Utility: **rm** -fir {*fileName*} *

The **rm** utility removes a file's label from the directory hierarchy. If the filename doesn't exist, an error message is displayed. The **-i** option prompts the user for confirmation before deleting a filename; press **y** to confirm your request and **n** otherwise. If *fileName* is a directory, the **-r** option causes all of its contents, including subdirectories, to be recursively deleted. The **-f** option inhibits all error messages and prompts.

FIGURE 2.26

Description of the **rm** command.

To remove every file in the "lyrics.draft" directory, I moved into the "lyrics.draft" directory and used **rm**:

```
$ cd lyrics.draft          ...move to "lyrics.draft" dir.
$ rm heart.ver1 heart.ver2 heart.ver3 heart.ver4 heart.ver5
$ ls                       ...nothing remains.
$ _
```

Now that all the files were erased, I moved back to my home directory and erased the draft directory:

```
$ cd                       ...move to my home directory.
$ rmdir lyrics.draft       ...this time it works.
$ _
```

As you'll see in Chapter 4, there's a much easier way to erase a collection of files when you're using a shell. I could have written the following instead:

```
$ cd lyrics.draft          ...move into "lyrics.draft" directory.
$ rm *                     ...erase all files in current dir.
```

Even better, I could have used the more advanced **-r** option of **rm** to delete the "lyrics.draft" directory and all of its contents with just one command:

```
$ cd                    ...move to my home directory.
$ rm -r lyrics.draft    ...recursively delete directory.
$ _
```

PRINTING A FILE: lp/lpstat/cancel

Now that the hard work was done, I wanted to obtain a printout of my lyrics to sing from. I used the UNIX print utility called **lp**, which works as shown in Figure 2.27. **lp** causes a numbered print job to be started for the specified files. You may find the status of a particular job or printer by using the **lpstat** utility, which works as shown in Figure 2.28.

Utility: **lp** [-d *destination*] [-n *copies*] { *fileName* }*

lp prints the named files to the printer specified by the **-d** option. If no files are specified, standard input is printed instead. By default, one copy of each file is printed, although this action may be overridden by using the -n option.

FIGURE 2.27

Description of the **lp** command.

Utility: **lpstat** *[destination]*

lpstat displays the status of all print jobs sent to any printer with the **lp** command. If a printer destination is specified, **lpstat** reports queue information for that printer only. **lpstat** displays information about the user, information about the name and size of the job, and a print request ID.

FIGURE 2.28

Description of the **lpstat** command.

If, for some reason, you wish to cancel a print job, you may do so by using the **cancel** utility shown in Figure 2.29.

> *Utility*: **cancel** { *request-ID* }+
>
> **cancel** removes all of the specified jobs from the printer queue. If you're a superuser, then you may cancel any queued job.

FIGURE 2.29

Description of the **cancel** command.

You will need the request ID displayed by **lpstat**. You may obtain a list of the printers on your system from your system administrator.

In the following example, I started by ordering a printout of "heart.final" from the "lwcs" printer. I then decided to order two more copies and obtained a printer status. Finally, I changed my mind and canceled the last print job. The commands to do all this are as follows:

```
$ lp -d lwcs heart.final      ...order a printout.
request id is lwcs-37 (1 file)
$ lpstat lwcs             ...look at the printer status.
printer queue for lwcs
lwcs-36        ables       priority 0  Mar 18 17:02 on lwcs
      inventory.txt                    457 bytes
lwcs-37        glass       priority 0  Mar 18 17:04 on lwcs
      heart.final                      213 bytes
$ lp -n 2 -d lwcs heart.final      ...order two more copies.
request id is lwcs-38 (1 file)
$ lpstat lwcs             ...look at the printer status again.
printer queue for lwcs
lwcs-37        glass       priority 0  Mar 18 17:04 on lwcs
      heart.final                      213 bytes
lwcs-38        glass       priority 0  Mar 18 17:05 on lwcs
      heart.final     2 copies         213 bytes
$ cancel lwcs-38          ...remove the last job.
request "lwcs-38" cancelled
$ _
```

In the next example, I used the keyboard to compose a quick message for the printer:

```
$ lp -d lwcs                ...print from standard input.
Hi there,
This is a test of the print facility.
- Graham
^D                          ...end of input.
request id is lwcs-42 (standard input)
$ _
```

PRINTING A FILE: lpr/lpq/lprm

The commands above are on most UNIX systems and come from the System V family of UNIX. BSD UNIX provided its own print commands, which are still supported in many versions of UNIX with a strong BSD background as well as in Linux. These commands cover the same basic functions of printing, checking the queue, and canceling the job, but have different names and arguments.

To print my file by using such a system, I employ the **lpr** utility, which works as shown in Figure 2.30. **lpr** causes a numbered print job to be started for the specified files. You may find the status of a particular job or printer by using the **lpq** utility, which works as shown in Figure 2.31.

Utility: **lpr** –m [-P*printer*] [-#*copies*] { *fileName* }*

lpr prints the named files to the printer specified by the **–P** option. If no printer is specified, the printer in the environment variable $PRINTER is used. (For more information about environment variables, refer to Chapter 4.) If no files are specified, standard input is printed instead. By default, one copy of each file is printed, although this may be overridden using the **-#** option. The **–m** option causes mail to be sent to you when printing is complete.

FIGURE 2.30

Description of the **lpr** command.

Utility: **lpq** –l [-P*printer*] { *job#* }* {*userId* }*

lpq displays the status of jobs on the printer specified by the **–P** option. If no printer is specified, the printer in the environment variable $PRINTER is used. **lpq** displays information pertaining to the specified jobs or the jobs of the specified users. If no jobs or users are specified, the statuses of all jobs on the specified printer are displayed. The **–l** option generates extra information.

FIGURE 2.31

Description of the **lpq** command.

If, for some reason, you wish to cancel a print job, you may do so by using the **lprm** utility shown in Figure 2.32. You may obtain a list of the printers on your system from your system administrator.

> *Utility:* **lprm** [-P*printer*] [-] { *job#* }* { *userId* }*
>
> **lprm** cancels all of the specified jobs on the printer specified by the **–P** option. If no printer is specified, the printer in the environment variable $PRINTER is used. The – option cancels all of the print jobs started by you. If you are the superuser, you may cancel all of the jobs owned by a particular individual by specifying his or her user id.

FIGURE 2.32

Description of the **lprm** command.

As in our previous example, I started by ordering a printout of "heart.final" from the "lwcs" printer. I then decided to order two more copies and obtained a printer status. Finally, I changed my mind and canceled the last print job. The commands are as follows:

```
$ lpr -Plwcs heart.final          ...order a printout.
$ lpq -Plwcs glass                ...look at the printer status.
lwcs is ready and printing
Rank    Owner  Job  Files         Total Size
active  glass  731  heart.final   213 bytes
$ lpr -#2 -Plwcs heart.final      ...order two more copies.
$ lpq -Plwcs glass                ...look at the printer status again.
lwcs is ready and printing
Rank    Owner  Job  Files         Total Size
active  glass  731  heart.final   213 bytes
active  glass  732  heart.final   426 bytes
$ lprm -Plwcs 732                 ...remove the last job.
centaur: dfA732vanguard dequeued
centaur: cfA732vanguard.utdallas.edu dequeued
$ _
```

In the next example, I used the keyboard to compose a quick message for the printer and requested that I be notified by e-mail upon completion of the job:

```
$ lpr -m -Plwcs              ...print from standard input.
Hi there,
This is a test of the print facility.
- Graham
^D                          ...end of input.
$                           ...wait a little.
$ mail                      ...read my mail.
Mail version SMI 4.0 Sat Oct 13 20:32:29 PDT 1990 Type ? for help.
>N 1 daemon@utdallas.edu Fri Jan 31 16:59  15/502  printer job
& 1                         ...read the first mail message.
From: daemon@utdallas.edu
```

```
To: glass@utdallas.edu
Subject: printer job
Date: Wed, 18 Mar 1998 18:04:32 -0600
Your printer job (stdin)
Completed successfully
& q                          ...quit out of mail.
$ _
```

COUNTING THE WORDS IN A FILE: wc

I was quite interested in finding out how many characters, words, and lines were in the "heart.final" file (even though printing it gave me a byte count). To do this, I used the **wc** utility, which works as shown in Figure 2.33. Here's an example of **wc**:

```
$ wc heart.final          ...obtain a word count.
       9         43     213 heart.final
$ _
```

Utility: **wc** -lwc { *fileName* }*

The **wc** utility counts the lines, words, or characters in a list of files. If no files are specified, standard input is used instead. The **-l** option requests a line count, the **-w** option requests a word count, and the **-c** option requests a character count. If no options are specified, then all three counts are displayed. A word is defined by a sequence of characters surrounded by tabs, spaces, or newlines.

FIGURE 2.33

Description of the **wc** command.

FILE ATTRIBUTES

Now that I've introduced you to some of the common file-oriented utilities, it's time to look at the various file attributes. I used **ls** to obtain a long listing of "heart.final," and got the following output:

```
$ ls -lgsF heart.final
1 -rw-r--r-- 1   glass cs   213   Jan 31 00:12   heart.final
$ _
```

Each field is the value of a file attribute, described in Figure 2.34.

Field #	Field value	Meaning
1	1	the number of blocks of physical storage occupied by the file
2	-rw-r--r--	the type and permission mode of the file, which indicates who can read, write, and execute the file
3	1	the hard link count (discussed in Chapter 3)
4	glass	the username of the owner of the file
5	cs	the group name of the file
6	213	the size of the file, in bytes
7	Jan 31 00:12	the time that the file was last modified
8	heart.final	the name of the file

FIGURE 2.34

File attributes.

The next few sections describe the meaning of the individual fields, in increasing order of difficulty.

File Storage

The number of blocks of physical storage is shown in field 1 and is useful if you want to know how much actual disk space a file is using. It's possible to create sparse files that seem to be very large in terms of field 6, but actually take up very little physical storage. Sparse files are discussed in detail in Chapter 13.

Filenames

The name of the file is shown in field 8. A UNIX filename may be up to 255 characters in length. You may use any printable[2] characters you want in a filename except the slash (/), although I recommend that you avoid the use of any character that is special to a shell (like <, >, *, ?, or the tab), as these can confuse both the user and the shell. Unlike some operating systems, there's no requirement that a file end in an extension such as ".c" and ".h," although many UNIX utilities (e.g., the C compiler) will accept only files that end with a particular suffix. Thus, the filenames "heart" and "heart.final" are both perfectly valid. The only filenames that you definitely *can't* choose are "." and "..", as these are predefined filenames that correspond to your current working directory and its parent directory, respectively.

---

[2]Some nonprintable characters are valid in filenames, but can result in unexpected behavior when displayed or used, so their use is discouraged.

File Modification Time

Field 7 shows the time that the file was last modified and is used by several utilities. For example, the **make** utility, described in Chapter 12, uses the last modification time of files to control its dependency checker. The **find** utility, described in Chapter 3, may be used to find files on the basis of their last modification time.

File Owner

Field 3 tells you the owner of the file. Every UNIX process has an owner, which is typically the same as the username of the person who started it. For example, my login shell is owned by "glass," which is my username. Whenever a process creates a file, the file's owner is set to the process' owner. This means that every file that I create from my shell is owned by "glass," the owner of the shell itself. Chapter 13 contains more information on processes and ownership.

Note that while the text string known as the username is typically how we refer to a user, internally UNIX represents this as an integer known as the *user ID*. The username is easier for humans to understand than a numeric ID. Therefore, I will refer to the textual name as *username* and use *user ID* to refer to the numeric value itself.

File Group

Field 5 shows the file's group. Every UNIX user is a member of a group. This membership is initially assigned by the system administrator and is used as part of the UNIX security mechanism. For example, my group name is "cs." Every UNIX process also belongs to a specific group, usually the same as that of the user which started the process. My login shell belongs to the group name "cs." Because each file created by a process is assigned to the same group as that of the process that created the file, every file that I create from my shell has the group name "cs." Chapter 13 contains more information on processes and groups. The use of groups in relation to the UNIX security mechanism is described in the next few sections.

As with the user ID, the group is usually referenced by the text string name, but is represented internally as an integer value called the *group ID*. Therefore, I will refer to the textual name as *group name* and use *group ID* to refer to the numeric value itself.

File Types

Field 2 describes the file's type and permission settings. For convenience, here's the output from the previous **ls** example:

```
1 -rw-r--r--  1  glass cs  213  Jan 31 00:12  heart.final
```

The first character of field 2 indicates the type of the file, which is encoded as shown in Figure 2.35. In the example, the type of "heart.final" is indicated as a regular file. You'll encounter symbolic links in Chapter 3 pipes and sockets in Chapter 13, and buffered and unbuffered special files in Chapter 14.

Character	File type
-	regular file
d	directory file
b	buffered special file (such as a disk drive)
c	unbuffered special file (such as a terminal)
l	symbolic link
p	pipe
s	socket

FIGURE 2.35

File types.

A file's type can often be determined by using the file utility, which works as shown in Figure 2.36. For example, when I ran **file** on "heart.final," I saw this:

```
$ file heart.final                    ...determine the file type.
heart.final: ascii text
$ _
```

Utility: **file** { *fileName* }+

The **file** utility attempts[3] to describe the contents of the *fileName* arguments, including the language that any text is written in. When using **file** on a symbolic link file, **file** reports on the file that the link is pointing to, rather than the link itself.

FIGURE 2.36

Description of the **file** command.

File Permissions

The next nine characters of field 2 indicate the file's permission settings. In the current example, the permission settings are "rw-r--r--":

```
1 -rw-r--r--  1  glass cs  213  Jan 31 00:12 heart.final
```

These nine characters should be thought of as being arranged in three groups of three characters, as shown in Figure 2.37, where each cluster of three letters has the same format. If a dash occurs instead of a letter, then permission is denied. The meaning of

---

[3]While **file** is quite useful, it is not 100% accurate and can be fooled by some file formats.

See umask setting
pg 46, pg 178

User (owner)	Group	Others
rw-	r--	r--

Read permission	Write permission	Execute permission
r	w	x

FIGURE 2.37

File permissions.

	Regular file	Directory file	Special file
read	The process may change the contents.	The process may read the directory (i.e., list the names of the files that it contains).	The process may read from the file, using the read () system call.
write	The process may change the contents.	The process may add files to or remove files from the directory.	The process may write to the file, using the write () system call.
execute	The process may execute the file (which makes sense only if the file is a program)	The process may access files in the directory or any of its subdirectories.	No meaning.

FIGURE 2.38

Permission meanings for file types.

the read, write, and execute permissions depends on the type of the file, as shown in Figure 2.38.

When a process executes, it has four values related to file permissions:

1. a *real* user ID
2. an *effective* user ID
3. a *real* group ID
4. an *effective* group ID

When you log in, your login shell process has its real and effective user IDs set to your own user ID and its real and effective group IDs set to your group ID. When a process runs, the file permissions apply as follows:

- If the process' effective user ID is the same as the owner of the file, the **User** permissions apply.

- If the process' effective user ID is different from the owner of the file, but its effective group ID matches the file's group ID, then the **Group** permissions apply.
- If neither the process' effective user ID nor the process' effective group ID matches, the **Others** permissions apply.

The permission system is therefore a three-tier arrangement that allows you to protect your files from general users, but at the same time allows access by certain groups. Later on in the chapter, I'll illustrate the use of permission settings to good effect and describe the utilities that are used to alter them.

Note that only a process' effective user and group IDs affect its permissions; its real user and group IDs are only used for accounting purposes. Note also that a process' access rights ordinarily depend on who *executes* the process and not on who *owns* the executable file. Sometime, though, this is undesirable. For example, there is a game called **rogue** that comes with some UNIX systems and that maintains a file of the best scores of previous players. Obviously, the **rogue** process must have permission to alter this file when it is executing, but the player that executes **rogue** should not. This seems impossible on the basis of the permission rules that I just described. To get around the problem, the designers of UNIX added two special file permissions called "*set user ID*" and "*set group ID.*" When an executable file with "set user ID" permission is executed, the process' effective user ID becomes that of the executable file. Similarly, when an executable file with "set user ID" permission is executed, the process' effective group ID is copied from the executable file. In both cases, the real user or group ID is unaffected. In the case of the **rogue** game, the executable file and the score file are both owned by the user "rogue," and the **rogue** executable file has "set user ID" permission. The score file has only write permission for its owner, thus protecting general users from modifying it. When a player executes **rogue**, the player process executes with the effective user ID of rogue and thus is able to modify the score file.

"Set user ID" and "set group ID" permissions are indicated by an "s" instead of an "x" in the user and group clusters, respectively. They may be set using the **chmod** utility, described shortly, and by the chmod () system call, described in Chapter 13.

Here are a few other notes relating to file permissions:

- When a process creates a file, the default permissions given to that file are modified by a special value called the *umask*. The value of umask is usually set to a sensible default, so we will wait to discuss it further in Chapter 4.
- The superuser automatically has all access rights, regardless of whether they're granted or not.
- It's perfectly possible, although unusual, for the owner of a file to have fewer permissions than the group or anyone else.

Hard Link Count

Field 3 shows the file's hard link count, which indicates how many labels in the hierarchy are pointing to the same physical file. Hard links are rather advanced and are discussed in conjunction with the **ln** utility in Chapter 3.

GROUPS

Now that you've read about file permissions, it's time to see how they can come in handy. Recall that the "heart.final" file's user and group names were "glass" and "cs," respectively, inherited from my login shell:

```
$ ls -lg heart.final
-rw-r--r--  1  glass  cs   213  Jan 31 00:12 heart.final
$ _
```

The original permission flags allow anyone to read the file, but only the owner to write it. What I really wanted to do was set up a new group called "music" and allow anyone in the group to read my work. I, the owner, would retain read and write permissions, and anyone else would be denied all access rights.

The only way to create a new group is to ask the system administrator to add it. The actual way that a new group is added is described in Chapter 15. After a new group is added, any user who wants to be a part of that group must also ask the system administrator. At this time, I mailed a request to the system administrator for a new "music" group and asked for myself and my friend Tim to be added to the group. When I received a confirmation of the request, it was time to update my file attributes.

LISTING YOUR GROUPS: GROUPS

Before changing my file's group setting, I wanted to confirm that I was now an official member of the "music" group. The **groups** utility allows you to list all of the groups of which you're a member, and it works as shown in Figure 2.39. Here's what I saw when I executed **groups**:

Utility: **groups** [*userId*]

When invoked with no arguments, the **groups** utility displays a list of all the groups of which you are a member. If the name of a user is specified, a list of that user's groups is displayed.

FIGURE 2.39

Description of the **groups** command.

```
$ groups                 ...list my groups.
cs      music
$ _
```

CHANGING A FILE'S GROUP: chgrp

The first step toward protecting my lyrics was to change the group name of "heart.final" from "cs" to "music." I did this by using the **chgrp** utility, which works as shown in Figure 2.40. I used **chgrp** like this:

```
$ ls -lg heart.final
-rw-r--r-- 1 glass   cs       213 Jan 31 00:12 heart.final
$ chgrp music heart.final     ...change the group.
$ ls -lg heart.final          ...confirm it changed.
-rw-r--r-- 1 glass  music 213 Jan 31 00:12 heart.final
$ _
```

Utility: **chgrp** -R *groupname* { *fileName* }*

The **chgrp** utility allows a user to change the group of files that he or she owns. A superuser can change the group of any file. All of the files that follow the *groupname* argument are affected. The **-R** option recursively changes the group of the files in a directory.

FIGURE 2.40

Description of the **chgrp** command.

You may also use **chgrp** to change the group of a directory.

CHANGING A FILE'S PERMISSIONS: chmod

Now that the file's group was changed, it was necessary to update its permissions in order to deny all access rights to general users. To do this, I used the **chmod** utility, which works as shown in Figure 2.41. To remove read permission from others, I used **chmod** as follows:

```
$ ls -lg heart.final              ...before.
-rw-r--r-- 1 glass        music 213 Jan 31 00:12  heart.final
$ chmod o-r heart.final           ...remove read for others.
$ ls -lg heart.final              ...after.
-rw-r--1 glass      music 213 Jan 31 00:12          heart.final
$ _
```

Figure 2.42 shows some other examples of the use of **chmod**. I recommend that you protect your login directory from unauthorized access by not granting write permission for

Utility: **chmod** -R *change* { , *change* }*{ *fileName* }+

The **chmod** utility changes the modes of the specified files according to the *change* parameters, which may take any of the forms

clusterSelection+newPermissions (add permissions)

clusterSelection-newPermissions (subtract permissions)

and

clusterSelection=newPermissions (assign permissions absolutely)

where *clusterSelection* is any combination of

- u (user/owner)
- g (group)
- o (others)
- a (all)

and *newPermissions* is any combination of

- r (read)
- w (write)
- x (execute)
- s (set user ID/set group ID) *— see pg 46*

The **-R** option recursively changes the modes of the files in directories. (See the text that follows for examples.) Changing a directory's permission settings doesn't change the settings of the files that the directory contains.

FIGURE 2.41

Description of the **chmod** command.

anyone but yourself and by restricting read and execute permission to yourself and members of your group. Here's an example of how to do that:

```
$ cd                       ...change to home directory.
$ ls -ld .                 ...list attributes of home dir.
drwxr-xr-x 45 glass     4096 Apr 29 14:35 .
$ chmod o-rx               ...update permissions.
$ ls -ld                   ...confirm.
drwxr-x--- 45 glass     4096 Apr 29 14:35  .
$ _
```

Requirement	Change parameters
Add group write permission.	g+w
Remove user read and write permission.	u-rw
Add execute permission for user, group, and others.	a+x
Give the group just read permission.	g=r
Add write permission for user, and remove read permission from group.	u+w, g-r

FIGURE 2.42

File permission specifications for the **chmod** command.

Note that I used the **-d** option of **ls** to ensure that the attributes of my home directory, rather than the attributes of its files, were displayed.

The **chmod** utility allows you to specify the new permission setting of a file as an octal number. Each octal digit represents a permission triplet. For example, if you wanted a file to have the permission settings

```
rwxr-x---
```

then the octal permission setting would be 750, calculated as shown in Figure 2.43. The octal permission setting would be supplied to **chmod** as follows:

```
$ chmod 750 .          ...update permissions.
$ ls -ld               ...confirm.
drwxr-x--- 45 glass     4096 Apr 29 14:35   .
$ _
```

	User	Group	Others
setting	rwx	r-x	--
binary	111	101	000
octal	7	5	0

FIGURE 2.43

Permissions of 750 for the **chmod** command.

CHANGING A FILE'S OWNER: chown

If, for some reason, you ever want to relinquish ownership of a file, you may do so by using the **chown** utility, which works as shown in Figure 2.44. Some versions of UNIX allow only a superuser to change the ownership of a file, whereas some allow the owner to reassign ownership to another user. The latter is generally not allowed on a system in which disk quotas (limiting disk space for each user) are in effect. Several occasions when the system administrator needs to use **chown** are described in Chapter 15.

Utility: **chown** -R *newUserId* { *fileName* }+

The **chown** utility allows a superuser to change the ownership of files. All of the files that follow the *newUserId* argument are affected. The **-R** option recursively changes the owner of the files in directories.

FIGURE 2.44

Description of the **chown** command.

If I were a superuser, I could have executed the following sequence of commands to change the ownership of "heart.final" to "tim" and then back to "glass" again:

```
$ ls -lg heart.final        ...before.
-rw-r---- 1 glass  music 213  Jan 31 00:12 heart.final
$ chown tim heart.final     ...change the owner to "tim".
$ ls -lg heart.final        ...after.
-rw-r---- 1 tim    music 213  Jan 31 00:12 heart.final
$ chown glass heart.final   ...change the owner back.
$ _
```

CHANGING GROUPS: newgrp

If you're a member of several groups and then you create a file, to what group does the file belong? Well, although you may be a member of several groups, only one of them is your *effective* group at any given time. When a process creates a file, the group ID of the file is set to the process' *effective* group ID. This means that when you create a file from the shell, the group ID of the file is set to the effective group ID of your shell. In the sample session currently under discussion, I was a member of the "cs" and "music" groups, and my login shell's effective group name was "cs."

The system administrator is the person who chooses which one of your groups is used as your login shell's effective group ID. The only way to permanently alter your login shell's effective group ID is to ask the system administrator to change it. However, you may create a shell with a different effective group ID by using the **newgrp** utility, which works as shown in Figure 2.45.

Utility: **newgrp** [-] [*groupname*]

The **newgrp** utility, when invoked with a group name as an argument, creates a new shell with an effective group ID corresponding to the group name. The old shell sleeps until you exit the newly created shell. You must be a member of the group that you specify. If you use a dash (-) instead of a filename as the argument, a shell is created with the same settings as the shell that was created when you logged into the system.

FIGURE 2.45

Description of the **newgrp** command.

In the next example, I created a file called "test1" from my login shell, which had an effective group of "cs." I then created a temporary shell with an effective group of "music," and after that I created a file called "test2." Finally, I terminated the shell and went back to the original shell and obtained a long listing of both files:

```
$ date > test1          ...create from a "cs" group shell.
$ newgrp music          ...create a "music" group shell.
$ date > test2          ...create from a "music" group shell.
^D                      ...terminate the new shell.
$ ls -lg test1 test2    ...look at each file's attributes.
-rw-r--r--  1  glass  cs     29 Jan 31 22:57  test1
-rw-r--r--  1  glass  music  29 Jan 31 22:57  test2
$ _
```

POETRY IN MOTION: EPILOGUE

During the now-completed "Poetry in Motion" series of examples, you were introduced to many useful UNIX concepts and utilities. I recommend that you try them out thoroughly before progressing further through this book; doing so will help you retain and understand the UNIX basics. The remainder of the chapter covers the two most popular UNIX editors and explains how you can alter your terminal settings so that they work correctly. It also contains some information on using the UNIX e-mail system.

DETERMINING YOUR TERMINAL'S TYPE: tset

Several UNIX utilities, including the two standard editors **vi** and **emacs**, need to "know" what kind of terminal you're using so that they can control the screen correctly. The type of your terminal is stored by your shell in something called an *environment variable*. (See Chapter 4.) You may think of environment variables as being rather like global variables that hold strings.

Before **vi** or **emacs** can work correctly, your shell's TERM environment variable must be set to your terminal type. Common settings for this variable include "vt100" and "vt52." There are several ways to set TERM:

- Your shell start-up file, described in the next section, can set TERM directly by containing a line of the form 'setenv TERM vt100' (C shell) or 'TERM=vt100 ; export TERM' (for Bourne, Korn, and Bash shells). This method of setting TERM is practical only if you know the type of your terminal in advance and you always log into the same terminal.

- Your shell start-up file can invoke the **tset** utility, which looks at the communications port that you're connected to and then examines a special file called "/etc/ttytab," which contains a table of port–terminal mappings. In most cases, **tset** can find out what kind of terminal you're using from this table and set TERM accordingly. If **tset** can't find the terminal type, it can be told to prompt you for that information when you log in.
- You can manually set TERM from a shell.

The rest of this section describes the operation of **tset**. Before using **vi** or **emacs**, you should be sure to read the section that follows, which describes the operation of a related utility called **stty**.

The best way to set TERM is to use **tset** from your login shell. **tset** works as shown in Figure 2.46. The "/etc/ttytab" file contains lines of the following form:

see pg 55, 20

Utility: **tset** -s [-ec] [-ic] {-m *portId*:[?]*terminalType*}*

tset is a utility that tries to determine your terminal's type and then resets it for standard operation.

If the **-s** option is not used, **tset** assumes that your terminal type is already stored in the TERM environment variable. **tset** then resets the type, using terminal capability information stored in "/etc/termcap" or the *terminfo* database, depending on your version of UNIX.

If you use the **-s** option, **tset** examines the "/etc/ttytab" file and tries to map your terminal's port to a terminal type. If the type is found, **tset** initializes your terminal with an appropriate initialization sequence from the "/etc/termcap" file. The **-s** option also causes **tset** to generate shell commands to standard output. When executed, these commands cause the TERM and TERMCAP environment variables to be set properly. **tset** uses the contents of the SHELL environment variable to determine which kind of shell commands to generate. Filename expansion must be temporarily inhibited during the execution of the command sequence that **tset** generates, since there could be special characters that might be misinterpreted by the shell. Examples of this inhibition follow shortly.

FIGURE 2.46
Description of the **tset** command.

> The **-e** option sets the terminal's erase character to *c* in place of the default *Control-H* setting. Control characters may be indicated either by typing the character directly or by preceding the character by a ^ (i.e., use ^h to indicate *Control-H*).
>
> The **-i** option sets the terminal's interrupt character to *c* in place of the default *Control-C* setting. Control characters may be indicated as described in the previous paragraph.
>
> The "/etc/ttytab" mappings may be overridden or supplemented by using the **-m** option. The sequence "*-m pp:tt*" tells **tset** that if the terminal's port type is *pp*, then it should assume that the terminal is of type *tt*. If a question mark (?) is placed after the colon (:), **tset** displays *tt* and asks the user either to press *Enter* to confirm that the terminal type is indeed *tt* or to enter the actual terminal type that **tset** should use.

FIGURE 2.46   (*Continued*)

```
tty0f "usr/etc getty std.9600"   vt100      off local
ttyp0 none                       network    off secure
ttyp1 none                       network    off secure
```

The first field contains the names of ports, and the third field contains the names of terminal types. For example, if I was logged on via port tty0f, my terminal type would be read from this file as a vt100. In environments in which terminals are *hardwired* (i.e., directly connected to a specific port), this convention works nicely, since the terminal is always on the same port. In a network environment, it doesn't work very well, as we will see shortly. In the following example, I found out my actual port name by using the **tty** utility (described in Chapter 3) and then examined the output from the **tset** command:

```
$ tty                       ...display my terminal's port id.
/dev/ttyp0
$ tset -s                   ...call tset.
set noglob;                 ...shell commands generated by tset.
TERM=network;
export TERM;
TERMCAP='sa;cent;network:li#24:co#80:am:do=^J: ';
export TERMCAP;
unset noglob;
Erase is Ctrl-H
$ _
```

The previous example is provided only to illustrate how **tset** does its stuff. To actually make **tset** change the TERM and TERMCAP variables, which, after all, is the reason for using it in the first place, you must "eval" its output. The *eval* shell command is described fully in the next chapter. Here's a more realistic example of **tset**:

```
    $ set noglob            ...temporarily inhibit filename expansion.
 *  $ eval 'tset -s'        ...evaluate output from tset.
    Erase is Backspace      ...message from tset.
    $ unset noglob          ...reenable filename expansion.
    $ echo $TERM            ...look at the new value of TERM.
    network                 ...the terminal type that tset found.
    $ _
```

Unfortunately, the terminal type *network* is not very useful, as it assumes that my terminal has almost no capabilities at all. The **tset** command may be presented with a rule that tells it, "If the terminal type is discovered to be network, assume that the terminal is a vt100 and prompt the user for confirmation." Here is the variation of **tset** that does this:

```
    $ set noglob                     ...disable filename expansion.
 *  $ eval 'tset -s -m 'network:vt100''         ...provide rule.
    TERM = (vt100) <Enter>     ...I pressed the Enter key.
    Erase is Backspace
    $ unset noglob             ...reenable filename expansion.
    $ echo $TERM               ...display new TERM setting.
    vt100                      ...this is the terminal type that tset used.
    $ _
```

In sum, it's wise to contain a command in your shell's start-up file that calls **tset** to set your terminal type. Shell start-up files are described in Chapter 4. The simplest form of **tset** is the following:

C shell

```
    setenv TERM vt100
    tset
```

Bourne/Korn/Bash shell

```
    TERM=vt100; export TERM
    tset
```

The more sophisticated form of **tset** searches the "/etc/ttytab" file for your terminal type and should look somewhat like this:

C shell

```
    set noglob
    eval 'tset -s -m 'network:?vt100''
    unset noglob
```

Bourne/Korn/Bash shell

```
    eval 'tset -s -m 'network:?vt100''
```

CHANGING A TERMINAL'S CHARACTERISTICS: stty

All terminals have the ability to process certain characters in a special manner; these characters are called *metacharacters*. Examples of metacharacters include the backspace character and the *Control*-C sequence, which is used to terminate programs. The default metacharacter settings may be overridden by using the **stty** utility, which works as shown in Figure 2.47.

Utility: **stty** -a { *option* }* { *metacharacterString* <value>} *

The **stty** utility allows you to examine and set a terminal's characteristics. **stty** supports the modification of over 100 different settings, so I've listed only the most common ones here. Consult **man** for more details. To list a terminal's current settings, use the **-a** option. To alter a particular setting, supply one or more of the following options:

Option	Meaning
-echo	Don't echo typed characters.
echo	Echo typed characters.
-raw	Enable the special meaning of metacharacters.
raw	Disable the special meaning of metacharacters.
-tostop	Allow background jobs to send output to the terminal.
tostop	Stop background jobs that try to send output to the terminal.
sane	Set the terminal characteristics to sensible default values.

You may also set the mapping of a metacharacter by following the name of its corresponding string with its new value. A control character may be indicated by preceding the character with a ^ or by typing a \, followed by the actual control character itself. Here are the common metacharacter strings, together with their meanings:

Option	Meaning
erase	Backspace one character.
kill	Erase all of the current line.
lnext	Don't treat the next character as if it were a special character.
susp	Suspend the current process temporarily.
intr	Terminate (interrupt) the foreground job with no core dump.
quit	Terminate the foreground job with a core dump.
stop	Stop/restart terminal output.
eof	End of input.

FIGURE 2.47

Description of the **stty** command.

see pg 20

Here's an example of **stty** in action:

```
$ stty -a                    ...display current terminal settings.
speed 38400 baud, 24 rows, 80 columns
parenb -parodd cs7 -cstopb -hupcl cread -clocal -crtscts
-ignbrk brkint ignpar -parmrk -inpck istrip -inlcr -igncr icrnl -iuclc
ixon -ixany -ixoff imaxbel
isig iexten icanon -xcase echo echoe echok -echonl -noflsh -tostop
echoctl -echoprt echoke
opost -olcuc onlcr -ocrnl -onocr -onlret -ofill -ofdel
erase  kill  werase  rprnt  flush  lnext  susp  intr  quit  stop  eof
^H    ^U       ^W      ^R      ^O     ^V      ^Z/^Y  ^C       ^\      ^S/^Q  ^D
$ stty erase ^b            ...set erase key to Control-B.
$ stty erase ^h            ...set erase key to Control-H
$ _
```

Invoke **stty** from your shell's start-up file if your favorite metacharacter mappings differ from the norm. **stty** is useful in building shells that need to turn keyboard echoing on and off; an example of such a script is included in Chapter 7. Here's an example that uses **stty** to turn off keyboard echoing:

```
$ stty -echo       ...turn echoing off.
$ stty echo        ...turn echoing back on again.
$ _
```

Note that the last line of input (*stty echo*) would not ordinarily be seen, due to the inhibition of echoing caused by the preceding line!

Now that you've seen how to set your terminal type and alter its settings, it's time to take a look at the two most popular UNIX editors: **vi** and **emacs**.

EDITING A FILE: vi

The two most popular UNIX text editors are **vi** and **emacs**. It's handy to be reasonably proficient in **vi**, which is found on nearly every version of UNIX. By contrast, **emacs** is not shipped with every version (although it is available with *almost* every version). This section and the next contain enough information about each editor to allow you to perform essential editing tasks. They also contain references to other books for obtaining more advanced information.

Starting vi

Bill Joy of Sun Microsystems, Inc., originally developed the **vi** editor for BSD UNIX while he was at the University of California at Berkeley. **vi** proved so popular in the UNIX world that it later was adopted as a standard utility for System V and most other versions of UNIX. Today, **vi** is found on virtually every UNIX system. **vi** stands for visual editor.

To start **vi** with a blank slate, enter the command **vi** without any parameters. To edit an existing file, supply the name of the file as a command line parameter. When your screen is initialized, blank lines are indicated by tildes (~). **vi** then enters *command mode* and awaits instructions. To conserve space, I'll draw screens that are only six lines long. For example, when I executed **vi** with no parameters, I saw the screen shown in Figure 2.48.

```
~

~

~

~

~

~
```

FIGURE 2.48

Example of the screen when starting **vi**.

Command mode is one of the two modes that **vi** may be in; the other mode is called *text entry mode*. Since it's easier to describe command mode when there's some text on the screen, I'll start by describing text entry mode.

Text Entry Mode

To enter text entry mode from command mode, press one of the keys shown in Figure 2.49. Each key enters you into text entry mode in a slightly different way, also shown in the figure. Any text that you enter at this point will be displayed on the screen. To move to the next line, press the *Enter* key. You may use the backspace key to delete the last character that you entered. *You may not move around the screen with the cursor keys when you're in text entry mode.* In text entry mode, cursor keys are interpreted as regular ASCII characters, and their control codes are entered as normal text. This takes many users by surprise, so beware.

Key	Action
i	Text is inserted in front of the cursor.
I	Text is inserted at the beginning of the current line.
a	Text is added after the cursor.
A	Text is added to the end of the current line.
o	Text is added after the current line.
O	Text is inserted before the current line.
R	Text is replaced (overwritten).

FIGURE 2.49

Text input commands in **vi**.

To go from command mode to text entry mode, press the *Esc*, or *Escape*, key.

To enter a short four-line poem, I pressed the **a** key to add characters in text entry mode, entered the text of the poem, and then pressed the *Esc* key to return to command mode. Figure 2.50 shows what I ended up with.

I always remember standing in the rains,

On a cold and damp september,

Brown Autumn leaves were falling softly to the ground,

Like the dreams of a life as they slide away.

~

~

FIGURE 2.50

Editing a file with **vi**.

The next section describes the editing features of vi that allowed me to change this poem to something a little more appealing.

Command Mode

To edit text, you must enter command mode. To travel from text entry mode to command mode, press the *Esc* key. If you accidentally press the *Esc* key when you are in command mode, nothing bad happens. (Depending on your terminal settings, you may hear a beep or bell which tells you that you are already in command mode.)

vi's editing features are selected by pressing special character sequences. For example, to erase a single word, position the cursor at the beginning of a particular word and press the **d** key and then the **w** key (**d**elete **w**ord).

Some editing features require parameters and are accessed by pressing the colon (:) key, followed by the command sequence, followed by the *Enter* key. When the colon key is pressed, the remainder of the command sequence is displayed at the bottom of the screen. In the next example, the Enter key is indicated as *<Enter>*. The characters < and > act as delimiters and should not be entered. For example, to delete lines 1 through 3, you'd enter the following command sequence:

```
:1,3d<Enter>
```

Some editing features, such as the block delete command that I just described, act upon a range of lines. **vi** accepts a couple of formats for a line range:

- To select a single line, state its line number.
- To select a block of lines, state the first and last line numbers inclusively, separated by a comma.

vi allows you to use $ to denote the line number of the last line in the file and . to denote the line number of the line currently containing the cursor. **vi** also allows you to use arithmetic expressions when stating line numbers. For example, the sequence

```
:.,.+2d<Enter>
```

would delete the current line and the two lines that follow it. Figure 2.51 shows some other examples of line ranges.

Range	Selects
1,$	all of the lines in the file
1,.	all of the lines from the start of the file to the current line, inclusive
.,$	all of the lines from the current line to the end of the file, inclusive
.-2	the single line that's two lines before the current line

FIGURE 2.51

Specifying a line range in **vi**.

[handwritten notes: $ – end of file; 0 – start of file; $ – last line; end of line; . – current line; 0 – beginning of line]

In what follows, the term *<range>* indicates a range of lines in the format just described.

Memory Buffer and Temporary Files

As you edit your file, **vi** stores a copy of it in memory and makes the changes you specify to that copy of your file. The disk file is not modified until you explicitly tell **vi** to write the file or you exit **vi** with one of the commands that also writes the file (discussed shortly). For this reason, I recommend that you not spend hours and hours editing a file without either writing or exiting **vi** and getting back in on a regular basis. If your system were to crash (for whatever reason) while you were editing, all changes you made since the last time you either wrote the file or started **vi** would be lost.

Even if the system does crash while you are editing, all may not be lost. **vi** also uses a temporary file to manage the in-memory copy of your file while you edit. (If your file is very large, it won't all be kept in memory at the same time.) **vi** may be able to recover the file using the **–r** argument ("vi –r filename"). Some versions of UNIX will even send you an e-mail message telling you how to recover the contents of the file you were editing. While this is a nice feature, it is much safer to not depend on it and just write the file periodically. Even though today's UNIX systems are much more reliable, it is still wise to save your work often.

Common Editing Features

The most common **vi** editing features can be grouped into the following categories:

- moving the cursor
- deleting text
- replacing text
- pasting text
- searching through text
- searching and replacing text
- saving or loading files
- miscellaneous (including how to quit **vi**)

These categories are described and illustrated in the subsections that follow, using the sample poem that I entered at the start of this section.

Cursor Movement

Figure 2.52 shows the common cursor movement commands. For example, to insert the word "Just" before the word "Like" on the fourth line, I moved the cursor to the fourth line, pressed the **i** key to enter text entry mode, entered the text, and pressed the *Esc* key to return to command mode. To move the cursor to the fourth line, I used the key sequence :4<*Enter*> (or I could have used 4G).

Movement	Key sequence
Up one line	<cursor up> or **k**
Down one line	<cursor down> or **j**
Right one character	<cursor right> or **l** (will not wrap around)
Left one character	<cursor left> or **h** (will not wrap around)
To start of line	^
To end of line	$
Back one word	b
Forward one word	w
Forward to end of current word	e
To top of screen	H
To middle of screen	M
To bottom of screen	L
Down a half screen	*Control*-D

FIGURE 2.52

Cursor movement commands in **vi**.

Forward one screen	*Control*-F
Up a half screen	*Control*-U
Back one screen	*Control*-B
To line *nn*	:*nn*<*Enter*> (*nn***G** also works)
To end of file	**G**

FIGURE 2.52 (*Continued*)

Deleting Text

Figure 2.53 shows the common text deletion commands. For example, to delete the word "always," I typed :1<Enter> to move to the start of line 1, pressed **w** to move forward one word, and then typed the letters **dw**. To delete the trailing "s" on the end of "rains" on the first line, I moved my cursor over the letter "s" and then pressed the **x** key. My poem now looked like Figure 2.54.

Item to delete	Key sequence
Character	Position the cursor over the character and then press x.
Word	Position the cursor at start of the word and then press dw.
Line	Position the cursor anywhere in the line and then press dd. (Typing a number ahead of dd will cause **vi** to delete the specified number of lines, beginning with the current line.)
Current position to end of current line	Press D.
Block of lines	:<*range*>**d**<*Enter*>

FIGURE 2.53

Commands that delete text in **vi**.

I remember standing in the rain,

On a cold and damp september,

Brown Autumn leaves were falling softly to the ground,

Just Like the dreams of a life as they slide away.

~

~

FIGURE 2.54

Our file after deleting some text.

Replacing Text

CW <new word> Esc

Figure 2.55 shows the common text replacement commands. For example, to replace the word "standing" by "walking," I moved to the start of the word and typed the letters **cw**. I then typed the word "walking" and pressed the *Esc* key. To replace the lowercase "s" of "september" by an uppercase "S," I positioned the cursor over the "s," pressed the **r** key, and then pressed the "S" key.

Item to replace	Key sequence
Character	Position the cursor over the character, press **r**, and then type the replacement character.
Word	Position the cursor at start of the word, press **cw**, and then type the replacement text followed by *Esc*.
Line	Position the cursor anywhere in line, press **cc**, and then type the replacement text followed by *Esc*.

FIGURE 2.55

Commands that replace text in **vi**.

I then performed a few more tidy-up operations, replacing "damp" by "dark," "slide" by "slip," and the "L" of "like" by "l". Figure 2.56 shows the final version of the poem.

> I remember walking in the rain,
>
> On a cold and dark September,
>
> Brown Autumn leaves were falling softly to the ground,
>
> Just like the dreams of a life as they slip away.
>
> ~
>
> ~

FIGURE 2.56

Our file after replacing text.

Pasting Text

vi maintains a paste buffer that may be used for copying and pasting text between areas of a file. Figure 2.57 shows the most common pasting operations. For example, to copy the first two lines into the paste buffer and then paste them after the third line, I entered the following two commands:

```
:1,2y
:3pu
```

Action	Key sequence
Copy (yank) lines into paste buffer.	:*<range>***y***<Enter>*
Copy (yank) current line into paste buffer.	Y
Insert (put) paste buffer after current line.	**p** or **:pu***<Enter>* (contents of paste buffer are unchanged)
Insert paste buffer after line *nn*.	:*nn***pu***<Enter>* (contents of paste buffer are unchanged)

FIGURE 2.57

vi commands that paste text.

The poem then looked like Figure 2.58.

I remember walking in the rain,

On a cold and dark September,

Brown Autumn leaves were falling softly to the ground,

I remember walking in the rain,

On a cold and dark September,

Just like the dreams of a life as they slip away.

FIGURE 2.58

Our file after pasting text.

To restore the poem, I typed **:4,5d***<Enter>*.

Searching

vi allows you to search forward and backward through a file, relative to the current line, for a particular substring. Figure 2.59 shows the most common search operations. The trailing "/" and "?" in the first two searches are optional. (**vi** figures out what you mean when you type *Enter*, but using "/" and "?" is a good habit to adopt, since you can add other commands after those symbols, rather than simply hitting *Enter*.)

Action	Key sequence
Search forward from current position for string *sss.*	/*sss*/<Enter>
Search backward from current position for string *sss.*	?*sss*?<Enter>
Repeat last search.	n
Repeat last search in the opposite direction.	N

FIGURE 2.59

Search commands in **vi**.

For example, I searched for the substring "ark" from line 1 of the poem by entering the following commands:

```
:1<Enter>
/ark/<Enter>
```

vi positioned the cursor at the start of the substring "ark" located in the word "dark" on the second line, as shown in Figure 2.60

I remember walking in the rain,

On a cold and dark September,

Brown Autumn leaves were falling softly to the ground,

Just like the dreams of a life as they slip away.

~

~

FIGURE 2.60

Searching in **vi**.

Searching and Replacing

You may perform a global "search-and-replace" operation by using the commands shown in Figure 2.61. For example, to replace every occurrence of the substring "re" by "XXX," I entered the command displayed in Figure 2.62.

Search + Replace

Action	Key sequence
Replace the first occurrence of *sss* on each line with *ttt*.	:*<range>*s/ *sss*/ *ttt*/*<Enter>*
Relace every occurrence of *sss* on each line with *ttt* (global replace).	:*<range>*s/ *sss*/ *ttt*/**g***<Enter>*

FIGURE 2.61

Searching and replacing in **vi**.

\ ~ esc character

I XXXmember walking in the rain,

On a cold and dark September,

Brown Autumn leaves weXXX falling softly to the ground,

Just like the dXXXams of a life as they slip away.

~

EX: :1,$s/re/XXX/g   — search + replace, from line 1 to end of file, "re" with "XXX", globally (all)

FIGURE 2.62

Example of searching and replacing in **vi**.

Saving and Loading Files

Figure 2.63 shows the most common save and load file commands. For example, I saved the poem in a file called "rain.doc" by entering the command displayed in Figure 2.64.

Action	Key sequence
Save file as <name>.	:**w** *<name>* *<Enter>* w! ~ force write (ignore file permissions)
Save file with current name.	:**w***<Enter>*
Save file with current name and exit.	:**wq***<Enter>* (**ZZ** also works)
Save only certain lines to another file.	:*<range>* **w** *<name>* *<Enter>*
Read in contents of another file at current position.	:**r** *<name>* *<Enter>*
Edit file <name> instead of current file.	:**e** *<name>* *<Enter>*
Edit next file on initial command line.	:**n***<Enter>*

FIGURE 2.63

Commands that write to and read from files in **vi**.

> I remember walking in the rain,
>
> On a cold and dark September,
>
> Brown Autumn leaves were falling softly to the ground,
>
> Just like the dreams of a life as they slip away.
>
> ~
>
> :w rain.doc

FIGURE 2.64

Example of writing a buffer to a file in **vi**.

vi tells you how many bytes a file occupies when you save it. Note that you can't accidentally quit **vi** without saving the current file. If you place more than one file on the command line when you first invoke **vi**, **vi** starts by loading up the first file. You may edit the next file by using the key sequence **:n**.

Miscellaneous

Figure 2.65 shows the most common miscellaneous commands, including the commands for quitting **vi**. *Control*-L is particularly useful for refreshing the screen if a message pops up and messes up your screen or if some static interferes with your modem connection during a **vi** session.

Action	Key sequence
Redraw screen.	*Control*-L
Undo the last operation.	**u**
Undo multiple changes made on the current line.	**U**
Join the next line with the current line.	**J**
Repeat the last operation.	**.**
Execute *command* in a subshell and then return to **vi**.	**:!**<*command*> <*Enter*>
Execute *command* in a subshell and read its output into the edit buffer at the current position.	**:r !**<*command*> <*Enter*>
Quit **vi** if work is saved.	**:q**<*Enter*>
Quit **vi** and discard unsaved work.	**:q!**<*Enter*>

FIGURE 2.65

Miscellaneous **vi** commands.

Finally, to quit **vi** after saving the final version of the poem, I typed the command illustrated in Figure 2.66

I remember walking in the rain,

On a cold and dark September,

Brown Autumn leaves were falling softly to the ground,

Just like the dreams of a life as they slip away.

~

:*q*

FIGURE 2.66

Quitting **vi**.

Customizing vi

vi can be customized by setting options that determine its behavior in certain situations. The complete list of available options varies, depending on the version and platform, but we will discuss the most often used options.

The ":set" command is used to set and unset **vi**'s options. After typing ":set all", you will see a list of all the options supported by your version of **vi** and their current settings. Settings are either toggled (on or off) or set to a numeric or string value. The most commonly used options are shown in Figure 2.67.

Option	Description	Default setting
autoindent	When set, subsequent lines you type are indented the same amount as the previous line.	off
ignorecase	When set, during searches and substitutions, the upper- and lowercase characters both satisfy the criteria required for a match.	off
number	When set, **vi** displays line numbers on the left-hand side of the screen.	off
showmode	Causes **vi** to indicate when you are in a text input mode (open, insert, append, or replace), rather than the normal command mode.	off
showmatch	Causes **vi** to briefly move the cursor back to the opening parenthesis or brace when you type the matching closing one.	off

FIGURE 2.67

Commands to customize **vi**.

To turn autoindent on, type ":set autoindent<Enter>". To turn autoindent off again, type ":set noautoindent<Enter>".

Keeping Your Customizations

You don't want to have to type every ":set" command you want every time you enter **vi**. You would quickly decide that most settings weren't worth that much effort. But you can create a special file in your home directory that **vi** recognizes, and you can put your preferred settings there. Then, every time you run **vi**, your settings will be the way you want them (and you can always modify the file as you find others you like).

To set autoindent and ignorecase every time we run **vi**, create a file called ".exrc". (Note that the filename begins with a period: this is a special convention that we will see again later when we look at command shells.) In that file, put the following lines:

```
set autoindent
set ignorecase
set nonumber
```

We don't really need to set "nonumber," since its initial value is "off," but the example shows how you would turn an option off if the default was that it was set.

Now every time you start **vi**, autoindent and ignorecase will be set.

For More Information

For more information about **vi**, I recommend Christian (1988).

Editing a File: emacs

Emacs (Editor MACroS) is a popular editor that is found on many UNIX systems (and for those in which it is not included, a version is probably available for download on the Internet). Emacs had its start in the Lisp-based artificial intelligence community. In 1975, Richard Stallman and Guy Steele wrote the original version that has evolved into the version now distributed for free and in source code form through the Free Software Foundation (FSF). Open Source and the Free Software Foundation are discussed further in Chapter 16.

Starting emacs

To start **emacs** with a blank file, enter the command **emacs** with no parameters. To edit an existing file, specify its name as a command line parameter. Assuming that you supply no parameters, your screen will initially look something like Figure 2.68, depending on your version of **emacs**.

```
GNU Emacs 19.34.1

Copyright (C) 1996 Free Software Foundation, Inc.

Type C-x C-c to exit Emacs.

Type C-h for help; C-x u to undo changes.

Type C-h t for a tutorial on using Emacs.


– Emacs: *scratch*                    (Fundamental) --- All -----------
```

FIGURE 2.68

Example of starting **emacs**.

I'll draw screens that are only about six lines long to conserve space. The second-from-bottom line is called the *mode line* and contains information in the following left-to-right order:

- If the first three dashes contain a **, then the current file has been modified.
- The name that follows "Emacs:" is the name of the current file. If no file is currently loaded, the name *scratch* is used instead.
- The current editing mode is then shown between parentheses. In this case, it's *Fundamental*, which is the standard editing mode.
- The next entry indicates your relative position in the file as a percentage of the entire file. If the file is very small and fits completely on the screen, then *All* is displayed. If you're at the top or the bottom of a file, then *Top* and *Bot* are respectively displayed.

emacs Commands

Unlike **vi**, **emacs** doesn't distinguish between text entry mode and command mode. To enter text, simply start typing. The initial **emacs** welcome banner automatically disappears when you type the first letter. Long lines are not automatically broken, so you must press the *Enter* key when you wish to start a new line. Lines longer than the width of the screen are indicated by a \ character at the end of the screen, with the remainder of the line "wrapped" onto the next line, as shown in Figure 2.69.

```
This is a very long line that illustrates the way that unbroken lines a \

re displayed.

This is a much shorter line.


– Emacs: *scratch*(Fundamental) -- All -----------
```

FIGURE 2.69

How **emacs** wraps long lines.

emacs's editing features are accessed via either a control sequence or a metasequence. I'll indicate control sequences by appending the prefix *Control-* to the name of the key. For example, the sequence

```
Control-H t
```

means "Press and hold the Control key and then press the **H** key. (For control sequences, it doesn't matter whether you use uppercase or lowercase, so I suggest that you use lowercase, as it's easier.) Then release both keys and press the **t** key on its own." Similarly, metasequences use the *Esc* key. For example, the sequence

```
Esc x
```

means "Press the *Esc* key (but don't hold it) and then press the **x** key." The next few sections contain many examples of **emacs** command sequences. If you ever accidentally press *Esc* followed by *Esc*, **emacs** warns you that you're trying to do something advanced and suggests that you press the **n** key to continue. Unless you're a seasoned **emacs** user, it's good advice.

Getting Out of Trouble

Whenever you're learning a new editor, it's quite easy to get lost and confused. Here are a couple of useful command sequences to return you to a sane state:

- The command sequence *Control-*G terminates any **emacs** command, even if it's only partially entered, and returns **emacs** to a state in which it's waiting for a new command.
- The command sequence *Control-*X **1** closes all **emacs** windows except your main file window. This action is useful, as several **emacs** options create a new window to display information, and it's important to know how to close them once you've read their contents.

Getting Help

There are several ways to obtain help information about **emacs**. One of the best ways to get started with **emacs** is to read the self-describing help tutorial. I suggest that you do this before anything else. To read the tutorial, use the command sequence *Control-*H **t**. The tutorial will appear and give you directions on how to proceed.

Leaving emacs

To leave **emacs** and save your file, use *Control-*X *Control-*C. If you haven't saved your file since it was last modified, you'll be asked whether you want to save it.

emacs Modes

emacs supports several different modes for entering text, including Fundamental, Lisp Interaction, and C. Each mode supports special features that are customized for the particular kind of text that you're editing. **emacs** starts in Fundamental mode by default; I'll use that mode during my description of **emacs**. For more information about modes, consult the **emacs** tutorial.

Entering Text

To enter text, simply start typing. For example, Figure 2.70 shows a short four-line poem.

The next section describes the editing features of **emacs** that allowed me to change this poem to something a little better.

There is no need for fear in the night,

You know that your Mommy is there,

To watch over her babies and hold them tight,

When you are in her arms you can feel her sigh all night.

—Emacs: *scratch*   (Fundamental) --- All ---------

FIGURE 2.70

Entering text in **emacs**.

Common Editing Features

The most common **emacs** editing features can be grouped into the following categories:

- moving the cursor
- deleting, pasting, and undoing text
- searching through text
- searching and replacing text
- saving and loading files
- miscellaneous

These categories are described and illustrated in the subsections that follow, using the sample poem that I entered at the start of this section.

Moving the Cursor

Figure 2.71 shows the common cursor movement commands. For example, to insert the words "worry or" before the word "fear" on the first line, I moved the cursor to the first line of the file by typing *Esc* < and then moved forward several words by using the *Esc* **f** sequence. I then typed in the words, which were automatically inserted at the current cursor position.

Deleting, Pasting, and Undoing

Figure 2.72 shows the common deletion commands. Whenever an item is deleted, **emacs** "remembers" it in an individual "kill buffer." A list of kill buffers is maintained

Movement	Key sequence
Up one line	*Control*-P (previous)
Down one line	*Control*-N (next)
Right one character	*Control*-F (forward, wraps around)
Left one character	*Control*-B (backward, wraps around)
To start of line	*Control*-A (a is first letter)
To end of line	*Control*-E (end)
Back one word	*Esc* **b** (back)
Forward one word	*Esc* **f** (forward)
Down one screen	*Control*-V
Up one screen	*Esc* **v**
Start of file	*Esc* <
End of file	*Esc* >

FIGURE 2.71

Moving the cursor in **emacs**.

so that deleted items may be retrieved long after they have been removed from the display. To retrieve the last killed item, use *Control*-Y. After you have typed *Control*-Y, you may type *Esc* **y** to replace the retrieved item with the previously deleted item. Every time you type *Esc* **y**, the retrieved item moves one step back through the kill buffer list.

You may append the next deleted item onto the end of the last kill buffer, rather than create a new buffer, by typing *Esc Control*-W immediately prior to the delete command. This tack is useful if you wish to cut different bits and pieces out of a file and then paste them all together back into one place.

Item to delete	Key sequence
Character before cursor	<delete> key
Character after cursor	*Control*-D
Word before cursor	*Esc* <delete>
Word after cursor	*Esc* **d**
To end of current line	*Control*-K
Sentence	*Esc* **k**

FIGURE 2.72

Deleting, pasting, and undoing in **emacs**.

You may undo editing actions one at a time by typing *Control-X* **u** for each action that you wish to undo.

Figure 2.73 shows a summary of the kill buffer and undo commands.

Action	Key sequence
Insert last kill buffer.	*Control-Y*
Retrieve previous kill.	*Esc* **y**
Append next kill.	*Esc Control-W*
Undo.	*Control-X* **u**

FIGURE 2.73

The kill buffer in **emacs**.

Searching

emacs allows you to perform something called an *incremental search*. To search forward from your current cursor position for a particular sequence of letters, type *Control-S*. The prompt "I-search:" is displayed on the bottom line of the screen, indicating that **emacs** wants you to enter the string that you wish to search for. As you enter the character sequence, **emacs** searches to find the string nearest to your initial cursor position that matches what you've entered so far; in other words, partial substrings are found as you enter the full string. To terminate the search and leave your cursor at its current position, press *Esc*. If you delete characters in the full string before pressing the *Esc* key, **emacs** moves back to the first match of the remaining substring. To repeat a search, don't press *Esc*, but instead press *Control-S* to search forward or *Control-R* to search backward. Figure 2.74 shows a summary of the searching commands.

Action	Key sequence
Search foward for *str*.	*Control-S str*
Search backward for *str*.	*Control-R str*
Repeat last search forward.	*Control-S*
Repeat last search backward.	*Control-R*
Leave search mode.	*Esc*

FIGURE 2.74

Searching in **emacs**.

Search and Replace

To perform a global search and replace, type *Esc* **x**, followed by the string "repl s", followed by *Enter*. **emacs** will prompt you for the string to replace. Enter the string and press *Enter*. **emacs** will prompt you for the replacement string. Enter the string and press *Enter*. **emacs** then performs the global text substitution.

Saving and Loading Files

To save your current work to a file, type *Control-X Control-S*. If your work hasn't been associated with a filename yet, you are prompted for one. Your work is then saved into its associated file.

To edit another file, type *Control-X Control-F*. You are prompted for the new filename. If the file already exists, its contents are loaded into **emacs**; otherwise, the file is created.

To save your file and then quit **emacs**, type *Control-X Control-C*.

Figure 2.75 shows a summary of the save and load commands.

Action	Key sequence
Save current work.	*Control-X Control-S*
Edit another file.	*Control-X Control-F*
Save work and then quit.	*Control-X Control-C*

FIGURE 2.75

Saving and loading files in **emacs**.

Miscellaneous

To redraw the screen, type *Control-L*. To place **emacs** into autowrap mode, which automatically inserts line breaks when words flow past the end of a line, type *Esc* **x** auto-fill-mode and press *Enter*. To leave this mode, repeat the command.

For More Information

For more information about **emacs**, I recommend Roberts (1991).

ELECTRONIC MAIL: mail/mailx

This last section of the current chapter contains information about how to use the UNIX electronic mail system. It's handy to be able to use **mail** from the very beginning, as it's a convenient way to ask the system administrator and other seasoned users questions about UNIX. The name is **mail** on some versions of UNIX and **mailx** on others. For the purposes of this section, I shall refer to both of them as **mail**.

mail has a large number of features, so in accordance with the initial aim of this book, I shall describe only what I consider to be the most useful ones; consult **man** for more information. Figure 2.76 provides a description of **mail**.

Utility: **mail** -H [-f *fileName*] { *userId*]*

mail allows you to send and read mail. If a list of usernames is supplied, mail reads standard input, mails it to the specified users, and then terminates. Usernames can be a combination of the following forms:

- a local user name (i.e., login name)
- an Internet address of the form name@hostname.domain
- a filename
- a mail group

Internet addresses are described in Chapter 9, and mail groups are described shortly.

If no usernames are specified, **mail** assumes that you wish to read mail from a folder. The folder "/var/mail/<username>", where <username> is your own username, is read by default, although this action may be overridden by using the **-f** option. **mail** prompts you with an & and then awaits commands. The **-H** option lists the headers from your mail folder, but does not enter the command mode. A list of the most useful command mode options is contained in the next few pages.

When **mail** is invoked, it begins by reading the contents of the mail start-up file, which may contain statements that customize the **mail** utility. By default, mail reads the file ".mailrc" in your home directory, although the name of this file may be overridden by setting the environment variable MAILRC. Environment variables are discussed in Chapter 4.

There are a large number of customizable options. The most important one is the ability to define mail groups (also sometimes called aliases), which are variables that denote a group of users. To specify a mail group, place a line of the form

```
group name {userId}+
```

into the **mail** start-up file. You may then use *name* as an alias for the specified list of users, either on the command line or in command mode.

FIGURE 2.76

Description of the **mail** command.

Figure 2.77 lists the most useful **mail** commands that are available from command mode.

Command	Meaning
?	Display help.
copy [*mesgList*] [*fileName*]	Copy messages into *fileName* without marking them as "saved."
delete [*mesgList*]	Delete specified messages from the system mailbox.
file [*fileName*]	Read mail from mailbox *fileName*. If no filename is given, display the name of the current mailbox, together with the number of bytes and messages that the mailbox contains.
headers [*message*]	Display a screen of message headers that include *message*.
mail { *userId* }+	Send mail to specified users.
print [*mesgList*]	Display specified messages, using **more**.
quit	Exit **mail**.
reply [*mesgList*]	Mail response to senders of message list.
save [*mesgList*] [*fileName*]	Save specified messages to *fileName*. If no filename is given, save them in a file called "mbox" in your home directory by default.

FIGURE 2.77

mail commands.

In Figure 2.77, *mesgList* describes a collection of one or more mail messages, using the syntax shown in Figure 2.78.

Syntax	Meaning
.	current message
nn	message number *nn*
^	first undeleted message
$	last message
*	all messages
nn-mm	messages numbered *nn* through *mm*, inclusive
user	all messages from user

FIGURE 2.78

Message designators in **mail**.

As you'll see in the examples that follow, these **mail** commands may be invoked by their first letter only (i.e., you can use "p" instead of "print.")

Sending Mail

The easiest way to send mail is to enter the mail directly from the keyboard and terminate the message by pressing *Control-D* on a line of its own:

```
$ mail tim                 ...send some mail to the local user tim.
Subject: Mail Test         ...enter the subject of the mail
Hi Tim,
 How is Amanda doing?
- with best regards from Graham
^D                         ...end of input; standard input is sent as mail.
$ _
```

I wanted to create a mail group called "music" that would allow me to send mail to all of the people in my band. To do this, I created the following file called ".mailrc" in my home directory:

```
group music jeff richard kelly bev
```

This allowed me to send mail as follows:

```
$ mail music               ...send mail to each member of the group.
Subject: Music
Hi guys
 How about a jam sometime?
- with best regards from Graham.
^D                         ...end of input.
$ _
```

For mail messages that are more than just a few lines long, it's a good idea to compose the message via a text editor, save it in a named file, and then redirect the input of **mail** from the file:

```
$ mail music < jam.txt     ...send jam.txt as mail.
$ _
```

To send mail to users on the Internet, use the standard Internet addressing scheme described in Chapter 9.

```
$ mail glass@utdallas.edu < mesg.txt     ...send it.
$ _
```

Reading Mail

When mail is sent to you, it is stored in a file called "/var/mail/<username>", where <username> is your login name. Files that hold mail are termed "mail folders." For example, my own incoming mail is held in the mail folder "/var/mail/glass." To read a mail folder, type **mail**, followed by an optional folder specifier. You are notified if no mail is currently present:

```
$ mail       ...try reading my mail from the default folder.
No mail for glass
$ _
```

If mail is present, **mail** displays a list of the incoming mail headers and then prompts you with an ampersand. Press *Enter* to read each message in order, and press **q**(uit) to exit mail. The mail that you read is appended by default to the mail folder "mbox" in your home directory, which may be read at a later time by typing the following in your home directory:

```
$ mail -f mbox          ...read mail saved in the mbox folder.
```

In the examples that follow, I've deleted some of **mail's** verbose information so that the output would fit into a reasonable amount of space. In the following example, I read two pieces of mail from my friend Tim and then exited **mail**:

```
$ ls -l /var/mail/glass       ...see if mail is present.
-rw---- 1 glass               758 May  2 14:32 /var/mail/glass
$ mail                        ...read mail from default folder.
Mail version SMI 4.0 Thu Oct 11 12:59:09 PDT 1990
Type ? for help.
"/var/mail/glass": 2 messages 2 unread
>U  1 tim@utdallas.edu Sat May  2 14:32 11/382  Mail test
 U  2 tim@utdallas.edu Sat May  2 14:32 11/376  Another
& <Enter>               ...press enter to read message #1.
From tim@utdallas.edu Sat Mar 14 14:32:33 1998
To: glass@utdallas.edu
Subject: Mail test
hi there
& <Enter>               ...press enter to read message #2.
From tim@utdallas.edu Sat Mar 14 14:32:33 1998
To: glass@utdallas.edu
Subject: Another
hi there again
& <Enter>               ...press enter to read next message.
At EOF                  ...there are none!
& q                     ...quit mail.
Saved 2 messages in /home/glass/mbox
$ _
```

To see the headers of the messages in your mail folder without entering **mail's** command mode, use the **-H** option:

```
$ mail -H                     ...peek at my mail folder.
>U  1 tim@utdallas.edu Sat May  2 14:32 11/382  Mail test
 U  2 tim@utdallas.edu Sat May  2 14:32 11/376  Another
$ _
```

To respond to a message after reading it, use the **r**(eply) option. To save a message to a file, use the **s**(ave) option. If you don't specify a message **list**, **mail** selects the current message by default. Here's an example:

```
& 15                              ...read message #15.
From ssmith@utdallas.edu Tue Mar 17 23:27:11 1998
To: glass@utdallas.edu
Subject: Re:  come to a party
The SIGGRAPH party begins Thursday NIGHT at 10:00 PM!!
Hope you don't have to teach Thursday night.
& r                               ...reply to ssmith.
To: ssmith@utdallas.edu
Subject: Re:  come to a party
Thanks for the invitation.
- see you there
^D                                ...end of input.
& s ssmith.party                  ...save the message from ssmith.
"ssmith.party" [New file] 27/1097
& q                               ...quit from mail.
$ _
```

A word of caution is in order: In some mailers, the default "r" replies to the sender and "R" replies to everyone who received the original message. Others are the other way around, with "R" replying to the sender and "r" replying to everyone. Until you know which way your mailer works, be careful with your replies so that you don't annoy everyone on a public distribution list (or worse, say something you didn't intend for public consumption!).

It's quite possible that you'll receive quite a bit of "junk mail"; to delete messages that aren't worth reading, use the d(elete) option:

```
& d1-15        ...delete messages 1 thru 15 inclusive.
& d*           ...delete all remaining messages.
```

Contacting the System Administrator

The system administrator's mailing address is usually "root" or, possibly, "sysadmin." Typically, the alias "postmaster" should direct mail to the person in charge of e-mail-related issues.

CHAPTER REVIEW

Checklist

In this chapter, I described

- how to obtain a UNIX account
- how to log in and out of a UNIX system
- the importance of changing your password
- the function of a shell

- how to run a utility
- how to obtain on-line help
- the special terminal metacharacters
- the most common file-oriented utilities
- two UNIX editors
- how to set up your terminal correctly
- how to send electronic mail

Quiz

1. What is one way that hackers try to break UNIX security?
2. What's the best kind of password?
3. What UNIX command do you use to change the name or location of a file?
4. Is UNIX case sensitive?
5. Name the four most common UNIX command shells.
6. Why are shells better suited than C programs to some tasks?
7. How do you terminate a process?
8. How do you indicate the end of input when entering text from the keyboard?
9. How do you terminate a shell?
10. What term is given to the current location of a process?
11. What attributes does every file have?
12. What is the purpose of groups?
13. How do permission flags relate to directories?
14. Who may change the ownership of a file?

Exercises

2.1 Obtain the Internet mailing address of an acquaintance in another country, and send him or her e-mail. How long does it take to get there? Does the travel time seem reasonable? [level: *easy*]

2.2 Why may a process have only *one* current group? [level: *medium*]

2.3 Design a file security mechanism that alleviates the need for the "set user ID" feature. [level: *hard*]

2.4 Even seemingly trivial inventions such as a flashing cursor and a scrolling window have been granted patents. Many software designers construct programs, only to find that they have unintentionally reinvented someone else's patented invention. Do you think that patents are fair, and if not, can you think of a better mechanism to protect intellectual property? [level: *hard*]

Project

Send mail to the system administrator and set up two new groups for yourself. Experiment with the group-related utilities and explore the permissions system. [level: easy]

CHAPTER 3

UNIX Utilities for Power Users

MOTIVATION

In addition to the common file-oriented UNIX utilities, there are plenty of other utilities that process text, schedule commands, archive files, and sort files. This chapter contains descriptions and examples of the utilities that will be most useful in increasing your productivity.

PREREQUISITES

In order to understand this chapter, you should already have read the first two chapters of the text. It also helps if you have access to a UNIX system so that you can try out the various utilities that I discuss.

OBJECTIVES

In this chapter, I'll show you how to use about 30 useful utilities.

PRESENTATION

The information herein is presented in the form of several sample UNIX sessions.

UTILITIES

The chapter introduces the following utilities, listed in alphabetical order:

at	crypt	gzip	tar
awk	diff	ln	time
biff	dump	mount	tr
cmp	egrep	od	ul

compress	fgrep	perl	umount
cpio	find	sed	uncompress
cron	grep	sort	uniq
crontab	gunzip	su	whoami

In addition to describing these standard UNIX utilities, this chapter will also provide a brief introduction to Perl, because, while it does not come with many versions of UNIX, it has become an integral part of many UNIX environments.

INTRODUCTION

The utilities we will be discussing may be logically grouped into sets as shown in Figure 3.1. We will examine each group in turn, describing its members and illustrating their operational worked-out examples. Note that, while most of these utilities exist in all versions of UNIX, this is not true for every version.

Section	Utilities
filtering files	egrep, fgrep, grep, uniq
sorting files	sort
comparing files	cmp, diff
archiving files	tar, cpio, dump
searching for files	find
scheduling commands	at, cron, crontab
programmable text processing	awk, perl
hard and soft links	ln
switching users	su
checking for mail	biff
transforming files	compress, crypt, gunzip, gzip, sed, tr, ul, uncompress
looking at raw file contents	od
mounting file systems	mount, umount
identifying shells	whoami
document preparation	nroff, spell, style, troff
timing execution of a command	time

FIGURE 3.1

Advanced UNIX utilities.

FILTERING FILES

There are many times when it's handy to be able to filter the contents of a file, selecting only those lines that match certain criteria. The utilities that do this include the following:

- **egrep**, **fgrep**, and **grep**, which filter out all lines that do not contain a specified pattern
- **uniq**, which filters out duplicate adjacent lines

Filtering Patterns: `egrep`/`fgrep`/`grep`

egrep, **fgrep**, and **grep** allow you to scan a file and filter out all of the lines that don't contain a specified pattern. These utilities are similar in nature, the main difference being the kind of text patterns that each can filter. I'll begin by describing the common features of all three and then finish up by illustrating the differences. Figure 3.2 provides a brief synopsis of the three utilities.

[handwritten annotations: Show context ☆ / grep -n -B3 -A3 pattern filename or wildcard --color=auto]

Utility: **grep** -hilnvw *pattern* {*fileName*}*

fgrep -hilnvwx *string* {*fileName*}*

egrep -hilnvw *pattern* {*fileName*}*

[handwritten annotations on right side:
-n - include line #
-i - ignore case
-l - list file names only
-v - include all lines that don't match
-w - match whole words only
-m 1 - show only one line per file
-c - show count of matches for each file]

grep (Global or Get Regular Expression and Print) is a utility that allows you to search for a pattern in a list of files. If no files are specified, it searches standard input instead. *pattern* may be a regular expression. All lines that match the pattern are displayed as standard output. If more than one file is specified, each matching line that is displayed is preceded by the name of the file in which it is found, unless the **-h** option is specified. The **-n** option causes each such matching line to be preceded by its line number. The **-i** option causes the case of the patterns to be ignored. The **-l** option displays a list of the files that contain the specified pattern. The **-v** option causes **grep** to display all of the lines that don't match the pattern. The **-w** option restricts matching to whole words only. **fgrep** (Fixed grep) is a fast version of **grep** that can search only for fixed strings. **egrep** (Extended grep) supports matching with regular expressions. **fgrep** also supports the **-x** option, which outputs only lines that are exactly equal to *string*.

For more information about regular expressions, consult the Appendix.

FIGURE 3.2

Description of the **grep** command.

To obtain a list of all the lines in a file that contain a string, follow **grep** by the string and the name of the file to scan. Here's an example:

```
$ cat grepfile                    ...list the file to be filtered.
Well you know it's your bedtime,
So turn off the light,
Say all your prayers and then,
Oh you sleepy young heads dream of wonderful things,
Beautiful mermaids will swim through the sea,
And you will be swimming there too.
$ grep the grepfile               ...search for the word "the".
So turn off the light,
Say all your prayers and then,
Beautiful mermaids will swim through the sea,
And you will be swimming there too.
$ _
```

Notice that words that contain the string "the" also satisfy the matching condition. Here's an example of the use of the **-w** and **-n** options:

```
$ grep -wn the grepfile  ...be more particular this time!
2:So turn off the light,
5:Beautiful mermaids will swim through the sea,
$ _
```

To display only those lines in a file that don't match, use the **-v** option, as shown in the following example:

```
$ grep -wnv the grepfile      ...reverse the filter.
1:Well you know it's your bedtime,
3:Say all your prayers and then,
4:Oh you sleepy young heads dream of wonderful things,
6:And you will be swimming there too.
$ _
```

If you specify more than one file to search, each line that is selected is preceded by the name of the file in which it appears. In the following example, I searched my C source files for the string "x". (See Chapter 4 for a description of the shell file wildcard mechanism.)

```
$ grep -w x *.c        ...search all files ending in ".c".
a.c:test (int x)
fact2.c:long factorial (x)
fact2.c:int x;
fact2.c:  if ((x == 1) ,, (x == 0))
fact2.c:    result = x * factorial (x-1);
$ grep -wl x *.c    ...list names of matching files.
a.c
fact2.c
$ _
```

fgrep, **grep**, and **egrep** all support the options that I've described so far. However, they differ from each other in that each allows a different kind of text pattern to be matched, as shown in Figure 3.3. For information about regular expressions and extended regular expressions, consult the Appendix.

Utility	Kind of pattern that may be searched for
fgrep	fixed string only
grep	regular expression
egrep	extended regular expression

FIGURE 3.3

The differences in the **grep** command family.

To illustrate the use of **grep** and **egrep** regular expressions, let's examine a piece of text followed by the lines of text that would match various regular expressions. When **egrep** or **grep** is used, regular expressions should be placed inside single quotes to prevent interference from the shell. In the examples shown in Figures 3.4 and 3.5, the portion of each line of this sample text that satisfies the regular expression is italicized:

```
Well you know it's your bedtime,
So turn off the light,
Say all your prayers and then,
Oh you sleepy young heads dream of wonderful things,
Beautiful mermaids will swim through the sea,
And you will be swimming there too.
```

Matching Patterns

grep Pattern	Lines that match
.nd	Say all your prayers *and* then, *any char before*
	Oh you sleepy young heads dream of *wonderful* things,
	And you will be swimming there too.
^.nd	*And* you will be swimming there too. *Lines that begin with*

FIGURE 3.4

Pattern matching in **grep**.

sw.*ng	And you will be *swimming* there too.
[A-D]	*Beautiful* mermaids will swim through the sea,
	And you will be swimming there too.
\.	And you will be swimming there too.
a.	*Say* all your prayers and then,
	Oh you sleepy young he*ads* dream of wonderful things,
	Be*au*tiful mermaids will swim through the sea,
a.$	Beautiful mermaids will swim through the *sea,*
[a-m]nd	Say all your prayers *and* then,
[^a-m]nd	Oh you sleepy young heads dream of *wond*erful things, *And* you will be swimming there too.

FIGURE 3.4   (*Continued*)

egrep Pattern	Lines that match
s.*w	Oh you *sleepy young heads dream of* wonderful things, Beautiful mermaids *will swim* through the sea, And you will be *sw*imming there too.
s.+w	Oh you *sleepy young heads dream of* wonderful things, Beautiful mermaids *will sw*im through the sea,
off|will	So turn *off* the light, Beautiful mermaids *will* swim through the sea, And you *will* be swimming there too.
im*ing	And you will be swimming there too.
im?ing	<no matches>

FIGURE 3.5

Pattern matching in **egrep**.

Removing Duplicate Lines: `uniq`

The **uniq** utility displays a file with all of its identical adjacent lines replaced by a single occurrence of the repeated line. **uniq** works as shown in Figure 3.6.

Utility: **uniq** -c -number [*inputfile* [*outputfile*]]

uniq is a utility that displays its input file with all adjacent repeated lines collapsed to a single occurrence of the repeated line. If an input file is not specified, standard input is read. The **-c** option causes each line to be preceded by the number of occurrences that were found. If *number* is specified, then *number* fields of each line are ignored.

FIGURE 3.6

Description of the **uniq** command.

Here's an example:

```
$ cat animals            ...look at the test file.
cat   snake
monkey   snake
dolphin   elephant
dolphin   elephant
goat   elephant
pig   pig
pig   pig
monkey   pig
$ uniq animals           ...filter out duplicate adjacent lines.
cat   snake
monkey   snake
dolphin   elephant
goat   elephant
pig   pig
monkey   pig
$ uniq -c animals        ...display a count with the lines.
   1 cat   snake
   1 monkey   snake
   2 dolphin   elephant
   1 goat   elephant
   2 pig   pig
   1 monkey   pig
$ uniq -1 animals        ...ignore first field of each line.
cat   snake
dolphin   elephant
pig   pig
$ _
```

SORTING FILES: sort

The **sort** utility sorts a file in ascending or descending order on the basis of one or more *sort fields*. It works as shown in Figure 3.7. Individual fields are ordered lexicographically,

---

Utility: **sort** -tc -r { *sortField*-bfMn }* { *fileName* }*

sort is a utility that sorts lines in one or more files on the basis of specified sorting criteria. By default, lines are sorted into ascending order. The **-r** option specifies descending order instead. Input lines are split into fields separated by spaces or tabs. To specify a different field separator, use the **-t** option. By default, all of a line's fields are considered when the sort is being performed. This convention may be overridden by specifying one or more sort fields, whose format is described later in this section. Individual sort fields may be customized by following them with one or more options. The **-f** option causes **sort** to ignore the case of the field. The **-M** option sorts the field in month order. The **-n** option sorts the field in numeric order. The **-b** option ignores leading spaces.

FIGURE 3.7

Description of the **sort** command.

which means that corresponding characters are compared on the basis of their ASCII value. (See 'man ascii' for a list of all characters and their corresponding values.) Two consequences of this convention are that an uppercase letter is "less" than its lowercase equivalent and a space is "less" than a letter. In the following example, I sorted a text file in ascending order and descending order, using the default ordering rule:

```
$ cat sortfile                    ...list the file to be sorted.
jan   Start chapter 3   10th
Jan   Start chapter 1   30th
 Jan  Start chapter 5   23rd
 Jan  End chapter 3   23rd
Mar   Start chapter 7   27
 may  End chapter 7   17th
Apr   End Chapter 5   1
 Feb  End chapter 1   14
$ sort sortfile                   ...sort it.
 Feb  End chapter 1   14
 Jan  End chapter 3   23rd
 Jan  Start chapter 5   23rd
 may  End chapter 7   17th
Apr   End Chapter 5   1
Jan   Start chapter 1   30th
Mar   Start chapter 7   27
jan   Start chapter 3   10th
$ sort -r sortfile                ...sort it in reverse order.
jan   Start chapter 3   10th
Mar   Start chapter 7   27
Jan   Start chapter 1   30th
Apr   End Chapter 5   1
```

```
may   End chapter 7   17th
Jan   Start chapter 5   23rd
Jan   End chapter 3   23rd
Feb   End chapter 1   14
$ _
```

To sort on a particular field, you must specify the starting field number with the use of a + prefix, followed by the noninclusive stop field number with a - prefix. Field numbers start at index 0. If you leave off the stop field number, all fields following the start field are included in the sort. In the next example, I sorted the text file from the preceding example on the first field only, which is the number zero:

```
$ sort +0 -1 sortfile              ...sort on first field only.
 Feb   End chapter 1   14
 Jan   End chapter 3   23rd
 Jan   Start chapter 5   23rd
 may   End chapter 7   17th
Apr   End Chapter 5   1
Jan   Start chapter 1   30th
Mar   Start chapter 7   27
jan   Start chapter 3   10th
$ _
```

Note that the leading spaces were counted as being part of the first field, which resulted in a strange sorting sequence. In addition, I would have preferred the months to be sorted in correct order, with "Jan" before "Feb", and so forth. The **-b** option ignores leading blanks and the **-M** option sorts a field on the basis of month order. Here's an example that worked better:

```
$ sort +0 -1 -bM sortfile          ...sort on first month.
 Jan   End chapter 3   23rd
 Jan   Start chapter 5   23rd
Jan   Start chapter 1   30th
jan   Start chapter 3   10th
 Feb   End chapter 1   14
Mar   Start chapter 7   27
Apr   End Chapter 5   1
 may   End chapter 7   17th
$ _
```

The sample text file was correctly sorted by month, but the dates were still out of order. You may specify multiple sort fields on the command line to deal with this problem. The **sort** utility first sorts all of the lines on the basis of the first sort specifier and then uses the second sort specifier to order lines that the first specifier judged to be equal in rank. Therefore, to sort the sample text file by month and date, it had to first be sorted using the first field and then sorted again using the fifth field. In addition, the fifth field had to be sorted numerically with the **-n** option.

```
$ sort +0 -1 -bM +4 -n sortfile
jan   Start chapter 3   10th
 Jan   End chapter 3   23rd
 Jan   Start chapter 5   23th
Jan   Start chapter 1   30th
 Feb   End chapter 1   14
Mar   Start chapter 7   27
Apr   End Chapter 5   1
 may   End chapter 7   17th
$ _
```

Characters other than spaces often delimit fields. For example, the "/etc/passwd" file contains user information stored in fields separated by colons. You may use the **-t** option to specify an alternative field separator. In the following example, I sorted a file based on fields separated by : characters.

```
$ cat sortfile2                          ...look at the test file.
jan:Start chapter 3:10th
Jan:Start chapter 1:30th
Jan:Start chapter 5:23rd
Jan:End chapter 3:23rd
Mar:Start chapter 7:27
may:End chapter 7:17th
Apr:End Chapter 5:1
Feb:End chapter 1:14
$ sort -t: +0 -1 -bM +2 -n sortfile2     ...colon delimiters.
jan:Start chapter 3:10th
Jan:End chapter 3:23rd
Jan:Start chapter 5:23rd
Jan:Start chapter 1:30th
Feb:End chapter 1:14
Mar:Start chapter 7:27
Apr:End Chapter 5:1
may:End chapter 7:17th
$ _
```

sort contains several other options that are too detailed to describe here. I suggest that you use the **man** utility to find out more about them.

COMPARING FILES

The following two utilities allow you to compare the contents of two files:

- **cmp,** which finds the first byte that differs between two files
- **diff,** which displays all the differences and similarities between two files

Testing for Sameness: cmp

The **cmp** utility determines whether two files are the same. It works as shown in Figure 3.8. In the following example, I compared the files "lady1," "lady2," and "lady3":

```
$ cat lady1                ...look at the first test file.
Lady of the night,
I hold you close to me,
And all those loving words you say are right.
$ cat lady2                ...look at the second test file.
Lady of the night,
I hold you close to me,
And everything you say to me is right.
$ cat lady3                ...look at the third test file.
Lady of the night,
I hold you close to me,
And everything you say to me is right.
It makes me feel,
I'm so in love with you.
Even in the dark I see your light.
$ cmp lady1 lady2          ...files differ.
lady1 lady2 differ: char 48, line 3
$ cmp lady2 lady3          ...file2 is a prefix of file3.
cmp: EOF on lady2
$ cmp lady3 lady3          ...files are exactly the same.
$ _
```

Utility: **cmp** -ls *fileName1 fileName2* [*offset1*] [*offset2*]

cmp is a utility that tests two files for equality. If *fileName1* and *fileName2* are exactly the same, then **cmp** returns the exit code 0 and displays nothing; otherwise, **cmp** returns the exit code 1 and displays the offset and line number of the first mismatched byte. If one file is a prefix of the other, then the EOF message for the file that is shorter is displayed. The **-l** option displays the offset and values of all mismatched bytes. The **-s** option causes all output to be inhibited. The optional values *offset1* and *offset2* specify the starting offsets in *fileName1* and *fileName2*, respectively, and that the comparison should begin.

FIGURE 3.8

Description of the **cmp** command.

The **-l** option displays the byte offset and values of every byte that doesn't match. Here's an example:

```
$ cmp -l lady1 lady2   ...display bytes that don't match.
   48 141 145
   49 154 166
```

```
   . . .
   81 145   56
   82   40   12
cmp: EOF on lady2         ...lady2 is smaller than lady1.
$ _
```

File Differences: `diff`

The **diff** utility compares two files and displays a list of editing changes that would convert the first file into the second file. It works as shown in Figure 3.9. There are three kinds of editing changes: adding lines (a), changing lines (c), and deleting lines (d). Figure 3.10 shows the format that **diff** uses to describe each kind of edit. Note that

---

Utility: **diff** -i -d*flag fileName1 fileName2*

diff is a utility that compares two files and outputs a description of their differences. (See the rest of this section for information on the format of this output.) The **-i** flag makes **diff** ignore the case of the lines. The **-D** option causes **diff** to generate output designed for the C preprocessor.

FIGURE 3.9

Description of the **diff** command.

Additions

firstStart **a** secondStart, secondStop

> lines from the second file to add to the first file

Deletions

firstStart, firstStop **d** lineCount

< lines from the first file to delete

Changes

firstStart, firstStop **c** secondStart, secondStop

< lines in the first file to be replaced

--

> lines in the second file to be used for the replacement

FIGURE 3.10

The meaning of output produced by **diff**.

firstStart and *firstStop* denote line numbers in the first file and *secondStart* and *secondStop* denote line numbers in the second file.

In the following example, I compared several text files in order to observe their differences:

```
$ cat lady1              ...look at the first test file.
Lady of the night,
I hold you close to me,
And all those loving words you say are right.
$ cat lady2              ...look at the second test file.
Lady of the night,
I hold you close to me,
And everything you say to me is right.
$ cat lady3              ...look at the third test file.
Lady of the night,
I hold you close to me,
And everything you say to me is right.
It makes me feel,
I'm so in love with you.
Even in the dark I see your light.
$ cat lady4              ...look at the fourth test file.
Lady of the night,
I'm so in love with you.
Even in the dark I see your light.
$ diff lady1 lady2                     ...compare lady1 and lady2.
3c3
< And all those loving words you say are right.
---
> And everything you say to me is right.
$ diff lady2 lady3                     ...compare lady2 and lady3.
3a4,6
> It makes me feel,
> I'm so in love with you.
> Even in the dark I see your light.
$ diff lady3 lady4                     ...compare lady3 and lady4.
2,4d1
< I hold you close to me,
< And everything you say to me is right.
< It makes me feel,
$ _
```

The **-D** option of **diff** is useful for merging two files into a single file that contains C pre-processor directives. Each version of the file can be re-created by using the **cc** compiler with suitable options and macro definitions. The following commands are illustrative:

```
$ diff -Dflag lady3 lady4    ...look at the output.
Lady of the night,
#ifndef flag                       ...preprocessor directive.
I hold you close to me,
And everything you say to me is right.
```

```
It makes me feel,
#endif flag                       ...preprocessor directive.
I'm so in love with you.
Even in the dark I see your light.
$ diff -Dflag lady2 lady4 > lady.diff   ...store output.
$ cc -P lady.diff                 ...invoke the preprocessor.
$ cat lady.i                      ...look at the output.
Lady of the night,
I hold you close to me,
And everything you say to me is right.
$ cc -Dflag -P lady.diff          ...obtain the other version.
$ cat lady.i                      ...look at the output.
Lady of the night,
I'm so in love with you.
Even in the dark I see your light.
$ _
```

FINDING FILES: **find**

The **find** utility can do much more than simply locate a named file; it can perform actions on a set of files that satisfy specific conditions. For example, you can use **find** to erase all of the files belonging to a user *tim* that haven't been modified for three days. Figure 3.11 provides a formal description of **find**, and Figure 3.12 describes the syntax of *expression*.

Utility: **find** *pathList expression*

The **find** utility recursively descends through *pathList* and applies *expression* to every file. The syntax of *expression* is described in Figure 3.12.

FIGURE 3.11

Description of the **find** command.

Expression	Value/action
-name *pattern*	True if the file's name matches *pattern*, which may include the shell metacharacters *, [ ], and ?.
-perm *oct*	True if the octal description of the file's permission flags are exactly equal to *oct*.
-type *ch*	True if the type of the file is *ch* (b = block, c = char, etc.).

FIGURE 3.12

find expressions.

-user *userId*	True if the owner of the file is *userId*.
-group *groupId*	True if the group of the file is *groupId*.
-atime *count*	True if the file has been accessed within *count* days.
-mtime *count*	True if the contents of the file have been modified within *count* days.
-ctime *count*	True if the contents of the file have been modified within *count* days or if any of the file's attributes have been altered.
-exec *command*	True if the exit code from executing *command* is 0. *command* must be terminated by an escaped semicolon (\;). If you specify {} as a command line argument, it is replaced by the name of the current file.
-print	Prints out the name of the current file and returns true.
-ls	Displays the current file's attributes and returns true.
-cpio *device*	Writes the current file in cpio format to *device* and returns true. (cpio format is defined in a subsequent section.)
!*expression*	Returns the logical negation of *expression*.
expr1 [-a] *expr2*	Short-circuits and. If *expr1* is false, it returns false and *expr2* is not executed. If *expr1* is true, it returns the value of *expr2*.
expr1 -o *expr2*	Short-circuits or. If *expr1* is true, it returns true. If *expr 1* is false, it returns the value of *expr2*.

FIGURE 3.12   (*Continued*)

Here are some examples of **find** in action:

```
$ find . -name '*.c' -print          ...print c source files in the
                                      ...current directory or any of
                                      ...its subdirectories.
./proj/fall.89/play.c
./proj/fall.89/referee.c
./proj/fall.89/player.c
./rock/guess.c
./rock/play.c
./rock/player.c
./rock/referee.c
$ find . -mtime 14 -ls       ...ls modified files
                             ...during the last 14 days.
```

```
-rw-r--r--  1 glass  cs 14151 May  1 16:58 ./stty.txt
-rw-r--r--  1 glass  cs    48 May  1 14:02 ./myFile.doc
-rw-r--r--  1 glass  cs    10 May  1 14:02 ./rain.doc
-rw-r--r--  1 glass  cs 14855 May  1 16:58 ./tset.txt
-rw-r--r--  1 glass  cs 47794 May  2 10:56 ./mail.txt
$ find . -name '*.bak' -ls -exec rm {} \;
                    ...ls and then remove all files
                    ...that end with ".bak".
-rw-r--r--  1 glass  cs     9 May 16 12:01 ./a.bak
-rw-r--r--  1 glass  cs     9 May 16 12:01 ./b.bak
-rw-r--r--  1 glass  cs 15630 Jan 26 00:14 ./s6/gosh.bak
-rw-r--r--  1 glass  cs 18481 Jan 26 12:59 ./s6/gosh2.bak
$ find . \( -name '*.c' -o -name '*.txt' \) -print
                    ...print the names of all files that
                    ...end in ".c" or ".txt".
./proj/fall.89/play.c
./proj/fall.89/referee.c
./proj/fall.89/player.c
./rock/guess.c
./rock/play.c
./rock/player.c
./rock/referee.c
./stty.txt
./tset.txt
./mail.txt
$ _
```

ARCHIVES

There are a number of reasons that you might want to save some files to a secondary storage medium such as a disk or tape:

- for daily, weekly, or monthly backups
- for transport between nonnetworked UNIX sites
- for posterity

UNIX possesses a family of three utilities, each of which has its own strengths and weaknesses, that allow you to archive files. In my opinion, it would be much better to have a single, powerful, general-purpose archive utility, but no standard utility has these qualities. Here is a list of the utilities, together with a brief description of them:

- **cpio,** which allows you to save directory structures to a single backup volume. **cpio** is handy for saving small quantities of data, but the single-volume restriction makes it useless for large backups.
- **tar,** which allows you to save directory structures to a single backup volume. **tar** is especially designed to save files to tape, so it always archives files at the end of

the storage medium. As with **cpio**, the single-volume restriction makes **tar** unusable for large backups.

- **dump,** which allows you to save a file system to multiple backup volumes. **dump** is especially designed for doing total and incremental backups, but restoring individual files with it is tricky. (*Note*: In many System V-based versions of UNIX, the **ufsdump** program is equivalent to **dump**.)

Copying Files: `cpio`

The **cpio** utility allows you to create and access special cpio-format files. These special-format files are useful for backing up small subdirectories, thereby avoiding the heavy-duty **dump** utility. Unfortunately, the **cpio** utility is unable to write special-format files to multiple volumes, so the entire backup file must be able to reside on a single storage medium. If it cannot, use the **dump** utility instead. **cpio** works as shown in Figure 3.13.

Utility: **cpio** -ov

  cpio -idtu *patterns*

  cpio -pl *directory*

cpio allows you to create and access special cpio-format files.

The **-o** option takes a list of filenames from standard input and creates a cpio-format file that contains a backup of the files with those filenames. The **-v** option causes the name of each file to be displayed as it's copied.

The **-i** option reads a cpio-format file from standard input and re-creates all of the files from the input channel whose names match a specified pattern. By default, older files are not copied over younger files. The **-u** option causes unconditional copying. The **-d** option causes directories to be created if they are needed during the copy process. The **-t** option causes a table of contents to be displayed instead of performing the copy.

The **-p** option takes a list of filenames from standard input and copies the contents of the files to a named directory. This option is useful for copying a subdirectory to another place, although most uses of **-p** can be performed more easily using the **cp** utility with the **-r** (recursive) option. Whenever possible, the **-l** option creates links instead of actually making physical copies.

FIGURE 3.13

Description of the **cpio** command.

To demonstrate the **-o** and **-i** options, I created a backup version of all the C source files in my current directory, deleted the source files, and then restored them. The commands for doing this are as follows:

```
$ ls -l *.c            ...list the files to be saved.
-rw-r--r--  1 glass     172 Jan  5 19:44 main1.c
-rw-r--r--  1 glass     198 Jan  5 19:44 main2.c
-rw-r--r--  1 glass     224 Jan  5 19:44 palindrome.c
-rw-r--r--  1 glass     266 Jan  5 23:46 reverse.c
$ ls *.c | cpio -ov > backup   ...save in "backup".
main1.c
main2.c
palindrome.c
reverse.c
3 blocks
$ ls -l backup           ...examine "backup".
-rw-r--r--  1 glass    1536 Jan  9 18:34 backup
$ rm *.c                  ...remove the original files.
$ cpio -it < backup       ...restore the files.
main1.c
main2.c
palindrome.c
reverse.c
3 blocks
$ ls -l *.c            ...confirm their restoration.
-rw-r--r--  1 glass     172 Jan  5 19:44 main1.c
-rw-r--r--  1 glass     198 Jan  5 19:44 main2.c
-rw-r--r--  1 glass     224 Jan  5 19:44 palindrome.c
-rw-r--r--  1 glass         266 Jan  5 23:46 reverse.c
$ _
```

To back up all of the files, including subdirectories, that match the pattern "*.c", use the output from the **find** utility as the input to **cpio**. The **-depth** option of **find** recursively searches for matching patterns. In the following example, note that I escaped the * character in the argument to the **-name** option so that it was not expanded by the shell:

```
$ find . -name \*.c -depth -print | cpio -ov > backup2
main1.c
main2.c
palindrome.c
reverse.c
tmp/b.c
tmp/a.c
3 blocks
$ rm -r *.c              ...remove the original files.
$ rm tmp/*.c             ...remove the lower-level files.
$ cpio -it < backup2     ...restore the files.
main1.c
main2.c
```

```
palindrome.c
reverse.c
tmp/b.c
tmp/a.c
3 blocks
$ _
```

To demonstrate the **-p** option, I used the **find** utility to obtain a list of all the files in my current directory that were modified in the last two days and then copied those files into the parent directory. Without using the **-l** option, the files were physically copied, resulting in a total increase in disk usage of 153 blocks. Using the **-l** option, however, linked the files, resulting in no disk usage at all. This is shown in the following example:

```
$ find . -mtime -2 -print | cpio -p ..      ...copy
153 blocks
$ ls -l ../reverse.c         ...look at the copied file.
-rw-r--r--  1 glass       266 Jan  9 18:42 ../reverse.c
$ find . -mtime -2 -print | cpio -pl ..    ...link
0 blocks
$ ls -l ../reverse.c         ...look at the linked file.
-rw-r--r--  2 glass       266 Jan  7 15:26  ../reverse.c
$ _
```

Tape Archiving: `tar`

The **tar** utility was designed specifically for maintaining an archive of files on a magnetic tape. When you add a file to an archive file using **tar**, the file is *always* placed at the end of the archive file, since you cannot modify the middle of a file that is stored on tape. If you're not archiving files to a tape, I suggest that you use the **cpio** utility instead. Figure 3.14 shows how **tar** works.

Utility: **tar** -cfrtuvx [*tarFileName*] *fileList*

tar allows you to create and access special tar-format archive files. The **-c** option creates a tar-format file. The name of the tar-format file is "/dev/rmt0" by default. (This may vary with different versions of UNIX.) However, the default may be overriden by setting the $TAPE environment variable or by using the **-f** option followed by the required filename. The **-v** option encourages verbose output. The **-x** option allows you to extract named files, and the **-t** option generates a table of contents. The **-r** option unconditionally appends the listed files to the archived file. The **-u** option appends only files that are more recent than those already archived. If the file list contains directory names, the contents of the directories are appended or extracted recursively.

FIGURE 3.14

Description of the **tar** command.

In the following example, I saved all of the files in the current directory to the archive file "tarfile":

```
$ ls                           ...look at the current directory.
main1*      main2       palindrome.c      reverse.h
main1.c     main2.c     palindrome.h      tarfile
main1.make  main2.make  reverse.c         tmp/
$ ls tmp                       ...look in the "tmp" directory.
a.c         b.c
$ tar -cvf tarfile .    ...archive the current directory.
a ./main1.c 1 blocks
a ./main2.c 1 blocks
...
a ./main2 48 blocks
a ./tmp/b.c 1 blocks
a ./tmp/a.c 1 blocks
$ ls -l tarfile    ...look at the archive file "tarfile".
-rw-r--r--  1 glass    65536 Jan 10 12:44 tarfile
$ _
```

To obtain a table of contents of a **tar** archive, use the **-t** option, as shown in the following example:

```
$ tar -tvf tarfile          ...look at the table of contents.
rwxr-xr-x   496/62         0 Jan 10 12:44 1998 ./
rw-r--r--   496/62       172 Jan 10 12:41 1998 ./main1.c
rw-r--r--   496/62       198 Jan  9 18:36 1998 ./main2.c
...
rw-r--r--   496/62     24576 Jan  7 15:26 1998 ./main2
rwxr-xr-x   496/62         0 Jan 10 12:42 1998 ./tmp/
rw-r--r--   496/62         9 Jan 10 12:42 1998 ./tmp/b.c
rw-r--r--   496/62         9 Jan 10 12:42 1998 ./tmp/a.c
$
```

To unconditionally append a file to the end of a tar archive, use the **-r** option followed by a list of files or directories to append. Notice in the following example that the tar archive ended up holding two copies of "reverse.c":

```
$ tar -rvf tarfile reverse.c            ...unconditionally append.
a reverse.c 1 blocks
$ tar -tvf tarfile                  ...look at the table of contents.
rwxr-xr-x   496/62         0 Jan 10 12:44 1998 ./
rw-r--r--   496/62       172 Jan 10 12:41 1998 ./main1.c
...
rw-r--r--   496/62       266 Jan  9 18:36 1998 ./reverse.c
...
rw-r--r--   496/62       266 Jan 10 12:46 1998 reverse.c
$ _
```

To append a file only if it isn't in the archive or if it has been modified since it was last archived, use the **-u** option instead of **-r**. In the following example, note that "reverse.c" was not archived, because it hadn't been modified:

```
$ tar -rvf tarfile reverse.c      ...unconditionally append.
a reverse.c 1 blocks
$ tar -uvf tarfile reverse.c      ...conditionally append.
$ _
```

To extract a file from an archive file, use the **-x** option followed by a list of files or directories. If a directory name is specified, it is recursively extracted, as shown in the following example:

```
$ rm tmp/*                  ...remove all files from "tmp".
$ tar -vxf tarfile ./tmp ...extract archived "tmp" files.
x ./tmp/b.c, 9 bytes, 1 tape blocks
x ./tmp/a.c, 9 bytes, 1 tape blocks
$ ls tmp                    ...confirm restoration.
a.c         b.c
$ _
```

Unfortunately, **tar** doesn't support pattern matching of the name list, so to extract files that match a particular pattern, be crafty and use **grep** as part of the command sequence, like this:

```
$ tar -xvf tarfile `tar -tf tarfile | grep '.*\.c'`
x ./main1.c, 172 bytes, 1 tape blocks
x ./main2.c, 198 bytes, 1 tape blocks
x ./palindrome.c, 224 bytes, 1 tape blocks
x ./reverse.c, 266 bytes, 1 tape blocks
x ./tmp/b.c, 9 bytes, 1 tape blocks
x ./tmp/a.c, 9 bytes, 1 tape blocks
$ _
```

If you change into another directory and then extract files that were stored using relative pathnames, the names are interpreted as being relative to the current directory. In the following example, I restored "reverse.c" from the previously created tar file to a new directory "tmp2":

```
$ mkdir tmp2                    ...create a new directory.
$ cd tmp2                       ...move there.
$ tar -vxf ../tarfile reverse.c   ...restore single file.
x reverse.c, 266 bytes, 1 tape blocks
x reverse.c, 266 bytes, 1 tape blocks
$ ls -l                         ...confirm restoration.
total 1
-rw-r--r--  1 glass       266 Jan 10 12:48 reverse.c
$ _
```

Note that each copy of "reverse.c" overwrote the previous one, so that the latest version was the one that was left intact.

Incremental Backups: `dump` and `restore`

The dump and restore commands came from the Berkeley version of UNIX, but have been added to most other versions. (In many System V-based versions of UNIX, they are **ufsdump** and **ufsrestore**.) Here's a system administrator's typical backup strategy:

- Perform a weekly total-file system backup.
- Perform a daily incremental backup, storing only those files that were changed since the last incremental backup.

This kind of backup strategy is supported nicely by the **dump** and **restore** utilities.

dump works as shown in Figure 3.15. Here's an example that performs a level-0 dump of the file system on /dev/da0 to the tape drive /dev/rmt0 with verification:

```
$ dump 0 fv /dev/rmt0 /dev/da0
```

Utility: **dump** [*level*] [f *dumpFile*] [v] [w] *fileSystem*

    dump [*level*] [f *dumpFile*] [v] [w] {*fileName*}+

The **dump** utility has two forms. The first form copies files from the specified file system to *dumpFile*, which is "/dev/rmt0" by default. (This may vary in different versions of UNIX.) If the dump level is specified as n, then all of the files that have been modified since the last dump at a lower level than n are copied. For example, a level-0 dump will always dump all files, whereas a level-2 dump will dump all of the files modified since the last level-0 or level-1 dump. If no dump level is specified, the dump level is set to 9. The **v** option causes **dump** to verify each volume of the medium after it is written. The **w** option causes **dump** to display a list of all the file systems that need to be dumped, instead of performing a backup.

    The second form of **dump** allows you to specify the names of files to be dumped.

    Both forms prompt the user to insert or remove the dump medium when necessary. For example, a large system dump to a tape drive often requires an operator to remove a full tape and replace it with an empty one.

    When a dump is performed, information about the dump is recorded in the "/etc/dumpdates" file for use by future invocations of **dump**.

FIGURE 3.15

Description of the **dump** command.

The **restore** utility allows you to restore files from a **dump** backup, and it works as shown in Figure 3.16. In the following example, I used **restore** to extract a couple of previously saved files from the dump device "/dev/rmt0":

```
$ restore -x f /dev/rmt0 wine.c hacking.c
```

Utility: **restore** -irtx [f *dumpFile*] {*fileName*}*

The **restore** utility allows you to restore a set of files from a previous dump file. If *dumpFile* is not specified, "/dev/rtm0" is used by default. (Again, this could vary in different versions of UNIX.) The **-r** option causes every file on *dumpFile* to be restored into the current directory, so use this option with care. The **-t** option causes a table of contents of *dumpFile* to be displayed, instead of restoring any files. The **-x** option causes **restore** to restore only those files with specified filenames from *dumpFile*. If a filename is the name of a directory, its contents are recursively restored.

    The **-i** option causes **restore** to read the table of contents of *dumpFile* and then enter an interactive mode that allows you to choose the files that you wish to restore. For more information on this interactive mode, consult **man restore**.

FIGURE 3.16

Description of the **restore** command.

SCHEDULING COMMANDS

The following two utilities allow you to schedule commands to be executed at a later point in time:

- **crontab**, which allows you to create a scheduling table that describes a series of jobs to be executed on a periodic basis
- **at**, which allows you to schedule jobs to be executed on a one-time basis

Periodic Execution: `cron/crontab`

The **crontab** utility allows you to schedule a series of jobs to be executed on a periodic basis. It works as shown in Figure 3.17. To use **crontab**, you must prepare an input file that contains lines of the format

```
minute   hour   day   month   weekday   command
```

Utility: **crontab** *crontabName*

    crontab -ler [*userName*]

crontab is the user interface to the UNIX cron system. When used without any options, the crontab file (see text) called *crontabName* is registered, and its commands are executed according to the specified timing rules. The **-l** option lists the contents of a registered crontab file. The **-e** option edits and then registers a registered crontab file. The **-r** option unregisters a registered crontab file. The **-l, -e,** and **-r** options may be used by a superuser to access another user's crontab file by supplying the user's name as an optional argument. The anatomy of a crontab file is described in the text.

FIGURE 3.17

Description of the **crontab** command.

Field	Valid value
minute	0–59
hour	0–23
day	1–31
month	1–12
weekday	1–7 (1 = Mon, 2 = Tue, 3 = Wed, 4 = Thu, 5 = Fri, 6 = Sat, 7 = Sun)
command	any UNIX command

FIGURE 3.18

crontab field meanings and values.

where the values of each field are as shown in Figure 3.18. Files of this nature are called "crontab" files. Whenever the current time matches a line's description, the associated command is executed by the shell specified in the SHELL environment variable. A Bourne shell is used if this variable is not set. If any of the first five fields contains an asterisk (*) instead of a number, the field always matches. The standard output of the command is automatically sent to the user via **mail**. Any characters following a % are copied into a temporary file and used as the command's standard input. Here is a sample crontab file that I created in my home directory and called "crontab.cron":

```
$ cat crontab.cron             ...list the crontab file.
0   8   *   *   1     echo Happy Monday Morning
*   *   *   *   *     echo One Minute Passed > /dev/tty1
```

```
30 14 1  * 1      mail users % Jan Meeting At 3pm
$ _
```

The first line mails me "Happy Monday Morning" at 8:00 A.M. every Monday. The next line echoes "One Minute Passed" every minute to the device "/dev/tty1", which happens to be my terminal. The last line sends mail to all users on January 1 at 2:30 P.M. to remind them of an impending meeting.

A single process called "cron" is responsible for executing the commands in registered crontab files in a timely fashion. The process is started when the UNIX system is booted and does not stop until the UNIX system is shut down. Copies of all registered crontab files are stored in the directory "/var/spool/cron/crontabs".

To register a crontab file, use the **crontab** utility with the name of the crontab file as the single argument:

```
$ crontab crontab.cron    ...register the crontab file.
$ _
```

If you already have a registered crontab file, the new one is registered in place of the old one. To list the contents of your registered crontab, use the **-l** option. To list someone else's registered crontab file, add his or her, name as an argument. Only a superuser can use this option. In the following example, note that one of my previously registered crontab file entries triggered coincidentally after I used the **crontab** utility:

```
$ crontab -l    ...list contents of current crontab file.
0  8  *  *  1      echo Happy Monday Morning
*  *  *  *  *      echo One Minute Passed > /dev/tty1
30 14  1  * 1      mail users % Jan Meeting At 3pm
$ One Minute Passed  - ...output from one crontab command.
$ _
```

To edit your crontab file and then resave it, use the **-e** option. To unregister a crontab file, use the **-r** option:

```
$ crontab -r            ...un-register my crontab file.
$ _
```

A superuser may create files called "cron.allow" and "cron.deny" in the "/var/spool/cron" directory in order, respectively, to enable and inhibit individual users from using the crontab facility. Each file consists of a list of user names on separate lines. If neither of the files exists, only a superuser may use **crontab**. If "cron.deny" is empty and "cron.allow" doesn't exist, all users may use **crontab**.

One-Time Execution: `at`

The **at** utility allows you to schedule one-time commands or scripts. It works as shown in Figure 3.19. In the following example, I scheduled an **at** script to send a message to

---

Utility: **at** -csm *time* [*date* [, *year*]] [+*increment*] [*script*]

      at -r {*jobId*}+

      at -l {*jobId*}*

at allows you to schedule one-time commands or scripts. It supports a flexible format for time specification. The **-c** and **-s** options allow you to specify that commands are run by a C shell and Bourne shell, respectively. The **-m** option instructs **at** to send you mail when the job is completed. If no script name is specified, **at** takes a list of commands from standard input. The **-r** option removes the specified jobs from the **at** queue, and the **-l** option lists the pending jobs. A job is removed from the **at** queue after it has executed.

    time is in the format HH or HHMM, followed by an optional am/pm specifier, and *date* is spelled out using the first three letters of the day or month. The keyword "now" may be used in place of the time sequence. The keywords "today" and "tomorrow" may be used in place of *date*. If no *date* is supplied, then **at** uses the following rules:

- If *time* is after the current time, then *date* is assumed to be "today".
- If *time* is before the current time, then *date* is assumed to be "tomorrow".

The stated time may be augmented by an *increment*, which is a number, followed by "minutes", "hours", "days", "weeks", "months", or "years".

    A script is executed by the shell specified by the SHELL environment variable, or a Bourne shell if this variable is not set. All standard output from an **at** script is mailed to the user.

FIGURE 3.19

Description of the **at** command.

my terminal "/dev/tty1":

```
$ cat at.csh          ...look at the script to be scheduled.
#! /bin/csh
echo at done > /dev/tty1         ...echo output to terminal.
$ date                           ...look at current time.
Sat Jan 10 17:27:42 CST 1998
$ at now + 2 minutes at.csh      ...schedule script to
                                  ... execute in 2 minutes
job 2519 at Sat Jan 10 17:30:00 1998
$ at -l                          ...look at the at schedule.
```

```
      2519 a        Sat Jan 10 17:30:00 1998
$ _
at done                 ...output from scheduled script.
$ at 17:35 at.csh       ...schedule the script again.
job 2520 at Sat Jan 10 17:35:00 1998
$ at -r 2520                 ...deschedule.
$ at -l                      ...look at the at schedule.
$ _
```

Here are some more examples of valid **at** time formats:

```
0934am Sep 18 at.csh
9:34 Sep 18 , 1994 at.csh
11:00pm tomorrow at.csh
now + 1 day at.csh
9pm Jan 13 at.csh
10pm Wed at.csh
```

If you omit the command name, **at** displays a prompt and then waits for a list of commands to be entered from standard input. To terminate the command list, press *Control*-D. Here's an example:

```
$ at 8pm      ...enter commands to be scheduled from keyboard.
at> echo at done > /dev/ttyp1
at> ^D            ...end-of-input.
job 2530 at Sat Jan 10 17:35:00 1998
$ _
```

You may program a script to reschedule itself by calling **at** within the script:

```
$ cat at.csh        ...a script that reschedules itself.
#! /bin/csh
date > /dev/tty1
# Reschedule script
at now + 2 minutes at.csh
$ _
```

A superuser may create files called "at.allow" and "at.deny" in the "/var/spool/cron" directory in order, respectively, to enable and to inhibit individual users from using the **at** facility. Each file should consist of a list of user names on separate lines. If neither file exists, only a superuser may use **at**. If "at.deny" is empty and "at.allow" doesn't exist, all users may use **at**.

PROGRAMMABLE TEXT PROCESSING: awk

The **awk** utility scans one or more files and performs an action on all of the lines that match a particular condition. The actions and conditions are described by an **awk** program and range from the very simple to the complex.

awk got its name from the combined first letters of its authors' surnames: Aho, Weinberger, and Kernighan. It borrows its control structures and expression syntax from the C language. If you already know C, then learning **awk** is quite straightforward.

awk is a comprehensive utility—so comprehensive, in fact, that there's a book on it! Because of this, I've attempted to describe only the main features and options of **awk**; however, I think that the material I describe in this section will allow you to write a good number of useful **awk** applications. Figure 3.20 provides a synopsis of **awk**.

Utility: **awk** -Fc [-f *fileName*] *program* {*variable=value*}*{*fileName*}*

awk is a programmable text-processing utility that scans the lines of its input and performs actions on every line that matches a particular criterion. An **awk** program may be included on the command line, in which case it should be surrounded by single quotes; alternatively, it may be stored in a file and specified using the **-f** option. The initial values of variables may be specified on the command line. The default field separators are tabs and spaces. To override this default, use the **-F** option followed by the new field separator. If no filenames are specified, **awk** reads from standard input.

FIGURE 3.20

Description of the **awk** command.

awk Programs

An **awk** program may be supplied on the command line, but it's much more common to place it in a text file and specify the file using the **-f** option. If you decide to place an **awk** program on the command line, surround it by single quotes.

When **awk** reads a line, it breaks it into fields that are separated by tabs or spaces. The field separator may be overridden by using the **-F** option, as you'll see later in the section. An **awk** program is a list of one or more commands of the form

```
[ condition ] [ \{ action \} ]
```

where *condition* is either

- the special token BEGIN or END

or

- an expression involving any combination of logical operators, relational operators, and regular expressions and *action* is a list of one or more of the following kinds of C-like statements, terminated by semicolons:

- **if** (conditional) statement [**else** statement]
- **while** (conditional) statement
- **for** (expression; conditional; expression) statement
- **break**
- **continue**
- variable=expression
- **print** [list of expressions] [> expression]
- **printf** format [, list of expressions] [> expression]
- **next** (skips the remaining patterns on the current line of input)
- **exit** (skips the rest of the current line)
- { list of statements }

action is performed on every line that matches *condition*. If *condition* is missing, *action* is performed on every line. If *action* is missing, then all matching lines are simply sent to standard output. The statements in an **awk** program may be indented and formatted using spaces, tabs, and newlines.

[handwritten annotations: $0 — entire line / $1 — first field of current line / $n — n'th field of current line / NF — number of fields on current line]

Accessing Individual Fields

The first field of the current line may be accessed by $1, the second by $2, and so forth. $0 stands for the entire line. The built-in variable **NF** is equal to the number of fields in the current line. In the following example, I ran a simple **awk** program on the text file "float" to insert the number of fields into each line:

```
$ cat float                       ...look at the original file.
Wish I was floating in blue across the sky,
My imagination is strong,
And I often visit the days
When everything seemed so clear.
Now I wonder what I'm doing here at all...
$ awk '{ print NF, $0 }' float    ...execute the command.
9 Wish I was floating in blue across the sky,
4 My imagination is strong,
6 And I often visit the days
5 When everything seemed so clear.
9 Now I wonder what I'm doing here at all...
$ _
```

Begin and End

The special condition BEGIN is triggered before the first line is read, and the special condition END is triggered after the last line has been read. When expressions are listed in a print statement, no space is placed between them, and a newline is printed by default. The built-in variable FILENAME is equal to the name of the input file. In the following example, I ran a program that displayed the first, third, and last fields of every line:

```
$ cat awk2                      ...look at the awk script.
BEGIN { print "Start of file:", FILENAME }
{ print $1 $3 $NF }      ...print 1st, 3rd, and last field.
END { print "End of file" }
$ awk -f awk2 float             ...execute the script.
Start of file: float
Wishwassky,
Myisstrong,
Andoftendays
Whenseemedclear.
Nowwonderall...
End of file
$ _
```

Operators

When commas are placed between the expressions in a **print** statement, a space is printed. All of the usual C operators are available in **awk**. The built-in variable **NR** contains the line number of the current line. In the next example, I ran a program that displayed the first, third, and last fields of lines 2..3 of "float":

```
$ cat awk3                  ...look at the awk script.
NR > 1 && NR < 4 { print NR, $1, $3, $NF }
$ awk -f awk3 float         ...execute the script.
2 My is strong,
3 And often days
$ _
```

Variables

awk supports user-defined variables. There is no need to declare a variable. A variable's initial value is a null string or zero, depending on how you use the variable. In the next example, the program counted the number of lines and words in a file as it echoed the lines to standard output:

```
$ cat awk4                  ...look at the awk script.
BEGIN { print "Scanning file" }
{
 printf "line %d: %s\n", NR, $0;
 lineCount++;
 wordCount += NF;
}
END { printf "lines = %d, words = %d\n", lineCount, wordCount }
$ awk -f awk4 float     ...execute the script.
Scanning file
```

```
line 1: Wish I was floating in blue across the sky,
line 2: My imagination is strong,
line 3: And I often visit the days
line 4: When everything seemed so clear.
line 5: Now I wonder what I'm doing here at all...
lines = 5, words = 33
$ _
```

Control Structures

awk supports most of the standard C control structures. In the following example, I printed the fields in each line backward:

```
$ cat awk5               ...look at the awk script.
{
  for (i = NF; i >= 1; i--)
    printf "%s ", $i;
    printf "\n";
}
$ awk -f awk5 float      ...execute the script.
sky, the across blue in floating was I Wish
strong, is imagination My
days the visit often I And
clear. so seemed everything When
all... at here doing I'm what wonder I Now
$ _
```

Extended Regular Expressions

The condition for matching lines can be an extended regular expression, which is defined in the appendix of this book. Regular expressions must be placed between slashes (/). In the next example, I displayed all of the lines that contained a "t" followed by an "e," with any number of characters in between (for the sake of clarity, I've italicized the character sequences of the output lines that satisfied the condition):

```
$ cat awk6               ...look at the script.
/t.*e/ { print $0 }
$ awk -f awk6 float      ...execute the script.
Wish I was floating in blue across the sky,
And I often visit the days
When everything seemed so clear.
Now I wonder what I'm doing here at all...
$ _
```

Condition Ranges

A condition may be two expressions separated by a comma. In this case, **awk** performs *action* on every line from the first line that matches the first condition to the next line that satisfies the second condition, as shown in the following example:

```
$ cat awk7                    ...look at the awk script.
/strong/ , /clear/ { print $0 }
$ awk -f awk7 float    ...execute the script.
My imagination is strong,
And I often visit the days
When everything seemed so clear.
$ _
```

Field Separators

If the field separators are not spaces, use the **-F** option to specify the separator character. In the next example, I processed a file whose fields were separated by colons:

```
$ cat awk3                    ...look at the awk script.
NR > 1 && NR < 4 { print $1, $3, $NF }
$ cat float2                  ...look at the input file.
Wish:I:was:floating:in:blue:across:the:sky,
My:imagination:is:strong,
And:I:often:visit:the:days
When:everything:seemed:so:clear.
Now:I:wonder:what:I'm:doing:here:at:all...
$ awk -F: -f awk3 float2     ...execute the script.
My is strong,
And often days
$ _
```

Built-In Functions

awk supports several built-in functions, including exp (), log (), sqrt (), int (), and substr ().
The first four functions work just like their standard C counterparts. The substr (str, x,
y) function returns the substring of *str* from the *x*th character and extending *y* characters. Here's an example of the operation of, and output from, these functions:

```
$ cat test                 ...look at the input file.
1.1 a
2.2 at
3.3 eat
4.4 beat
$ cat awk8                 ...look at the awk script.
{
 printf "$1 = %g ", $1;
 printf "exp = %.2g ", exp ($1);
 printf "log = %.2g ", log ($1);
 printf "sqrt = %.2g ", sqrt ($1);
 printf "int = %d ", int ($1);
 printf "substr (%s, 1, 2) = %s\n", $2, substr($2, 1, 2);
}
$ awk -f awk8 test         ...execute the script.
$1 = 1.1 exp = 3 log = 0.095 sqrt = 1 int = 1 substr (a, 1, 2) = a
```

```
$1 = 2.2 exp = 9 log = 0.79 sqrt = 1.5 int = 2 substr (at, 1, 2) = at
$1 = 3.3 exp = 27 log = 1.2 sqrt = 1.8 int = 3 substr (eat, 1, 2) = ea
$1 = 4.4 exp = 81 log = 1.5 sqrt = 2.1 int = 4 substr (beat, 1, 2) = be
$ _
```

HARD AND SOFT LINKS: ln

The **ln** utility allows you to create both hard links and symbolic (soft) links between files. It works as shown in Figure 3.21. In the following example, I added a new label,

---

Utility: **ln** -sf *original* [*newLink*]

　　　ln -sf {*original*} + *directory*

ln is a utility that allows you to create hard links or symbolic (soft) links to existing files.

To create a hard link between two regular files, specify the existing file label as the *original* filename and the new file label as *newLink*. Both labels will then refer to the same physical file, and this arrangement will be reflected in the hard link count shown by the **ls** utility. The file can then be accessed via either label and is removed from the file system only when all of its associated labels are deleted. If *newLink* is omitted, the last component of *original* is assumed. If the last argument is the name of a directory, then hard links are made from that directory to all of the specified original filenames. Hard links may not span file systems.

The **-s** option causes **ln** to create symbolic links, resulting in a new file that contains a pointer (by name) to another file. A symbolic link may span file systems, since there is no explicit connection to the destination file other than the name. Note that if the file pointed to by a symbolic link is removed, the symbolic link file still exists, but will result in an error if accessed.

The **-f** option allows a superuser to create a hard link to a directory.

For further information about how hard links are represented in the file system, see the discussion of UNIX file systems in Chapter 14.

FIGURE 3.21

Description of the **ln** command.

"hold", to the file referenced by the existing label, "hold.3" (note that the hard link count field was incremented from one to two when the hard link was added and then back to one again when the hard link was deleted):

```
$ ls -l              ...look at the current directory contents.
total 3
-rw-r--r--  1 glass          124 Jan 12 17:32 hold.1
-rw-r--r--  1 glass           89 Jan 12 17:34 hold.2
-rw-r--r--  1 glass           91 Jan 12 17:34 hold.3
$ ln hold.3 hold      ...create a new hard link.
$ ls -l              ...look at the new directory contents.
total 4
-rw-r--r--  2 glass           91 Jan 12 17:34 hold
-rw-r--r--  1 glass          124 Jan 12 17:32 hold.1
-rw-r--r--  1 glass           89 Jan 12 17:34 hold.2
-rw-r--r--  2 glass           91 Jan 12 17:34 hold.3
$ rm hold            ...remove one of the links.
$ ls -l              ...look at the updated directory contents.
total 3
-rw-r--r--  1 glass          124 Jan 12 17:32 hold.1
-rw-r--r--  1 glass           89 Jan 12 17:34 hold.2
-rw-r--r--  1 glass           91 Jan 12 17:34 hold.3
$ _
```

A series of hard links may be added to an existing directory if the directory's name is specified as the second argument of **ln**. In the following example, I created links in the "tmp" directory to all of the files matched by the pattern "hold.*":

```
$ mkdir tmp           ...create a new directory.
$ ln hold.* tmp   ...create a series of links in "tmp".
$ ls -l tmp           ...look at the contents of "tmp".
total 3
-rw-r--r--  2 glass          124 Jan 12 17:32 hold.1
-rw-r--r--  2 glass           89 Jan 12 17:34 hold.2
-rw-r--r--  2 glass           91 Jan 12 17:34 hold.3
$ _
```

A hard link may not be created from a file on one file system to a file on a different file system. To get around this problem, create a *symbolic* link instead. A symbolic link may span file systems. To create a symbolic link, use the **-s** option of **ln**. In the following example, I tried to create a hard link from my home directory to the file "/usr/include/stdio.h". Unfortunately, that file was on a different file system, so **ln** failed. However, **ln** with the **-s** option succeeded. When **ls** is used with the **-F** option, symbolic links are preceded by the character @. By default, **ls** displays the contents of the symbolic link; to obtain information about the file that the link refers to, use the **-L** option.

```
$ ln /usr/include/stdio.h stdio.h        ...hard link.
ln: stdio.h: Cross-device link
$ ln -s /usr/include/stdio.h stdio.h    ...symbolic link.
$ ls -l stdio.h                          ...examine the file.
lrwxrwxrwx  1 glass  20 Jan 12 17:58 stdio.h -> /usr/include/stdio.h
$ ls -F                                  ...@ indicates a sym. link.
stdio.h@
```

```
$ ls -1L stdio.h              ...look at the link itself.
-r--r--r--  1 root        1732 Oct 13  1998 stdio.h
$ cat stdio.h                        ...look at the file.
# ifndef FILE
#define     BUFSIZ    1024
#define SBFSIZ   8
extern      struct    iobuf {
...
$ _
```

IDENTIFYING SHELLS: `whoami`

Let's say that you come across a vacated terminal and there's a shell prompt on the screen. Obviously, someone was working on the UNIX system and forgot to log off. You wonder curiously who that person was. To solve the mystery, you can use the **whoami** utility, shown in Figure 3.22, which displays the name of the owner of a shell. For example, when I executed **whoami** at my terminal, I saw this:

```
$ whoami
glass
$ _
```

Utility: **whoami**

Displays the name of the owner of a shell.

FIGURE 3.22

Description of the **whoami** command.

SUBSTITUTING A USER: `su`

A lot of people think that **su** abbreviates "superuser," but it doesn't. Instead, it abbreviates "substitute user" and allows you to create a subshell owned by another user. It works as shown in Figure 3.23. Here's an example of the use of **su**:

```
$ whoami          ...find out my current user ID.
glass
$ su              ...substitute user.
Password: <enter super-user password here>
$ whoami          ...confirm my current user ID has changed.
root
$ ... perform super-user tasks here
$ ^D              ...terminate the child shell.
$ whoami          ...confirm current user ID is restored.
glass
$ _
```

Utility: **su** [-] [*userName*] [*args*]

su creates a temporary shell with *userName's* real and effective user and group IDs. If *userName* is not specified, "root" is assumed, and the new shell's prompt is set to a pound sign (#) as a reminder. While you're in the subshell, you are effectively logged on as that user; when you terminate the shell with a *Control*-D, you are returned to your original shell. Of course, you must know the other user's password to use this utility. The SHELL and HOME environment variables are set from *userName's* entry in the password file. If *userName* is not "root", the USER environment variable is also set. The new shell does not go through its login sequence unless the - option is supplied. All other arguments are passed as command-line arguments to the new shell.

FIGURE 3.23

Description of the **su** command.

CHECKING FOR MAIL: `biff`

The UNIX shells check for incoming mail periodically. This means that several minutes may pass between the receipt of mail at your mailbox and the shell's notification to your terminal. To avoid this delay, you may enable instant mail notification by using the **biff** utility, which works as shown in Figure 3.24. Here's an example of **biff**:

```
$ biff          ...display current biff setting.
biff is n
$ biff y         ...enable instant mail notification.
$ biff          ...confirm new biff setting.
biff is y
$ _
```

Utility: **biff** [y|n]

The **biff** utility allows you to enable and disable instant mail notification. To see your current biff setting, use **biff** with no parameters. Use **y** to enable instant notification and **n** to disable it. Why is this utility called **biff**? The woman at the University of California at Berkeley who wrote the utility for BSD UNIX named it after her dog Biff, who always barked when the mailman brought the mail.

FIGURE 3.24

Description of the **biff** command.

TRANSFORMING FILES

The following utilities, among others, perform a transformation on the contents of a file:

- **compress/uncompress** and **gzip/gunzip**, which convert a file into a space-efficient intermediate format and then back again. These utilities are useful for saving disk space.
- **crypt**, which encodes a file so that other users can't understand it.
- **sed**, a general-purpose programmable stream editor that edits a file according to a previously prepared set of instructions.
- **tr**, which maps characters from one set to another. This utility is useful for performing simple mappings, such as converting a file from uppercase to lowercase.
- **ul**, which converts embedded underline sequences in a file to a form suitable for a particular terminal.

Compressing Files: `compress/uncompress` and `gzip/gunzip`

The **compress** utility encodes a file into a more compact format, to be decoded later with the use of the **uncompress** utility. The two utilities work as shown in Figure 3.25.

Utility: **compress** -cv {*fileName*}+

   uncompress -cv {*fileName*}+

compress replaces a file with its compressed version, appending a ".Z" suffix. The **-c** option sends the compressed version to standard output rather than overwriting the original file. The **-v** option displays the amount of compression that takes place.

   uncompress reverses the effect of **compress**, re-creating the original file from its compressed version.

FIGURE 3.25

Description of the **compress** and **uncompress** commands.

compress is useful for reducing your disk space and packing more files into an archived file. Here's an example:

```
$ ls -l palindrome.c reverse.c   ...examine the originals.
-rw-r--r-- 1 glass              224 Jan 10 13:05 palindrome.c
-rw-r--r-- 1 glass              266 Jan 10 13:05 reverse.c
$ compress -v palindrome.c reverse.c    ...compress them.
palindrome.c: Compression: 20.08% -- replaced with palindrome.c.Z
reverse.c: Compression: 22.93%   -- replaced with reverse.c.Z
$ ls -l palindrome.c.Z reverse.c.Z
-rw-r--r-- 1 glass              179 Jan 10 13:05 palindrome.c.Z
-rw-r--r-- 1 glass              205 Jan 10 13:05 reverse.c.Z
$ uncompress -v *.Z              ...restore the originals.
palindrome.c.Z:   -- replaced with palindrome.c
```

```
reverse.c.Z:        -- replaced with reverse.c
$ ls -l palindrome.c reverse.c            ...confirm.
-rw-r--r--  1 glass              224 Jan 10 13:05 palindrome.c
-rw-r--r--  1 glass              266 Jan 10 13:05 reverse.c
$ _
```

The **compress** and **uncompress** utilities incorporate an algorithm that was already patented at the time the utilities were written (although many were unaware of the fact). When the owner began to defend the patent, either a royalty fee had to be paid for the use of the two utilities or they had to be removed from systems. Many UNIX vendors chose to adopt the GNU utility known as **gzip**, which works in much the same way as **compress**, but uses a different, unrestricted algorithm. **gzip** and **gunzip** are described in Figure 3.26. The following example of their use is virtually identical to that shown earlier for **compress** and **uncompress**:

```
$ ls -l palindrome.c reverse.c
 -rw-r--r--  1 ables            224 Jul  1 14:14 palindrome.c
 -rw-r--r--  1 ables            266 Jul  1 14:14 reverse.c
$ gzip -v palindrome.c  reverse.c
palindrome.c:             34.3% -- replaced with palindrome.c.gz
reverse.c:                39.4% -- replaced with reverse.c.gz
$ ls -l palindrome.c.gz reverse.c.gz
 -rw-r--r--     1 ables        178 Jul  1 14:14 palindrome.c.gz
 -rw-r--r--     1 ables        189 Jul  1 14:14 reverse.c.gz
$ gunzip -v *.gz
palindrome.c.gz:          34.3% -- replaced with palindrome.c
reverse.c.gz:             39.4% -- replaced with reverse.c
$ ls -l palindrome.c reverse.c
 -rw-r--r--     1 ables        224 Jul  1 14:14 palindrome.c
 -rw-r--r--     1 ables        266 Jul  1 14:14 reverse.c
$ _
```

Utility: **gzip** -cv {*fileName*}+

     gunzip -cv {*fileName*}+

gzip replaces a file with its compressed version, appending a ".gz" suffix. The **-c** option sends the compressed version to standard output rather than overwriting the original file. The **-v** option displays the amount of compression that takes place. **gunzip** can uncompress a file created by either **gzip** or **compress**.

    Gzip and gunzip are available from the GNU Web site

```
http://www.gnu.org/software/gzip/gzip.html
```

You may download them if they don't already exist on your system.

FIGURE 3.26

Description of the **gzip** and **gunzip** commands.

File Encryption: `crypt`

The **crypt** utility creates a key-encoded version of a text file. The only way to retrieve the original text from the encoded file is by executing **crypt** with the same key that was used to encode the file. Figure 3.27 shows how it works. Here's an example of the use of **crypt**:

```
$ cat sample.txt                              ...list original.
Here's a file that will be encrypted.
$ crypt agatha < sample.txt > sample.crypt
                                   ...agatha is the key.
$ rm sample.txt                        ...remove original.
$ crypt agatha < sample.crypt > sample.txt    ...decode.
$ cat sample.txt  ...list original.
Here's a file that will be encrypted.
$ _
```

Utility: **crypt** [*key*]

crypt performs one of following two duties:

- If the standard input is regular text, an encoded version of the text is sent to standard output, using *key* as the encoding key.
- If the standard input is encoded text, a decoded version of the text is sent to standard output, using *key* as the decoding key.

If *key* is not specified, **crypt** prompts you for a key that you must enter from your terminal. The key that you enter is not echoed. If you supply *key* on the command line, beware: A **ps** listing will show the value of *key*.

    crypt uses a coding algorithm similar to the one that was used in the German "Enigma" machine.

FIGURE 3.27

Description of the **crypt** command.

Stream Editing: `sed`

The stream **ed**itor utility **sed** scans one or more files and performs an editing action on all of the lines that match a particular condition. The actions and conditions may be stored in a **sed** script. **sed** is useful for performing simple, repetitive editing tasks.

    sed is a fairly comprehensive utility. Because of this, I've attempted to describe only its main features and options; however, I think that the material I describe in this section will allow you to write a good number of useful **sed** scripts.

Figure 3.28 provides a synopsis of **sed**.

Utility: **sed** [-e *script*] [-f *scriptfile*] {*fileName*}*

sed is a utility that edits an input stream according to a script that contains editing commands. Each editing command is separated by a newline and describes an action and a line or range of lines to perform the action upon. A **sed** script may be stored in a file and executed by using the **-f** option. If a script is placed directly on the command line, it should be surrounded by single quotes. If no files are specified, **sed** reads from standard input.

FIGURE 3.28

Description of the **sed** command.

sed Commands

A **sed** script is a list of one or more of the commands shown in Figure 3.29, separated by newlines. The following rules apply to the use of **sed** commands:

1. *address* must be either a line number or a regular expression. A regular expression selects all of the lines that match the expression. You may use $ to select the last line.

Command syntax	Meaning
address **a** *text*	Append *text* after the line specified by *address*.
addressRange **c** *text*	Replace the text specified by *addressRange* with *text*.
addressRange **d**	Delete the text specified by *addressRange*.
address **i** *text*	Insert *text* after the line specified by *address*.
address **r** *name*	Append the contents of the file *name* after the line specified by *address*.
addressRange **s**/*expr*/*str*/	Substitute the first occurrence of the regular expression *expr* by the string *str*.
addressRange **a**/*expr*/*str*/**g**	Substitute every occurrence of the regular expression *expr* by the string *str*.

FIGURE 3.29

Editing commands in **sed**.

2. *addressRange* can be a single address or a couple of addresses separated by commas. If two addresses are specified, then all of the lines between the first line that matches the first address and the first line that matches the second address are selected.

3. If no address is specified, then the command is applied to all of the lines.

Substituting Text

In the next example, I supplied the **sed** script on the command line. The script inserted a couple of spaces at the start of every line. The command are as follows:

```
$ cat arms                  ...look at the original file.
People just like me,
Are all around the world,
Waiting for the loved ones that they need.
And with my heart,
I make a simple wish,
Plain enough for anyone to see.
$ sed 's/^/  /' arms > arms.indent   ...indent the file.
$ cat arms.indent                    ...look at the result.
  People just like me,
  Are all around the world,
  Waiting for the loved ones that they need.
  And with my heart,
  I make a simple wish,
  Plain enough for anyone to see.
$ _
```

To remove all of the leading spaces from a file, use the substitute operator in the reverse fashion, as shown in the following example:

```
$ sed 's/^ *//' arms.indent    ...remove leading spaces.
People just like me,
Are all around the world,
Waiting for the loved ones that they need.
And with my heart,
I make a simple wish,
Plain enough for anyone to see.
$ _
```

Deleting Text

The following example illustrates a script that deleted all of the lines that contained the regular expression 'a':

```
$ sed '/a/d' arms           ...remove all lines containing an 'a'.
People just like me,
$ _
```

To delete only those lines that contain the *word* 'a', I surrounded the regular expression by escaped angled brackets ($\backslash <$ and $\backslash >$):

```
$ sed '/\<a\>/d' arms
People just like me,
Are all around the world,
Waiting for the loved ones that they need.
And with my heart,
Plain enough for anyone to see.
$ _
```

Inserting Text

In the next example, I inserted a copyright notice at the top of the file by using the insert command. Notice that I stored the **sed** script in a file and executed it by using the **-f** option:

```
$ cat sed5                   ...look at the sed script.
1i\
Copyright 1992, 1998, & 2002 by Graham Glass\
All rights reserved\
$ sed -f sed5 arms           ...insert a copyright notice.
Copyright 1992, 1998, & 2002 by Graham Glass
All rights reserved
People just like me,
Are all around the world,
Waiting for the loved ones that they need.
And with my heart,
I make a simple wish,
Plain enough for anyone to see.
$ _
```

Replacing Text

To replace lines, use the change function. In the following example, I replaced the group of lines 1..3 with a censored message:

```
$ cat sed6                   ...list the sed script.
1,3c\
Lines 1-3 are censored.
$ sed -f sed6 arms           ...execute the script.
Lines 1-3 are censored.
And with my heart,
I make a simple wish,
Plain enough for anyone to see.
$ _
```

To replace individual lines with a message rather than an entire group, supply a separate command for each line:

```
$ cat sed7                    ...list the sed script.
1c\
Line 1 is censored.
2c\
Line 2 is censored.
3c\
Line 3 is censored.
$ sed -f sed7 arms            ...execute the script.
Line 1 is censored.
Line 2 is censored.
Line 3 is censored.
And with my heart,
I make a simple wish,
Plain enough for anyone to see.
$ _
```

Inserting Files

In the following example, I inserted a message after the last line of the file:

```
$ cat insert              ...list the file to be inserted.
The End
$ sed '$r insert' arms            ...execute the script.
People just like me,
Are all around the world,
Waiting for the loved ones that they need.
And with my heart,
I make a simple wish,
Plain enough for anyone to see.
The End
$ _
```

Multiple Sed Commands

This example illustrates the use of multiple **sed** commands. I inserted a '≪' sequence at the start of each line and appended a '≫' sequence to the end of each line:

```
$ sed -e 's/^/<< /' -e 's/$/ >>/' arms
<< People just like me, >>
<< Are all around the world, >>
<< Waiting for the loved ones that they need. >>
<< And with my heart, >>
<< I make a simple wish, >>
<< Plain enough for anyone to see. >>
$ _
```

Translating Characters: tr

The **tr** utility maps the characters in a file from one character set to another. It works as shown in Figure 3.30. Here are some examples of **tr** in action:

Utility: **tr** -cds *string1 string2*

tr maps all of the characters in its standard input from the character set *string1* to the character set *string2*. If the length of *string2* is less than the length of *string1*, *string2* is padded by repeating its last character; in other words, the command '*tr abc de*' is equivalent to '*tr abc dee*'.

A character set may be specified using the [ ] notation of shell filename substitution:

- To specify the character set *a*, *d*, and *f*, simply write them as a single string: *adf*.

- To specify the character set *a* through *z*, separate the start and end characters by a dash: *a–z*.

By default, **tr** replaces every character of standard input in *string1* with its corresponding character in *string2*.

The **-c** option causes *string1* to be complemented before the mapping is performed. *Complementing* a string means that it is replaced by a string that contains every ASCII character except those in the original string. The net effect of this action is that every character of standard input that *does not* occur in *string1* is replaced.

The **-d** option causes every character in *string1* to be deleted from standard input.

The **-s** option causes every repeated output character to be condensed into a single instance.

FIGURE 3.30

Description of the **tr** command.

```
$ cat go.cart              ...list the sample input file.
go cart
racing
$ tr a-z A-Z < go.cart     ...translate lower to uppercase.
GO CART
RACING
$ tr a-c D-E < go.cart         ...replace abc by DEE.
go EDrt
rDEing
$ tr -c a X < go.cart      ...replace every non-a with X.
XXXXaXXXXXaXXXXX$          ...even last newline is replaced.
$ tr -c a-z '\012' < go.cart   ...replace non-alphas with
go                                ...ASCII 12 (newline).
cart
racing
$ tr -cs a-z '\012' < go.cart ...repeat, but condense
go                                   ...repeated newlines.
cart
racing
```

```
$ tr -d a-c < go.cart          ...delete all a-c characters.
go rt
ring
$ _
```

Converting Underline Sequences: ul

The **ul** utility transforms a file that contains underlining characters so that it appears correctly on a particular type of terminal. This is useful with commands like **man** that generate underlined text. **ul** works as shown in Figure 3.31.

Utility: **ul** -t*terminal* {*filename*}*

ul is a utility that transforms underline characters in its input so that they will be displayed correctly on the specified terminal. If no terminal is specified, the one defined by the TERM environment variable is assumed. The "/etc/termcap" file (or terminfo database) is used by **ul** to determine the correct underline sequence.

FIGURE 3.31

Description of the **ul** command.

As an example of the use of **ul** with **man**, let's say that you want to use the **man** utility to produce a document that you wish to print on a simple ASCII-only printer. The **man** utility generates underline characters for your current terminal, so to filter the output to make it suitable for a dumb printer, pipe the output of **man** through **ul** with the "dumb" terminal setting. Here's an example:

```
$ man who | ul -tdumb > man.txt
$ head man.txt              ...look at the first 10 lines.
WHO(1)                   USER COMMANDS                     WHO(1)
NAME
    who - who is logged in on the system
SYNOPSIS
    who [ who-file ] [ am i ]
$ _
```

Looking at Raw File Contents: od

The octal dump utility, **od**, allows you to see the contents of a nontext file in a variety of formats. It works as shown in Figure 3.32. In the following example, I displayed the contents of the "/bin/od" executable as octal numbers and then as characters starting from location 1000 (octal):

Utility: **od** -acbcdfhilox *fileName* [*offset*[.][b]]

od displays the contents of *fileName* in a form specified by one of the following options:

OPTION	MEANING
-a	Interpret bytes as characters, and print as ASCII names (i.e., 0 = nul).
-b	Interpret bytes as unsigned octal.
-c	Interpret bytes as characters, and print in C notation (i.e., 0 = \0).
-d	Interpret two-byte pairs as unsigned decimal.
-f	Interpret four-byte pairs as floating point.
-h	Interpret two-byte pairs as unsigned hexadecimal.
-i	Interpret two-byte pairs as signed decimal.
-l	Interpret four-byte pairs as signed decimal.
-o	Interpret two-byte pairs as unsigned octal.
-s[n]	Look for strings of minimum length *n* (default 3), terminated by null characters.
-x	Interpret two-byte pairs as hexadecimal.

By default, the contents are displayed as a series of octal numbers. *offset* specifies where the listing should begin. If *offset* ends in **b**, then it is interpreted as a number of blocks; otherwise, it is interpreted as an octal number. To specify a hex number, precede it by **x**; to specify a decimal number, end it with a period.

FIGURE 3.32

Description of the **od** command.

```
$ od /bin/od          ...dump the "/bin/od" file in octal.
0000000  100002 000410 000000 017250 000000 003630 000000 006320
0000020  000000 000000 000000 020000 000000 000000 000000 000000
0000040  046770 000000 022027 043757 000004 021002 162601 044763
0000060  014004 021714 000002 000410 045271 000000 020746 063400
0000100  000006 060400 000052 044124 044123 027402 047271 000000
0000120  021170 047271 000000 021200 157374 000014 027400 047271
0000140  000002 000150 054217 027400 047271 000002 000160 047126
...
$ od -c /bin/od 1000    ...dump "/bin/od" as characters.
0001000   H   x  \0 001   N   @  \0 002  \0  \0   /   u   s   r   /   l
0001020   i   b   /   l   d   .   s   o  \0   /   d   e   v   /   z   e
0001040   r   o  \0  \0  \0  \0  \0 030   c   r   t   0   :       n   o
```

```
0001060          /  u  s  r  /  l  i  b  /  l  d  .  s  o  \n
0001100  \0 \0 \0  %  c  r  t  0  :     /  u  s  r  /  l
0001120  i  b  /  l  d  .  s  o     m  a  p  p  i  n  g
0001140     f  a  i  l  u  r  e  \n \0 \0 \0 \0 023  c  r
0001160  t  0  :     n  o     /  d  e  v  /  z  e  r  o
0001200  \n \0 200 \0 \0 002 200 \0 \0 022 \0 \0 \0 007 \0 \0
...
$ _
```

You may search for strings of a minimum length by using the -s option. Any series of characters followed by an ASCII null is considered to be a string. Here's an example:

```
$ od -s7 /bin/od    ...search for strings 7 chars or more.
0000665 \fN^Nu o
0001012 /usr/lib/ld.so
0001031 /dev/zero
0001050 crt0: no /usr/lib/ld.so\n
0001103 %crt0: /usr/lib/ld.so mapping failure\n
...
$ _
```

Mounting File Systems: mount/umount

A superuser may extend the file system by using the **mount** utility, which works as shown in Figure 3.33. In the next example, I spliced the file system contained on the

---

Utility: **mount** -o*options* [*deviceName directory*]

   umount *deviceName*

mount is a utility that allows you to "splice" a device's file system into the root hierarchy. When used without any arguments, **mount** displays a list of the currently mounted devices. To specify special options, follow **-o** by a list of valid codes, among which are **rw**, which mounts a file system for read/write, and **ro**, which mounts a file system for read only. The **umount** utility unmounts a previously mounted file system.

FIGURE 3.33

Description of the **mount** and **unmount** commands.

"/dev/dsk2" device onto the "/usr" directory. Notice that before I performed the mount, the "/usr" directory was empty; after the mount, the files stored on the "/dev/dsk2" device appeared inside this directory. The commands are as follows:

```
$ mount            ...list the currently mounted devices.
/dev/dsk1 on /  (rw)
$ ls /usr             .../usr is currently empty.
$ mount /dev/dsk2 /usr   ...mount the /dev/dsk2 device.
$ mount            ...list the currently mounted devices.
/dev/dsk1 on /  (rw)
/dev/dsk2 on /usr (rw)
$ ls /usr    ...list the contents of the mounted device.
bin/      etc/     include/  lost+found/  src/     ucb/
demo/     games/   lib/      pub/         sys/     ucblib/
dict/     hosts/   local/    spool/       tmp/
$ _
```

To unmount a device, use the **umount** utility. In the following example, I unmounted the "/dev/dsk2" device and then listed the "/usr" directory:

```
$ umount /dev/dsk2 ...unmount the device.
$ mount            ...list the currently mounted devices.
/dev/dsk1 on /  (rw)
$ ls /usr          ...note that /usr is empty again.
$ _
```

The files were no longer accessible.

Identifying Terminals: `tty`

The **tty** utility identifies the name of your terminal. It works as shown in Figure 3.34. In the following example, my login terminal was the special file "/dev/ttyp0":

```
$ tty        ...display the pathname of my terminal.
/dev/ttyp0
$ _
```

Utility: **tty**

tty displays the pathname of your terminal. It returns zero if its standard input is a terminal; otherwise, it returns 1.

FIGURE 3.34

Description of the **tty** command.

Text Formatting: `nroff/troff/style/spell`

One of the first uses of UNIX was to support the text-processing facilities at Bell Laboratories. Several utilities, including **nroff**, **troff**, **style**, and **spell**, were created expressly for text formatting. Although these utilities were reasonable in their time, they have been made virtually obsolete by far more sophisticated tools whereby what you see is what you get (WYSIWYG). For example, **nroff** requires you to manually place special commands such as ".pa" inside a text document in order for it to format correctly, whereas modern tools allow you to do this graphically.

For more information about these old-style text-processing utilities, see Sobell (1994).

Timing Execution: `time`

It is sometimes useful to know how long it takes to run a specific command or program (or, more to the point, to know how long it takes relative to how long something else takes). The *time* utility can be used to report the execution time of any specified UNIX command. It works as shown in Figure 3.35. Here is an example:

```
$ time sort allnames.txt >sortednames.txt

real     0m 4.18s
user     0m 1.85s
sys      0m 0.14s
$ _
```

Utility: **time** *command-line*

The **time** command can be used to report the execution time of any UNIX command specified by *command-line*. Time is reported in both elapsed time and CPU time. (CPU time is expressed as two values: user time and system time.)

FIGURE 3.35

Description of the **time** command.

This command tells us that it took nearly 4.2 seconds of "wall clock" time to sort our file, whereas the total CPU time used was 1.99 seconds.

The **time** command is particularly useful in testing programs or scripts on small amounts of data whereby you can't "feel" the difference in the time required because they run so fast, but you know that when you run the scripts on your large amount of "real data," you'll want your program to be as efficient as possible.

ROLLING YOUR OWN PROGRAMS: Perl

We've seen that when what you needed to do required combining two or more of the UNIX utilities, you had to write a shell script in one of the shell languages we examined in earlier chapters. Shell scripts are slower than C programs, since they are interpreted instead of compiled, but they are also much easier to write and debug. C programs allow you to take advantage of many more UNIX features, but generally require more time both to write and to modify.

In 1986, Larry Wall found that shell scripts weren't enough and that C programs were overkill for many purposes. He set out to write a scripting language that would be the best of both worlds. The result was the Practical Extraction Report Language (Perl). The language addressed many of the problems Larry had generating reports and other text-oriented functions, although it also provided easy access to many other UNIX facilities to which shell scripts do not provide access.

The Perl language syntax will look familiar to shell and C programmers, since much of the syntax was taken from elements of both. I can only hope to give you a high-level view of Perl here. Like **awk**, entire books have been written on Perl that describe it in detail. (See, e.g., Medinets, 1996 and Wall, 1996.) That level of detail is beyond the scope of this book, but by after having your appetite what with an introduction, I'm sure you'll want to find out more about Perl.

Getting Perl

Although Perl is used in most UNIX environments, it often does not come with your native UNIX distribution, as it is not strictly part of UNIX. If your UNIX software vendor does not bundle Perl, you'll have to download it and install it yourself.

The best source for all things Perl is

```
http://www.perl.com
```

This site contains distributions of Perl for various platforms in the "downloads" section, as well as documentation and links to many other useful resources.

One huge advantage of implementing tools in Perl is the language's availability on most major platforms, including most versions of UNIX, Windows, and MacOS. You do have to watch out for inconsistencies in system calls and system locations of data files, but your code will require very few changes to run properly on different platforms.

The biggest advantage of Perl is that it is free. Perl is licensed by a variation of the GNU Public License known as the Artistic License. This does not affect any code you write in Perl. You are free to use and distribute your own code in any way you see fit, and you generally don't need to worry about redistributing Perl for someone else to be able to run your code, since Perl is so freely available.

Printing Text

Without the ability to print output, most programs wouldn't accomplish much. So in the UNIX tradition, I'll start our Perl script examples with one that prints a single line:

```
print "hello world.\n";
```

Just from this simple example, you can infer that each line in Perl must end with a semi-colon (;). Also, note that "\n" is used (as it is in the C programming language) to print a newline character at the end of the line.

Variables, Strings, and Integers

To write useful programs, of course, requires the ability to assign and modify values such as strings and integers. Perl provides variables much as the shells do. These variables can be assigned any type of value; Perl keeps track of the type for you. The major difference between Perl variables and shell variables is that, in Perl, the dollar sign is not simply used to expand the value of a variable, but is *always* used to denote the variable. Even when assigning a value to a variable, as in the code

```
$i = 3;
```

you put the $ on the variable. This is probably the most difficult adjustment for seasoned shell programmers to make.

In addition to all of the "typical" mathematical operators (addition, subtraction, and so forth), integers also support a *range operator*, "..", which is used to specify a range of integers. This is useful in building a loop around a range of values, as we will see later.

As in most languages, strings in Perl are specified by text in quotation marks. Strings also support a concatenation operator, ".", which puts strings together. Here's an example:

```
print 1, 2, 3..15, "\n";     # range operator
print "A", "B", "C", "\n";   # strings
$i = "A" . "B" ;             # concatenation operator
print "$i", "\n" ;
```

These lines generate the following output:

```
123456789101112131415
ABC
AB
```

You can see that each value, and only each value, is printed, giving you control over all spacing.

Arrays

Most programming languages provide *arrays*, which are lists of data values. Arrays in Perl are quite simple to use, as they are dynamically allocated. (You don't have to define how large they will be, and if you use more than the space currently allocated, Perl will allocate more space and enlarge the array.) The syntax is probably new, however. Rather than using a dollar sign, as you do with Perl variables, an array is denoted by an at sign (@), as follows:

```
@arr = (1,2,3,4,5);
```

This line defines the array "arr" and puts five values into it. You could also define the same array with the line

```
@arr = (1..5);
```

which uses the range operator with integers.

You can access a single element with a subscript in brackets, as in the line

```
print @arr[0],"\n";
```

As with most array implementations, the first element is numbered zero. Using the previous definition, this line would print "1", since that's the first value.

If you print an array without subscripts, all defined values are printed. If you use the array name without a subscript in a place where a scalar value is expected, the number of elements in the array is used, as shown in the following example:

```
@a1 = (1);            # array of 1 element
@a2 = (1,2,3,4,5);    # array of 5 elements
@a3 = (1..10);        # array of 10 elements

print @a1, " ", @a2, " ", @a3, "\n";

print @a1[0], " ", @a2[1], " ", @a3[2], "\n";

# using as scalar will yield number of items
print @a2 + @a3, "\n";
```

When executed, this code will result in the following output:

```
1 12345 12345678910
1 2 3
15
```

A special type of array provided in Perl is the *associative array.* Whereas you specify an index or a position of a normal array with an integer between zero and the maximum size of the array, an associative array can have indices in any order and of any value. Consider, for example, an array of month names. You can define an array called $month with the 12 values "January", "February", and so on. (Since arrays begin with index 0, you either remember to subtract one from your index or you define an array of 13 values and ignore $month[0], starting instead with $month[1] = "January").

But what if you are reading month names from the input and want to look up the numeric value. You could use a **for** loop to search through the array until you found the value that matched the name you read, but that requires extra code. Wouldn't it be nice if you could just index into the array with the name? With an associative array you can, in the following way:

```
@month{'January'} = 1;
@month{'February'} = 2;
             .
             .
             .
             .
```

Then you can read in the month name and access its numeric value via the code

```
$monthnum = $month{$monthname};
```

without having to loop through the array and search for the name. Rather than setting up the array one element at a time, as we did in the precedings example, you can define it at the beginning of your Perl program like this:

```
%month = ("January", 1, "February", 2, "March", 3,
          "April", 4, "May", 5, "June", 6,
          "July", 7, "August", 8, "September", 9,
    "October", 10, "November", 11, "December", 12);
```

The set of values that can be used in an associative array (also called the keys to the array) is returned as a regular array by a call to the Perl function **keys()**:

```
@monthnames = keys(%month);
```

If you attempt to use an invalid value as a key, a null or zero (depending on how you use the value) will be returned.

Mathematical and Logical Operators

Once you have your variables assigned, the next thing you usually want to do with them is change their values. Most operations on values are familiar from C programming. The typical operators of addition, subtraction, multiplication, and division are +, −, *, and /, respectively, for both integers and real numbers. Integers also support the C constructs to increment and decrement before and after a value is used, and they support logical ANDs and ORs as well. In the following example, note that I have to backslash the $ used as text in a print statement, since want, not the value of the variable in those places, but the name with the $ appended to it as a prefix:

```
$n = 2;
print ("\$n=", $n, "\n");

$n = 2 ; print ("increment after \$n=", $n++, "\n");
$n = 2 ; print ("increment before \$n=", ++$n, "\n");
$n = 2 ; print ("decrement after \$n=", $n--, "\n");
$n = 2 ; print ("decrement before \$n=", --$n, "\n");

$n = 2;                         # reset
print ("\$n+2=", $n + 2, "\n");
print ("\$n-2=", $n - 2, "\n");
print ("\$n*2=", $n * 2, "\n");
print ("\$n/2=", $n / 2, "\n");

$r = 3.14;              # real number
print ("\$r=", $r, "\n");

print ("\$r*2=", $r * 2, "\n"); # double
print ("\$r/2=", $r / 2, "\n"); # cut in half
print ("1 && 1 -> ", 1 && 1, "\n");
print ("1 && 0 -> ", 1 && 0, "\n");
print ("1 || 1 -> ", 1 || 1, "\n");
print ("1 || 0 -> ", 1 || 0, "\n");
```

This script generates the following output:

```
$n=2
increment after $n=2
increment before $n=3
decrement after $n=2
decrement before $n=1
$n+2=4
$n-2=0
$n*2=4
$n/2=1
$r=3.14
$r*2=6.28
$r/2=1.57
1 && 1 -> 1
1 && 0 -> 0
1 || 1 -> 1
1 || 0 -> 1
```

String Operators

Operations on string types are more complex than the integers just discussed and usually require the use of string functions (discussed later). The only simple operation that makes sense for a string (since you can't add it to or subtract it from anything else) is concatenation. Strings are concatenated with the "." operator. Here's an example:

```
$firstname = "Graham";
$lastname = "Glass";
$fullname = $firstname . " " . $lastname;
print "$fullname\n";
```

This code results in the output

```
Graham Glass
```

However, several simple matching operations are available for strings:

```
if ($value =~ /abc/) { print "contains 'abc'\n"};
$value =~ s/abc/def/;     # change 'abc' to 'def'
$value =~ tr/a-z/A-Z/;    # translate to upper case
```

The experienced UNIX user will recognize the substitution syntax from **vi** and **sed**, as well as the translation syntax based on the UNIX **tr** command.

Comparison Operators

You'll also want operators to compare values with one another. Comparison operators, as shown in Figure 3.36, are the usual suspects. In the case of greater than or less than

Operation	Numeric Values	String Values
Equal to	==	eq
Not equal to	!=	ne
Greater than	>	gt
Greater than or equal to	>=	ge
Less than	<	lt
Less than or equal to	<=	le

FIGURE 3.36

Perl comparison operators.

comparisons with strings, these operations compare the strings' sorting order. In most cases, you're concerned with comparing strings for equivalence (or the lack thereof).

If, While, For, and Foreach Loop Constructs

An essential part of any programming language is the ability to execute different statements, depending on the value of a variable, and create loops for repetitive tasks or indexing through array values. "If" statements and "while" loops in Perl are similar to those in the C language.

In an "if" statement, a comparison operator is used to compare two values, and different sets of statements are executed, depending on the result of the comparison (true or false):

```
$i = 0;
if ( $i == 0 ) {
    print "it's true\n";
} else {
    print "it's false\n";
}
```

This script results in "it's true" being printed. As with C, other comparison operators can be != (is not equal to), < (is less than), and > (is greater than), among others.

You could also loop with a "while" statement and print the text until the comparison is no longer true:

```
while ( $i == 0 ) {
    print "it's true\n";
    $i++;
}
```

Of course, the comparison will be true the next time through the loop, since $i was incremented.

Perl also handles both "for" loops from C and "foreach" loops from the C shell. Here's an example:

```
for ($i = 0 ; $i < 10 ; $i++ ) {
    print $i, " ";
}
print "\n";
```

This script counts from 0 to 9, prints the value (without a newline until the end), and generates the following output:

```
0 1 2 3 4 5 6 7 8 9
```

A "foreach" loop looks like this:

```
foreach $n (1..15) {
    print $n, " ";
}
print "\n";
```

This script generates about what you would expect:

```
1 2 3 4 5 6 7 8 9 10 11 12 13 14 15
```

File I/O

One big improvement in Perl over shell scripts is the ability to route input and output to specific files rather than just the standard input, output, or error channels. You still can access standard input and output as follows:

```
while (@line=<stdin>) {
    foreach $i (@line) {
        print "->", $i;        # also reads in EOL
    }
}
```

This script will read each line from the standard input and print it. However, perhaps you have a specific data file you wish to read from. Here's how you do it:

```
$FILE="info.dat";
open (FILE);               # name of var, not eval
@array = <FILE>;
close (FILE);
foreach $line (@array) {
    print "$line";
}
```

This Perl script opens "info.dat" and reads all its lines into the array called "array" (clever name, wouldn't you say?). It then does the same as the previous script and prints out each line.

Functions

To be able to separate various tasks a program performs, especially if the same task is needed in several places, a language needs to provide a *subroutine* or *function* capability. The Korn shell provides a weak type of function implemented through the command interface, and it is the only major shell that provides functions at all. Of course, the C language provides functions, but script writers had a harder time of it before Perl came along.

Perl functions are simple to use, although the syntax can get complicated. The following simple example of a Perl function will give you the idea:

```
sub pounds2dollars {
    $EXCHANGE_RATE = 1.54;    # modify when necessary
    $pounds = $_[0];
    return ($EXCHANGE_RATE * $pounds);
}
```

This function changes a value specified in pounds sterling (British money) into U. S. dollars (given an exchange rate of $1.54 to the pound, which can be modified as necessary). The special variable $_[0] references the first argument of the function. To call the function, our Perl script would look like this:

```
$book = 3.0;       # price in British pounds
$value = pounds2dollars($book);
print "Value in dollars = $value\n";
```

When we run this script (which includes the Perl function at the end), we get

```
Value in dollars = 4.62
```

In the next section, we'll see an example of a function that returns more than one value.

Library Functions

One capability that is conspicuously absent from shell scripting is that of making UNIX system calls. By contrast, Perl provides an interface to many UNIX system calls. The interface is via Perl library functions, not directly through the system call library; therefore, its use is dependent on the implementation and version of Perl, and you should consult the documentation for your version for specific information. When an interface is available, it is usually very much like it's C library counterpart.

Without even realizing it, we've already looked at a few Perl functions in previous sections when we saw the use of **open()**, **close()**, and **print()**. Another simple example of a useful system-level function is

```
exit(1);
```

used to exit a Perl program and pass the specified return code to the shell. Perl also provides a special exit function to print a message to **stdout** and exit with the current error code:

```
open(FILE) or die("Cannot open file.");
```

Thus, if the call to **open()** fails, the **die()** function will be executed, causing the error message to be written to **stdout** and the Perl program to exit with the error code returned by the failure from **open()**.

Some string functions to assist in manipulating string values are **length()**, **index()**, and **split()**. The command

```
$len = length($fullname);
```

sets the **$len** variable to the length of the text stored in the string variable **$fullname**. To locate one string inside another, use

```
$i = index($fullname, "Glass");
```

The value of **$i** will be zero if the string begins with the text you specify as the search string (the second argument). To divide up a line of text on the basis of a delimiting character (e.g., if you want to separate the tokens from the UNIX password file into its various parts), use

```
($username, $password, $uid, $gid, $name, $home, $shell)
                             = split(/:/, $line)
```

In this case, the **split()** function returns an array of values found in the string denoted by **$line** and separated by a colon. We have specified separate variables in which to store each item in this array so that we can use the values more easily than indexing into an array.

The following common function provides your Perl program with the time and date:

```
($s, $m, $h, $dy, $mo, $yr, $wd, $yd, $dst) = gmtime();
$mo++;        # month begins counting at zero
$yr+= 1900;      # Perl returns years since 1900
print "The date is $mo/$dy/$yr.\n";
print "The time is $h:$m:$s.\n";
```

The preceding code produces the following result:

```
The date is 4/25/2002.
The time is 13:40:27.
```

Note that gmtime() returns nine values. The Perl syntax is to specify these values in parentheses (as you would if you were assigning multiple values to an array).

Command-Line Arguments

Another useful capability is to be able to pass command-line arguments to a Perl script. Shell scripts provide a very simple interface to command-line arguments, while C programs provide a slightly more complex (but more flexible) interface. The Perl interface is somewhere in between, as shown in the following example:

```
$n = $#ARGV+1;  # number of arguments (beginning at zero)
print $n, " args: \n";
for ( $i = 0 ; $i < $n ; $i++ ) {
    print "   @ARGV[$i]\n";
}
```

This Perl script prints the number of arguments that were supplied in the **perl** command (after the name of the Perl script itself) and then prints out each argument on a separate line.

We can modify our pounds-to-dollars script from before to allow a value in British pounds to be specified on the command line as follows:

```
if ( $#ARGV < 0 ) {  # if no argument given
    print "Specify value in to convert to dollars\n";
    exit
}
$poundvalue = @ARGV[0];  # get value from command line

$dollarvalue = pounds2dollars($poundvalue);
print "Value in dollars = $dollarvalue\n";

sub pounds2dollars {
    $EXCHANGE_RATE = 1.54;    # modify when necessary

    $pounds = $_[0];
    return ($EXCHANGE_RATE * $pounds);
}
```

A Real-World Example

All of the foregoing brief examples should have given you the flavor of how Perl works, but so far we haven't done anything that's really very useful. So let's take what we've seen and write a Perl script to print out a table of information about a loan. We define a command with the syntax shown in Figure 3.37.

Utility: **loan** -a amount -p payment -r rate

loan prints a table, given a loan amount, an interest rate, and a payment to be made each month. The table shows how many months will be required to pay off the loan, as well as how much interest and principal will be paid each month. All arguments are required.

FIGURE 3.37

Description of the **loan** command written in Perl.

The Perl script loan.pl is available on-line (see the preface for more information) and looks like this:

```
# show loan interest

$i=0;
while ( $i < $#ARGV) {                    # process args
    if ( @ARGV[$i] eq "-r" ) {
        $RATE=@ARGV[++$i];                # interest rate
    } else {
        if ( @ARGV[$i] eq "-a" ) {
            $AMOUNT=@ARGV[++$i]; # loan amount
        } else {
            if ( @ARGV[$i] eq "-p" ) {
                $PAYMENT=@ARGV[++$i];     # payment amount
            } else {
                print "Unknown argument (@ARGV[$i])\n";
                exit
            }
        }
    }
    $i++;
}

if ($AMOUNT == 0 || $RATE == 0 || $PAYMENT == 0) {
    print "Specify -r rate -a amount -p payment\n";
    exit
}

print "Original balance: \$$AMOUNT\n";
print "Interest rate:    ${RATE}%\n";
print "Monthly payment:  \$$PAYMENT\n";
print "\n";
print "Month\tPayment\tInterest\tPrincipal\tBalance\n\n";
```

```
$month=1;
$rate=$RATE/12/100;          # get actual monthly percentage rate
$balance=$AMOUNT;
$payment=$PAYMENT;

while ($balance > 0) {
# round up interest amount
    $interest=roundUpAmount($rate * $balance);
    $principal=roundUpAmount($payment - $interest);
    if ( $balance < $principal ) {     # last payment
        $principal=$balance;           # don't pay too much!
        $payment=$principal + $interest;
    }
    $balance = roundUpAmount($balance - $principal);
    print
"$month\t\$$payment\t\$$interest\t\t\$$principal\t\t\$$balance\n";
    $month++;
}
sub roundUpAmount {
#
# in: floating point monetary value
# out: value rounded (and truncated) to the nearest cent
#

    $value=$_[0];

    $newvalue = ( int ( ( $value * 100 ) +.5 ) ) / 100;

    return ($newvalue);
}
```

If I want to pay $30 a month on my $300 credit card balance and the interest rate is 12.9% APR, my payment schedule looks like this:

```
Original balance: $300
Interest rate:    12.5%
Monthly payment:  $30
```

Month	Payment	Interest	Principal	Balance
1	$30	$3.13	$26.87	$273.13
2	$30	$2.85	$27.15	$245.98
3	$30	$2.56	$27.44	$218.54
4	$30	$2.28	$27.72	$190.82
5	$30	$1.99	$28.01	$162.81
6	$30	$1.7	$28.3	$134.51
7	$30	$1.4	$28.6	$105.91
8	$30	$1.1	$28.9	$77.01
9	$30	$0.8	$29.2	$47.81
10	$30	$0.5	$29.5	$18.31
11	$18.5	$0.19	$18.31	$0

So I find that it will take 11 months to pay off the balance at $30 per month, but the last payment will be only $18.31. If I want to pay the card off faster than that, I know I need to raise my monthly payment!

CHAPTER REVIEW

Checklist

In this chapter, I described utilities that

- filter files
- sort files
- compare files
- archive files
- find files
- schedule commands
- support programmable text processing
- create hard and soft links
- substitute users
- check for mail
- transform files
- look at raw file contents
- mount file systems
- prepare documents

I also described writing Perl scripts.

Quiz

1. Under what circumstances would you archive files using **tar**?
2. How would you convert the contents of a file to uppercase?
3. What is the difference between **cmp** and **diff**?
4. Describe what it means to "mount" a file system.
5. Which process serves the **crontab** system?
6. What additional functionality does an *extended* regular expression have?
7. What are the main differences between **sed** and **awk**?
8. How did **awk** get its name?
9. Under what circumstances would you use a symbolic link instead of a hard link?
10. What are the drawbacks of using a symbolic link?
11. What is meant by an *incremental* backup, and how would you perform one?
12. What are some ways that Perl makes script programming easier to write than conventional shell scripts?

Exercises

3.1 Perform some timing tests on **grep** and **fgrep** to determine the advantage of using **fgrep**'s speed. [level: *easy*]

3.2 Ask the system administrator to demonstrate the use of **tar** to produce a backup tape of your files. [level: *easy*]

3.3 Use **crontab** to schedule a script that removes your old core files at the start of each day. [level: *medium*]

Projects

1. Write a command pipeline that compresses the contents of a file and then encrypts it, using a known key, and writes the result to a new file. What is the corresponding command pipeline to take this encrypted file and decrypt and uncompress it to produce the original file? [level: *easy*]

2. Write a command pipeline to find files in a directory hierarchy (e.g. your home directory) that have not been accessed for 30 days and compress them. [level: *medium*]

3. Modify the **loan** Perl script so that you can pass a list of payments to it rather than using the same payment amount every month. [level: *medium*]

C H A P T E R   4

The UNIX Shells

MOTIVATION

A shell is a program that sits between you and the raw UNIX operating system. There are four shells that are commonly supported by UNIX vendors: the Bourne shell (sh), the Korn shell (ksh), the C shell (csh), and the Bourne Again shell (bash). All of these shells share a common core set of operations that make life in the UNIX system a little easier. For example, all of the shells allow the output of a process to be stored in a file or "piped" to another process. They also allow the use of wildcards in filenames, so it's easy to say things like "list all of the files whose names end with the suffix '.c'." This chapter describes all of the common core shell facilities; Chapters 5 through 8 describe the special features of each individual shell.

PREREQUISITES

In order to understand this chapter, you should have already read Chapter 1 and Chapter 2. Some of the utilities that I mention are described fully in Chapter 3. It also helps if you have access to a UNIX system so that you can try out the various features that I discuss.

OBJECTIVES

In this chapter, I'll explain and demonstrate the common shell features, including I/O redirection, piping, command substitution, and simple job control.

PRESENTATION

The information is presented in the form of several sample UNIX sessions. If you don't have access to a UNIX account, march through the sessions anyway, and perhaps you'll be able to try them out later.

UTILITIES

The chapter introduces the following utilities, listed in alphabetical order:

chsh	kill	ps
echo	nohup	sleep

SHELL COMMANDS

Also introduced are the following shell commands, listed in alphabetical order:

echo	kill	umask
eval	login	wait
exec	shift	
exit	tee	

INTRODUCTION

A shell is a program that is an interface between a user and the raw operating system. It makes basic facilities such as multitasking and piping easy to use, as well as adding useful file-specific features, like wildcards and I/O redirection. There are four common shells in use:

- the Bourne shell (sh)
- the Korn shell (ksh)
- the C shell (csh)
- the Bourne Again shell (bash)

The shell that you use is a matter of taste, power, compatibility, and availability. For example, the C shell is better than the Bourne shell for interactive work, but slightly worse in some respects for script programming. The Korn shell was designed to be upward compatible with the Bourne shell, and it incorporates the best features of the Bourne and C shells, plus some more of its own. Bash also takes a "best of all worlds" approach, including features from all the other major shells. The Bourne shell comes with absolutely every version of UNIX. The others come with most versions these days, but you might not always find your favorite. Bash probably ships with the fewest versions of UNIX, but is available for the most. (Chapter 8 has information on downloading Bash if it doesn't come with your particular version of UNIX.)

SHELL FUNCTIONALITY

This chapter describes the common core of functionality that all four shells provide. Figure 4.1 illustrates the relationships among the shells. A hierarchy diagram is a useful way to illustrate the features shared by the four shells—so nice, in fact, that I use the same kind of hierarchy chart (Figure 4.2) throughout the rest of the book. The remainder of this chapter describes each component of the hierarchy in detail.

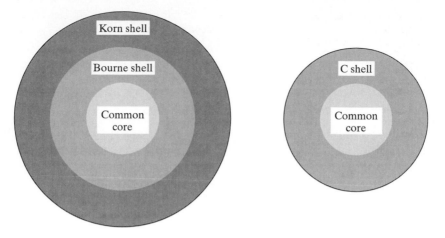

FIGURE 4.1

The relationship of shell functionality.

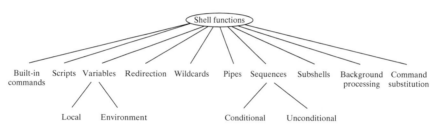

FIGURE 4.2

Core shell functionality.

SELECTING A SHELL

chsh = change shell , see 2/50 sh command pg 122

2nd bash
2nd ksh, pg 211
2nd csh, pg 256

When you are provided a UNIX account, the system administrator chooses a shell for you. To find out which shell was chosen for you, look at your prompt. If you have a "%" prompt, you're probably in a C shell. The other shells use "$" as the default prompt. When I wrote this chapter, I used a Bourne shell, but it really doesn't matter, since the facilities that I'm about to describe are common to all four shells. However, when studying the later chapters, you will want to select the particular shell described in each.

To change your default login shell, use the **chsh** utility, which works as shown in Figure 4.3. In order to use **chsh**, you must know the full pathnames of the four shells. The names are shown in Figure 4.4. In the following example, I changed my default login shell from a Bourne shell to a Korn shell:

```
% chsh                    ...change the login shell from sh to ksh.
Changing login shell for glass
Old shell: /bin/sh        ...pathname of old shell is displayed.
```

```
New shell: /bin/ksh          ...enter full pathname of new shell.
% ^D                         ...terminate login shell.


login: glass                 ...log back in again.
Password:                    ...secret.
$ _                          ...this time I'm in a Korn shell.
```

Another way to find out the full pathname of your login shell is to type the following:

```
$ echo $SHELL    ...display the name of my login shell.
/bin/ksh         ...full pathname of the Korn shell.
$ _
```

Utility: **chsh**

chsh allows you to change your default login shell. It prompts you for the full pathname of the new shell, which is then used as your shell for subsequent logins.

FIGURE 4.3

Description of the **chsh** command.

Shell	Full pathname
Bourne	/bin/sh
Korn	/bin/ksh
C	/bin/csh
Bash	/bin/bash

FIGURE 4.4

Common shell locations.

This example illustrated the *echo* shell command and a shell variable called SHELL. Both of these new facilities—echoing and variables—are discussed later in the chapter.

SHELL OPERATIONS

When a shell is invoked, either automatically during a login or manually from a keyboard or script, it follows a preset sequence:

1. It reads a special start-up file, typically located in the user's home directory, that contains some initialization information. Each shell's start-up sequence is different, so I'll leave the specific details to later chapters.

2. It displays a prompt and waits for a user command.
3. If the user enters a Control-D character on a line of its own, this is interpreted by the shell as meaning "end of input" and causes the shell to terminate; otherwise, the shell executes the user's command and returns to step 2.

Commands range from simple utility invocations, such as

```
$ ls
```

to complex-looking pipeline sequences, such as

```
$ ps -ef | sort | ul -tdumb | lp
```

If you ever need to enter a command that is longer than a line on your terminal, you may terminate a portion of the command with a backslash (\) character, and the shell then allows you to continue the command on the next line:

```
$ echo this is a very long shell command and needs to \
be extended with the line continuation character. Note \
that a single command may be extended for several lines.
this is a very long shell command and needs to be extended with the line
continuation character. Note that a single command may be extended for
several lines.
$ _
```

EXECUTABLE FILES VERSUS BUILT-IN COMMANDS

Most UNIX commands invoke utility programs that are stored in the directory hierarchy. Utilities are stored in files that have execute permission. For example, when you type

```
$ ls
```

the shell locates the executable program called "ls," which is typically found in the "/bin" directory, and executes it. (The way that the shell finds a utility is described later in the chapter.) In addition to its ability to locate and execute utilities, the shell contains several built-in commands, which it recognizes and executes internally. I'll describe two of the most useful ones, *echo* and *cd*, now.

Displaying Information: echo

The built-in echo command displays its arguments to standard output. It works as shown in Figure 4.5. All of the shells we will see contain this built-in function, but you may also invoke the utility called **echo** (usually found in /bin) instead. This is sometimes useful, since some arguments and subtle behavior may vary among the different built-ins and it can be confusing if you write scripts in more than one of these shells. (We'll look at writing shell scripts shortly.)

Shell Command: **echo** {*arg*}*

echo is a built-in shell command that displays all of its arguments to standard output. By default, it appends a newline to the output.

FIGURE 4.5

Description of the *echo* shell command.

Changing Directories: cd

The built-in *cd* command changes the current working directory of the shell to a new location and was described fully in Chapter 2.

METACHARACTERS

Some characters receive special processing by the shell and are known as *metacharacters*. All four shells share a core set of common metacharacters, whose meanings are shown in Figure 4.6. When you enter a command, the shell scans it for metacharacters and

Symbol	Meaning
>	Output redirection; writes standard output to a file.
>>	Output redirection; appends standard output to a file.
<	Input redirection; reads standard input from a file.
*	File substitution wildcard; matches zero or more characters.
?	File substitution wildcard; matches any single character.
[...]	File substitution wildcard; matches any character between brackets.
`command`	Command substitution; replaced by the output from *command*.
|	Pipe symbol; sends the output of one process to the input of another.
;	Used to sequence commands.
|	Conditional execution; executes a command if the previous one failed.
&&	Conditional execution; executes a command if the previous one succeeded.

FIGURE 4.6

Shell metacharacters.

(...)	Groups commands.
&	Runs a command in the background.
#	All characters that follow, up to a newline, are ignored by the shell and programs (i.e., signifies a comment).
$	Expands the value of a variable.
\	Prevents special interpretation of the next character.
≪ *tok*	Input redirection; reads standard input from script, up to *tok*.

FIGURE 4.6   (*Continued*)

processes them specially. When all metacharacters have been processed, the command is finally executed. To turn off the special meaning of a metacharacter, precede it with a \ character. Here's an example:

```
$ echo hi > file          ...store output of echo in "file".
$ cat file                ...look at the contents of "file".
hi
$ echo hi \> file         ...inhibit > metacharacter.
hi > file                 ...> is treated like other characters.
$ _                       ...and output comes to terminal instead
```

This chapter describes the meaning of each metacharacter in the order in which it was listed in Figure 4.6.

REDIRECTION

The shell redirection facility allows you to do the following:

- store the output of a process to a file (*output redirection*)
- use the contents of a file as input to a process (*input redirection*)

Let's have a look at each facility, in turn.

Output Redirection

Output redirection is handy because it allows you to save a process' output into a file so it can be listed, printed, edited, or used as input to a future process. To redirect output, use either the > or ≫ metacharacter. The sequence

```
$ command > fileName
```

> – create/overwrite
>> – append

sends the standard output of *command* to the file with name *fileName*. The shell creates the file with name *fileName* if it doesn't already exist or overwrites its previous contents if it already exists. If the file already exists and doesn't have write permission, an error occurs. In the next example, I created a file called "alice.txt" by redirecting the output of the **cat** utility. Without parameters, **cat** simply copies its standard input—which in this case is the keyboard—to its standard output:

```
$ cat > alice.txt                  ...create a text file.
In my dreams that fill the night,
I see your eyes,
^D                                 ...end-of-input.
$ cat alice.txt                    ...look at its contents.
In my dreams that fill the night,
I see your eyes,
$ _
```

The sequence

```
$ command >> fileName
```

append

appends the standard output of *command* to the file with name *fileName*. The shell creates the file with name *fileName* if it doesn't already exist. In the following example, I appended some text to the existing "alice.txt" file:

overwrite

```
$ cat > alice.txt                  ...append to the file.
And I fall into them,
Like Alice fell into Wonderland.
^D                                 ...end-of-input.
$ cat alice.txt                    ...look at the new contents.
In my dreams that fill the night,
I see your eyes,
And I fall into them,
Like Alice fell into Wonderland.
$ _
```

By default, both forms of output redirection leave the standard error channel connected to the terminal. However, both shells have variations of output redirection that allow them to redirect the standard error channel. The C, Korn, and Bash shells also provide protection against accidental overwriting of a file due to output redirection. (These facilities are described in later chapters.)

Input Redirection

Input redirection is useful because it allows you to prepare a process' input and store it in a file for later use. To redirect input, use either the < or ≪ metacharacter. The sequence

```
$ command < fileName
```

executes *command*, using the contents of the file *fileName* as its standard input. If the file doesn't exist or doesn't have read permission, an error occurs. In the following example, I sent myself the contents of "alice.txt" via the **mail** utility:

```
$ mail glass < alice.txt                    ...send myself mail.
$ mail                                       ...look at my mail.
Mail version SMI 4.0 Sat Oct 13 20:32:29 PDT 1990  Type ? for help.
>N  1 glass@utdallas.edu Mon Feb  2 13:29   17/550
& 1                                          ...read message #1.
From: Graham Glass <glass@utdallas.edu>
To: glass@utdallas.edu
In my dreams that fill the night,
I see your eyes,
And I fall into them,
Like Alice fell into Wonderland
& q                                          ...quit mail.
$ _
```

When the shell encounters a sequence of the form

See pg 167

```
$ command << word
```

it copies its standard input up to, but not including, the line starting with *word* into a buffer and then executes *command*, using the contents of the buffer as its standard input. This facility, which is utilized almost exclusively to allow shell programs (*scripts*) to supply the standard input to other commands as in-line text, is revisited in more detail later on in the chapter.

FILENAME SUBSTITUTION (WILDCARDS)

All shells support a wildcard facility that allows you to select files from the file system that satisfy a particular name pattern. Any word on the command line that contains at least one of the wildcard metacharacters is treated as a pattern and is replaced by an alphabetically sorted list of all the matching filenames. This act of pattern replacement is called *globbing*. The wildcards and their meanings are as shown in Figure 4.7.

Wildcard	Meaning
*	Matches any string, including the empty string.
?	Matches any single character.
[..]	Matches any one of the characters between the brackets. A range of characters may be specified by separating a pair of characters by a dash.

FIGURE 4.7

Shell wildcards.

You may prevent the shell from processing the wildcards in a string by surrounding the string with single quotes (apostrophes) or double quotes. (See "Quoting" later in the chapter for more details.) A / character in a filename must be matched explicitly. Here are some examples of wildcards in action:

```
$ ls -FR               ...recursively list my current directory.
a.c    b.c   cc.c  dir1/  dir2/


dir1:
d.c  e.e


dir2:
f.d  g.c
$ ls *.c                   ...any text followed by ".c".
a.c    b.c    cc.c
$ ls ?.c                   ...one character followed by ".c".
a.c  b.c
$ ls [ac]*                 ...any string beginning with "a" or "c".
a.c    cc.c
$ ls [A-Za-z]*             ...any string beginning with a letter.
a.c    b.c    cc.c
$ ls dir*/*.c              ...all ".c" files in "dir*" directories.
dir1/d.c  dir2/g.c
$ ls */*.c                 ...all ".c" files in any subdirectory.
dir1/d.c  dir2/g.c
$ ls *2/?.? ?.?
a.c    b.c    dir2/f.d  dir2/g.c
$ _
```

The result of a pattern that has no matches is shell specific. Some shells have a mechanism for turning off wildcard replacement.

PIPES

The shell allows you to use the standard output of one process as the standard input of another process by connecting the processes together via the pipe (|) metacharacter. The sequence

```
$ command1 | command2
```

causes the standard output of *command1* to "flow through" to the standard input of *command2*. Any number of commands may be connected by pipes. A sequence of commands chained together in this way is called a *pipeline*. Pipelines support one of the basic UNIX philosophies, which is that large problems can often be solved by a chain of smaller processes, each performed by a relatively small, reusable utility. The standard error channel is not piped through a standard pipeline, although some shells support this capability.

In the following example, I piped the output of the **ls** utility to the input of the **wc** utility to count the number of files in the current directory (see Chapter 2 for a description of **wc**):

```
$ ls                                 ...list the current directory.
a.c    b.c    cc.c    dir1    dir2
$ ls | wc -w                         ...count the entries.
    5
$ _
```

Figure 4.8 is an illustration of a pipeline.

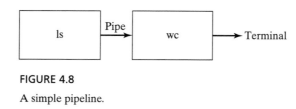

FIGURE 4.8

A simple pipeline.

In the next example, I piped the contents of the "/etc/passwd" file into the **awk** utility to extract the first field of each line. The output of **awk** was then piped to the sort utility, which sorted the lines alphabetically. The result was a sorted list of every user on the system. The commands are as follows (the **awk** utility is described fully in Chapter 3):

```
$ head -4 /etc/passwd        ...look at the password file.
root:eJ2S1OrVe8mCg:0:1:Operator:/:/bin/csh
nobody:*:65534:65534::/:
daemon:*:1:1::/:
sys:*:2:2::/:/bin/csh
$ cat /etc/passwd | awk -F: '{ print $1 }' | sort
audit
bin
daemon
glass
ingres
news
nobody
root
sync
sys
tim
uucp
$ _
```

Figure 4.9 is an illustration of a pipeline that sorts.

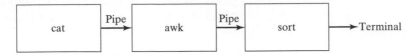

FIGURE 4.9

A pipeline that sorts.

There's a very handy utility called **tee** that allows you to copy the output of a pipe to a file while still allow sing that output to flow down the pipeline. As you might have guessed, the name of this utility comes from the "T" connections that plumbers use. Figure 4.10 shows how **tee** works. In the following example, I copied the output of **who** to a file called "who.capture" and also let the output pass through to **sort**:

```
$ who | tee who.capture | sort
ables     ttyp6    May  3 17:54 (gw.waterloo.com)
glass     ttyp0    May  3 18:49 (bridge05.utdalla)
posey     ttyp2    Apr 23 17:44 (blackfoot.utdall)
posey     ttyp4    Apr 23 17:44 (blackfoot.utdall)
$ cat who.capture            ...look at the captured data.
glass     ttyp0    May  3 18:49 (bridge05.utdalla)
posey     ttyp2    Apr 23 17:44 (blackfoot.utdall)
posey     ttyp4    Apr 23 17:44 (blackfoot.utdall)
ables     ttyp6    May  3 17:54 (gw.waterloo.com)
$
```

Utility: **tee** -ia {fileName}+

The **tee** utility copies its standard input to the specified files and to its standard output. The **-a** option causes the input to be appended to the files, rather than overwriting them. The **-i** option causes interrupts to be ignored.

FIGURE 4.10

Description of the **tee** command.

Notice that the output is captured directly from the **who** utility before the list is sorted.

COMMAND SUBSTITUTION

A command surrounded by grave accents (`) is executed, and its standard output is inserted in the command in its place. Any newlines in the output are replaced with spaces, as in the following examples:

```
$ echo the date today is `date`
the date today is Mon Feb 2 00:41:55 CST 1998
$ _
```

It's possible to do some crafty things by combining pipes and command substitution. For example, the **who** utility (described in Chapter 9) produces a list of all the users on the system, and the **wc** utility (described in Chapter 2) counts the number of words or lines in its input. By piping the output of **who** to the **wc** utility, it's possible to count the number of users on the system:

```
$ who              ...look at the output of who.
posey     ttyp0   Jan 22 15:31    (blackfoot:0.0)
glass     ttyp3   Feb  3 00:41    (bridge05.utdalla)
huynh     ttyp5   Jan 10 10:39    (atlas.utdallas.e)
$ echo there are `who | wc -l` users on the system
there are 3 users on the system
$ _
```

The output of command substitution may be used as part of another command. For example, the **vi** utility allows you to specify, on the command line, a list of files to be edited. These files are then visited by the editor one after the other. The **grep** utility, described in Chapter 3, has a **-l** option which returns a list of all the files on the command line that contain a specified pattern. By combining these two features via command substitution and using the following single command, it's possible to specify that **vi** be invoked for all files ending in ".c" that contain the pattern "debug":

```
$ vi `grep -l debug *.c`
```

SEQUENCES

If you enter a series of simple commands or pipelines separated by semicolons, the shell will execute them in sequence, from left to right. This facility is useful for type-ahead (and think-ahead) addicts who like to specify an entire sequence of actions at once. Here's an example:

```
$ date; pwd; ls    ...execute three commands in sequence.
Mon Feb  2 00:11:10 CST 1998
/home/glass/wild
a.c    b.c    cc.c   dir1   dir2
$ _
```

Each command in a sequence may be individually I/O redirected, as shown in the following example:

```
$ date > date.txt; ls; pwd > pwd.txt
a.c        b.c        cc.c       date.txt  dir1       dir2
```

```
$ cat date.txt              ...look at output of date.
Mon Feb  2 00:12:16 CST 1998
$ cat pwd.txt               ...look at output of pwd.
/home/glass
$ _
```

Conditional Sequences

Every UNIX process terminates with an exit value. By convention, an exit value of 0 means that the process completed successfully, and a nonzero exit value indicates failure. All built-in shell commands return 1 if they fail. You may construct sequences that make use of this exit value as follows:

- If you specify a series of commands separated by && tokens, the next command is executed only if the previous command returns an exit code of 0.
- If you specify a series of commands separated by || tokens, the next command is executed only if the previous command returns a nonzero exit code.

The && and || metacharacters therefore mirror the operation of their counterpart C operators.

For example, if the C compiler **cc** compiles a program without fatal errors, it creates an executable program called "a.out" and returns an exit code of 0; otherwise, it returns a nonzero exit code. The following conditional sequence compiles a program called "myprog.c" and executes the "a.out" file only if the compilation succeeds:

```
$ cc myprog.c && a.out
```

The following example compiles a program called "myprog.c" and displays an error message if the compilation fails:

```
$ cc myprog.c || echo compilation failed.
```

Exit codes are discussed in more detail toward the end of the chapter.

GROUPING COMMANDS

Commands may be grouped by placing them between parentheses, which causes them to be executed by a child shell (*subshell*). The commands in a given group share the same standard input, standard output, and standard error channels, and the group may be redirected and piped as if it were a simple command. Here are some examples:

```
$ date; ls; pwd > out.txt       ...execute a sequence
Mon Feb  2 00:33:12 CST 1998    ...output from date.
a.c        b.c                  ...output from ls.
$ cat out.txt                   ...only pwd was redirected.
/home/glass
$ (date; ls; pwd) > out.txt     ...group and then redirect.
```

```
$ cat out.txt                    ...all output was redirected.
Mon Feb  2 00:33:28 CST 1998
a.c
b.c
/home/glass
$ _
```

BACKGROUND PROCESSING

— see nohup (pg 170) for how to ensure bgnd tasks continue to run after you log off

If you follow a simple command, pipeline, sequence of pipelines, or group of commands with the & metacharacter, a subshell is created to execute the commands as a background process that runs concurrently with the parent shell and does not take control of the keyboard. Background processing is therefore very useful for performing several tasks simultaneously, as long as the background tasks do not require keyboard input. In windowed environments, it's more common to run each command within its own window than to run many commands in one window using the background facility. When a background process is created, the shell displays some information that may be employed to control the process at a later stage. The exact format of this information is shell specific.

In the next example, I executed a **find** command in the foreground to locate the file called "a.c". This command took quite a while to execute, so I decided to run the next **find** command in the background. The shell displayed the background process' unique process ID number and then immediately gave me another prompt, allowing me to continue my work. Note that the output of the background process continued to be displayed at my terminal, which was inconvenient. In the next few sections, I'll show you how you can use the process ID number to control the background process and how to prevent background processes from messing up your terminal. The following are the commands to locate the file "a.c":

```
$ find . -name a.c -print      ...search for "a.c".
./wild/a.c
./reverse/tmp/a.c
$ find . -name b.c -print &     ...search in the background.
27174                           ...process ID number
$ date                          ...run "date" in the foreground.
./wild/b.c                      ...output from background "find".
Mon Feb  2 18:10:42 CST 1998        ...output from date.
$ ./reverse/tmp/b.c             ...more from background "find"
      ...came after we got the shell prompt so we don't
      ...get another one.
```

You may specify several background commands on a single line by separating each command with an ampersand, as shown in the following example:

```
$ date & pwd &          ...create two background processes.
27310                       ...process ID of "date".
27311                       ...process ID of "pwd".
```

```
/home/glass                         ...output from "date".
$ Mon Feb  2 18:37:22 CST 1998      ...output from "pwd".
$ _
```

REDIRECTING BACKGROUND PROCESSES

Redirecting Output

To prevent the output of a background process from arriving at your terminal, redirect its output to a file. In the next example, I redirected the standard output of the **find** command to a file called "find.txt". As the command was executing, I watched it grow via the **ls** command:

```
$ find . -name a.c -print > find.txt &
27188                        ...process ID of "find".
$ ls -l find.txt             ...look at "find.txt".
-rw-r--r--  1 glass           0 Feb  3 18:11 find.txt
$ ls -l find.txt             ...watch it grow.
-rw-r--r--  1 glass          29 Feb  3 18:11 find.txt
$ cat find.txt                    ...list "find.txt".
./wild/a.c
./reverse/tmp/a.c
$ _
```

Another alternative is to mail the output to yourself, as shown in the following example:

```
$ find . -name a.c -print | mail glass &
27193
$ cc program.c                           ...do other useful work.
$ mail                                   ...read my mail.
Mail version SMI 4.0 Sat Oct 13 20:32:29 PDT 1990  Type ? for help.
>N  1 glass@utdallas.edu Mon Feb  3 18:12    10/346
& 1
From: Graham Glass <glass@utdallas.edu>
To: glass@utdallas.edu
./wild/a.c                      ...the output from "find".
./reverse/tmp/a.c
& q
$ _
```

Some utilities also produce output on the standard error channel, which must be redirected *in addition* to standard output. The next chapter describes in detail how this is done, but here is an example of how it is done in the Bourne and Korn shells just in case you're interested:

```
$ man ps > ps.txt &              ...save documentation in background.
27203
$ Reformatting page.  Wait       ...shell prompt comes here.
```

[handwritten annotations: "2 = std error device", "1 = std output device", "& = runs a bgnd process"]

```
done                                  ...standard error messages.
man ps > ps.txt 2>&1 &                ...redirect error channel too.
27212
$ _                                   ...all output is redirected.
```

[handwritten: "redirect std error → std out"]

Redirecting Input

When a background process attempts to read from a terminal, the terminal automatically sends it an error signal, which causes it to terminate. In the next example, I ran the **chsh** utility in the background. It immediately issued the "Login shell unchanged" message and terminated, never bothering to wait for any input. I then ran the **mail** utility in the background, which similarly issued the message "No message !?!". The commands are as follows:

```
$ chsh &                        ...run "chsh" in background.
27201
$ Changing NIS login shell for glass on csservr1.
Old shell: /bin/sh
New shell: Login shell unchanged.     ...didn't wait.

mail glass &                    ...run "mail" in background.
27202
$ No message !?!                ...don't wait for keyboard input.
```

SHELL PROGRAMS: SCRIPTS

[handwritten: "chmod +x filename"]

Any series of shell commands may be stored inside a regular text file for later execution. A file that contains shell commands is called a *script*. Before you can run a script, you must give it execute permission by using the **chmod** utility. Then, to run the script, you only need to type its name. Scripts are useful for storing commonly used sequences of commands and range in complexity from simple one-liners to full-blown programs. The control structures supported by the languages built into the shells are sufficiently powerful to enable scripts to perform a wide variety of tasks. System administrators find scripts particularly useful for automating repetitive administrative tasks, such as warning users when their disk usage goes beyond a certain limit.

When a script is run, the system determines which shell the script was written for and then executes the shell, using the script as its standard input. The system decides which shell the script is written for by examining the first line of the script. Here are the rules that it uses:

- If the first line is just a #, then the script is interpreted by the shell from which it was executed as a command.
- If the first line is of the form #! *pathName*, then the executable program *pathName* is used to interpret the script. *(it uses the shell you specify)*
- If neither of the first two rules applies, then the script is interpreted by a Bourne shell.

[handwritten: "Bourne shell is default shell for scripts"]

 # = comment line, except 1st line

If a # appears on any line other than the first, all characters up to the end of that line are treated as a comment. Scripts should be liberally commented in the interests of maintainability.

When you write your own scripts, I recommend that you use the #! form to specify which shell the script is designed for, as that form is unambiguous and doesn't require the reader to be aware of the default rules.

Here is an example that illustrates the construction and execution of two scripts, one for the C shell and the other for the Korn shell:

```
$ cat > script.csh              ...create the C shell script.
#!/bin/csh
# This is a sample C shell script.
echo -n the date today is      # in csh, -n omits newline
date         # output today's date.
^D                             ...end-of-input.
$ cat > script.ksh              ...create the Korn shell script.
#!/bin/ksh
# This is a sample Korn shell script.
echo "the date today is \c"     # in ksh, \c omits the nl
date         # output today's date.
^D                              ...end-of-input.
$ chmod +x script.csh script.ksh       ...make them executable.
$ ls -1F script.csh script.ksh         ...look at attributes.
-rwxr-xr-x  1 glass         138 Feb  1 19:46 script.csh*
-rwxr-xr-x  1 glass         142 Feb  1 19:47 script.ksh*
$ script.csh                    ...execute the C shell script.
the date today is Sun Feb  1 19:50:00 CST 1998
$ script.ksh                    ...execute the Korn shell script.
the date today is Sun Feb  1 19:50:05 CST 1998
$ _
```

The ".csh" and ".ksh" extensions of my scripts are used only for clarity; scripts can be called anything at all and don't even need an extension.

Note the usage of "\c" and "-n" in the preceding examples of the **echo** command. Different versions of "/bin/echo" use one or the other to omit the newline. It may also depend on the shell being used: If the shell has a built-in *echo* function, then the specifics of "/bin/echo" won't matter. You'll want to experiment with your particular shell and echo combination; it isn't quite as simple as I implied in the preceding comments.

SUBSHELLS

When you log into a UNIX system, you execute an initial login shell. This shell executes any simple commands that you enter. However, there are several circumstances under which your current (*parent*) shell creates a new (*child*) shell to perform some tasks:

- When a grouped command such as (ls; pwd; date) is executed, the parent shell creates a child shell to execute the grouped commands. If the command is not executed in the background, the parent shell sleeps until the child shell terminates.
- When a script is executed, the parent shell creates a child shell to execute the commands in the script. If the script is not executed in the background, the parent shell sleeps until the child shell terminates.
- When a background job is executed, the parent shell creates a child shell to execute the background commands. The parent shell continues to run concurrently with the child shell.

A child shell is called a *subshell*. Just like any other UNIX process, a subshell has its own current working directory, so *cd* commands executed in a subshell do not affect the working directory of the parent shell:

```
$ pwd              ...display my login shell's current dir.
/home/glass
$ (cd /; pwd)      ...the subshell moves and executes pwd.
/                  ...output comes from the subshell.
$ pwd              ...my login shell never moved.
/home/glass
$ _
```

Every shell contains two data areas: an environment space and a local variable space. A child shell inherits a copy of its parent's environment space and a clean local variable space, as shown in Figure 4.11.

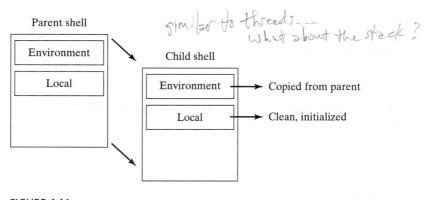

FIGURE 4.11

Child shell data spaces.

VARIABLES

A shell supports two kinds of variables: *local* and *environment* variables. Both hold data in a string format. The main difference between them is that when a shell invokes a subshell, the child shell gets a copy of its parent shell's environment variables, but not its local variables. Environment variables are therefore used for transmitting useful information between parent shells and their children.

Every shell has a set of predefined environment variables that are usually initialized by the start-up files described in later chapters. Similarly, every shell has a set of predefined local variables that have special meanings to the shell. Other environment and local variables may be created as needed and are particularly useful in writing scripts. Figure 4.12 shows a list of the predefined environment variables that are common to all shells.

Name	Meaning
$HOME	the full pathname of your home directory
$PATH	a list of directories to search for commands
$MAIL	the full pathname of your mailbox
$USER	your username
$SHELL	the full pathname of your login shell
$TERM	the type of your terminal

FIGURE 4.12

Predefined shell variables.

The syntax for assigning variables differs among shells, but the way that you access the variables is the same: If you append the prefix $ to the name of a variable, this token sequence is replaced by the shell with the value of the named variable.

To create a variable, simply assign it a value; a variable does not have to be declared. The details of how variables are assigned are left to the chapters on specific shells, but for now it's enough to know that the syntax for assigning a variable in the Bourne, Korn, and Bash shells is as follows:

```
variableName=value              ...place no spaces around the =.
```

In the following example, I displayed the values of some common shell environment variables:

```
$ echo HOME = $HOME, PATH = $PATH       ...list two variables.
HOME = /home/glass, PATH = /bin:/usr/bin:/usr/sbin
$ echo MAIL = $MAIL                            ...list another.
MAIL = /var/mail/glass
```

```
$ echo USER = $USER, SHELL = $SHELL, TERM=$TERM
USER = glass, SHELL = /bin/sh, TERM=vt100
$ _
```

The next example illustrates the difference between local and environment variables. I assigned values to two local variables and then made one of them an environment variable by using the Bourne shell *export* command (described fully in Chapter 5). I then created a child Bourne shell and displayed the values of the variables that I had assigned in the parent shell. Note that the value of the environment variable was copied into the child shell, but the value of the local variable was not. Finally, I typed a *Control-D* to terminate the child shell and restart the parent shell, and then I displayed the original variables. The commands are as follows:

```
$ firstname=Graham        ...set a local variable.
$ lastname=Glass          ...set another local variable.
$ echo $firstname $lastname   ...display their values.
Graham Glass
$ export lastname         ...make "lastname" an environment var.
$ sh                      ...start a child shell; the parent sleeps.
$ echo $firstname $lastname   ...display values again.
Glass                     ...note that firstname wasn't copied.
$ ^D                      ...terminate child; the parent awakens.
$ echo $firstname $lastname   ...they remain unchanged.
Graham Glass
$ _
```

Figure 4.13 shows several common built-in variables that have a special meaning. The first special variable is especially useful for creating temporary filenames, and the rest are handy for accessing command-line arguments in shell scripts. Here's an example that illustrates all of the common special variables:

```
$ cat script.sh                               ...list the script.
echo the name of this script is $0
echo the first argument is $1
echo a list of all the arguments is $*
echo this script places the date into a temporary file
echo called $1.$$
date > $1.$$        # redirect the output of date.
ls $1.$$            # list the file.
rm $1.$$            # remove the file.
$ script.sh paul ringo george john    ...execute it.
the name of this script is script.sh
the first argument is paul
a list of all the arguments is paul ringo george john
this script places the date into a temporary file
called paul.24321
paul.24321
$ _
```

[Handwritten annotations in right margin:]
$0 = arg 0 = command name
$1 = arg 1
$2 = arg 2
: etc
$* = list of all args (after 0)
$$ = process Id

[Handwritten note at bottom:] its John, Paul, George and Ringo !

Name	Meaning
$$	The process ID of the shell.
$0	The name of the shell script (if applicable).
$1..$9	$n refers to the nth command line argument (if applicable).
$*	A list of all the command-line arguments.

FIGURE 4.13

Special built-in shell variables.

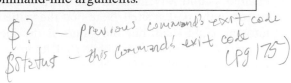

$? — previous command's exit code
$status — this command's exit code (pg 175)

QUOTING

Oftentimes, you want to inhibit the shell's wildcard replacement, variable substitution, or command substitution mechanisms. The shell's quoting system allows you to do just that. Here's the way it works:

- Single quotes (') inhibit wildcard replacement, variable substitution, and command substitution.
- Double quotes (") inhibit wildcard replacement only.
- When quotes are nested, only the outer quotes have any effect.

The following example illustrates the difference between the two kinds of quotes:

```
$ echo 3 * 4 = 12          ...remember, * is a wildcard.
3 a.c b.c c.c 4 = 12
$ echo "3 * 4 = 12"          ...double quotes inhibit wildcards.
3 * 4 = 12
$ echo '3 * 4 = 12'          ...single quotes inhibit wildcards.
3 * 4 = 12
$ name=Graham
```

By using single quotes (apostrophes) around the text, we inhibit all wildcard replacement, variable substitution, and command substitution:

```
$ echo 'my name is $name - date is `date`'
my name is $name and the date is `date`
```

By using double quotes around the text, we inhibit wildcard replacement, but allow variable and command substitution:

```
$ echo "my name is $name - date is `date`"
my name is Graham - date is Mon Feb  2 23:14:56 CST 1998
$ _
```

HERE DOCUMENTS   (pg 153)

Earlier in the chapter, I briefly mentioned the ≪ metacharacter. I delayed its full description until now, as it's really used only in conjunction with scripts and variables. When the shell encounters a sequence of the form

```
$ command << word
```

it copies its own standard input up to, but not including, the line starting with *word* into a shell buffer and then executes *command*, using the contents of the buffer as its standard input. Obviously, you should choose a sensible value for *word* that is unusual enough not to occur naturally in the text that follows. If no line containing just *word* is encountered, the Bourne and Korn shells stop copying input when they reach the end of the script, whereas the C shell issues an error message. All references to shell variables in the copied text are replaced by their values. The most common use of the ≪ metacharacter is to allow scripts to supply the standard input of other commands as in-line text, rather than having to use auxiliary files. Scripts that use ≪ are sometimes called *here documents*. Here's an example of a here document:

```
$ cat here.sh             ...look at an example of a "here" doc.
mail $1 << ENDOFTEXT
Dear $1,
 Please see me regarding some exciting news!
 - $USER
ENDOFTEXT
echo mail sent to $1
$ here.sh glass           ...send mail to myself using the script.
mail sent to glass
$ mail                    ...look at my mail.
Mail version SMI 4.0 Sat Oct 13 20:32:29 PDT 1990  Type ? for help.
>N  1 glass@utdallas.edu Mon Feb  2 13:34   12/384
& 1                       ...read message #1.
From: Graham Glass <glass@utdallas.edu>
To: glass@utdallas.edu

Dear glass,
 Please see me regarding some exciting news!

 - glass
& q                                    ...quit out of mail.
$ _
```

JOB CONTROL   - ps, kill, wait

Convenient multitasking is one of UNIX's best features, so it's important to be able to obtain a listing of your current processes and control their behavior. The following two utilities and one built-in command allow you to do this:

- **ps,** which generates a list of processes and their attributes, including their names, process ID numbers, controlling terminals, and owners

- **kill,** which allows you to terminate a process on the basis of its ID number
- **wait,** which allows a shell to wait for one of its child processes to terminate

Process Status: ps

The **ps** utility allows you to monitor the status of processes. It works as shown in Figure 4.14. In the next example, I made use of the **sleep** utility to delay a simple echo statement and placed the command in the background. I then executed the ps utility to obtain a list of my shell's associated processes. Each "sh" process was a Bourne shell process; one of them was my login shell, and the other one was the subshell created to execute the command group. The commands are as follows:

```
$ (sleep 10; echo done) &      ...delayed echo in background.
27387                          ...the process ID number.
$ ps                           ...obtain a process status list.
  PID TTY      TIME CMD
27355 pts/3    0:00 -sh        ...the login shell.
27387 pts/3    0:00 -sh        ...the subshell.
27388 pts/3    0:00 sleep 10   ...the sleep.
27389 pts/3    0:00 ps         ...the ps command itself!
$ done              ...the output from the background process.
```

Utility: **ps** -efl_x

ps generates a listing of <u>process status</u> information. By default, the output is limited to processes created by your current shell. The **-e** option instructs **ps** to include all processes that are currently running. The **–f** option causes **ps** to generate a full listing. The **–l** option generates a long listing. The meaning of each **ps** column is described in the text. *–x lists all processes with/without control terminals, pg 171 (includes background processes)*

FIGURE 4.14

Description of the **ps** command.

For the record, Figure 4.15 provides a description of the **sleep** utility.

Utility: **sleep** *seconds*

The **sleep** utility sleeps for the specified number of seconds and then terminates.

FIGURE 4.15

Description of the **sleep** command.

The meanings of the common column headings of **ps** output are shown in Figure 4.16. The S field encodes the process' state, as shown in Figure 4.17. The meanings of

Column	Meaning
S	the process state
UID	the effective user ID of the process
PID	the process ID
PPID	the parent process ID
C	the percentage of CPU time that the process used in the last minute
PRI	the priority of the process
SZ	the size of the process' data and stack in kilobytes
STIME	the time the process was created, or the date if it was created before today
TTY	the controlling terminal
TIME	the amount of CPU time used so far (MM:SS)
CMD	the name of the command

FIGURE 4.16

ps output column meanings.

Letter	Meaning
O	running on a processor
R	runnable
S	sleeping
T	suspended
Z	zombie process

FIGURE 4.17

Process state codes reported by **ps**.

most of these terms are described later in the book; only the R and S fields will make sense right now. Here's an example of some user-oriented output from **ps:**

```
$ (sleep 10; echo done) &
27462
$ ps -f                   ...request user-oriented output.
     UID    PID  PPID  C    STIME TTY        TIME CMD
   glass   731   728  0 21:48:46 pts/5     0:01 -ksh
   glass   831   830  1 22:27:06 pts/5     0:00 sleep 10
   glass   830   731  0 22:27:06 pts/5     0:00 -ksh
$ done                    ...output from previous command
```

If you're interested in tracking the movements of other users on your system, try the **-e** and **-f** options of **ps:**

```
$ ps -ef              ...list all user's processes.
  UID  PID PPID C  STIME  TTY TIME CMD
root    0    0 0 18:58:16 ?  0:01 sched
root    1    0 0 18:58:19 ?  0:01 /etc/init -
root    2    0 0 18:58:19 ?  0:00 pageout
root    3    0 1 18:58:19 ?  0:53 fsflush
root  198    1 0 18:59:38 ?  0:00 /usr/sbin/nscd
root  178    1 0 18:59:35 ?  0:00 /usr/sbin/syslogd
root  302    1 0 18:59:58 ?  0:00 /usr/lib/saf/sac
root  125    1 0 18:59:14 ?  0:00 /usr/sbin/rpcbind
root  152    1 0 18:59:29 ?  0:01 /usr/sbin/inetd -s
root  115    1 0 18:59:13 ?  0:00 /usr/sbin/in.routed -q
root  127    1 0 18:59:15 ?  0:00 /usr/sbin/keyserv
root  174    1 0 18:59:34 ?  0:00 /etc/automountd
glass 731  728 0 21:48:46 p5 0:01 -ksh
$ _
```

In Chapter 6, I describe a utility called "track" that makes use of these options to monitor other users. The Bourne and Korn shells automatically terminate background processes when you log out, whereas the C and Bash shells allow them to continue. If you're using a Bourne or Korn shell and you want to make a background process immune from this effect, use the **nohup** utility to protect it. **nohup** works as shown in Figure 4.18.

Utility: **nohup** *command*   — No Hangup — prevents process from terminating

The **nohup** utility executes *command* and makes it immune to the hangup (HUP) and terminate (TERM) signals. The standard output and error channels of *command* are automatically redirected to a file called "nohup.out," and the process' priority value is increased by 5, thereby reducing its priority. This utility is ideal for ensuring that background processes are not terminated when your login shell is exited.

FIGURE 4.18

Description of the **nohup** command.

If you execute a command using **nohup**, log out, and then log back in again, you won't see the command on the output of a regular **ps**. This is because a process loses its control terminal when you log out and continues to execute without it. To include a list of all the processes without control terminals in a **ps** output, use the **-x** option. Here's an example of this effect:

```
$ nohup sleep 10000 &      ...nohup a background process.
27406
Sending output to 'nohup.out'  ...message from "nohup".
$ ps                            ...look at processes.
 PID TT STAT  TIME COMMAND
27399 p3 S      0:00 -sh (sh)
27406 p3 S N    0:00 sleep 10000
27407 p3 R      0:00 ps
$ ^D                            ...log out.

UNIX(r) System V Release 4.0
login: glass                    ...log back in.
Password:                       ...secret.
$ ps                   ...the background process is not seen.
 PID TT STAT  TIME COMMAND
27409 p3 S      0:00 -sh (sh)
27411 p3 R      0:00 ps
$ ps -x                ...the background process may be seen.
 PID   TT   STAT  TIME  COMMAND
27406   ?    IN   0:00  sleep 10000
27409  p3    S    0:00  -sh (sh)
27412  p3    R    0:00  ps -x
$ _
```

For more information about control terminals, see Chapter 13.

Signaling Processes: `kill`

If you wish to terminate a process before it is completed, use the **kill** command. The Korn and C shells contain a built-in command called **kill**, whereas the Bourne shell invokes the standard utility instead. Both versions of **kill** support the functionality described in Figure 4.19. In the following example, I created a background process and then killed it. To confirm the termination, I obtained a **ps** listing. The commands are as follows:

```
$ (sleep 10; echo done) &&       ...create background process.
27390                            ...process ID number.
$ kill 27390                     ...kill the process.
$ ps                             ...it's gone!
 PID TT STAT  TIME COMMAND
27355 p3 S      0:00 -sh (sh)
27394 p3 R      0:00 ps
$ _
```

Utility/Shell Command: **kill** [-signalId] {pid}+

    kill –l   *Always try just a kill first, before using*
                                          Kill –9

kill sends the signal with code signalId to the list of numbered processes. signalId may be the number or name of a signal. By default, **kill** sends a TERM signal (number 15), which causes the receiving processes to terminate. To obtain a list of the valid signal names, use the **-l** option. To send a signal to a process, you must either own it or be a superuser. (For more information about signals, see Chapter 13.)

   Processes may protect themselves from all signals except the KILL signal (number 9). Therefore, to ensure a kill, send signal number 9. (Note that sending a KILL will not allow a process to clean up and terminate normally, as many programs do when they receive a TERM signal.)

   The kill utility (as opposed to the Korn and C shell built-ins) allows you to specify 0 as the *pid*, which causes all of the processes associated with the shell to be terminated. Chapter 6 contains information on the advanced features of the built-in kill command.

(margin handwriting: why use Kill –9 or Kill –KILL)

FIGURE 4.19

Description of the **kill** command.

The next example illustrates the use of the **-l** option and a named signal. The signal names are listed in numeric order, starting with signal 1:

```
$ kill -l                        ...list the signal names.
HUP INT QUIT ILL TRAP ABRT EMT FPE KILL BUS SEGV SYS PIPE ALRM TERM URG
STOP TSTP CONT CHLD TTIN TTOU IO XCPU XFSZ VTALRM PROF WINCH LOST USR1
USR2
$ (sleep 10; echo done) &
27490                            ...process ID number.
$ kill -KILL 27490       ...kill the process with signal #9.
$ _
```

Finally, here's an example of the **kill** utility's ability to kill all of the processes associated with the current shell:

```
$ sleep 30 & sleep 30 & sleep 30 &        ...create three.
27429
27430
27431
$ kill 0                                  ...kill them all.
27431 Terminated
27430 Terminated
27429 Terminated
$ _
```

Waiting for Child Processes: `wait`

A shell may wait for one or more of its child processes to terminate by executing the built-in **wait** command, which works as shown in Figure 4.20. In the following example, the shell waited until both background child processes terminated before continuing:

```
$ (sleep 30; echo done 1) &          ...create a child process.
24193
$ (sleep 30; echo done 2) &          ...create a child process.
24195
$ echo done 3; wait; echo done 4     ...wait for children.
done 3
done 1                               ...output from first child.
done 2                               ...output from second child.
done 4
$ _
```

Shell Command: **wait** [*pid*]

wait causes the shell to suspend operation until the child process with the specified process ID number terminates. If no arguments are supplied, the shell waits for all of its child processes to terminate.

FIGURE 4.20

Description of the *wait* shell command.

This facility is generally useful only in advanced shell scripts.

FINDING A COMMAND: $PATH

When a shell processes a command, it first checks to see whether the command is a built-in; if it is, the shell executes it directly. *echo* is an example of a built-in shell command:

```
$ echo some commands are executed directly by the shell
some commands are executed directly by the shell
$ _
```

If the command in question isn't a built-in command, the shell checks whether it begins with a / character. If it does, the shell assumes that the first token is the absolute pathname of a command and tries to execute the file with the stated name. If the file doesn't exist or isn't an executable file, an error occurs:

```
$ /bin/ls                    ...full pathname of the ls utility.
script.csh  script.ksh
```

```
$ /bin/nsx               ...a non-existent filename.
/bin/nsx: not found
$ /etc/passwd                    ...the name of the password file.
/etc/passwd: Permission denied    ...it's not executable.
$ _
```

3) If the command in question isn't a built-in command or a full pathname, the shell searches the directories whose names are stored in the PATH environment variable. Each directory in the PATH variable is searched (from left to right) for an executable file matching the command name. If a match is found, the file is executed. If a match isn't found in any of the directories, or if the file that matches is not executable, an error occurs. If PATH is not set or is equal to the empty string, then only the current directory is searched. The contents of the PATH variable may be changed using the methods described in later chapters, thereby allowing you to tailor the search path to your needs. The original search path is usually initialized by the shell's start-up file and typically includes all of the standard UNIX directories that contain executable utilities. Here are some examples:

```
$ echo $PATH
/bin:/usr/bin:/usr/sbin    ...directories searched.
$ ls                       ...located in "/bin".
script.csh   script.ksh
$ nsx                      ...not located anywhere.
nsx: not found
$ _
```

OVERLOADING STANDARD UTILITIES

Users often create a "bin" subdirectory in their home directory and place this subdirectory *before* the traditional "bin" directories in their PATH setting. Doing so allows them to overload default UNIX utilities with their own "home-brewed" versions, since those versions will be located by the search process before their standard counterparts are. If you choose to do this, you should take great care, as scripts that are run from a shell are programmed to use standard utilities, and they might be "confused" by the nonstandard utilities that actually get executed. In the following example, I inserted my own "bin" directory into the search path sequence and then overrode the standard "ls" utility with my own version:

```
$ mkdir bin        ...make my own personal "bin" directory.
$ cd bin           ...move into the new directory.
$ cat > ls         ...create a script called "ls".
echo my ls
^D                 ...end-of-input.
$ chmod +x ls      ...make it executable.
$ echo $PATH       ...look at the current PATH setting.
```

```
/bin:/usr/bin:/usr/sbin
$ echo $HOME          ...get pathname of my home directory.
/home/glass
$ PATH=/home/glass/bin:$PATH   ...update.
$ ls                  ...call "ls".
my ls                 ...my own version overrides "/bin/ls".
$ _
```

Note that only this shell and its child shells would be affected by the change to PATH; all other shells would be unaffected.

TERMINATION AND EXIT CODES

Every UNIX process terminates with an exit value. By convention, an exit value of 0 means that the process completed successfully, and a nonzero exit value indicates failure. All built-in commands return 1 if they fail. In the Bourne, Korn, and Bash shells, the special shell variable $? always contains the value of the previous command's exit code. In the C shell, the $status variable holds the exit code. In the following example, the **date** utility succeeded, whereas the **cc** and **awk** utilities failed:

```
$ date                     ...date succeeds.
Sat Feb  2 22:13:38 CST 2002
$ echo $?                  ...display its exit value.
0                          ...indicates success.
$ cc prog.c           ...compile a non-existent program.
cpp: Unable to open source file 'prog.c'.
$ echo $?                  ...display its exit value.
1                          ...indicates failure.
$ awk                 ...use awk illegally.
awk: Usage: awk [-Fc] [-f source | 'cmds'] [files]
$ echo $?                  ...display its exit value.
2                          ...indicates failure.
$ _
```

Any script that you write should always explicitly return an exit code. To terminate a script, use the built-in *exit* command, which works as shown in Figure 4.21. If a shell doesn't include an explicit *exit* statement, the exit value of the last command is returned by default. The script in the following example returned an exit value of 3:

```
$ cat script.sh              ...look at the script.
echo this script returns an exit code of 3
exit 3
$ script.sh                  ...execute the script.
this script returns an exit code of 3
$ echo $?                    ...look at the exit value.
3
$ _
```

> *Shell Command*: **exit** *number*
>
> *exit* terminates the shell and returns the exit value *number* to its parent process. If *number* is omitted, the exit value of the previous command is used.

FIGURE 4.21

Description of the *exit* shell command.

The next chapter contains some examples of scripts that make use of a command's exit value.

COMMON CORE BUILT-INS

A large number of built-in commands are supported by the four shells, but only a few are common to all. This section describes the most useful common core built-in commands.

eval

The *eval* command works as shown in Figure 4.22. In the following example, I executed the result of the *echo* command, which caused the variable x to be set:

```
$ echo x=5          ...first execute an echo directly.
x=5
$ eval `echo x=5` ...execute the result of the echo.
$ echo $x                 ...confirm that x was set to 5.
5
$ _
```

> *Shell Command*: **eval** *command*
>
> The *eval* shell command executes the output of *command* as a regular shell command. It is useful in processing the output of utilities that generate shell commands (e.g., **tset**).

FIGURE 4.22

Description of the *eval* shell command.

For a more complex example, see the description of **tset** in Chapter 2.

exec

The *exec* command works as shown in Figure 4.23. In the following example, I "ex-ec'ed" the **date** command from my login shell, which caused the **date** utility to run and then my login process to terminate:

```
$ exec date                    ...replace shell process by date process.
Sun Feb  1 18:55:01 CDT 1998       ...output from date.
login: _                           ...login shell is terminated.
```

Shell Command: **exec** *command*

The *exec* shell command causes the shell's image to be replaced with *command* in the process' memory space. If *command* is successfully executed, the shell that performed the *exec* ceases to exist. If that shell was a login shell, then the login session is terminated when *command* terminates.

FIGURE 4.23

Description of the *exec* shell command.

shift

The *shift* command works as shown in Figure 4.24. In the following example, I wrote a C shell script to display its arguments before and after a shift.

```
$ cat shift.csh                      ...list the script.
#!/bin/csh
echo first argument is $1, all args are $*
shift
echo first argument is $1, all args are $*
$ shift.csh a b c d                  ...run with four arguments.
first argument is a, all args are a b c d
first argument is b, all args are b c d
$ shift.csh a                        ...run with one argument.
first argument is a, all args are a
first argument is , all args are
$ shift.csh                ...run with no arguments.
first argument is , all args are
shift: No more words       ...error message.
$ _
```

Shell Command: **shift**

The *shift* shell command causes all of the positional parameters $2..$n to be renamed $1..$(n-1) and $1 to be lost. It is particularly handy in shell scripts when they are cycling through a series of command line parameters. If there are no positional arguments left to shift, an error message is displayed.

FIGURE 4.24

Description of the *shift* shell command.

umask

When a C program creates a file, it supplies the file's original permission settings as an octal parameter to the system call open(). For example, to create a file with read and write permission for the owner, group, and others, the program would execute a system call such as this one:

```
fd = open ("myFile", OCREAT | ORDWR, 0666);
```

For information on the encoding of permissions as octal numbers, see Chapter 2. For information on the open() system call, see Chapter 13. When the shell performs redirection (using the ">" character), it employs a system call sequence similar to the one shown in the preceding example to construct a file with octal permission 666. However, if you try creating a file by using redirection with the ">" character, you'll probably end up with a file that has a permission setting of 644 octal, as shown in the following example:

```
$ date > date.txt
$ ls -l date.txt
-rw-r--r--  1 glass      29 May  3 18:56 date.txt
$ _
```

[handwritten margin note: for Linux, default umask is root - 022 regular users - 002]

The reason for this difference in permission is that every UNIX process contains a special quantity called a *umask* value, which is used to restrict the permission settings that it requests when a file is created. The default umask value of a shell is 022 octal. The set bits of a umask value mask out the set bits of a requested permission setting. In the preceding example, the requested permission 666 was masked with 022 to produce the final permission, 644, as shown in Figure 4.25.

	owner			group			others		
	r	w	x	r	w	x	r	w	x
original	1	1	0	1	1	0	1	1	0
mask	0	0	0	0	1	0	0	1	0
final	1	1	0	1	0	0	1	0	0

[handwritten: 666 / 022 umask / 644 / (XOR)]

FIGURE 4.25

Bit-by-bit example of the effect of the umask setting.

If a file already exists before something is redirected to it, the original file's permission values are retained and the umask value is ignored.

Figure 4.26 shows how the *umask* command may be used to manipulate the umask value. In the following example, I changed the umask value to 0 and then created a new file to illustrate its effect:

```
$ umask                  ...display current umask value.
22                       ...mask write permission of group/others.
```

```
$ umask 0            ...set umask value to 0.
$ date > date2.txt   ...create a new file.
$ ls -l date2.txt
-rw-rw-rw-  1 glass    29 May  3 18:56 date2.txt
$ _
```

Shell Command: **umask** [*octalValue*]

The *umask* shell command sets the shell's umask value to the specified octal number, or displays the current umask value if the argument is omitted. A shell's umask value is retained until changed. Child processes inherit their umask value from their parents.

FIGURE 4.26

Description of the *umask* shell command.

CHAPTER REVIEW

Checklist

In this chapter, I described

- the common functionality of the four major shells
- the common shell metacharacters
- output and input redirection
- filename substitution
- pipes
- command substitution
- command sequences
- grouped commands
- the construction of scripts
- the difference between local and environment variables
- the two different kinds of quotes
- basic job control
- the mechanism that the shell uses to find commands
- several core built-in commands

Quiz

1. Can you change your default shell?
2. What UNIX command is used to change your current directory?
3. How can you enter commands that are longer than one line?
4. What is the difference between a built-in command and a utility?

5. How can you make a script executable?
6. What is the strange term that is sometimes given to filename substitution?
7. Describe a common use for command substitution.
8. Describe the meaning of the terms *parent shell*, *child shell*, and *subshell*.
9. How do you think the **kill** command got its name?
10. Describe a way to override a standard utility.
11. What is a good *umask* value, and why?

Exercises

4.1 Write a script that prints the current date, your user name, and the name of your login shell. [level: *easy*]

4.2 Experiment with the *exec* command by writing a series of three shell scripts called "a.sh," "b.sh," and "c.sh", each of which displays its name, executes **ps**, and then *exec*'s the next script in the sequence. Observe what happens when you start the first script by executing exec a.sh. [level: *medium*]

4.3 Why is the file that is created in the following session unaffected by the umask value? [level: *medium*]

```
$ ls -l date.txt
-rw-rw-rw-  1 glass     29 Aug 20 21:04 date.txt
$ umask 0077
$ date > date.txt
$ ls -l date.txt
-rw-rw-rw-  1 glass     29 Aug 20 21:04 date.txt
$ _
```

4.4 Write a script that creates three background processes, waits for them all to complete, and then displays a simple message. [level: *medium*]

Project

Compare and contrast the UNIX shell features with the graphical shells available on Windows. Which do you think is better? [level: *medium*]

C H A P T E R   5

The Bourne Shell

the default shell for script files,
if no other shell is specified
on line one , pg 161

See $SHELL env. var , pg 146

See pg 146 for
general comparison

See chsh (change shell,
pg 147)

See ^D — terminates shell,
pg 149

MOTIVATION

The Bourne shell, written by Stephen Bourne, was the first popular UNIX shell and is available on all UNIX systems. It supports a fairly versatile programming language and is a subset of the more powerful Korn shell that is described in Chapter 6. Knowledge of the Bourne shell will therefore allow you to understand the operation of many scripts that have already been written for UNIX, as well as preparing you for the more advanced Korn shell.

PREREQUISITES

You should have already read Chapter 4 and experimented with some of the core shell facilities.

OBJECTIVES

In this chapter, I'll explain and demonstrate the Bourne-specific facilities, including the use of environment and local variables, the built-in programming language, and advanced I/O redirection.

PRESENTATION

The information is presented in the form of several sample UNIX sessions.

UTILITIES

The chapter introduces the following utilities, listed in alphabetical order:

expr   test

SHELL COMMANDS

The following shell commands, listed in alphabetical order, are introduced:

break	for..in..do..done	set
case..in..esac	if..then..elif..fi	trap
continue	read	while..do..done
export	readonly	

INTRODUCTION

The Bourne shell supports all of the core shell facilities described in Chapter 4, plus the following other facilities:

- several ways to set and access variables
- a built-in programming language that supports conditional branching, looping, and interrupt handling
- extensions to the existing redirection and command sequence operations
- several new built-in commands

These facilities are diagram shown in Figure 5.1.

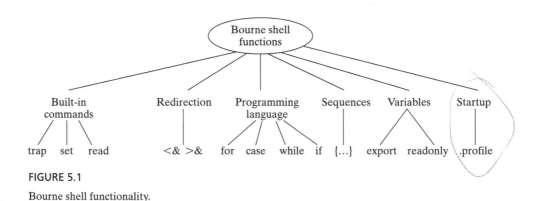

FIGURE 5.1

Bourne shell functionality.

START-UP

The Bourne shell is a regular C program whose executable file is stored as "/bin/sh". If your chosen shell is "/bin/sh," an interactive Bourne shell is invoked automatically when you log into UNIX. You may also invoke a Bourne shell manually from a script or from a terminal by using the command **sh** (which has several command-line options, described at the end of the chapter).

When an interactive Bourne shell is started, it searches for a file called ".profile" in the user's home directory. If it finds the file, it executes all of the shell commands that the file contains. Then, regardless of whether ".profile" was found, an interactive

Bourne shell displays its prompt and awaits user commands. The standard Bourne shell prompt is $, although it may be changed by setting the local variable PS1, described later in the chapter. (Note that noninteractive Bourne shells do not read any start-up files.)

One common use of ".profile" is to initialize environment variables such as TERM, which contains the type of your terminal, and PATH, which tells the shell where to search for executable files. Here's an example of a Bourne shell ".profile" startup file:

```
TERM=vt100                      # Set terminal type.
export TERM                     # Copy to environment.
# Set path and metacharacters
stty erase "^?" kill "^U" intr "^C" eof "^D"
PATH='.:$HOME/bin:/bin:/usr/sbin:/usr/bin:/usr/local/bin'
```

VARIABLES

The Bourne shell can perform the following variable-related operations:

- simple assignment and access
- testing of a variable for existence
- reading a variable from standard input
- making a variable read only
- exporting a local variable to the environment

The Bourne shell also defines several local and environment variables in addition to those mentioned in Chapter 4.

Creating/Assigning a Variable

The Bourne shell syntax for assigning a value to a variable is

```
{name=value}+
```

If a variable doesn't exist, it is implicitly created; otherwise, its previous value is over-written. A newly created variable is always local, although it may be turned into an environment variable by means of a method I'll describe shortly. To assign a value that contains spaces, surround the value by quotes. Here's an example:

```
$ firstName=Graham lastName=Glass age=29   ...assign vars.
$ echo $firstName $lastName is $age
Graham Glass is 29                              ...simple access.
$ name=Graham Glass                             ...syntax error.
Glass: not found
$ name="Graham Glass"      ...use quotes to built strings.
$ echo $name                                    ...now it works.
Graham Glass
$ _
```

Accessing a Variable

The Bourne shell supports the access methods shown in Figure 5.2. If a variable is accessed before it is assigned a value, it returns a null string.

Syntax	Action
$name	Replaced by the value of *name*.
${name}	Replaced by the value of *name*. This form is useful if the expression is immediately followed by an alphanumeric character that would otherwise be interpreted as part of the variable name.
${name−word}	Replaced by the value of *name* if set and *word* otherwise.
${name+word}	Replaced by *word* if *name* is set and nothing otherwise.
${name=word}	Assigns *word* to the variable *name* if *name* is not already set and then is replaced by the value of *name*.
${name?word}	Replaced by name if *name* is set. If *name* is not set, *word* is displayed to the standard error channel and the shell is exited. If *word* is omitted, then a standard error message is displayed instead.

FIGURE 5.2

Bourne shell special variables.

I personally find these techniques for accessing variables to be "hack" methods of dealing with certain conditions, so I hardly ever use them. However, it's good to be able to understand code that uses them. The following examples illustrate each access method. In the first example, I used braces to append a string to the value of a variable:

```
$ verb=sing              ...assign a variable.
$ echo I like $verbing   ...there's no variable "verbing".
I like
$ echo I like ${verb}ing    ...now it works.
I like singing
$ _
```

Here's an example that uses command substitution to set the variable startDate to the current date if it's not already set to that:

```
$ startDate=${startDate-`date`}    ...if not set, run date.
$ echo $startDate                  ...look at its value.
Tue Wed 4 06:56:51 CST 1998
$ _
```

In the next example, I set the variable x to a default value and printed its value, all at the same time:

```
$ echo x = ${x=10}        ...assign a default value.
x = 10
$ echo $x                 ...confirm the variable was set.
10
$ _
```

In the following example, I displayed messages on the basis of whether certain variables were set:

```
$ flag=1                              ...assign a variable.
$ echo ${flag+'flag is set'}         ...conditional message #1.
flag is set
$ echo ${flag2+'flag2 is set'}       ...conditional message #2.
                                     ...result is null

$ _
```

In the next example, I tried to access an undefined variable called grandTotal and received an error message instead:

```
$ total=10                            ...assign a variable.
$ value=${total?'total not set'}     ...accessed OK.
$ echo $value                                 ...look at its value.
10
$ value=${grandTotal?'grand total not set'}  ...not set.
grandTotal: grand total not set
$ _
```

In the final example, I ran a script that used the same access method as the previous example. Note that the script terminated when the access error occurred:

```
$ cat script.sh                    ...look at the script.
value=${grandTotal?'grand total is not set'}
echo done           # this line is never executed.
$ script.sh                        ...run the script.
script.sh: grandTotal: grand total is not set
$ _
```

Reading a Variable from Standard Input

The *read* command allows you to read variables from standard input. It works as shown in Figure 5.3. If you specify just one variable, the entire line is stored in the variable. Here's a sample script that prompts a user for his or her full name:

```
$ cat script.sh                    ...list the script.
echo "Please enter your name: \c"
read name                          # read just one variable.
```

```
          echo your name is $name          # display the variable.
          $ script.sh                              ...run the script.
          Please enter your name: Graham Walker Glass
          your name is Graham Walker Glass      ...whole line was read.
          $ _
```

Shell Command: **read** {*variable*}+

read reads one line from standard input and then assigns successive words from the line to the specified variables. Any words that are left over are assigned to the last named variable.

FIGURE 5.3

Description of the *read* shell command.

Here's an example that illustrates what happens when you specify more than one variable:

```
          $ cat script.sh                       ...list the script.
          echo "Please enter your name: \c"
          read firstName lastName       # read two variables.
          echo your first name is $firstName
          echo your last name is $lastName
          $ script.sh                           ...run the script.
          Please enter your name: Graham Walker Glass
          your first name is Graham             ...first word.
          your last name is Walker Glass        ...the rest.
          $ script.sh                           ...run it again.
          Please enter your name: Graham
          your first name is Graham             ...first word.
          your last name is                     ...only one.
          $ _
```

Exporting Variables

The *export* command allows you to mark local variables for export to the environment. It works as shown in Figure 5.4. Although it's not necessary, I tend to use uppercase letters

---

Shell Command: **export** {*variable*}+

export marks the specified variables for export to the environment. If no variables are specified, a list of all the variables marked for export during the shell session is displayed.

FIGURE 5.4

Description of the *export* shell command.

to name environment variables. The **env** utility, described in Figure 5.5, allows you to modify and list such variables. In the following example, I created a local variable called DATABASE, which I then marked for export. When I created a subshell, a copy of the environment variable was inherited:

```
$ export                    ...list my current exports.
export TERM                 ...set in my ".profile" startup file.
$ DATABASE=/dbase/db        ...create a local variable.
$ export DATABASE           ...mark it for export.
$ export                    ...note that it's been added.
export DATABASE
export TERM
$ env                       ...list the environment.
DATABASE=/dbase/db
HOME=/home/glass
LOGNAME=glass
PATH=:/usr/ucb:/bin:/usr/bin
SHELL=/bin/sh
TERM=vt100
USER=glass
$ sh                        ...create a subshell.
$ echo $DATABASE            ...a copy was inherited.
/dbase/db
$ ^D                        ...terminate subshell.
$ _
```

Utility: **env** {*variable = value*}* [*command*]

env assigns values to specified environment variables and then executes an optional command using the new environment. If no variables or command is specified, a list of the current environment is displayed.

FIGURE 5.5

Description of the **env** command.

Read-only Variables

The *readonly* command allows you to protect variables against modification. It works as shown in Figure 5.6. In the following example, I protected a local variable from modification, exported the variable, and then showed that its copy did not inherit the read-only status:

```
$ password=Shazam           ...assign a local variable.
$ echo $password            ...display its value.
Shazam
$ readonly password         ...protect it.
$ readonly                  ...list all readonly variables.
```

```
      readonly password
      $ password=Phoombah                  ...try to modify it.
      password: is read only
      $ export password                    ...export the variable.
      $ password=Phoombah                  ...try to modify it.
      password: is read only
      $ sh                                 ...create a subshell.
      $ readonly                   ...the exported password is not readonly.
      $ echo $password                     ...its value was copied correctly.
      Shazam
      $ password=Alacazar                  ...but its value may be changed.
      $ echo $password                     ...echo its value.
      Alacazar
      $ ^D                                 ...terminate the subshell.
      $ echo $password                     ...echo original value.
      Shazam
      $ _
```

Shell Command: **readonly** {*variable*}*

readonly makes the specified variables read only, protecting them against future modification. If no variables are specified, a list of the current read-only variables is displayed. Copies of exported variables do not inherit their read-only status.

FIGURE 5.6

Description of the *readonly* shell command.

Predefined Local Variables

In addition to the core predefined local variables, the Bourne shell defines the local variables shown in Figure 5.7. Here's a small shell script that illustrates the first three variables. In this example, the C compiler (**cc**) was invoked on a file that didn't exist, and therefore the system returned a failure exit code.

```
      $ cat script.sh                      ...list the script.
      echo there are $# command line arguments: $@
      cc $1                    # compile the first argument.
      echo the last exit value was $?   # display exit code.
      $ script.sh nofile tmpfile          ...execute the script.
      there are 2 command line arguments: nofile tmpfile
      cc: Warning: File with unknown suffix (nofile) passed to ld
      ld: nofile: No such file or directory
      the last exit value was 4           ...cc errored.
      $ _
```

Name	Value
$@	an individually quoted list of all the positional parameters
$#	the number of positional parameters
$?	the exit value of the last command
$!	the process ID of the last background command
$-	the current shell options assigned from the command line or by the built-in set command (see later)
$$	the process ID of the shell in use

FIGURE 5.7

Bourne predefined local variables.

The next example illustrates how $! may be used to kill the last background process:

```
$ sleep 1000 &             ...create a background process.
29455                      ...process ID of background process.
$ kill $!                  ...kill it!
29455 Terminated
$ echo $!                  ...the process ID is still remembered.
29455
$ _
```

Predefined Environment Variables

In addition to the core predefined environment variables (listed in Chapter 2), the Bourne shell defines the environment variables shown in Figure 5.8. Here's a small example that illustrates the first three predefined environment variables. I set my prompt to something different by assigning a new value to PS1 and changed the delimiter character to a colon, saving the previous value in a local variable. Finally, I set PS2 to a new value and illustrated a situation in which the secondary prompt is displayed.

```
$ PS1="sh? "               ...set a new primary prompt.
sh? oldIFS=$IFS            ...remember the old value of IFS.
sh? IFS=":"                ...change the word delimiter to a colon.
sh? ls:*.c                 ...this executes OK!
badguy.c    number.c    open.c    trunc.c    writer.c
fact2.c     number2.c   reader.c  who.c
sh? IFS=$oldIFS                   ...restore the old value of IFS.
sh? string="a long\              ...assign a string over 2 lines
> string"                  ...">" is the secondary prompt.
sh? echo $string           ...look at the value of "string".
a long string
```

```
sh? PS2="??? "                      ...change the secondary prompt.
sh? string="a long\                 ...assign a long string.
??? string"                     ..."???" is new secondary prompt.
sh? echo $string                    ...look at the value of "string".
a long string
sh? _
```

Name	Value
$IFS	When the shell tokens a command line prior to its execution, it uses the characters in this variable as delimiters. IFS usually contains a space, a tab, and a newline character.
$PS1	This variable contains the value of the command-line prompt, $ by default. To change the prompt, simply set PS1 to a new value.
$PS2	This variable contains the value of the secondary command-line prompt (> by default) that is displayed when more input is required by the shell. To change the prompt, set PS2 to a new value.
$SHENV	If this variable is not set, the shell searches the user's home directory for the ".profile" start-up file when a new shell is created. If the variable is set, then the shell searches the directory specified by SHENV.

FIGURE 5.8

Bourne shell predefined environment variables.

ARITHMETIC

Although the Bourne shell itself doesn't support arithmetic directly, the **expr** utility does and is used as described in Figure 5.9. The following example illustrates some of the functions of **expr** and makes plentiful use of command substitution:

```
$ x=1                               ...initial value of x.
$ x=`expr $x + 1`                   ...increment x.
$ echo $x
2
$ x=`expr 2 + 3 \* 5`               ...* before +.
$ echo $x
17
$ echo `expr \( 2 + 3 \) \* 5`      ...regroup.
25
$ echo `expr length "cat"`          ...find length of "cat".
3
$ echo `expr substr "donkey" 4 3`   ...extract a substring.
key
```

```
$ echo `expr index "donkey" "ke"`        ...locate a substring.
4
$ echo `expr match "smalltalk" '.*lk'`...attempt a match.
9
$ echo `expr match "transputer" '*.lk'`      ...attempt match.
0
$ echo `expr "transputer" : '*.lk'`          ...attempt a match.
0
$ echo `expr \( 4 \> 5 \)`                    ...is 4 > 5 ?
0
$ echo `expr \( 4 \> 5 \) \/ \( 6 \< 7 \)`   ...4>5 or 6<7?
1
$ _
```

Utility: **expr** *expression*

expr evaluates *expression* and sends the result to standard output. All of the components of *expression* must be separated by blanks, and all of the shell metacharacters must be escaped by a \. *expression* may yield a numeric or string result, depending on the operators that it contains. The result of *expression* may be assigned to a shell variable by the appropriate use of command substitution.

    expression may be constructed by applying the following binary operators to integer operands, grouped in decreasing order of precedence:

OPERATOR	MEANING
* / %	multiplication, division, remainder
+ −	addition, subtraction
= > >= < <= !=	comparison operators
&	logical and
|	logical or

Parentheses may be used to explicitly control the order of evaluation. (They also must be escaped.) **expr** supports the following string operators as well:

OPERATOR	MEANING
string : regularExpression **match** *string regularExpression*	Both forms return the length of *string* if both sides match, and each returns zero otherwise.

FIGURE 5.9

Description of the **expr** command.

substr string start length	Returns the substring of *string*, starting from index *start* and consisting of *length* characters.
index string charList	Returns the index of the first character in *string* that appears in *charList*.
length string	Returns the length of *string*.

The format of *regularExpression* is defined in the appendix.

FIGURE 5.9   (*Continued*)

CONDITIONAL EXPRESSIONS

The control structures described in the next section often branch, depending on the value of a logical expression—that is, an expression that evaluates to true or false. The **test** utility supports a substantial set of UNIX-oriented expressions that are suitable for most occasions. It works as shown in Figure 5.10. A **test** expression may take the forms shown in Figure 5.11 **test** is very picky about the syntax of expressions; the spaces shown in this table are *not* optional. For examples of **test**, see the next section, which uses them in a natural context.

Utility: **test** *expression*

    [*expression*]   (equivalent form on some UNIX systems)

test returns a zero exit code if *expression* evaluates to true; otherwise, it returns a nonzero exit status. The exit status is typically used by shell control structures for branching purposes.

    Some Bourne shells support **test** as a built-in command, in which case they support the second form of evaluation as well. The brackets of the second form must be surrounded by spaces in order to work.

    (See the text for a description of the syntax of *expression*.)

FIGURE 5.10

Description of the **test** command.

Form	Meaning
-b *filename*	True if *filename* exists as a block special file.
-c *filename*	True if *filename* exists as a character special file.
-d *filename*	True if *filename* exists as a directory.
-f *filename*	True if *filename* exists as a nondirectory.
-g *filename*	True if *filename* exists as a "set group ID" file.
-h *filename*	True if *filename* exists as a symbolic link.
-k *filename*	True if *filename* exists and has its "sticky bit" set.
-l *string*	The length of *string*.
-n *string*	True if *string* contains at least one character.
-p *filename*	True if *filename* exists as a named pipe.
-r *filename*	True if *filename* exists as a readable file.
-s *filename*	True if *filename* contains at least one character.
-t *fd*	True if file descriptor *fd* is associated with a terminal.
-u *filename*	True if *filename* exists as a "set user ID" file.
-w *filename*	True if *filename* exists as a writable file.
-x *filename*	True if *filename* exists as an executable file.
-z *string*	True if *string* contains no characters.
str1 = *str2*	True if *str1* is equal to *str2*.
str1! = *str2*	True if *str1* is not equal to *str2*.
string	True if *string* is not null.
int1 -eq *int2*	True if integer *int1* is equal to integer *int2*.
int1 -ne *int2*	True if integer *int1* is not equal to integer *int2*.
int1 -gt *int2*	True if integer *int1* is greater than integer *int2*.
int1 -ge *int2*	True if integer *int1* is greater than or equal to integer *int2*.
int1 -lt *int2*	True if integer *int1* is less than integer *int2*.
int1 -le *int2*	True if integer *int1* is less than or equal to integer *int2*.
! *expr*	True if *expr* is false.
expr1 -a *expr2*	True if *expr1* and *expr2* are both true.
expr1 -o *expr2*	True if *expr1* or *expr2* are true.
\(*expr* \)	Escaped parentheses are used for grouping expressions.

FIGURE 5.11

test command expressions.

CONTROL STRUCTURES

The Bourne shell supports a wide range of control structures that make the shell suitable as a high-level programming tool. Shell programs are usually stored in scripts and are commonly used to automate maintenance and installation tasks. The next few subsections describe the control structures in alphabetical order; they assume that you are already familiar with at least one high-level programming language.

case .. in .. esac

The case command supports multiway branching based on the value of a single string, It has the syntax described in Figure 5.12. Here's an example of a script called "menu.sh" that makes use of a *case* control structure (this script is also available on-line; see the preface for information):

```
#! /bin/sh
echo menu test program
stop=0                          # reset loop termination flag.
while test $stop -eq 0          # loop until done.
do
 cat << ENDOFMENU               # display menu.
 1   : print the date.
 2, 3: print the current working directory.
 4   : exit
ENDOFMENU
 echo
 echo 'your choice? \c'         # prompt.
 read reply                     # read response.
 echo
 case $reply in                 # process response.
   "1")
     date                       # display date.
     ;;
   "2"|"3")
     pwd                        # display working directory.
     ;;
   "4")
     stop=1                     # set loop termination flag.
     ;;
   *)                           # default.
     echo illegal choice        # error.
     ;;
 esac
 done
```

case *expression* **in**
pattern {|*pattern*}*)
list
;;
esac

expression is an expression that evaluates to a string, *pattern* may include wildcards, and *list* is a list of one or more shell commands. You may include as many pattern–list associations as you wish. The shell evaluates *expression* and then compares it with each pattern in turn, from top to bottom. When the first matching pattern is found, its associated list of commands is executed, and then the shell skips to the matching **esac**. A series of patterns separated by "or" symbols (|) is all associated with the same list. If no match is found, then the shell skips to the matching **esac**.

FIGURE 5.12

Description of the *case* shell command.

Here's the output from the "menu.sh" script:

```
$ menu.sh
menu test program
    1   : print the date.
    2, 3: print the current working directory.
    4   : exit
your choice? 1
Thu Feb  5 07:09:13 CST 1998
    1   : print the date.
    2, 3: print the current working directory.
    4   : exit
your choice? 2
/home/glass
    1   : print the date.
    2, 3: print the current working directory.
    4   : exit
your choice? 5
illegal choice
    1   : print the date.
    2, 3: print the current working directory.
    4   : exit
your choice? 4
$ _
```

for .. do .. done

The *for* command allows a list of commands to be executed several times, using a different value of the loop variable during each iteration. Its syntax is shown in Figure 5.13. Here's an example of a script that uses a *for* control structure:

```
$ cat for.sh                        ...list the script.
for color in red yellow green blue
do
 echo one color is $color
done
$ for.sh                            ...execute the script.
one color is red
one color is yellow
one color is green
one color is blue
$ _
```

---

for *name* [**in** {*word*}*]
do
   list
done

The **for** command loops the value of the variable *name* through each *word* in the word list, evaluating the commands in *list* after each iteration. If no word list is supplied, $@ ($1..) is used instead. A *break* command causes the loop to end immediately, and a *continue* command causes the loop to jump immediately to the next iteration.

FIGURE 5.13

Description of the *for* shell command.

if .. then .. fi

The *if* command supports nested conditional branches. It has the syntax shown in Figure 5.14. Here's an example of a script that uses an *if* control structure:

```
$ cat if.sh                                ...list the script.
echo 'enter a number: \c'
read number
if [ $number -lt 0 ]
```

```
then
  echo negative
elif [ $number -eq 0 ]
then
  echo zero
else
  echo positive
fi
$ if.sh                          ...run the script.
enter a number: 1
positive
$ if.sh                          ...run the script again.
enter a number: -1
negative
$ _
```

---

if *list1*
then
  list2
elif *list3*   ...optional, **elif** part may be repeated several times.
then
  list4
else   ...optional, **else** part may occur zero or one times.
  list5
fi

The commands in *list1* are executed. If the last command in *list1* succeeds, the commands in *list2* are executed. If the last command in *list1* fails and there are one or more *elif* components, then a successful command list following an *elif* causes the commands following the associated *then* to be executed. If no successful lists are found and there is an *else* component, the commands following the *else* are executed.

FIGURE 5.14

Description of the *if* shell command.

trap

The *trap* command allows you to specify a command that should be executed when the shell receives a signal of a particular value. Its syntax is shown in Figure 5.15. Here's an example of a script that uses the *trap* control structure:

```
$ cat trap.sh                          ...list the script.
trap 'echo Control-C; exit 1' 2   # trap Ctl-C (signal #2)
while  1
do
  echo infinite loop
  sleep 2                              # sleep for two seconds.
done
$ trap.sh                              ...execute the script.
infinite loop
infinite loop
^C                           ...I typed a Control-C here.
Control-C                    ...displayed by the echo command.
$ _
```

Shell command: **trap**. [[*command*] {*signal*} +]

The *trap* command instructs the shell to execute *command* whenever any of the numbered signals *signal* is received. If several signals are received, they are trapped in numeric order. If a signal value of 0 is specified, then *command* is executed when the shell terminates. If *command* is omitted, then the traps of the numbered signals are reset to their original values. If *command* is an empty string, then the numbered signals are ignored. If *trap* is executed with no arguments, a list of all the signals and their *trap* settings are displayed. (For more information on signals and their default actions, see Chapter 13.)

FIGURE 5.15

Description of the *trap* shell command.

Note that when *Control-C* was typed, the shell executed the *echo* command followed by the exit command.

until .. do .. done

The *until* command executes one series of commands as long as another series of commands fails. It has the syntax shown in Figure 5.16. Here's an example of a script that uses an *until* control structure:

```
$ cat until.sh                         ...list the script.
x=1
until [ $x -gt 3 ]
do
  echo x = $x
```

```
  x=`expr $x + 1`
done
$ until.sh                    ...execute the script.
x = 1
x = 2
x = 3
$ _
```

---

until *list1*
do
  list2
done

The *until* command executes the commands in *list1* and ends if the last command in *list1* succeeds; otherwise, the commands in *list2* are executed and the process is repeated. If *list2* is empty, the *do* keyword should be omitted. A *break* command causes the loop to end immediately, and a *continue* command causes the loop to jump immediately to the next iteration.

FIGURE 5.16

Description of the *until* shell command.

while .. done

The *while* command executes one series of commands as long as another series of commands succeeds. Its syntax is shown in Figure 5.17. Here's an example of a script that uses a *while* control structure to generate a small multiplication table:

```
$ cat multi.sh                           ...list the script.
if [ "$1" -eq "" ]; then
    echo "Usage: multi number"
    exit
fi
x=1                                 # set outer loop value
while [ $x -le $1 ]                 # outer loop
do
   y=1                        # set inner loop value
   while [ $y -le $1 ]
   do                               # generate one table entry
     echo `expr $x \* $y` "   \c"
     y=`expr $y + 1`                      # update inner loop count
```

```
      done
      echo                              # blank line
      x=`expr $x + 1`            # update outer loop count
done
$ multi.sh 7                           ...execute the script.
1       2       3       4       5       6       7
2       4       6       8       10      12      14
3       6       9       12      15      18      21
4       8       12      16      20      24      28
5       10      15      20      25      30      35
6       12      18      24      30      36      42
7       14      21      28      35      42      49

$ _
```

---

while *list1*
do
  list2
done

The *while* command executes the commands in *list1* and ends if the last command in *list1* fails; otherwise, the commands in *list2* are executed and the process is repeated. If *list2* is empty, the *do* keyword should be omitted. A *break* command causes the loop to end immediately, and a *continue* command causes the loop to jump immediately to the next iteration.

FIGURE 5.17

Description of the *while* shell command.

SAMPLE PROJECT: `track`

To illustrate a good percentage of the capabilities of the Bourne shell, I'll present a small project that I call "track." This script tracks a user's log-ins and log-outs, generating a simple report of the user's sessions. The script utilizes the following utilities:

- **who**, which displays a listing of the current users of the system
- **grep**, which filters text for lines that match a specified pattern
- **diff**, which displays the differences between two files
- **sort**, which sorts a text file
- **sed**, which performs preprogrammed edits on a file
- **expr**, which evaluates an expression
- **cat**, which lists a file

- **date**, which displays the current time
- **rm**, which removes a file
- **mv**, which moves a file
- **sleep**, which pauses for a specified number of seconds

grep, **diff**, **sort**, and **sed** are described in Chapter 3; **who** is described in Chapter 9. The usage of **track** is as shown in Figure 5.18. Here's an example of **track** at work:

```
$ track -n3 ivor -t200    ...track ivor's sessions.
track report for ivor:    ...initial output.
login          ivor              ttyp3    Feb  5 06:53
track report for ivor:    ...ivor logged out.
logout         ivor              ttyp3    Feb  5 06:55
^C                        ...terminate program using Control-C.
stop tracking             ...termination message.
$ _
```

Script: **track** [-n*count*] [-t*pause*] *userId*

track monitors the specified user's login and logout sessions. Every *pause* number of seconds, **track** scans the system and makes a note of who is currently logged in. If the specified user has logged in or logged out since the last scan, this information is displayed to standard output. **track** operates until *count* scans have been completed. By default, *pause* is 20 seconds and *count* is 10,000 scans. **track** is usually executed in the background, with its standard output redirected.

FIGURE 5.18

Description of the **track** shell script.

The implementation of **track** consists of three files:

- "track," the main Bourne shell script
- "track.sed," a **sed** script for editing the output of the **diff** utility
- "track.cleanup," a small script that cleans up temporary files at the end

The operation of **track** may be divided into three pieces:

- It parses the command line and sets the values of three local variables: user, pause, and loopCount. If any errors occur, a usage message is displayed and the script terminates.
- It then sets two traps: one to trap the script's termination and the other to trap an INT (*Control*-C) or a QUIT (*Control*-\) signal. The latter trap invokes the former trap by executing an explicit exit, so the cleanup script always gets called,

regardless of how the script terminates. The cleanup script takes the process ID of the main script as its single argument and removes the temporary files that **track** uses for its operation.

- The script then loops the specified number of times, storing a filtered list of the current users in a temporary file called ".track.new.$$," where $$ is the process ID of the script itself. This file is then compared against the last version of the same output, stored in ".track.old.$$." If a line is in the new file, but not in the oldone, the user must have logged in; if a line is in the old file, but not in the newone, the user must have logged out. If the output file from **diff** is of nonzero length, it is massaged into a suitable form by **sed** and displayed. The script then pauses for the specified number of seconds and continues to loop.

The output from two "**diff**'ed" **who** outputs is illustrated by the following session:

```
$ cat track.new.1112              ...the new output from who.
glass                 ttyp0         Feb  4 23:04
glass                 ttyp2         Feb  4 23:04
$ cat track.old.1112              ...the old output from who.
glass                 ttyp0         Feb  4 23:04
glass                 ttyp1         Feb  4 23:06
$ diff track.new.1112 track.old.1112      ...the changes.
2c2
< glass                 ttyp2         Feb  4 23:04
---
> glass                 ttyp1         Feb  4 23:06
$ _
```

The **sed** script "track.sed" removes all lines that start with a digit or "---" and then substitutes "<" for a login and ">" for a logout. Here is a listing of the three source files (which are also available on-line; see the preface for more information):

track.sed

```
/^[0-9].*/d
/^---/d
s/^</login/
s/^>/logout/
```

track.cleanup

```
echo stop tracking
rm -f .track.old.$1 .track.new.$1 .track.report.$1
```

track

```
pause=20        # default pause between scans
loopCount=10000 # default scan count
error=0         # error flag
for arg in $*   # parse command line arguments
do
```

```
  case $arg in
    -t*)            # time
      pause=`expr substr $arg 3 10`       # extract number
      ;;
    -n*)            # scan count
      loopCount=`expr substr $arg 3 10` # extract number
      ;;
    *)
      user=$arg                          # user name
      ;;
  esac
done
if [ ! "$user" ]         # check a user ID was found
then
  error=1
fi
if [ $error -eq 1 ]      # display error if error(s) found
then
  cat << ENDOFERROR      # display usage message
usage: track [-n#] [-t#] userId
ENDOFERROR
  exit 1                 # terminate shell
fi
trap 'track.cleanup $$; exit $exitCode' 0  # trap on exit
trap 'exitCode=1; exit' 2 3              # trap on INT/QUIT
> .track.old.$$            # zero the old track file.
count=0                    # number of scans so far
while [ $count -lt $loopCount ]
do
  who | grep $user | sort > .track.new.$$   # scan system
  diff .track.new.$$ .track.old.$$ | \
              sed -f track.sed > .track.report.$$
  if [ -s .track.report.$$ ]        # only report changes
  then                              # display report
    echo track report for ${user}:
    cat .track.report.$$
  fi
  mv .track.new.$$ .track.old.$$  # remember current state
  sleep $pause                    # wait a while
  count=`expr $count + 1`         # update scan count
done
exitCode=0                        # set exit code
```

MISCELLANEOUS BUILT-INS

The Bourne shell supports several specialized built-in commands. I have already described several of them, such as those related to control structures and job control, in other sections of the chapter. This section contains an alphabetical list of the rest, together with a brief description.

Read Command: .

To execute the contents of a text file from within a shell's environment (i.e., not by starting a subshell, as you do when executing a shell script), use a period followed by the name of the file. The file does not have to have execute permission. This command is handy if you make modifications to your ".profile" file and wish to reexecute it. The following command sequence illustrative:

```
$ cat .profile        ...assume ".profile" was just edited.
TERM=vt100
export TERM
$ . .profile          ...re-execute it.
$ _
```

Note that, since a subshell is not created to execute the contents of the file, any local variables that the file sets are those of the current shell.

null Command

The *null* command is usually used in conjunction with the control structures listed earlier in the chapter and performs no operation, as shown in Figure 5.19. It is often used in case structures to denote an empty set of statements associated with a particular switch.

Shell Command: **null**

The *null* command performs no operation.

FIGURE 5.19

Description of the *null* shell command.

Setting Shell Options: `set`

The *set* command allows you to control several shell options. Its syntax is shown in Figure 5.20. Figure 5.21 shows a list of the *set* options. The next example shows a brief script that makes use of these options. The **-x** and **-v** options are useful in debugging a shell script, as they cause the shell to display lines both before and after the variable, wildcard, and command substitution metacharacters are processed. I recommend that you always use these options when testing scripts. Here is the relevant code:

```
$ cat script.sh                   ...look at the script.
set -vx a.c       # set debug trace and overwrite $1.
ls $1             # access first positional parameter.
```

```
set -                # turn off trace.
echo goodbye $USER
echo $notset
set -u      # unset variables will generate an error now.
echo $notset       # generate an error.
$ script.sh b.c                    ...execute the script.
ls $1                              ...output by -v option.
+ ls a.c                           ...output by -x option.
a.c                                ...regular output.
set -                              ...output by -v option.
+ set -                            ...output by -x option.
goodbye glass                      ...regular output.
script.sh: notset: parameter not set  ...access unset variable.
$ _
```

Shell Command: **set** -ekntuvx $\{arg\}*$

set allows you to choose the shell options that are displayed in Figure 5.21. Any remaining arguments are assigned to the positional parameters $1, $2, and so forth, overwriting their current values.

FIGURE 5.20

Description of the *set* shell command.

Option	Meaning
e	If the shell is not executing commands from a terminal or a start-up file, and a command fails, then execute an ERR trap and exit.
n	Accept but do not execute commands. This flag does not affect interactive shells.
t	Execute the next command and then exit.
u	Generate an error when an unset variable is encountered.
v	Echo shell commands as they are read.
x	Echo shell commands as they are executed.
-	Turns off the x and v flags and treat further - characters as arguments.

FIGURE 5.21

set shell command options.

ENHANCEMENTS

In addition to possessing the new facilities that have already been described, the Bourne shell enhances the following areas of the common core:

- redirection
- sequenced commands

Redirection

Besides employing the common core redirection facilities, the Bourne shell allows you to duplicate, close, and redirect arbitrary I/O channels. You may associate the standard input file descriptor (0) with file descriptor n by using the following syntax:

```
$ command <& n    ...associate standard input.
```

Similarly, you may associate the standard output file descriptor (1) with file descriptor n by using the following syntax:

```
$ command >& n    ... associate standard output.
```

To close the standard input and standard output channels, use this syntax:

```
$ command <&-    ...close stdin and execute command.
$ command >&-    ...close stdout and execute command.
```

You may precede any redirection metacharacters, including the Bourne-specific ones just described, by a digit to indicate the file descriptor that should be used instead of 0 (for input redirection) or 1 (for output redirection). It's fairly common to redirect file descriptor 2, which corresponds to the standard error channel.

The next example illustrates the use of the foregoing redirection facilities. The **man** utility always writes a couple of lines to the standard error channel: "Reformatting page. Wait" when it begins and "done" when it ends. If you redirect only standard output, these messages are seen on the terminal. To redirect the standard error channel to a separate file, use the "2>" redirection sequence; to send it to the same place as standard output, use the "2>&1" sequence, as shown in the following commands:

```
$ man ls > ls.txt    ...send standard output to "ls.txt".
Reformatting page.  Wait... done   ...from standard error.
$ man ls > ls.txt 2> err.txt   ...send error to "err.txt".
$ cat err.txt                  ...look at the file.
Reformatting page.  Wait... done
$ man ls > ls.txt 2>&1   ...associate stderr with stdout.
$ head -1 ls.txt      ...look at first line of "ls.txt".
Reformatting page.
$ _
```

Sequenced Commands

When a group of commands is placed between parentheses, the commands are executed by a subshell. The Bourne shell also lets you group commands by placing them between braces, in which case they are still redirectable and "pipeable" as a group, but are executed directly by the parent shell. A space must be left after the opening brace, and a semicolon must precede the closing brace.

In the following example, the first *cd* command didn't affect the current working directory of my login shell, since it executed inside a subshell, but the second *cd* command *did*:

```
$ pwd                    ...display current working directory.
/home/glass
$ (cd /; pwd; ls | wc -l)  ...count files with subshell.
/
      22
$ pwd                         ...my shell didn't move.
/home/glass
$ { cd /; pwd; ls | wc -l; } ...count files with shell.
/
      22
$ pwd                         ...my shell moved.
/
$ _
```

COMMAND LINE OPTIONS

The Bourne shell supports the command-line options shown in Figure 5.22.

Option	Meaning
-c *string*	Create a shell to execute the command *string*.
-s	Create a shell that reads commands from standard input and sends shell messages to the standard error channel.
-i	Create an interactive shell; like the -s option, except that the SIGTERM, SIGINT, and SIGQUIT signals are all ignored. (For information about signals, consult Chapter 13.)

FIGURE 5.22

Bourne shell command-line options.

CHAPTER REVIEW

Checklist

In this chapter, I described

- the creation of a Bourne shell start-up file
- the creation and access of shell variables
- arithmetic
- conditional expressions
- six control structures
- a sample project for tracking user login sessions
- some miscellaneous built-in commands
- several enhancements to the core facilities

Quiz

1. Who wrote the Bourne shell?
2. Describe a common use of the built-in variable $$.
3. What is the easiest way to reexecute your ".profile" file?
4. What is the method used to have a shell variable defined in a subshell (i.e., to pass the value to the subshell)?
5. What debugging features does the Bourne shell provide?

Exercises

5.1 Write a **shhelp** utility that works as follows:

Utility: **shhelp** [-k] {*command*}*

shhelp lists help about the specified Bourne shell command. The **-k** option lists every command that **shhelp** knows about.

Here's an example of **shhelp** in action:

```
$ shhelp null              ...ask for help about null.
The null command performs no operation.
$ _
```

Make sure that your utility displays a suitable error message if *command* is not a valid command. I suggest that the text of each command's help message be kept in a separate file, rather than being stored inside the **shhelp** script. If you do decide to place it all inside a script, try using the "here" document facility. [level: *easy*]

5.2   Write a utility called **junk** that satisfies the following specification:

Utility: **junk** [-l] [-p] {*fileName*}*

junk is a replacement for the **rm** utility. Rather than removing files, it moves them into the subdirectory ".junk" in your home directory. If ".junk" doesn't exist, it is automatically created. The **-l** option lists the current contents of the ".junk" directory, and the **-p** option purges ".junk".

---

working example is given as a Korn shell script on pgs 249-251

Here's an example of junk at work:

```
$ ls -l reader.c        ...list existing file.
-rw-r--r--  1 glass     2580 May  4 19:17 reader.c
$ junk reader.c         ...junk it!
$ ls -l reader.c        ...confirm that it was moved.
reader.c not found
$ junk badguy.c         ...junk another file.
$ junk -l        ...list contents of "junk" directory.
-rw-r--r--  1 glass       57 May  4 19:17 badguy.c
-rw-r--r--  1 glass     2580 May  4 19:17 reader.c
$ junk -p                    ...purge junk.
$ junk -l                    ...list junk.
$ _
```

Remember to comment your script liberally. [level: *medium*]

5.3   Modify the **junk** script so that it is menu driven. [level: *easy*]

Projects

1. Write a crafty script called **ghoul** that is difficult to kill; when it receives a SIG-INT (from a *Control*-C), it should create a copy of itself before dying. Thus, every time an unwary user tries to kill a ghoul, another ghoul is created to take its place! Of course, **ghoul** can still be killed by a SIGKILL (-9) signal. [level: *medium*]

2. Build a phone book utility that allows you to access and modify an alphabetical list of names, addresses, and telephone numbers. Use the utilities described in Chapter 3, such as **awk** and **sed**, to maintain and edit the file of phone-book information. [level: *hard*]

3. Build a process management utility that allows you to kill processes on the basis of their CPU usage, user ID, total elapsed time, and so forth. This kind of utility would be especially useful to system administrators. (See Chapter 15.) [level: *hard*]

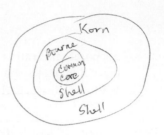

Korn
Bourne
Common
Core
Shell
Shell

CHAPTER 6

The Korn Shell

See also:

- $SHELL, pg 148
- General comparison with other shells, pg 146
- chsh, pg 147
- ^D, pg 149

MOTIVATION

The Korn shell, written by David Korn, is a powerful superset of the Bourne shell and offers improvements in job control, command line editing, and programming features. It's rapidly becoming the industry favorite and looks likely to be the UNIX shell of choice for many years to come.

PREREQUISITES

You should already have read Chapter 5 and experimented with the Bourne shell.

OBJECTIVES

In this chapter, I explain and demonstrate the Korn-specific facilities.

PRESENTATION

The information is presented in the form of several sample UNIX sessions.

SHELL COMMANDS

The following shell commands, listed in alphabetical order, are introduced:

alias	jobs	select
bg	kill	typeset
fc	let	unalias
fg	print	
function	return	

INTRODUCTION

The Korn shell supports all of the Bourne shell facilities described in Chapter 5 plus the following new features:

- command customization, using aliases
- access to previous commands via a history mechanism (through vi-like and emacs-like command line editing features)
- functions
- advanced job control
- several new built-in commands and several enhancements to existing commands

The new facilities are shown in Figure 6.1.

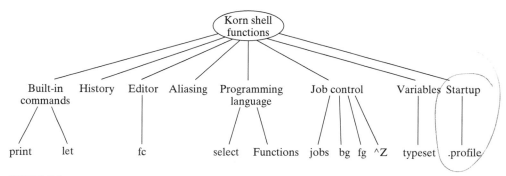

FIGURE 6.1

Korn shell functionality.

START-UP

The Korn shell is a regular C program whose executable file is stored as "/bin/ksh." If your chosen shell is "/bin/ksh", an interactive Korn shell is invoked automatically when you log into UNIX. You may also invoke a Korn shell manually from a script or from a terminal by using the command **ksh**, which has several command line options that are described at the end of the chapter.

When a Korn shell is invoked, the start-up sequence is different for interactive shells and non-interactive shells, as shown in Figure 6.2. The value $ENV is usually set to $HOME/.kshrc in the $HOME/.profile script. After reading the start-up files, an interactive Korn shell displays its prompt and awaits user commands. The standard Korn shell prompt is $, although it may be changed by setting the local variable PS1 described in the previous chapter. Here's an example of a Korn shell ".profile" script, which is executed exactly once at the start of every login session:

```
TERM=vt100; export TERM          # my terminal type.
ENV=~/.kshrc; export ENV         # environment filename.
```

```
HISTSIZE=100; export HISTSIZE # remember 100 commands.
MAILCHECK=60; export MAILCHECK  # seconds between checks.
set -o ignoreeof             # don't let Control-D log me out.
set -o trackall              # speed up file searches.
stty erase '^H'              # set backspace character.
tset                             # set terminal.
```

Step	Shell type	Action
1	interactive only	Execute commands in "/etc/profile" if it exists.
2	interactive only	Execute commands in $HOME/.profile if it exists.
3	both	Execute commands in $ENV if it exists.

FIGURE 6.2

Korn shell start-up sequence.

Some of these commands won't mean much to you right now, but their meaning will become clear as the chapter progresses.

Here's an example of a Korn shell ".kshrc" script, which typically contains useful Korn-shell-specific information required by all shells, including those created purely to execute scripts:

```
PATH='.:~/bin:/bin:/usr/bin:/usr/local/bin:/gnuemacs'
PS1='! $ ';export PS1    # put command number in prompt.
alias h="fc -l"            # set up useful aliases.
alias ll="ls -l"
alias rm="rm -i"
alias cd="cdx"
alias up="cdx .."
alias dir="/bin/ls"
alias ls="ls -aF"
alias env="printenv|sort"

# function to display path and directory when moving
function cdx
{
 if 'cd' "$@"
 then
   echo $PWD
   ls -aF
 fi
}
```

Every Korn shell, including all subshells, executes this script when it begins.

ALIASES

The Korn shell allows you to create and customize your own commands by using the *alias* command, which works as shown in Figure 6.3. Here's an example of *alias* in action:

```
$ alias dir='ls -aF'    ...register an alias.
$ dir                   ...same as typing "ls -aF".
./          main2.c     p.reverse.c         reverse.h
../          main2.o     palindrome.c        reverse.old
$ dir *.c               ...same as typing "ls -aF *.c".
main2.c     p.reverse.c palindrome.c
$ alias dir             ...definition of "dir".
dir=ls -aF
$ _
```

> *Shell Command:* **alias** [-tx] [*word* [= *string*]]
>
> *alias* supports a simple form of command line customization. If you alias *word* to be equal to *string* and then later enter a command beginning with *word*, the first occurrence of *word* is replaced by *string*, and then the command is reprocessed. If you don't supply *word* or *string*, a list of all the current shell aliases is displayed. If you supply only *word*, then the string currently associated with the alias *word* is displayed. If you supply *word* and *string*, the shell adds the specified alias to its collection of aliases. If an alias already exists for *word*, it is replaced. If the replacement string begins with *word*, it is not reprocessed for aliases, in order to prevent infinite loops. If the replacement string ends with a space, then the first word that follows is processed for aliases.

FIGURE 6.3

Description of the *alias* shell command.

In the following example, I defined a command in terms of itself:

```
$ alias ls='ls -aF'     ...no problem.
$ ls *.c                ...same as typing "ls -aF *.c".
main2.c     p.reverse.c         palindrome.c
$ alias dir='ls'        ...define "dir" in terms of "ls".
$ dir                   ...same as typing "ls -aF".
./          main2.c     p.reverse.c         reverse.h
../          main2.o     palindrome.c        reverse.old
$ _
```

Aliasing Built-In Commands

All built-in commands may be aliased, except for *case, do, done, elif, else, esac, fi, for, function, if, select, then, time, until, while, {,* and *}.*

Removing an Alias

To remove an alias, use the *unalias* command, which works as shown in Figure 6.4.
Here's an example of the use of *unalias*:

```
$ alias dir              ...look at an existing alias.
dir=ls
$ unalias dir            ...remove the alias.
$ alias dir              ...try looking at the alias again.
dir alias not found
$ _
```

Shell Command: **unalias** {*word*}+

unalias removes all the specified aliases.

FIGURE 6.4

Description of the *unalias* shell command.

Predefined Aliases

For convenience, the shell predefines the aliases shown in Figure 6.5. The uses of these
aliases will become more apparent as the chapter progresses. For example, the "r" alias
is particularly useful, allowing you to recall previous commands without having to use
the tedious sequence "fc -e -".

Alias	Value
false	let 0
functions	typeset -f
history	fc -l
integer	typeset -i
nohup	nohup
r	fc -e -
true	:
type	whence -v
hash	alias -t

FIGURE 6.5

Korn shell predefined aliases.

Some Useful Aliases

Figure 6.6 presents a grab bag of useful aliases that I've gathered from various sources. For some other interesting aliases, see "Aliases" in Chapter 7.

Alias	Value
rm	rm -i This causes rm to prompt for confirmation.
mv	mv -i This causes mv to prompt for confirmation.
ls	ls -aF This causes ls to display more information.
env	printenv | sort This displays a sorted list of the environment variables.
ll	ls -l This allows you to obtain a long directory listing more conveniently.

FIGURE 6.6

Some useful aliases.

Tracked Aliases

One common use of aliases is as a shorthand for full pathnames, to avoid the lookup penalty of the standard search mechanism as it scans the directories specified by $PATH. You may arrange for the full pathname replacement to occur automatically by making use of the *tracked alias* facility. All aliases listed with the **-t** option are flagged as tracked aliases, and the standard search mechanism is used to set their initial value. From then on, a tracked alias is replaced by its value, thereby avoiding the search time. If no aliases follow the **-t** option, a list of all the currently tracked aliases is displayed. Here's an example:

```
$ alias -t page     ...define a tracked alias for page.
$ alias -t          ...look at all tracked aliases.
page=/usr/ucb/page      ...its full pathname is stored.
$ _
```

The "-o trackall" option of *set* (described later in the chapter) tells the shell to track all commands automatically, as shown in the following example:

```
$ set -o trackall      ...all commands are now tracked.
$ date                 ...execute date.
```

```
Fri Feb  6 00:54:44 CST 1998
$ alias -t                 ...look at all tracked aliases.
date=/bin/date             ...date is now tracked.
page=/usr/ucb/page
$ _
```

Since the value of a tracked alias is dependent on the value of $PATH, the values of all tracked aliases are reevaluated every time the PATH variable is changed. If PATH is unset, the values of all tracked aliases are set to null, but remain tracked.

Sharing Aliases

To make an alias available to a child shell, you must mark the alias as an *export alias* by using the **-x** option of *alias*. All aliases listed with the **-x** option are flagged as export aliases. If no aliases follow the **-x** option, a list of all currently exported aliases is displayed. Note that if the value of an alias is changed in a child shell, it does not affect the value of the original alias in the parent shell. Here's an example of the use of the export alias:

```
$ alias -x mroe='more'   ...add an export alias.
$ alias -x               ...list exported aliases.
autoload=typeset -fu     ...a standard alias.
...                      ...other aliases are listed here.
ls=ls -F
mroe=more                ...the alias I just added.
...                      ...other aliases are listed here.
type=whence -v
vi=/usr/ucb/vi
$ cat test.ksh           ...a script using the new alias.
mroe main2.c
$ test.ksh               ...run the script. mroe works!
/* MAIN2.C */

#include #stdio.h,
#include "palindrome.h"

main ()
{
  printf ("palindrome (\"cat\") = %d\n",
                       palindrome ("cat"));
  printf ("palindrome (\"noon\") = %d\n",
                       palindrome ("noon"));
}
$ _
```

HISTORY

The Korn shell keeps a record of commands entered from the keyboard so that they may be edited and re-executed at a later stage. This facility is known as a *history* mechanism. The built-in command *fc* (**fix c**ommand) gives you access to history. There are two forms of *fc*. The first, simpler form allows you to re-execute a specified set of previous commands, and the second, more complex form allows you edit them before reexecution.

Numbered Commands

When you're using history, it's very handy to arrange for your prompt to contain the number of the command that you're about to enter. To do this, set the primary prompt variable (PS1) to contain a ! character:

```
$ PS1='! $ '          ...set PS1 to contain a !.
103 $ _                ...prompt for command #103.
```

Storage of Commands

The Korn shell records the last $HISTSIZE commands in the file $HISTFILE. If the environment variable HISTSIZE is not set, a default value of 128 is used. If HISTFILE is not set or the named file is not writable, then the file $HOME/.sh_history is used by default. All the Korn shells that specify the same history file will share it. Therefore, as long as you don't change the value of $HISTFILE during a login session, the commands entered during that session are available as history at the next session. In the following example, I examined the history file where commands are stored:

```
$ echo $HISTSIZE                  ...set in ".profile".
100
$ echo $HISTFILE                  ...not set previously.
$ tail -3 $HOME/.sh_history  ...display last 3 lines.
echo $HISTSIZE
echo $HISTFILE
tail -3 $HOME/.sh_history
$ _
```

Command Reexecution

The *fc* command allows you to reexecute previous commands. The first, simpler form of *fc* works as shown in Figure 6.7. Here's an example of *fc* in action:

```
360 $ fc -e - ech     ...last command starting with "ech".
echo $HISTFILE
361 $ fc -e - FILE=SIZE ech   ...replace "FILE" by "SIZE".
echo $HISTSIZE
100
362 $ fc -e - 360                ...execute command # 360.
echo $HISTFILE
363 $ _
```

The token "r" is a predefined alias for "fc -e -", which allows for the following more convenient way to reexecute commands:

```
364 $ alias r          ...look at "r"'s alias.
r=fc -e 365
```

```
365 $ r 364              ...execute command # 364.
alias r
r=fc -e -
366 $ _
```

Shell Command: **fc** -e - [*old=new*] *prefix*

This form of the *fc* command reexecutes the previous command beginning with *prefix* after optionally replacing the first occurrence of the string *old* by the string *new*. *prefix* may be a number, in which case the numbered event is reexecuted.

FIGURE 6.7

Description of the *fc* shell command used for reexecuting a command.

Editing Commands

The Korn shell allows you to preedit commands before they are reexecuted by using a more advanced form of the *fc* command, which works as shown in Figure 6.8. The following example illustrates the method of editing and reexecution:

```
371 $ whence vi              ...find the location of "vi".
/usr/ucb/vi
372 $ FCEDIT=/usr/ucb/vi    ...set FCEDIT to full path.
373 $ fc 371                 ...edit command # 371.
...enter vi, edit the command to say "whence ls", save, quit vi
whence ls                    ...display edited commands.
/bin/ls                      ...output from edited command.
374 $ fc 371 373             ...edit commands # 371..373.
...enter vi and edit a list of the last three commands.
...assume that I deleted the first line, changed the remaining
...lines to read "echo -n hi" and "echo there", and then quit.
echo -n "hi "                ...display edited commands.
echo there
hi there                     ...output from edited commands.
375 $ _
```

Shell Command: **fc** [*-e editor*] [*-nlr*] [*start*] [*end*]

This form of *fc* invokes the editor called *editor* upon the specified range of commands. When the editor is exited, the edited range of commands is executed. If *editor* is not specified, then the editor whose pathname is stored in the environment

---

FIGURE 6.8

Description of the *fc* shell command used for command editing.

variable FCEDIT is used. The value $FCEDIT is "/bin/ed" by default, and I *don't* recommend that you use this default. I personally prefer "/usr/ucb/vi" (the full pathname of the **vi** editor on my system), since I'm most familiar with the UNIX **vi** editor. If no other options are specified, the editor is invoked upon the previous command.

When you enter the editor, you may edit the command(s) as you wish and then save the text. When you exit the editor, the Korn shell automatically echoes and executes the saved version of the command(s).

To specify a particular command either by its index or by its prefix, supply the number or the prefix as the value of *start*, but don't supply a value for *end*. To specify a range of commands, set the value of *start* to select the first command in the series, and set the value of *end* to select the last command in the series. If a negative number is supplied, it's interpreted as an offset to the current command.

The **-l** option causes the selected commands to be displayed, but not executed. In this case, if no command series is specified, the last 16 commands are listed. The **-r** option reverses the order of the selected commands, and the **-n** option inhibits the generation of command numbers when they are listed.

FIGURE 6.8   (*Continued*)

Here's an example of the use of the **-l** option:

```
376 $ fc -l 371 373       ...list commands with numbers.
371 $ whence vi
372 $ FCEDIT=/usr/ucb/vi
373 $ fc 371
377 $ fc -6                ...edit command # 371.
...edit command to say "whence ls" and then quit.
whence ls                 ...display edited command.
/bin/ls                   ...output by command.
378 $ _
```

EDITING COMMANDS

The Korn shell contains simplified built-in versions of the **vi**, **gmacs**, and **emacs** editors that may be used to edit the current command or previous commands. To select one of these built-in editors, set either the VISUAL or the EDITOR variable to a string that ends in the name of one of the editors. In the following example, I selected the **vi** editor:

```
380 $ VISUAL=vi    ...select the built-in "vi" editor.
381 $ _
```

The Built-In vi Editor

The description that follows assumes that you are familiar with the **vi** editor. If you're not, consult the description of the **vi** editor in Chapter 2.

To edit the current line, press the *Esc* key to enter the built-in **vi** editor's control mode, and then make the required changes. To enter append or insert mode from control mode, press the **a** key or the **i** key, respectively. To go back to control mode from either of these modes, press the *Esc* key. To reexecute the command, press the *Enter* key. Be warned that if you type a *Control*-D inside the editor, it terminates the shell, not just the editor.

In control mode, key sequences fall into one of the following categories:

- standard **vi** key sequences (described in Chapter 2.)
- additional movement
- additional searching
- filename completion
- alias replacement

Additional Movement

The cursor up (**k** or −) and cursor down (**j** or +) keys select the previous and next commands, respectively, in the history list. This allows you to easily access history from within the built-in editor. To load a command with a particular number, enter command mode and then enter the number of the command, followed by the **G** key. Here's an example:

```
125 $ echo line 1
line 1
126 $ echo line 2
line 2
127 $ ...at this point, I pressed the Esc key followed by
      ...k twice (up, up). This loaded command #125 onto
      ...the command line, which I then executed by
      ...pressing the Enter key.
line 1
128 $ ...at this point, I pressed Esc followed by 125G.
      ...This loaded command #125 onto the command line,
      ...which I then executed by pressing the Enter key.
line 1
129 $ _
```

Additional Searching

The standard search mechanisms /*string* and ?*string* search backward and forward, respectively, through history. Here's an example:

```
127 $ echo line 1
line 1
```

```
138 $ echo line 2
line 2
139 $ ...at this point, I pressed the Esc key followed
        ...by /ech, which loaded the last command
        ...containing "ech" onto the command line.
        ...Then I pressed n to continue the search to
        ...the next command that matched. Finally, I
        ...pressed the Enter key to execute the command.
line 1
$ _
```

Filename Completion

If you type an asterisk (*) in control mode, it is appended to the word that the cursor is over and is then processed as if it were a wildcard by the filename substitution mechanism. If no match occurs, a beep is sounded; otherwise, the word is replaced by an alphabetical list of all the matching filenames, and the editor enters input mode automatically. Here's an example:

```
114 $ ls m*
m             m3           main.c            mbox
m1            madness.c    main.o            mon.out
m2            main         makefile          myFile
115 $ ls ma   ...at this point I pressed the Esc key
              ...the * key, and then the Enter key.
115 $ ls madness.c main main.c main.o makefile
madness.c    main.c             makefile
main         main.o
116 $ _
```

If you type an equals sign (=) in control mode, the editor displays a numbered list of all the files that have the current word as a prefix and then redraws the command line:

```
116 $ ls ma        ...at this point I pressed the Esc key
                   ...and then the = key.
1) madness.c
2) main
3) main.c
4) main.o
5) makefile
116 $ ls ma_       ...back to the original command line.
```

If you type a \ in control mode, the editor attempts to complete the current filename in an unambiguous way. If a completed pathname matches a directory, a / is appended; otherwise, a space is appended. Here's an example:

```
116 $ ls ma     ...at this point I pressed the Esc key
                ...and then the \ key.
```

```
                    ...No completion was performed, since "ma"
                    ...is a prefix of more than one file.
      116 $ ls mak  ...at this point I pressed the Esc key
                    ...and then the \ key. The editor
                    ...completed the name to be "makefile".
      116 $ ls makefile _
```

Alias Replacement

If you find yourself typing the same pattern again and again from the editor, you can make good use of the alias replacement mechanism. If you give _letter_ an alias of _word_, the sequence @_letter_ is replaced by _word_ when you're in command mode. In the following example, the letter **i** at the start of the alias causes the built-in editor to go into insert mode, and the literal _Esc_ at the end of the string causes it to leave **vi** mode:

```
      123 $ alias _c='icommon text^['     ...^[ was Control-V
                                          ...followed by Esc
      124 $ echo          ...at this point I pressed Esc followed by @c.
      124 $ echo common text_
```

The Built-In emacs/gmacs Editor

This description assumes that you are familiar with the **emacs** editor. If you're not, consult the description of the **emacs** editor in Chapter 2.

Most of the **emacs** key sequences are supported. You may move the cursor and manipulate text by using the standard **emacs** key sequences. To reexecute the command, press the _Enter_ key.

The main difference between the built-in editor and standard **emacs** is that the cursor-up, cursor-down, search forward, and search backward key sequences operate on the history list. For example, the cursor-up key sequence, _Control_-P, displays the previous command on the command line. Similarly, the search backward key sequence, _Control_-R _string_, displays the most recent command that contains _string_.

ARITHMETIC

The _let_ command allows you to perform arithmetic. It works as shown in Figure 6.9. Here are some examples:

```
      $ let x = 2 + 2         ...expression contains spaces.
      ksh: =: syntax error    ...no spaces or tabs allowed!
      $ let x=2+2             ...OK.
      $ echo $x
      4
      $ let y=x*4             ...don't place $ before variables.
      $ echo $y
      16
      $ let x=2#100+2#100     ...add two numbers in base 2.
```

```
$ echo $x
4                                    ...number is displayed in base 10.
$ _
```

Shell Command: **let** *expression*

The *let* command performs double-precision integer arithmetic and supports all of the basic math operators using the standard precedence rules. Here they are, grouped in descending order of precedence:

OPERATOR	MEANING
–	unary minus
!	logical negation
* / %	multiplication, division, remainder
+ –	addition, subtraction
<= >= <>	relational operators
== !=	equality, inequality
=	assignment

All of the operators associate from left to right, except for the assignment operator. Expressions may be placed between parentheses to modify the order of evaluation. The shell doesn't check for overflow, so beware! Operands may be integer constants or variables. When a variable is encountered, it is replaced by its value, which in turn may contain other variables. You may explicitly override the default base (10) of a constant by using the format *base#number* where *base* is a number between 2 and 36. You must not put spaces or tabs between the operands or operators. You must not place a $ in front of variables that are part of an expression.

FIGURE 6.9

Description of the *let* shell command.

Preventing Metacharacter Interpretation

Unfortunately, the shell interprets several of the standard operators, such as <, >, and *, as metacharacters, so they must be quoted or preceded by a backslash (\) to inhibit their special meaning. To avoid this inconvenience, there is an equivalent form of *let* that automatically treats all of the tokens as if they were surrounded by double quotes and allows you to use spaces around tokens. The token sequence

```
(( list ))
```

is equivalent to

```
let " list "
```

Note that double quotes do not prevent the expansion of variables. I personally *always* use the (( )) syntax instead of *let*. Here's an example:

```
$ (( x = 4 ))              ...spaces are OK.
$ (( y = x * 4 ))
$ echo $y
16
$ _
```

Return Values

If an expression evaluates to zero, its return code is one; otherwise it is zero. The return code may be used by decision-making control structures, such as an *if* statement, as in this example:

```
$ (( x = 4 ))          ...assign x to 4.
$ if (( x > 0 ))       ...OK to use in a control structure.
> then
>   echo x is positive
> fi
x is positive          ...output from control structure.
$ _
```

For simple arithmetic tests, I recommend using ((..)) instead of **test** expressions.

TILDE SUBSTITUTION

Any token of the form *~name* is subject to *tilde substitution*. The shell checks the password file to see whether *name* is a valid user name and, if it is, replaces the *~name* sequence with the full pathname of the user's home directory. If *name* isn't a valid user name, the *~name* sequence is left unchanged. Tilde substitution occurs *after* aliases are processed. Figure 6.10 shows a list of the tilde substitutions, including the special cases ~+ and ~−.

Tilde sequence	Replaced by
~	$HOME
~*user*	home directory of *user*
~/*pathname*	$HOME/*pathname*
~+	$PWD (current working directory)
~−	$OLDPWD (previous working directory)

FIGURE 6.10

Tilde substitutions in the Korn shell.

The predefined local variables PWD and OLDPWD are described later in the chapter. Here are some examples of tilde substitution:

```
$ pwd
/home/glass              ...current working directory.
$ echo ~
/home/glass              ...my home directory.
$ cd /                   ...change to root directory.
$ echo ~+
/                        ...current working directory.
$ echo ~-
/home/glass              ...previous working directory.
$ echo ~dcox
/home/dcox               ...another user's home directory.
$ _
```

MENUS: `select`

The *select* command allows you to create simple menus and has the syntax shown in Figure 6.11. The *select* command displays a numbered list of the words specified by the *in* clause to the standard error channel, displays the prompt stored in the special variable PS3, and then waits for a line of user input. When the user enters a line, it is stored in the predefined variable REPLY, and then one of the following three things occurs:

- If the user entered one of the listed numbers, *name* is set to that number, the commands in list are executed, and the user is prompted for another choice.
- If the user entered a blank line, the selection is displayed again.
- If the user entered an invalid choice, *name* is set to null, the commands in list are executed, and then the user is prompted for another choice.

---

select *name* [**in** {*word*}+]
do
list
done

FIGURE 6.11

Description of the *select* shell command.

The next example is a recoding of the menu selection example from Chapter 5. It replaces the while loop and termination logic with a simpler *select* command. The commands are as follows:

```
$ cat menu.ksh            ...list the script.
echo menu test program
```

```
    select reply in "date" "pwd" "pwd" "exit"
    do
     case $reply in
       "date")
          date
          ;;
       "pwd")
          pwd
          ;;
       "exit")
          break
          ;;
       *)
          echo illegal choice
          ;;
     esac
    done
    $ menu.ksh                  ...execute the script.
    menu test program
    1) date
    2) pwd
    3) pwd
    4) exit
    #? 1
    Fri Feb  6 21:49:33 CST 1998
    #? 5
    illegal choice
    #? 4
    $ _
```

FUNCTIONS

The Korn shell allows you to define functions that may be invoked as shell commands. Parameters passed to functions are accessible via the standard positional parameter mechanism. Functions must be defined before they are used. There are two ways to define a function, as shown in Figure 6.12. I personally favor the second form, because it looks more like the C language. To invoke a function, supply its name followed by the appropriate parameters. For obvious reasons, the shell does not check the number or type of the parameters. Here's an example of a script that defines and uses a function that takes no parameters:

```
$ cat func1.ksh           ...list the script.
message ()  # no-parameter function.
{
 echo hi
 echo there
}
i=1
```

```
while (( i <= 3 ))
do
 message    # call the function.
 let i=i+1 # increment loop count.
done
$ func1.ksh             ...execute the script.
hi
there
hi
there
hi
there
$ _
```

---

function *name*

{

list of commands

}

or the keyword **function** may be omitted:

name ()

{

list of commands.

}

FIGURE 6.12

The Korn shell *function* declaration.

Using Parameters

As I mentioned previously, parameters are accessible via the standard positional mechanism. Here's an example of a script that passes parameters to a function:

```
$ cat func2.ksh            ...list the script.
f ()
{
 echo parameter 1 = $1      # display first parameter.
 echo parameter list = $*   # display entire list.
}
# main program.
f 1                         # call with 1 parameter.
f cat dog goat              # call with 3 parameters.
```

```
$ func2.ksh                    ...execute the script.
parameter 1 = 1
parameter list = 1
parameter 1 = cat
parameter list = cat dog goat
$ _
```

Returning from a Function

The *return* command returns the flow of control back to the caller. It has the syntax shown in Figure 6.13. When *return* is used without an argument, the function call returns immediately with the exit code of the last command that was executed in the function; otherwise, it returns with its exit code set to *value*. If a *return* command is executed from the main script, it's equivalent to an *exit* command. The exit code is accessible from the caller via the $? variable. Here's an function that multiplies its arguments and returns the result:

```
$ cat func3.ksh            ...list the script.
f ()  # two-parameter function.
{
  (( returnValue = $1 * $2 ))
  return $returnValue
}
# main program.
f 3 4                      # call function.
result=$?                  # save exit code.
echo return value from function was $result
$ func3.ksh                ...execute the script.
return value from function was 12
$ _
```

---

return [*value*]

FIGURE 6.13

Korn shell function *return* statement.

Context

A function executes in the same context as the process that calls it. This means that the function and the process share the same variables, current working directory, and traps. The only exception is the "trap on exit": A function's "trap on exit" executes when the function returns.

Local Variables

The *typeset* command (described in more detail later in the chapter) has some special function-oriented facilities. Specifically, a variable created using the *typeset* function is limited in scope to the function in which it is created and all of the functions that the defining function calls. If a variable of the same name already exists, its value is over-written and replaced when the function returns. This property is similar (but not iden-tical) to the scoping rules in most traditional high-level languages. Here's an example of a function that uses *typeset* to declare a local variable:

```
$ cat func4.ksh              ...list the script.
f ()   # two-parameter function.
{
   typeset x                  # declare local variable.
   (( x = $1 * $2 ))          # set local variable.
   echo local x = $x
   return $x
}
# main program.
x=1                           # set global variable.
echo global x = $x            # display value before function call.
f 3 4                         # call function.
result=$?                     # save exit code.
echo return value from function was $result
echo global x = $x            # value of global after function.
$ func4.ksh                   ...execute the script.
global x = 1
local x = 12
return value from function was 12
global x = 1
$ _
```

Recursion

With careful thought, it's perfectly possible to write recursive functions. Following are two sample scripts that implement a recursive version of *factorial ()*. The first uses the exit code to return the result, and the second uses standard output to echo the result. Note that these scripts are available on-line. (See the preface for more information.)

Recursive Factorial, Using Exit Code

```
factorial ()        # one-parameter function
{
 if (( $1 <= 1 ))
 then
    return 1                       # return result in exit code.
 else
    typeset tmp                    # declare two local variables.
    typeset result
    (( tmp = $1 - 1 ))
    factorial $tmp                 # call recursively.
    (( result = $? * $1 ))
```

```
      return $result              # return result in exit code.
   fi
}
# main program.
factorial 5                       # call function
echo factorial 5 = $?             # display exit code.
```

Recursive Factorial, Using Standard Output

```
factorial ()        # one-parameter function
{
 if (( $1 <= 1 ))
 then
    echo 1                        # echo result to standard output.
 else
    typeset tmp             # declare two local variables.
    typeset result
    (( tmp = $1 - 1 ))
    (( result = `factorial $tmp` * $1 ))
    echo $result       # echo result to standard output.
 fi
}
#
echo factorial 5 = `factorial 5`     # display result.
```

Sharing Functions

To share the source code of a function among several scripts, place the code in a separate file and then read it, using the "." built-in command at the start of the scripts that use the function. In the following example, assume that the source code of one of the previous factorial scripts was saved in a file called "fact.ksh":

```
$ cat.ksh                      ...list the script.
. fact.ksh                     # read function source code.
echo factorial 5 = `factorial 5`   # call the function.
$ func6.ksh                        ...execute the script.
factorial 5 = 120
$ _
```

ENHANCED JOB CONTROL

In addition to the Bourne shell job control facilities, the Korn shell supports the commands shown in Figure 6.14. These facilities are available only on UNIX systems that support job control. The next few sections contain a description of each job control facility and examples of their use. The job control features of the Korn shell that are about to be described are identical to those of the C shell.

Command	Function
jobs	lists your jobs
bg	places a specified job into the background
fg	places a specified job into the foreground
kill	sends an arbitrary signal to a process or job

FIGURE 6.14

Korn shell job control commands.

Jobs

The *jobs* shell command displays a list of all the shell's jobs. It works as shown in Figure 6.15. Here's an example of *jobs* in action:

```
$ jobs                              ...no jobs right now.
$ sleep 1000 &                  ...start a background job.
[1] 27128
$ man ls | ul -tdumb > ls.txt &   ...another bg job.
[2] 27129
$ jobs -l                           ...list current jobs.
[2] + 27129  Running      man ls | ul -tdumb > ls.txt &
[1] - 27128  Running      sleep 1000 &
$ _
```

Shell Command: **jobs** [-l]

jobs displays a listing of all the shell's jobs. When used with the **-l** option, process IDs are added to the listing. The syntax of each line of output is

job# [+|-]   *PID   Status   Command*

where a + means that the job was the last job to be placed into the background and a − means that the job was the second-to-last job to be placed into the background. *Status* may be one of the following:

- Running
- Stopped (suspended)

FIGURE 6.15

Description of the *jobs* shell command.

> - Terminated (killed by a signal)
> - Done (zero exit code)
> - Exit (nonzero exit code)
>
> The only real significance of the + and − is that they may be used when specifying the job in a later command. (See "Specifying a Job," next.)

FIGURE 6.15   (*Continued*)

Specifying a Job

The *bg, fg,* and *kill* commands allow you to specify a job, using one of the forms shown in Figure 6.16.

Form	Specifies
%integer	the job number *integer*
%prefix	the job whose name starts with *prefix*
%+	the job that was last referenced
%%	same as %+
%-	the job that was referenced second to last

FIGURE 6.16

Job specifications in the Korn shell.

bg

The *bg* shell command resumes the specified job as a background process. It works as shown in Figure 6.17. In the next example, I started a foreground job and then decided that it would be better to run it in the background. I suspended the job using *Control*-Z and then resumed it in the background. The command I used is as follows:

```
$ man ksh | ul -tdumb > ksh.txt    ...start in foreground.
^Z                                 ...suspend it.
[1] + Stopped           man ksh | ul -tdumb > ksh.txt
$ bg %1                       ...resume it in background.
[1]    man ksh | ul -tdumb > ksh.txt&
$ jobs                             ...list current jobs.
[1] + Running           man ksh | ul -tdumb > ksh.txt
$ _
```

> *Shell Command:* **bg** [*%job*]
>
> *bg* resumes the specified job as a background process. If no job is specified, the last referenced job is resumed.

FIGURE 6.17

Description of the *bg* shell command.

fg

The *fg* shall command resumes the specified job as the foreground process. It works as shown in Figure 6.18. In the following example, I brought a background job into the foreground, using *fg*:

```
$ sleep 1000 &                    ...start a background job.
[1]   27143
$ man ksh | ul -tdumb > ksh.txt &  ...start another.
[2]   27144
$ jobs                            ...list the current jobs.
[2] +  Running              man ksh | ul -tdumb > ksh.txt &
[1] -  Running              sleep 1000 &
$ fg %ma                          ...bring job to foreground.
man ksh | ul -tdumb > ksh.txt  ...command is redisplayed.
$ _
```

> *Shell Command:* **fg** [*%job*]
>
> *fg* resumes the specified job as the foreground process. If no job is specified, the last referenced job is resumed.

FIGURE 6.18

Description of the *fg* shell command.

kill

The *kill* shell command sends the specified signal to the specified job or processes. It works as shown in Figure 6.19. The following example contains a couple of kills:

```
$ kill -l                     ...list all kill signals.
1) HUP           12) SYS            23) STOP
2) INT           13) PIPE           24) TSTP
3) QUIT          14) ALRM           25) CONT
4) ILL           15) TERM           26) TTIN
5) TRAP          16) USR1           27) TTOU
```

```
    6) ABRT              17) USR2             28) VTALRM
    7) EMT               18) CHLD             29) PROF
    8) FPE               19) PWR              30) XCPU
    9) KILL              20) WINCH            31) XFSZ
    10) BUS              21) URG
    11) SEGV             22) POLL
$ man ksh | ul -tdumb > ksh.txt &    ...start a bg job.
[1]    27160
$ kill -9 %1              ...kill it via a job specifier.
[1] + Killed             man ksh | ul -tdumb > ksh.txt &
$ man ksh | ul -tdumb > ksh.txt &    ...start another.
[1]    27164
$ kill -KILL 27164          ...kill it via a process ID.
[1] + Killed             man ksh | ul -tdumb > ksh.txt &
$ _
```

Shell Command: **kill** [-l] [*-signal*] { *process* | *%job* }+

kill sends the specified signal to the specified job or processes. A process is specified by its PID number. A signal may be specified either by its number or symbolically, by removing the "SIG" prefix from its symbolic constant in "/usr/include/sys/signal.h." To obtain a list of signals, use the **-l** option. If no signal is specified, the TERM signal is sent. If the TERM or HUP signal is sent to a suspended process, it is sent the CONT signal, which causes the process to resume.

FIGURE 6.19

Description of the *kill* shell command.

ENHANCEMENTS

In addition to the new facilities that have already been described, the Korn shell offers some enhancements to the Bourne shell in the following areas:

- redirection
- pipes
- command substitution
- variable access
- extra built-in commands

Redirection

The Korn shell supplies a minor extra redirection facility: the ability to strip leading tabs off of "here" documents. Figure 6.20 shows the augmented syntax. If *word* is preceded by a -, then leading tabs are removed from the lines of input that follow. Here's an example:

```
$ cat <<- ENDOFTEXT
>           this input contains
>      some leading tabs
> ^D
this input contains
some leading tabs
$ _
```

---

command ≪ [-] *word*

FIGURE 6.20

Redirection with a "here" document in the Korn shell.

This command example allows "here" text in a script to be indented to match the near-by shell commands, without affecting how the text is used.

Pipes

The |& operator supports a simple form of concurrent processing. When a command is followed by |&, it runs as a background process whose standard input and output channels are connected to the original parent shell via a two-way pipe. When the original shell generates output using a *print -p* command (discussed later in the chapter), the output is sent to the child shell's standard input channel. When the original shell reads input using a *read -p* command (also discussed later in the chapter), the input is taken from the child shell's standard output channel. Here's an example:

```
$ date |&                       ...start child process.
[1]   8311
$ read -p theDate        ...read from standard output of child.
[1] + Done    date |&       ...child process terminates.
$ echo $theDate             ...display the result.
Sun May 10 21:36:57 CDT 1998
$ _
```

Command Substitution

In addition to the older method of command substitution—surrounding the command with grave accents—the Korn shell allows you to perform command substitution via the syntax shown in Figure 6.21. Note that the $ that immediately precedes the open parentheses is part of the syntax and is *not* a prompt. Here's an example:

```
$ echo there are $(who | wc -1) users on the system
there are 6 users on the system
$ _
```

```
$( command )
```

FIGURE 6.21

Command substitution in the Korn shell.

To substitute the contents of a file into a shell command, you may use **$(<file)** as a faster form of **$(cat file).**

Variables

The Korn shell supports the following additional variable facilities:

- more flexible access methods
- more predefined local variables
- more predefined environment variables
- simple arrays
- a *typeset* command for formatting the output of variables

Flexible Access Methods

In addition to the variable-access methods supported by the Bourne shell, the Korn shell supports some more complex access methods, as shown in Figure 6.22. Here are some examples:

```
$ fish='smoked salmon'          ...set a variable.
$ echo ${#fish}      ...display the length of the value.
13
$ cd dir1                        ...move to directory.
$ echo $PWD     ...display the current working directory.
/home/glass/dir1
$ echo $HOME
/home/glass
$ echo ${PWD#$HOME/}            ...remove leading $HOME/
dir1
$ fileName=menu.ksh            ...set a variable.
$ echo ${fileName%.ksh}.bak   ...remove trailing ".ksh"
menu.bak                       ...and add ".bak".
$ _
```

Syntax	Action
${#*name*}	Replaced by the length of the value of *name*.
${#*name*[*]}	Replaced by the number of elements in the array *name*.

FIGURE 6.22

Korn shell variable access methods.

${name:+word} ${name:=word} ${name:?word} ${name:+word}	Work like their counterparts that do not contain a :, except that *name* must be set *and* nonnull, instead of just set.
${name#pattern} ${name##pattern}	Removes a leading *pattern* from *name*. The expression is replaced by the value of *name* if *name* doesn't begin with *pattern*, and with the remaining suffix if it does begin with *pattern*. The first form removes the smallest matching pattern, and the second form removes the largest matching pattern.
${name%pattern} ${name%%pattern}	Removes a trailing *pattern* from *name*. The expression is replaced by the value of *name* if *name* doesn't end with *pattern*, and with the remaining suffix if it does end with *pattern*. The first form removes the smallest matching pattern, and the second form removes the largest matching pattern.

FIGURE 6.22   (*Continued*)

Predefined Local Variables

In addition to supporting the common predefined local variables, the Korn shell supports the variables shown in Figure 6.23. Here are some examples of these other predefined variables:

```
$ echo hi there      ...display a message to demonstrate $_.
hi there
$ echo $_            ...display last arg of last command.
there
$ echo $PWD          ...display the current working dir.
/home/glass
$ echo $PPID         ...display the shell's parent pid .
27709
$ cd /               ...move to the root directory.
$ echo $OLDPWD       ...display last working directory.
/home/glass
$ echo $PWD          ...display current working directory.
/
$ echo $RANDOM $RANDOM  ...display two random numbers.
32561 8323
$ echo $SECONDS      ...display seconds since shell began.
918
```

```
$ echo $TMOUT          ...display the timeout value
0                      ...no timeout selected.
$ _
```

Name	Value
$_	The last parameter of the previous command.
$PPID	The process ID number of the shell's parent.
$PWD	The current working directory of the shell.
$OLDPWD	The previous working directory of the shell.
$RANDOM	A random integer.
$REPLY	Set by a *select* command.
$SECONDS	The number of seconds since the shell was invoked.
$CDPATH	Used by the *cd* command.
$COLUMNS	Sets the width of the edit window for the built-in editors.
$EDITOR	Selects the type of built-in editor.
$ENV	Selects the name of the Korn shell start-up file.
$FCEDIT	Defines the editor that is invoked by the fc command.
$HISTFILE	The name of the history file.
$HISTSIZE	The number of history lines to remember.
$LINES	Used by *select* to determine how to display the selections.
$MAILCHECK	Tells the shell how many seconds to wait before checking mail again. The default value is 600.
$MAILPATH	This should be set to a list of filenames, separated by colons. The shell checks these files for modification every $MAILCHECK seconds.
$PS3	The prompt used by the *select* command, #? by default.
$TMOUT	If set to a number greater than zero, and if more than $TMOUT seconds elapse between commands, the shell terminates.
$VISUAL	Selects the type of built-in editor.

FIGURE 6.23

Korn shell predefined local variables.

One-dimensional Arrays

The Korn shell supports simple one-dimensional arrays. To create an array, simply assign a value to a variable name, using a subscript between 0 and 511 in brackets. Array elements are created as needed. The syntax is shown in Figure 6.24. If you omit *subscript*, the value 0 is the default. Here's an example that uses a script to display the squares of the numbers between 0 and 9:

```
$ cat squares.ksh                       ...list the script.
i=0
while (( i < 10 ))
do
  (( squares[$i] = i * i ))  ...assign individual element.
  (( i = i + 1 ))            ...increment loop counter.
done
echo 5 squared is ${squares[5]}  ...display one element.
echo list of all squares is ${squares[*]} ...display all.
$ squares.ksh                           ...execute the script.
5 squared is 25
list of all squares is 0 1 4 9 16 25 36 49 64 81
$ _
```

To set the value of an array element, use

name[*subscript*]=*value*

To access the value of an array element, use

${*name*[*subscript*]}

FIGURE 6.24

Korn shell array definition and use.

typeset

The *typeset* shell command allows the creation and manipulation of variables. It works as shown in Figure 6.25. Figure 6.26 lists the options used with *typeset*, and the sections that follow illustrate their usage. I've split the descriptions up into related sections to make things a little easier.

Shell Command: **typeset** { - HLRZfilrtux [*value*] [*name* [=*word*]]}*

typeset allows the creation and manipulation of variables. It allows variables to be formatted, converted to an internal integer representation for speedier

FIGURE 6.25

Description of the *typeset* shell command.

arithmetic, made read only, made exportable, and switched between lowercase and uppercase.

Every variable has an associated set of flags that determine its properties. For example, if a variable has its "uppercase" flag set, it will always map its contents to uppercase, *even when they are changed.* The options to *typeset* operate by setting and resetting the various flags associated with named variables. When an option is preceded by -, it causes the appropriate flag to be turned *on*. To turn a flag *off* and reverse the sense of the option, precede the option by a + instead of a -.

FIGURE 6.25   (*Continued*)

Option	Meaning
L	Turn the L flag on and turn the R flag off. Left justify *word* and remove leading spaces. If the width of *word* is less than *name's* field width, then pad *word* with trailing spaces. If the width of *word* is greater than *name's* field width, then truncate *word's* end to fit. If the Z flag is set, leading zeroes are also removed.
R	Turn the R flag on and turn the L flag off. Right justify word and remove trailing spaces. If the width of *word* is less than *name's* field width, then pad *word* with leading spaces. If the width of *word* is greater than *name's* field width, then truncate *word's* end to fit.
Z	Right justify word and pad with zeroes if the first nonspace character is a digit and the L flag is off.

FIGURE 6.26

Formatting with the *typeset* shell command.

Formatting

In all of the formatting options, the field width of *name* is set to *value* if present; otherwise, it is set to the width of *word*.

Case

With the case options, the value can be converted to upper- or lowercase as shown in Figure 6.27. Here's an example that left justifies all the elements in an array and then displays them in uppercase:

```
$ cat justify.ksh        ...list the script.
wordList[0]='jeff'       # set three elements.
wordList[1]='john'
wordList[2]='ellen'
typeset -uL7 wordList     # typeset all elements in array.
echo ${wordList[*]}       # beware! shell removes non-quoted spaces
echo "${wordList[*]}"     # works OK.
$ justify.ksh            ...execute the script.
```

```
JEFF JOHN ELLEN
JEFF    JOHN    ELLEN
$ _
```

Option	Meaning
l	Turn the l flag on and turn the u flag off. Convert *word* to lowercase.
u	Turn the u flag on and turn the l flag off. Convert *word* to uppercase.

FIGURE 6.27

Changing the case of characters with the *typeset* shell command.

Type

The type of value stored can be set using the type options shown in Figure 6.28. In the next example, I modified a previous example by declaring the squares array to be an array of integers. This made the script run faster. The code is as follows:

```
$ cat squares.ksh          ...list the script.
typeset -i squares  # declare array integers (for speed).
i=0
while (( i < 10 ))
do
  (( squares[$i] = i * i ))
  (( i = i + 1 ))
done
echo 5 squared is ${squares[5]}
echo list of all squares is ${squares[*]}
$ squares.ksh              ...execute the script.
5 squared is 25
list of all squares is 0 1 4 9 16 25 36 49 64 81
$ _
```

Option	Meaning
i	Store *name* internally as an integer for arithmetic speed. Set the output base to *value* if specified; otherwise, use the *base* of *word*.
r	Flag the named variables as read only.
x	Flag the named variables as exportable.

FIGURE 6.28

Setting the type of values with the *typeset* shell command.

Miscellaneous

Two additional miscellaneous *typeset* shell command options are shown in Figure 6.29. In the following example, I selected the function *factorial ()* to be traced using the **-ft** option, and then I ran the script:

```
$ cat func5.ksh              ...list the script.
factorial ()                 # one-parameter function
{
 if (( $1 <= 1 ))
 then
    return 1
 else
    typeset tmp
    typeset result
    (( tmp = $1 - 1 ))
    factorial $tmp
    (( result = $? * $1 ))
    return $result
 fi
}
#
typeset -ft factorial        ...select a function trace.
factorial 3
echo factorial 3 = $?
$ func5.ksh                  ...execute the script.
+ let   3 <= 1               ...debugging information.
+ typeset tmp
+ typeset result
+ let   tmp = 3 - 1
+ factorial 2
+ let   2 <= 1
+ typeset tmp
+ typeset result
+ let   tmp = 2 - 1
+ factorial 1
+ let   1 <= 1
+ return 1
+ let   result = 1 * 2
+ return 2
+ let   result = 2 * 3
+ return 6
factorial 3 = 6
$ _
```

Option	Meaning
f	The only flags allowed in conjunction with this option are **t**, which sets the trace option for the named functions, and **x**, which displays all functions with the x attribute set.
t	Tags name with the token *word*.

FIGURE 6.29

Miscellaneous *typeset* shell command options.

typeset with No Named Variables

If no variables are named, then the names of all the parameters that have the specified flags set are listed. If no flags are specified, then a list of all the parameters and their flag settings are listed. Here's an example:

```
$ typeset      ...display a list of all typeset variables.
export NODEID
export PATH
...
leftjust 7 t
export integer MAILCHECK
$ typeset -i  ...display list of integer typeset vars.
LINENO=1
MAILCHECK=60
...
$ _
```

Built-Ins

The Korn shell enhances the following built-in commands:

- *cd*
- *set*
- *print* (an enhancement of the Bourne shell *echo* command)
- *read*
- *test*
- *trap*

cd

The Korn shell's version of *cd* supports several new features. It works as shown in Figure 6.30. Here's an example of *cd* in action:

```
$ CDPATH=.:/usr  ...set my CDPATH.
$ cd dir1        ...move to "dir1", located under ".".
$ pwd
/home/glass/dir1
$ cd include     ...move to "include", located in "/usr".
$ pwd            ...display the current working dir.
/usr/include
$ cd -           ...move to my previous directory.
$ pwd            ...display the current working dir.
/home/glass/dir1
$ _
```

Shell Command: **cd** { *name* }
                      cd *oldName newName*

The first form of the *cd* command is processed as follows:

- If *name* is omitted, the shell moves to the home directory specified by $HOME.
- If *name* is equal to −, the shell moves to the previous working directory that is kept in $OLDPWD.
- If *name* begins with a /, the shell moves to the directory whose full name is *name*.
- If *name* begins with anything else, the shell searches through the directory sequence specified by $CDPATH for a match and then moves the shell to the matching directory. The default value of $CDPATH is null, which causes *cd* to search only the current directory.

If the second form of *cd* is used, the shell replaces the first occurrence of the token *oldName* with the token *newName* in the current directory's full pathname. Then the shell attempts to change to the new pathname. The shell always stores the full pathname of the current directory in the variable PWD. The current value of $PWD may be displayed by using the built-in command *pwd*.

FIGURE 6.30

Description of the *cd* shell command.

set

The *set* command allows you to set and unset flags that control shellwide characteristics Figure 6.31 shows how it works. Figure 6.32 shows a list of the options used with *set*.

Shell Command: **set** [+-aefhkmnostuvx] [+-o *option*] {*arg*} *

The Korn shell version of *set* supports all of the Bourne *set* features, plus a few more. The various features of *set* do not fall naturally into categories, so I'll just list each one together with a brief description. An option preceded by a + instead of a − reverses the sense of the description.

FIGURE 6.31

Description of the *set* shell command.

Option	Meaning
a	All variables that are created are automatically flagged for export.
f	Disable filename substitution.
h	All non-built-in commands are automatically flagged as tracked aliases.
m	Place all background jobs in their own unique process group and display a notification of completion. This flag is automatically set for interactive shells.
n	Accept, but do not execute, commands. This flag has no effect on interactive shells.
o	This option is described separately in the text.
p	Set $PATH to its default value, causing the start-up sequence to ignore the $HOME/.profile file and read "/etc/suid_profile" instead of the $ENV file. This flag is set automatically whenever a shell is executed by a process in "set user ID" or "set group ID" mode. For more information on "set user ID" processes, see Chapter 13.
s	Sort the positional parameters.
--	Do not change any flags. If no arguments follow, all of the positional parameters are unset.

FIGURE 6.32

set shell command options.

The o Option

The **o** option of *set* takes an argument. The argument frequently has the same effect as one of the other flags used with *set*. If no argument is supplied, the current settings are displayed. Figure 6.33 shows a list of the valid arguments and their meanings. Note that I can set the **ignoreeof** option in my ".profile" script to protect myself against accidental *Control*-D logouts:

```
set -o ignoreeof
```

Option	Meaning
allexport	Equivalent to the a flag.
errexit	Equivalent to the e flag.
bgnice	Background processes are executed at a lower priority.

FIGURE 6.33

set -o arguments.

emacs	Invokes the built-in **emacs** editor.
gmacs	Invokes the built-in **gmacs** editor.
ignoreeof	Don't exit on *Control*-D. **exit** must be used instead.
keyword	Equivalent to the k flag.
markdirs	Append trailing / to directories generated by filename substitution.
monitor	Equivalent to the m flag.
noclobber	Prevents redirection from truncating existing files.
noexec	Equivalent to the n flag.
noglob	Equivalent to the f flag.
nolog	Do not save function definitions in history file.
nounset	Equivalent to the u flag.
privileged	Same as **-p**.
verbose	Equivalent to the v flag.
trackall	Equivalent to the h flag.
vi	Invokes the built-in **vi** editor.
viraw	Characters are processed as they are typed in **vi** mode.
xtrace	Equivalent to the x flag.

FIGURE 6.33 (*Continued*)

print

The *print* command is a more sophisticated version of *echo* and allows you to send output to an arbitrary file descriptor. It works as shown in Figure 6.34. Here's an example:

```
121 $ print -u2 hi there        ...send output to stderr.
hi there
122 $ print -s echo hi there  ...append to history.
124 $ r 123                    ...recall command #123.
echo hi there
hi there
125 $ print -R -s hi there     ...treat "-s" as an arg.
-s hi there
126 $ _
```

Shell Command: **print** -npsuR [*n*] { *arg* } *

By default, *print* displays its arguments to standard output, followed by a newline. The **-n** option inhibits the newline, and the **-u** option allows you to specify a single-digit file descriptor n for the output channel. The **-s** option causes the output to be appended to the history file instead of to an output channel. The **-p** option causes the output to be sent to the shell's two-way pipe channel. The **-R** option causes all further words to be interpreted as arguments.

FIGURE 6.34

Description of the *print* shell command.

read

The Korn shell's *read* command is a superset of the Bourne shell's *read* command. It works as shown in Figure 6.35. Here's an example:

```
$ read 'name?enter your name '
enter your name Graham
$ echo $name
Graham
$ _
```

Shell Command: **read** -prsu [*n*] [*name?prompt*] { *name* } *

The Korn shell *read* works just like the Bourne shell *read*, except for the following new features:

- The **-p** option causes the input line to be read from the shell's two-way pipe.
- The **-u** option causes the file descriptor *n* to be used for input.
- If the first argument contains a ?, the remainder of the argument is used as a prompt.

FIGURE 6.35

Description of the *read* shell command.

test

The Korn shell version of *test* accepts several new operators, as shown in Figure 6.36. The Korn shell also supports a more convenient syntax for *test*, as shown in Figure 6.37. I prefer the more modern form of *test* that uses the double brackets, as it allows me to write more readable programs. Here's an example of this newer form of *test* in action:

```
$ cat test.ksh           ...list the script.
i=1
while [[ i -le 4 ]]
do
 echo $i
 (( i = i + 1 ))
done
$ test.ksh               ...execute the script.
1
2
3
4
$ _
```

Operator	Meaning
-L *fileName*	Return true if *fileName* is a symbolic link.
file1 -nt *file2*	Return true if *file1* is newer than *file2*.
file1 -ot *file2*	Return true if *file1* is older than *file2*.
file1 -ef *file2*	Return true if *file1* is the same file as *file2*.

FIGURE 6.36

Test operators unique to the Korn shell *test* shell command.

[[*testExpression*]]

which is equivalent to

test *textExpression*

FIGURE 6.37

Two forms of *test* in the Korn shell.

trap

The Korn shell's *trap* command is a superset of the Bourne shell's *trap* command. It works as shown in Figure 6.38. In the following example, I set the EXIT trap inside a function to demonstrate local function traps:

```
$ cat trap.ksh                        ...list the script.
f ()
{
 echo 'enter f ()'
 trap 'echo leaving f...' EXIT    # set a local trap
 echo 'exit f ()'
}
```

```
# main program.
trap 'echo exit shell' EXIT      # set a global trap.
f                                # invoke the function f ().
$ trap.ksh                       ...execute the script.
enter f ()
exit f ()
leaving f...                     ...local EXIT is trapped.
exit shell                       ...global EXIT is trapped.
$ _
```

Shell Command: **trap** [*command*] [*signal*]

The Korn shell *trap* works just like the Bourne shell *trap*, except for the following features:

- If arg is -, then all of the specified signals are reset to their initial values.
- If an EXIT or 0 signal is given to a *trap* inside a function, then *command* is executed when the function is exited.

FIGURE 6.38

Description of the *trap* shell command.

SAMPLE PROJECT: JUNK

To illustrate some of the Korn shell capabilities, I present a Korn shell version of the "junk" script project that was suggested at the end of chapter 5. The **junk** utility is defined in Figure 6.39. The Korn shell script that follows uses a function to process error messages and uses an array to store filenames. The rest of the functionality should be pretty easy to follow from the embedded comments. (The shell script is available online. See the preface for more information.)

Utility: **junk** -lp { *fileName* }*

junk is a replacement for the **rm** utility. Rather than removing files, it moves them into the subdirectory ".junk" in your home directory. If ".junk" doesn't exist, it is automatically created. The **-l** option lists the current contents of the ".junk" directory, and the **-p** option purges ".junk".

FIGURE 6.39

Description of the **junk** shell script.

junk

```
#! /bin/ksh
# junk script
# Korn shell version
```

```
# author: Graham Glass
# 9/25/91
#
# Initialize variables
#
fileCount=0      # the number of files specified.
listFlag=0       # 1 if list option (-)used.
purgeFlag=0      # 1 if purge (-p) option used.
fileFlag=0       # 1 if at least one file is specified.
junk=~/.junk     # the name of the junk directory.
#
error ()
{
#
# Display error message and quit
#
cat << ENDOFTEXT
Dear $USER, the usage of junk is as follows:
 junk -p means "purge all files"
 junk -l means "list junked files"
 junk <list of files, to junk them
ENDOFTEXT
exit 1
}
#
# Parse command line
#
for arg in $*
do
  case $arg in
    "-p")
      purgeFlag=1
      ;;
    "-l")
      listFlag=1
      ;;
    -*)
      echo $arg is an illegal option
      ;;
    *)
      fileFlag=1
      fileList[$fileCount]=$arg      # append to list
      let fileCount=fileCount+1
      ;;
  esac
done
#
# Check for too many options
#
let total=$listFlag+$purgeFlag+$fileFlag
if (( total != 1 ))
then
 error
```

```
fi
#
# If junk directory doesn't exist, create it
#
if [[ ! (-d $junk) ]]
then
 'mkdir' $junk          # quoted just in case it's aliased.
fi
#
# Process options
#
if (( listFlag == 1 ))
then
 'ls' -lgF $junk        # list junk directory.
 exit 0
fi
#
if (( purgeFlag == 1 ))
then
 'rm' $junk/*           # remove files in junk directory.
 exit 0
fi
#
if (( fileFlag == 1 ))
then
 'mv' ${fileList[*]} $junk   # move files to junk dir.
 exit 0
fi
#
exit 0
```

Here's some sample output from **junk**:

```
$ ls *.ksh                          ...list some files to junk.
fact.ksh*    func5.ksh*      test.ksh*    trap.ksh*
func4.ksh*   squares.ksh*    track.ksh*
$ junk func5.ksh func4.ksh      ...junk a couple of files.
$ junk -l                       ...list my junk.
total 2
-rwxr-xr-x 1 gglass apollocl  205 Feb  6 22:44 func4.ksh*
-rwxr-xr-x 1 gglass apollocl  274 Feb  7 21:02 func5.ksh*
$ junk -p                       ...purge my junk.
$ junk -z                       ...try a silly option.
-z is an illegal option
Dear glass, the usage of junk is as follows:
 junk -p means "purge all files"
 junk -l means "list junked files"
 junk <list of files> to junk them
$ _
```

THE RESTRICTED SHELL

There is a variation of the Korn shell called the *restricted* Korn shell that provides every Korn shell feature, except that

- You may not change directory.
- You may not redirect output using > or ≫ .
- You may not set the SHELL, ENV, or PATH environment variables.
- You may not use absolute pathnames.

These restrictions become active only *after* the shell's ".profile" and $ENV files have been executed. Any scripts executed by the restricted Korn shell are interpreted by their associated shell and are not restricted in any way.

The restricted Korn shell is a regular C program whose executable file is stored as "/bin/rksh". If your chosen shell is "/bin/rksh", an interactive restricted Korn shell is invoked automatically when you log into UNIX. You may also invoke a restricted Korn shell manually from a script or from a terminal by using the command **rksh**.

System administrators use the restricted shell to provide users with a limited access to UNIX features as follows:

- They write a series of regular Korn shell scripts that enable users to access the features that they (the users) wish to use.
- They place these scripts into a read-only directory, typically called something like "/usr/local/rbin".
- They set up the restricted user's ".profile" file so that $PATH contains only "/usr/local/rbin" and a few other select directories.
- They change the user's entry in the password file (discussed in Chapter 15), so that the user's login shell is "/bin/rksh".

COMMAND LINE OPTIONS

If the first command line argument is a -, the Korn shell is started as a login shell. In addition to this, the Korn shell supports the Bourne shell command line options, the flags of the built-in *set* command (including **-x** and **-v**), and the options listed in Figure 6.40.

Option	Meaning
-r	Make the Korn shell a restricted Korn shell.
fileName	Execute the shell commands in *fileName* if the -s option is not used. *fileName* is $0 within the *fileName* script.

FIGURE 6.40

Korn shell command line options.

CHAPTER REVIEW

Checklist

In this chapter, I described

- the creation of a Korn shell start-up file
- aliases and the history mechanism
- the built-in **vi** and **emacs** line editors
- arithmetic
- functions
- advanced job control
- several enhancements to inherited Bourne shell commands

Quiz

1. Who wrote the Korn shell?
2. Why is the alias mechanism useful?
3. How can you reedit and reexecute previous commands?
4. Does the Korn shell support recursive functions?
5. Describe the modern syntax of the *test* command.

Exercises

6.1 Rewrite the **junk** script of this chapter so that it is menu driven. Use the *select* command. [level: *easy*]

6.2 Write a function called **dateToDays** that takes three parameters—a month string such as Sep, a day number such as 18, and a year number such as 1962—and returns the number of days from January 1, 1900, to the date. [level: *medium*]

6.3 Write a set of functions that emulate the directory stack facilities of the C shell (described in the next chapter). Use environment variables to hold the stack and its size. [level: *medium*]

6.4 Build a script called **pulse** that takes two parameters: the name of a script and an integer. **pulse** should execute the specified script for the specified number of seconds, suspend the script for the same number of seconds, and continue this cycle until the script is finished. [level: *hard*]

Projects

1. Write a skeleton script that allows system administration tasks to be performed automatically from a menu-driven interface. Useful tasks to automate include the following:

   - automatic deletion of core files
   - automatic warnings to those who use a lot of CPU time or disk space
   - automatic archiving

Don't worry about making the tasks do anything just yet; we'll fill that in at the end of Chapter 15. For now, concentrate on making the menu and task selection work properly, and just use the **echo** or **print** commands to print out what would happen for each selection. [level: *easy*]

2. Write an alias manager script that allows you to choose DOS emulation, VMS emulation, or no emulation. [level: *medium*]

# CHAPTER 7

The C Shell

MOTIVATION

The C shell was written after the Bourne shell and adheres more closely to the C language syntax and control structures. The first shell to support advanced job control the C shell became a favorite of early UNIX developers. Many C shell users are changing over to the Korn and Bash shells because of their additional features and availability, but the C shell still remains popular.

PREREQUISITES

You should already have read Chapter 4 and experimented with some of the core shell facilities.

OBJECTIVES

In this chapter, I explain and demonstrate the C-shell-specific facilities.

PRESENTATION

The information is presented in the form of several sample UNIX sessions and a small project.

SHELL COMMANDS

The chapter introduces the following shell commands, listed in alphabetical order:

alias	nice	source
chdir	nohup	stop
dirs	notify	suspend
foreach..end	onintr	switch..case..endsw
glob	popd	unalias
goto	pushd	unhash

hashstat	rehash	unset
history	repeat	unsetenv
if..then..else..endif	set	while..end
logout	setenv	

INTRODUCTION

The C shell supports all of the core shell facilities described in Chapter 4, plus the following new features:

- several ways to set and access variables
- a built-in programming language that supports conditional branching, looping, and interrupt handling
- command customization using aliases
- access to previous commands via a history mechanism
- advanced job control
- several new built-in commands and several enhancements to existing commands

These new facilities are illustrated in the hierarchy diagram shown in Figure 7.1.

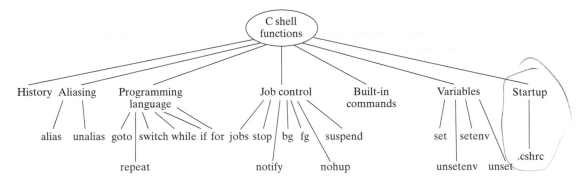

FIGURE 7.1

C shell functionality.

START-UP

The C shell is a regular C program whose executable file is stored as "/bin/csh". If your chosen shell is "/bin/csh", an interactive C shell is invoked automatically when you log into UNIX. You may also invoke a C shell manually from a script or from a terminal by using the command **csh**, which has several command line options that are described at the end of the chapter.

When a C shell is started as a login shell, a global login initialization file, which applies to all users, may also be executed if it is present. This file is useful for setting up environment variables (such as PATH) so that they contain information about the local environment. The name of the file varies from one version of UNIX to another, but it is generally something like "/.login" or "/etc/login."

Step	Shell type	Action
1	both	Execute commands in $HOME/.cshrc if it exists.
2	login only	Execute commands in global login initialization file if it exists.
3	login only	Execute commands in $HOME/.login if it exists.

FIGURE 7.2

C shell start-up sequence.

When a C shell is invoked, the start-up sequence is different for login shells and nonlogin shells, as shown in Figure 7.2. Note that the ".cshrc" file is run before either type of login initialization file. This may seem counterintuitive, and it has been the cause of much unexpected behavior when users are crafting their initialization files. The way to keep things straight is to remember that the C shell always runs its own initialization file immediately upon starting and then determines whether the shell is a login shell, which would require running the other initialization files.

Once an interactive shell starts and finishes running all the appropriate initialization files, it displays its prompt and awaits user commands. The standard C shell prompt is %, although it may be changed by setting the local variable $prompt, described shortly.

The ".login" file typically contains commands that set environment variables such as TERM, which contains the type of your terminal, and PATH, which tells the shell where to search for executable files. Put things in your ".login" file that need to be set only once (environment variables whose values are inherited by other shells) or that make sense only for an interactive session (such as specifying terminal settings). Here's an example of a ".login" file:

```
echo -n "Enter your terminal type (default is vt100): "
set termtype = $<
set term = vt100
if ("$termtype" != "") set term = "$termtype"
unset termtype
set path=(. /bin /usr/bin /usr/local/bin )
stty erase "^?" kill "^U" intr "^C" eof "^D" crt crterase
set cdpath = (~)
set history = 40
set notify
set prompt = "! % "
set savehist = 32
```

The ".cshrc" file generally contains commands that set common aliases (discussed later) or anything else that applies only to the current shell. The "rc" suffix stands for "**run** **c**ommands." Here's an example of a ".cshrc" file:

```
alias emacs /usr/local/emacs
alias h history
alias ll ls -l
alias print prf -pr pb1-2236-lp3
```

```
alias ls ls -F
alias rm rm -i
alias m more
```

VARIABLES

The C shell supports local and environment variables. A local variable may hold either one value, in which case it's called a *simple* variable, or more than one value, in which case it's termed a *list*. This section describes the C shell facilities that support variables.

Creating and Assigning Simple Variables

To assign a value to a simple variable, use the built-in *set* command described in Figure 7.3. Here are some examples:

```
% set flag          ...set "flag" to a null string.
% echo $flag             ...nothing is printed, as it's null.

% set color = red ...set "color" to the string "red".
% echo $color
red
% set name = Graham Glass      ...beware! Must use quotes.
% echo $name               ...only the first string was assigned.
Graham
% set name = "Graham Glass"    ...now it works as expected.
% echo $name
Graham Glass
% set        ...display a list of all local variables.
argv  ()
cdpath       /home/glass
color        red
cwd          /home/glass
flag
...
name         Graham Glass
term         vt100
user         glass
% _
```

---

set {*name* [=*word*]}*

If no arguments are supplied, a list of all the local variables is displayed. If *word* is not supplied, *name* is set to a null string. If the variable *name* doesn't exist, it is implicitly created.

FIGURE 7.3

Description of the *set* shell command.

Accessing a Simple Variable

In addition to the simple variable access syntax (*$name*), the C shell supports the complex access methods shown in Figure 7.4. Some examples follow that illustrate these access methods. In the first example, I used braces to append a string to the value of a variable:

```
% set verb = sing
% echo I like $verbing
verbing: Undefined variable.
% echo I like ${verb}ing
I like singing
% _
```

Syntax	Action
${*name*}	Replaced by the value of *name*. This form is useful if the expression is immediately followed by an alphanumeric character that would otherwise be interpreted as part of the variable's name.
${*?name*}	Replaced by 1 if *name* is set and 0 otherwise.

FIGURE 7.4

Accessing C shell variables.

In the following example, I used a variable as a simple flag in a conditional expression:

```
% cat flag.csh          ...list the script.
#
set flag                ...set "flag" to a null string.
if (${?flag}) then      ...branch if "flag" is set.
 echo flag is set
endif
% flag.csh              ...execute the script.
flag is set
% _
```

Creating and Assigning List Variables

To assign a list of values to a variable, use the built-in *set* command with the syntax shown in Figure 7.5. Here's an example:

```
% set colors = ( red yellow green )     ...set to a list.
% echo $colors                           ...display entire list.
red yellow green
% _
```

Accessing a List Variable

The C shell supports a couple of ways to access a list variable. Both of these methods have two forms, the second of which is surrounded by braces. The second form is useful

---

set {*name* = ({ *word*}*) }*

If the named variable doesn't exist, it is created implicitly. The named variable is assigned to a copy of the specified list of words.

FIGURE 7.5

Description of the *set* shell command setting a list variable.

Syntax	Action
$name[*selector*] ${name[*selector*]}	Both forms are replaced by the element of *name* whose index is specified by the value of *selector*, which may either be a single number, a range of numbers in the format *start-end*, or an asterisk*. If *start* is omitted, 1 is assumed. If *end* is omitted, the index of the last element is assumed. If a * is supplied, then all of the elements are selected. The first element of a list has index 1.
$#name ${#name}	Both forms are replaced by the number of elements in *name*.

FIGURE 7.6

Accessing C shell list variables.

if the expression is immediately followed by an alphanumeric character that would otherwise be interpreted as part of the variable's name. Figure 7.6 provides a description of the two access methods. Here are some examples:

```
% set colors = ( red yellow green )    ...set to a list.
% echo $colors[1]                ...display first element.
red
% echo $colors[2-3]              ...display 2nd and 3rd.
yellow green
% echo $colors[4]                ...illegal access.
Subscript out of range.
% echo $#colors                  ...display size of list.
3
% _
```

Building Lists

To add an element to the end of a list, set the original list equal to itself plus the new element, surrounded by parentheses; if you try to assign the new element directly, you'll get an error message. The following example illustrates some list manipulations:

```
% set colors = ( red yellow green )    ...set to a list.
% set colors[4] = pink                 ...try to set the 4th.
Subscript out of range.
% set colors = ( $colors blue )        ...add to the list.
% echo $colors                              ...it works!
red yellow green blue
% set colors[4] = pink                 ...OK, since 4th exists.
% echo $colors
red yellow green pink
% set colors = $colors black    ...don't forget to use ().
% echo $colors                         ...only the first was set.
red
$ set girls = ( sally georgia )        ...build one list.
$ set boys = ( harry blair )           ...build another.
$ set both = ( $girls $boys )          ...add the lists.
$ echo $both                           ...display the result.
sally georgia harry blair
% _
```

Predefined Local Variables

In addition to the common predefined local variables, the C shell defines the variables shown in Figure 7.7. Here's a small shell script that uses the $< variable to obtain a user response:

```
% cat var5.csh                             ...list the script.
#
echo -n "please enter your name: "
set name = $<      # take a line of input.
echo hi $name, your current directory is $cwd
% var5.csh                                 ...execute the script.
please enter your name: Graham
hi Graham, your current directory is /home/glass
% _
```

Name	Value
$?0	1 if the shell is executing commands from a named file; 0 otherwise.
$<	The next line of standard input, fully quoted.
$argv	A list that contains all of the positional parameters: $argv[1] is equal to $1.
$cdpath	The list of alternative directories that *chdir* uses for searching purposes.

FIGURE 7.7

C shell predefined local variables.

$cwd	The current working directory.
$echo	Set if the -x command line option is active.
$histchars	May be used to override the default history metacharacters. The first character is used in place of ! for history substitutions, and the second is used in place of ^ for quick command reexecution.
$history	The size of the history list.
$home	The shell's home directory.
$ignoreeof	Prevents the shell from terminating when it gets a *Control-D*.
$mail	A list of the files to check for mail. By default, the shell checks for mail every 600 seconds (10 minutes). If the first word of $mail is a number, the shell uses this value instead.
$noclobber	Prevents existing files from being overridden by > and nonexistent files from being appended to by >>.
$noglob	Prevents wildcard expansion.
$nonomatch	Prevents an error from occurring if no files match a wildcard filename.
$notify	By default, the shell notifies you of changes in job status just before a new prompt is displayed. If $notify is set, the change in status is displayed immediately when it occurs.
$path	Used by the shell for locating executable files.
$prompt	The shell prompt.
$savehist	The number of commands to save in the history file.
$shell	The full pathname of the log-in shell.
$status	The exit code of the last command.
$time	If this is set, any process that takes more than the specified number of seconds will cause a message to be displayed that indicates process statistics.
$verbose	Set if the -v command line option is used.

FIGURE 7.7   (*Continued*)

Creating and Assigning Environment Variables

To assign a value to an environment variable, use the built-in command *setenv* described in Figure 7.8. Here's an example of *setenv*:

```
% setenv TERM vt52              ...set my terminal type.
% echo $TERM                    ...confirm.
vt52
% _
```

---

setenv *name word*

If the named variable doesn't exist, it is created implicitly; otherwise, it is overwritten. Note that environment variables always hold exactly one value; there is no such thing as an environment list.

FIGURE 7.8

Description of the *setenv* shell command.

Predefined Environment Variables

In addition to the common predefined environment variables, the C shell supports the variable shown in Figure 7.9.

Name	Value
$LOGNAME	the shell owner's user ID

FIGURE 7.9

C shell predefined environment variables.

EXPRESSIONS

The C shell supports string, arithmetic, and file-oriented expressions.

String Expressions

The C shell supports the string operators shown in Figure 7.10. If either operand is a list, then the first element of the list is used for the comparison. The script in the following example employed the string-matching technique to infer a user's response:

```
% cat expr1.csh                    ...list the script.
#
echo -n "do you like the C shell? " #prompt.
set reply = $<                     # get a line of input.
if ($reply == "yes") then          #check for exact match.
```

```
        echo you entered yes
      else if ($reply =~ y*) then              #check for inexact match.
        echo I assume you mean yes
      endif
      % expr1.csh                              ...execute the script.
      do you like the C shell? yeah
      I assume you mean yes
      % _
```

Operator	Meaning
= =	Return true if the string operands are exactly equal.
!=	Return true if the string operands are unequal.
=~	Like = =, except that the right operand may contain wildcards.
!~	Like !=, except that the right operand may contain wildcards.

FIGURE 7.10

C shell string operators.

Arithmetic Expressions

The C shell supports the arithmetic operators shown in Figure 7.11 in descending order of precedence. These operators work just like their standard C counterparts, except that they can operate only on integers. Expressions may be enclosed in parentheses to control the order of evaluation. When an arithmetic expression is evaluated, a null

Operator(s)	Meaning
-	unary minus
!	logical negation
* / %	multiplication, division, remainder
+ -	addition, subtraction
<< >>	bitwise left shift, bitwise right shift
<= >= <>	relational operators
= = !=	equality, inequality
& ^		bitwise and, bitwise xor, bitwise or
|| &&	logical or, logical and

FIGURE 7.11

C shell arithmetic operators.

string is equivalent to zero. Any expression that uses the &, &&, ||, |, <, >, <<, or >> operator must be enclosed in parentheses to prevent the shell from interpreting these characters in a special manner. Here's a sample script that uses a couple of operators:

```
% cat expr3.csh                           ...list the script.
#
set a = 3
set b = 5
if ($a > 2 && $b > 4) then
  echo expression evaluation seems to work
endif
% expr3.csh                       ...execute the script.
expression evaluation seems to work
% _
```

You may not use the *set* command to assign the result of an expression to a variable. Instead, use the built-in @ command, which has the forms shown in Figure 7.12. Here are some examples:

```
% set a = 2 * 2    ...you can't use set for assignment.
set: Syntax error.
% @ a = 2 * 2               ...use @ instead.
% echo $a
4
% @ a = $a + $a    ...add two variables.
% echo $a
8
% set flag = 1
% @ b = ($a && $flag)    ...need ()s because of &&.
% echo $b
1
% @ b = ($a && $flag)
% echo $b
0
% _
```

USE	MEANING
@	list all of the shell variables
@*variable op expression*	set *variable* to *expression*
@*variable*[*index*]*op expression*	set *index*th element of *variable* to *expression*
where *op* is =, +=, -=, *=, or /=.	

FIGURE 7.12

Forms of the C shell command "@".

You may also increment or decrement a variable by using ++ or --, as in the following commands:

```
% set value = 1
% @ value ++
% echo $value
2
% _
```

File-Oriented Expressions

To make file-oriented decisions a little easier to program, the C shell supports several file-specific expressions of the form shown in Figure 7.13. A description of each option

---

-option *fileName*

where 1 (true) is returned if the selected option is true and 0 (false) is returned otherwise. If *fileName* does not exist or is inaccessible, all options return 0.

FIGURE 7.13

Description of C shell file-oriented expression.

is shown in Figure 7.14. Here's an sample script that uses the **-w** option to determine whether a file is writable:

```
% cat expr4.csh                    ...list the script.
#
echo -n "enter the name of the file you wish to erase: "
set filename = $<           # get a line of input.
if (! (-w "$filename")) then  # check I have access.
  echo you do not have permission to erase that file.
else
  rm $filename
  echo file erased
endif
% expr4.csh                    ...execute the script.
enter the name of the file you wish to erase: /
you do not have permission to erase that file.
% _
```

Option	Meaning
r	Shell has read permission for *fileName*.
w	Shell has write permission for *fileName*.
x	Shell has execute permission for *fileName*.
e	*fileName* exists.
o	*fileName* is owned by the same user as the shell process.
z	*fileName* exists and is zero bytes in size.
f	*fileName* is a regular file (not a directory or special file).
d	*fileName* is a directory file (not a regular or special file).

FIGURE 7.14

Options used in file-oriented expressions.

FILENAME COMPLETION

Like the Korn shell, the C shell provides a way to avoid typing a long filename on a command line. (This feature was introduced during the evolution of the C shell, so older versions may not provide such functionality.)

To turn on the file completion function, you need to set the filec variable:

```
% set filec
```

Now, whenever you type part of a filename, you can type the *Escape* key, and if the part of the filename you have typed so far uniquely identifies a file, the rest of the name will be added automatically. If the text does not uniquely identify a file, no text will be modified and you may hear a beep or tone. You can also type a * to see a list of the filenames that currently match the part of the name you have typed. Here's an example:

```
% ls -al .log*            ...typed Escape, nothing so typed *
.login      .logout
% ls -al .login           ...shell retyped, I added "i" and
                          ...Escape and the "n" was added.
```

ALIASES

The C shell allows you to create and customize your own commands by using the built-in command *alias*, which works as shown in Figure 7.15. Here's an example of *alias* in action:

Shell Command: **alias** [*word* [*string*]]

alias supports a simple form of command line customization. If you alias *word* to be equal to *string* and then enter a command beginning with *word*, the first occurrence of *word* is replaced by *string* and the command is reprocessed.

If you don't supply *word* or *string*, a list of all the current shell aliases is displayed. If you supply just *word*, then the string currently associated with the alias *word* is displayed. If you supply *word* and *string*, the shell adds the specified alias to its collection of aliases. If an alias already exists for *word, word* is replaced.

If the replacement string begins with *word*, it is not reprocessed for aliases, in order to prevent infinite loops. If the replacement string contains *word* elsewhere, an error message is displayed when the alias is executed.

FIGURE 7.15

Description of the *alias* shell command.

```
$ alias dir 'ls -aF'      ...register an alias.
$ dir                     ...same as typing "ls -aF".
./          main2.c       p.reverse.c        reverse.h
../          main2.o       palindrome.c       reverse.old
$ dir *.c                 ...same as typing "ls -aF *.c".
main2.c      p.reverse.c           palindrome.c
$ alias dir  ...look at the value associated with "dir".
ls -aF
$ _
```

In the following example, I aliased a word in terms of itself:

```
% alias ls 'ls -aF'      ...define "ls" in terms of itself.
% ls *.c                 ...same as typing "ls -aF *.c".
main2.c          p.reverse.c         palindrome.c
% alias dir 'ls'         ...define "dir" in terms of "ls".
% dir                    ...same as typing "ls -aF".
./          main2.c       p.reverse.c        reverse.h
../          main2.o       palindrome.c       reverse.old
% alias who 'date; who'          ...infinite loop problem.
% who
Alias loop.
% alias who 'date; /bin/who'  ...full path avoids error
% who                          ...works fine now.
Fri Feb 13 23:33:37 CST 1998
glass                    ttyp0         Feb 13 23:30    (xyplex2)
% _
```

Removing an Alias

To remove an alias, use the built-in command *unalias*, which works as shown in Figure 7.16.

Shell Command: **unalias** *pattern*

unalias removes all of the aliases that match *pattern*. If *pattern* is *, then all aliases are removed.

FIGURE 7.16

Description of the *unalias* shell command.

Useful Aliases

Figure 7.17 provides a list of useful aliases, together with a brief description of each one. I keep these aliases in my ".cshrc" file.

Sharing Aliases

To make an alias available to a subshell, place its definition in the shell's ".cshrc" file.

Alias	Value
cd	cd \!*; set prompt = "$cwd \!>"; ls
	This changes your prompt so that it contains both the current working directory and the latest command number. (See "history" later in the list for more details.)
ls	ls -F
	This causes **ls** to include extra file information.
rm	rm -i
	This causes **rm** to ask for confirmation.
rm	mv \!* ~/tomb
	This causes **rm** to move a file into a special "tomb" directory instead of removing the file.
h	history
	This shows you a list of previously used commands by typing just one letter.

FIGURE 7.17

Useful C shell aliases.

vi	(mesg n; /bin/vi \!*; mesg y) This stops people from sending you messages while you're in the vi editor.
mroe	more This corrects a common spelling error when using the **more** command.
ls-l	ls -l This corrects a common spelling error when using the **ls** command.
ll	ls -l This allows you to obtain a long directory listing more conveniently.

FIGURE 7.17   (*Continued*)

Parameterized Aliases

An alias may refer to arguments in the original, "prealiased" command by using the history mechanism described in the next section. The original command is treated as if it were the previous command. The useful alias for *cd* that I mentioned makes good use of this facility; the \!* part of the alias is replaced by all of the arguments in the original command. The ! is preceded by a \ to inhibit its special meaning during the assignment of the alias:

```
alias cd 'cd \!*; set prompt = "$cwd \! > "; ls'
```

HISTORY

The C shell keeps a record of the commands you enter from the keyboard so that they may be edited and reexecuted at a later stage. This facility is sometimes known as a *history* mechanism. The ! metacharacter gives you access to history.

Numbered Commands

When you're using *history*, it's very handy to arrange for your prompt to contain the number of the command you're about to enter. To do this, insert the \! character sequence into your prompt:

```
% set prompt = '\! % '    ...include event num in prompt.
1 % echo Genesis          ...this command is event #1.
Genesis
2 % _                     ...the next command will be event #2.
```

Storage of Commands

A C shell records the last $history commands during a particular session. If $history is not set, a default value of 1 is used. If you want the next session to be able to access these commands set the $savehist variable. If you do this, the last $savehist commands are maintained in the file specified by the HISTFILE variable (which usually defaults to $HOME/.history, but may vary with versions of UNIX). A history file is shared by all of the interactive C shells created by the same user, unless HISTFILE is purposely set to a unique value in each different shell. In the following example, I instructed my shell to remember the last 40 commands in my history list and to store the last 32 commands between sessions:

```
2 % set history = 40      ...remember the last 40 commands.
40
3 % set savehist = 32     ...save 32 across sessions.
32
4 % _
```

Reading History

To obtain a listing of a shell's history, use the built-in command *history*, which works as shown in Figure 7.18. Here's an example:

```
4 % alias h history                ...make a useful alias.
5 % h                              ...list current history.
  1 set prompt = '\! % '
  2 set history = 40
  3 set savehist = 32
  4 alias h history
  5 h
6 % h -r 3          ...list last 3 commands in reverse order.
  6 h 3
  5 h
  4 alias h history
7 % _
```

Shell Command: **history** [-rh] [*number*]

history allows you to access a shell's history list. If no parameters are supplied, this command lists the last $history commands. The **-r** option causes the history list to be listed in reverse order, and the **-h** option inhibits the display of event numbers. "history" is usually aliased to "h" for speed.

FIGURE 7.18

Description of the *history* shell command.

Command Reexecution

To reexecute a previous command, use the ! metacharacter in one of the forms shown in Figure 7.19. These sequences may appear anywhere in a command line, although

Form	Action
!!	Replaced with the text of the most recent command.
!*number*	Replaced with the text of the command with the specified event number.
!*prefix*	Replaced with the text of the most recent command that started with *prefix*.
!?*substring*?	Replaced with the text of the most recent command that contained *substring*.

FIGURE 7.19

Command reexecution in the C shell.

they're usually used in isolation. The recalled command is echoed to the terminal before it is executed. The value of *prefix* or *substring* may not contain a space. The special meaning of ! is not inhibited by any kind of quote, but may be inhibited by preceding it with a space, tab, =, (, or \. Here are some examples:

```
41 % echo event 41        ...a simple echo.
event 41
42 % echo event 42        ...another simple echo.
event 42
43 % !!                   ...re-execute last command.
echo event 42             ...echo command before re-execution.
event 42
44 % !41                  ...re-execute command #41.
echo event 41             ...echo command before re-execution.
event 41
45 % !ec          ...re-execute command starting with "ec".
echo event 41             ...echo command before re-execution.
event 41
46 % _
```

Accessing Pieces of History

You may access a portion of a previous command by using history *modifiers*, which are a collection of options that may immediately follow an event specifier. Each modifier returns a single token or range of tokens from the specified event. Figure 7.20 provides a list of the modifiers. The colon before the ^, $, and * options is optional. To use one of

Modifier	Token(s) returned
:0	first
:number	(number+1)th
:start-end	(*start*+1)th through to (*end*+1)th
:^	first
:$	last
:*	second through last

FIGURE 7.20

C shell history modifiers.

these modifiers on the most recent command, you may precede the modifier by "!!" or just "!". Here are some examples:

```
48 % echo I like horseback riding     ...original line.
I like horseback riding
49 % !!:0 !!:1 !!:2 !!:4              ...access specified arguments.
echo I like riding
I like riding
50 % echo !48:1-$                      ...access range of arguments.
echo I like horseback riding
I like horseback riding
51 % _
```

Accessing Portions of Filenames

If a history modifier refers to a filename, it may be further modified in order to access a particular portion of the name. The existing modifiers may be followed immediately by the filename modifiers shown in Figure 7.21. In the following example, I

Modifier	Part of file	Portion of the specified fileName that is returned
:h	head	the filename minus the trailing pathname
:r	root	the filename minus the trailing .* suffix
:e	extension	the trailing .* suffix
:t	tail	the filename minus the leading directory path

FIGURE 7.21

C shell filename modifiers.

accessed various portions of the original filename by using the aforesaid filename access facility:

```
53 % ls /usr/include/stdio.h              ...the original.
/usr/include/stdio.h
54 % echo !53:1:h                         ...access head.
echo /usr/include
/usr/include
55 % echo !53:1:r                         ...access root.
echo /usr/include/stdio
/usr/include/stdio
56 % echo !53:1:e                         ...access extension.
echo h
h
57 % echo !53:1:t                         ...access tail.
echo stdio.h
stdio.h
% _
```

History Substitution

The substitution modifier is replaced by the specified portion of a previous event after a textual substitution is performed. The syntax is shown in Figure 7.22. Here's an example:

```
58 % ls /usr/include/stdio.h         ...the original.
/usr/include/stdio.h
58 % echo !58:1:s/stdio/signal/      ...perform substitution.
echo /usr/include/signal.h
/usr/include/signal.h
59 % _
```

!*event*:s/*pat1*/*pat2*/

This sequence is replaced by the specified event after replacing the first occurrence of *pat1* by *pat2*.

FIGURE 7.22

Description of C shell history substitution.

CONTROL STRUCTURES

The C shell supports a wide range of control structures that make the language suitable as a high-level programming tool. Shell programs are usually stored in scripts and are commonly used to automate maintenance and installation tasks.

Several of the control structures require several lines to be entered. If such a control structure is entered from the keyboard, the shell prompts you with a ? for each additional line until the control structure is ended, at which point it executes.

Following is a description of each control structure, in alphabetical order. I made the C shell examples correspond closely to the Bourne shell examples so that you can compare and contrast the two shells.

foreach .. end

The *foreach* command allows a list of commands to be executed repeatedly, each time using a different value for a named variable. The syntax is shown in Figure 7.23. Here's an example of a script that uses a *foreach* control structure:

```
% cat foreach.csh                          ...list the script.
#
foreach color (red yellow green blue)    # four colors
 echo one color is $color
end
% foreach.csh                              ...execute the script.
one color is red
one color is yellow
one color is green
one color is blue
% _
```

---

foreach *name* (*wordList*)

  commandList

end

The *foreach* command iterates the value of *name* through each variable in *wordList*, executing the list of commands *commandList* after each assignment. A *break* command causes the loop to end immediately, and a *continue* command causes the loop to jump immediately to the next iteration.

FIGURE 7.23

Description of the *foreach* shell command.

goto

The *goto* command allows you to jump unconditionally to a named label. To declare a label, simply start a line with the name of the label, followed immediately by a colon. Figure 7.24 shows the syntax of a *goto* command. Use *goto*s sparingly, to

> **goto** *name*
>
> where a label of the form exists later on in the script.
>
> *name:*
>
> When a *goto* statement is encountered, control is transferred to the line following the location pointed to by the label. Note that the label may precede or follow the *goto* statement, even if the command is entered from the keyboard.

FIGURE 7.24

Description of the *goto* shell command.

avoid nasty "spaghettilike" code (even if you like spaghetti). Here's an example of a simple *goto*:

```
% cat goto.csh                    ...list the script.
#
echo gotta jump
goto endOfScript                  # jump
echo I will never echo this
endOfScript:                      # label
echo the end
% goto.csh                        ...execute the script.
gotta jump
the end
% _
```

if .. then .. else .. endif

There are two forms of the *if* command. The first form supports a simple one-way branch and has the syntax shown in Figure 7.25. Here is an example of this form of *if*:

```
% if (5 > 3) echo five is greater than 3
five is greater than three
% _
```

> **if** (*expr*) *command*
>
> This form of the *if* command evaluates *expr* and, if *expr* is true (nonzero), executes *command*.

FIGURE 7.25

Description of the **if** shell command in its simple form.

> **if (*expr1*) then**
>   *list1*
> **else if (*expr2*) then**
>   *list2*
> **else**
>   *list3*
> **endif**
>
> The *else* and *else if* portions of this command are optional, but the terminating *endif* is not. *expr1* is executed. If *expr1* is true, the commands in *list1* are executed and the *if* command is done. If *expr1* is false and there are one or more *else if* components, then a true expression following an *else if* causes the commands following the associated *then* to be executed and the *if* command to finish. If no true expressions are found and there is an *else* component, the commands following the *else* are executed.

FIGURE 7.26

Description of the *if* shell command with *else* clauses.

The second form of the *if* command supports alternative branching. Its general syntax is shown in Figure 7.26. Here's an example of the second form of *if*:

```
% cat if.csh                  ...list the script.
#
echo -n 'enter a number: '    # prompt user.
set number = $<               # read a line of input.
if ($number < 0) then
  echo negative
else if ($number == 0) then
  echo zero
else
  echo positive
endif
% if.csh                      ...execute the script.
enter a number: -1
negative
% _
```

onintr

The *onintr* command allows you to specify a label that should be jumped to when the shell receives a SIGINT signal. This signal is typically generated by a *Control*-C from

> **onintr** [- | *label*]
>
> The *onintr* command instructs the shell to jump to *label* when SIGINT is received. If the - option is used, SIGINTs are ignored. If no options are supplied, the shell's original SIGINT handler is restored.

FIGURE 7.27

Description of the *onintr* shell command.

the keyboard and is described in more detail in Chapter 13. The syntax of *onintr* is shown in Figure 7.27. Here's an example:

```
% cat onintr.csh              ...list the script.
#
onintr controlC              # set Control-C trap.
while (1)
  echo infinite loop
  sleep 2
end
controlC:
echo control C detected
% onintr.csh                 ...execute the script.
infinite loop
infinite loop
^C                           ...press Control-C.
control C detected
% _
```

repeat

The *repeat* command allows you to execute a single command a specified number of times. Its syntax is shown in Figure 7.28. Here is an example of the use of *repeat*:

```
% repeat 2 echo hi there          ...display two lines.
hi there
hi there
% _
```

> **repeat** *expr command*
>
> The *repeat* command evaluates *expr* and then executes *command* the resultant number of times.

FIGURE 7.28

Description of the *repeat* shell command.

---

switch (*expr*)

case *pattern1*:

  list

 breaksw

case *pattern2*:

case *pattern3*:

  list2

 breaksw

default:

  defaultList

endsw

---

expr is an expression that evaluates to a string, *pattern1/pattern2/pattern3* may include wildcards, and *list1/list2/defaultList* are lists of one or more shell commands. The shell evaluates *expr* and then compares it with each pattern in turn, from top to bottom. When the first matching pattern is found, its associated list of commands is executed, and then the shell skips to the matching *endsw*. If no match is found and a default condition is supplied, then *defaultList* is executed. If no match is found and no default condition exists, then execution continues from the command following the matching *endsw*.

FIGURE 7.29

Description of the *switch* shell command.

switch .. case .. endsw

The *switch* command supports multiway branching based on the value of a single expression. Figure 7.29 shows the general form of a *switch* construct. Here's an example of a script called "menu.csh" that makes use of a *switch* control structure:

```
#
echo menu test program
set stop = 0             # reset loop termination flag
while ($stop == 0)       # loop until done
 cat << ENDOFMENU        # display menu
 1   : print the date.
 2, 3: print the current working directory
 4   : exit
ENDOFMENU
 echo
```

```
        echo -n 'your choice? '      # prompt
        set reply = $<               # read response
        echo ""
        switch ($reply)              # process response
          case "1":
            date                     # display date
            breaksw
          case "2":
          case "3":
            pwd                      # display working directory
            breaksw
          case "4":
            set stop = 1             # set loop termination flag
            breaksw
          default:                   # default
            echo illegal choice      # error
            breaksw
        endsw
      end
```

Here's the output from the "menu.csh" script:

```
% menu.csh
menu test program
 1   : print the date.
 2, 3: print the current working directory
 4   : exit
your choice? 1
Sat Feb 14 00:50:26 CST 1998
 1   : print the date.
 2, 3: print the current working directory
 4   : exit
your choice? 2
/home/glass
 1   : print the date.
 2, 3: print the current working directory
 4   : exit
your choice? 5
illegal choice
 1   : print the date.
 2, 3: print the current working directory
 4   : exit
your choice? 4

% _
```

while .. end

The built-in *while* command allows a list of commands to be executed repeatedly, as long as a specified expression evaluates to true (nonzero). The syntax is shown in

> **while** (*expr*)
>
>   *commandlist*
>
> **end**
>
> The *while* command evalutes the expression *expr* and, if it is true, proceeds to execute every command in *commandlist* and then repeats the process. If *expr* is false, the while loop terminates, and the script continues to execute from the command following the end. A *break* command causes the loop to end immediately, and a *continue* command causes the loop to jump immediately to the next iteration.

FIGURE 7.30

Description of the *while* shell command.

Figure 7.30. Here's an example of a script that uses a *while* control structure to generate a small multiplication table:

```
% cat multi.csh              ...list the script.
#
set x = 1                    # set outer loop value
while ($x <= $1)             # outer loop
  set y = 1                  # set inner loop value
  while ($y <= $1)           # inner loop
    @ v = $x * $y            # calculate entry
    echo -n $v "      "      # display entry
    @ y ++                   # update inner loop counter
  end
  echo ""                    # newline
  @ x ++                     # update outer loop counter
end
% multi.csh 7                ...execute the script.
1       2       3       4       5       6       7
2       4       6       8       10      12      14
3       6       9       12      15      18      21
4       8       12      16      20      24      28
5       10      15      20      25      30      35
6       12      18      24      30      36      42
7       14      21      28      35      42      49
% _
```

SAMPLE PROJECT: JUNK

To illustrate some of the C shell capabilities we have discussed, I present a C shell version of the "junk" script project that was suggested at the end of Chapter 5. Figure 7.31 gives a definition of the **junk** utility about to be described.

Utility: **junk** -lp { *fileName* }*

junk is a replacement for the **rm** utility. Rather than removing files, **junk** moves them into the subdirectory ".junk" in your home directory. If ".junk" doesn't exist, it is automatically created. The **-l** option lists the current contents of the ".junk" directory, and the **-p** option purges ".junk".

FIGURE 7.31

Description of the **junk** shell script.

The C shell script that follows uses a list variable to store filenames. The rest of the functionality is evident from the embedded comments. The shell script is available on-line. (See the preface for more information.) Here is the code:

Junk

```
#! /bin/csh
# junk script
# author: Graham Glass
# 9/25/91
#
# Initialize variables
#
set fileList = ()          # a list of all specified files.
set listFlag = 0           # set to 1 if -l option is specified.
set purgeFlag = 0  # 1 if -p option is specified.
set fileFlag = 0   # 1 if at least one file is specified.
set junk = ~/.junk         # the junk directory.
#
# Parse command line
#
foreach arg ($*)
 switch ($arg)
   case "-p":
     set purgeFlag = 1
     breaksw
    case "-l":
     set listFlag = 1
     breaksw
    case -*:
     echo $arg is an illegal option
     goto error
     breaksw
    default:
     set fileFlag = 1
     set fileList = ($fileList $arg) # append to list
     breaksw
  endsw
```

```
end
#
# Check for too many options
#
@ total = $listFlag + $purgeFlag + $fileFlag
if ($total != 1) goto error
#
# If junk directory doesn't exist, create it
#
if (!(-e $junk)) then
 'mkdir' $junk
endif
#
# Process options
#
if ($listFlag) then
 'ls' -lgF $junk               # list junk directory.
 exit 0
endif
#
if ($purgeFlag) then
 'rm' $junk/*       # remove contents of junk directory.
 exit 0
endif
#
if ($fileFlag) then
 'mv' $fileList $junk          # move files to junk directory.
 exit 0
endif
#
exit 0
#
# Display error message and quit
#
error:
cat << ENDOFTEXT
Dear $USER, the usage of junk is as follows:
 junk -p means "purge all files"
 junk -l means "list junked files"
 junk <list of files> to junk them
ENDOFTEXT
exit 1
```

ENHANCEMENTS

In addition to the new facilities that have already been described, the C shell enhances the common core shell facilities in the following areas:

- a shortcut for command reexecution
- the {} metacharacters

- filename substitution
- redirection
- piping
- job control

Command Reexecution: A Shortcut

It's quite common to want to reexecute the previous command with a slight modification. For example, say you misspelled the name of a file. Instead of "fil.txt", you meant to type "file.txt". There's a convenient shorthand way to correct such a mistake. If you type the command

```
^pat1^pat2
```

then the previous command is reexecuted after the first occurrence of *pat1* is replaced by *pat2*. This shortcut procedure applies only to the previous command. Here's an example:

```
% ls -l fil.txt              ...whoops!
ls: File or directory "fil.txt" is not found.
% ^fil^file                  ...quick correction.
ls -l file.txt               ...OK.
-rw-r-xr-x   1 ables      410 Jun  6 23:58 file.txt
% _
```

Metacharacters: {}

You may use braces around filenames to save typing common prefixes and suffixes. The notation

```
a{b,c}d
```

is replaced with

```
abd acd
```

In the following example, I copied the C header files "/usr/include/stdio.h" and "/usr/include/signal.h" (which have a common prefix and suffix) into my home directory:

```
% cp /usr/include/{stdio,signal}.h .     ...copy two files.
% _
```

Filename Substitution

In addition to the common filename substitution facilities, the C shell supports two new features: the ability to disable filename substitution and the ability to specify what action should be taken if a pattern has no matches.

Disabling Filename Substitution

To disable filename substitution, set the $noglob variable. If this is done, wildcards lose their special meaning. The $noglob variable is not set by default. Here's an example:

```
% echo a* p*              ...one wildcard pair matches: p*
prog1.c      prog2.c      prog3.c      prog4.c
% set noglob             ...inhibit wildcard processing.
% echo a* p*
a* p*
% _
```

No Match Situations

If several patterns are present in a command and at least one of them has a match, then no error occurs. However, if none of the patterns has a match, the shell issues an error message by default. If the $nonomatch variable is set and no matches occur, then the original patterns are used as is. The $nonomatch variable is not set by default. Here's an example:

```
% echo a* p*              ...one wildcard pair matches: p*.
prog1.c      prog2.c      prog3.c      prog4.c
% echo a* b*              ...no wildcards match.
echo: No match.          ...error occurs by default.
% set nonomatch          ...set special nonomatch variable.
% echo a* b*             ...wildcards lose their special meaning.
a* b*                    ...no error occurs.
% _
```

Redirection

In addition to the common redirection facilities, the C shell supports a couple of enhancements: the ability to redirect the standard error channel and the ability to protect files against accidental overwrites.

Redirecting the Standard Error Channel

To redirect the standard error channel in addition to the standard output channel, simply append an ampersand (&) to the > or >> redirection operator, as shown in the following example:

```
% ls -l a.txt b.txt >list.out      ...ls sends errors to stderr
ls: File or directory "b.txt" is not found.
% ls -l a.txt b.txt >& list.out    ...also redirect stderr
% _
```

Although there's no easy way to redirect just the error channel, it can be done by using the following "trick":

```
(process1 > file1) >& file2
```

This trick works by redirecting the standard output from *process1* to *file1* (which can be "/dev/null" if you don't want to save the output), allowing only the standard errors to leave the command group. The command group's output and error channels are then redirected to *file2*.

Protecting Files Against Accidental Overwrites

You may protect existing files from accidental overwrites, and nonexistent files from being accidentally appended to, by setting the $noclobber variable. If a shell command tries to perform either action, it fails and issues an error message. Note that regular system calls such as write () are unaffected. $noclobber is not set by default. Here's an example:

```
% ls -l errors              ...look at existing file.
-rw-r-xr-x   1 glass      225 Feb 14 10:59 errors
% set noclobber             ...protect files.
% ls a.txt >& errors        ...cannot overwrite.
errors: File exists.
% _
```

To temporarily override the effect of $noclobber, append a ! character to the redirection operator:

```
% ls a.txt >&! errors         ...existing file is overwritten.
% _
```

Piping

In addition to supporting the common piping facilities, the C shell allows you to pipe the standard output and standard error channel from *process1* to *process2*, using the syntax shown in Figure 7.32. In the following example, I piped the standard output and error channels from the **ls** utility to **more**:

```
% ls -l a.txt b.txt |& more    ...pipe stdout and stderr.
ls: File or directory "b.txt" is not found.
-rw-r-xr-x   1 ables       988 Dec  7 06:27 a.txt
% _
```

Although there's no direct way to pipe *just* the error channel, it can be done by using a "trick" similar to the one used previously to pipe only the error channel to a file:

```
(process1 > file) |& process2
```

---

process1 |& process2

FIGURE 7.32

Example of piping both stdout and stderr.

This trick works by redirecting the standard output from *process1* to *file* (which can be "/dev/null" if you don't want to save the output), allowing only the standard errors to leave the command group. The command group's output and error channels are then piped to *process2*, but because the standard output is now empty, the result is only the standard error output.

Job Control

The job control facilities of the C shell are the same as the Korn shell's, with the following additional built-in commands:

- *stop*
- *suspend*
- *nice*
- *nohup*
- *notify*

stop

To suspend a specified job, use the *stop* command described in Figure 7.33.

suspend

The *suspend* command is described in Figure 7.34.

Shell Command: **stop** { *%job* }*

stop suspends the jobs that are specified, using the same standard job specifier format described in Chapter 6. If no arguments are supplied, the most recently referenced job is suspended.

FIGURE 7.33

Description of the *stop* shell command.

Shell Command: **suspend**

suspend suspends the shell that invokes it. It makes sense to do this only when the shell is a subshell of the log-in shell, and it is most commonly done to suspend a shell invoked by the **su** or **script** utilities.

FIGURE 7.34

Description of the *suspend* shell command.

nice

To set the priority level of the shell or a command, use the *nice* command described in Figure 7.35. For more information about process priorities, see Chapter 13.

Shell Command: **nice** [+l- *number*] [*command*]

nice runs *command* with priority level *number*. In general, the higher the priority, the slower the process will run. Only a superuser can specify a negative priority level. If the priority level is omitted, 4 is assumed. If no arguments are specified, the shell's priority level is set.

FIGURE 7.35

Description of the *nice* shell command.

nohup

To protect a command from a hang-up, use the built-in *nohup* command as described in Figure 7.36.

Shell Command: **nohup** [*command*]

nohup executes *command* and protects it from a hang-up. If no arguments are supplied, then all further commands executed from the shell are protected. Note that all background commands are automatically "nohup'ed" in the C shell.

FIGURE 7.36

Description of the *nohup* shell command.

notify

Normally, the shell notifies you of a change in a job's state just before displaying a new prompt. If you want immediate (asynchronous) notification of job state changes, use the built-in *notify* command described in Figure 7.37.

Shell Command: **notify** { *%job* }*

notify instructs the shell to inform you immediately when the specified jobs change state. Jobs must be specified in accordance with the standard job specifier format described in Chapter 6. If no job is specified, the most recently referenced job is used. To enable immediate notification of all jobs, set the $notify variable.

FIGURE 7.37

Description of the *notify* shell command.

Terminating a Login Shell

The *logout* command terminates a login shell. Unlike *exit*, *logout* cannot be used to terminate an interactive subshell. You may therefore terminate a login C shell in one of the following three ways:

- Type a *Control*-D on a line by itself (as long as $ignoreeof is not set).
- Use the built-in *exit* command.
- Use the built-in *logout* command.

Here's an example:

```
% set ignoreeof       ...set to prevent ^D exit.
% ^D                  ...won't work now.
Use "logout" to logout.
% logout              ...a better way to log out.
login: _
```

When a login C shell is terminated, it searches for "finish-up" files. The commands in each such file, if found, are executed in sequence. The user's finish-up file is $HOME/.logout, and it is executed if found. Then, any global finish-up file is executed. The name of this file might be "/etc/logout" or "/.logout", depending on your version of UNIX.

A finish-up file typically contains commands for cleaning up temporary directories, performing other such cleanup operations, and issuing a goodbye message.

If a nonlogin C shell is terminated by using *exit* or *Control*-D, no finish-up files are executed.

BUILT-INS

The C shell provides the following extra built-ins:

- *chdir*
- *glob*
- *source*

chdir

The *chdir* shell command is described in Figure 7.38.

glob

The *glob* shell command is described in Figure 7.39.

source

When a script is executed, it is interpreted by a subshell. Any aliases or local-variable assignments performed by the script therefore have no effect on the original shell. If

---

Shell Command: **chdir** [*path*]

chdir works in the same way as *cd*, changing your current working directory to the specified directory.

FIGURE 7.38

Description of the *chdir* shell command.

Shell Command: **glob** { *arg* }

glob works in the same way as *echo*, printing a list of *args* after they have been processed by the shell metacharacter mechanisms. The difference is that the args in the list are delimited by nulls (ASCII 0) instead of spaces in the final output. This makes the output ideally suited for use by C programs that accept strings terminated by null characters.

FIGURE 7.39

Description of the *glob* shell command.

Shell Command: **source** [-h] *fileName*

source causes a shell to execute every command in the script called *fileName* without invoking a subshell. The commands in the script are placed in the history list only if the **-h** option is used. It is perfectly valid for *fileName* to contain further *source* commands. If an error occurs during the execution of *fileName*, control is returned to the original shell.

FIGURE 7.40

Description of the *source* shell command.

you want a script to be interpreted by the current shell and thus affect that shell, use the built-in *source* command described in Figure 7.40. In the following example, I used *source* to reexecute an edited ".login" file:

```
% vi .login                     ...edit my .login file.
...
% source .login                 ...re-execute it.
Enter your terminal type (default is vt100): vt52
% _
```

The only other way to reexecute the file would have been to log out and then log back in again.

THE DIRECTORY STACK

The C shell allows you to create and manipulate a directory stack, which makes life a little easier when you're flipping back and forth between a small working set of directories. To push a directory onto the directory stack, use the *pushd* command described in Figure 7.41. To pop a directory from the directory stack, use the *popd* command, which works as described in Figure 7.42. The *dirs* command, described in Figure 7.43, lets you see the contents of the directory stack. Here are some examples of directory stack manipulation:

```
% pwd                ...I'm in my home directory.
/home/glass
% pushd /            ...go to root directory, push home dir.
/ ~                  ...displays directory stack automatically.
% pushd /usr/include    ...push another directory.
/usr/include / ~
% pushd           ...swap two stack elements, go back to root.
/ /usr/include ~
% pushd           ...swap them again, go back to "/usr/include".
/usr/include / ~
% popd                    ...pop a directory, go back to root.
/ ~
% popd                    ...pop a directory, go back to home.
~
% _
```

Shell Command: **pushd** [+*number* | *name*]

pushd pushes the specified directory onto the directory stack and works like this:

- When *name* is supplied, the current working directory is pushed onto the stack and the shell moves to the named directory.
- When no arguments are supplied, the top two elements of the directory stack are swapped.
- When *number* is supplied, the *number*th element of the directory stack is rotated to the top of the stack and becomes the current working directory. The elements of the stack are numbered in ascending order, with the top as number 0.

FIGURE 7.41

Description of the *pushd* shell command.

Shell Command: **popd** [+*number*]

popd pops a directory from the directory stack and works like this:

- When no argument is supplied, the shell moves to the directory that's on the top of the directory stack and then pops it.
- When a *number* is supplied, the shell moves to the *number*th directory on the stack and discards it.

FIGURE 7.42

Description of the *popd* shell command.

Shell Command: **dirs**

dirs lists the current directory stack.

FIGURE 7.43

Description of the *dirs* shell command.

The Hash Table

As described in Chapter 4, the PATH variable is used when one is searching for an executable file. To speed up this process, the C shell stores an internal data structure, called a *hash table*, that allows the directory hierarchy to be searched more quickly. The hash table is constructed automatically whenever the ".cshrc" file is read. In order for the hash table to work correctly, however, it must be reconstructed whenever $PATH is changed or whenever a new executable file is added to any directory in the $PATH sequence. The C shell takes care of the first case automatically, but *you* must take care of the second.

If you add or rename an executable file in any of the directories in the $PATH sequence, except for your current directory, you should use the *rehash* command to instruct the C shell to reconstruct the hash table. If you wish, you may use the *unhash* command to disable the hash table facility, thereby slowing down the search process.

The *hashstat* command may be used to examine the effectiveness of the hashing system. However, the output of this command doesn't mean anything unless you're familiar with hashing algorithms.

In the next example, I added a new executable file into the directory "~/bin", which was in my search path. The shell couldn't find the file until I performed a *rehash*. Here are the commands:

```
% pwd                    ...I'm in my home directory.
/home/glass
% echo $PATH             ...list my PATH variable.
.:/home/glass/bin:/usr/bin:/usr/local/bin:/bin:
```

```
% cat > bin/script.csh          ...create a new script.
#
echo found the script
^D                              ...end-of-input.
% chmod +x bin/script.csh       ...make executable.
% script.csh                    ...try to run it.
script.csh: Command not found.
% rehash                        ...make the shell rehash.
% script.csh                    ...try to run it again.
found the script                ...success!
% hashstat                      ...display hash statistics.
5 hits, 6 misses, 45%
% _
```

COMMAND LINE OPTIONS

If the first command line argument is a -, the C shell is started as a login shell. In addition to this feature, the C shell supports the command line options shown in Figure 7.44.

Option	Meaning
-c *string*	Creates a shell to execute the command *string*.
-e	Terminates shell if any command returns a nonzero exit code.
-f	Starts shell, but doesn't search for or read commands from ".cshrc".
-i	Creates an interactive shell; like the -s option, except that the SIGTERM, SIGINT, and SIGQUIT messages are all ignored.
-n	Parses commands, but does not execute them; for debugging only.
-s	Creates a shell that reads commands from standard input and sends shell messages to the standard error channel.
-t	Reads and executes a single line from standard input.
-v	Causes $verbose to be set (described earlier).
-V	Like -v, except that $verbose is set before ".cshrc" is executed.
-x	Causes the $echo variable to be set (described earlier).
-X	Like -x, except that $echo is set before ".cshrc" is read.
fileName	Executes the shell commands in *fileName* if none of the -c, -i, -s, or -t options is used. *fileName* is $0 within the *fileName* script.

FIGURE 7.44

C shell command line options.

CHAPTER REVIEW

Checklist

In this chapter, I described

- the creation of a C shell start-up file
- simple variables and lists
- expressions, including integer arithmetic
- aliases and the history mechanism
- several control structures
- enhanced job control
- several new built-in commands

Quiz

1. Why do you think integer expressions must be preceded by an @ sign?
2. What's a good way to correct a simple typing mistake on the previous command?
3. What's the function of the {} metacharacters?
4. Describe the differences between the *set* and *setenv* built-in commands.
5. How do you protect files from accidental overwrites?
6. How do you protect scripts from *Control-C* interrupts?

Exercises

7.1 Write a C shell version of the **track** script that was described in Chapter No, 5. [level: *easy*]

7.2 Write a utility called **hunt** that acts as a front end to **find**; **hunt** takes the name of a file as its single parameter and displays the full pathname of every matching filename, searching downwards from the current directory. [level: *medium*]

Project

Study the current trends in object-oriented programming, and then design an object-oriented shell (a C++ shell?). [level: *hard*]

# CHAPTER 8

The Bourne Again Shell

MOTIVATION

Bash, a.k.a. the Bourne Again Shell, originally written by Brian Fox of the Free Software Foundation, is the newest, and is quickly becoming the most popular, UNIX shell. Bash is an attempt to create a "best of all shells" that not only provides backward compatibility with the Bourne Shell, but also includes the most useful features of both the C Shell and the Korn Shell. Another advantage is that Bash, as an Open Software product, is freely available, can be found in all Linux distributions, and can be downloaded and installed on just about any version of UNIX if it isn't already present there. (See Chapter 16 for more information on Open Software.)

PREREQUISITES

You should have already read Chapter 4 and experimented with some of UNIX's core shell facilities. I recommend that you also read Chapter 5, since all of the information there is also applicable to Bash.

OBJECTIVES

In this chapter, I'll explain and demonstrate the facilities of Bash that are unique or different from previously discussed shells. Everything covered in Chapter 5 works in Bash, and much of the material in Chapters 6 and 7 is also applicable to Bash.

PRESENTATION

The information in the chapter is presented in the form of several sample UNIX sessions.

SHELL COMMANDS

The following shell commands, listed in alphabetical order, are described:

alias	if..then..elif..then..else..fi	set
builtin	jobs	source
case..in..esac	kill	unalias
declare	local	unset
dirs	popd	until..do..done
export	pushd	while..do..done
for..do..done	readonly	
history	select	

INTRODUCTION

Bash is the shell of choice on Linux systems. (See Chapter 16 for more information on Linux.) Bash implements all the core facilities described in Chapter 4 and is compatible with the Bourne Shell (so Bourne Shell scripts run under Bash) described in Chapter 5. Bash conforms to the POSIX standard for command shells (IEEE 1003.2). Although Bash attempts to conform to both **sh** and **csh** functionality and syntax, when there is a conflict, expect **sh** syntax to prevail. The following features of Bash are new or a bit different from what has been discussed in previous chapters:

- variable manipulation
- command-line processing, aliases, and history
- arithmetic, conditional expressions, control structures
- directory stack
- job control
- shell functions

Getting Bash

Bash is available for nearly every version of UNIX and is even available for Windows platforms. The GNU Bash web site is

```
http://www.gnu.org/software/bash/bash.html
```

You can find Bash source code at

```
ftp://ftp.gnu.org/pub/gnu/bash
```

Bash for Windows can be found at[1]

```
http://www.cygwin.com
```

---

[1]To install any or all components of the Cygwin tools, click on the "install" icon, which downloads and runs setup.exe. This takes you through the process whereby you can select Bash, as well as any other parts of Cygwin you wish to install.

The *Bash Reference Manual* is also available on-line, at

```
http://www.gnu.org/manual/bash
```

If your UNIX system doesn't already have Bash, you should download the proper package for your particular UNIX platform, build it, and install it in /bin. Note that you must have superuser privileges in order to install a program in a system directory. However, you can install one in your own directory and run it manually. (If you do this, there may be security issues that prevent you from making the program your login shell, however.)

START-UP

Like other shells, Bash is a UNIX program. When a new Bash shell starts, it executes commands in the file ".bashrc" in the home directory of the user running the shell. The one exception to this is when Bash is started as a login shell, in which case it runs the commands in the file ".bash_profile" in the user's home directory instead. So if you want your ".bashrc" file to be executed in your login shell as well, you have to add the following code to your ".bash_profile" file:

```
if [ -f ~/.bashrc ]; then
    . ~/.bashrc
fi
```

We'll see how and why this code works later in the chapter. The code is often found by default in ".bash_profile" files on a system.

In addition to using the ".bashrc" and ".bash-profile" files, the system administrator can put initialization commands appropriate for all users in the file "/etc/profile", which Bash will also read and execute. Note that Bash will read the "/etc/profile" file first, before running any initialization files belonging to the user.

VARIABLES

As with most shells, Bash allows the creation and use of shell variables for the following purposes:

- Value assignment and access
- Defining and using lists of values
- Testing a value or testing for the existence of a variable
- Reading or writing a variable's value

Creating and Assigning a Simple Variable

The Bash syntax for assigning a value to a simple variable is similar to that of other shells. It is shown in Figure 8.1. Here are some examples:

```
$ teamname="Denver Broncos"
$ gameswon=12
$ gameslost=3
```

{name=value}+

FIGURE 8.1

Example of assigning a simple variable.

The *set* built-in command can be used to set and display shell settings and to display the value of shell variables. The *set* built-in has many arguments and uses; we'll discuss them as necessary. Its simplest use is to display shell variables and their values, as shown in Figure 8.2. Here's an example:

```
$ set
gameslost=3
gameswon=12
teamname="Denver Broncos"
$ _
```

Shell command: **set**

The *set* built-in displays all variables set in the shell.

FIGURE 8.2

Example of the *set* built-in to display shell variables and values.

Other output that *set* would produce has been omitted for clarity. Later, we'll see other ways that *set* can be used to define shell behavior.

Accessing Simple Variables

Accessing the value of simple variables is also the same as in other shells, as shown in Figure 8.3. With the variables set in the previous section, one might use the following command to summarize a team's season record:

$name	Value of the variable *name* is used.
${name}	Value of the variable *name* is used next to other characters where the name of the variable might be misinterpreted.

FIGURE 8.3

Accessing the value of a simple variable.

```
$ echo "The $teamname went ${gameswon}-${gameslost} last year."
The Denver Broncos went 12-3 last year.
```

Creating and Assigning a List Variable

List variables, or arrays, are similar to those in the C Shell. Bash, however, provides a more explicit method for defining an array, with the *declare* built-in command, described in Figure 8.4, although using a variable in the form of an array will also work. Here is an example of how you might create a list of teams:

```
$ declare -a teamnames
$ teamnames[0]="Dallas Cowboys"
$ teamnames[1]="Washington Redskins"
$ teamnames[2]="New York Giants"
```

In practice, if you omit the *declare* command, the other lines will still work as expected.

Shell command: **declare** [–ax] [*listname*]

If the named variable does not already exist, it is created. If an array name is omitted when **–a** is used, *declare* will display all currently defined arrays and their values. If the **–x** option is used, the variable is exported to subshells. *declare* writes its output in a format that can be used again as input commands. This is useful when you want to create a script that sets variables as they are set in your current environment.

FIGURE 8.4

Example of the *declare* shell command.

Accessing List Variables

Once you build a list of values, you will want to use them for something. When accessing array values, you can always put braces around the variable name to distinguish it explicitly from other text that might be around it (to prevent the shell from trying to use other text as part of the variable name). This convention is shown in Figure 8.5. The braces are required when one uses arrays to distinguish between

${name[index]}	Access the *index*th element of the array $name
${name[*]} or ${name[@]}	Access all elements of the array $name
${#name[*]} or ${#name[@]}	Access the number of elements in the array $name

FIGURE 8.5

Accessing the value(s) of a list variable.

other shell operators. Suppose, for example, we have our list of 32 NFL teams stored as $teamname[0] .. $teamname[31]. One might use this information this way:

```
$ echo "There are ${#teamnames[*]} teams in the NFL"
There are 32 teams in the NFL

$ echo "They are: ${teamnames[*]}"
```

Building Lists

You can build an array or list variable in one of two ways. If you know how many elements you will need, you can use the *declare* built-in command to define the space and assign the values to specific locations in the list. If you don't know, or don't care, how many elements will be in the list, you can simply list them, and they will be added in the order you specify. For example, to define our list of NFL teams, of which we know (at least today) there are 32, you might define it as follows:

```
$ declare -a teamnames
$ teamnames[0]="Dallas Cowboys"
$ teamnames[1]="Washington Redskins"
$ teamnames[2]="New York Giants"
  ...
$ teamnames[31]="Houston Texans"
```

This can also be done in the following single (though long) command:

```
$ declare -a teamnames
$ teamnames=([0]="Dallas Cowboys" \
             [1]="Washington Redskins" \
  ...
             [31]="Houston Texans")
```

The backslash is used to tell the shell that the command is continued on the next line.
Even though we know the number of teams ahead of time, it isn't really necessary to know this to define the array. We could instead have done it this way:

```
$ teamnames = ("Dallas Cowboys" "Washington Redskins" \
               "New York Giants" "New York Jets"   \
  ...
               "Houston Texans")
```

Note that if you have populated the array sparsely (i.e., if you have not assigned values in consecutive locations, but have skipped around), then when you ask for the number of values in the array, the number value will be the actual number of populated elements, not the largest index defined. The following example is illustrative:

```
$ mylist[0]=27
$ mylist[5]=30
$ echo ${#mylist[*]}                    ...number of elements in mylist[]
2
$ declare -a
declare -a mylist='([0]="27" [5]="30")'
$ _
```

Destroying Lists

List variables can be deallocated, or destroyed, using the *unset* built-in described in Figure 8.6. If you have finished using an array, you can deallocate the space used by the array by destroying it completely. It is more likely, however, that you will want to remove a specific element in the array, as follows:

```
$ unset teamnames[17]
```

Now our array contains 31 names instead of 32.

Shell command: **unset** *name*

unset *name*[*index*]

Deallocates the specified variable or element in the list variable.

FIGURE 8.6

Description of the *unset* shell command.

Exporting Variables

In all shells, variables are local to the specific shell and, unless otherwise specified, are not passed to subshells. You must export a shell variable in the relevant Bourne or Korn shells for its value to still be set in a subshell. The *export* built-in is supported in Bash as it is in the Bourne Shell, or the **–x** option to the *declare* built-in, as we saw earlier, will also export a variable to a subshell. In the C shell, a variable must be created as an "environment" variable in order to be accessible in a subshell.

Bash provides a shell option that allows you to specify that, by default, all shell variables are to be exported to any subshells created. Shell options are defined with the *set* built-in, described in Figure 8.7.

Shell command: **set** –o allexport

Tell the shell to export all variables to subshells.

FIGURE 8.7

Example of the *set* built-in to export all variables.

Predefined Variables

Like most shells, Bash defines some variables when it starts. In addition to common predefined variables, Bash defines the variables shown in Figure 8.8.

Name	Value
BASH	The full path name of the Bash executable file
BASH_ENV	Location of Bash's start-up file (default is ~/.bashrc)
BASH_VERSION	Version string
BASH_VERSINFO	A read-only array of version information
DIRSTACK	Array defining the directory stack (discussed later)
EUID	Read-only value of effective user ID of user running Bash (UNIX only)
HISTFILE	Location of file containing shell history (default ~/.bash_history)
HISTSIZE	Maximum number of commands in history (default is 500)
HISTFILESIZE	Maximum number of lines allowed in history file (default is 500)
HOSTNAME	Hostname of machine on which Bash is running
HOSTTYPE	Type of host on which Bash is running
MAILCHECK	How often (seconds) to check for new mail
OSTYPE	Operating system of machine on which Bash is running
PPID	Read-only process ID of the parent process of Bash
SHLVL	Level of shell (incremented once each time a Bash process is started; shows how deeply the shell is nested)
UID	Read-only value of user ID of user running Bash (UNIX only)

FIGURE 8.8

Bash predefined variables.

COMMAND SHORTCUTS

Bash provides a few ways to shorten commands and arguments you type at the keyboard.

Aliases

As with the C Shell and Korn Shell, Bash allows you to define your own commands with the *alias* built-in command, described in Figure 8.9. Bash aliases work very much like Korn Shell aliases, as shown in the following example:

```
$ alias dir="ls -aF"
$ dir
./              main2.c          p.reverse.c       reverse.h
../             main2.o          palindrome.c      reverse.old
$ dir *.c
main2.c         p.reverse.c      palindrome.c
$
```

Shell Command: **alias** [-p] [word[=string]]

If you alias a new command word equal to string, then when you type the command word, the string will be used in its place (and any succeeding arguments will be appended to string), and the command will be evaluated. In the usage "alias *word*", any alias defined for word will be printed. Its simplest usage, "alias", will print all defined aliases. If the **–p** argument is used, the aliases are printed in a format suitable for input to the shell. (So if you've manually set up aliases you like, you can write them to a file to include in your .bashrc file.)

FIGURE 8.9

Description of the *alias* shell command.

To cause an alias to no longer have a special definition, use the *unalias* built-in described in Figure 8.10. You might wish to undefine an alias when you want to return to the normal behavior of a command that you usually alias to a different behavior. (For instance, in the foregoing example, you might no longer want *dir* to use the **ls** command because there is another **dir** command in the system.)

Shell Command: **unalias** [-a] {word}+

Remove the specified alias(es). If "-a" is used, remove all aliases.

FIGURE 8.10

Description of the *unalias* shell command.

Command History

Like the C Shell and the Korn Shell, Bash maintains a historical record of the commands you type. With the commands maintained in this history, you can selectively re-execute commands or cause them to be modified and then executed with the changes in them.

Storage of Commands

Commands you have typed to the shell are stored in a history file defined by the $HISTFILE shell variable. By default, the value specifies the file ".bash_history" in the user's home directory. This file can hold a maximum of $HISTFILESIZE entries; the default value is 500.

Reading Command History

To see your shell history, use the built-in *history* command described in Figure 8.11.

Shell Command: **history** [-c] [*n*]

Print out the shell's current command history. If a numeric value n is specified, show only the last n entries in the history list. If "-c" is used, clear the history list.

FIGURE 8.11

Description of the *history* shell command.

Command Reexecution

Bash honors the "!" metacharacter to reexecute commands from the history list in the same way the C Shell does, so C Shell users will be quite comfortable with the symbol. The Bash reexecution meta characters are shown in Figure 8.12.

Form	Action
!!	Replaced with the text of the most recent command.
!*number*	Replaced with command number *number* in the history list.
!-*number*	Replaced with the text of the command *number* commands back from the end of the list (!-1 is equivalent to !!).
!*prefix*	Replaced with the text of the most recent command that started with *prefix*.
!?*substring*?	Replaced with the text of the most recent command that contained *substring*.

FIGURE 8.12

Command reexecution metacharacters in Bash.

History Substitution

Sometimes you want to do more than simply reexecute a command that you have previously used. For example, you may want to modify the command slightly (change a filename or a single argument to a long command). The simplest form of history substitution is the same as in the C Shell and is shown in Figure 8.13. This form is useful

---

^*string1*^*string2*^

Substitute *string2* for *string1* in the previous command and execute it.

FIGURE 8.13

Description of simple history substitution in Bash.

when you make a minor mistake in a command and don't want to have to retype the entire command. The following commands are illustrative:

```
$ lp financial_report_july_2001.txt
lp: File not found.
$ ^2001^2002^
lp financial_report_july_2002.txt
request id is lwcs-37 (1 file)
$ _
```

Or perhaps you wish to substitute something in an earlier command (because you have issued other commands to find out what was wrong, so now the command you want to repeat isn't the most recent command in the history list). Figure 8.14 shows how to do this. Here's an example:

```
$ lp financial_report_july_2001.txt
lp: file not found.
$ ls
financial_report_july_2002.txt          financial_report_may_2002.txt
financial_report_june_2002.txt
$ !lp:s/2002/2001/
request id is lwcs-37 (1 file)
$ _
```

!*command*:s/*string1*/*string2*/

string2 is substituted for *string1* in the most recent command that begins with the text specified by *command*.

FIGURE 8.14

Example of more complex history substitution in Bash.

Command Editing

Bash provides a fairly sophisticated command-editing capability, much like that of the Korn Shell. Both **emacs** and **vi** styles of editing are supported; **emacs** is the default. Since, in **emacs**, you are always in text input mode, you can type **emacs** movement characters anytime you are typing a command. So, for example, if you've left out a word, you can back up with *Control-B* and insert it. To access your history list of previous commands, you can use *Control-P* to move "up" as if your history list were a file. Most other **emacs** movement commands are supported in Bash. (See the section "Editing A File: Emacs" in Chapter 2 for more information.)

Bash also allows **vi** users the same luxury, but it must be set by using the *set* built-in described in Figure 8.15. Because **vi** has two modes, "command mode" and "text

---

Shell command: **set** –o vi

Tell the shell to use **vi**-style command editing. If you ever want to return to the default **emacs**-style, substitute "emacs" for "vi" in the command..

FIGURE 8.15

Example of the *set* built-in to set the command line edit style.

input mode," while you are typing a normal command, Bash treats you as if you are in text input mode. Therefore, to access the **vi** command-editing features, you have to hit the *ESCAPE* key, just as you would in **vi** to get back into command mode. Once you do that, you can move around the same way you would in **vi** (using "h" to back up in the command and "k" to back up to previous commands in the history list). (See the section "Editing A File: Vi" in Chapter 2 for more information).

Autocompletion

Bash can complete a filename, command name, username, or shell variable name that you've begun typing if you've typed enough to uniquely identify it. To have Bash attempt to complete the current argument of your command, type the *TAB* character. If matching filenames are available, but the text you've typed does not identify one completely, text that the possible names have in common will be filled in to the point where they no longer have characters in common. This gives you the option of having the shell fill in long filenames where only a few characters at the end are different (like a sequence number or a date). Then you can type only the part that is unique to the file you wish to access.

ARITHMETIC

Arithmetic operations are easier in Bash than in the Bourne shell. What you have to use the **expr** utility to accomplish, you can do with built-in commands in Bash. Not only does this require less typing, but it also executes faster in Bash shell scripts.

To perform an arithmetic operation in Bash, you simply put the operation inside a set of double parentheses, as shown in Figure 8.16. Common numeric operations include those listed in Figure 8.17.

((*operation*))

FIGURE 8.16

Syntax of an arithmetic operation.

+, -	Addition, subtraction
++, --	Increment, decrement
*, /, %	Multiplication, division, remainder
**	Exponentiation

FIGURE 8.17

Arithmetic operators.

Integer arithmetic is faster than floating-point arithmetic. If you know that your variable will always be an integer (such as a counter or an array index), you can use the *declare* built-in, described in Figure 8.18, to declare it to be an integer.

Shell command: **declare** –i *name*

This form of *declare* defines the variable *name* as an integer.

FIGURE 8.18

Using the *declare* built-in to define a variable as an integer.

After we look at some simple conditional expressions, we'll combine them into a simple math script.

CONDITIONAL EXPRESSIONS

You can compare values (usually stored in shell variables) with each other and branch to different commands, depending on the outcome of the comparison. (In the next section, on control structures, we'll see how you control what you do after the comparison.)

Like arithmetic operations, arithmetic tests are enclosed in double parentheses. The types of comparisons you can make are shown in Figure 8.19.

<=, >=, <, >	Less than or equal to, greater than or equal to, less than, greater than comparisons
==, !=	Equal to, not equal to
!	Logical NOT
&&	Logical AND
||	Logical OR

FIGURE 8.19

Arithmetic conditional operators.

Arithmetic Tests

These comparisons make it simple to do a bit of math in a Bash script. We'll count up to 20 and test to see what numbers divide into 20 evenly (don't worry too much about the *while* construct just yet; we'll see it a bit later):

```
$ cat divisors.bash
#!/bin/bash
#
declare -i testval=20
declare -i count=2              # start at 2, 1 always works

while (( $count <= $testval )); do
  (( result = $testval % $count ))
  if (( $result == 0 )); then    # evenly divisible
    echo " $testval is evenly divisible by $count"
  fi
  (( count++ ))
done
$ bash divisors.bash
 20 is evenly divisible by 2
 20 is evenly divisible by 4
 20 is evenly divisible by 5
 20 is evenly divisible by 10
 20 is evenly divisible by 20
$ _
```

String Comparisons

The Bash string conditional operators are shown in Figure 8.20.

-n *string*	True if length of string is nonzero
-z *string*	True if length of string is zero
string1 == *string2*	True if strings are equal
string1 != *string2*	True if strings are not equal

FIGURE 8.20

String conditional operators.

File-Oriented Expressions

Figure 8.21 lists the Bash file-oriented conditional operators. A simple example of a file operation might be the following:

```
$ cat owner.bash
#!/bin/bash
#

if [ -O /etc/passwd ]; then
    echo "you are the owner of /etc/passwd."
else
    echo "you are NOT the owner of /etc/passwd."
fi
$ bash owner.bash
you are NOT the owner of /etc/passwd.
$_
```

-a *file*	True if the file exists
-b *file*	True if the file exists and is a block special file
-c *file*	True if the file exists and is a character special file
-d *file*	True if the file exists and is a directory
-e *file*	True if the file exists
-f *file*	True if the file exists and is a regular file
-g *file*	True if the file exists and its set-group-id bit is set
-k *file*	True if the file exists and its "sticky" bit is set

FIGURE 8.21

File-oriented conditional operators.

-p *file*	True if the file exists and is a named pipe
-r *file*	True if the file exists and is readable
-s *file*	True if the file exists and has a size greater than zero
-t *fd*	True if the file descriptor is open and refers to the terminal
-u *file*	True if the file exists and its set-user-id bit is set
-w *file*	True if the file is writable
-x *file*	True if the file exists and is executable
-O *file*	True if the file exists and is owned by the effective user id of the user
-G *file*	True if the file exists and is owned by the effective group id of the user
-L *file*	True if the file exists and is a symbolic link
-N *file*	True if the file exists and has been modified since it was last read
-S *file*	True if the file exists and is a socket
file1 –nt *file2*	True if *file1* is newer than *file2*
file1 –ot *file2*	True if *file1* is older than *file2*
file1 –ef *file2*	True if *file1* and *file2* have the same device and inode numbers

FIGURE 8.21   (*Continued*)

CONTROL STRUCTURES

To take advantage of the preceding comparisons, you can use various commands that control what command is executed next. These control structures are similar to ones found in the Bourne, Korn, and C Shells. Although they can be used in the interactive Bash shell, they are most often used in writing Bash shell scripts.

case .. in .. esac

The *case* statement lets you specify multiple actions to be taken when the value of a variable matches one or more values. The statement is described in Figure 8.22. A section of Bash shell script that uses the *case* statement to print out the home location of the NFL teams listed in our earlier example might look like this:

```
case ${teamname[$index]} in
    "Dallas Cowboys") echo "Dallas, TX" ;;
    "Denver Broncos") echo "Denver, CO" ;;
```

```
    "New York Giants"|"New York Jets") echo "New York, NY";;
        . . .
    *) echo "Unknown location" ;;
  esac
```

Shell command: **case** *word* **in** *pattern* {| *pattern* }*) *commands* ; ; **esac**

Execute the commands specified by *commands* when the value of *word* matches the pattern specified by *pattern*. The ")" indicates the end of the list of patterns to match. The ";;" is required to indicate the end of the commands to be executed.

FIGURE 8.22

Description of the *case* shell command.

Note the special use of the pattern "*" as the last pattern. If the script goes through all the patterns without finding a match, the pattern "*" will catch this situation. It is permissible to not match any patterns, in which case none of the commands will be executed.

if .. then .. elif .. then .. else .. fi

The *if* statement, described in Figure 8.23, will look familiar to Bourne and Korn Shell users. This construct lets you compare two or more values and branch to a block of

---

Shell command: **if**

if *test1*; **then**
  commands1;
[**elif** *test2*; **then**
  commands2;]
[**else** *commands3*;]
fi

test1 is a conditional expression (previously discussed) that, if true, causes the commands specified by *commands1* to be executed. If *test1* tests false, then if an "elif" structure is present, the next test, *test2*, is evaluated ("else if"). If *test2* evaluates to true, then the commands in *commands2* are executed. The "else" construct is used when you want to run commands after a test has evaluated to false.

FIGURE 8.23

Description of the *if* shell command.

commands, depending on how the values relate to each other. As an example, let's assume a special case for a couple of our NFL teams when we print information about them. We might determine which file of information to print like this:

```
# $index has been set to some arbitrary team in the list
#
if [ "${teamname[$index]}" == "Minnesota Vikings" ]; then
    cat "vikings.txt"       # print "special" info
elif [ "${teamname[$index]}" == "Chicago Bears" ]; then
    cat "bears.txt"         # ditto
else
    cat "nfl.txt"   # for everyone else, print the standard
fi
```

for .. do .. done

The *for* construct, described in Figure 8.24, is best used when you have a known set of items over which you wish to iterate (e.g., a list of hostnames, filenames, or something

---

Shell command: **for** *name* **in** *word* { *word* }* ; **do** *commands* ; **done**

Perform *commands* for each *word* in a list, with $name containing the value of the current *word*.

FIGURE 8.24

Description of the *for* shell command.

of that sort). You might use a comparison to jump out of such a loop, or you might simply wish to process each item in the list sequentially. The simplest example might be to print all text files in the current directory:

```
$ for file in *.txt
do
  lp $file
done
request id is lwcs-37 (1 file)
request id is lwcs-37 (1 file)
request id is lwcs-37 (1 file)
$ _
```

while/until .. do .. done

The *while* and *until* constructs, shown in Figure 8.25, work in a similar fashion, performing a loop while or until a test condition is met ("while" in case the condition is

> *Shell command:* **while** *test* ; **do** *commands* ; **done**
>
> **until** *test* ; **do** *commands* ; **done**
>
> In a *while* statement, perform *commands* as long as the expression *test* evaluates to true. In an *until* statement, perform *commands* as long as the expression *test* evaluates to false (i.e., until *test* is true).

FIGURE 8.25

Description of the *while* and *until* shell commands.

initially true and you want to loop until it becomes false, "until" in case the condition is initially false and you want to loop until it becomes true). These constructs are useful when you don't know exactly when the status of the test condition will be changed.

DIRECTORY STACK

Bash provides a directory stack similar to that offered by the C Shell, with a few improvements. One improvement is that the entire stack is stored in the string array $DIRSTACK, allowing easy access to any item in the stack from a Bash shell script.

To push the current directory onto the directory stack and change to a new directory, use the *pushd* built-in command described in Figure 8.26. When it's time to return to a previous directory, use the *popd* built-in, described in Figure 8.27, to retrieve previous locations, and change directories there. In addition to contents of the stack being available in the $DIRSTACK shell variable, the *dirs* built-in command, described in Figure 8.28, will print (or empty) the contents of the directory stack.

> *Shell command:* **pushd** [-n] [*dir*]
>
> *pushd* saves the current directory as the most recent addition to (i.e., on top of) the directory stack. A subsequent *popd* will retrieve this directory. Then *pushd* changes directories to the one that is specified. If no new directory is specified, the current directory and the top directory on the stack are swapped (i.e., you pop the current top of the stack and change directories there, and then you push the directory you were in onto the stack). If the **–n** argument is present, do not change to the new directory, but simply push the current directory onto the stack.

FIGURE 8.26

Description of the *pushd* shell command.

> *Shell command:* **popd** [-n]
>
> *popd* retrieves the last directory that was pushed onto the stack and changes directory to that location. The entry is removed from the stack. If the **–n** argument is present, do not change to the new directory, but simply remove it from the top of the stack.

FIGURE 8.27

Description of the *popd* shell command.

> *Shell command:* **dirs** [-cp]
>
> If no arguments are given, *dirs* simply prints out the contents of the directory stack. The **–p** option causes the directories to be printed one per line. The **–c** option causes the directory stack to be cleared.

FIGURE 8.28

Description of the *dirs* shell command.

JOB CONTROL

Bash adds a few capabilities for job control beyond those described in Chapter 6. If you skipped over the Korn Shell, I suggest you go back and read the section on "Enhanced Job Control" to supplement this section.

Job control allows you to suspend and resume the execution of a process begun from the Bash command line. As with the Korn Shell and C Shell, typing Control-Z while a process is running will suspend it. You can then use the *fg* or *bg* shell command to resume the process in the background or foreground, respectively. The specification of the job is the same as in the Korn Shell, with the two additional options shown in Figure 8.29. The specifier must uniquely identify a job. If more than one job matches

Form	Specifies
%name	Refers to a process whose name begins with *name*.
%?name	Refers to a process where *name* appears anywhere in the command line

FIGURE 8.29

Additional job specifiers in Bash.

> *Shell command*: **jobs** [-lrs]
>
> *jobs* displays a list of all the shell's jobs. When *jobs* is used with the **-l** option, process IDs are included in the listing. If the **-r** option is used, list only currently running jobs. If the **-s** option is used, list only currently stopped jobs.

FIGURE 8.30

Description of the *jobs* shell command.

> *Shell command*: **kill** [-s *signame*] [-n *signum*] *jobspec* or *pid*
>
> *kill* sends the specified signal to the specified process. Either *jobspec* (e.g., "%1") or a process ID is required. If the **-s** option is used, *signame* is a valid signal name (e.g., SIGINT). If the **-n** option is used, *signum* is the signal number. If neither **-s** nor **-n** is used, a SIGTERM signal is sent to the process.

FIGURE 8.31

Description of the *kill* shell command.

the specifier, Bash reports an error. Otherwise, the *fg*, *bg*, and *wait* commands work the same as they do in the Korn shell. The *jobs* and *kill* shell built-ins work a bit differently in Bash, as shown in Figures 8.30 and 8.31.

FUNCTIONS

Bash functions are syntactically the same as functions in the Korn Shell. If you skipped over the Korn Shell, go back and read the "Functions" section of Chapter 6. Bash makes a couple of valuable additions to the use of functions that we'll see here.

Functions can be exported to subshells in Bash with the use of the *export* built-in, described in Figure 8.32. Bash also provides a built-in command called *local* which restricts a variable so that it is local only to the current function (i.e., its value cannot be passed to a subshell). The command *local* is described in Figure 8.33.

> *Shell command*: **export** –f *functionname*
>
> The *export* built-in command used with the **-f** option exports a function to a subshell in the same way that exported shell variable values are exported to subshells.

FIGURE 8.32

Description of the *export* shell command used to export a function.

Shell command: **local** *name*[=*value*]

The *local* built-in command defines a variable so that it is local only to the current function. A variable name can be listed, or a value can be assigned in the same statement.

FIGURE 8.33

Description of the *local* shell command.

Shell command: **builtin** [*command* [*args*]]

The *builtin* shell built-in runs the named shell built-in *command* and passes it *args* if present. This command is useful when you are writing a shell function that has the same name as an existing built-in, but within the function you still want to run the built-in rather than recursively call the function.

FIGURE 8.34

Description of the *builtin* shell command.

A useful command for writing functions is the *builtin* built-in command, shown in Figure 8.34.

MISCELLANEOUS BUILT-IN COMMANDS

Bash includes many other built-in commands, some that it borrows from other shells for compatibility. A few of the more useful ones are described in Figures 8.35, 8.36, and 8.37.

The *set* built-in also has several other options we have not previously discussed. Figure 8.38 lists the most useful options of *set*, both ones that we have seen previously and ones we have not seen previously:

Shell command: **readonly**

readonly is used to prevent the value of a shell variable from being changed. In Bash, this can also be accomplished with *declare –r*. The use of *readonly* is the same as it is in both the Bourne and Korn shells and is described in Chapter 5.

FIGURE 8.35

Description of the *readonly* shell command.

Shell command: **select**

select is used to generate menu prompts. The *select* built-in works the same way as the *select* built-in in the Korn shell and is described in Chapter 6.

FIGURE 8.36

Description of the *select* shell command.

Shell command: **source** *file*

         . *file*

source and "." can be used to run a shell script in the current shell. This is useful for rerunning a .profile or .bashrc file after making a modification to it. The *source* built-in is the same as the *source* built-in in the C shell. The "." usage is the same as it is in the Bourne and Korn shells.

FIGURE 8.37

Description of the *source* and "." shell commands.

-o allexport | -a	Export all created or modified variables and functions.
-o emacs	Set command edit style to behave like **emacs**.
-o ignoreeof	Interactive shell will not exit on EOF (e.g., if you typed *Control-D* by accident).
-o noclobber | -C	Prevent output redirection from overwriting existing files.
-o noglob | -f	Disable filename substitution (a.k.a. "globbing").
-o posix	Cause Bash behavior to adhere to the POSIX 1003.2 Shell standard.
-o verbose | -v	Print shell input lines as they are read (useful for debugging scripts).
-o vi	Set command edit style to behave like **vi**.

FIGURE 8.38

Some of the *set* built-in options.

COMMAND LINE OPTIONS

Bash supports many command line options. Some of the most useful ones are shown in Figure 8.39.

-c *string*	Run *string* as a shell command
-s	Read commands from standard input
--login	Make Bash your login shell. This is useful if you can't set Bash to be your login shell with **chsh**.
--noprofile	Ignore Bash profile files (systemwide and user versions).
--norc	Ignore Bash rc files (~/.bashrc).
--posix	Run in Posix mode (same as *set –o posix*)
--verbose | -v	Print shell input lines as they are read (same as *set –o verbose*).

FIGURE 8.39

Some Bash command line options.

CHAPTER REVIEW

Checklist

In this chapter, I described

- Bash start-up files
- using shell variables
- using aliases, the history mechanism, and command line editing
- Bash arithmetic, conditionals, and control structures
- using the directory stack
- Bash's implementation of job control
- Bash shell functions

Quiz

1. Why does the fact that Bash provides arithmetic capability natively improve the run time of shell scripts so dramatically?
2. Why are braces ({}) required around list variables?
3. Do all Bourne Shell scripts work in Bash?
4. Do all Bash scripts work in the Korn Shell?
5. What shell variable contains the directory stack?

Exercise

The **track** script presented in Chapter 5 runs as is under Bash. However, it makes use of the **expr** UNIX command to do its arithmetic calculations. Modify **track** to use Bash arithmetic, and compare its speed of execution with that of the original version. You may wish to use the UNIX **time** command (described in Chapter 3) to measure the differences if nothing "feels" significantly different. [level: *easy*]

Project

Write a Bash script called **mv** (which replaces the UNIX command **mv**) that tries to rename the specified file (using the UNIX command **mv**), but if the destination file exists, instead creates an index number—a sort of version number—to append to the destination file. So if I type

```
$ mv a.txt b.txt
```

but b.txt already exists, **mv** will move the file to b.txt.1. Note that if b.txt.1 already exists, you must rename the file to b.txt.2, and so on, until you can successfully rename the file with a name that does not already exist. [level: *medium*]

CHAPTER 9

Networking

MOTIVATION

One of the most significant advantages of UNIX over other competing systems during its origin was that it was one of the first operating systems to provide access to widely distributed local networks, as well as to the large Internet network that spans the globe. Today, millions of users and programs share information on these networks for a myriad of reasons, from distributing large computational tasks to exchanging a good recipe for lasagna. To make the best use of these network resources, you should understand the utilities that manage the exchange of information. This chapter describes the most useful network utilities. While these utilities are applicable to both local networks and the Internet, I will defer most specific Internet-related topics until Chapter 10.

PREREQUISITES

In order to understand this chapter, you should already have read Chapters 1 and 2. It also helps if you have access to a UNIX system so that you can try out the various utilities that I discuss.

OBJECTIVES

In this chapter, I'll show you how to find out what's on the network, how to talk to other users, how to copy files across a network, and how to execute processes on other computers on the network.

PRESENTATION

The chapter begins with an overview of network concepts and terminology and then describes the UNIX network utilities.

COMMANDS

The following utilities, listed in alphabetical order, are introduced:

finger	rsh	w
ftp	rusers	wall
hostname	rwho	who
mesg	talk	whois
rcp	telnet	write
rlogin	users	

ping :

INTRODUCTION

A network is an interconnected system of cooperating computers. Through a network, you can share resources with other users via an ever-increasing number of network applications, such as Web browsers and electronic mail messaging systems.

There has been a huge explosion of UNIX network use in the 1990s. For example, the client–server paradigm described in Chapter 1 has been adopted by many of the major computer corporations and relies heavily on the operating system's network capabilities to distribute the workload between the server and its clients.

In order to prepare yourself for the advent of widespread networking, it's important to know the following subjects:

- common network terminology
- how networks are built
- how to talk to other people on the network
- how to use other computers on the network

This chapter covers all of these issues and more.

BUILDING A NETWORK

One of the best ways to understand how modern networks work is to look at how they evolved. Imagine that two people in an office want to hook their computers together so that they can share data. The easiest way to do this is to connect a cable between their serial ports. This is the simplest form of *local area network* (LAN), and it requires virtually no special software or hardware. When one computer wants to send information to the other, it simply sends the information out of its serial port: This arrangement is shown in Figure 9.1.

FIGURE 9.1

The simplest LAN.

Ethernets

To make things a little more interesting, let's assume that another person wants to tie into the other two guys' existing network. With three computers in the network, we need an addressing scheme so that the computers can be differentiated. We would also like to keep the number of connections down to a minimum. The most common implementation of this kind of LAN is called an *Ethernet®*. Ethernet is a hardware standard defining cabling, signaling, and behavior that allow data to pass across a length of wire. The data format is defined by *network protocols* that we'll look at a bit later. The Ethernet standard was originally developed by Xerox Corporation and works like this:

- Each computer contains an Ethernet card, which is a special piece of hardware that has a unique Ethernet address.
- Every computer's Ethernet card is connected to the same single piece of wire.
- When a computer wishes to send a message to another computer with a particular Ethernet address, it broadcasts the message onto the Ethernet, together with Ethernet header and trailer information that contains the Ethernet destination address. Only the Ethernet card whose address matches the destination address accepts the message.
- Two computers trying to broadcast to the Ethernet at the same time results in what is known as a *collision*. When a collision occurs, both computers wait a random period of time and then try again. Figure 9.2 shows a diagram of an Ethernet. Ethernet networks can transmit data on the order of tens or hundreds of megabytes per second.

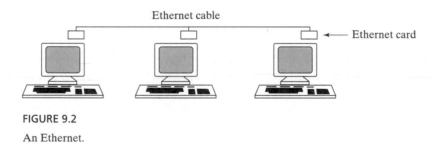

Ethernet cable

Ethernet card

FIGURE 9.2

An Ethernet.

Bridges

Let's assume that the Ethernet in the office works so well that the people in the office next door build themselves an Ethernet, too. How does one computer on one Ethernet talk to another computer on another Ethernet? One solution might be to connect a special bit of hardware called a *bridge* between the networks. A bridge (see Figure 9.3) passes an Ethernet message between the different *segments* (wires) of the network as if both segments were a single Ethernet network cable. A bridge is used when you need

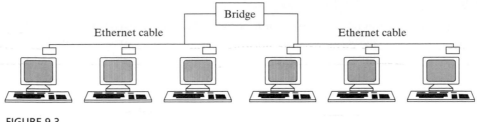

FIGURE 9.3

A bridge.

to extend a network past the allowed length of a single section of wire. (The length is limited by degradation of the signal over a distance.)

Routers

The use of bridges facilitates the construction of small serially linked sections of Ethernet, but it's a pretty inefficient way to link together large numbers of networks. For example, suppose that a corporation has four LANs that it wishes to interconnect in an efficient way. Stringing them all together with bridges would cause data to pass across the "middle" sections to get to the ends when hosts on those middle sections have no interest in the data. To pass data directly from the originating network to the destination network, a *router* can be used. A router (see Figure 9.4) is a device that hooks together two or more networks and automatically routes incoming messages to the correct network.

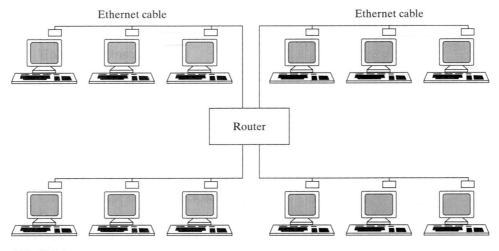

FIGURE 9.4

A router.

Gateways

The final stage in network evolution occurs when many corporations wish to connect their local area networks together into a single, large wide area network (WAN). To do this, several high-capacity routers called *gateways* are placed throughout the country, and each corporation ties its LAN into the nearest gateway. The arrangement is shown in Figure 9.5.

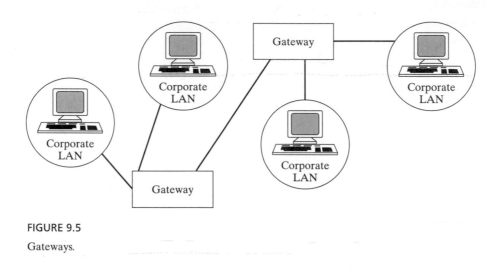

FIGURE 9.5

Gateways.

INTERNETWORKING

In order for a collection of LANs and WANs to be able to route information among themselves, they must agree upon a networkwide addressing and routing scheme. This large-scale interconnection of different networks is known as *internetworking*. Any group of two or more networks connected together may properly be called an internet. However, the largest and best known such network has become known as *the* Internet.

Universities, large corporations, government offices, and military sites all have computers that are part of the Internet. The computers are generally linked together by high-speed data links. The largest of these computer systems are joined together to form what is known as the *backbone* of the Internet. Other, smaller establishments link their LANs to the backbone via gateways.

Packet Switching

Today's digital computer networks are *packet switched* networks. When one node on the network sends a message to another node, the message is split up into small packets, each of which can be routed independently (i.e., switched) through the network.

Packets contain special information that allows them to be recombined at the destination. They also contain information for routing purposes, including the address of the source and destination nodes. The combined set of protocols is called the Transmission Control Protocol and Internet Protocol (TCP/IP) protocol suite. UNIX interprocess communication (IPC) uses TCP/IP to allow UNIX processes on different machines to "talk" to each other.

Internet Addresses

Hosts on the Internet, as well as many private internets, also use TCP/IP to send data. While it is most popularly implemented on Ethernet networks, TCP/IP can also be used on other types of networks. This makes it useful for connecting different types of networks, because not all computers are connected by Ethernet. For example, some LANs may use the IBM Token Ring system. The IP addressing system therefore uses a hardware-independent labeling scheme: The bridges, routers and gateways transmit messages based purely on their destination IP address, which is mapped to a physical hardware address only when the message reaches the destination host's LAN. Thus, the computer sending the message does not need to understand hardware-specific information about the computer to which the message is to be sent.

The IP addressing mechanism works the same, regardless of whether you actually connect your computers to the Internet. When an organization sets up a LAN that is to be part of the Internet, it must get a unique address range assigned to its computers, a process we will learn about in Chapter 10. For now, let's assume we're using a local IP network.

An IP address is a 32-bit value that is written as four dot-separated numbers, each number representing 8 of the 32 bits of the address. Because each part represents an 8-bit value, the maximum value it may have is 255.

Due to the explosive growth of the Internet, the seemingly endless supply of 32-bit addresses is quickly being used up. The current IP protocol standard (IP version 4) is being modified to allow larger addresses. IPv6 will define 128-bit IP addresses so that many more addresses can be assigned. (See Chapter 16 for more information on IPv6.)

Naming

Numeric IP addresses are not very convenient for humans to use to access remote computers. Humans are much more used to naming things (e.g., people, pets, and cars). So we have taken to naming our computers as well.

When a *host name* is assigned to a particular computer, a correlation can be established between the name and the computer's numeric IP address. That way, a user can type the name to reference the computer, and the software can translate the name to an IP address automatically.

The mapping of IP addresses to local host names is kept by the LAN's system administrator in a file called "/etc/hosts". To show you what this looks like, here's a small section of the file from UT Dallas:

```
129.110.41.1    manmax03
129.110.42.1    csservr2
129.110.43.2    ncube01
```

```
129.110.43.128   vanguard
129.110.43.129   jupiter
129.110.66.8     neocortex
129.110.102.10   corvette
```

Routing

The Internet Protocol performs two kinds of routing: static and dynamic. Static routing information is kept in the file "/etc/route" and is of the form "You may get to the destination DEST via the gateway GATE with X hops." When a router has to forward a message, it can use the information in this file to determine the best route. Dynamic routing information is shared between hosts via the "/etc/routed" or "/etc/gated" daemons.[1] These programs constantly update their local routing tables on the basis of information gleaned from network traffic, and they periodically share their information with other neighboring daemons.

Security

Several UNIX networking utilities allow a user with accounts on more than one machine to execute a command on one of these machines from another. For example, I have an account on both the "csservr2" and "vanguard" machines at UT Dallas. To execute the **date** command on the "vanguard" machine from the "csservr2" machine, I can use the **rsh** utility (discussed later in the chapter) as follows:

```
$ rsh vanguard date     ...execute date on vanguard.
```

The interesting thing about **rsh** and a few other utilities is that they are able to obtain a shell on the remote host *without requiring a password.* They can do this because of a UNIX facility called *machine equivalence.* If, in your home directory, you create a file called ".rhosts" that contains a list of host names, then any user with the same user ID as your own may log into your account from these hosts without supplying a password. Both my "csservr2" and "vanguard" home directories contain a file ".rhosts" that contains the following lines:

```
csservr2.utdallas.edu
vanguard.utdallas.edu
```

We must use the "official" hostname, which includes the Internet domain, in the ".rhosts" file. (I discuss Internet domains in Chapter 10.)

This capability of obtaining a shell without having to use a password allows me to execute remote commands from either computer without any hassle. UNIX also allows a system administrator to list globally equivalent machines in the file "/etc/hosts.equiv". Global equivalence means that *any* user on the listed machines can log into the local

---

[1]A daemon is a fancy term for a constantly running background process that is normally started when the system is booted.

host without a password. For example, if the "vanguard" "/etc/hosts.equiv" file contained the lines

```
csservr2.utdallas.edu
vanguard.utdallas.edu
```

then any user on "csservr2" could log into the "vanguard" or execute a remote command on it without citing a password. Global equivalence should be used with great care (if ever).

Ports and Common Services

When one network host talks to another, it does so via a set of numbered ports. Every host supports some standard ports for common uses and allows application programs to create other ports for transient communication. The file "/etc/services" contains a list of the standard ports. Here's a snippet from the UT Dallas file:

```
echo        7/tcp
discard     9/tcp           sink null                    80 = HTTP
systat      11/tcp          users                        443 = HTTPS
daytime     13/tcp
ftp-data    20/tcp
ftp         21/tcp
telnet      23/tcp
smtp        25/tcp          mail
time        37/tcp          timeserver
rlp         39/udp          resource
whois       43/tcp
finger      79/tcp
sunrpc      111/tcp
exec        512/tcp
login       513/tcp
```

The description of the **telnet** utility later in this chapter contains some examples in which I connected to some of these standard ports.

Network Programming

The UNIX interprocess communication allows you to communicate with other programs at a known IP address and port. The facility is described near the end of Chapter 13, together with the full source code for an "Internet shell" that can pipe and redirect data to other Internet shells on different hosts.

USERS

UNIX networking is all about moving around the network and talking to other people. Therefore, one of the most basic things to learn is how to find out who's on a particular host. There are several utilities that do this, each with its own strengths:

- **users**, which lists all of the users on your local host
- **rusers**, which lists all of the users on your local network

- **who,** which is like users, except that it gives you more information
- **rwho,** which is like **rusers**, except that it gives you more information
- **w,** which is like **who**, except that it gives you *even more* information
- **whois,** which allows you to obtain information about major Internet sites
- **hostname,** which displays your local host's name.

Listing Users: `users/rusers`

The **users** and **rusers** utilities simply list the current users of your local host and local network, respectively, as described in Figures 9.6 and 9.7.

Here's an example of **users** and **rusers** in action:

```
$ users            ...display users on the local host.
glass posey
$ rusers -al       ...display users on the local network.
csservr4.utd posey
vanguard.utd huynh posey datta venky
csservr2.utd posey glass
$ _
```

Utility: **users**

users displays a simple, terse list of the users on your local host.

FIGURE 9.6

Description of the **users** command.

Utility: **rusers** -a { *host* }*

rusers displays a list of the users on your local network. By default, all of the machines on the network are interrogated, although you may override this default by supplying a list of host names. **rusers** works by broadcasting a request for information to all of the hosts and then displaying the responses as they arrive. In order for a host to respond, it must be running the **rusersd** daemon. (See Chapter 15 for more information about daemons.)

FIGURE 9.7

Description of the **rusers** command.

More User Listings: `who`/`rwho`/`w`

The **who** and **rwho** utilities, described in Figures 9.8 and 9.9, respectively, supply a little more information than the **users** and **rusers** utilities do. Here's an example of **who**:

```
$ who              ... list all users currently on local host.
posey       ttyp0   May 15 16:31 (blackfoot.utdall)
glass       ttyp2   May 17 17:00 (bridge05.utdalla)
$ who am i                   ...list myself.
csservr2!glass      ttyp2    May 17 17:00 (bridge05.utdalla)
$ who /var/adm/wtmp        ...examine the who file.
lcui        ttyp2   May 17 12:48 (bridge05.utdalla)
juang       ttyp3   May 17 12:49 (annex.utdallas.e)
            ttyp3   May 17 12:52
            ttyp2   May 17 12:57
weidman     ttyp2   May 17 16:25 (annex.utdallas.e)
            ttyp2   May 17 16:33
glass       ttyp2   May 17 17:00 (bridge05.utdalla)
$ _
```

Utility: **who** [*whoFile*] [am i]

By default, **who** displays a list of every user on your local host. If you supply the arguments "am i", **who** describes only yourself.

Whenever a user logs in or out, the file "/var/adm/wtmp" is updated with information about the user's login session. You may give the name of this file (or a file in the same format) as the *whoFile* argument, in which case **who** decodes the information in the file and presents it in the typical **who** format.

FIGURE 9.8

Description of the **who** command.

Utility: **rwho**

rwho is just like **who**, except that it displays a list of the users logged onto all of the remote hosts on your local network.

FIGURE 9.9

Description of the **rwho** command.

Utility: **w** { *UserId* }*

w displays a list that describes what each specified user is doing. In other words, **w** is almost the same as **who**.

FIGURE 9.10

Description of the **w** command.

The **w** utility is just as easy to use as the **who** utility and is described in Figure 9.10. Here's an example:

```
$ w              ...obtain more detailed information than who.
 5:27pm  up 11 days, 11 mins,  3 users,  load average: 0.08, 0.03, 0.01
User      tty         login@  idle   JCPU   PCPU  what
posey     ttyp0    Fri 4pm 2days      1            -csh
glass     ttyp2       5:00pm   1      13     1  w
$ w glass   ...examine just myself.
 5:27pm  up 11 days, 11 mins,  3 users,  load average: 0.08, 0.03, 0.01
User      tty         login@  idle   JCPU   PCPU  what
glass     ttyp2       5:00pm          13     1  w glass
$ _
```

Your Own Host Name: `hostname`

To find out the name of your local host, use **hostname**, described in Figure 9.11. Here's an example:

```
$ hostname           ...display my host's name.
csservr2
$ _
```

Utility: **hostname** [*hostName*]

When used with no parameters, **hostname** displays the name of your local host. A superuser may change this name by supplying the new host name as an argument, which is usually done automatically in the "/etc/rc.local" file. (For more information about this file, see Chapter 15.)

FIGURE 9.11

Description of the **hostname** command.

Personal Data: `finger`

Once you've obtained a list of the people on your system, it's handy to be able to learn a little bit more about them. The **finger** utility, described in Figure 9.12, allows you to do this. I recommend that you create your own ".plan" and ".project" files in your home directory so that people can "finger" *you* back. Have fun!

Utility: **finger** { *UserId* }*

finger displays information about a list of users that is gleaned from the following sources:

- The user's home directory, start-up shell, and full name are read from the password file "/etc/passwd".
- If the user supplies a file called ".plan" in his/her home directory, the contents of the file are displayed as the user's "plan".
- If the user supplies a file called ".project" in his/her home directory, the contents of the file are displayed as the user's "project".

If no user IDs are listed, **finger** displays information about every user that is currently logged on. You may finger a user on a remote host by using the "@" protocol, in which case the remote host's finger daemon is used to reply to the local finger's request.

FIGURE 9.12

Description of the **finger** command.

In the following example, I fingered everyone on the system and then fingered myself:

```
$ finger                    ...finger everyone on the system.
Login       Name      TTY Idle   When     Where
posey    John Posey    p0   2d Fri 16:31  blackfoot.utdall
glass    Graham Glass  p2      Sun 17:00  bridge05.utdalla
$ finger glass              ...finger myself.
Login name: glass                In real life: Graham Glass
Directory: /home/glass           Shell: /bin/ksh
On since May 17 17:00:47 on ttyp2 from bridge05.utdalla
No unread mail
Project: To earn an enjoyable, honest living.
Plan: To work hard and have fun and not notice the difference.
$ _
```

In the next example, I listed the three sources of **finger's** information about me:

```
$ cat .plan                    ...list the ".plan" file.
To work hard and have fun and not notice any difference.
$ cat .project                 ...list the ".project" file.
To earn an enjoyable, honest living.
$ grep glass /etc/passwd  ...look at the password file.
glass:##glass:496:62:Graham Glass:/home/glass:/bin/ksh
$ _
```

In this final example, I used **rusers** to get a listing of the remote users and then performed a remote **finger** to learn all about Susan:

```
$ rusers                       ...look at remote users.
csservr4.utd posey
vanguard.utd huynh posey datta venky
centaur.utda susan
csservr2.utd posey posey lcui glass
$ finger susan@centaur         ...do a remote finger.
[centaur.utdallas.edu]
Login name: susan              In real life: Susan Marsh
Directory: /home/susan         Shell: /bin/csh
On since May 11 11:00:55 on console   1 day Idle Time
New mail received Fri May 15 19:24:01 1998;
 unread since Fri May 15 16:40:28 1998
No Plan.
$ _
```

COMMUNICATING WITH USERS

The following utilities allow you to communicate with a user:

- **write**, which allows you to send individual lines to a user, one at a time
- **talk**, which allows you to have an interactive split-screen two-way conversation
- **wall**, which allows you to send a message to everyone on the local host
- **mail**, which allows you to send mail messages

The **mail** utility was described in Chapter 2; it supports the full standard Internet addressing scheme. The rest of these utilities are described in this section, together with a simple utility called **mesg** that allows you to shield yourself from other people's messages.

Shielding Yourself from Communication: `mesg`

The **write, talk,** and **wall** utilities communicate with other users by writing directly to their terminals. You may disable the ability of other users to write to your terminal by

---

Utility: **mesg** [n | y]

mesg allows you to prevent other users from writing to your terminal. It works by modifying the write permission of your tty device. The **n** and **y** arguments respectively disable and enable writes. If no arguments are supplied, your current status is displayed.

FIGURE 9.13

Description of the **mesg** command.

using the **mesg** utility, described in Figure 9.13. In the following example, **mesg** prevented me from receiving a **write** message:

```
$ mesg n          ...protect terminal.
$ write glass     ...try to write to myself.
write: You have write permission turned off
$ _
```

Sending a Line at a Time: `write`

The **write** command, described in Figure 9.14, is a simple utility that allows you to send one line at a time to a named user. In the following example, I received a **write** message from my friend Tim and then initiated my own **write** command to respond to him. We used the -o- (over) and -oo- (over and out) conventions for synchronization:

Utility: **write** *userId* [*tty*]

write copies its standard input, one line at a time, to the terminal associated with *userId*. If the user is logged onto more than one terminal, you may specify the particular tty as an optional argument.

> The first line of input that you send to a user via **write** is preceded by the message
>
> Message from yourHost!yourId on yourTty

so that the receiver may initiate a **write** command to talk back to you. To exit **write**, type *Control*-D on a line of its own. You may disable writes to your terminal by using **mesg**.

FIGURE 9.14

Description of the **write** command.

```
$
Message from tim@csservr2 on ttyp2 at 18:04
hi Graham -o-                              ...from tim.
$ write tim                    ...initiate a reply.
hi Tim -o-                              ...from me.
don't forget the movie later -oo-       ...from tim.
OK -oo-                                  ...from me.
^D                             ...end of my input.
$ _
```

Although you can have a two-way conversation using **write**, it's awfully clumsy. A better way is to use the **talk** utility.

Interactive Conversations: `talk`

The **talk** utility, described in Figure 9.15, allows you to have a two-way conversation across a network. This is a fun utility that is worth exploring with a friend.

Utility: **talk** *userId* [*tty*]

The **talk** command allows you to talk to another user on the network via a split-screen interface. If the user is logged onto more than one terminal, you may choose a particular terminal by supplying a specific tty name.

To talk to someone, type the following at your terminal:

```
$ talk theirUserId@theirHost
```

This causes the following message to appear on the recipient's screen:

```
Message from TalkDaemon@theirHost...
talk: connection requested by yourUserId@yourHost
talk: respond with: talk yourUserId@yourHost
```

If the recipient agrees to your invitation, he or she will type the following at the shell prompt:

```
$ talk yourUserIdKyourHost
```

At this point, your screen divides into two portions, one containing your keyboard input and the other containing the other guy's. Everything that you type is echoed at the other guy's terminal, and vice versa. To redraw the screen if it ever gets messed up, type *Control*-L. To quit **talk**, press *Control*-C.

To prevent other people from talking to you, use the **mesg** utility.

FIGURE 9.15

Description of the **talk** command.

Messages to Everyone: `wall`

If you ever have something important to say to the world (or at least to everyone on your local host), **wall** is the way to say it. **wall** stands for "write all," and allows you to broadcast a message as described in Figure 9.16. In the following example, I sent a one-liner to everyone on the local host (including myself):

```
$ wall                          ...write to everyone.
this is a test of the broadcast system
^D                              ...end of input.
Broadcast Message from glass@csservr2 (ttyp2) at 18:04 ...
this is a test of the broadcast system
$ _
```

Utility: **wall** [*fileName*]

wall copies its standard input (or the contents of *fileName* if supplied) to the terminals of every user on the local host, preceding it with the message "Broadcast Message...' If a user has disabled communication with terminals by using **mesg**, the message will not be received unless the user of **wall** is a superuser.

FIGURE 9.16

Description of the **wall** command.

The **wall** command is most often used by system administrators to send users important, timely information (such as "System going down in five minutes!").

DISTRIBUTING DATA

A very basic kind of remote operation is the transmission of files, and once again UNIX has several utilities which do that:

- **rcp** (remote copy) allows you to copy files between your local UNIX host and another remote UNIX host.
- **ftp** (file transfer protocol or program) allows you to copy files between your local UNIX host and any other host (including a non-UNIX host) that supports the File Transfer Protocol. **ftp** is thus more powerful than **rcp**.
- **uucp** (unix-to-unix copy) is similar to **rcp**, and allows you to copy files between any two UNIX hosts.

Copying Files between Two UNIX Hosts: `rcp`

rcp, described in Figure 9.17, allows you to copy files between UNIX hosts. In the following example, I copied the file "original.txt" from the remote "vanguard" host to a file called "new.txt" on my local "csservr2" host and then copied the file "original2.txt" from my local host to the file "new2.txt" on the remote host:

```
$ rcp vanguard:original.txt new.txt          ...remote to local.
$ rcp original2.txt vanguard:new2.txt        ...local to remote.
$ _
```

Utility: **rcp** -p *originalFile newFile*

  rcp -pr {*fileName*}+*directory*

rcp allows you to copy files between UNIX hosts. Both your local host and the remote host must be registered as equivalent machines. (See the discussion of security earlier in this chapter for more information.) To specify a remote file on *host*, use the syntax

```
host:pathName
```

If *pathName* is relative, it's interpreted as being relative to your home directory on the remote host. The **-p** option tries to preserve the last modification time, last access time, and permission flags during the copy. The **-r** option causes any file that is a directory to be recursively copied.

FIGURE 9.17

Description of the **rcp** command.

Copying Files between Non-UNIX Hosts: `ftp`

The File Transfer Protocol is a generic protocol for the transmission of files and is supported by many machines. You can therefore use it to transfer files from your local UNIX host to any other kind of remote host, as long as you know the Internet address of the remote host's ftp server. Users of non-UNIX computers often use **ftp** for transferring files between UNIX and their own system. Figure 9.18 provides a brief description of **ftp**, and Figure 9.19 lists the most useful **ftp** commands that are available from its command mode. In the following example, I copied "writer.c" from the remote host "vanguard" to my local host and then copied "who.c" from my local host to the remote host:

```
$ ftp vanguard        ...open ftp connection to "vanguard".
Connected to vanguard.utdallas.edu.
vanguard FTP server (SunOS 5.4) ready.
Name (vanguard:glass): glass        ...login
```

```
Password required for glass.
Password:                          ...secret!
User glass logged in.
ftp> ls                 ...obtain directory of remote host.
PORT command successful.
ASCII data connection for /bin/ls (129.110.42.1,4919) (0 bytes).
...                     ...lots of files were listed here.
uniq
upgrade
who.c
writer.c
ASCII Transfer complete.
1469 bytes received in 0.53 seconds (2.7 Kbytes/s)
ftp> get writer.c              ...copy from remote host.
PORT command successful.
ASCII data connection for writer.c (129.110.42.1,4920) (1276 bytes).
ASCII Transfer complete.
local: writer.c remote: writer.c
1300 bytes received in 0.012 seconds (1e+02 Kbytes/s)
ftp> !ls                 ...obtain directory of local host.
reader.c    who.c       writer.c
ftp> put who.c          ...copy file to remote host.
PORT command successful.
ASCII data connection for who.c (129.110.42.1,4922).
ASCII Transfer complete.
ftp> quit                 ...disconnect.
Goodbye.
$ _
```

Utility: **ftp** -n [*hostName*]

ftp allows you to manipulate files and directories on both your local host and a remote host. If you supply a remote host name, **ftp** searches the ".netrc" file to see if the remote host has an anonymous **ftp** account (i.e., one without a password). If it does, it uses that account to log you into the remote host. If it doesn't have an anonymous account, it assumes that you have an account on the remote host and prompts you for its user ID and password. If the login is successful, **ftp** enters its command mode and displays the prompt "ftp>". If you don't supply a remote host name, **ftp** enters its command mode immediately, and you must use the open command to connect to a remote host.

The **-n** option prevents **ftp** from attempting the initial automatic login sequence.

ftp's command mode supports many commands for file manipulation. The most common of these commands are described in the text. You may abort file transfers without quitting **ftp** by pressing *Control-C*.

FIGURE 9.18

Description of the **ftp** command.

Command	Meaning
!*command*	Executes *command* on local host.
append *localFile remoteFile*	Appends the local file *localFile* to the remote file *remoteFile*.
bell	Causes a beep to be sounded after every file transfer.
bye	Shuts down the current remote host connection and then quits **ftp**.
cd *remoteDirectory*	Changes your current remote working directory to *remoteDirectory*.
close	Shuts down the current remote host connection.
delete *remoteFile*	Deletes *remoteFile* from the remote host.
get *remoteFile* [*localFile*]	Copies the remote file *remoteFile* to the local file *localFile*. If *localFile* is omitted, it is given the same name as the remote file.
help [*command*]	Displays help about *command*. If *command* is omitted, a list of all **ftp** commands is displayed.
lcd *localDirectory*	Changes your current local working directory to *localDirectory*.
ls *remoteDirectory*	Lists the contents of your current remote working directory.
mkdir *remoteDirectory*	Creates *remoteDirectory* on the remote host.
open *hostName* [*port*]	Attempts a connection to the host with name *hostName*. If you specify an optional port number, **ftp** assumes that this port is an **ftp** server.
put *localFile* [*remoteFile*]	Copies the local file *localFile* to the remote file *remoteFile*. If *remoteFile* is omitted, it is given the same name as the local file.
pwd	Displays your current remote working directory.
quit	Same as **bye**.
rename *remoteFrom remoteTo*	Renames a remote file from *remoteFrom* to *remoteTo*.
rmdir *remoteDirectory*	Deletes the remote directory *remoteDirectory*.

FIGURE 9.19

Commands within the **ftp** program.

DISTRIBUTING PROCESSING

The power of distributed systems becomes striking when you start moving around a network and logging into different hosts. Some hosts supply limited passwordless accounts with user IDs like "guest" so those explorers can roam the network without causing any harm, although this practice is fading away as more people abuse the privilege. These days, you almost always have to have an account on a remote computer in order to log into a network. Three utilities for distributed access are

- **rlogin**, which allows you to log in to a remote UNIX host,
- **rsh**, which allows you to execute a command on a remote UNIX host, and
- **telnet**, which allows you to execute commands on any remote host that has a telnet server.

Of these, **telnet** is the most flexible, since there are other systems in addition to UNIX that support telnet servers.

Remote Logins: `rlogin`

To log into a remote host, use **rlogin**, described in Figure 9.20. In the following example, I logged into the remote host "vanguard" from my local host "csservr2", executed

---

Utility: **rlogin** -ec [-l *userId*] *hostName*

rlogin attempts to log you into the remote host *hostName*. If you don't supply a user ID by using the **-l** option, your local user ID is used during the login process.

If the remote host isn't set as an equivalent of your local host in your "$HOME/.rhost" file, you are asked for your password on the remote host.

Once you are connected, your local shell goes to sleep and the remote shell starts to execute. When you're finished with the remote log-in shell, terminate it in the normal fashion (usually with *Control*-D), and your local shell will then awaken.

There are a few special "escape commands" you may type that have a special meaning; each is preceded by the escape character, which is a tilde (~) by default. You may change this escape character by following the **-e** option with the preferred escape character. Here is a list of the escape commands:

SEQUENCE	MEANING
~.	Disconnect immediately from remote host.
~susp	Suspend remote login session. Restart remote login using **fg**.
~dsusp	Suspend input half of remote login session, but still echo output from login session to your local terminal. Restart remote login using **fg**.

FIGURE 9.20

Description of the **rlogin** command.

the **date** utility, and then disconnected:

```
$ rlogin vanguard                      ...remote login.
Last login: Tue May 19 17:23:51 from csservr2.utdallas
vanguard% date            ...execute a command on vanguard.
Wed May 20 18:50:47 CDT 1998
vanguard% ^D              ...terminate the remote login shell.
Connection closed.
$ _                       ...back home again at csservr2!
```

Executing Remote Commands: `rsh`

If you want to execute just a single command on a remote host, **rsh** is much handier than **rlogin**. Figure 9.21 shows how it works. In the following example, I executed the **hostname** utility on both my local "csservr2" host and the remote "vanguard" host:

```
$ hostname               ...execute on my local host.
csservr2
$ rsh vanguard hostname ...execute on the remote host.
vanguard
$ _
```

Utility: **rsh** [-l *userId*] *hostName* [*command*]

rsh attempts to create a remote shell on the host *hostName* to execute *command*. **rsh** copies its standard input to *command* and copies the standard output and errors from *command* to its own standard output and error channels. Interrupt, quit, and terminate signals are forwarded to *command*, so you may use *Control-C* on a remote command. **rsh** terminates immediately after *command* terminates.

   If you do not supply a user ID by using the **-l** option, your local user ID is used during the connection. If no command is specified, **rsh** gives you a remote shell by invoking **rlogin**.

   Quoted metacharacters are processed by the remote host; all others are processed by the local shell.

FIGURE 9.21

Description of the **rsh** command.

Remote Connections: `telnet`

telnet allows you to communicate with any remote host on the Internet that has a **telnet** server. Figure 9.22 shows how it works. In the following example, I used **telnet** to

---

Utility: **telnet** [*host* [*port*]]

telnet establishes a two-way connection with a remote port. If you supply a host name, but not a port specifier, you are automatically connected to a **telnet** server on the specified host, which typically allows you to log into the remote machine. If you don't even supply a host name, **telnet** goes directly into command mode (in the same fashion as **ftp**).

What happens after the connection is complete depends on the functionality of the port you're connected to. For example, port 13 of any Internet machine will send you the time of day and then disconnect, whereas port 7 will echo ("ping") back to you anything that you enter from the keyboard.

To enter command mode after you've established a connection, press the sequence *Control-*], which is the **telnet** escape sequence. This causes the command mode prompt to be displayed. The following commands, among others, are accepted:

COMMAND	MEANING
close	Close current connection.
open *host* [*port*]	Connect to *host* with optional *port* specifier.
quit	Exit **telnet**.
z	Suspend **telnet**.
?	Print summary of **telnet** commands.

Therefore, to terminate a **telnet** connection, press *Control-*], followed by the command **quit**.

FIGURE 9.22

Description of the **telnet** command.

emulate the **rlogin** functionality by omitting an explicit port number with the **open** command:

```
$ telnet                        ...start telnet.
telnet> ?                       ...get help.
Commands may be abbreviated.  Commands are:
close       close current connection
display     display operating parameters
mode        try to enter line-by-line or character-at-a-time mode
open        connect to a site
quit        exit telnet
send        transmit special characters ('send ?' for more)
set         set operating parameters ('set ?' for more)
status      print status information
toggle      toggle operating parameters ('toggle ?' for more)
z           suspend telnet
```

```
?                print help information
telnet> open vanguard          ...get a login shell from vanguard.
Trying 129.110.43.128 ...
Connected to vanguard.utdallas.edu.
Escape character is '^]'.
SunOS 5.4 (vanguard)
login: glass                   ...enter my user ID.
Password:                      ...secret!
Last login: Tue May 19 17:22:45 from csservr2.utdalla
***  For assistance, send mail to UNIXINFO.
Tue May 19 17:23:21 CDT 1998
Erase is Backspace
vanguard% date                 ...execute a command.
Tue May 19 17:23:24 CDT 1998
vanguard% ^D          ...disconnect from remote host.
Connection closed by foreign host.
$ _                            ...telnet terminates.
```

You may specify the host name directly on the command line if you like, as follows:

```
$ telnet vanguard          ...specify host name on command line.
Trying 129.110.43.128 ...
Connected to vanguard.utdallas.edu.
Escape character is '^]'.

SunOS 5.4 (vanguard)
login: glass                   ...enter user ID, etc...
```

You may use **telnet** to try out some of the standard port services that I described earlier in the chapter. For example, port 13 prints the day and time on the remote host and then immediately disconnects:

```
$ telnet vanguard 13   ...what's the remote time & day?
Trying 129.110.43.128 ...
Connected to vanguard.utdallas.edu.
Escape character is '^]'.
Tue May 19 17:26:32 1998
Connection closed by foreign host   ...telnet terminates.
$ _
```

Similarly, port 79 allows you to enter the name of a remote user and obtain finger information:

```
$ telnet vanguard 79 ...manually perform a remote finger.
Trying 129.110.43.128 ...
Connected to vanguard.utdallas.edu.
Escape character is '^]'.
glass                              ...enter the user ID.
Login name: glass         In real life: Graham Glass
Directory: /home/glass    Shell: /bin/csh
```

```
Last login Tue May 19 17:23 on from csservr2.utdalla
No unread mail
No Plan.
Connection closed by foreign host.   ...telnet terminates.
$ _
```

When system administrators are testing a network, they often use port 7 to check host connections. Port 7 echoes everything that you type back to your terminal and is sometimes known as a "ping-port." Here's an example:

```
$ telnet vanguard 7                 ...try a ping.
Trying 129.110.43.128 ...
Connected to vanguard.utdallas.edu.
Escape character is '^]'.
hi                                  ...my line.
hi                                  ...the echo.
there
there
^]                                  ...escape to command mode.
telnet> quit                        ...terminate connection.
Connection closed.
$ _
```

telnet accepts numeric Internet addresses as well as symbolic names, as shown in the following example:

```
$ telnet 129.110.43.128 7    ... vanguard's numeric addr.
Trying 129.110.43.128 ...
Connected to 129.110.43.128.
Escape character is '^]'.
hi                           ...my line.
hi                           ...the echo.
^]                           ...escape to command mode.
telnet> quit                 ...disconnect.
Connection closed.
$ _
```

NETWORK FILE SYSTEM: NFS

In order to make good use of UNIX network capabilities, Sun Microsystems introduced a public-domain specification for a network file system (NFS). NFS supports the following useful features:

- It allows several local file systems to be mounted into a single network file hierarchy that may be transparently accessed from any host. To support this capability, NFS includes a remote mounting facility.

- A remote procedure call (RPC) is used by NFS to allow one machine to make a procedure call to another machine, thereby encouraging distributed computation.
- NFS supports a host-neutral external data representation (XDR) scheme which allows programmers to create data structures that may be shared by hosts with different byte-ordering and word lengths.

NFS is very popular and is used on most machines that run UNIX. (See Nemeth, 2000, for more details on NFS.)

FOR MORE INFORMATION...

If you've enjoyed this overview of UNIX networking and you wish to find out more, Stevens (1998), Anderson (1995), and the network section of Nemeth (2000) are excellent sources.

CHAPTER REVIEW

Checklist

In this chapter, I described

- the main UNIX network concepts and terminology
- utilities for listing users and communicating with them
- utilities for manipulating remote files
- utilities for obtaining remote login shells and executing remote commands

Quiz

1. What's the difference between a bridge, a router, and a gateway?
2. What's a good way for a system administrator to tell people about important events?
3. Why is **ftp** more powerful than **rcp**?
4. Describe some uses of common ports.
5. What does *machine equivalence* mean and how can you make use of it?

Exercises

9.1 Try out **rcp** and **rsh** as follows:

- Copy a single file from your local host to a remote host by using **rcp**.
- Using **rsh**, obtain a shell on the remote host, and edit the file that you just copied.

- Exit the remote shell, using *exit*.
- Using **rcp**, copy the file from the remote host back to the local host.

[level: *easy*]

9.2 Use **telnet** to obtain the time of day at several remote host sites. Are the times accurate relative to each other? [level: *medium*]

Project

Write a shell script that operates in the background on two machines and which ensures that the contents of a named directory on one machine is always a mirror image of another named directory on the other machine. [level: *hard*]

# CHAPTER 10

The Internet

nslookup
bind

MOTIVATION

The Internet is probably the most visible aspect of computing in the history of the industry. What started out as a network tool to connect university and government users has grown into a huge entity used by millions of people worldwide. Even the most computer-illiterate person in the United States has at least heard of the Internet. Much of the appeal of having a home computer nowadays is to be able to access information on the Internet. This chapter will provide you with a solid understanding of what the Internet is and what you can do with it.

PREREQUISITES

While you don't really have to understand the nuts and bolts of the Internet Protocol (discussed in Chapter 9) to benefit from the current chapter, the more familiar you are with generic UNIX networking issues, the more of the chapter you will find helpful.

OBJECTIVES

After reading this chapter, you will have a solid understanding of what the Internet is, how it came about, how it works, and what you can use it for.

PRESENTATION

To really understand any topic, an understanding of its history is critical. I will first describe how the Internet came to be what it is today, given its inauspicious start. After a survey of the tools that you use to access information on the Internet, I will also discuss where the future may take Internet users.

THE EVOLUTION OF THE INTERNET

As the local networks we looked at in Chapter 9 began to grow larger and to be connected together, an evolution began. First, some companies linked their own LANs via private connections. Others transferred data across a network implemented on the public telephone network. Ultimately, network research funded by the U. S. government brought it all together.   *Al Gore invented the Internet?*

It may sound hard to believe, but what we know today as "the Internet" was almost inevitable. Although the prototype of the Internet began in a computer lab, and at the time most thought only high-powered computer scientists would ever use it, the way we stored and utilized information almost dictated that we find a better way to move the information from one place to another.

Now when I watch television and see web page addresses at the end of commercials for mainstream products, I know that the Internet has truly reached common usage. Not only do high-tech companies maintain web pages, but even cereal companies have web sites. One may argue about the usefulness of some of these sites, but the fact that they exist tells us a great deal about how society has embraced the new technology.

It makes you wonder how we got here and where we might go with it all.

In the Beginning: The 1960s

In the 1960s, human beings were about to reach the moon, society was going through upheavals on several fronts, and technology was changing more rapidly than ever before. The Advanced Research Projects Agency (ARPA) of the Department of Defense was attempting to develop a computer network to connect government computers (and some government contractors' computers) together. As with so many advances in our society, some of the motivation (and funding) came from a government that hoped to leverage an advance for military or defensive capability. High-speed data communication might be required to help win a war at some point. Our interstate highway system (another kind of network) has its roots in much the same type of motivation.

In the 1960s, mainframe computers still dominated computing, and they would for some time to come. Removable disk packs, small cartridge tapes, and compact disc technology were still in the future. Moving data from one of these mainframe computers to another usually required writing the data on a bulky tape device or some large disk, physically carrying that medium to the other mainframe computer, and loading the data onto that computer. Although this was, of course, done, it was extremely inconvenient.

A Network Connection   During the time computer networking was still in its infancy, local networks existed also and were the inspiration for what would ultimately become the Internet. During 1968 and 1969, ARPA experimented with connections between a few government computers. The basic architecture was a 50-kb dedicated telephone circuit connected to a machine at each site called an Interface Message Processor (IMP). Conceptually, this is not unlike your personal Internet connection today if you consider that your modem does the job of the IMP. (Of course, the IMP was a much more complex device than a modem.) At each site, the IMP then connected to the computer or computers that needed to access the network.

The ARPANET   The ARPANET was born in September 1969, when the first four IMPs were installed at the University of Southern California, Stanford Research Institute, the University of California at Santa Barbara, and the University of Utah. All of these sites had significant numbers of ARPA contractors. The success of the initial experiments among the four sites generated a great deal of interest on the part of ARPA, as well as in the academic community. Computing would never be the same.

Standardizing the Internet: The 1970s

The problem with the first connections to the ARPANET was that each IMP was, to some degree, custom designed for each site, depending on the operating systems and network configurations of its other computer. Much time and effort had been expended to get the network up to four sites. Hundreds of sites would require hundreds of times that much custom work if it were done in the same fashion.

It became clear that if all the computers connected to the network in the same way and used the same software protocols, they could all connect to each other more efficiently and with much less effort at each site. But at the time, different computer vendors supplied their own operating systems with their own hardware, and there was very little in the way of standardization to help them interact or cooperate. What was required was a set of standards that could be implemented in software on different systems, so that they could share data in a form that the different computers could still "understand."

Although the genesis of standard networking protocols began in the 1970s, it would be 1983 before all members of the ARPANET used them exclusively.

The Internet Protocol Family   In the early 1970s, researchers began to design the Internet Protocol. The word "internet" was used, since it was more generic (at the time) than ARPANET, which referred to a specific network. The word "internet" referred to the generic internetworking of computers to allow them to communicate.

The Internet Protocol is the fundamental software mechanism that moves data from one place to another across a network. Data to be sent is divided into *packets*, which are the basic data units used on a digital computer network. IP does not guarantee that any single packet will arrive at the other end or in what order the packets will arrive, but it does guarantee that if the packet arrives, it will arrive unchanged from the original packet at the source. This property may not seem very useful at first, but stay with me for a moment.

TCP/IP   Once you can transmit a packet to another computer and know that if it arrives at all, it will be correct, other protocols can be added "on top" of the basic IP to provide more functionality. The Transmission Control Protocol (TCP) is the protocol most often used with IP. (Together, the two are referred to as TCP/IP.) As the name implies, TCP controls the actual transmission of the stream of data packets. TCP adds sequencing and acknowledgement information to each packet, and each end of a TCP "conversation" cooperates to make sure that the data stream which is received is reconstructed in the same order as the original. When a single packet fails to arrive at the other end due to some failure in the network, the receiving TCP software figures this out, because the packet's sequence number is missing. The software can contact the sender and have it send the packet again. Alternatively, the sender, having likely not received an acknowledgment of the receipt of the packet in question, will eventually retransmit the packet on its own, assuming that it was not received. If the packet was received and only the acknowledgment was lost, the TCP software, upon receiving a second copy, will drop it, since it has already received the first one. The receiver will still send the acknowledgment the sending TCP software was waiting for.

TCP is a connection-oriented protocol. An application program opens a TCP connection to another program on another computer, and the two machines send data back and forth to each other. When they have completed their work, they close down the connection. If one end (or a network break) closes the connection unexpectedly, this is considered an error by the other end.

UDP/IP   Another useful protocol that cooperates with IP is the User Datagram Protocol (UDP) (sometimes semi-affectionately called the Unreliable Datagram Protocol). UDP provides a low-overhead method for delivering short messages over IP, but does not guarantee their arrival. On some occasions, an application needs to send status information to another application (such as a management agent sending status information to a network or systems management application), but the information is not of critical importance. If it does not arrive, either it will be sent again later or it may not be necessary, in each and every instance, for the data to be received by the application. Of course, this assumes that any failure is due to some transient condition and that "next time" the method will work. If it fails all the time, that would imply that a network problem exists that might not become apparent.

In a case like this, the overhead required to open and maintain a TCP connection is more work than is really necessary. You just want to send a short status message. You don't really care whether the other end gets it (since, if it doesn't, it probably will get the next one), and you certainly don't want to wait around for receipt of the message to be acknowledged. So an unreliable protocol fits the bill nicely.

Internet Addressing   When an organization is setting up a LAN that it wishes to be part of the Internet, it requests a unique Internet IP address from the Network Information Center (NIC). The number that is allocated depends on the size of the organization:

- A huge organization, such as a country or very large corporation, is allocated a Class A address—a number that is the first 8 bits of a 32-bit IP address. The organization is then free to use the remaining 24 bits to label its local hosts. The NIC rarely allocates these Class A addresses, since each one uses up a lot of the total 32-bit number space.

- A medium-sized organization, such as a midsize corporation, is allocated a Class B address. A Class B address is a number that is the first 16 bits of a 32-bit IP address. The organization can then use the remaining 16 bits to label its local hosts.

- A small organization is allocated a Class C address, which is the first 24 bits of a 32-bit IP address.

For example, the University of Texas at Dallas is classified as a medium-sized organization, and its LAN was allocated the 16-bit number 33134. IP addresses are written as a series of four 8-bit numbers, with the most significant byte written first. All computers on the UT Dallas LAN therefore have an IP address of the form 129.110.XXX.YYY,[1] where XXX and YYY are numbers between 0 and 255.

Internet Applications   Once a family of protocols existed that allowed easy transmission of data to a remote network host, the next step was to provide application programs that took advantage of these protocols. The first applications to be used with TCP/IP were two programs that were in wide use even before TCP/IP was used on the ARPANET: **telnet** and **ftp**. (See Chapter 9.)

The **telnet** program was (and still is) used to connect to another computer on a network in order to login and use that computer from your local computer or terminal. This feature was quite useful in those days of high-priced computing resources. Then, your organization might not have its own supercomputer, but you might have access to one at another site. Telnet allows you to login remotely without having to travel to the other site.

The **ftp** program was used to transfer files back and forth. While **ftp** is still available today, most people use web browsers or network file systems to move data files from one computer to another.

Rearchitecting and Renaming the Internet: The 1980s

As more universities and government agencies began using the ARPANET, word of its usefulness spread. Soon corporations were getting connected. At first, because of the funding involved, a corporation had to have some kind of government contract in order to qualify. Over time, this requirement was enforced less and less.

With growth came headaches. As with a local network, the smaller any network is, the fewer nodes that are connected, and the easier it is to administer. As the network grows, the complexity of managing the whole thing grows as well. It became clear that the growth rate the ARPANET was experiencing would soon outpace the Defense Department's ability to manage the network.

The rate of addition of new hosts now required modifications to the network host table on a daily basis. Also, each ARPANET site had to download new host tables every day if it wished to have up-to-date tables. In addition, the number of available host names was dwindling, since each name had to be unique across the entire network.

Domain Name Service   Enter the Domain Name Service (DNS). Together with the Berkeley Internet Name Daemon (BIND), DNS proposed a hierarchy of domain naming of network hosts and the method for providing address information to anyone on the network as requested.

In the new system, top-level domain names were established under which each network site could establish a subdomain. The DOD would manage the top-level domains

---

[1]129 * 256 + 110 = 33134.

and delegate management of each subdomain to the entity or organization that registered the domain. The DNS/BIND software provided the method for any network site to do a lookup of network address information for a particular host.

Let's look at a real-world example of how a host name is resolved to an address. One of the most popular top-level domains is **com**, so we'll use that in our example, as most people will be familiar with it. The DOD maintained the server for the **com** domain. All subdomains registered in the **com** domain were "known" to the DOD server. When another network host needed an address for a host name under the **com** domain, it queried the **com** name server.

If you attempted to make a connection to snoopy.hp.com, your machine would not know the IP address, because there was no information in your local host table for snoopy.hp.com. Your machine would contact the domain name server for the **com** domain to ask it for the address. That server, however "knows" only the address for the **hp.com** name server; it does not need to know everything under that domain. But since **hp.com** is registered with the **com** name server, it can query the **hp.com** name server for the address[2]. Once a name server that has authority for the **hp.com** domain is contacted, an address for **snoopy.hp.com** (or a message that the host does not exist) is returned to the requestor.

Up to this point, every host name on the ARPANET was just a name, like **utexas** for the ARPANET host at the University of Texas. Under the new system, that machine would be renamed to be a member of the **utexas.edu** domain. However, this change could not be made everywhere overnight. So for a time, a default domain **.arpa** was established. By default, all hosts began to be known under that domain (hence, **utexas** changed its name to **utexas.arpa**). Once a site had taken that single step, it was easier for it to become a member of its "real" domain, since most of the pain involved implementing software that "understood" the domain name system.

Once the ARPANET community adopted this system, all kinds of problems were solved. Suddenly, a host name had to be unique only within a subdomain. Accordingly, just because HP had a machine called snoopy didn't mean that someone at the University of Texas couldn't also use that name, since snoopy.hp.com and snoopy.utexas.edu were different names. This had not been such a big problem when only mainframe computers were connected to the network, but the era of exploding growth of workstations was quickly approaching, and the problem would only have gotten bigger. The other big advantage was that a single networkwide host table no longer had to be maintained and updated on a daily basis. Each site kept its own local host tables up to date and would simply query the name server when an address for a host at another site was needed. By querying other name servers, you were guaranteed to receive the most up-to-date information.

---

[2]Two options are available in the protocols. The first is that the requesting machine may be redirected to a "more knowledgeable" host and may then make follow-up requests until it obtains the information it needs. The other possibility is that the original machine may make a single request, and each subsequent machine that doesn't have the address can make a follow-up request of the more knowledgeable host on behalf of the original host. This is a configuration option in the domain resolution software and has no effect on how many requests are made or on the efficiency of the requests.

Name	Category
biz	business
com	commercial
edu	educational
gov	governmental
mil	military
net	network service provider
org	nonprofit organization
XX	two-letter country code

FIGURE 10.1

Common top-level domain names.

The top-level domains encountered most often are shown in Figure 10.1.

For example, the LAN at University of Texas at Dallas was allocated the name "utdallas.edu". Once an organization has obtained its unique IP address and domain name, it may use the rest of the IP number to assign addresses to the other hosts on the LAN.

You can see what addresses your local DNS server returns for specific host names with the **nslookup** command, available on most UNIX systems and described in Figure 10.2. **nslookup** is most useful for obtaining addresses of machines in your own network. Machines at other sites around the Internet are often behind firewalls, so the address you get back may not be directly usable. However, **nslookup** is good for finding out whether domain names or Web servers (machines that would need to be outside the firewall for the public to access) within domains are valid. You might see

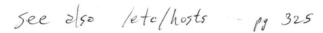

Utility: **nslookup** [hostname or address]

nslookup contacts the local Name Service and requests the IP address for a given host name. Some versions also allow you to do a reverse lookup in which, by specifying an IP address, you receive the host name for that address. If **nslookup** is run with no arguments, you enter an interactive session in which you can submit multiple commands. (Use ^D to exit.)

FIGURE 10.2

Description of the **nslookup** command.

the following type of output from **nslookup**:

```
$ nslookup www.hp.com
Server:   localhost
Address:  127.0.0.1

Non-authoritative answer:
Name:     www.hp.com
Addresses:  192.151.52.217, 192.151.52.187, 192.151.53.86,
            192.6.118.97, 192.6.118.128, 192.6.234.8

$ nslookup www.linux.org
Server:   localhost
Address:  127.0.0.1

Non-authoritative answer:
Name:     www.linux.org
Address:  198.182.196.56
$ _
```

The first thing reported by **nslookup** is the name and IP address of the DNS server being used for the query. In this case, the machine on which we are running **nslookup** is also running **bind**. After that, we are provided the current IP address(es) for the host name we requested. When a host name doesn't exist or the DNS server can't (or won't) provide the address, we see something like this:

```
$ nslookup
Server:   localhost
Address:  127.0.0.1

> xyzzy
Server:   localhost
Address:  127.0.0.1

*** localhost can't find xyzzy: Non-existent host/domain
> ^D
$ _
```

DOD Lets Go   Like a parent whose child has grown up and needs its independence, the Department of Defense was coming to a point where its child, the ARPANET, needed to move out of the house and be on its own. The DOD originally started the network as a research project—a proof of concept. The network became valuable, so the DOD continued to run it and manage it. But as membership grew, managing the network took more and more resources and provided the DOD fewer and fewer payoffs as more entities not related to the DOD got connected. It was time for the Department of Defense to get out of the network management business.

[handwritten margin note: Al Gore >92 in !]

In the late 1980s, the National Science Foundation (NSF) began to build NSFNET. Taking an approach to large-scale networking that was unique at the time in that it was constructed as a "backbone" network to which other regional networks would connect, NSFNET was originally intended to link supercomputer centers.

Using the same types of equipment and protocols as those making up the ARPANET, NSFNET provided an alternative medium with much freer and easier access than the government-run ARPANET. To most people, except the programmers and managers involved, the ARPANET appears to have mutated into the Internet of today. In reality, connections to NSFNET (and its regional networks) were created and ARPANET connections were severed, but because of the sharing of naming conventions and appearances, the change was much less obvious to the casual user.

The end result was a network that worked (from the user's point of view) the same as the ARPANET had, but that was made up of many more corporations and nongovernment agencies. More importantly, this new network was not funded by government money, but rather was surviving on private funding from those using it.

The Web: The 1990s

The 1990s saw the Internet come into popular use. Although it had grown consistently since its inception, it was still predominately a world belonging to computer users and programmers. Two things happened to spring the Internet on an unsuspecting public: the continued proliferation of personal computers in the home and one amazingly good idea.

[handwritten margin note: Web browser –]

The "Killer App"   Again, timing played a role in the history of the Internet. The network itself was growing and being used by millions of people, but was still not considered mainstream. The more sophisticated home users were getting connected to the Internet via a connection to their employer's network or by subscribing to a company that provided access to the Internet. These companies came to be known as Internet Service Providers (ISPs). In the early 1990s, only a handful of these providers existed, as only a few people recognized that there was a business in providing Internet access to anyone who wanted it.

Then came Mosaic. Mosaic was the first "browser" and was conceived by software designers at the National Center for Supercomputing Applications (NCSA) at the University of Illinois at Urbana–Champaign. With Mosaic, a computer user could access information from other sites on the Internet without having to use the complicated and nonintuitive tools that were popular at the time (e.g., **telnet, ftp**).

Mosaic was (and browsers in general are) an application that displays a page of information both textually and graphically. It displays information described by a page description language called HyperText Markup Language (HTML). The most revolutionary aspect of HTML was that of a *hyperlink*—a way to link information in one place in a document to other information in another part of the document (or, more generically, in another document).

By designing a page with HTML, you could display information and include links to other parts of the page or to other pages at other sites that contained related information. This approach created a document that could be "navigated" to allow users to obtain the specific information in which they were interested, rather than having to read or search the document in a sequential fashion, as was typical at the time.

Almost overnight, servers sprang up across the Internet and provided information that could be viewed by Mosaic. Now, rather than maintaining an anonymous FTP site, a site could maintain its publicly accessible information in a much more presentable format. Anonymous FTP sites usually required that users accessing them know what they were trying to find or, at best, that they get the README file which would help them find what they wanted. With a server that provided HTML, users could simply point and click with a mouse and be taken to the page containing the information they sought.

Of course, not all this magic happened automatically: Each site that maintained any information for external users had to set up a server and format the information. But this was not significantly more work than providing the information via anonymous FTP. Early on, as people switched from providing information via FTP-based tools to using web-based tools, the two alternatives were comparable in terms of the amount of effort required to make data available. As sites have become more sophisticated, the work required has increased, but the payoff in presentation has also increased.

Some of the people involved in the early releases of Mosaic later formed Netscape Communications, Inc., where they applied the lessons they had learned from early browser development and produced Netscape, the next generation in browsers. Since then, browsers, led by Netscape and Microsoft Internet Explorer, have become sophisticated applications that introduce significant advances to both browsing and publishing every year.

The Web vs. the Internet   The word "web" means many different things to different people in different contexts and causes as much confusion as it conveys information. Before Mosaic and other browsers, there was just the Internet, which, we have already seen, is simply a worldwide network of computers. This in itself can be diagrammed as a web of network connections. But that is not what the word "web" means here.

When Mosaic, using HTML, provided the capability of jumping around from one place to another on the Internet, yet another conceptual "web" emerged. Not only is my computer connected to several others forming a web, but now my HTML document is also connected to several others (by hyperlinks), creating a virtual spider web of information. This is the "web" that gave rise to the terms "web pages" and "web browsing."

When someone talks about "the Web" today, they usually mean the Internet itself. Alternatively (especially when the term is lowercased), they may mean the web of information available on the Internet. Although not originally intended that way, the nomenclature "the Web" and "the Internet" are often used interchangeably nowadays. However, in its original, lowercase usage, "the web" refers to the information that is available from the infrastructure of the Internet.

Accessibility   A few ISPs had sprung up even as "the Web" was coming into existence. Once the concept of "the Web" gained visibility, it seemed that suddenly

Internet vs. internet, Web vs. web

everyone wanted to get on the Internet. While electronic mail was always usable and remains one of the most talked-about services provided by access to the Internet, web browsing had the visibility and the public relations appeal to win over the general public.

All of a sudden, the average person saw useful (or at least fun) things he or she could get from being connected to the Internet; it was no longer solely the domain of computer geeks. For better or worse, the Internet would change rapidly. More people, more information, and more demand caused the Internet to burgeon in usage and availability. Of course, with more people come more inexperienced people and more congestion; popularity is always a double-edged sword.

Another factor allowing the general public to have access to the Internet has been the geometric increase in modem speeds. While large companies have direct connections to the Internet, most private connections are dial-up connections over home phone lines requiring modems. When the top modem speed was 2400 bytes per second (bps), which wasn't all that long ago, downloading a web page would have been intolerably slow. As modem speeds have increased to 100 kbps and high-speed digital lines have become economical for home use, it has become much more reasonable to have more than just a terminal using a dial-up connection.

Most private connections can be had for between $10 and $60 per month, depending on their speed and usage. A bill for Internet service that is comparable to a cable TV bill or a phone bill is tolerable; the general public probably would not have accepted a bill that was an order of magnitude higher than other utility bills.

Changes in the Internet As the public has played a larger and larger part in the evolution of the Internet, some of the original spirit of the Internet has changed. The Internet was first developed "just to prove that it could be done," not as a profit-making enterprise. The original spirit of the Internet, especially in its ARPANET days, was that information and software should be free to others with similar interests and objectives. Much of the early code that ran the Internet (the IP protocol suite and tools such as **ftp** and **telnet**) was given away by its authors and was modified by others who contributed their changes back to the authors for "the greater good." This was probably what allowed the Internet to grow and thrive in its youth. However, today business is conducted over the Internet, and much of the information is accessible for a fee. This is not to say that everybody is out to do nothing but make money or even that making money is bad. But it represents a significant change in the culture of the Internet.

The Internet needed the "free spirit" origins that it had, but now that mainstream society is using it, it is only natural that it change so that economics plays an increasing role. Advertising on web sites is common, and some sites require each user to pay a subscription fee in order to be able to login to gain access to information. Commerce over the Internet (such as on-line ordering of goods and services, including on-line information) is expected to continue to grow long into the future.

Security Entire books exist concerning Internet security (e.g., Cheswick (1994)). In the future, as more commercial activity takes place across the Internet, the need for security and concerns about the security of the operations that take place on the Internet will only increase.

In general, a single transfer of data is responsible for its own security. In other words, if you are making a purchase, the vendor will probably use secure protocols to acquire pertinent information from you (such as a credit card number).

Four major risks confront an Internet Web server or surfer: information copying, information modification, impersonation, and denial of service. Encryption services can prevent copying or modifying information. User education can help minimize impersonation.

The most feared (and, ironically, the least frequently occurring) risk is the copying of information that travels across the network. The Internet is a public network, and therefore, information that is sent "in the clear" (not encrypted) can, in theory, be copied by someone between the sender and the recipient. In reality, since information is divided into packets that may or may not travel the same route to their destination, it is often impractical to try to eavesdrop in order to obtain useful information.

Modification of information that is in transit has the same problem as eavesdropping, with the additional problem of actually making the modification. While not impossible, it is a very difficult problem and usually not worth the effort.

Impersonation of a user, either through a login interface or an e-mail message, is probably the most common type of security breach. Users often do not safeguard their passwords. Once another person knows someone's username and password, that person can login and have all the same rights and privileges as the legitimate user. Unfortunately, it is trivial to send an e-mail message with forged headers to make it appear that the message came from another user. Close examination can usually authenticate the header, but this can still lead to confusion, especially if an inexperienced user receives the message. One might also impersonate another network host by claiming to use the same network address. This is known as *spoofing*: it is not a trivial exercise, but an experienced network programmer or administrator can pull it off.

A denial-of-service attack occurs when an outside source sends a huge amount of information to a server with the aim of overloading it and compromising its capability to do its job. The server gets so bogged down that it either becomes unusable or completely crashes so that no one can use it.

Copyright   One of the biggest challenges in the development of information exchange on the Internet is that of copyright. In traditional print media, time is required to reproduce information, and proof of that reproduction will exist. In other words, if I reprint someone else's text without his or her permission, the copy I create would prove the action. On the Internet, information can be reproduced literally at the speed of light. In the amount of time it takes to copy a file, a copyright can be violated with very little evidence of the action left behind.

Censorship   In any environment where information can be distributed, there will be those who want to be able to limit who can gain access to what information. If the information is mine and I want to limit your access to it, this is called my right to privacy. If the information is someone else's and I want to limit your access to it, it is called censorship.

This is not to say that censorship is bad. As with so much in our society, the idea alone is not the problem; rather, the interpretation of the idea is. Censorship on the

Internet is, to put it mildly, a complex issue. Governments and organizations may try to limit certain kinds of access to certain kinds of materials (often with the best of intentions). The problem is that, since the Internet is a worldwide resource, local laws have very little jurisdiction over it. How can a law in Nashville be applied to a web server in Sydney? Moreover, even if the web server *is* doing something illegal, who will prosecute the case?

Misinformation   As much of a problem as copyrighted or offensive material may be, much more trouble is caused by information that is simply incorrect. Since no one has the authority to approve or validate information put on the net, anyone can publish anything. This is great for free speech, but humans tend to believe information they see in print. I can't tell you how many stories I've heard about people acting on information they found on the Web that turned out to be misleading or wrong. How much credence would you give to a rumor you were told by someone you didn't know? That's how much you should give to information you pick up from the Web, at least when you aren't sure of the source.

"Acceptable Use"   Many ISPs have an acceptable-use policy you must adhere to in order to use their services. Over time, this may well solve many of the problems the Internet has had since its formative years. Most acceptable-use policies request that users behave themselves and not do anything illegal or abusive to other users. This includes sending harassing e-mail, copying files that don't belong to you, and so on.

There is a perceived anonymity[3] of users of the Internet. If you send me an e-mail message that I disagree with, it may be difficult for me to walk over to you and yell at you personally. I might have to settle for YELLING AT YOU IN E-MAIL.[4] Because of this, people tend to behave in ways they would not in person. As the Internet and its users grow up, this problem should lessen.

USING TODAY'S INTERNET

In the past, using the Internet meant keeping track of a collection of commands and ftp sites. You had to keep track of the resources, as well as the method of accessing them.

Today, almost everything you access on the Internet is web based—that is, accessible via a *web browser*. Many web browsers have been written, but by far the most common browser for UNIX computers is Netscape, written by Netscape Communications. Much like any other window-based program, a web browser is a program with menu buttons, a control area, and a display area. You type in or select a web address, and the browser sends the request to the specified computer on the network (either the

---

[3] I say "perceived" here because it is actually possible to find most people if you're willing to do enough work. Even people who have filtered threatening e-mail through "anonymous e-mail" services have been found by law enforcement. ISPs will cooperate with the authorities when arrest warrants are involved!

[4] Text in all caps is typically interpreted as the written equivalent to speaking the words in a loud voice. This does not include those few users who still use computers or terminals that can only generate uppercase characters.

local network or the Internet) and displays the information that is returned in the window. I won't go into detail about how to use Netscape or any other browser, since trying it yourself is the best way to learn about web browsing. In general, all browsers have a place to type in a web address, a way to view your browser's *history*, web addresses you've previously visited, and buttons to help you move backward or forward in this list. Most browsers allow you to save or print information and store web addresses in a list of "bookmarks" so that you can return to a site in the future without having to remember and retype its address.

URLs

A *web page* is what is displayed in a browser window when you type in a particular web address. The address is called a Uniform Resource Locator (URL). For example, the URL for the Prentice Hall web site is

```
http://www.prenhall.com
```

The components of a URL are the protocol to use to obtain the web page, the Internet address or hostname of the computer on which the page resides, an optional port number, and an optional filename. In the case of the Prentice Hall URL, the port number and filename were omitted, and the browser assumed port 80 and requested the "root" (/) file within the web server document tree (not the same as the root of the UNIX file system).

The most common protocol is HyperText Transport Protocol (**http**), which is the protocol for accessing HTML information. An encrypted channel, Secure HTTP, specified with **https**, is used for pages or transactions involving confidential information (e.g., credit card numbers). Most web browsers also support the **ftp** protocol, which gives you a GUI-based way of accessing anonymous ftp sites through your browser. (See Chapter 11 for a discussion of the Graphical User Interface, or GUI.) If no protocol is specified, most browsers will assume that "http://" goes on the front of the URL, so you can usually leave that off when manually typing in a URL.

Typically, when you load a particular web page into your browser, you are presented with a nicely formatted page containing information and other highlighted text or icons (hyperlinks) that you can click on to be taken to other related web pages, possibly part of the current web site or possibly managed by a completely different organization. The hyperlink is the fundamental concept at the heart of the World Wide Web. It results in a web of information, each page containing links to many other pages. Since many web pages containing related information have links to each other, the result is a "web" of links all over the Internet.

Web Searches

So now that you have a browser window and can access web sites, how do you find the information you want? I could list some of the thousands of sites I know that contain interesting information, but by the time this book is published, many of the sites I listed might not be available anymore. Rather than just giving you a fish, I'd rather show you how to fish so that you can find anything you might need on your own.

There are more than a few web "search engines" on the Internet. These are sites that build and continuously update their database of web pages and keyword indices relating to those pages. Normally, their services are free; the pages that show you results of a search usually have advertising on them that sponsors pay for to support the cost of running the site.

Some common search engines, in alphabetical order, are as follows:

- `www.altavista.com`
- `www.excite.com`
- `www.google.com`
- `www.infoseek.com`
- `www.lycos.com`
- `www.webcrawler.com`
- `www.yahoo.com`

I have my own preferences and so will you. Your favorite may depend on the speed of the response, the layout of the information, the quality of what the engine finds, the ease with which you can build a query, or some of the other services the site may offer.

Today, there are so many sites on the Internet that the biggest problem with using a search engine is building a specific enough query so that you don't get thousands of links, most of which aren't what you really want.

If you are trying to find a "regular company," you can often get lucky by guessing. A URL of the form

```
http://www.companyname.com
```

probably works more often than it doesn't.

Finding Users and Domains

The NIC provides web-page access to the database of registered Internet users and Internet domains. The user database does not contain a listing of every Internet user; rather, it lists only users who have registered with the NIC. This usually includes system and network administrators who manage domain information for a site.

The NIC's web site is

```
http://www.internic.net
```

and its web page can point you to the resources you can use to perform all sorts of searches for domain and Internet information.

Factors Affecting Future Use

Will the Internet continue to grow as it has so far? The only factor limiting its use before was accessibility. This problem has been solved by ISPs and high-speed dial-up and broadband connections. Today, millions of people access the Internet every day. Some use it to send and receive e-mail and read bulletin boards. Some use it to look up information of all kinds on corporate and educational institution web servers. Many use the Internet to order products. As convenience becomes a priority in people's busy lives, Internet access may prove to be the most efficient way of finding information, even at the local level.

With millions of people using the Internet now, and with more expected, advertisers are eager to get their message to this new market. As web servers and applications become more sophisticated, advertisers will be able to target their message to only those users who are interested. This is an advantage to both the merchant and the customer, since it helps reduce the information overload we are already suffering from these days.

CHAPTER REVIEW

Checklist

In this chapter, I described

- the history of the Internet
- protocols used on the Internet
- applications that access the Internet
- the Domain Name Service used on the Internet
- the World Wide Web, web browsing, and web searching

Quiz

1. Why does the NIC allocate very few Class A addresses?
2. What is the difference between the http and https protocols?
3. If you were looking for Sun Microsystems' web page, what address would you try first?
4. What are the two most significant differences between the TCP and UDP protocols?

Exercises

10.1 Pick some companies you know, and try to access their web pages with URLs you make up in the form of www.company.com. [level: *easy*]

10.2 Connect to the "www.internic.net" web site and explore it to find out what kinds of services the NIC provides. Look up information about your domain name (or your ISP's domain name). [level: *medium*]

Project

Pretend you want to buy the latest CD of your favorite group, but you don't know of an Internet site that sells them. (There are several.) Do a web search with several keywords (e.g., *music*, *CD*, *purchase*, and the name of the group). See if you can find a way to buy the CD and explore some of the other sites that come up to find out why they satisfied your search so that you know how to make a better search next time. [level: *medium*]

CHAPTER 11

Windowing Systems

MOTIVATION

Virtually all UNIX computers now employ some form of windowing system. The vast majority of these systems are based on MIT's *X Window System*. A familiarity with the X Window System should allow you to function on virtually any UNIX-based window system in use today.

PREREQUISITES

Since the X Window System takes advantage of several UNIX networking facilities, you should have read or should be familiar with the issues discussed in Chapter 9 prior to reading this chapter.

OBJECTIVES

In the current chapter, I will provide you with a general overview of the X Window System and how to use some of its most common features. I will show you how the system can improve your productivity. Many other books (e.g., Quercia, 1993; OSF, 1992; and Fountain, 2000) go into much greater detail about this complicated subject. The goal here is to give you enough information to get you started using the X Window System and to give you an understanding upon which to build.

PRESENTATION

First, I will present a brief history of window systems in general. Then we will examine the X Window System, what it looks like, how it works, and the UNIX commands involved in using it.

UTILITIES

This chapter includes a discussion of the following utilities, listed in alphabetical order:

xbiff	xhost	xterm
xclock	xrdb	

INTRODUCTION

In the early days of UNIX systems, a character terminal was the only interface to the system. You logged in and did all your work in a single, character-based session. If you were lucky, you had a terminal with "smart" cursor capabilities permitting full-screen manipulations (which allowed screen-oriented text editing or debugging). Usually, you simply had a line-oriented terminal on which you typed in a line of text (a command) and got back one or more lines of text in response. And you were happy to have it instead of the punch cards you used before that!

Graphical User Interfaces

As computer systems became more sophisticated, bit-mapped displays (whereby each bit on the screen can be turned on or off, rather than simply displaying a character in a certain space) allowed user interfaces to become more sophisticated. The *Graphical User Interface* (GUI, often pronounced "gooey") was born. The first computer with a semi-well-known GUI was the Xerox STAR. This computer was purely a text-processing system and was the first to use the icon representing a document that looked like a page with one corner folded over. The Xerox STAR had icons for folders, documents, and printers on a *desktop* (the screen) rather than a command-line-driven interface, as had been the norm to that time.

The ability to click on a picture of a document to edit it and the ability to to drag it onto the top of a printer icon to print it, rather than having to remember what the commands were to perform these functions, was, at that time, revolutionary. Some of the engineers from Xerox moved on to Apple Computer and worked on the Apple Lisa, which led to development of the Macintosh.

UNIX also got into the GUI act. Sun Microsystems introduced Suntools early in the history of SunOS (the predecessor to Solaris, Sun's current version of UNIX). Suntools allowed multiple terminal windows on the same screen with a cut-and-paste ability between them. At first, there were only a few applications that provided real GUI functionality. A performance meter could graphically display system performance statistics rather than show them as numbers on a chart. The **mailtool** program allowed you to read e-mail with something other than the traditional **/bin/mail** program.

But under conventional windowing systems, an application could display information only on the screen of the computer on which the application was running. The next step in the evolution was still to come.

MIT

In 1984, the Massachusetts Institute of Technology released the X Window System. Recognizing the usefulness of windowing systems, but being unimpressed with what

UNIX vendors had provided, students at MIT, in a move comparable to the BSD movement at Berkeley, set out to write a windowing system of their own. Initially, Digital Equipment Corporation helped fund Project Athena, where X had its origins.

The revolutionary idea behind the X Window System, which has yet to be rivaled in any modern computer system, is the distinction between the functions of client and server in the process of drawing an image on a computer screen. Unlike most windowing systems, X is defined by a network protocol, replacing the traditional procedure call interface. Thus, rather than simply having an application draw its image directly to the screen, as previous window systems had done, the X Window System split the two functions apart. The X server takes care of drawing on, and managing the contents of, the computer's bit-mapped display and communicating with all clients who wish to draw on the screen. An X client doesn't draw directly to a screen, but communicates with an X server running on the computer where the screen on which it wishes to draw is located. By allowing this communication to take place between two processes on the same machine, or via a network connection between two processes on different machines, suddenly you have the capability of drawing graphics on a different screen. This opens the door to all sorts of new possibilities (as well as security problems).

The X Window System is often referred to simply as "X" or "X11," referring to its most recent major version. At the time of this writing, X11 is in its sixth release; hence, the complete reference is X11R6. For the latest information about the X Window System, see the Open Group's X.Org Consortium web site at

```
http://www.x.org
```

X SERVERS

An *X server* starts up and "takes over" the bit-mapped display on a computer system. This may happen automatically when a user logs in, or it may happen when the user executes a command to do so, depending on the implementation.

Usually, at the time the X server starts, one or two *X clients* are also started. X Clients are programs that will communicate with one or more X servers in order to communicate with a user. Some other program must be started that will allow the user access to the system. (A screen being driven by an X server, but not running any application, would not allow you to do anything on it.) A terminal window and a window manager are generally the types of programs you start here, as we will see later.

On systems that don't start an X server for you at login time, there is usually a command such as **xinit** or **xstart** that you can either type manually or add to your login or profile script so that it will be started automatically when you log in.

Screen Geometry

The layout of the screen is called *geometry*. A bit-mapped display has a certain size measured in pixels—the dots on a display that can be set to "on" or "off" (white or black) or to some color value. A small screen might be 600 × 480 (a typical low-resolution PC monitor). A larger screen might be 1280 × 1000 pixels, or even larger for very high resolution graphics screens.

Screen geometry is specified either by referencing a specific position on the screen (e.g., 500 × 200) or by referencing positions relative to a corner of the screen. Position +0+0 is the upper left corner of the screen and −0−0 is the lower right corner (−0+0 is the upper right, +0−0 the lower left). Therefore, +500+500 would be 500 pixels away from the upper left corner of the screen in both the X and Y directions. We will see examples of this when we discuss X clients.

Security and Authorization

As you may have guessed by now, the ability to scribble on any computer screen in your network could lead to security problems, not so much because the act of writing on someone else's screen is anything more than annoying if the recipient does not want it, but because I/O to an X server is just that—input and output. Write access to an X server also gives you the ability to query that system for a current copy of the display or even keyboard input.

Because of this, the X Window System has a certain amount of security built into the X server. It isn't highly rated security, but it is enough to keep the casual snoop from gaining unauthorized access. By default, the X server running on any computer system allows only X clients on that same system to talk to it. The X server does not accept connections from "foreign" X clients without knowing who they are. This causes the default configuration of an X server to be very much like a conventional window system, where only applications running on that computer can write to its display. In order to take advantage of the network capabilities of the X Window System, you have to allow outside access.

The **xhost** command (an X client) is used to allow X clients on other systems to display to your system. It works as shown in Figure 11.1. For example,

```
xhost +bluenote
```

will allow X clients running on the computer called "bluenote" to write to the display on the system on which the **xhost** utility was run. Later, when whatever you needed to run is finished, you can prohibit access with the command

```
xhost -bluenote
```

Utility: **xhost** [+|-][*hostname*]

The **xhost** command allows or denies access to the X server on a system. With no arguments, **xhost** prints its current settings and which hosts (if any) have access. By specifying only +, you can give access to all hosts; by specifying only -, you can deny access to all hosts. When a host name is specified after a + or -, access is granted or denied, respectively, to that host.

FIGURE 11.1

Description of the **xhost** command.

In a secure environment where you aren't afraid of other systems writing to your display, you can allow any X client on the network to write to your display with the command

```
xhost +
```

You can also take away access from all X clients with

```
xhost -
```

X WINDOW MANAGERS

All this ability to write to a display isn't really very useful if you just sit there and watch windows pop up and go away, but you can't do anything with them. This is where window managers come in. A window manager is a program (an X client) that communicates with the X server and with the keyboard and mouse on the system. It provides the interface for the user to give instructions to the X server about what to do with the windows.

Although window managers are usually run on the same computer as the display they manage, this is not a requirement. If you have a special X window manager that runs only on one specific type of computer, it is possible to set it up to manage your workstation from a remote computer. Of course, there are inherent problems involved in doing this. For example, what if the remote machine running the window manager or the entire network went down? Your X server would no longer be managed, because it could not communicate with the window manager, and your keyboard and mouse probably would not respond (at least properly) to your input. But the fact that the system could still operate is a testament to the flexibility of the X Window System architecture.

One of the important features provided by a window manager is the "look and feel" of the desktop. The look and feel of the interior of a window depends on the application creating the window. While all window managers provide similar basic functionality, the appearance of each can vary widely.

Focus

The most important job of a window manager is to maintain window *focus*, the term used to describe which window is currently selected or active. If you type on the keyboard, the window with focus is where the data will be sent. Focus is what allows you to move from one window to another and to do multiple things in different windows. Generally, a window with focus has a different border than the other windows, although it may be configured not to be different in that regard.

Window focus can be configured so that it is set when a window border or title bar is selected or simply when the mouse pointer is moved onto the window, depending on your preference.

Program Start-Up

Most window managers provide a *pull-down menu* capability that can be customized to allow you to start different, often-used applications. For example, if your pointer is on the root window (the desktop itself, not an application window) and you click and hold down a mouse button, most window managers will bring up a menu of things that you can select to perform a function. This list usually includes functions like starting a new terminal window or exiting the window manager. The specific functions vary from one window manager to another and can be heavily customized. Different mouse buttons can be customized to bring up different lists of functions. Figure 11.2 shows an example of a window.

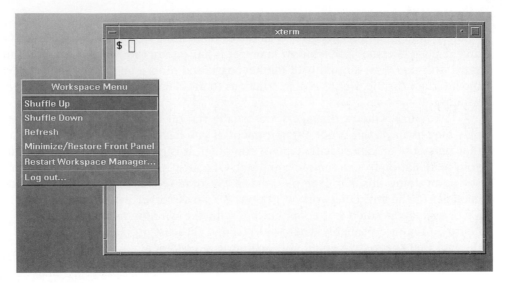

FIGURE 11.2

A window and a root window pull-down menu.

Open and Closed Windows

The window manager also takes care of displaying active windows and positioning icons which represent windows that are not open. If you start a new terminal window and are finished with it, but don't want to terminate it because you may need it later, you can close the terminal window. The window manager will create an icon on the desktop that represents the terminal window program, but it won't take up much space. You will still be able to see it and you can click (or perhaps double-click, depending on the window manager you use) on the icon later to have the window restored (reopened). The program itself is still running while its window is represented by an icon, but the window is conveniently out of your way. The X server itself knows nothing of this function, as you will see if you ever kill your window manager. (If you do, all of your icons will pop their windows open all over your screen!). Figure 11.3 shows a desktop with an open window and icons.

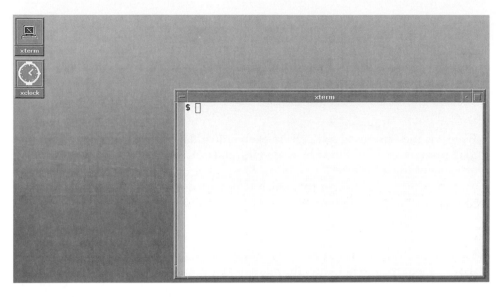

FIGURE 11.3

A desktop with an open window and icons.

Choices of Window Managers

Many different window managers are available for X servers. Most are based on the Motif standard, developed by the Open Software Foundation. Several window managers have a common lineage from the original Motif window manager. Many implement a *virtual desktop*, which provides an area of desktop that is larger than the area the on-screen real estate supports. The window manager then helps you manage which section of the larger virtual desktop is displayed on the screen.

The most common window managers (in alphabetical order) include the following:

- **dtwm:** The Desktop Window Manager, part of the Common Desktop Environment (CDE), similar to **vuewm**, but supporting a virtual desktop
- **fvwm:** A free, virtual window manager, written by Robert Nation, that became very popular in the Linux community
- **kwm:** The K Window Manager, used with the K Desktop Environment (KDE)
- **mwm:** The Motif Window Manager, the original window manager
- **olwm/olvwm:** Sun Microsystems' OpenLook Window Manager and OpenLook Virtual Window Manager
- **twm/tvtwm:** Tom's Window Manager and Tom's Virtual Window Manager, written by Tom LaStrange to correct some of the things he didn't like about Motif
- **vuewm:** Hewlett-Packard's VUE Window Manager

For the sake of simplicity, I will use the Motif Window Manager as the generic window manager, since the aspects of windows that are of interest are common to all of these window managers. The Motif Window Manager provides additional components of a window that the application (X client) does not have to worry about. For example, Motif draws a border around a window that can be selected with the mouse to change focus onto the window, move (drag) the window, or change its size. The window border contains a title and buttons allowing it to be moved, resized, minimized (replaced with an icon), made to fill the entire screen, or terminated.

Widgets

Widget is the term used to describe each individual component of an X window. Buttons, borders, and scrolling boxes are all widgets. Each X tool kit can define its own set of widgets. Since we are focusing on Motif environments, we will concern ourselves with only the Motif widget set, which is provided to the application program via the Motif *Application Programming Interface* (API).

Menus

Menu buttons provide GUI access to functions afforded by the application. Often, these functions are not directly related to the contents of any particular window. (Rather, they do things like opening files, setting options, and exiting a program.) Menu buttons are found along the top of a window, as shown in Figure 11.4.

Push Buttons

Push buttons can be laid out in any fashion required by an application. A typical example is the OK/Cancel *dialog box* (an additional window that pops up with new information or one that queries the user for more information). Figure 11.5 shows a sample dialog box.

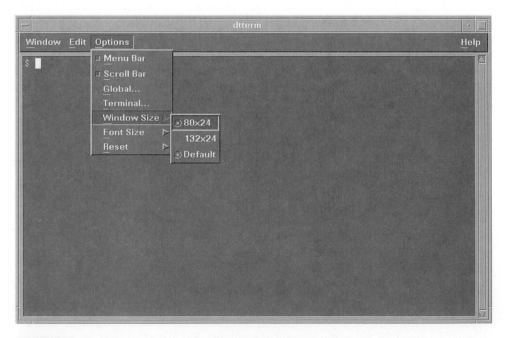

FIGURE 11.4

A pull-down menu.

FIGURE 11.5

A dialog box with push buttons.

Check Boxes and Radio Buttons

Check boxes and *radio buttons* are input-gathering widgets. Check boxes are a yes-or-no type of button. If checked, they indicate "true," "yes," or "present," depending on the context of the statement. Radio buttons are a collection of mutually exclusive selections: When one is selected, any others that were selected are deselected (like the buttons on a car radio). Check boxes and radio buttons are shown in Figure 11.6.

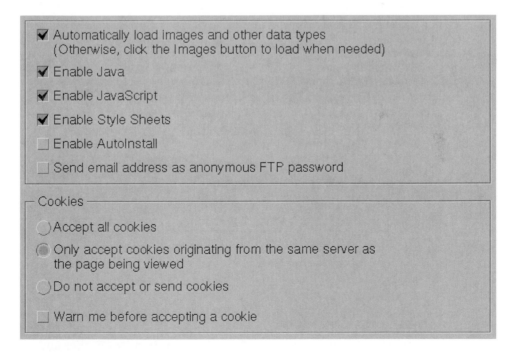

FIGURE 11.6

Check boxes and radio buttons.

Scroll Bars

Scroll bars allow you to scroll back and forth in a window or a part of a window. Scrolling is useful when a lot of text is involved, but a short display area is available, so that not all the text fits. Scroll bars may be either horizontal or vertical. Vertical scroll bars are generally on the right side of a window (as in Figure 11.7). Horizontal scroll bars are usually along the bottom of a window.

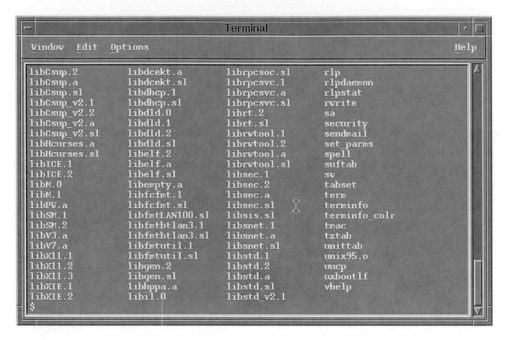

FIGURE 11.7

A terminal window with a scroll bar.

MOTIF WINDOW MANAGER FUNCTIONS

Functions performed on windows and icons on the desktop under the Motif Window Manager are similar to functions and icons belonging to other X Window System window managers, although some details might vary slightly.

Bringing Up the Root Menu

The root menu contains the basic functions needed to control your X session. The default list includes starting a terminal window, moving the focus to another window, and exiting the window manager. The root menu is customizable and is often heavily customized to add frequently used X applications so that they are easy to start. It is possible to have a different menu brought up for each of the different mouse buttons.

Opening a Window

Open (or "maximize") a window by double-clicking on the icon representing the closed window.

Closing a Window

Close (or "minimize") a window by clicking on the close tab in the window border. You can also pull down a menu with a "Close" selection by selecting the window border. In addition, most window managers provide a way to define a keyboard shortcut that can be used when the focus is on the window.

Moving a Window

Move a window by selecting the window border and dragging the window to the new location by holding down the middle mouse button. A window border pull-down menu also usually has a "Move" selection.

Resizing a Window

Resize a window by selecting the resize border area of any corner or border of the window with the left mouse button and dragging the window to the new size. By dragging a corner, both the X and Y sizes are modified. When selecting a top, bottom, or side border and dragging it, the window size is modified in only one direction.

Raising or Lowering a Window

A window can be raised to the top (over other windows) simply by selecting its border. This action also sets the focus on that window.

Bringing Up a Window Menu

The window manager can supply a menu for each window. The menus generally list one or more of the functions just discussed, but can also be customized. To bring up the window menu, you can either click on the menu button in the upper left corner of the window or hold down the right mouse button anywhere in the window border or title bar.

CLIENT APPLICATIONS

Every program that writes to the screen of an X server is known as an X client. Many useful X clients are included with the X Window System.

We next examine a few of the simplest X clients—the ones beginners tend to use first when they are learning the X Window System. You should consult the *man* page for each program to find out about optional arguments that can be used to customize the client program.

xclock

The **xclock** X client is described in Figure 11.8. The **xclock** command can be started by hand or in your initialization file. Figure 11.9 shows an xclock client.

Utility: **xclock** [-digital]

The **xclock** command provides a simple clock on your desktop. The default is an analog clock (with sweeping hands). If the **-digital** argument is specified, a digital clock is displayed instead.

FIGURE 11.8

Description of the **xclock** X client.

FIGURE 11.9

An xclock client.

xbiff

The **xbiff** X client, described in Figure 11.10, is basically an X Window System version of the Berkeley UNIX **biff** program that tells you when you have new mail. As mentioned

---

Utility: **xbiff**

The **xbiff** command displays a mailbox icon on the desktop. If the user running **xbiff** has no new mail, the flag is down (like a real roadside mailbox). When mail is delivered, the flag goes up and the icon may change color.

FIGURE 11.10

Description of the **xbiff** X client.

earlier, one of the developers at the University of California at Berkeley was said to have had a dog named Biff that always barked when the postman came by. Many other such X client commands have been written to do more sophisticated types of notifications, but **xbiff** is the original. Figure 11.11 shows the use of **xbiff**.

xterm

The **xterm** X client is probably the most commonly used X client among UNIX users. It provides a terminal interface window to the system. Early windowing system users used their X terminals mostly to provide multiple terminal interfaces into the system to consolidate monitors on their desktop. As X clients become more sophisticated, **xterm** was used less and less, but it is still quite useful if you use the

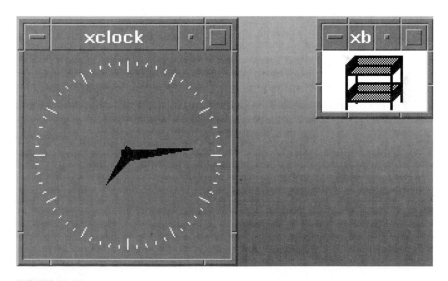

FIGURE 11.11

Two views of the xbiff client.

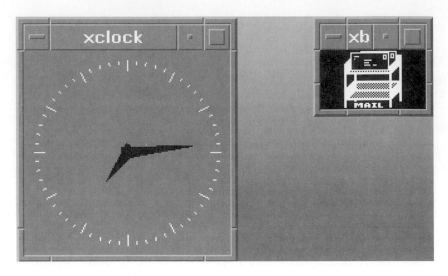

FIGURE 11.11 (*Continued*)

Utility: **xterm** [-C]

The **xterm** command starts a terminal window on the desktop. If the **-C** argument is included, the terminal window will receive console messages. This feature is useful for preventing console messages from being written across the screen on a system in which the bit-mapped display is also the console device.

FIGURE 11.12

Description of the **xterm** X client.

UNIX shell interface. We saw an example of the use of **xterm** earlier in the chapter. **xterm** has a myriad of arguments allowing the window's size, color, and font to be defined at the command line. (See the **man** page for **xterm** for details.) The **xterm** X client is described in Figure 11.12.

STANDARD X CLIENT ARGUMENTS

Most X clients accept standard arguments that allow the X client's size and position to be customized when started.

Geometry

X client geometry is specified by the *–geometry* argument. You can specify not only the size of the client, but the offset position where it will appear on the screen. The general format is "*XxY*" for the position, followed by "*+X+Y*" for the offset position. For example, to start an **xclock** positioned 10 pixels in each direction from the upper right-hand corner of the screen and 100 pixels in both width and height, you would use the command

```
$ xclock -geometry 100x100-10+10
```

Note that the value of the *-geometry* argument is a single shell token. (There are no spaces embedded in it.)

Foreground and Background

Foreground and background colors can be set with the **–foreground** and **–background** arguments. The following **xterm** command will create a terminal window with cyan (a light shade of blue) letters on a black background:

```
$ xterm -foreground cyan -background black
```

I find this combination of colors very easy to work with, but everyone has his or her own favorites.

Title

The **–title** argument sets the title in the title bar of a window. This feature is often useful for labeling one of many terminal windows used during a remote log-in session to another machine to help keep the windows straight. The command for doing this would be something like

```
$ xterm -title "Remote access to mail server"
```

Iconic

The **–iconic** argument is used to start an X client, but to have the window closed (minimized) so that only the icon representing it shows up on the desktop. This is useful for an application that you will be using, but don't necessarily want to use the moment it starts up (like a mail reader or web browser).

ADVANCED TOPICS

Some of the topics we will examine here fall into one or more of the previous sections, but you need a good foundation before we discuss these more complex capabilities of the X Window System.

Copy and Paste

The *copy-and-paste* function is one of the more useful features of the X Window System. The ability to select text in one window and copy it to another window without having to retype it is a great time-saver. I am discussing the topic outside the scope of the window manager because, even though it "feels" like the window manager provides the capability, it is actually provided by the X server itself. You can prove this by using copy and paste even when no window manager is running.

To copy text into the copy-and-paste text buffer, you simply click and, while holding down the left mouse button with the pointer set at one end of the text you wish to select, drag it to the other end. (You can do this either forward or backward.) When you release the mouse button, the highlighted text has been copied to the buffer (unlike a PC, which requires you to tell it to copy the highlighted text to the buffer). You then go to the window where you wish to paste the text, click the middle mouse button (or both mouse buttons at once on a system that only has two buttons), and the text will be inserted. Some applications insert the text at the current cursor position while others insert it at the point where you click the middle mouse button. The feature is application specific.

In the example shown in Figure 11.13, I executed a **who** command to find out who was logged into the system. To copy-and-paste the line showing Graham's log-in, I moved the mouse pointer to the beginning of the line and dragged the mouse to the end of the line before letting go. This highlighted the text and put it in the copy-and-paste buffer. Then, when I sent an e-mail message to Graham, I clicked on the middle mouse button (or both left and right buttons at the same time on a two-button mouse) to paste the text into the mail message at the current point.

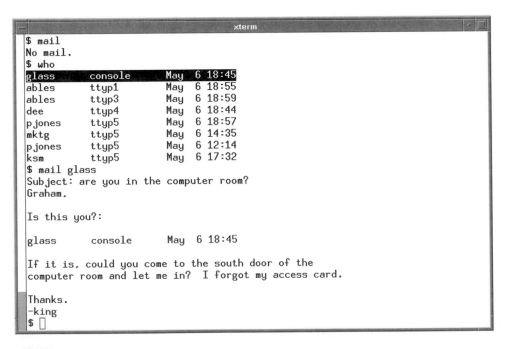

FIGURE 11.13

A copy-and-paste example.

Networking Capabilities

I mentioned earlier that the X Window System is a networked windowing system and that it is possible to display information from an X client running on one computer to an X server running on another. This capability is fundamental to the X design and is quite simple to use from any X client by specifying the **-display** argument. The argument tells the X client which X server to contact to display its widgets. By default, the display is the local machine on which the client is running. To start an **xterm** on the host "savoy," use an **xterm** command such as

```
$ xterm -display savoy:0.0
```

The specification of ":0.0" is a method of uniquely identifying a display and an X server running on the computer. While it is possible to run multiple X servers, as well as having multiple monitors connected to a single computer, in general usage, each computer will have only one monitor and will be running only one X server, so the value ":0.0" will almost always denote this configuration. The default display name for the local system would be "unix:0.0" or perhaps ":0.0" without a host name. The "unix" name has the special meaning of "the local computer" and therefore will not work remotely if you actually have a local host called "unix."

If I type the command

```
$ xterm -display bluenote.utexas.edu:0.0
```

and if the user on bluenote has used the **xhost** command to allow access to the machine on which I typed this command, then the X terminal window that is created will be displayed on bluenote.utexas.edu.

Application Resources

Application *resources* are both a Pandora's box of detail and one of the most revolutionary aspects of the X Window System. X Resources allow users to customize the look and feel of their desktops and the applications they run to a degree that no other window system provides. Here we will take a quick look at the most basic parts of using X resources. I strongly urge you to read the chapter titled "Setting Resources" in Quercia (1993) for exhaustive details.

How Resources Work

Every application, including the window manager itself, can take advantage of X Resources. An X resource is a text string, like a variable name, and a value, which is set as part of the X server. The value of a resource is tied to a specific widget. When the X server draws a particular widget, it looks up the value(s) associated with the widget in its list of resources and sets the described attribute appropriately.

For example, consider the hypothetical application called **xask**. This application is simply a dialog box containing a text message (a question) and two buttons: "yes" and "no." It might be defined with (at least) the following resources:

```
xask.Button.yes.text
xask.Button.no.text
```

The application may have default values in case these resources are not set. With no resources set, when you run **xask**, you might see a window like the one shown in Figure 11.14.

FIGURE 11.14

The mythical **xask** application.

But what if you would rather have something more interesting than "yes" and "no" for choices? Maybe you need to change the language used by the application, but you do not wish to have a separate version for each language. The answer is to customize the values with X resources. In our example, we'll set the following resources for **xask**:

```
xask.Button.yes.text: Sure
xask.Button.no.text:  No way
```

Of course, this is a trivial example, but you see the power of X resources. By setting the foregoing values to those resources in the X server, the next time you run **xask**, you see the window shown in Figure 11.15. If I set these X resources on my X server and run **xask**, and you do not set any resources on your X server and run the exact same copy of **xask**, we will each see a different window!

X resources are used to set things like sizes, colors, fonts, and values of text strings. While these are typical, there is really no limit to what you could allow to be customized in an application. Every X application uses some number of X resources,

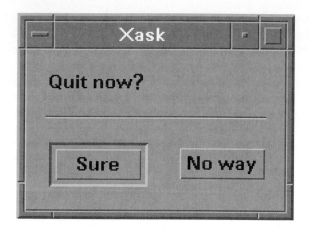

FIGURE 11.15

The **xask** application with customized X resources.

and they should be defined in the documentation for the application. The larger (more complex) the application, the more resources it will use. For instance, the Motif window manager has what seems like an endless number of resources that allow you to customize nearly everything about it.

Defining Resources

Once you know what resources you want to set, how do you do it? X resources are resources of the X server; therefore, they are set on the machine on which the X server runs. There are many ways to load resources into an X server. The most manual method of accessing the X resource database in the X server is with the **xrdb** command, described in Figure 11.16.

Utility: **xrdb** [*-query|-load|-merge|-remove*] [*filename*]

The **xrdb** command provides access to the X Resource database for the X server. Used with the **-query** argument, **xrdb** prints the resources defined in the X server. The **-load** argument causes new resource information to be loaded into the resource database, replacing the previous information. If a filename is specified, the resource information is loaded from that file, otherwise the Standard Input channel is read to find the resource information. The **-merge** argument loads new resource information, similarly to the **-load** argument's operation, except that existing information is not removed. (Information about duplicate resources is overwritten.) Finally, the **-remove** argument clears out the X server's resource database.

FIGURE 11.16

Description of the **xrdb** command.

You can add or remove individual or groups of resources anytime you wish. However, manually adding and removing X resources gets tedious very quickly. What we really want is a way to specify a resource that will apply every time we run a given application. We do this by setting up a default resource file called .Xdefaults. This file is an initialization file recognized by the X server program when run by the user. Upon start-up, the X server loads all resources listed in the file. For example, if we always wanted our **xask** program to use the more casual text in the response buttons, as in our earlier example, we could enter those resources into our .Xdefaults file, and the next time we start the X server, these resources will be set. Note that we could also run **xrdb** on our .Xdefaults file itself to load or reload the aforesaid resources at any time.

If you customize a great number of resources in many applications, putting all of these customized resource lines in your .Xdefaults file, over time you will find that the file gets extremely large. While this isn't a real problem, it makes the contents of the file harder to manage. Also, some applications come with a default set of resources that specify the default attributes of widgets used by the application, rather than setting these default values in the code itself. In this case, we need a way to load those resources into the X server when we run the application.

Specifying a directory where X resources are kept allows the X server to load multiple resource files. Lists of resources for an application are stored in a file named so that the application will find it. (This is usually the same name as the application, but it is defined by the application itself.) In this way, resources can be managed more easily, since each file will contain only the resources for one application. You may find tens or even hundreds of files in this directory, but each file will be of a manageable size.

In our previous **xask** example, we might put our resources in a file called Xask that we know is used by the application. Then, all we need is a way to tell the application where to look for this file. We do that by defining a shell variable called XAP-PLRESDIR (X application resource directory). In the C-shell, this should be an environment variable so that child shells inherit the value. In Bourne-based shells, this variable should be exported when it is set.

Configuration and Start-Up

It may seem strange that I left this section until now, but trying to run the X Window System without any idea about how it works sometimes proves to be quite an impediment. Knowing the relationship between the X server and the client and knowing where the window manager fits into the picture should make the section seem simple. The details of starting X also vary from platform to platform and implementation to implementation.

xinit and .xinitrc

When running the "generic" X Window System distribution from MIT, you log into the UNIX computer the way you normally do. You can then type the **xinit** command to start the X server, or you might have this command in your shell initialization file.

The **xinit** command starts the X server and runs commands found in a shell script file called .xinitrc. In this file, you can specify any application that you wish to be started when the X server starts. Typical commands found in the .xinitrc file are xterms and mail programs or perhaps your favorite Web browser. You will also start up your window manager of choice here.

The real trick to setting up a proper .xinitrc is to understand that your X server runs the commands in this file like a shell script, and when the script finishes (i.e., all the commands have completed), the X server terminates. This is a key point. Often, people put commands in their .xinitrc file and use the "&"to fork off the processes (run them in the background). But they also do this with the last command in the list. In this case, the .xinitrc script exits and the X server terminates. The appearance is that the X server starts, starts up applications, and then abruptly exits. The reason is that the last application started in the .xinitrc file should *not* be started in the background with the "&" on the end of the command! Then, when this particular application exits, the X server itself exits.

Some people choose to make this "last application" the window manager (**mwm**). Advanced users sometimes make this last command the special "console" terminal window, because they want to be able to stop and start their window manager without the X server terminating. In that case, to cause the X server to exit, you would simply terminate (type "exit" or *Control-D* in) your console window. In the following sample .xinitrc file, **mwm** is started last and is not put into the background, so the execution of the script stops there as long as **mwm** is running. When you exit your window manager, execution of your .xinitrc script continues to the end, and when the script terminates, then your X server also exits, as the following commands indicate:

```
$ cat .xinitrc
xbiff &
mailtool &
xterm -C &
mwm
$ _
```

This whole discussion may sound simple, but this simple idea has caused more than its share of grief for the novice X Window System user!

mwm and .mwmrc

Just as .xinitrc is the start-up file for **xinit**, .mwmrc is the initialization file for **mwm**. When starting the Motif Window Manager, the window manager must be instructed how to map mouse buttons, what to do when you click on various widgets, and, in general, how to behave. Usually, your account will be provided with a default copy of the .mwmrc file, which you may edit to customize.

Within the .mwmrc file, all the pull-down menus that will be available to you are defined. This is the one way you can do anything useful when the X server is running without starting other applications (in your .xinitrc). Over time, you may find certain applications so useful that you add a command to start them to your pull-down menus defined here so that you can start them with a mouse click. (You should consult OSF, 1992, for all the details you need to know regarding customizing your .mwmrc file.)

A (LIMITED) SURVEY OF OTHER X-COMPATIBLE DESKTOPS

Three major UNIX desktops are in use today: CDE, KDE, and Gnome. Older desktops such as VUE and OpenWindows figure into the history of the UNIX desktop, so we mention them, but they are no longer used in many UNIX environments.

CDE

With companies developing their own implementations of X servers and adding their own bells and whistles to them, it became clear that X environments were getting very complicated and diverse. Hewlett-Packard, IBM, SunSoft, and Novell got together to define a new X implementation that could be shared and used by all UNIX platforms. The Common Desktop Environment (CDE) was the result.

CDE's outward appearance is very much like that of VUE, although there are also OpenWindows influences apparent throughout. CDE is also Motif based, like VUE, and has a login and session manager. CDE does not provide any great technological leap over OpenWindows, VUE, or even X itself. What it provides is, as its name implies, a common environment, shared by major UNIX vendors and available to UNIX users on different UNIX platforms. CDE was the first UNIX desktop to be adopted by several UNIX vendors.

Gnome

The GNU Network Object Model Environment (Gnome) is the GNU Project's contribution to the UNIX desktop. As with other GNU software, it is freely available and runs on most UNIX hardware platforms. While it now comes with many commercial distributions of UNIX and Linux, it can also be found at

```
http://www.gnome.org
```

Gnome's goal is to provide an easy-to-use desktop for beginning users without tying the hands of experienced users.

KDE

Much like Gnome, KDE, the K Desktop Environment, is an Open Source, freely available UNIX desktop developed by a loose group of programmers around the world. KDE is also available for just about every version of UNIX and Linux and can be found at

```
http://www.kde.org
```

KDE attempts to provide an interface similar to those of MacOS and Windows desktops to encourage the adoption of UNIX or Linux in home and office desktop environments (where MacOS and Windows have traditionally dominated).

OpenWindows

Acknowledging that its original windowing system, Suntools, was not the right answer, Sun abandoned it and developed its own X-based window system called OpenWindows. While based on X and capable of running X clients, OpenWindows provided a new "look and feel" and a new widget set (and, of course, a new set of applications). The new style was called OpenLook. While Sun users and the Open Software Foundation embraced the Open Look style and OpenWindows, it never really took off in the rest of the X community.

VUE

Hewlett-Packard also wanted to improve on the original X concept while staying compatible with generic X clients. The HP Visual User Environment (VUE) implemented an X server, a new desktop design, and a new start-up paradigm.

VUE provided a login screen so that the user never saw a generic UNIX login or shell prompt on the terminal. VUE ran when the computer started, and it turned control over to the user's initialization files when he or she logged in. VUE also provided a useful set of default files so that the environment worked well initially, but it could still be customized by the experienced X user. Where, with generic X, the user had to edit initialization files to modify the behavior of the window system, VUE provided many methods for modifying behavior via the GUI, which was easier for the average user to work with.

CHAPTER REVIEW

Checklist

In this chapter, I described

- what a Graphical User Interface does
- MIT's X Window System
- X servers, X clients, and X widgets
- the Motif window manager
- X application resources

Quiz

1. Which command is used to change access permissions on an X server?
2. Which Motif widget would you use in a window wherein you want to give users a choice among several options, but they can choose only one?
3. What is the X application argument used to cause the application's window to show up on a different computer's screen?

4. What attribute about an X server allows you to change the appearance of an X application without having to modify the program?

Exercises

11.1 Explain why a window manager is an X client. [level: *easy*]

11.2 Suppose that your window manager has exited and you cannot get focus in a window to type a command to bring up a new window manager. (Suppose also that you have no root menu button that starts a new window manager.) Explain how you might still be able to use *copy-and-paste* with your existing windows to execute a command. [level: *hard*]

Project

Use the **xrdb** command to print the resource database of a running X server. Study the output to learn what types of applications use which types of resources. [level: *medium*]

# CHAPTER 12

C Programming Tools

MOTIVATION

The most commonly used programming languages on UNIX systems are C and C++. This isn't surprising, since UNIX was written in C and many versions come with a standard C compiler. Most UNIX utilities and many commercial products are written in C or C++. It's therefore likely that you will find knowledge about writing, compiling, and running C programs very useful. Of course, UNIX supports many other popular programming languages, but this chapter applies primarily to the C language and its supporting tools, because these are so fundamental to UNIX environments.

PREREQUISITES

The chapter assumes that you already know C and have compiled programs on at least one platform. For example, many readers may have used the Borland or Microsoft C compiler.

OBJECTIVES

In this chapter, I describe the tools that support the various different stages of program development: compilation, debugging, maintaining libraries, profiling, and source code control.

PRESENTATION

The C programming environment is introduced in a natural fashion, with plenty of examples and small programs.

UTILITIES

This section introduces the following utilities, listed in alphabetical order:

admin	ld	sact
ar	lint	strip
cc	lorder	touch
comb	make	tsort
dbx	prof	unget
get	prs	
help	ranlib	

THE C LANGUAGE

The C language can be found in two main forms: K&R C and ANSI C. K&R, named for Brian Kernighan and Dennis Ritchie, the authors of the first popular C programming text, defines C as it was in the early days of UNIX. Some now refer to this as "Classic C." The American National Standards Institute defined a C standard of its own, adding some useful features and defining exact syntax for existing, but not well-defined, features. Most compilers support both standards.

Before we get into any source code, I'd like to make an important point: *The source code in this book does not conform to the ANSI C standard*. This is unfortunate, because ANSI C contains several nice syntactic and type-checking facilities that encourage maintainable and readable programs. The reason that I did not use these features is that several major corporations and universities that I know of firsthand support only K&R C. In order to make my source code as portable and useful as possible, I tailored the code to the most reasonable lowest common denominator. I didn't enjoy doing this, as I'm a professional software developer as well as an author, and it really goes against my grain. In fact, I'd rather have written all of the code in C++, but that's another story.

C COMPILERS

Until recently, a C compiler was a standard component in UNIX, especially UNIX versions that came with source code. (How else would you modify the code and create a new kernel?) Unfortunately, some vendors have chosen to "unroll" the C compilers from their UNIX distributions and sell them separately. Depending on your needs, you should check on this in any version of UNIX you are considering using. However, even if your version of UNIX no longer ships a C compiler, you have an alternative, thanks to the GNU Project: GNU C (gcc) and GNU C++ (g++) are freely available C and C++ compilers, respectively, on most UNIX platforms at the GNU Compiler Collection web site,

```
http://www.gnu.org/software/gcc/gcc.html
```

SINGLE-MODULE PROGRAMS

Let's examine a C program[1] that performs a simple task: reversing a string. To begin with, I'll show you how to write, compile, link, and execute a program that solves the problem using a single source file. Then I'll explain why it's better to split the program up into several independent modules, and I'll show you how to do that. Here's a source code listing of the first version of the reverse program:

```
1   /* REVERSE.C */
2
3   #include <stdio.h>
4
5   /* Function Prototype */
6   reverse ();
7
8   /***********************************************************/
9
10  main ()
11
12  {
13    char str [100]; /* Buffer to hold reversed string */
14
15    reverse ("cat", str); /* Reverse the string "cat" */
16    printf ("reverse ("cat") = %s\n", str); /* Display result */
17    reverse ("noon", str); /* Reverse the string "noon" */
18    printf ("reverse ("noon") = %s\n", str); /* Display Result */
19  }
20
21  /***********************************************************/
22
23  reverse (before, after)
24
25  char *before; /* A pointer to the source string */
26  char *after; /* A pointer to the reversed string */
27
28  {
29    int i;
30    int j;
31    int len;
32
33    len = strlen (before);
34
35    for (j = len - 1; i = 0; j >= 0; j--; i++) /* Reverse loop */
36      after[I] = before[j];
```

---

[1]Most of the examples used in this chapter are available on-line. (See the preface for more information.)

```
37
38    after[len] = NULL; /* NULL terminate reversed string */
39   }
```

Compiling a C Program

To write and run the reverse program, I first created a subdirectory called "reverse" inside my home directory and then created the file "reverse.c", using the UNIX **emacs** editor. I then compiled the C program with the **cc** utility.

To prepare an executable version of a single, self-contained program, follow **cc** with the name of the source code file, which must end in a ".c" suffix. **cc** doesn't produce any output when the compilation is successful. By default, **cc** creates an executable file called "a.out" in the current directory. To run the program, type "a.out". Any errors that are encountered are sent to the standard error channel, which is connected by default to your terminal's screen.

Here's what happened when I compiled my program:

```
$ mkdir reverse    ...create subdirectory for source code.
$ cd reverse
$ ... I created the file reverse.c using emacs.
$ cc reverse.c            ...compile source.
"reverse.c", line 16: syntax error at or near variable name "cat"
"reverse.c", line 18: syntax error at or near variable name "noon"
"reverse.c", line 35: syntax error at or near symbol ;
"reverse.c", line 35: syntax error at or near symbol )
$ _
```

As you can see, **cc** found a number of compile-time errors, listed together with their causes as follows:

- The errors on lines 16 and 18 were due to an inappropriate use of double quotes within double quotes.
- The errors on line 35 were due to an invalid use of a semicolon (;).

Since these errors were easy to correct, I copied the error-laden "reverse.c" file to a file called "reverse.old1.c" and then removed the compile-time errors via **emacs**. I left the original file in the directory so that I could see the evolution of my programming attempts.

A Listing of the Corrected Reverse Program

Here is the second, corrected version of the reverse program, with the lines containing the errors that I corrected in italics:

```
1   /* REVERSE.C */
2
3   #include <stdio.h>
4
```

```
 5   /* Function Prototype */
 6   reverse ();
 7
 8   /*****************************************************************/
 9
10   main ()
11
12   {
13     char str [100]; /* Buffer to hold reversed string */
14
15     reverse ("cat", str); /* Reverse the string "cat" */
16     printf ("reverse (\"cat\") = %s\n", str); /* Display */
17     reverse ("noon", str); /* Reverse the string "noon" */
18     printf ("reverse (\"noon\") = %s\n", str); /* Display */
19   }
20
21   /*****************************************************************/
22
23   reverse (before, after)
24
25   char *before; /* A pointer to the source string */
26   char *after; /* A pointer to the reversed string */
27
28   {
29     int i;
30     int j;
31     int len;
32
33     len = strlen (before);
34
35     for (j = len - 1, i = 0; j >= 0; j--, i++) /* Reverse loop */
36       after[i] = before[j];
37
38     after[len] = NULL; /* NULL terminate reversed string */
39   }
```

Running a C Program

After compiling the second version of "reverse.c", I ran it by typing the name of the executable file, "a.out". As you can see, the answers were correct:

```
$ cc reverse.c                ...compile source.
$ ls -l reverse.c a.out       ...list file information.
-rwxr-xr-x  1 glass       24576 Jan5 16:16 a.out*
-rw-r--r--  1 glass         439 Jan5 16:15 reverse.c
$ a.out                       ...run program.
reverse ("cat") = tac
reverse ("noon") = noon
$ _
```

Overriding the Default Executable Name

The name of the default executable file, "a.out", is rather cryptic, and an "a.out" file produced by a subsequent compilation would overwrite the one that I just produced. To avoid both problems, it's best to use the **-o** option with **cc**, which allows you to specify the name of the executable file that you wish to create:

```
$ cc reverse.c -o reverse     ...call the executable "reverse".
$ ls -l reverse
-rwxr-xr-x  1 glass        24576 Jan  5 16:19 reverse*
$ reverse                     ...run the executable "reverse".
reverse ("cat") = tac
reverse ("noon") = noon
$ _
```

MULTIMODULE PROGRAMS

The trouble with the way that I built the reverse program is that the reverse function cannot easily be used in other programs. For example, let's say that I wanted to write a function that returns 1 if a string is a palindrome and 0 otherwise. (A palindrome is a string that reads the same forward and backward; for example, "noon" is a palindrome, but "nono" is not.) I could use the reverse function to implement my palindrome function. One way to do this is to cut and paste reverse () into the palindrome program, but this is a poor technique for at least three reasons:

- Performing a cut-and-paste operation is slow.
- If we came up with a better piece of code for performing a reverse operation, we'd have to replace every copy of the old version with the new version, which is a maintenance nightmare.
- Each copy of reverse () soaks up disk space.

As I'm sure you realize, there's a better way to share functions.

Reusable Functions

A better strategy for sharing reverse () is to remove it from the reverse program, compile it separately, and then link the resultant object module into whichever programs you wish to use it with. This technique avoids all three of the problems listed in the previous section and allows the function to be used in many different programs. Functions with this property are termed *reusable*.

Preparing a Reusable Function

To prepare a reusable function, create a module that contains the source code of the function, together with a header file that contains the function's prototype. Then compile the source code module into an object module by using the **-c** option of **cc**. An object module contains machine code, together with information, in the form of a symbol table, that allows the module to be combined with other object modules when an executable file is being created. Here are the listings of the new "reverse.c" and "reverse.h" files:

reverse.h

```
1   /* REVERSE.H */
2
3   reverse (); /* Declare but do not define this function */
```

reverse.c

```
1   /* REVERSE.C */
2
3   #include <stdio.h>
4   #include "reverse.h"
5
6   /***************************************************************/
7
8   reverse (before, after)
9
10  char *before; /* A pointer to the original string */
11  char *after; /* A pointer to the reversed string */
12
13  {
14     int i;
15     int j;
16     int len;
17
18     len = strlen (before);
19
20     for (j = len - 1, i = 0; j >= 0; j--, i++) /* Reverse loop */
21        after[i] = before[j];
22
23     after[len] = NULL; /* NULL terminate reversed string */
24  }
```

Here's a listing of a main program that uses reverse ():

main1.c

```
1   /* MAIN1.C */
2
3   #include <stdio.h>
4   #include "reverse.h" /* Contains the prototype of reverse () */
5
6   /***************************************************************/
7
8   main ()
9
```

```
10  {
11     char str [100];
12
13     reverse ("cat", str); /* Invoke external function */
14     printf ("reverse (\"cat\") = %s\n", str);
15     reverse ("noon", str); /* Invoke external function */
16     printf ("reverse (\"noon\") = %s\n", str);
17  }
```

Compiling and Linking Modules Separately

To compile each source code file separately, use the **-c** option of **cc**. This creates a separate object module for each source code file, each with a ".o" suffix. The following commands are illustrative:

```
$ cc -c reverse.c          ...compile reverse.c to reverse.o.
$ cc -c main1.c            ...compile main1.c to main1.o.
$ ls -l reverse.o main1.o
-rw-r--r--  1 glass         311 Jan  5 18:24 main1.o
-rw-r--r--  1 glass         181 Jan  5 18:08 reverse.o
$ _
```

Alternatively, you can list all of the source code files on one line:

```
$ cc -c reverse.c main1.c        ...compile each .c file to .o file.
$ _
```

To link them all together into an executable called "main1", list the names of all the object modules after the **cc** command:

```
$ cc reverse.o main1.o -o main1   ...link object modules.
$ ls -l main1                      ...examine the executable.
-rwxr-xr-x  1 glass        24576 Jan  5 18:25 main1*
$ main1                            ...run the executable.
reverse ("cat") = tac
reverse ("noon") = noon
$ _
```

The Stand-Alone Loader: ld

When **cc** is used to link several object modules, it transparently invokes the UNIX stand-alone loader, **ld**, to do the job. The loader is better known as the *linker*. Although most C programmers never need to invoke **ld** directly, it's wise to know a little bit about it. Figure 12.1 describes the **ld** utility.

Utility: **ld** -n { -L*path* }* { *objModule* }* { *library* }* {-l*x*}* [-o *outputFile*]

ld links together the specified object and library modules to produce an executable file. You may override the default name of the executable file, "a.out", by using the **-o** option. If you wish to create a stand-alone executable file (as opposed to a dynamic link module, which is beyond the scope of this book), then you should specify the **-n** option.

When **ld** encounters an option of the form **-l*x***, it searches the standard directories "/lib", "/usr/lib", and "/usr/local/lib" for a library with the name "libx.a". To insert the directory *path* into this search path, use the **-L*path*** option.

The **ld** command (even more than most other UNIX commands) varies wildly from version to version. I strongly suggest that you consult the documentation for your version of UNIX when using **ld**.

FIGURE 12.1

Description of the **ld** command.

If you link a C program manually, it's important to specify the C run-time object module, "/lib/crt0.o", as the first object module, and to specify the standard C library, "/lib/libc.a", as a library module. Here's an example:

```
$ ld -n /lib/crt0.o main1.o reverse.o -lc -o main1 ...manual link.
$ main1                                         ...run program.
reverse ("cat") = tac
reverse ("noon") = noon
$ _
```

Reusing the Reverse Function

Now that you've seen how the original reverse program may be built out of a couple of modules, let's use the reverse module again to build the palindrome program. Here are the header and source code listing of the palindrome function:

palindrome.h

```
1   /* PALINDROME.H */
2
3   int palindrome (); /* Declare but do not define */
```

palindrome.c

```
1   /* PALINDROME.C */
2
3   #include "palindrome.h"
4   #include "reverse.h"
```

```
 5  #include <string.h>
 6
 7  /******************************************************************/
 8
 9  int palindrome (str)
10
11  char *str;
12
13  {
14    char reversedStr [100];
15    reverse (str, reversedStr); /* Reverse original */
16    return (strcmp (str, reversedStr) == 0); /* Compare the two */
17  }
```

Here's the source code of the program "main2.c" that tests the palindrome function ():

```
 1  /* MAIN2.C */
 2
 3  #include <stdio.h>
 4  #include "palindrome.h"
 5
 6  /******************************************************************/
 7
 8  main ()
 9
10  {
11    printf ("palindrome (\"cat\") = %d\n", palindrome ("cat"));
12    printf ("palindrome (\"noon\") = %d\n", palindrome ("noon"));
13  }
```

The way to combine the "reverse", "palindrome", and "main2" modules is as we did before; compile the object modules and then link them. We don't have to recompile "reverse.c", as it hasn't changed since the "reverse.o" object file was created.

```
$ cc -c palindrome.c              ...compile palindrome.c to palindrome.o.
$ cc -c main2.c                   ...compile main2.c to main2.o.
$ cc reverse.o palindrome.o main2.o -o main2    ...link them all.
$ ls -l reverse.o palindrome.o main2.o main2
-rwxr-xr-x  1 glass      24576 Jan  5 19:09 main2*
-rw-r--r--  1 glass        306 Jan  5 19:00 main2.o
-rw-r--r--  1 glass        189 Jan  5 18:59 palindrome.o
-rw-r--r--  1 glass        181 Jan  5 18:08 reverse.o
$ main2                           ...run the program.
palindrome ("cat") = 0
palindrome ("noon") = 1
$ _
```

Maintaining Multimodule Programs

Several different issues must be considered in maintaining multimodule systems:

1. What ensures that object modules and executable files are kept up to date?
2. What stores the object modules?
3. What tracks each version of source and header files?

Fortunately, there are UNIX utilities that address each problem. Here is an answer to each question:

A1. **make**, the UNIX file dependency system

A2. **ar**, the UNIX archive system

A3. **sccs**, the UNIX source code control system

THE UNIX FILE DEPENDENCY SYSTEM: make

You've now seen how several independent object modules may be linked into a single executable file. You've also seen that the same object module may be linked to several different executable files. Although multi-module programs are efficient in terms of reusability and disk space, they must be carefully maintained. For example, let's assume that we change the source code of "reverse.c" so that it uses pointers instead of array subscripts. This would result in a faster reverse function. In order to update the two main program executable files, "main1" and "main2", manually, we'd have to perform the following steps, in order:

1. Recompile "reverse.c".
2. Link "reverse.o" and "main1.o" to produce a new version of "main1".
3. Link "reverse.o" and "main2.o" to produce a new version of "main2".

Similarly, imagine a situation where a **#define** statement in a header file is changed. All of the source code files that directly or indirectly include the file must be recompiled, and then all of the executable modules that refer to the changed object modules must be relinked.

Although this might not seem like a big deal, imagine a system with a thousand object modules and 50 executable programs. Remembering all of the relationships among the headers, source code files, object modules, and executable files would be a nightmare. One way to avoid this problem is to use the UNIX **make** utility, which allows you to create a *makefile* that contains a list of all interdependencies for each executable file. Once such a file is created, re-creating the executable file is easy: You just use the **make** command

```
$ make -f makefile
```

Figure 12.2 provides synopsis of **make**.

Utility: **make** [-f *makefile*]

make is a utility that updates a file on the basis of a series of dependency rules stored in a special format, "make file". The **-f** option allows you to specify your own **make** filename; if none is specified, the name "makefile" is assumed.

FIGURE 12.2

Description of the **make** command.

Make Files

To use the **make** utility to maintain an executable file, you must first create a make file. This file contains a list of all the interdependencies that exist between the files that are used to create the executable file. A make file may have any name; I recommend that you name it by taking the name of the executable file and adding the suffix ".make". Thus, the name of the make file for "main1" would be called "main1.make". In its simplest form, a make file contains rules of the form shown in Figure 12.3, where *targetList* is a list of target files and *dependencyList* is a list of files that the files in *targetList* depend on. *commandList* is a list of zero or more commands, separated by newlines, that reconstruct the target files from the dependency files. Each line in *commandList* must start with a tab character. Rules must be separated by at least one blank line.

---

targetList:dependencyList

    commandList

FIGURE 12.3

make dependency specification.

For example, let's think about the file interdependencies related to the executable file "main1". This file is built out of two object modules: "main1.o" and "reverse.o". If either file is changed, then "main1" may be reconstructed by linking the files, using the **cc** utility. Therefore, one rule in "main1.make" would be

```
main1:      main1.o reverse.o
            cc main1.o reverse.o -o main1
```

This line of reasoning must now be carried forward to the two object files. The file "main1.o" is built from two files: "main1.c" and "reverse.h". (Remember that any file which is either directly or indirectly **#included** in a source file is effectively part of that file.) If either file is changed, then "main1.o" may be reconstructed by compiling "main1.c". Here, therefore, are the remaining rules in "main1.make":

```
main1.o:     main1.c reverse.h
             cc -c main1.c
reverse.o:   reverse.c reverse.h
             cc -c reverse.c
```

The Order of Make Rules

The order of make rules is important. The **make** utility creates a "tree" of interdependencies by initially examining the first rule. Each target file in the first rule is a root node of a dependency tree, and each file in its dependency list is added as a leaf of each root node. In our example, the initial tree would look like Figure 12.4.

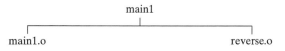

FIGURE 12.4

Initial **make** dependency tree.

The **make** utility then visits each rule associated with each file in the dependency list and performs the same actions. In our example, the final tree would, therefore, look like Figure 12.5.

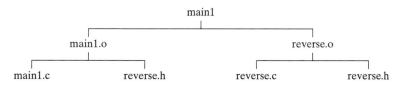

FIGURE 12.5

Final **make** dependency tree.

Finally, the **make** utility works up the tree from the bottom leaf nodes to the root node, looking to see if the last modification time of each child node is more recent than the last modification time of its immediate parent node. For every case where this is so, the associated parent's rule is executed. If a file is not present, its rule is executed regardless of the last modification times of its children. To illustrate the order in which the nodes would be examined, I've numbered the diagram shown in Figure 12.6.

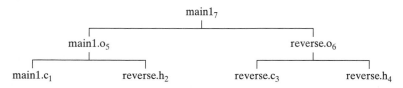

FIGURE 12.6

make ordering.

Executing a Make

Once a make file has been created, you're ready to run **make** to re-create the executable file whose dependency information is specified by the make file. To show you how this works, I deleted all of the object modules and the executable file to force every command list to execute. When I then performed the make, here's what I saw:

```
$ make -f main1.make      ...make executable up-to-date.
cc -c main1.c
cc -c reverse.c
cc main1.o reverse.o -o main1
$ _
```

Notice that every make rule was executed, in the exact order shown in Figure 12.6. Since I created a second executable file when I made the palindrome program, I also fashioned a second make file, called "main2.make". Here it is:

```
main2:          main2.o reverse.o palindrome.o
                cc main2.o reverse.o palindrome.o -o main2
main2.o:        main2.c palindrome.h
                cc -c main2.c
reverse.o:      reverse.c reverse.h
                cc -c reverse.c
palindrome.o:   palindrome.c palindrome.h reverse.h
                cc -c palindrome.c
```

When I performed a make using this file, I saw the following output:

```
$ make -f main2.make      ...make executable up-to-date.
cc -c main2.c
cc -c palindrome.c
cc main2.o reverse.o palindrome.o -o main2
$ _
```

Notice that "reverse.c" was not recompiled. This is because the previous make had already created an up-to-date object module, and **make** recompiles files only when necessary.

Make Rules

The make files that I've shown you so far are larger than they need to be. This is because some of the make rules that I supplied are already known by the **make** utility in a more general way. For example, note that several of the rules are of the form

```
xxx.o:      reverse.c reverse.h
            cc -c xxx.c
```

where xxx varies among rules. The **make** utility contains a predefined rule similar to

```
.c.o:
          /bin/cc -c -O $<
```

This cryptic-looking rule tells the **make** utility how to create an object module from a C source code file. The existence of this general rule allows me to leave off the C recompilation rule. Here, therefore, is a sleeker version of "main2.make":

```
main2:          main2.o reverse.o palindrome.o
                cc main2.o reverse.o palindrome.o -o main2
main2.o:        main2.c palindrome.h
reverse.o:      reverse.c reverse.h
palindrome.o:   palindrome.c palindrome.h reverse.h
```

The **make** utility also includes other inference rules. For example, **make** "knows" that the name of an object module and its corresponding source code file are usually related. It uses this information to infer standard dependencies. For example, it deduces that "main2.o" is dependent on "main2.c", and thus you may leave this information off the dependency list. Here is an even sleeker version of "main2.make":

```
main2:          main2.o reverse.o palindrome.o
                cc main2.o reverse.o palindrome.o -o main2
main2.o:        palindrome.h
reverse.o:      reverse.h
palindrome.o:   palindrome.h reverse.h
```

Writing Your Own Rules

Unfortunately, the method for writing your own rules, or even understanding the ones that already exist, is beyond the scope of this book. For more information, consult one of the sources listed under the heading "Other Make Facilities" later in the chapter.

Touch

To confirm that the new version of the make file worked, I requested a **make** and obtained the following output:

```
$ make -f main2.make
'main2' is up to date.
$ _
```

Obviously, since I'd already performed a successful **make**, another one wasn't going to trigger any rules! To force a **make** for testing purposes, I used a handy utility called **touch**, which makes the last modification time of all the named files equal to the current system time. Figure 12.7 gives a brief synopsis of **touch**.

Utility: **touch** -c { *fileName* }+

touch updates the last modification and access times of the named files to equal the current time. By default, if a specified file doesn't exist, it is created with zero size. To prevent this, use the **-c** option.

FIGURE 12.7

Description of the **touch** command.

I **touch**ed the file "reverse.h", which subsequently caused the recompilation of several source files:

```
$ touch reverse.h        ...fool make.
$ make -f main2.make
/bin/cc -c -O reverse.c
/bin/cc -c -O palindrome.c
cc main2.o reverse.o palindrome.o -o main2
$ _
```

Macros

The **make** utility supports primitive macros. If you specify a line of the form shown in Figure 12.8 at the top of a make file, every occurrence of $(token) in the make file is replaced with *replacementText*. In addition to containing rules, the standard rules file contains default definitions of macros such as CFLAGS, which are used by some of the built-in rules. For example, the rule that tells the **make** utility how to update an object file from a C source file looks like this:

```
.c.o:
            /bin/cc -c $(CFLAGS) $<
```

---

token = replacementText

FIGURE 12.8

A macro in **make**.

The standard rules file contains a line of the form

```
CFLAGS =     -O
```

If you wanted to recompile a suite of programs by using the **-p** option of **cc**, you would override the default value of CFLAGS at the top of the make file and use the **-p** option in the final call to **cc** in the "main2" rule, like this:

```
CFLAGS =          -p
main2:            main2.o reverse.o palindrome.o
```

```
                        cc -p main2.o reverse.o palindrome.o -o main2
main2.o:                palindrome.h
reverse.o:              reverse.h
palindrome.o:           palindrome.h reverse.h
```

To recompile the suite of programs, I used the **touch** utility to force recompilation of all the source files:

```
$ touch *.c        ...force make to recompile everything.
$ make -f main2.make
/bin/cc -c -p main2.c
/bin/cc -c -p palindrome.c
/bin/cc -c -p reverse.c
cc -p main2.o reverse.o palindrome.o -o main2
$ _
```

Other Make Facilities

make is a rather complicated utility and includes provisions for handling libraries and inference rules. Information on all but the library facilities is included in this book, and many other books contain less information about **make** than this one, so I suggest that you consult the UNIX **man** pages for more details.

THE UNIX ARCHIVE SYSTEM: ar

A medium-sized C project typically uses several hundred object modules. Specifying that many object modules in a make file rule can get rather tedious, so I recommend that you learn how to use the UNIX archive utility, **ar**, to organize and group your object modules. An archive utility, sometimes known as a *librarian*, allows you to perform the following tasks:

- creating a special archive format file ending in a ".a" suffix
- adding, removing, replacing, and appending any kind of file to an archive
- obtaining an archive's table of contents

Figure 12.9 gives synopsis of **ar**.

Utility: **ar** *key archiveName* { *fileName* }*

ar allows you to create and manipulate archives. *archiveName* is the name of the archive file that you wish to access, and it should end with a ".a" suffix. *key* may be one of the following:

    d   deletes a file from an archive
    q   appends a file onto the end of an archive, even if it's already present

---

FIGURE 12.9

Description of the **ar** command.

r	adds a file to an archive if it isn't already there, or replaces the current version if it is
t	displays an archive's table of contents to standard output
x	copies a list of files from an archive into the current directory
v	generates verbose output

FIGURE 12.9   (*Continued*)

When a set of object modules is stored in an archive file, it may be accessed from the **cc** compiler and the **ld** loader simply by supplying the name of the archive file as an argument. Any object modules that are needed from the archive file are automatically linked as necessary. This greatly reduces the number of parameters these utilities require when linking large numbers of object modules.

The rest of this section gives examples of each **ar** option.

Creating an Archive

An archive is automatically created when the first file is added. Therefore, to see how an archive is created, read the next section, "Adding a File."

Adding a File

To add a file to (or replace a file in) a named archive, use the **ar** utility with the **r** option, as shown in Figure 12.10. This option adds all of the specified files to the archive file *archiveName*, replacing files if they already exist. If the archive file doesn't exist, it is automatically created. The name of the archive should have a ".a" suffix.

ar r *archiveName* { *fileName* }+

FIGURE 12.10

Adding or replacing a file in an archive.

Appending a File

To append a file to a named archive, use the **ar** utility with the **q** option, as shown in Figure 12.11. This option appends all of the specified files to the archive file *archiveName*, regardless of whether they do or do not already exist. If the archive file doesn't exist, it is automatically created. The **q** option is handy if you know that the file isn't already present, as it enables **ar** to avoid searching through the archive.

ar q *archiveName* { *fileName* }+

FIGURE 12.11

Appending a file to an archive.

Obtaining a Table of Contents

To obtain a table of contents of an archive, use the **ar** utility with the **t** option, as shown in Figure 12.12.

```
ar t archiveName
```

FIGURE 12.12

Listing the table of contents of an archive.

Deleting a File

To delete a list of files from an archive, use the **ar** utility with the **d** option, as shown in Figure 12.13.

```
ar d archiveName { fileName }+
```

FIGURE 12.13

Deleting files from an archive.

Extracting a File

To copy a list of files from an archive to the current directory, use the **ar** utility with the **x** option, as shown in Figure 12.14. If you don't specify a list of files, then all of the files in the archive are copied.

```
ar x archiveName { fileName }+
```

FIGURE 12.14

Extracting a file from an archive.

Maintaining an Archive from the Command Line

The next example illustrates how an archive may be built and manipulated from the command line, using the object modules built earlier in the chapter. Later, I'll show how a library can be maintained automatically from a make file.

First, I built an archive file called "string.a" to hold all of my string-related object modules. Next, I added each module in turn, using the **r** option. Finally, I demonstrated the various **ar** options. The commands are as follows:

```
$ cc -c reverse.c palindrome.c main2.c      ...create object files.
$ ls *.o                                     ...confirm.
main2.o      palindrome.o          reverse.o
$ ar r string.a reverse.o palindrome.o       ...add to an archive.
ar: creating string.a
$ ar t string.a                              ...obtain a table of contents.
```

```
                 reverse.o
                 palindrome.o
                 $ cc main2.o string.a -o main2          ...link the object modules.
                 $ main2                                 ...execute the program.
                 palindrome ("cat") = 0
                 palindrome ("noon") = 1
                 $ ar d string.a reverse.o               ...delete a module.
                 $ ar t string.a                         ...confirm deletion.
                 palindrome.o
                 $ ar r string.a reverse.o               ...put it back again.
                 $ ar t string.a                         ...confirm addition.
                 palindrome.o
                 reverse.o
                 $ rm palindrome.o reverse.o             ...delete originals.
                 $ ls *.o                                ...confirm.
                 main2.o
                 $ ar x string.a reverse.o               ...copy them back again.
                 $ ls *.o                                ...confirm.
                 main2.oreverse.o
                 $ _
```

Maintaining an Archive by Using Make

Although an archive can be built and maintained from the command line, it's much
better to use **make**. To refer to an object file inside an archive, place the name of the
object file inside parentheses, preceded by the name of the archive. The **make** utility
has built-in rules that take care of the archive operations automatically. Here is the updated "main2.make" file that uses archives instead of plain object files:

```
main2:          main2.o string.a(reverse.o) string.a(palindrome.o)
                cc main2.o string.a -o main2
main2.o:        palindrome.h
string.a(reverse.o):     reverse.h
string.a(palindrome.o): palindrome.h reverse.h
```

Here is the output from a make performed with the use of the foregoing file:

```
$ rm *.o                          ...remove all object modules.
$ make -f main2.make              ...perform a make.
cc -c main2.c
cc -c reverse.c
ar rv string.a reverse.o          ...object module is saved.
a - reverse.o
ar: creating string.a
rm -f reverse.o                   ...original is removed.
cc -c palindrome.c
ar rv string.a palindrome.o
a - palindrome.o
rm -f palindrome.o
cc main2.o string.a -o main2      ...access archived object modules.
$ _
```

Notice that the built-in make rules automatically removed the original object file once it had been copied into the archive.

Ordering Archives

The built-in make rules do not maintain any particular order in an archive file. On most systems, this is fine, since the **cc** and **ld** utilities are able to extract object modules and resolve external references regardless of order. However, on some older systems, this is unfortunately not the case. Instead, if an object module A contains a function that calls a function in an object module B, then B must come before A in the link sequence. If A and B are in the same library, then B must appear before A in the library. If your system is one of these older types, then you'll probably get the following error at the end of the make shown in the previous example:

```
ld: Undefined symbol
    _reverse
*** Error code 2
make: Fatal error: Command failed for target 'main2'
```

This cryptic error occurs because "reverse.o" contains a call to palindrome () in "palindrome.o", which means that "reverse.o" should be *after* "palindrome.o" in the archive, but it isn't. To resolve the error, you must either reorder the modules in the archive, using the **lorder** and **tsort** utilities, or use **ranlib** as described in the next section. In the following example, I created a new ordered version of the old archive and then renamed it to replace the original:

```
$ ar cr string2.a elorder string.a | tsort'         ...order archive.
$ ar t string.a                                      ...old order.
reverse.o
palindrome.o
$ ar t string2.a                                     ...new order.
palindrome.o
reverse.o
$ mv string2.a string.a                 ...replace old archive.
$ make -f main2d.make                   ...try make again.
cc main2.o string.a -o main2
$ _
```

The make file then worked correctly.

For more information on **lorder** and **tsort**, use the **man** facility.

Creating a Table of Contents: `ranlib`

On older systems in which this ordering is a problem, you can help the linker to resolve out-of-order object modules by adding a table of contents to each archive, using the **ranlib** utility described in Figure 12.15. (If **ranlib** does not exist on your system, then you don't need to worry about ordering.)

> *Utility*: **ranlib** { *archive* }+
>
> **ranlib** adds a table of contents to each specified archive. (It does this by inserting an entry called _.SYMDEF into the archive.)

FIGURE 12.15

Description of the **ranlib** command.

In the next example, the unresolved reference error was due to an out-of-order sequence of object modules in the "string.a" archive. **cc** reminded me that I should add a table of contents, so I followed its recommendation. As you can see, the link was successful:

```
$ ar r string.a reverse.o palindrome.o    ...this order causes problems.
ar: creating string.a
$ cc main2.o string.a -o main2            ...compile fails.
ld: string.a: warning: archive has no table of contents; add one using
ranlib(1)
ld: Undefined symbol
  _reverse
$ ranlib string.a                         ...add table of contents.
$ cc main2.o string.a -o main2            ...no problem.
$ main2                                   ...program runs fine.
palindrome ("cat") = 0
palindrome ("noon") = 1
$ _
```

Shared Libraries

Static libraries work just fine for many applications. However, as the speed of processors has increased and the price of memory has come down, code has become more complex. Thus, programs linked with large archive libraries now produce very large executable files. (A small program that creates a single X window can be a megabyte when linked with the required X libraries.)

To reduce the size of the object code you generated, you can link your program with a *shared library* instead. A shared (or dynamic) library is associated with a compiled program, but its functions are loaded in dynamically as they are needed rather than all at once at load time. The resulting object code is smaller because it does not include the text of the library, as it does when linked with a static library.

The one disadvantage of using a shared library is that your object code will have been written for a specific version of the library. If the code is changed, but no interfaces are modified, then your program will benefit from the newer library that works better. However, if changes are made to library interfaces, then when your program links with the newer version of the library at run time, problems may (and probably will) result. It is therefore important to be aware of changes in supporting libraries when writing an application.

The **ld** command includes arguments that allow you to instruct it to build a shared library (on systems that support such libraries), rather than a static library, when it runs. These arguments vary in different versions of UNIX, and you should check your documentation. The most common form is **-shared**. You can also instruct **ld** to link with either static or dynamic libraries by using the **-B** argument (-Bstatic or -Bdynamic). Depending on your C compiler, the **cc** command may have one of these (or different) arguments to allow you to create a shared library at compile time.

THE UNIX SOURCE CODE CONTROL SYSTEM: SCCS

To maintain a large project properly, it's important to be able to store, access, and protect all of the versions of source code files. For example, if I decided to change reverse () to use pointers for efficiency reasons, it would be nice if I could easily go back and see how the source file looked *before* the changes were made. Similarly, it's important to be able to "lock out" other users from altering a file while you're actively modifying it. Here is an outline of how the UNIX source code control system SCCS works:

- When you create the original version of a function, you convert it into an "SCCS" format file using the **admin** utility. An SCCS format file is stored in a special way and may not be edited or compiled in the usual manner. The file contains information about the time and the user creating it. Future modifications will contain information about the changes that have been made from the previous version.
- Whenever you wish to edit an SCCS format file, you must first "check out" the latest version of the file, using the **get** utility. This creates a standard-format text file that you may edit and compile. The **get** utility also allows you to obtain a previous version of a file.
- When the new version of the file is complete, you must return it to the SCCS file by means of the **delta** utility. This command optimizes the storage of the sccs file by saving only the differences between the old version and the new version. The **get** utility does not allow anyone else to check out the file until you return it.
- The **sact** utility allows you to see the current editing activity on a particular SCCS file.

SCCS also contains the utilities **help**, **prs**, **comb**, **what**, and **unget**. Before we investigate the more advanced SCCS options, let's look at a sample session. In so doing, however, be warned that some systems vary in the way that SCCS works; I suggest that you consult **man** to see if the SCCS examples in this text tally with your own system's version of SCCS. Note that I discuss SCCS because it comes with most versions of UNIX. Other source code control software that may better suit your needs is available, both free from the Internet [e.g., GNU's Revision Control System (RCS)] and commercially for a price.

Creating an SCCS File

Utility: **admin** -i*name* -fl*list* -dl*list* -e*name* -a*name* *sccsfile*

admin is an SCCS utility that allows you to create and manipulate an SCCS format file. The **-i** option creates a file called *sccsfile* from the file *name*. *sccsfile* should have a ".s" prefix. The **-fl** and **-dl** options respectively allow you to lock and unlock a set of listed releases. The **-a** and **-e** options respectively allow you to add and subtract named users from the list of users that are able to obtain an editable version of the SCCS file. Once the SCCS file has been created, you may delete the original. If you get an error from any SCCS-related utility, invoke the SCCS **help** utility, with the code of the message as its argument.

FIGURE 12.16

Description of the SCCS **admin** command.

To create an SCCS file, use the **admin** utility, which works as shown in Figure 12.16. In the following example, I created an SCCS version of the "reverse.c" source file:

```
$ ls -l reverse.c                      ...look at the original.
-rw-r--r--   1 gglass            266 Jan  7 16:37 reverse.c
$ admin -ireverse.c s.reverse.c        ...create an SCCS file.
No id keywords (cm7)
$ help cm7                             ...get help on "cm7".
cm7: "No id keywords"
No SCCS identification keywords were substituted for. You may not have
any keywords in the file, in which case you can ignore this warning. If
this message came from delta then you just made a delta without any
keywords. If this message came from get then the last time you made a
delta you changed the lines on which they appeared. It's a little late
to be telling you that you messed up the last time you made a delta, but
this is the best we can do for now, and it's better than nothing.
This isn't an error, only a warning.
$ ls -l s.reverse.c                    ...look at the SCCS file.
-r--r--r--   1 gglass            411 Jan  7 17:39 s.reverse.c
$ rm reverse.c                         ...remove the original.
$ _
```

Figure 12.17 gives a synopsis of the **help** utility.

Utility: **help** { *message* }+

help is an SCCS utility that displays an explanation of the named key messages. Key messages are generated by other SCCS utilities in cases of warnings or fatal errors.

FIGURE 12.17

Description of the SCCS **help** command.

Checking Out a File

To make a read-only copy of an SCCS file, use the **get** utility described in Figure 12.18. In the following example, I checked out a read-only copy of the latest version of the "reverse.c" file:

```
$ get s.reverse.c        ...check out a read-only copy.
1.1                      ...version number.
29 lines                 ...number of lines in file.
No id keywords (cm7)
$ ls -l reverse.c        ...look at the copy.
-r--r--r--   1 gglass        266 Jan  7 18:04 reverse.c
$ _
```

Utility: **get** -e -p -r*revision sccsfile*

get is an SCCS utility that checks out a revision of a file from its SCCS counterpart. If no version number is supplied, the latest version is checked out. If the **-e** option is used, the file is modifiable and should be returned to the SCCS file by using **delta**; otherwise, it is read only and should not be returned. The **-p** option causes a read-only copy of the file to be displayed to standard output; no file is created.

FIGURE 12.18

Description of the SCCS **get** command.

The **get** command displays the version number of the file that is being checked out; in this case, it's the default, version 1.1. A version number is of the form *release.delta*. Note that Every time a change is saved to an SCCS file, the delta number is incremented automatically. The release number is changed only explicitly, with the use of the **get** utility. I'll show you how to create a new release a little later.

When you obtain a read-only version of an SCCS file, it may not be edited, and nothing is done to prevent anyone else from accessing the file. To check out an editable version of an SCCS file, use the **-e** option. This creates a writable file and prevents multiple "gets". The following commands illustrate the use of **-e**:

```
$ get -e s.reverse.c        ...check out a writeable version.
1.1
new delta 1.2               ...editable version is 1.2.
29 lines
$ ls -l reverse.c           ...look at it.
-rw-r-xr-x   1 gglass        266 Jan  7 18:05 reverse.c
$ get -e s.reverse.c        ...version is locked.
ERROR [s.reverse.c]: writable ereverse.c' exists (ge4)
$ _
```

Monitoring SCCS Activity

The **sact** utility displays a list of the current activity related to a named file. It works as shown in Figure 12.19. Here's the output of **sact** from the previous example:

```
$ sact s.reverse.c    ...monitor activity on "reverse.c".
1.1 1.2 gglass 98/01/07 18:05:11
$ _
```

Utility: **sact** { *sccsfile* }+

sact is an SCCS utility that displays the current editing activity on the named SCCS files. The output contains the version of the existing delta, the version of the new delta, the identity of the user that checked out the file with **get -e,** and the date and time that the **get -e** was executed.

FIGURE 12.19

Description of the SCCS **sact** command.

Undoing a Checkout and Returning a File

If you perform a **get** and then wish that you hadn't, you may undo the **get** by using the **unget** utility, which works as described in Figure 12.20. In the following example, assume that I had just performed a **get** on "reverse.c" and then changed my mind:

```
$ ls -l reverse.c           ...look at checked out file.
-rw-r-xr-x    1 gglass        266 Jan  7 18:05 reverse.c
$ unget s.reverse.c         ...return it.
1.2                         ...version of returned file.
$ ls -l reverse.c           ...original is gone.
reverse.c not found
$ sacts.reverse.c           ...original activity is gone.
No outstanding deltas for: s.reverse.c
$ _
```

Utility: **unget** -r*revision* -n { *sccsfile* }+

unget is an SCCS utility that reverses the effect of a previous **get. unget** restores the SCCS file to its former state, deletes the non-SCCS version of the file, and unlocks the file for other people to use. If several revisions are currently being edited, use the **-r** option to specify which revision you wish to **unget**. By default, **unget** moves the file back into the SCCS file. The **-n** option causes **unget** to *copy* the file instead, leaving the checked-out version in place.

FIGURE 12.20

Description of the SCCS **unget** command.

Creating a New Delta

Let's say that you check out an editable version of "reverse.c" and change it so that it uses pointers instead of array subscripts. Here is a listing of the new version:

```
1   /* REVERSE.C */
2
3   #include <stdio.h>
4   #include "reverse.h"
5
6
7   reverse (before, after)
8
9   char *before;
10  char *after;
11
12  {
13     char* p;
14
15     p = before + strlen (before);
16
17     while (p-- != before)
18        *after++ = *p;
19
20     *after = NULL;
21  }
```

When the new version of the file is saved, you must return it to the SCCS file by using the **delta** command, which works as shown in Figure 12.21. Here's an example:

```
$ delta s.reverse.c   ...return the modified checked out version.
comments? converted the function to use pointers    ...comment.
No id keywords (cm7)
1.2                     ...new version number.
5 inserted              ...description of modifications.
7 deleted
16 unchanged
$ ls -l reverse.c     ...the original was removed.
reverse.c not found
$ _
```

Utility: **delta** -r*revision* -n { *sccsfile* }+

delta is an SCCS utility that returns a checked-out file back to the specified SCCS file. The new version's delta number is equal to the old delta number plus one. As a

---

FIGURE 12.21

Description of the SCCS **delta** command.

> bonus, **delta** describes the changes that you made to the file. **delta** prompts you for a comment before returning the file. If the same user has two outstanding versions and wishes to return one of them, the **-r** option must be used to specify the revision number. By default, a file is removed after it is returned. The **-n** option prevents this.

FIGURE 12.21   (*Continued*)

Obtaining a File's History

To get a listing of an SCCS file's modification history, use the **prs** utility, which works as shown in Figure 12.22. Here's an example:

```
$ prs s.reverse.c        ...display the history.
s.reverse.c:
D 1.2 98/01/07 18:45:47 gglass 2 1        00005/00007/00016
MRs:
COMMENTS:
converted the function to use pointers
D 1.1 98/01/07 18:28:53 gglass 1 0        00023/00000/00000
MRs:
COMMENTS:
date and time created 98/01/07 18:28:53 by gglass
$ _
```

> *Utility:* **prs** -r*revision* { *sccsfile* }+
>
> **prs** is an SCCS utility that displays the history associated with the named SCCS files. By default, all of a file's history is displayed. You may limit the output to a particular version by using the **-r** option. The numbers in the right-hand column of the output refer to the number of lines inserted, deleted, and remaining unchanged, respectively.

FIGURE 12.22

Description of the SCCS **prs** command.

SCCS Identification Keywords

Several special character sequences can be placed in a source file and processed by **get** when read-only copies of a version are obtained. Figure 12.23 shows a few of the most common sequences. It's handy to place these sequences in a comment at the top of a source file. The comment won't affect your source code program and will be visible when the file is read. The next section contains an example of how the special character sequences are used.

Sequence	Replaced with
%M%	the name of the source code file
%I%	the release.delta.branch.sequence number
%D%	the current date
%H%	the current hour
%T%	the current time

FIGURE 12.23

SCCS identification keyword sequences.

Creating a New Release

To create a new release of an SCCS file, specify the new release number via the **-r** option of **get**. The new release number is based on the most recent version of the previous release. In the following example, I created release 2 of the "reverse.c" file and inserted the SCCS identification keywords described in the previous section:

```
$ get -e -r2 s.reverse.c        ...check out version 2.
1.2                             ...previous version number.
new delta 2.1                   ...new version number.
21 lines
$ vi reverse.c                  ...edit the writeable copy.
... I added the following lines at the top of the program:
/*
  Module: %M%
 SCCS Id: %I%
    Time: %D% %T%
*/
... and then saved the file.
$ delta s.reverse.c             ...return the new version.
comments? added SCCS identification keywords
2.1
6 inserted
0 deleted
21 unchanged
$ get -p s.reverse.c            ...display the file to standard output.
2.1
/* REVERSE.H */
/*
  Module: reverse.c
 SCCS Id: 2.1
    Time: 98/01/07 22:32:38
*/
... rest of file
$ _
```

Note that the keywords were replaced when I obtained a read-only copy of version 2 later in the example.

Checking Out Read-Only Copies of Previous Versions

To check out a version other than the latest, use the -r option of **get** to specify the version number. For example, let's say that I wanted to obtain a read-only copy of version 1.1 of "reverse.c". Here's how it's done:

```
$ get -r1.1 s.reverse.c      ...check out version 1.1.
1.1
23 lines
$ _
```

Checking Out Editable Copies of Previous Versions

If you want to obtain an editable copy of a previous version, use the -e or -r option of **get**. Let's say that I wanted to obtain an editable copy of version 1.1 of "reverse.c". The version of the editable copy cannot be 1.2, since that version already exists. Instead, **get** creates a new "branch" off the 1.1 version numbered 1.1.1.1, as shown in Figure 12.24. Deltas added to this branch are numbered 1.1.1.2, 1.1.1.3, etc. Here's an example:

```
$ get -e -r1.1 s.reverse.c   ...get a branch off version 1.1.
1.1
new delta 1.1.1.1
23 lines
$ _
```

FIGURE 12.24

Delta branching.

Editing Multiple Versions

You may simultaneously edit multiple revisions of a file; you must, however, specify the revision number of the file that you're returning when you perform the **delta**. You must also rename the copy when you obtain another copy, since all copies are given the same name. In the following example, I obtained a copy of version 1.1 and version 2.1 for editing and then saved them both:

```
$ get -e -r1.1 s.reverse.c      ...edit a new version based on 1.1.
1.1
new delta 1.1.1.1
23 lines
$ mv reverse.c reverse2.c        ...rename version 1.1.1.1.
```

```
$ get -e -r2.1 s.reverse.c    ...edit a new version based on 2.1.
2.1
new delta 2.2
27 lines
$ sact s.reverse.c            ...view sccs activity.
1.1 1.1.1.1 gglass 98/01/07 22:42:26
2.1 2.2 gglass 98/01/07 22:42:49
$ delta s.reverse.c           ...ambiguous return.
comments? try it
ERROR [s.reverse.c]: missing -r argument (de1)
$ delta -r2.1 s.reverse.c     ...return modified version 2.1.
comments? try again
2.2
0 inserted
0 deleted
27 unchanged
$ mv reverse2.c reverse.c     ...rename other version.
$ delta s.reverse.c           ...unambiguous return.
comments? save it
No id keywords (cm7)
1.1.1.1
0 inserted
0 deleted
23 unchanged
$ sact s.reverse.c
No outstanding deltas for: s.reverse.c
$ _
```

Deleting Versions

You may remove a delta from an SCCS file, as long as it's a leaf node on the SCCS version tree. To do this, use the **rmdel** utility, which works as shown in Figure 12.25. In the example shown in Figure 12.26, I wasn't allowed to delete version 1.1, as it's not a leaf node, but I was allowed to delete version 1.1.1.1. The accompanying commands are as follows:

```
$ rmdel -r1.1 s.reverse.c     ...try removing non-leaf node 1.1.
ERROR [s.reverse.c]: not a 'leaf' delta (rc5)
$ rmdel -r1.1.1.1 s.reverse.c     ...remove leaf node 1.1.1.1.
$ _
```

Utility: **rmdel** -r*revision sccsfile*

rmdel removes the specified version from an SCCS file, as long as it's a leaf node.

FIGURE 12.25

Description of the SCCS **rmdel** command.

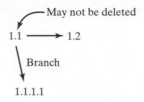

FIGURE 12.26

Only leaf nodes may be deleted.

Compressing SCCS Files

You may compress an SCCS file and remove any unnecessary deltas by using the **comb** utility, which works as shown in Figure 12.27. In the next example, assume that "s.reverse.c" contained several different versions. I compressed it into a smaller file containing just the latest version:

```
$ comb s.reverse.c > comb.out     ...generate script.
$ cat comb.out                    ...look at the script.
trap "rm -f COMB$$ comb$$ s.COMB$$; exit 2" 1 2 3 15
get -s -k -r2.3 -p s.reverse.c > COMB$$
...other lines go here.
rm comb$$
rm -f s.reverse.c
mv s.COMB$$ s.reverse.c
admin -dv s.reverse.c
$ chmod +x comb.out               ...make the script executable.
$ comb.out                        ...execute the script.
$ prs s.reverse.c                 ...look at the history.
s.reverse.c:
D 2.3 98/01/08 15:35:53 gglass 1 0   00028/00000/00000
MRs:
COMMENTS:
This was COMBined
$ _
```

Utility: **comb** { *sccsfile* }+

comb compresses an SCCS file so that it contains only the latest version of the source. Only the latest delta and the deltas that have branches remain. **comb** works by generating a Bourne shell script that must subsequently be run to perform the actual compression. The script is sent to standard output, so it must be saved and then executed.

FIGURE 12.27

Description of the SCCS **comb** command.

Restricting Access to SCCS Files

By default, a file may be checked out of an SCCS file by anyone. However, you may restrict access to one or more users (including groups of users) by using the **-a** and **-e** options to **admin**. The **-a** option may be followed by

- a user name, in which case the user is added to the list of users that may check out the file, and
- a group number, in which case any user in the group may check out the file

If the value is preceded by !, then the specified user is *denied* check-out rights. If you're using the C shell, be sure to escape the ! to prevent accidental reference to the history list. To remove a user from the list, use the **-e** option instead. Multiple **-a** and **-e** options may occur on a single command line. In the following example, I denied my own access rights and then restored them:

```
$ admin -a\!glass s.reverse.c       ...remove rights of user "glass".
$ get -e s.reverse.c                ...try to access.
2.3
ERROR [s.reverse.c]: not authorized to make deltas (co14)
$ admin -aglass s.reverse.c         ...restore access.
$ get -e s.reverse.c                ...no problem.
2.3
new delta 2.4
28 lines
$ unget s.reverse.c                 ...return file.
2.4
$ admin -atim s.reverse.c           ...add tim to user list.
$ admin -eglass s.reverse.c         ...deny "glass" access rights.
$ get -e s.reverse.c                ...try to access.
2.3
ERROR [s.reverse.c]: not authorized to make deltas (co14)
$ admin -aglass s.reverse.c         ...restore rights to "glass".
$ admin -a182 s.reverse.c           ...give access to group 182.
$ _
```

Locking Releases

You may prevent either a single release or all releases from being edited by using **admin** with the **-fl** and **-dl** options. To lock a particular release, follow **-fl** with the number of the release. To lock all releases, follow **-fl** with the letter "a". To release a lock, use the same rules, but with the **-dl** option. Here's an example:

```
$ admin -fla s.reverse.c            ...lock all releases.
$ get -e -r2.1 s.reverse.c          ...try to access.
2.1
ERROR [s.reverse.c]: SCCS file locked against editing (co23)
$ admin -dla s.reverse.c            ...release all locks.
$ get -e -r1.1 s.reverse.c          ...no problem.
```

```
1.1
new delta 1.1.1.1
21 lines
$ _
```

only for C prgms

THE UNIX PROFILER: prof

It's often handy to be able to see where a program is spending its time. For example, if a greater-than-expected amount of time is being spent in a particular function, it might be worth optimizing the function by hand for better performance. The **prof** utility allows you to obtain a program's profile. It works as shown in Figure 12.28. Here's an example of **prof** in action:

```
$ main2                     ...execute the program.
palindrome ("cat") = 0   ...program output.
palindrome ("noon") = 1
$ ls -l mon.out             ...list the monitor output.
-rw-r-xr-x    1 gglass       1472 Jan  8 17:19 mon.out
$ prof main2 mon.out    ...profile the program.
%Time Seconds Cumsecs  #Calls   msec/call  Name
 42.9   0.05    0.05                        rdpcs
 42.9   0.05    0.10    2002      0.025     reverse
 14.3   0.02    0.12    2002      0.008     palindrome
  0.0   0.00    0.12      1       0.        main
$ prof -l main2             ...order by name
%Time Seconds Cumsecs  #Calls   msec/call  Name
  0.0   0.00    0.05      1       0.        main
 14.3   0.02    0.07    2002      0.008     palindrome
 42.9   0.05    0.05                        rdpcs
 42.9   0.05    0.12    2002      0.025     reverse
$ _
```

After a profile has been viewed, you may decide to do some hand tuning and then obtain another profile.

Utility: **prof** -ln [*executableFile* [*profileFile*]]

prof is the standard UNIX profiler. It generates a table indicating the time spent processing each function and the number of calls to the function in the executable file *executableFile*, based on the performance trace stored in the file *profileFile*. If *profileFile* is omitted, "mon.out" is assumed. If *executableFile* is omitted, "a.out" is assumed. The executable file must have been compiled using the **-p** option of **cc**, which instructs the compiler to generate special code that writes a "mon.out" file when the program runs. The **prof** utility then looks at this output file after the

---

FIGURE 12.28

Description of the **prof** command.

program has terminated and displays the information contained therein. For information on how to make a file using the -p option, refer to the "make" section of this chapter. By default, the profile information is listed in descending order of time. The -l option orders the information by name, and the **-n** option orders the information by cumulative time.

FIGURE 12.28   (*Continued*)

DOUBLE-CHECKING PROGRAMS: lint

C has a handy utility called **lint**, described in Figure 12.29, that checks your program more thoroughly than **cc** does. If you're building a program out of several source modules, it's a good idea to specify them all on the same command line so that **lint** can check interactions among modules. Here's an example that demonstrates the difference between checking a single module and checking a number of modules:

```
$ lint reverse.c              ...check "reverse.c".
reverse defined( reverse.c(12) ), but never used
$ lint palindrome.c           ...check "palindrome.c".
palindrome defined( palindrome.c(12) ), but never used
reverse used( palindrome.c(14) ), but not defined
$ lint main2.c
...check "main2.c".
main2.c(11): warning: main() returns random value to invocation
environment
printf returns value which is always ignored
palindrome used( main2.c(9) ), but not defined
$ lint main2.c reverse.c palindrome.c
...check all modules together.
main2.c:
main2.c(11): warning: main() returns random value to invocation
environment
reverse.c:
palindrome.c:
Lint pass2:
printf returns value which is always ignored
$ _
```

> *Utility*: **lint** { *fileName* }*
>
> **lint** scans the specified source files and displays any potential errors that it finds.

FIGURE 12.29

Description of the **lint** command.

THE UNIX DEBUGGER: dbx

The UNIX debugger, **dbx**, allows you to debug a program symbolically. Although it's not as good as most professional debuggers on the market, **dbx** comes as a handy standard utility in most versions of UNIX. It includes the following facilities:

- single stepping
- breakpoints
- editing from within the debugger
- accessing and modifying variables
- searching for functions
- tracing

Utility: **dbx** *executableFilename*

dbx is a standard UNIX debugger. The named executable file is loaded into the debugger and a user prompt is displayed. To obtain information on the various **dbx** commands, enter **help** at the prompt.

FIGURE 12.30

Description of the **dbx** command.

Figure 12.30 gives a synopsis of **dbx**. To demonstrate **dbx**, let's debug the following recursive version of palindrome ():

```
1   /* PALINDROME.C */
2
3   #include "palindrome.h"
4   #include <string.h>
5
6
7   enum { FALSE, TRUE };
8
9
10  int palindrome (str)
11
12  char *str;
13
14  {
15     return (palinAux (str, 1, strlen (str)));
16  }
17
18  /*************************************************************/
19
20  int palinAux (str, start, stop)
```

```
21
22   char *str;
23   int start;
24   int stop;
25
26   }
27     if (start >= stop)
28         return (TRUE);
29     else if (str[start] != str[stop])
30         return (FALSE);
31     else
32         return (palinAux (str, start + 1, stop - 1));
33   }
```

Preparing a Program for Debugging

To debug a program, it must have been compiled using the **-g** option to **cc**, which places debugging information into the object module.

Entering the Debugger

Once a program has been compiled correctly, you may invoke **dbx**, with the name of the executable file as the first argument. **dbx** presents you with a prompt. I recommend that you enter **help** at the prompt to see a list of all the **dbx** commands:

```
$ dbx main2          ...enter the debugger.
dbx version sr10.3(4) of 7/6/90 17:52
reading symbolic information ...
Type 'help' for help.
(dbx) help          ...obtain help.
run [args]                    - begin execution of the program
stop at <line>                - suspend execution at the line
stop in <func>                - suspend execution when <func> is called
stop if <cond>                - suspend execution when <cond> is true
trace <line#>                 - trace execution of the line
trace <func>                  - trace calls to the function
trace <var>                   - trace changes to the variable
trace <exp> at <line#>        - print <exp> when <line> is reached
status                        - print numbered list of traces and stops in
                                effect
delete <#> [<#> ...]          - cancel trace or stop of each number given
cont                          - continue execution from where it stopped
step                          - execute one source line, stepping into functions
next                          - execute one source line, skipping over calls
return                        - continue until the current function returns
call <func>(<params>)         - execute the given function call
print <exp> [, <exp> ...]     - print the values of the expressions
where                         - print currently active procedures
whatis <name>                 - print the declaration of the name
assign <var> = <exp>          - assign the program variable the value of <exp>
```

```
dump <func>                - print all variables in the active function
list [<line#> ], <line#>>  - list source lines
use <directory-list>       - set the search path for source files
sh <command-line>          - pass the command line to the shell
quit                       - exit dbx
(dbx) _
```

Running a Program

To run your program, enter the **run** command, which runs the program to completion:

```
(dbx) run                ...run the program.
palindrome ("cat") = 0
palindrome ("noon") = 0
program exited
(dbx) _
```

Oops! The string "noon" is a palindrome, but my function thinks that it isn't. Time to delve into **dbx**.

Tracing a Program

To obtain a line-by-line **trace**, use the trace command. When any kind of trace is requested, **dbx** returns an index number that can be used by the **delete** command to turn off the trace. In continuing this example, I restarted the program from the beginning by using the **rerun** command:

```
(dbx) trace        ...request a trace.
[1] trace          ...request is #1.
(dbx) rerun        ...run the program from the start.
trace:      9    printf ("palindrome (\"cat\") = %d\n", palindrome
("cat"));
trace:     10    int palindrome (str)
trace:     15      return (palinAux (str, 1, strlen (str)));
trace:     20    int palinAux (str, start, stop)
trace:     27      if (start >= stop)
trace:     29      else if (str[start] != str[stop])
trace:     30        return (FALSE);
trace:     33    }
trace:     33    }
trace:     16    }
palindrome ("cat") = 0
trace:     10      printf ("palindrome (\"noon\") = %d\n", palindrome
("noon"));
trace:     10    int palindrome (str)
trace:     15      return (palinAux (str, 1, strlen (str)));
trace:     20    int palinAux (str, start, stop)
trace:     27      if (start >= stop)
trace:     29      else if (str[start] != str[stop])
trace:     30        return (FALSE);
```

```
trace:      33   }
trace:      33   }
trace:      16   }
palindrome ("noon") = 0
trace:      11   }
trace:      11   }
program exited
(dbx) _
```

Tracing Variables and Function Calls

A trace may be placed on a variable's value or a call to a particular function by adding parameters to the **trace** command. The syntax for **trace** is shown in Figure 12.31. Here's the output from **dbx** after three new traces were added and then the program was restarted:

```
(dbx) trace start in palinAux    ...trace the variable called "start".
[2] trace start in palinAux
(dbx) trace stop in palinAux     ...trace the variable called "stop".
[3] trace stop in palinAux
(dbx) trace palinAux             ...trace the function "palinAux".
[4] trace palinAux
(dbx) rerun                      ...run the program from the start.
trace:       9     printf ("palindrome (\"cat\") = %d\n", palindrome
("cat"));
trace:      10   int palindrome (str)
trace:      15     return (palinAux (str, 1, strlen (str)));
trace:      20   int palinAux (str, start, stop)
calling palinAux(str = "cat", start = 1, stop = 3) from function
palindrome.palindrome
trace:      27      if (start >= stop)
initially (at line 27 in "/home/glass/reverse/palindrome.c"): start = 1
initially (at line 27 in "/home/glass/reverse/palindrome.c"): stop = 3
trace:      29      else if (str[start] != str[stop])
trace:      30        return (FALSE);
trace:      33   }
trace:      33   }
trace:      16   }
palindrome ("cat") = 0
trace:      10     printf ("palindrome (\"noon\") = %d\n", palindrome
("noon"));
trace:      10   int palindrome (str)
trace:      15     return (palinAux (str, 1, strlen (str)));
trace:      20   int palinAux (str, start, stop)
after line 20 in "/home/glass/reverse/palindrome.c": stop = 4
calling palinAux(str = "noon", start = 1, stop = 4) from function
palindrome.palindrome
trace:      27      if (start ,= stop)
trace:      29      else if (str[start] != str[stop])
trace:      30        return (FALSE);
```

```
trace:      33   }
trace:      33   }
trace:      16   }
palindrome ("noon") = 0
trace:      11   }
trace:      11   }
program exited
(dbx) _
```

---

trace *variable* **in** *function*

and to trace a call to a named function, use the syntax:

trace *function*

FIGURE 12.31

The *trace* command in **dbx**.

The Bug

By now, the nature of the bug is fairly clear: The values of *start* and *stop* are incorrect, each being one greater than it should be. It's a very common error to forget that C array indices begin at zero rather than one. You may call up the editor specified by the $EDITOR environment variable by using the **edit** command. This is handy for correcting errors on the fly, although you must remember to recompile the program before debugging it again. Here is the correct version of the palindrome () function:

```
int palindrome (str)
char *str;
{
 return (palinAux (str, 0, strlen (str) - 1));
}
```

I'll end this section with a brief discussion of some useful miscellaneous **dbx** commands for setting breakpoints, single stepping, accessing variables, and listing portions of a program.

Breakpoints

To make **dbx** stop when it encounters a particular function, use the **stop** command. This allows you to run a program at full speed until the function that you wish to examine more closely is executed. The following dbx commands are illustrative:

```
(dbx) stop in palinAux          ...set breakpoint.
[7] stop in palinAux
(dbx) rerun                     ...run the program from the start.
trace:     9     printf ("palindrome (\"cat\") = %d\n", palindrome
("cat"));
```

```
trace:      10    int palindrome (str)
trace:      15       return (palinAux (str, 1, strlen (str)));
trace:      20    int palinAux (str, start, stop)
calling palinAux(str = "cat", start = 1, stop = 3) from function
palindrome.palindrome
[7] stopped in palinAux at line 27 in file
"/home/glass/reverse/palindrome.c"
  27      if (start >= stop)
(dbx) _
```

Single Stepping

To step through a program one line at a time, use the **step** command. This command causes **dbx** to redisplay its prompt immediately after each line of the program has been executed. The command is useful for high-resolution interrogation of a function. In the following example, I entered **step** after my program stopped at line 27:

```
(dbx) step          ...execute line after #27 and then stop.
trace:      29       else if (str[start] != str[stop])
initially (at line 29 in "/home/glass/reverse/palindrome.c"):
start = 1
initially (at line 29 in "/home/glass/reverse/palindrome.c"):
stop = 3
stopped in palinAux at line 29 in file
"/home/glass/reverse/palindrome.c"
  29      else if (str[start] != str[stop])
(dbx) _
```

Accessing Variables

To print the value of a particular variable at any time, use the **print** command. The **whatis** command displays a variable's declaration, and the **which** command tells you where the variable is declared. The **where** command displays a complete stack trace, and the **whereis** command tells you where a particular function is located. All of these commands appear in the following example:

```
(dbx) print start       ...display current value of start.
1
(dbx) whatis start      ...get type information.
int start;
(dbx) which start       ...find its location.
palindrome.palinAux.start
(dbx) where             ...obtain stack trace.
palinAux(str = "cat", start = 1, stop = 3), line 29 in
"/home/glass/reverse/palindrome.c"
palindrome.palindrome(str = "cat"), line 15 in
"/home/glass/reverse/palindrome.c"
main(), line 9 in "/home/glass/reverse/main2.c"
unix_$main() at 0x3b4e7a14
_start(), line 137 in "//garcon/unix_src/lang/sgs/src/crt0/crt0.c"
```

```
(dbx) whereis palinAux   ...locate a function.
palindrome.palinAux
(dbx) whereis start      ...locate a variable.
palindrome.palinAux.start
(dbx) _
```

Listing a Program

The **list** command allows you to list the first few lines of a function, and the / and ? commands allow you to search forwards and backwards through text, respectively, as shown in the following example:

```
(dbx) list palindrome          ...list ten lines.
    5
    6
    7    enum { FALSE, TRUE };
    8
    9
   10    int palindrome (str)
   11
   12    char* str;
   13
   14    {
   15      return (palinAux (str, 1, strlen (str)));
(dbx) list 10,20          ...list lines 10 thru 20.
   10    int palindrome (str)
   11
   12    char* str;
   13
   14    }
   15      return (palinAux (str, 1, strlen (str)));
   16    {
   17
   18    /*************************************************************/
   19
   20    int palinAux (str, start, stop)
   21
(dbx) ?palinAux            ...search backward for string "palinAux".
   20    int palinAux (str, start, stop)
(dbx) /palinAux            ...search forward for string "palinAux".
   32          return (palinAux (str, start + 1, stop - 1));
(dbx) _
```

Leaving the Debugger

To quit **dbx**, use the **quit** command:

```
(dbx) quit              ...leave the debugger.
$ _
```

You will now be back in your shell.

Summary

In this section, I've presented a smattering of the commonly used **dbx** commands. Utilized wisely, they can provide useful hints about the errors in your program. In my own opinion, **dbx** is actually a pretty poor debugger compared with some of the popular PC debuggers, such as Borland's Turbo Debugger, and advanced UNIX system debuggers, such as ObjectWorks\C++. On the positive side, at least **dbx** is available on most UNIX machines, which makes a rudimentary understanding of its operation handy.

WHEN YOU'RE DONE: strip

The debugger and profile utilities both require you to compile a program using special options, each of which adds code to the executable file. To remove this extra code after debugging and profiling are finished, use the **strip** utility, which works as shown in Figure 12.32. Here's an example of how much space you can save:

```
$ ls -l main2            ...look at original file.
-rwxr-xr-x   1 gglass     5904 Jan  8 22:18 main2*
$ strip main2            ...strip out spurious information.
$ ls -l main2            ...look at stripped version.
-rwxr-xr-x   1 gglass     3373 Jan  8 23:17 main2*
$ _
```

Synopsis: **strip** { *fileName* }+

strip removes all of the symbol table, relocation, debugging, and profiling information from the named files.

FIGURE 12.32

Description of the **strip** command.

CHAPTER REVIEW

Checklist

In this chapter, I described utilities that

- compile C programs
- manage the compilation of programs with many modules
- maintain archives
- maintain multiple versions of source code
- profile executable files
- debug executable files

Quiz

1. Why is it helpful to have a history of your source code?
2. What's the definition of a leaf node on an SCCS delta tree?
3. What's the benefit of the **-q** option of **ar**?
4. Can the **make** utility use object modules stored in an archive file?
5. What does the term "reusable function" mean?
6. Why would you profile an executable file?
7. Describe briefly what the **strip** utility does.

Exercises

12.1 Create a shared library with a simple function that returns an integer value. Then write a program to call the function and print its return value. After compiling and running the program, make a change to the library function, rebuild the library, and run the program again (without recompiling the main program). What happens if you rename the function in the shared library? [level: *easy*]

12.2 Compile "reverse.c" and "palindrome.c" and place them into an archive called "string.a". Write a main program in "prompt.c" that prompts the user for a string and then outputs 1 if the string is a palindrome and 0 otherwise. Create a make file that links "prompt.o" with the reverse () and palindrome () functions stored in "string.a". Use **dbx** to debug your code if necessary. [level: *medium*]

12.3 Try a modern debugger such as the Borland C++ source-level debugger. How does it compare with **dbx**? [level: *medium*].

Projects

1. Write a paper that describes how you would use the utilities presented in this section to help manage a 10-person computing team. [level: *medium*]
2. Replace the original version of palindrome () stored in "palindrome" with a pointer-based version. Use SCCS to manage the source code changes and **ar** to replace the old version in "string.a". [level: *medium*].

# CHAPTER 13

Systems Programming

MOTIVATION

If you're a C programmer and you wish to take advantage of the UNIX multitasking and interprocess communication facilities, it's essential that you have a good knowledge of the UNIX system calls.

PREREQUISITES

In order to understand this chapter, you should have a good working knowledge of C. For the Internet section of the chapter, it helps if you have read Chapters 9 and 10.

OBJECTIVES

In this chapter, I'll explain and demonstrate a majority of the UNIX system calls, including those which support I/O, process management, and interprocess communication.

PRESENTATION

The information is presented in the form of several sample programs, including a shell designed for the Internet. Most sample code is available on-line. (See the preface for more information.)

SYSTEM CALLS AND LIBRARY ROUTINES

The following system calls and library routines, listed in alphabetical order, are presented:

accept	fchown	inet_addr	perror
alarm	fcntl	inet_ntoa	pipe
bind	fork	ioctl	read
bzero	fstat	kill	setegid

see pg 669 for a listing of all system calls

chdir	ftruncate	lchown	seteuid
chmod	getdents	link	setgid
chown	getegid	listen	setpgid
close	geteuid	lseek	setuid
connect	getgid	lstat	signal
dup	gethostbyname	memset	socket
dup2	gethostname	mknod	stat
execl	getpgid	nice	sync
execlp	getpid	ntohl	truncate
execv	getppid	ntohs	unlink
execvp	getuid	open	wait
exit	htonl	pause	write
fchmod	htons		

INTRODUCTION

In order to make use of services such as file creation, process duplication, and inter-process communication, application programs must "talk" to the operating system. They can do this via a collection of routines called *system calls*, which are the programmer's functional interface to the UNIX kernel. System calls are just like library routines, except that they perform a subroutine call directly into the heart of UNIX.

UNIX system calls can be loosely grouped into the following three main categories:

- file management
- process management
- error handling

Interprocess communication (IPC) is, in fact, a subset of file management, since UNIX treats IPC mechanisms as special files. Figure 13.1 shows a diagram that illustrates the

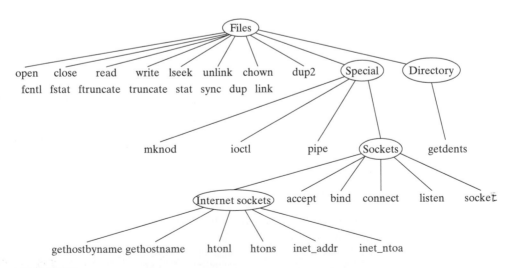

FIGURE 13.1

File management system call hierarchy.

file management system call hierarchy. The process management system call hierarchy includes routines for duplicating, differentiating, and terminating processes, as shown in Figure 13.2. The only system call that supports error handling is perror (), which I'll put in a hierarchy just to be consistent. This hierarchy is shown in Figure 13.3. In what

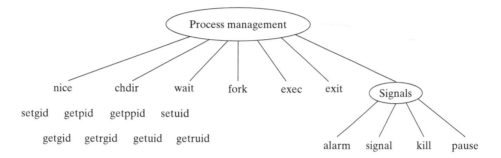

FIGURE 13.2

Process management system call hierarchy.

FIGURE 13.3

Error handling hierarchy.

follows, we cover the system calls shown in these hierarchy diagrams in the following order:

- **Error handling**. I start the chapter with a description of perror ().
- **Regular file management**. This includes information on how to create, open, close, read, and write regular files. We'll also see a short overview of STREAMS.
- **Process management**. Relevant here are how to duplicate, differentiate, suspend, and terminate processes. Multithreaded processes are discussed briefly.
- **Signals**. Although the signal facility could be considered a subtopic of either process management or interprocess communication, it's a significant enough topic to warrant a section of its own.
- **IPC**. Interprocess communication takes place via pipes (both unnamed and named) and sockets (including information about Internet sockets). Brief overviews of two newer IPC mechanisms found in some versions of UNIX— shared memory and semaphores—are presented.

The chapter ends with a source code listing and a discussion of a complete Internet shell, which is a shell that supports piping and redirection to other Internet shells on remote hosts. The Internet shell program uses most of the facilities described in this chapter.

ERROR HANDLING: perror ()

Most system calls are capable of failing in some way. For example, the open () system call will fail if you try to open a nonexistent file for reading. By convention, all system calls return −1 if an error occurs. However, this doesn't tell you much about *why* the error occurred; the open () system call can fail for one of several different reasons. If you want to deal with system call errors in a systematic way, you must know about the following two things:

- **errno**, a global variable that holds the numeric code of the last system call error
- perror (), a subroutine that describes system call errors

Every process contains a global variable called **errno**, which is originally set to zero when the process is created. When a system call error occurs, **errno** is set to the numeric code associated with the cause of the error. For example, if you try to open a file that doesn't exist for reading, **errno** is set to 2. The file "/usr/include/sys/errno.h" contains a list of the predefined error codes. Here's a snippet of this file:

```
#define      EPERM      1   /* Not owner */
#define      ENOENT     2   /* No such file or directory */
#define      ESRCH      3   /* No such process */
#define      EINTR      4   /* Interrupted system call */
#define      EIO        5   /* I/O error */
```

A successful system call never affects the current value of **errno**, and an unsuccessful system call always overwrites the current value of **errno**. To access **errno** from your program, include <errno.h>. The perror () subroutine converts the current value of **errno** into an English description and works as shown in Figure 13.4. Your program

---

Library Routine: void **perror** (char* *str*)

perror () displays the string *str*, followed by a colon, followed by a description of the last system call error. If there is no error to report, perror () displays the string "Error 0." Actually, perror () isn't a system call—it's a standard C library routine.

FIGURE 13.4

Description of the perror () library routine.

should check system calls for a return value of −1 and then deal with the situation immediately. One of the first things to do, especially during debugging, is to call perror () for a description of the error.

In the following example, I forced a couple of system call errors to demonstrate perror () and then demonstrated that **errno** retained the last system call error code even after a successful call was made: The only way to reset **errno** is to manually assign it to zero.

```
$ cat showErrno.c
#include <stdio.h>
```

```
#include <sys/file.h>
#include <errno.h>
main ()
{
 int fd;
  /* Open a non-existent file to cause an error */
 fd = open ("nonexist.txt", O_RDONLY);
 if (fd == -1) /* fd == -1 =, an error occurred */
   {
     printf ("errno = %d\n", errno);
     perror ("main");
   }
 fd = open ("/", O_WRONLY); /* Force a different error */
 if (fd == -1)
   {
     printf ("errno = %d\n", errno);
     perror ("main");
   }
 /* Execute a successful system call */
 fd = open ("nonexist.txt", O_RDONLY | O_CREAT, 0644);
 printf ("errno = %d\n", errno); /* Display after successful call */
 perror ("main");
 errno = 0; /* Manually reset error variable */
 perror ("main");
}
```

Don't worry about how open () works; I'll describe it later in the chapter. Here's the output from the program:

```
$ showErrno              ...run the program.
errno = 2
main: No such file or directory
errno = 21               ...even after a successful call
main: Is a directory
errno = 21
main: Is a directory
main: Error 0
$ _
```

REGULAR FILE MANAGEMENT

My description of file management system calls is split up into four main subsections:

- A primer that describes the main concepts behind UNIX files and file descriptors.
- A description of the basic file management system calls, using a sample program called "reverse" that reverses the lines of a file.
- An explanation of a few advanced system calls, using a sample program called "monitor," which periodically scans directories and displays the names of files within them that have changed since the last scan.

- A description of the remaining file management system calls, using some miscellaneous snippets of source code.

A File Management Primer

The file management system calls allow you to manipulate the full collection of regular, directory, and special files, including the following:

- disk-based files
- terminals
- printers
- interprocess communication facilities, such as pipes and sockets

In most cases, open () is used to initially access or create a file. If open () succeeds, it returns a small integer called a *file descriptor* that is used in subsequent I/O operations on that file. If open () fails, it returns −1. Here's a snippet of code that illustrates a typical sequence of events:

```
int fd; /* File descriptor */
...
fd = open (fileName, ...); /* Open file, return file descriptor */
if (fd == -1) { /* deal with error condition */ }
...
fcntl (fd, ...); /* Set some I/O flags if necessary */
...
read (fd, ...); /* Read from file */
...
write (fd, ...); /* Write to file */
...
lseek (fd, ...); /* Seek within file*/
...
close (fd); /* Close the file, freeing file descriptor */
```

When a process no longer needs to access an open file, it should close it, using the close () system call. All of a process' open files are automatically closed when the process terminates. Although this means that you may often omit an explicit call to close (), it's better programming practice to close your files.

File descriptors are numbered sequentially, starting from zero. By convention, the first three file descriptor values have a special meaning, as shown in Figure 13.5. For

Value	Meaning
0	standard input (stdin)
1	standard output (stdout)
2	standard error (stderr)

FIGURE 13.5

File descriptor values for standard I/O channels.

example, the printf () library function always sends its output by means of file descriptor 1, and scanf () always reads its input via file descriptor 0. When a reference to a file is closed, the file descriptor is freed and may be reassigned by a subsequent open (). Most I/O system calls require a file descriptor as their first argument so that they know which file to operate on.

A single file may be opened several times and may thus have several file descriptors associated with it, as shown in Figure 13.6. Each file descriptor has its own private

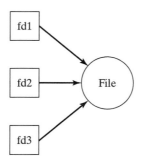

FIGURE 13.6

Many file descriptors, one file.

set of properties, such as the following, that have nothing to do with the file with which the descriptor is associated:

- A file pointer that records the offset in the file it is reading or writing. When a file descriptor is created, its file pointer is positioned at offset 0 in the file (the first character) by default. As the process reads or writes, the file pointer is updated accordingly. For example, if a process opened a file and then read 10 bytes from the file, the file pointer would end up positioned at offset 10. If the process then wrote 20 bytes, the bytes at offset 10..29 in the file would be overwritten, and the file pointer would end up positioned at offset 30.
- A flag that indicates whether the descriptor should automatically be closed if the process execs. [exec () is described later in the chapter.]
- A flag that indicates whether all of the output to the file should be appended to the end of the file.

In addition to these properties, the following ones are meaningful only if the file is a special file such as a pipe or a socket:

- A flag that indicates whether a process should block on input from the file if the file doesn't currently contain any input.
- A number that indicates a process ID or process group that should be sent a SIGIO signal if input becomes available on the file. (Signals and process groups are discussed later in the chapter.)

The system calls open () and fcntl () allow you to manipulate these flags and are described later.

Name	Function
open	opens/creates a file
read	reads bytes from a file into a buffer
write	writes bytes from a buffer to a file
lseek	moves to a particular offset in a file
close	closes a file
unlink	removes a file

FIGURE 13.7

UNIX system calls for basic I/O operations.

Utility: **reverse** -c [*fileName*]

reverse reverses the lines of its input and displays them to standard output. If no file name is specified, **reverse** reverses its standard input. When the **-c** option is used, **reverse** also reverses the characters in each line.

FIGURE 13.8

Description of the **reverse** program.

First Example: `reverse`

As a first example, I'll describe the most basic I/O system calls. Figure 13.7 shows a list of them, together with brief descriptions of their functions. To illustrate the use of these system calls, I'll use a small utility program called "reverse.c". As well as being a good vehicle for my presentation, it doubles as a nice example of how to write a UNIX utility. Figure 13.8 provides a description of reverse, an example of which is the following commands:

```
$ cc reverse.c -o reverse     ...compile the program.
$ cat test                    ...list the test file.
Christmas is coming,
The days that grow shorter,
Remind me of seasons I knew in the past.
$ reverse test                ...reverse the file.
Remind me of seasons I knew in the past.
The days that grow shorter,
Christmas is coming,
$ reverse -c test             ...reverse the lines too.
.tsap eht ni wenk I snosaes fo em dnimeR
,retrohs worg taht syad ehT
```

```
,gnimoc si samtsirhC
$ cat test | reverse        ...pipe output to "reverse".
Remind me of seasons I knew in the past.
The days that grow shorter,
Christmas is coming,
$ _
```

How reverse Works

The **reverse** utility works by performing two passes over its input. During the first pass, it notes the starting offset of each line in the file and stores this information in an array. During the second pass, it jumps to the start of each line in reverse order, copying it from the original input file to its standard output.

If no file name is specified on the command line, **reverse** reads from its standard input during the first pass and copies it into a temporary file for the second pass. When the program is finished, the temporary file is removed.

Figure 13.9 shows an overview of the program flow, together with a list of the functions that are associated with each action and a list of the system calls used by each step. What follows is a complete listing of "reverse.c," the source code of **reverse**. Skim through the code and then read the description of the system calls that follow. The code is also available on-line. (See the preface for more information.)

Step	Action	Functions	System calls
1	Parse command line.	parseCommandLine, processOptions	open
2	If reading from standard input, create temporary file to store input; otherwise open input file for reading.	pass1	open
3	Read from file in chunks, storing the starting offset of each line in an array. If reading from standard input, copy each chunk to the temporary file.	pass1, trackLines	read, write
4	Read the input file again, this time backwards, copying each line to standard output. Reverse the line if the -c option was chosen.	pass2, processLine, reverseLine	lseek
5	Close the file. Delete it if it is a temporary file.	pass2	close

FIGURE 13.9

Description of algorithm used in reverse.c.

reverse.c: Listing

```
1   #include <fcntl.h>  /* For file mode definitions */
2   #include <stdio.h>
3   #include <stdlib.h>
4
5
6   /* Enumerator */
7   enum { FALSE, TRUE }; /* Standard false and true values */
8   enum { STDIN, STDOUT, STDERR }; /* Standard I/O channel indices */
9
10
11  /* #define Statements */
12  #define BUFFER_SIZE    4096   /* Copy buffer size */
13  #define NAME_SIZE      12
14  #define MAX_LINES      100000 /* Max lines in file */
15
16
17  /* Globals */
18  char *fileName = NULL; /* Points to file name */
19  char tmpName [NAME_SIZE];
20  int charOption = FALSE; /* Set to true if -c option is used */
21  int standardInput = FALSE; /* Set to true if reading stdin */
22  int lineCount = 0; /* Total number of lines in input */
23  int lineStart [MAX_LINES]; /* Store offsets of each line */
24  int fileOffset = 0; /* Current position in input */
25  int fd; /* File descriptor of input */
26
27  /****************************************************************/
28
29  main (argc, argv)
30
31  int argc;
32  char* argv [];
33
34  {
35    parseCommandLine (argc,argv); /* Parse command line */
36    pass1 (); /* Perform first pass through input */
37    pass2 (); /* Perform second pass through input */
38    return (/* EXITSUCCESS */ 0); /* Done */
39  }
40
41  /****************************************************************/
42
43  parseCommandLine (argc, argv)
44
45  int argc;
46  char* argv [];
47
48  /* Parse command line arguments */
49
```

```
50  {
51    int i;
52
53    for (i= 1; i < argc; i++)
54      {
55        if(argv[i][0] == '-')
56          processOptions (argv[i]);
57        else if (fileName == NULL)
58          fileName= argv[i];
59        else
60          usageError (); /* An error occurred */
61      }
62
63    standardInput = (fileName == NULL);
64  }
65
66  /*************************************************************/
67
68  processOptions (str)
69
70  char* str;
71
72  /* Parse options */
73
74  {
75    int j;
76
77    for (j= 1; str[j] != NULL; j++)
78      {
79        switch(str[j]) /* Switch on command line flag */
80          {
81            case'c':
82              charOption = TRUE;
83              break;
84
85            default:
86              usageError ();
87              break;
88          }
89      }
90  }
91
92  /*************************************************************/
93
94  usageError ()
95
96  {
97    fprintf (stderr, "Usage: reverse -c [filename]\n");
98    exit (/* EXITFAILURE */ 1);
99  }
100
```

```
101   /***************************************************************/
102
103   pass1 ()
104
105   /* Perform first scan through file */
106
107   {
108     int tmpfd, charsRead, charsWritten;
109     char buffer [BUFFER_SIZE];
110
111     if (standardInput) /* Read from standard input */
112       {
113         fd = STDIN;
114         sprintf (tmpName, ".rev.%d",getpid ()); /* Random name */
115         /* Create temporary file to store copy of input */
116         tmpfd = open (tmpName, O_CREAT | O_RDWR, 0600);
117         if (tmpfd == -1) fatalError ();
118       }
119     else /* Open named file for reading */
120       {
121         fd = open (fileName, O_RDONLY);
122         if (fd == -1) fatalError ();
123       }
124
125     lineStart[0] = 0; /* Offset of first line */
126
127     while (TRUE) /* Read all input */
128       {
129         /* Fill buffer */
130         charsRead = read (fd, buffer, BUFFER_SIZE);
131         if (charsRead == 0) break; /* EOF */
132         if (charsRead == -1) fatalError (); /* Error */
133         trackLines (buffer, charsRead); /* Process line */
134         /* Copy line to temporary file if reading from stdin */
135         if (standardInput)
136           {
137             charsWritten = write (tmpfd, buffer, charsRead);
138             if(charsWritten != charsRead) fatalError ();
139           }
140       }
141
142     /* Store offset of trailing line, if present */
143     lineStart[lineCount + 1] = fileOffset;
144
145     /* If reading from standard input, prepare fd for pass2 */
146     if (standardInput) fd = tmpfd;
147   }
148
149   /***************************************************************/
150
```

```
151  trackLines (buffer, charsRead)
152
153  char* buffer;
154  int charsRead;
155
156  /* Store offsets of each line start in buffer */
157
158  {
159    int i;
160
161    for (i = 0; i < charsRead; i++)
162      {
163        ++fileOffset; /* Update current file position */
164        if (buffer[i] == '\n') lineStart[++lineCount] = fileOffset;
165      }
166  }
167
168  /*************************************************************/
169
170  int pass2 ()
171
172  /* Scan input file again, displaying lines in reverse order */
173
174  {
175    int i;
176
177    for (i = lineCount - 1; i >= 0; i--)
178      processLine (i);
179
180    close (fd); /* Close input file */
181    if (standardInput) unlink (tmpName); /* Remove temp file */
182  }
183
184  /*************************************************************/
185
186  processLine (i)
187
188  int i;
189
190  /* Read a line and display it */
191
192  {
193    int charsRead;
194    char buffer [BUFFER_SIZE];
195
196    lseek (fd, lineStart[i], SEEK_SET); /* Find the line and read it
*/
197    charsRead = read (fd, buffer, lineStart[i+1] - lineStart[i]);
198    /* Reverse line if -c option was selected */
199    if (charOption) reverseLine (buffer, charsRead);
```

```
200     write (1, buffer, charsRead); /* Write it to standard output */
201  }
202
203  /***************************************************************/
204
205  reverseLine (buffer, size)
206
207  char* buffer;
208  int size;
209
210  /* Reverse all the characters in the buffer */
211
212  {
213    int start = 0, end = size - 1;
214    char tmp;
215
216    if (buffer[end] == '\n') --end; /* Leave trailing newline */
217
218    /* Swap characters in a pairwise fashion */
219    while (start < end)
220      {
221        tmp = buffer[start];
222        buffer[start] = buffer[end];
223        buffer[end] = tmp;
224        ++start; /* Increment start index */
225        --end; /* Decrement end index */
226      }
227  }
228
229  /***************************************************************/
230
231  fatalError ()
232
233  {
234    perror ("reverse: "); /* Describe error */
235    exit (1);
236  }
```

Opening a File: `open` ( )

The **reverse** utility begins by executing parseCommandLine () [line 43], which sets various flags, depending on which options are chosen. If a filename is specified, the variable **fileName** is set to point to the name and **standardInput** is set to FALSE; otherwise, **fileName** is set to NULL and **standardInput** is set to TRUE. Next, pass1 () [line 103] is executed. Pass1 () performs one of the following actions:

- If **reverse** is reading from standard input, a temporary file is created with read and write permissions for the owner and no permissions for anyone else (octal mode 600). The file is opened in read/write mode and is used to store a copy of the standard input for use during pass 2. During pass 1, the input is taken from standard input, so the file descriptor **fd** is set to STDIN, defined to be 0 at the top of the program. Recall that standard input is always file descriptor zero.

- If **reverse** is reading from a named file, the file is opened in read-only mode so that its contents may be read during pass 1, using the file descriptor **fd**.

Each action uses the open () system call; the first action uses it to create a file, the second to access an existing file. The open () system call is described in Figure 13.10.

System Call: int **open** (char* *fileName*, int *mode* [, int *permissions*])

open () allows you to open or create a file for reading or writing. *fileName* is an absolute or relative pathname and *mode* is a bitwise OR of a read/write flag, with or without some miscellaneous flags. *permissions* is a number that encodes the value of the file's permission flags and should be supplied only when a file is being created. It is usually written using the octal encoding scheme described in Chapter 2. The *permissions* value is affected by the process' umask value, described in Chapter 4. The values of the predefined read/write and miscellaneous flags are defined in "/usr/include/fcntl.h". The read/write flags are as follows:

FLAG	MEANING
O_RDONLY	Open for read only.
O_WRONLY	Open for write only.
O_RDWR	Open for read and write.

The miscellaneous flags are as follows:

FLAG	MEANING
O_APPEND	Position the file pointer at the end of the file before each write ().
O_CREAT	If the file doesn't exist, create it and set the owner ID to the process' effective UID. The umask value is used when determining the initial permission flag settings.
O_EXCL	If O_CREAT is set and the file exists, then open () fails.
O_NONBLOCK (Called O_NDELAY on some systems)	This setting works only for named pipes. If set, an open for read only will return immediately, regardless of whether the write end is open, and an open for write only will fail if the read end isn't open. If clear, an open for read only or write only will block until the other end is also open.
O_TRUNC	If the file exists, it is truncated to length zero.

open () returns a nonnegative file descriptor if successful; otherwise, it returns –1.

FIGURE 13.10

Description of the open () system call.

Creating a File

To create a file, use the O_CREAT flag as part of the mode flags, and supply the initial file permission flag settings as an octal value. For example, lines 114–117 create a temporary file with read and write permission for the owner and then open the file for reading and writing:

```
114     sprintf (tmpName, ".rev.%d", getpid ()); /* Random name */
115     /* Create temporary file to store copy of input */
116     tmpfd = open (tmpName, O_CREAT | O_RDWR, 0600);
117     if (tmpfd == -1) fatalError ();
```

The getpid () function is a system call that returns the process' ID (PID) number, which is guaranteed to be unique. This is a handy way to generate unique temporary file names. [For more details on getpid (), see the "Process Management" section of the chapter.] Note that I chose the name of the temporary file to begin with a period so that it doesn't show up in an ls listing. Files that begin with a period are sometimes known as *hidden* files.

Opening an Existing File

To open an existing file, specify the mode flags only. Lines 121–122 open a named file for read only:

```
121     fd = open (fileName, O_RDONLY);
122     if (fd == -1) fatalError ();
```

Other Open Flags

The other more complicated flag settings for open (), such as O_NONBLOCK, are intended for use with the pipes, sockets, and STREAMS, all described later in the chapter. Right now, the O_CREAT flag is probably the only miscellaneous flag that you'll need.

Reading From a File: `read ()`

Once **reverse** has initialized the file descriptor **fd** for input, it reads chunks of input and processes them until the end of the file is reached. To read bytes from a file, **reverse** uses the read () system call, which works as shown in Figure 13.11. The read () system call performs low-level input and has none of the formatting capabilities of scanf (). The benefit of read () is that it bypasses the additional layer of buffering supplied by the C library functions and is therefore very fast. Although I could have read one character of input at a time, that would have resulted in a large number of system calls, thus slowing down the execution of my program considerably. Instead, I used read () to read up to BUFFER_SIZE characters at a time. BUFFER_SIZE was chosen to be a multiple of the disk block size, for efficient copying. Lines 130–132 perform the read and test the return result:

```
130     charsRead = read (fd, buffer, BUFFER_SIZE);
131     if (charsRead == 0) break; /* EOF */
132     if (charsRead == -1) fatalError (); /* Error */
```

System Call: ssize_t **read** (int *fd*, void* *buf*, size_t *count*)

Note: this synopsis describes how read () operates when reading a regular file. For information on reading from special files, see later sections of the chapter.

    read () copies *count* bytes from the file referenced by the file descriptor *fd* into the buffer *buf*. The bytes are read starting at the current file position, which is then updated accordingly.

    read () copies as many bytes from the file as it can, up to the number specified by *count*, and returns the number of bytes actually copied. If a read () is attempted after the last byte has already been read, it returns 0, which indicates end of file.

    If successful, read () returns the number of bytes that it read; otherwise, it returns –1.

FIGURE 13.11

Description of the read () system call.

As each chunk of input is read, it is passed to the trackLines () function. This function scans the input buffer for newlines and stores the offset of the first character in each line in the **lineStart** array. The variable **fileOffset** is used to maintain the current file offset. The contents of **lineStart** are used during the second pass.

Writing to a File: `write ()`

When **reverse** is reading from standard input, it creates a copy of the input for use during pass 2. To do this, it sets the file descriptor **tmpfd** to refer to a temporary file and then writes each chunk of input to the file during the read loop. To write bytes to a file, it uses the write () system call, which works as shown in Figure 13.12. The write () system call performs low-level output and has none of the formatting capabilities of printf (). The benefit of write () is that it bypasses the additional layer of buffering supplied by the C library functions and is therefore very fast. Lines 134–139 perform the write operation:

```
134     /* Copy line to temporary file if reading standard input */
135     if (standardInput)
136        {
137          charsWritten = write (tmpfd, buffer, charsRead);
138          if (charsWritten != charsRead) fatalError ();
139        }
```

System Call: ssize_t **write** (int *fd*, void* *buf*, size_t *count*)

Note: this synopsis describes how write () operates when writing to a regular file. For information on writing to special files, see later sections of this chapter.

write () copies *count* bytes from a buffer *buf* to the file referenced by the file descriptor *fd*. The bytes are written starting at the current file position, which is then updated accordingly. If the O_APPEND flag was set for *fd*, the file position is set to the end of the file before each write.

write () copies as many bytes from the buffer as it can, up to the number specified by *count*, and returns the number of bytes actually copied. Your process should always check the return value. If the return value isn't *count*, then the disk probably filled up and no space was left.

If successful, write () returns the number of bytes that were written; otherwise, it returns –1.

FIGURE 13.12

Description of the write () system call.

Moving in a File: `lseek ()`

Once the first pass is completed, the array **lineStart** contains the offsets of the first character of each line of the input file. During pass 2, the lines are read in reverse order and displayed to standard output. In order to read the lines out of sequence, the program makes use of lseek (), which is a system call that allows a descriptor's file pointer to be changed. Figure 13.13 describes lseek ().

System Call: off_t **lseek** (int *fd*, off_t *offset*, int *mode*)

lseek () allows you to change a descriptor's current file position. *fd* is the file descriptor, offset is a long integer, and mode describes how *offset* should be interpreted. The three possible values of mode are defined in "/usr/include/stdio.h" and have the following meanings:

VALUE	MEANING
SEEK_SET	*offset* is relative to the start of the file.
SEEK_CUR	*offset* is relative to the current file position.
SEEK_END	*offset* is relative to the end of the file.

lseek () fails if you try to move before the start of the file.

If successful, lseek () returns the current file position; otherwise, it returns –1.

On some systems, the modes are defined in "/usr/include/unistd.h."

FIGURE 13.13

Description of the lseek () system call.

Lines 196–197 seek until the start of a line and then read in all of the characters in the line. Note that the number of characters to read is calculated by subtracting the start offset of the next line from the start offset of the current line:

```
196    lseek (fd, lineStart[i], SEEK_SET); /* Find line and read it */
197    charsRead = read (fd, buffer, lineStart[i+1] - lineStart[i]);
```

If you want to find out your current location without moving, use an offset value of zero relative to the current position:

```
currentOffset = lseek (fd, 0, SEEK_CUR);
```

If you move past the end of the file and then perform a write (), the kernel automatically extends the size of the file and treats the intermediate file area as if it were filled with NULL (ASCII 0) characters. Interestingly enough, it doesn't allocate disk space for the intermediate area, which is confirmed by the following example:

```
$ cat sparse.c                    ...list the test file.
#include <fcntl.h>
#include <stdio.h>
#include <stdlib.h>
/**********************************************************/
main ()
{
  int i, fd;
   /* Create a sparse file */
  fd = open ("sparse.txt", O_CREAT | O_RDWR, 0600);
  write (fd, "sparse", 6);
  lseek (fd, 60006, SEEK_SET);
  write (fd, "file", 4);
  close (fd);
   /* Create a normal file */
  fd = open ("normal.txt", O_CREAT | O_RDWR, 0600);
  write (fd, "normal", 6);
  for (i = 1; i <= 60000; i++)
    write (fd, "/0", 1);
  write (fd, "file", 4);
  close (fd);
}
$ sparse                          ...execute the file.
$ ls -l *.txt                     ...look at the files.
-rw-r--r--    1 glass       60010 Feb 14 15:06 normal.txt
-rw-r--r--    1 glass       60010 Feb 14 15:06 sparse.txt
$ ls -s *.txt                     ...list their block usage.
  60 normal.txt*                  ...uses a full 60 blocks.
   8 sparse.txt*                  ...only uses 8 blocks.
$ _
```

Files that contain "gaps" like this are termed "sparse" files; for details on how they are actually stored, see Chapter 14.

Closing a File: `close ()`

When pass 2 is over, **reverse** uses the close () system call to free the input file descriptor. Figure 13.14 provides a description of close (). Line 180 contains the call to close ():

```
180    close (fd); /* Close input file */
```

System Call: int **close** (int *fd*)

close () frees the file descriptor *fd*. If *fd* is the last file descriptor associated with a particular open file, the kernel resources associated with the file are deallocated. When a process terminates, all of its file descriptors are automatically closed, but it's better programming practice to close a file when you're done with it. If you close a file descriptor that's already closed, an error occurs.

If successful, close () returns zero; otherwise, it returns –1.

FIGURE 13.14

Description of the close () system call.

Just because a file is closed does not guarantee that the file's buffers are immediately flushed to disk; for more information on file buffering, see Chapter 14.

Deleting a File: `unlink ()`

If **reverse** reads from standard input, it stores a copy of the input in a temporary file. At the end of pass 2, it removes this file, using the unlink () system call, which works as shown in Figure 13.15. Line 181 contains the call to unlink ():

```
181    if (standardInput) unlink (tmpName); /* Remove temp file */
```

For more information about hard links, see Chapter 14.

System Call: int **unlink** (const char* *fileName*)

unlink () removes the hard link from the name *fileName* to its file. If *fileName* is the last link to the file, the file's resources are deallocated. In this case, if any process' file descriptors are currently associated with the file, the directory entry is removed immediately, but the file is deallocated only after all of the file descriptors are closed. This means that an executable file can unlink itself during execution and still continue to completion.

If successful, unlink () returns zero; otherwise, it returns –1.

FIGURE 13.15

Description of the unlink () system call.

Second Example: `monitor`

This section contains a description of some more advanced system calls, listed in Figure 13.16. The use of these calls is demonstrated in the context of a program called **monitor**, which allows a user to monitor a series of named files and to obtain information whenever any of them are modified. Figure 13.17 gives a description of **monitor**.

Name	Function
stat	obtains status information about a file
fstat	works just like stat
getdents	obtains directory entries

FIGURE 13.16

Advanced UNIX I/O system calls.

Utility: **monitor** [-*t delay*] [-*l count*] { *fileName* }+

monitor scans all of the specified files every *delay* seconds and displays information about any of the specified files that were modified since the last scan. If *fileName* is a directory, all of the files inside that directory are scanned. File modification is indicated in one of three ways:

LABEL	**MEANING**
ADDED	Indicates that the file was created since the last scan. Every file in the file list is given this label during the first scan.
CHANGED	Indicates that the file was modified since the last scan.
DELETED	Indicates that the file was deleted since the last scan.

By default, **monitor** will scan forever, although you can specify the total number of scans by using the **-l** option. The default delay time is 10 seconds between scans, although this may be overridden by using the **-t** option.

FIGURE 13.17

Description of the **monitor** program.

In the following example, I monitored an individual file and a directory, storing the output of **monitor** into a temporary file:

```
% ls                              ...look at home directory.
monitor.c    monitor     tmp/
% ls tmp                          ...look at "tmp" directory.
b
```

```
% monitor tmp myFile.txt >& monitor.out &      ...start.
[1] 12841
% cat > tmp/a                    ...create a file in "~/tmp".
hi there
^D
% cat > myFile.txt               ...create "myFile.txt".
hi there
^D
% cat > myFile.txt               ...change "myFile.txt".
hi again
^D
% rm tmp/a                       ...delete "tmp/a".
% jobs                           ...look at jobs.
[1]  + Running            monitor tmp myFile.txt ,& monitor.out
% kill %1                        ...kill monitor job.
[1]     Terminated        monitor tmp myFile.txt ,& monitor.out
% cat monitor.out                ...look at output.
ADDED tmp/b size 9 bytes, mod. time = Sun Jan 18 00:38:55 1998
ADDED tmp/a size 9 bytes, mod. time = Fri Feb 13 18:51:09 1998
ADDED myFile.txt size 9 bytes, mod. time = Fri Feb 13 18:51:21 1998
CHANGED myFile.txt size 18 bytes, mod. time = Fri Feb 13 18:51:49 1998
DELETED tmp/a
% _
```

Notice how the contents of the "monitor.out" file reflected the additions, modifications, and deletions of the monitored file and directory.

How monitor Works

The **monitor** utility continually scans the specified files and directories for modifications. It uses the stat () system call to obtain status information about named files, including their type and most recent modification time, and uses the getdents () system call to scan directories. **Monitor** maintains a status table called **stats**, which holds the following information about each file that it finds:

- the name of the file
- the status information obtained by stat ()
- a record of whether the file was present during the current scan and the previous scan

During a scan, **monitor** processes each file as follows:

- If the file isn't currently in the scan table, it's added and the message "ADDED" is displayed.
- If the file is already in the scan table and has been modified since the last scan, the message "CHANGED" is displayed.

At the end of a scan, all entries that were present during the previous scan, but not during the current scan, are removed from the table and the message "DELETED" is displayed.

Following is a complete listing of "monitor.c", the source code of **monitor**. Skim through it and then read the description of the system calls that follow.

monitor.c: Listing

```
1   #include <stdio.h>              /* For printf, fprintf */
2   #include <string.h>             /* For strcmp */
3   #include <ctype.h>              /* For isdigit */
4   #include <fcntl.h>              /* For O_RDONLY */
5   #include <sys/dirent.h>         /* For getdents */
6   #include <sys/stat.h>           /* For IS macros */
7   #include <sys/types.h>          /* For modet */
8   #include <time.h>               /* For localtime, asctime */
9
10
11  /* #define Statements */
12  #define MAX_FILES          100
13  #define MAX_FILENAME       50
14  #define NOT_FOUND          -1
15  #define FOREVER            -1
16  #define DEFAULT_DELAY_TIME  10
17  #define DEFAULT_LOOP_COUNT  FOREVER
18
19
20  /* Booleans */
21  enum { FALSE, TRUE };
22
23
24  /* Status structure, one per file. */
25  struct statStruct
26    {
27      char fileName [MAX_FILENAME]; /* File name */
28      int lastCycle, thisCycle; /* To detect changes */
29      struct stat status; /* Information from stat () */
30    };
31
32
33  /* Globals */
34  char* fileNames [MAX_FILES]; /* One per file on command line */
35  int fileCount; /* Count of files on command line */
36  struct statStruct stats [MAX_FILES]; /* One per matching file */
37  int loopCount = DEFAULT_LOOP_COUNT; /* Number of times to loop */
38  int delayTime = DEFAULT_DELAY_TIME; /* Seconds between loops */
39
40  /****************************************************************/
41
42  main (argc, argv)
43
44  int argc;
45  char* argv [];
```

```
46
47  {
48    parseCommandLine (argc, argv); /* Parse command line */
49    monitorLoop (); /* Execute main monitor loop */
50    return (/* EXIT_SUCCESS */ 0);
51  }
52
53  /**************************************************************/
54
55  parseCommandLine (argc, argv)
56
57  int argc;
58  char* argv [];
59
60  /* Parse command line arguments */
61
62  {
63    int i;
64
65    for (i = 1; ( (i < argc) && (i < MAX_FILES) ); i++)
66      {
67        if (argv[i][0] ==  '-')
68          processOptions (argv[i]);
69        else
70          fileNames[fileCount++] = argv[i];
71      }
72
73    if (fileCount == 0) usageError ();
74  }
75
76  /**************************************************************/
77
78  processOptions (str)
79
80  char* str;
81
82  /* Parse options */
83
84  {
85    int j;
86
87    for (j = 1; str[j] != NULL; j++)
88      {
89        switch(str[j]) /* Switch on option letter */
90          {
91            case 't':
92              delayTime = getNumber (str, &j);
93              break;
94
```

```
 95              case 'l':
 96                 loopCount = getNumber (str, &j);
 97                 break;
 98            }
 99         }
100   }
101
102   /**************************************************************/
103
104   getNumber (str, i)
105
106   char* str;
107   int* i;
108
109   /* Convert a numeric ASCII option to a number */
110
111   {
112     int number = 0;
113     int digits = 0; /* Count the digits in the number */
114
115     while (isdigit (str[(*i) + 1])) /* Convert chars to ints */
116       {
117         number = number * 10 + str[++(*i)] - '0';
118         ++digits;
119       }
120
121     if (digits == 0) usageError (); /* There must be a number */
122     return (number);
123   }
124
125   /**************************************************************/
126
127   usageError ()
128
129   {
130     fprintf (stderr, "Usage: monitor -t<seconds> -l<loops>
{filename}+\n");
131     exit (/* EXIT_FAILURE */ 1);
132   }
133
134   /**************************************************************/
135
136   monitorLoop ()
137
138   /* The main monitor loop */
139
140   {
141     do
142       {
```

```
143           monitorFiles (); /* Scan all files */
144           fflush (stdout); /* Flush standard output */
145           fflush (stderr); /* Flush standard error */
146           sleep (delayTime); /* Wait until next loop */
147         }
148     while (loopCount == FOREVER || --loopCount > 0);
149   }
150
151   /**************************************************************/
152
153   monitorFiles ()
154
155   /* Process all files */
156
157   {
158     int i;
159
160     for (i = 0; i < fileCount; i++)
161       monitorFile (fileNames[i]);
162
163     for (i = 0; i< MAX_FILES; i++) /* Update stat array */
164       {
165         if (stats[i].lastCycle && !stats[i].thisCycle)
166           printf ("DELETED %s\n", stats[i].fileName);
167
168         stats[i].lastCycle = stats[i].thisCycle;
169         stats[i].thisCycle = FALSE;
170       }
171   }
172
173   /**************************************************************/
174
175   monitorFile (fileName)
176
177   char* fileName;
178
179   /* Process a single file/directory*/
180
181   {
182     struct stat statBuf;
183     mode_t mode;
184     int result;
185
186     result = stat (fileName, &statBuf); /* Obtain file status */
187
188     if (result == -1) /* Status was not available */
189       {
190         fprintf (stderr, "Cannot stat %s\n", fileName);
191         return;
192       }
```

```
193
194    mode = statBuf.st_mode; /* Mode of file */
195
196    if(S_ISDIR (mode)) /* Directory */
197      processDirectory (fileName);
198    else if (S_ISREG (mode) || S_ISCHR (mode) || S_ISBLK (mode))
199      updateStat (fileName, &statBuf); /* Regular file */
200  }
201
202  /****************************************************************/
203
204  processDirectory (dirName)
205
206  char* dirName;
207
208  /* Process all files in the named directory */
209
210  {
211    int fd, charsRead;
212    struct dirent dirEntry;
213    char fileName [MAX_FILENAME];
214
215    fd = open (dirName, O_RDONLY); /* Open for reading */
216    if (fd == -1) fatalError ();
217
218    while (TRUE) /* Read all directory entries */
219      {
220        charsRead = getdents(fd, &dirEntry, sizeof (struct dirent));
221        if (charsRead == -1) fatalError ();
222        if (charsRead == 0) break; /* EOF */
223        if (strcmp (dirEntry.d_name, ".") != 0&&
224            strcmp (dirEntry.d_name, "..") != 0) /* Skip . and .. */
225          {
226            sprintf (fileName, "%s/%s", dirName, dirEntry.d_name);
227            monitorFile (fileName); /* Call recursively */
228          }
229
230        lseek (fd, dirEntry.d_off, SEEK_SET); /* Find next entry */
231      }
232
233    close (fd); /* Close directory */
234  }
235
236  /****************************************************************/
237
238  updateStat (fileName, statBuf)
239
240  char* fileName;
241  struct stat* statBuf;
242
```

```
243  /* Add a status entry if necessary */
244
245  {
246    int entryIndex;
247
248    entryIndex = findEntry (fileName); /* Find existing entry */
249
250    if (entryIndex == NOT_FOUND)
251      entryIndex = addEntry (fileName, statBuf); /* Add new entry */
252    else
253      updateEntry (entryIndex, statBuf); /* Update existing entry */
254
255    if (entryIndex != NOT_FOUND)
256      stats[entryIndex].thisCycle = TRUE; /* Update status array */
257  }
258
259  /**************************************************************/
260
261  findEntry (fileName)
262
263  char* fileName;
264
265  /* Locate the index of a named filein the status array */
266
267  {
268    int i;
269
270    for (i = 0; i < MAX_FILES; i++)
271      if (stats[i].lastCycle &&
272          strcmp (stats[i].fileName, fileName) == 0) return (i);
273
274    return (NOT_FOUND);
275  }
276
277  /**************************************************************/
278
279  addEntry (fileName, statBuf)
280
281  char* fileName;
282  struct stat* statBuf;
283
284  /* Add a new entry into the status array */
285
286  {
287    int index;
288
289    index = nextFree (); /* Find the next free entry */
290    if (index == NOT_FOUND) return (NOT_FOUND); /* None left */
291    strcpy (stats[index].fileName, fileName); /* Add filename */
292    stats[index].status = *statBuf; /* Add status information */
```

```
293    printf ("ADDED "); /* Notify standard output */
294    printEntry (index); /* Display status information */
295    return (index);
296  }
297
298  /****************************************************************/
299
300  nextFree ()
301
302  /* Return the nextfree index in the status array */
303
304  {
305    int i;
306
307    for (i = 0; i < MAX_FILES; i++)
308      if (!stats[i].lastCycle && !stats[i].thisCycle) return (i);
309
310    return (NOT_FOUND);
311  }
312
313  /****************************************************************/
314
315  updateEntry (index, statBuf)
316
317  int index;
318  struct stat* statBuf;
319
320  /*Display information if the file has been modified */
321
322  {
323    if (stats[index].status.st_mtime != statBuf->st_mtime)
324      {
325        stats[index].status = *statBuf; /* Store stat information */
326        printf ("CHANGED "); /* Notify standard output */
327        printEntry (index);
328      }
329  }
330
331  /****************************************************************/
332
333  printEntry (index)
334
335  int index;
336
337  /* Display an entry of the status array */
338
339  {
340    printf ("%s ", stats[index].fileName);
341    printStat (&stats[index].status);
342  }
```

```
343
344   /**************************************************************/
345
346   printStat (statBuf)
347
348   struct stat* statBuf;
349
350   /* Display a status buffer */
351
352   {
353     printf ("size %lu bytes, mod. time = %s",  statBuf->st_size,
354               asctime (localtime (&statBuf->st_mtime)));
355   }
356
357   /**************************************************************/
358
359   fatalError ()
360
361   {
362     perror ("monitor: ");
363     exit (/* EXIT_FAILURE */ 1);
364   }
```

Obtaining File Information: `stat ()`

monitor obtains its file information by calling stat (), which works as shown in Figure 13.18. The **monitor** utility invokes stat () from monitorFile () [line 175] on line 186:

```
186     result = stat (fileName, &statBuf); /* Obtain file status */
```

System Call: int **stat** (const char* *name*, struct stat* *buf*)

int **lstat** (const char* *name*, struct stat* *buf*)

int **fstat** (int *fd*, struct stat* *buf*)

stat () fills the buffer *buf* with information about the file *name*. The **stat** structure is defined in "/usr/include/sys/stat.h". lstat() returns information about a symbolic link itself, rather than the file it references. fstat () performs the same function as stat (), except that it takes the file descriptor of the file to be "stat'ed" as its first parameter.

FIGURE 13.18

Description of the stat () system call.

The **stat** structure contains the following members:

NAME	MEANING
st_dev	the device number
st_ino	the inode number
st_mode	the permission flags
st_nlink	the hard-link count
st_uid	the user ID
st_gid	the group ID
st_size	the file size
st_atime	the last access time
st_mtime	the last modification time
st_ctime	the last status change time

There are some predefined macros defined in "/usr/include/sys/stat.h" that take **st_mode** as their argument and return true (1) for the following file types:

MACRO	RETURNS TRUE FOR FILE TYPE
S_IFDIR	directory
S_IFCHR	character special device
S_IFBLK	block special device
S_IFREG	regular file
S_IFFIFO	pipe

The time fields may be decoded with the standard C library asctime () and localtime () subroutines.

stat () and fstat () return 0 if successful and -1 otherwise.

FIGURE 13.18   (*Continued*)

monitor examines the mode of the file using the S_ISDIR, S_ISREG, S_ISCHR, and S_ISBLK macros, processing directory files, and other files as follows:

- If the file is a directory file, it calls processDirectory () [line 204], which applies monitorFile () recursively to each of its directory entries.

- If the file is a regular file, a character special file, or a block special file, **monitor** calls updateStat () [line 238], which either adds or updates the file's status entry. If the status changes in any way, updateEntry () [line 315] is called to display the file's new status. The decoding of the time fields is performed by the localtime () and asctime () routines in printStat () [line 346].

Reading Directory Information: `getdents ()`

processDirectory () [line 204] opens a directory file for reading and then uses getdents () to obtain every entry in the directory, as shown in Figure 13.19. processDirectory () is careful not to trace into the "." and ".." directories and uses lseek () to jump from one directory entry to the next. When the directory has been completely searched, it is closed.

System Call: int **getdents** (int *fd*, struct dirent* *buf*, int *structSize*)

getdents () reads the directory file with descriptor *fd* from its current position and fills the structure pointed to by *buf* with the next entry. The structure **dirent** is defined in "/usr/include/sys/dirent.h" and contains the following fields:

NAME	MEANING
d_ino	the inode number
d_off	the offset of the next directory entry
d_reclen	the length of the directory entry structure
d_nam	the length of the filename

getdents () returns the length of the directory entry when successful, 0 when the last directory entry has already been read, and −1 in the case of an error.

FIGURE 13.19

Description of the getdents () system call.

Some older systems use the getdirentries () system call instead of getdents (). The usage of getdirentries () differs somewhat from getdents (); see your system's man page for details.

Miscellaneous File Management System Calls

Figure 13.20 gives a brief description of some miscellaneous UNIX file management system calls.

Changing a File's Owner or Group: `chown ()` and `fchown ()`

chown () and fchown () change the owner or group of a file. They work as shown in Figure 13.21. In the following example, I changed the group of the file "test.txt" from "music" to "cs," which has group ID number 62 (for more information about group IDs and how to locate them, see Chapter 15):

Name	Function
chown	changes a file's owner or group
chmod	changes a file's permission settings
dup	duplicates a file descriptor
dup2	similar to dup
fchown	works just like chown
fchmod	works just like chmod
fcntl	gives access to miscellaneous file characteristics
ftruncate	works just like truncate
ioctl	controls a device
link	creates a hard link
mknod	creates a special file
sync	schedules all file buffers to be flushed to disk
truncate	truncates a file

FIGURE 13.20

UNIX file management system calls.

System Call: int **chown** (const char* *fileName*, uid_t *ownerId*, gid_t *groupId*)

　　　　　　int **lchown** (const char* *fileName*, uid_t *ownerId*, gid_t *groupId*)

　　　　　　int **fchown** (int *fd*, uid_t *ownerId*, gid_t *groupId*)

chown () causes the owner and group IDs of *fileName* to be changed to *ownerId* and *groupId*, respectively. A value of −1 in a particular field means that its associated value should remain unchanged. lchown() changes the ownership of a symbolic link itself, rather than the file the link references.

　　　Only a superuser can change the ownership of a file, and a user may change the group only to another group of which he or she is a member. If *fileName* is a symbolic link, the owner and group of the link are changed instead of the file that the link is referencing.

　　　fchown () is just like chown (), except that it takes an open descriptor as an argument instead of a filename.

　　　Both functions return −1 if unsuccessful and 0 otherwise.

FIGURE 13.21

Description of the chown (), lchown (), and fchown () system calls.

```
$ cat mychown.c                    ...list the file.
main ()
{
 int flag;
 flag = chown ("test.txt", -1, 62); /* Leave user ID unchanged */
 if (flag == -1) perror("mychown.c");
}
$ ls -lg test.txt                  ...examine file before.
-rw-r--r--  1 glass      music       3 May 25 11:42 test.txt
$ mychown                          ...run program.
$ ls -lg test.txt                  ...examine file after.
-rw-r--r--  1 glass      cs          3 May 25 11:42 test.txt
$ _
```

Changing a File's Permissions: `chmod ()` and `fchmod ()`

chmod () and fchmod () change a file's permission flags. They work as shown in Figure 13.22. In the following example, I changed the permission flags of the file "test.txt" to 600 octal, which corresponds to read and write permission for the owner only:

```
$ cat mychmod.c                    ...list the file.
main ()
{
 int flag;
 flag = chmod ("test.txt", 0600); /* Use an octal encoding */
 if (flag == -1) perror ("mychmod.c");
}
$ ls -l test.txt                   ...examine file before.
-rw-r--r--  1 glass          3 May 25 11:42 test.txt
$ mychmod                          ...run the program.
$ ls -l test.txt                   ...examine file after.
-rw-------  1 glass            3 May 25 11:42 test.txt
$ _
```

System Call: int **chmod** (const char* *fileName*, int *mode*)

        int **fchmod** (int *fd*, mode_t *mode*);

chmod () changes the mode of *fileName* to *mode*, usually an octal number as described in Chapter 2. The "set user ID" and "set group ID" flags have the octal values 4000 and 2000, respectively. To change a file's mode, you must either own it or be a superuser.

    fchmod () works just like chmod (), except that it takes an open file descriptor as an argument instead of a filename.

    Both functions return –1 if unsuccessful and 0 otherwise.

FIGURE 13.22

Description of the chmod () system call.

Duplicating a File Descriptor: dup () and dup2 ()

dup () and dup2 () allow you to duplicate file descriptors. They work as shown in Figure 13.23. Shells use dup2 () to perform redirection and piping. (For examples that show how this is done, see "Process Management" in this chapter, and study the Internet

---

System Call: int **dup** (int *oldFd*)

                int **dup2** (int *oldFd*, int *newFd*)

dup () finds the smallest free file descriptor entry and points it to the same file as *oldFd*. dup2 () closes *newFd* if it's currently active and then points it to the same file as *oldFd*. In both cases, the original and copied file descriptors share the same file pointer and access mode.

      Both functions return the index of the new file descriptor if successful and –1 otherwise.

FIGURE 13.23

Description of the dup () and dup2 () system calls.

shell at the end of the chapter. In the following example, I created a file called "test.txt" and wrote to it via four different file descriptors:

- The first file descriptor was the original descriptor.
- The second descriptor was a copy of the first, allocated in slot 4.
- The third descriptor was a copy of the first, allocated in slot 0, which was freed by the close (0) statement (the standard input channel).
- The fourth descriptor was a copy of descriptor 3, copied over the existing descriptor in slot 2 (the standard error channel).

```
$ cat mydup.c                    ...list the file.
#include <stdio.h>
#include <fcntl.h>
main ()
{
 int fd1, fd2, fd3;
  fd1 = open ("test.txt", O_RDWR | O_TRUNC);
 printf ("fd1 = %d\n", fd1);
 write (fd1, "what's", 6);
  fd2 = dup (fd1); /* Make a copy of fd1 */
 printf ("fd2 = %d\n", fd2);
 write (fd2, " up", 3);
  close (0); /* Close standard input */
 fd3 = dup (fd1); /* Make another copy of fd1 */
 printf ("fd3 = %d\n", fd3);
 write (0, " doc", 4);
```

```
    dup2 (3, 2); /* Duplicate channel 3 to channel 2 */
    write (2, "?\n", 2);
  }
$ mydup                   ...run the program.
fd1 = 3
fd2 = 4
fd3 = 0
$ cat test.txt            ...list the output file.
what's up doc?
$ _
```

File Descriptor Operations: `fcntl ()`

fcntl () directly controls the settings of the flags associated with a file descriptor. It works as shown in Figure 13.24. In the next example, I opened an existing file for writing and overwrote the initial few letters with the phrase "hi there." I then used fcntl () to set the file descriptor's APPEND flag, which instructed it to append all further

---

System Call: int **fcntl** (int *fd*, int *cmd*, int *arg*)

fcntl () performs the operation encoded by *cmd* on the file associated with the file descriptor *fd*. *arg* is an optional argument for *cmd*. Here are the most common values of *cmd*:

VALUE	OPERATION
F_SETFD	Set the close-on-exec flag to the lowest bit of *arg* (0 or 1).
F_GETFD	Return a number whose lowest bit is 1 if the close-on-exec flag is set and 0 otherwise.
F_GETFL	Return a number corresponding to the current file status flags and access modes.
F_SETFL	Set the current file status flags to *arg*.
F_GETOWN	Return the process ID or process group that is currently set to receive SIGIO/SIGURG signals. If the value returned is positive, it refers to a process ID. If it's negative, its absolute value refers to a process group.
F_SETOWN	Set the process ID or process group that should receive SIGIO/SIGURG signals to *arg*. The encoding scheme is as described for F_GETOWN.

fcntl () returns −1 if unsuccessful.

FIGURE 13.24

Description of the fcntl () system call.

writes. This caused "guys" to be placed at the end of the file, even though I moved the file position pointer back to the start with lseek (). The code is as follows:

```
$ cat myfcntl.c                    ...list the program.
#include <stdio.h>
#include <fcntl.h>
main ()
{
  int fd;
   fd = open ("test.txt", O_WRONLY); /* Open file for writing */
  write (fd, "hi there\n", 9);
  lseek (fd, 0, SEEK_SET); /* Seek to beginning of file */
  fcntl (fd, F_SETFL, O_WRONLY | O_APPEND); /* Set APPEND flag */
  write (fd, " guys\n", 6);
  close (fd);
}
$ cat test.txt                     ...list the original file.
here are the contents of
the original file.
$ myfcntl                          ...run the program.
$ cat test.txt                     ...list the new contents.
hi there
the contents of
the original file.
guys                               ...note that "guys" is at the end.
$ _
```

Controlling Devices: `ioctl ()`

Figure 13.25 describes the operation of ioctl ().

System Call: int **ioctl** (int *fd*, int *cmd*, int *arg*)

ioctl () performs the operation encoded by *cmd* on the file associated with the file descriptor *fd*. *arg* is an optional argument for *cmd*. The valid values of *cmd* depend on the device that *fd* refers to and are typically documented in the manufacturer's operating instructions. I therefore supply no examples for this system call.

ioctl () returns −1 if unsuccessful.

FIGURE 13.25

Description of the ioctl () system call.

Creating Hard Links: `link ()`

link () creates a hard link to an existing file. It works as shown in Figure 13.26. In the next example, I created the filename "another.txt" and linked it to the file referenced

---

System Call: int **link** (const char* *oldPath*, const char* *newPath*)

link () creates a new label, *newPath*, and links it to the same file as the label *oldPath*. The hard link count of the associated file is incremented by one. If *oldPath* and *newPath* reside on different physical devices, a hard link cannot be made and link () fails. For more information about hard links, see the description of **ln** in Chapter 3.
link () returns −1 if unsuccessful and 0 otherwise.

FIGURE 13.26

Description of the link () system call.

by the existing name, "original.txt". I then demonstrated that both labels were linked to the same file. The code is as follows:

```
$ cat mylink.c                      ...list the program.
main ()
{
  link ("original.txt", "another.txt");
}
$ cat original.txt                  ...list original file.
this is a file.
$ ls -l original.txt another.txt ...examine files before.
another.txt not found
-rw-r--r--  1 glass              16 May 25 12:18 original.txt
$ mylink                            ...run the program.
$ ls -l original.txt another.txt ...examine files after.
-rw-r--r--  2 glass              16 May 25 12:18 another.txt
-rw-r--r--  2 glass              16 May 25 12:18 original.txt
$ cat >> another.txt                   ...alter "another.txt".
hi
^D
$ ls -l original.txt another.txt    ...both labels reflect change.
-rw-r--r--  2 glass              20 May 25 12:19 another.txt
-rw-r--r--  2 glass              20 May 25 12:19 original.txt
$ rm original.txt                ...remove original label.
$ ls -l original.txt another.txt    ...examine labels.
original.txt not found
-rw-r--r--  1 glass              20 May 25 12:19 another.txt
$ cat another.txt          ...list contents via other label.
this is a file.
hi
$ _
```

Creating Special Files: mknod ( )

mknod () allows you to create a special file. It works as shown in Figure 13.27. For an example of mknod (), consult the section on named pipes later in the chapter.

System Call: int **mknod** (const char* *fileName*, mode_t *type*, dev_t *device*)

mknod () creates a new regular, directory, or special file called *fileName* whose type can be one of the following:

VALUE	MEANING
S_IFDIR	directory
S_IFCHR	character-oriented file
S_IFBLK	block-oriented file
S_IFREG	regular file
S_IFIFO	named pipe

If the file is a character- or block-oriented file, then the low-order byte of *device* should specify the minor device number, and the high-order byte should specify the major device number. (This can vary in different UNIX versions.) In other cases, the value of *device* is ignored. (For more information on special files, see Chapter 14.)

Only a superuser can use mknod () to create directories, character-oriented files, or block-oriented special files. It is typical now to use the mkdir () system call to create directories.

mknod () returns −1 if unsuccessful and 0 otherwise.

FIGURE 13.27

Description of the mknod () system call.

Flushing the File System Buffers: `sync` ()

sync () flushes the file system buffers. It works as shown in Figure 13.28.

System Call: void **sync** ()

sync () schedules all of the file system buffers to be written to disk. (For more information on the buffer system, consult Chapter 14.) sync () should be performed by any programs that bypass the file system buffers and examine the raw file system.

sync () always succeeds.

FIGURE 13.28

Description of the sync () system call.

Truncating a File: `truncate ()` and `ftruncate ()`

truncate () and ftruncate () set the length of a file. They work as shown in Figure 13.29. In the next example, I set the length of two files to 10 bytes; one of the files was originally shorter than that, and the other was longer. Here is the code:

```
$ cat truncate.c                      ...list the program.
main ()
{
  truncate ("file1.txt", 10);
  truncate ("file2.txt", 10);
}
$ cat file1.txt                       ...list "file1.txt".
short
$ cat file2.txt                       ...list "file2.txt".
long file with lots of letters
$ ls -l file*.txt                     ...examine both files.
-rw-r--r--  1 glass          6 May 25 12:16 file1.txt
-rw-r--r--  1 glass         32 May 25 12:17 file2.txt
$ truncate                            ...run the program.
$ ls -l file*.txt                     ...examine both files again.
-rw-r--r--  1 glass         10 May 25 12:16 file1.txt
-rw-r--r--  1 glass         10 May 25 12:17 file2.txt
$ cat file1.txt                       ..."file1.txt" is longer.
short
$ cat file2.txt                       ..."file2.txt" is shorter.
long file $ _
```

System Call: int **truncate** (const char* *fileName*, off_t *length*)

int **ftruncate** (int *fd*, off_t *length*)

truncate () sets the length of the file *fileName* to *length* bytes. If the file is longer than *length*, it is truncated. If it is shorter than length, it is padded with ASCII nulls.

ftruncate () works just like truncate (), except that it takes an open file descriptor as an argument instead of a filename.

Both functions return −1 if unsuccessful and 0 otherwise.

FIGURE 13.29

Description of the truncate () and ftruncate () system calls.

STREAMS

STREAMS is a newer and more generalized I/O facility that was introduced in System V UNIX. STREAMS are most often used to add device drivers to the kernel and provide an interface to the network drivers, among others.

Originally developed by Dennis Ritchie, one of the designers of UNIX, STREAMS provides a full-duplex (two-way) path between kernel space and user process space. The implementation of STREAMS is more generalized than previous I/O mechanisms, making it easier to implement new device drivers. One of the original motivations for STREAMS was to clean up and improve traditional UNIX character I/O sent to terminal devices.

System V-based versions of UNIX also include the Transport Layer Interface (TLI) networking interface to STREAMS drivers, a socketlike interface enabling the STREAMS-based network drivers to communicate with other socket-based programs.

Improvements over traditional UNIX I/O

Traditional UNIX character-based I/O evolved from the early days of UNIX. As with any complex software subsystem, over time, unplanned and poorly architected changes added yet more complexity. Some of the advantage of STREAMS comes simply from the fact that it is newer and can take advantage of lessons learned over the years. This yields a cleaner interface than was available before.

STREAMS also makes adding network protocols easier than having to write the whole driver and all its required parts from scratch. The device-dependent code has been separated into *modules* so that only the relevant part must be rewritten for each new device. Common I/O housekeeping code (e.g., buffer allocation and management) has been standardized so that each module can leverage services provided by the stream.

STREAMS processing involves sending and receiving *streams messages*, rather than just doing raw, character-by-character I/O. STREAMS also added flow control and priority processing.

Anatomy of a STREAM

Each STREAM has three parts:

- the **stream head**, an access point for a user application, for functions, and for data structures representing the STREAM
- **modules**—code to process data being read or written
- the **stream driver**, the back-end code that communicates with the specific device

All three run in kernel space, although modules can be added from user space.

The stream head provides the system call interface for a user application. A stream head is created by using the open () system call. The kernel manages any memory allocation required, the *upstream* and *downstream* flow of data, queue scheduling, flow control, and error logging.

Data written to the stream head from an application program are in the form of a message that is passed to the first module for processing. This module processes the message and passes the result to the second module. Processing and passing continue until the last module passes the message to the stream driver, which writes the data to the appropriate device. Data coming from the device take the same path in the reverse direction.

STREAM system calls

In addition to the I/O system calls we've already seen—ioctl (), open (), close (), read (), and write ()—the following system calls are useful with a stream:

- getmsg ()—get a message from a stream

- putmsg ()—put a message on a stream
- poll ()—poll one or more streams for activity
- isastream ()—find out whether a given file descriptor is a stream

PROCESS MANAGEMENT

A UNIX process is a unique instance of a running or runnable program. Every process in a UNIX system has the following attributes:

- some code (a. k. a. text)
- some data
- a stack
- a unique process ID (PID) number

When UNIX is first started, there's only one visible process in the system. This process is called "init," and is PID 1. The only way to create a new process in UNIX is to duplicate an existing process, so "init" is the ancestor of all subsequent processes. When a process duplicates, the parent and child processes are virtually identical (except for things like PIDs, PPIDs, and run times); the child's code, data, and stack are a copy of the parent's, and it even continues to execute the same code. A child process may, however, replace its code with that of another executable file, thereby differentiating itself from its parent. For example, when "init" starts executing, it quickly duplicates several times. Each of the duplicate child processes then replaces its code from the executable file called "getty," which is responsible for handling user logins. The process hierarchy therefore looks like that shown in Figure 13.30.

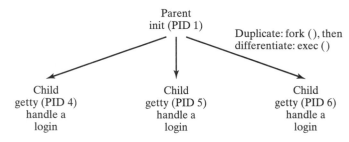

FIGURE 13.30

The initial process hierarchy.

When a child process terminates, its death is communicated to its parent so that the parent may take some appropriate action. It's common for a parent process to suspend until one of its children terminates. For example, when a shell executes a utility in the foreground, it duplicates into two shell processes; the child shell process replaces its code with that of the utility, whereas the parent shell waits for the child process to terminate. When the child terminates, the original parent process "awakens" and presents the user with the next shell prompt.

Figure 13.31 provides an illustration of the way that a shell executes a utility; I've indicated the system calls that are responsible for each phase of the execution. The Internet shell that I present later in the chapter has the basic process management facilities of classic UNIX shells and is a good place to look for some in-depth coding examples that utilize process-oriented system calls. In the meantime, let's look at some simple programs that introduce these system calls one by one. The next few subsections describe the system calls shown in Figure 13.32.

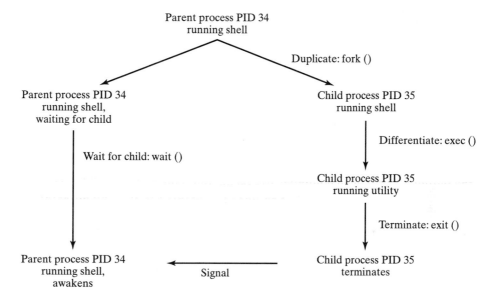

FIGURE 13.31

How a shell runs a utility.

Name	Function
fork	duplicates a process
getpid	obtains a process' ID number
getppid	obtains a parent process' ID number
exit	terminates a process
wait	waits for a child process
exec	replaces the code, data, and stack of a process

FIGURE 13.32

UNIX process-oriented system calls.

Creating a New Process: `fork` ()

A process may duplicate itself by using fork (), which works as shown in Figure 13.33. fork () is a strange system call, because one process (the original) calls it, but two processes (the original and its child) return from it. Both processes continue to run the same code concurrently, but have completely separate stack and data spaces.

System Call: pid_t **fork** (void)

fork () causes a process to duplicate. The child process is an almost exact duplicate of the original parent process; it inherits a copy of its parent's code, data, stack, open file descriptors, and signal table. However, the parent and child have different process ID numbers and parent process ID numbers.

    If fork () succeeds, it returns the PID of the child to the parent process and returns 0 to the child process. If fork () fails, it returns −1 to the parent process, and no child is created.

FIGURE 13.33

Description of the fork () system call.

Now, that reminds me of a great sci-fi story I read once, about a man who comes across a fascinating booth at a circus. The vendor at the booth tells the man that the booth is a matter replicator: Anyone who walks through the booth is duplicated. But that's not all: The original person walks out of the booth unharmed, but the duplicate person walks out onto the surface of Mars as a slave of the Martian construction crews. The vendor then tells the man that he'll be given a million dollars if he allows himself to be replicated, and the man agrees. He happily walks through the machine, looking forward to collecting the million dollars . . . and walks out onto the surface of Mars. Meanwhile, back on Earth, his duplicate is walking off with a stash of cash. The question is this: If you came across the booth, what would you do?

A process may obtain its own process ID and parent process ID numbers by using the getpid () and getppid () system calls, respectively. Figure 13.34 gives a synopsis

---

System Call: pid_t **getpid** (void)

        pid_t **getppid** (void)

getpid () and getppid () return a process' ID and parent process' ID numbers, respectively. They always succeed. The parent process ID number of PID 1 is 1.

FIGURE 13.34

Description of the getpid () and getppid () system calls.

of these calls. To illustrate the operation of fork (), here's a small program that duplicates and then branches, based on the return value of fork ():

```
$ cat myfork.c                      ...list the program.
#include <stdio.h>
main ()
{
 int pid;
 printf ("I'm the original process with PID %d and PPID %d.\n",
         getpid (), getppid ());
 pid = fork (); /* Duplicate. Child and parent continue from here */
 if (pid != 0) /* pid is non-zero, so I must be the parent */
    {
       printf ("I'm the parent process with PID %d and PPID %d.\n",
               getpid (), getppid ());
       printf ("My child's PID is %d\n", pid);
    }
 else /* pid is zero, so I must be the child */
    {
       printf ("I'm the child process with PID %d and PPID %d.\n",
               getpid (), getppid ());
    }
 printf ("PID %d terminates.\n", getpid () ); /* Both processes execute
this */
}
$ myfork                        ...run the program.
I'm the original process with PID 13292 and PPID 13273.
I'm the parent process with PID 13292 and PPID 13273.
My child's PID is 13293.
I'm the child process with PID 13293 and PPID 13292.
PID 13293 terminates.           ...child terminates.
PID 13292 terminates.           ...parent terminates.
$ _
```

The PPID of the parent refers to the PID of the shell that executed the "myfork" program.

Here is a warning: As you will soon see, it is dangerous for a parent to terminate without waiting for the death of its child. The only reason that the parent doesn't wait for its child to die in this example is because I haven't yet described the wait () system call!

Orphan Processes

If a parent dies before its child, the child is automatically adopted by the original "init" process, PID 1. To illustrate this feature, I modified the previous program by inserting a sleep statement into the child's code. This ensured that the parent process terminated before the child did. Here's the program and the resultant output:

```
$ cat orphan.c                       ...list the program.
#include <stdio.h>
main ()
```

```
{
  int pid;
   printf ("I'm the original process with PID %d and PPID %d.\n",
          getpid (), getppid ());
  pid = fork (); /* Duplicate. Child and parent continue from here */
  if (pid != 0) /* Branch based on return value from fork () */
    {
      /* pid is non-zero, so I must be the parent */
      printf ("I'm the parent process with PID %d and PPID %d.\n",
              getpid (), getppid ());
      printf ("My child's PID is %d\n", pid);
    }
  else
    {
      /* pid is zero, so I must be the child */
      sleep (5); /* Make sure that the parent terminates first */
      printf ("I'm the child process with PID %d and PPID %d.\n",
              getpid (), getppid ());
    }
   printf ("PID %d terminates.\n", getpid () ); /* Both processes execute
this */
}
$ orphan                       ...run the program.
I'm the original process with PID 13364 and PPID 13346.
I'm the parent process with PID 13364 and PPID 13346.
PID 13364 terminates.
I'm the child process with PID 13365 and PPID 1....orphaned!
PID 13365 terminates.
$ _
```

Figure 13.35 shows an illustration of the orphaning effect.

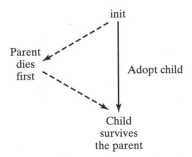

FIGURE 13.35

Process adoption.

Terminating a Process: `exit ()`

A process may terminate at any time by executing exit (), which works as shown in Figure 13.36. The termination code of a child process may be used for a variety of

---

System Call: void **exit** (int *status*)

exit () closes all of a process' file descriptors, deallocates its code, data, and stack, and then terminates the process. When a child process terminates, it sends its parent a SIGCHLD signal and waits for its termination code *status* to be accepted. Only the lower eight bits of *status* are used, so values are limited to 0–255. A process that is waiting for its parent to accept its return code is called a *zombie* process. A parent accepts a child's termination code by executing wait (), which is described shortly.

The kernel ensures that all of a terminating process' children are orphaned and adopted by "init" by setting their PPIDs to 1. The "init" process always accepts its children's termination codes.

exit () never returns.

FIGURE 13.36

Description of the exit () system call.

purposes by the parent process. Shells may access the termination code of their last child process via one of their special variables. For example, in the following code, the C shell stores the termination code of the last command in the variable $status:

```
% cat myexit.c                    ...list the program.
#include <stdio.h>
main ()
{
  printf ("I'm going to exit with return code 42\n");
  exit (42);
}
% myexit                          ...run the program.
I'm going to exit with return code 42
% echo $status                    ...display the termination code.
42
% _
```

In all other shells, the return value is returned in the special shell variable $?.

Zombie Processes

A process that terminates cannot leave the system until its parent accepts its return code. If its parent process is already dead, it'll already have been adopted by the "init" process, which always accepts its children's return codes. However, if a process' parent is alive, but never executes a wait (), the child process' return code will never be accepted and the process will remain a zombie. A zombie process doesn't have any code, data, or stack, so it doesn't use up many system resources, but it does continue to inhabit the system's fixed-size process table. Too many zombie processes can require the system administrator to intervene. (See Chapter 15 for more details.)

The next program created a zombie process, which was indicated in the output from the **ps** utility. When I killed the parent process, the child was adopted by "init" and allowed to rest in peace. Here is the code:

```
$ cat zombie.c                    ...list the program.
#include <stdio.h>
main ()
{
 int pid;
  pid = fork (); /* Duplicate */
  if (pid != 0) /* Branch based on return value from fork () */
    {
      while (1)  /* Never terminate, and never execute a wait () */
        sleep (1000);
    }
  else
    {
      exit (42); /* Exit with a silly number */
    }
}
$ zombie &      ...execute the program in the background.
[1] 13545
$ ps                              ...obtain process status.
 PID TT STAT   TIME COMMAND
13535 p2 S     0:00 -ksh (ksh) ...the shell.
13545 p2 S     0:00 zombie      ...the parent process.
13546 p2 Z     0:00 <defunct>  ...the zombie child.
13547 p2 R     0:00 ps
$ kill 13545                      ...kill the parent process.
[1]    Terminated          zombie
$ ps                      ...notice the zombie is gone now.
 PID TT STAT   TIME COMMAND
13535 p2 S     0:00 -ksh (ksh)
13548 p2 R     0:00 ps
$ _
```

Waiting for a Child: `wait ()`

A parent process may wait for one of its children to terminate and then accept its child's termination code by executing wait (), described in Figure 13.37. In the next example, the child process terminated before the end of the program by executing an exit () with return code 42. Meanwhile, the parent process executed a wait () and suspended until it received its child's termination code. At that point, the parent displayed information about its child's demise and executed the rest of the program. The code is as follows:

```
$ cat mywait.c                        ...list the program.
#include <stdio.h>
main ()
```

```
{
  int pid, status, childPid;
  printf ("I'm the parent process and my PID is %d\n", getpid ());
  pid = fork (); /* Duplicate */
  if (pid != 0) /* Branch based on return value from fork () */
    {
      printf ("I'm the parent process with PID %d and PPID %d\n",
              getpid (), getppid ());
      childPid = wait (&status); /* Wait for a child to terminate. */
      printf ("A child with PID %d terminated with exit code %d\n",
              childPid, status >> 8);
    }
  else
    {
      printf ("I'm the child process with PID %d and PPID %d\n",
              getpid (), getppid ());
      exit (42); /* Exit with a silly number */
    }
  printf ("PID %d terminates\n", getpid () );
}
$ mywait                          ...run the program.
I'm the parent process and my PID is 13464
I'm the child process with PID 13465 and PPID 13464
I'm the parent process with PID 13464 and PPID 13409
A child with PID 13465 terminated with exit code 42
PID 13465 terminates
$ _
```

System Call: pid_t **wait** (int* *status*)

wait () causes a process to suspend until one of its children terminates. A successful call to wait () returns the PID of the child that terminated and places a status code into *status* that is encoded as follows:

- If the rightmost byte of *status* is zero, the leftmost byte contains the low eight bits of the value returned by the child's exit () or return ().

- If the rightmost byte is nonzero, the rightmost seven bits are equal to the number of the signal that caused the child to terminate, and the remaining bit of the rightmost byte is set to 1 if the child produced a core dump.

If a process executes a wait () and has no children, wait () returns immediately with −1. If a process executes a wait () and one or more of its children are already zombies, wait () returns immediately with the status of one of the zombies.

FIGURE 13.37

Description of the wait () system call.

Differentiating a Process: exec ()

A process may replace its current code, data, and stack with those of another executable file by using one of the exec () family of system calls. When a process executes an exec (), its PID and PPID numbers stay the same—only the code that the process is executing changes. The exec () family works as shown in Figure 13.38. The members of the exec () family listed in the figure aren't really system calls: rather, they're C library functions that invoke the execve () system call. execve () is hardly ever used directly, as it contains some rarely used options.

Library Routine: int **execl** (const char* *path*, const char* *arg0*, const char* *arg1*, ..., const char* *argn*, NULL)

> int **execv** (const char* *path*, const char* *argv*[])
>
> int **execlp** (const char* *path*, const char* *arg0*, const char* *arg1*,..., const char* *argn*, NULL)
>
> int **execvp** (const char* *path*, const char* *argv*[])

The exec () family of library routines replaces the calling process' code, data, and stack from the executable file whose pathname is stored in *path*.

execl () is identical to execlp (), and execv () is identical to execvp (), except that execl () and execv () require the absolute or relative pathname of the executable file to be supplied, whereas execlp () and execvp () use the $PATH environment variable to find *path*.

If the executable file is not found, the system call returns –1; otherwise, the calling process replaces its code, data, and stack from the executable file and starts to execute the new code. A successful exec () never returns.

execl () and execlp () invoke the executable file with the string arguments pointed to by *arg1..argn*. *arg0* must be the name of the executable file itself, and the list of arguments must be terminated with a null.

execv () and execvp () invoke the executable file with the string arguments pointed to by *argv*[1]..*argv*[n], where *argv*[n+1] is NULL. *argv*[0] must be the name of the executable file itself.

FIGURE 13.38

Description of the execl (), execv (), execlp (), and execvp () library routines.

In the following example, the program displayed a small message and then replaced its code with that of the "ls" executable file:

```
$ cat myexec.c                    ...list the program.
#include <stdio.h>
main ()
{
  printf ("I'm process %d and I'm about to exec an ls -l\n", getpid ());
```

```
execl ("/bin/ls", "ls", "-l", NULL); /* Execute ls */
printf ("This line should never be executed\n");
}
$ myexec                        ...run the program.
I'm process 13623 and I'm about to exec an ls -l
total 125
-rw-r--r--  1 glass          277 Feb 15 00:47 myexec.c
-rwxr-xr-x  1 glass        24576 Feb 15 00:48 myexec
$ _
```

Note that the execl () was successful and therefore never returned.

Changing Directories: `chdir ()`

Every process has a *current working directory* that is used in processing a relative pathname. A child process inherits its current working directory from its parent. For example, when a utility is executed from a shell, its process inherits the shell's current working directory. To change a process' current working directory, use chdir (), which works as shown in Figure 13.39. In the following example, the process printed its current

---

System Call: int **chdir** (const char* *pathname*)

chdir () sets a process' current working directory to the directory *pathname*. The process must have execute permission from the directory to succeed.
   chdir () returns 0 if successful; otherwise, it returns –1.

FIGURE 13.39

Description of the chdir () system call.

---

working directory before and after executing chdir () by executing **pwd**, using the system () library routine:

```
$ cat mychdir.c              ...list the source code.
#include <stdio.h>
main ()
{
  system ("pwd"); /* Display current working directory */
  chdir ("/"); /* Change working directory to root directory */
  system ("pwd"); /* Display new working directory */
  chdir ("/home/glass"); /* Change again */
  system ("pwd"); /* Display again */
}
$ mychdir                    ...execute the program.
/home/glass
/
/home/glass
$ _
```

Changing Priorities: `nice ()`

Every process has a priority value between −20 and +19 that affects the amount of CPU time that the process is allocated. In general, the smaller the priority value, the faster the process will run. Only superuser and kernel processes (described in Chapter 14) can have a negative priority value, and login shells start with priority 0.

Library Routine: int **nice** (int *delta*)

nice () adds *delta* to a process' current priority value. Only a superuser may specify a *delta* that leads to a negative priority value. Valid priority values lie between −20 and +19. If a *delta* is specified that takes a priority value beyond a limit, the value is truncated to the limit.

   If nice () succeeds, it returns the new nice value; otherwise it returns −1. Note that this can cause problems, since a nice value of −1 is valid.

FIGURE 13.40

Description of the nice () library routine.

   A child process inherits its priority value from its parent and may change it by using nice (), described in Figure 13.40. In the following example, the process executed **ps** commands before and after a couple of nice () calls:

```
$ cat mynice.c                ...list the source code.
#include <stdio.h>
main ()
{
 printf ("original priority\n");
 system ("ps"); /* Execute a ps */
 nice (0); /* Add 0 to my priority */
 printf ("running at priority 0\n");
 system ("ps"); /* Execute another ps */
 nice (10); /* Add 10 to my priority */
 printf ("running at priority 10\n");
 system ("ps"); /* Execute the last ps */
}
$ mynice                      ...execute the program.
original priority
 PID TT STAT   TIME COMMAND
15099 p2 S     0:00 -sh (sh)
15206 p2 S     0:00 a.out
15207 p2 S     0:00 sh -c ps
15208 p2 R     0:00 ps
running at priority 0        ...adding 0 doesn't change it.
 PID TT STAT   TIME COMMAND
15099 p2 S     0:00 -sh (sh)
15206 p2 S     0:00 a.out
15209 p2 S     0:00 sh -c ps
15210 p2 R     0:00 ps
running at priority 10       ...adding 10 makes them run slower.
```

```
PID TT STAT   TIME COMMAND
15099 p2 S     0:00 -sh (sh)
15206 p2 S N   0:00 a.out
15211 p2 S N   0:00 sh -c ps
15212 p2 R N   0:00 ps
$ _
```

Note that when the process' priority value became nonzero, it was flagged with an "N" by **ps**, together with the **sh** and **ps** commands that it created due to the system () library call.

Accessing User and Group IDs

Figure 13.41 shows the system calls that allow you to read a process' real and effective IDs. Figure 13.42 shows the system calls that allow you to set a process' real and effective IDs.

System Call: uid_t **getuid** ()

        uid_t **geteuid** ()

        gid_t **getgid** ()

        gid_t **getegid** ()

getuid () and geteuid () return the calling process' real and effective user ID, respectively. getgid () and getegid () return the calling process' real and effective group ID, respectively. The ID numbers correspond to the user and group IDs listed in the "/etc/passwd" and "/etc/group" files.
    These calls always succeed.

FIGURE 13.41

Description of the getuid (), geteuid (), getgid (), and getegid () system calls.

Library Routine: int **setuid** (uid_t *id*)

        int **seteuid** (uid_t *id*)

        int **setgid** (gid_t *id*)

        int **setegid** (gid_t *id*)

seteuid () and (setegid ()) set the calling process' effective user (group) ID. setuid () and (setgid ()) set the calling process' effective and real user (group) IDs to the specified value.
    These calls succeed only if executed by a superuser or if *id* is the real or effective user (group) ID of the calling process. They return 0 if successful; otherwise, they return –1.

FIGURE 13.42

Description of the setuid (), seteuid (), setgid (), and setegid () library routines.

Sample Program: Background Processing

Next, we will examine a sample program that makes use of fork () and exec () to execute a program in the background. The original process creates a child to exec the specified executable file and then terminates. The orphaned child is automatically adopted by "init." Here is the code:

```
$ cat background.c                    ...list the program.
#include <stdio.h>
main (argc, argv)
int argc;
char* argv [];
{
  if (fork () == 0) /* Child */
    {
      execvp (argv[1], &argv[1]); /* Execute other program */
      fprintf (stderr, "Could not execute %s\n", argv[1]);
    }
}
$ background cc mywait.c   ...run the program.
$ ps                      ...confirm that "cc" is in background.
  PID TT STAT  TIME COMMAND
13664 p0 S     0:00 -csh (csh)
13716 p0 R     0:00 ps
13717 p0 D     0:00 cc mywait.c
$ _
```

Note how I craftily passed the argument list from main () to execvp () by passing &argv[1] as the second argument to execvp (). Note also that I used execvp () instead of execv () so that the program could use $PATH to find the executable file.

Sample Program: Disk Usage

The next programming example uses a novel technique for counting the number of nondirectory files in a hierarchy. When the program is started, its first argument must be the name of the directory to search. The program searches through each entry in the directory, spawning off a new process for each. Each child process either exits with 1 if its associated file is a nondirectory file or repeats the process, summing up the exit codes of its children and exiting with the total count. This technique is interesting, but silly: Not only does it create a large number of processes, which is not particularly efficient, but since it uses the termination code to return the file count, it's limited to an eight-bit total count. The code is as follows:

```
$ cat count.c                         ...list the program.
#include <stdio.h>
#include <fcntl.h>
#include <sys/dirent.h>
#include <sys/stat.h>
long processFile ();
```

```
long processDirectory ();
main (argc, argv)
int argc;
char* argv [];
{
 long count;
  count = processFile (argv[1]);
 printf ("Total number of non-directory files is %ld\n", count);
 return (/* EXIT_SUCCESS */ 0);
}
long processFile (name)
char* name;
{
 struct stat statBuf; /* To hold the return data from stat () */
 mode_t mode;
 int result;
  result = stat (name, &statBuf); /* Stat the specified file */
 if (result == -1) return (0); /* Error */
 mode = statBuf.st_mode; /* Look at the file's mode */
 if (S_ISDIR (mode)) /* Directory */
   return (processDirectory (name));
 else
   return (1); /* A non-directory file was processed */
}
long processDirectory (dirName)
char* dirName;
{
 int fd, children, i, charsRead, childPid, status;
 long count, totalCount;
 char fileName [100];
 struct dirent dirEntry;
  fd = open (dirName, O_RDONLY); /* Open directory for reading */
 children = 0; /* Initialize child process count */
  while (1) /* Scan directory */
   {
     charsRead = getdents (fd, &dirEntry, sizeof (struct dirent));
     if (charsRead == 0) break; /* End of directory */
     if (strcmp (dirEntry.d_name, ".") != 0 &&
        strcmp (dirEntry.d_name, "..") != 0)
       {
         if (fork () == 0) /* Create a child to process dir. entry */
           {
             sprintf (fileName, "%s/%s", dirName, dirEntry.d_name);
             count = processFile (fileName);
             exit (count);
           }
         else
           ++children; /* Increment count of child processes */
       }
```

```
          lseek (fd, dirEntry.d_off, SEEK_SET); /* Jump to next dir.entry */
      }
   close (fd); /* Close directory */
   totalCount = 0; /* Initialize file count */
   for (i = 1; i <= children; i++) /* Wait for children to terminate */
      {
         childPid = wait (&status); /* Accept child's termination code */
         totalCount += (status >> 8); /* Update file count */
      }
    return (totalCount); /* Return number of files in directory */
}
$ ls -F              ...list current directory.
a.out*          disk.c           fork         tmp/         zombie*
background      myexec.c         myfork.c     mywait.c
background.c    myexit.c         orphan.c     mywait*
count*          myexit*          orphan*      zombie.c
$ ls tmp             ...list only subdirectory.
a.out*          disk.c           myexit.c     orphan.c
background.c    myexec.c         myfork.c     mywait.c
zombie.c
$ count .            ...count regular files from ".".
Total number of non-directory files is 25
$ _
```

Threads

Multiple processes are expensive to create, either anew or by copying an existing process with the fork () system call. Often, a completely new process space is not necessary for a small, yet independent, task in a program. In fact, you may want separate tasks to be able to share some resources in a process, such as memory space, or to share an open device.

When multiprocessor systems became available, it was clear that UNIX needed a better way to take advantage of multiple processors without requiring a new process to be started in order to take advantage of the additional processor. A *thread* is an abstraction that allows multiple "threads of control" in a single process space. It can almost be thought of as a process within a process (almost). The thread model is similar to the UNIX process model in many ways.

Terminology among some thread implementations can be confusing. You may find the term "lightweight processes" used interchangeably with "thread," or you may find places where the two terms are used to distinguish subtle differences. In most cases, the idea of lighter weight (i.e., less expensive costs) is what is intended. For the purposes of our high-level examination, we will merely refer to *threads*.

Since the implementation of thread functionality varies widely in different versions of UNIX, to examine any one would unfairly ignore others, and a complete examination of all current implementations is beyond the scope of this introductory text. We therefore will examine UNIX thread functionality at a high level that is common to all implementations. I recommend that you consult the documentation for your version of UNIX for information on specific system calls.

Thread management

Four major functions make up the common thread management capabilities in most implementations:

- **create**—create a thread
- **join**—suspend and wait for a created thread to terminate (similar to the **wait**() system call between parent and child processes)
- **detach**—allow the thread to release its resources to the system when it finishes and not require a join (in this case, an exit value is not available)
- **terminate**—return resources to process

Thread synchronization

In a multithreaded environment, one or more threads can be created to handle specific tasks. If the tasks are unrelated, the threads can be initiated and run to completion. If any part of the task requires information from another task, processing among threads must be synchronized. Synchronization can often be accomplished via standard UNIX IPC mechanisms, but most threads libraries also provide synchronization primitives specific to the use of threads.

A *mutex* object can be used to manage **mut**ual **ex**clusion among threads. Mutex objects can be created, destroyed, locked, and unlocked. The attributes of a mutex object are shared among threads and are used to let other threads know the state of the thread the mutex object describes. Mutex objects can also be used in conjunction with *conditional variables*, which maintain a value (such as a threshold) to allow more precise management of thread synchronization.

Thread Safety

So now you've synchronized the various threads of control in your own program, but what about library functions they call? Does your code need to synchronize its use of a graphics library (for example) to make sure that two separate threads don't try to write to the same part of the screen at the same time? What about two threads that are using a math library to update shared data? You've synchronized your use of your variables, but do the math functions use any shared variables? Is the function reentrant (i.e., can more than one control point be used in the memory space of the function at the same time)?

By asking these questions, you are asking if the library is *thread safe*. Is it safe to call the functions in these libraries from a multithreaded program? It probably isn't hard to imagine the kinds of unforeseen problems that can crop up under these circumstances. Unless the vendor or author of the library claims that it is thread safe, you should assume that it is not and write your code accordingly (managing mutually exclusive access to the library among the various threads in your program).

Other process-related system calls that we've already examined may be affected by the implementation of threads. For example, each thread maintains its own stack, signal mask, and local storage area. Therefore, it may not always be obvious when a system call applies only to the thread or to the entire process running the thread. It will be important for you to find out what effects your implementation of threads may have on other UNIX system calls.

Redirection

When a process forks, the child inherits a copy of its parent's file descriptors. When a process execs, all file descriptors that do not close upon execution remain unaffected, including the standard input, output, and error channels. The UNIX shells use these two pieces of information to implement redirection. For example, say you type the command

```
$ ls > ls.out
```

at a terminal. To perform the redirection, the shell performs the following series of actions:

- The parent shell forks and then waits for the child shell to terminate.
- The child shell opens the file "ls.out," creating or truncating it as necessary.
- The child shell then duplicates the file descriptor of "ls.out" to the standard output file descriptor, number 1, and then closes the original descriptor of "ls.out". All standard output is therefore redirected to "ls.out".
- The child shell then exec's the ls utility. Since file descriptors are inherited during an exec (), all of the standard output of ls goes to "ls.out".
- When the child shell terminates, the parent resumes. The parent's file descriptors are unaffected by the child's actions, as each process maintains its own private descriptor table.

To redirect the standard error channel in addition to standard output, the shell would simply have to duplicate the "ls.out" descriptor twice—once to descriptor 1 and once to descriptor 2.

Following a small program that does approximately the same kind of redirection as a UNIX shell. When invoked with the name of a file as the first parameter and a command sequence as the remaining parameters, the program "redirect" redirects the standard output of the command to the named file. Here's the code:

```
$ cat redirect.c                    ...list the program.
#include <stdio.h>
#include <fcntl.h>
main (argc, argv)
int argc;
char* argv [];
{
  int fd;
   /* Open file for redirection */
  fd = open (argv[1], O_CREAT | O_TRUNC | O_WRONLY, 0600);
  dup2 (fd, 1); /* Duplicate descriptor to standard output */
  close (fd); /* Close original descriptor to save descriptor space */
  execvp (argv[2], &argv[2]); /* Invoke program; will inherit stdout */
  perror ("main"); /* Should never execute */
}
```

```
$ redirect ls.out ls -1      ...redirect "ls -1" to "ls.out".
$ cat ls.out                 ...list the output file.
total 5
-rw-r-xr-x    1 gglass          0 Feb 15 10:35 ls.out
-rw-r-xr-x    1 gglass        449 Feb 15 10:35 redirect.c
-rwxr-xr-x    1 gglass       3697 Feb 15 10:33 redirect
$ _
```

The Internet shell described at the end of this chapter has better redirection facilities than the standard UNIX shells; it can even redirect output to another Internet shell on a remote host.

SIGNALS

Programs must sometimes deal with unexpected or unpredictable events, such as any of the following:

- a floating-point error
- a power failure
- an alarm clock "ring" (discussed soon)
- the death of a child process
- a termination request from a user (i.e., a *Control*-C)
- a suspend request from a user (i.e., a *Control*-Z)

These kinds of events are sometimes called *interrupts,* since they must interrupt the regular flow of a program in order to be processed. When UNIX recognizes that such an event has occurred, it sends the corresponding process a signal. There is a unique, numbered signal for each possible event. For example, if a process causes a floating-point error, the kernel sends the offending process signal number 8, as shown in Figure 13.43. The kernel isn't the only one that can send a signal; any process can send any other process a signal, as long as it has permission. (The rules regarding permissions are discussed shortly.)

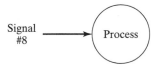

FIGURE 13.43

Floating-point error signal.

By means of a special piece of code called a *signal handler*, a programmer may arrange for a particular signal to be ignored or to be processed. In the latter case, the process that receives the signal suspends its current flow of control, executes the signal handler, and then resumes the original flow of control when the signal handler finishes.

By learning about signals, you can "protect" your programs from *Control*-C's, arrange for an alarm clock signal to terminate your program if it takes too long to perform a task, and learn how UNIX uses signals during everyday operations.

The Defined Signals

Signals are defined in "/usr/include/sys/signal.h." A programmer may choose for a particular signal to trigger a user-supplied signal handler, trigger the default kernel-supplied handler, or be ignored. The default handler usually performs one of the following actions:

- terminates the process and generates a core file (*dump*)
- terminates the process without generating a core image file (*quit*)
- ignores and discards the signal (*ignore*)
- suspends the process (*suspend*)
- resumes the process

A List of Signals

Figure 13.44 lists the System V predefined signals, along with their macro definitions, numeric values, default actions, and a brief description of each.

Macro	#	Default	Description
SIGHUP	1	quit	hang-up
SIGINT	2	quit	interrupt
SIGQUIT	3	dump	quit
SIGILL	4	dump	invalid instruction
SIGTRAP	5	dump	trace trap (used by debuggers)
SIGABRT	6	dump	abort
SIGEMT	7	dump	emulator trap instruction
SIGFPE	8	dump	arithmetic exception
SIGKILL	9	quit	kill (cannot be caught, blocked, or ignored)
SIGBUS	10	dump	bus error (bad format address)
SIGSEGV	11	dump	segmentation violation (out-of-range address)

FIGURE 13.44

Signals.

SIGSYS	12	dump	bad argument to system call
SIGPIPE	13	quit	write on a pipe or other socket with no one to read it
SIGALRM	14	quit	alarm clock
SIGTERM	15	quit	software termination signal (default signal sent by *kill*)
SIGUSR1	16	quit	user signal 1
SIGUSR2	17	quit	user signal 2
SIGCHLD	18	ignore	child status changed
SIGPWR	19	ignore	power fail or restart
SIGWINCH	20	ignore	window size change
SIGURG	21	ignore	urgent socket condition
SIGPOLL	22	exit	pollable event
SIGSTOP	23	quit	stopped (signal)
SIGSTP	24	quit	stopped (user)
SIGCONT	25	ignore	continued
SIGTTIN	26	quit	stopped (tty input)
SIGTTOU	27	quit	stopped (tty output)
SIGVTALRM	28	quit	virtual timer expired
SIGPROF	29	quit	profiling timer expired
SIGXCPU	30	dump	CPU time limit exceeded
SIGXFSZ	31	dump	file size limit exceeded

FIGURE 13.44   *(Continued)*

Terminal Signals

The easiest way to send a signal to a foreground process is by pressing *Control*-C or *Control*-Z from the keyboard. When the terminal driver (the piece of software that supports the terminal) recognizes a *Control*-C, it sends a SIGINT signal to all of the processes in the current foreground job. Similarly, *Control*-Z causes the driver to send a SIGTSTP signal to all of the processes in the current foreground job. By default, SIGINT terminates a process and SIGTSTP suspends a process. Later in this section, I'll show you how to perform similar actions from a C program.

Requesting an Alarm Signal: `alarm ()`

One of the simplest ways to see a signal in action is to arrange for a process to receive an alarm clock signal, SIGALRM, by using alarm (). The default handler for this signal displays the message "Alarm clock" and terminates the process. Figure 13.45 shows how alarm () works. Here's a small program that uses alarm (), together with its output:

```
$ cat alarm.c                  ...list the program.
#include <stdio.h>
main ()
{
 alarm (3); /* Schedule an alarm signal in three seconds */
 printf ("Looping forever...\n");
 while (1);
 printf ("This line should never be executed\n");
}
$ alarm                        ...run the program.
Looping forever...
Alarm clock                    ...occurs three seconds later.
$ _
```

The next section shows you how you override a default signal handler and make your program respond specially to a particular signal.

Library Routine: unsigned int **alarm** (unsigned int *count*)

alarm () instructs the kernel to send the SIGALRM signal to the calling process after *count* seconds. If an alarm had already been scheduled, it is overwritten. If *count* is 0, any pending alarm requests are cancelled.

alarm () returns the number of seconds that remain until the alarm signal is sent.

FIGURE 13.45

Description of the alarm () library routine.

Handling Signals: `signal ()`

The last sample program reacted to the alarm signal SIGALRM in the default manner. The signal () system call may be used to override the default action. It works as shown in Figure 13.46. I made the following changes to the previous program so that it caught and processed the SIGALRM signal efficiently:

- I installed my own signal handler, alarmHandler (), by using signal ().
- I made the while loop less draining on the time-sharing system by making use of a system call called pause (). The old version of the while loop had an empty code body that caused it to loop very fast and soak up CPU resources. The new version of the while loop suspends each time through the loop until a signal is received.

Library Routine: void (***signal** (int *sigCode*, void (*func*)(int))) (int)

signal () allows a process to specify the action that it will take when a particular signal is received. The parameter *sigCode* specifies the number of the signal that is to be reprogrammed, and *func* may be one of several values:

- SIG_IGN, which indicates that the specified signal should be ignored and discarded.
- SIG_DFL, which indicates that the kernel's default handler should be used.
- an address of a user-defined function, which indicates that the function should be executed when the specified signal arrives.

   The valid signal numbers are stored in "/usr/include/signal.h". The signals SIGKILL and SIGSTP may not be reprogrammed. A child process inherits the signal settings from its parent during a fork (). When a process performs an exec (), previously ignored signals remain ignored, but installed handlers are set back to the default handler.
   With the exception of SIGCHLD, signals are not stacked. This means that if a process is sleeping and three identical signals are sent to it, only one of the signals is actually processed.
   signal () returns the previous *func* value associated with *sigCode* if successful; otherwise, it returns –1.

FIGURE 13.46

Description of the signal () library routine.

Library Routine: int **pause** (void)

pause () suspends the calling process and returns when the calling process receives a signal. Pause () is most often used to wait efficiently for an alarm signal. It doesn't return anything useful.

FIGURE 13.47

Description of the pause () library routine.

Figure 13.47 provides a description of pause (). Here's the updated version of the program:

```
$ cat handler.c                        ...list the program.
#include <stdio.h>
#include <signal.h>
int alarmFlag = 0; /* Global alarm flag */
```

```
void alarmHandler (); /* Forward declaration of alarm handler */
/**************************************************************/
main ()
{
 signal (SIGALRM, alarmHandler); /* Install signal handler */
 alarm (3); /* Schedule an alarm signal in three seconds */
 printf ("Looping...\n");
 while (!alarmFlag) /* Loop until flag set */
   {
     pause (); /* Wait for a signal */
   }
 printf ("Loop ends due to alarm signal\n");
}
/**************************************************************/
void alarmHandler ()
{
 printf ("An alarm clock signal was received\n");
 alarmFlag = 1;
}
$ handler                          ...run the program.
Looping...
An alarm clock signal was received  ...occurs three seconds later.
Loop ends due to alarm signal
$ _
```

Protecting Critical Code and Chaining Interrupt Handlers

The same techniques that I just described may be used to protect critical pieces of code against *Control*-C attacks and other such signals. In these cases, it's common to save the previous value of the handler so that it can be restored after the critical code has executed. Here's the source code of a program that protects itself against SIGINT signals:

```
$ cat critical.c                    ...list the program.
#include <stdio.h>
#include <signal.h>
main ()
{
 void (*oldHandler) (); /* To hold old handler value */
  printf ("I can be Control-C'ed\n");
 sleep (3);
 oldHandler = signal (SIGINT, SIG_IGN); /* Ignore Control-C */
 printf ("I'm protected from Control-C now\n");
 sleep (3);
 signal (SIGINT, oldHandler); /* Restore old handler */
 printf ("I can be Control-C'ed again\n");
 sleep (3);
 printf ("Bye!\n");
}
$ critical                    ...run the program.
```

```
I can be Control-C'ed
^C                                  ...Control-C works here.
$ critical                          ...run the program again.
I can be Control-C'ed
I'm protected from Control-C now
^C                                  ...Control-C is ignored.
I can be Control-C'ed again
Bye!
$ _
```

Sending Signals: `kill ()`

A process may send a signal to another process by using the kill () system call. kill () is a misnomer, since many of the signals that it can send do not terminate a process. It's called kill () because of historical reasons: The main use of signals when UNIX was first designed was to terminate processes. kill () works as shown in Figure 13.48.

System Call: int **kill** (pid_t *pid*, int *sigCode*)

kill () sends the signal with value *sigCode* to the process with PID *pid*. kill () succeeds, and the signal is sent as long as at least one of the following conditions is satisfied:

- The sending process and the receiving process have the same owner.

- The sending process is owned by a superuser.

There are a few variations on the way that kill () works:

- If *pid* is 0, the signal is sent to all of the processes in the sender's process group.

- If *pid* is –1 and the sender is owned by a superuser, the signal is sent to all processes, including the sender.

- If *pid* is –1 and the sender is not a superuser, the signal is sent to all of the processes owned by the same owner as the sender, excluding the sending process.

- If *pid* is negative and not –1, the signal is sent to all of the processes in the process group. (Process groups are discussed later in the chapter.)

If kill () manages to send at least one signal successfully, it returns 0; otherwise, it returns –1.

FIGURE 13.48

Description of the kill () system call.

Death of Children

When a parent's child terminates, the child process sends its parent a SIGCHLD signal. A parent process often installs a handler to deal with this signal, which typically executes a wait () to accept the child's termination code and let the child "de-zombify."[1]

Alternatively, the parent can choose to ignore SIGCHLD signals, in which case the child de-zombifies automatically. One of the socket programs that follows later in the chapter makes use of this feature.

The next example illustrates a SIGCHLD handler and allows a user to limit the amount of time that a command takes to execute. The first parameter of "limit" is the maximum number of seconds that is allowed for execution, and the remaining parameters are the command itself. The program works by performing the following steps:

1. The parent process installs a SIGCHLD handler that is executed when its child process terminates.
2. The parent process forks a child process to execute the command.
3. The parent process sleeps for the specified number of seconds. When it wakes up, it sends its child process a SIGINT signal to kill it.
4. If the child terminates before its parent finishes sleeping, the parent's SIGCHLD handler is executed, causing the parent to terminate immediately.

Here are the source code and sample output from the program:

```
$ cat limit.c                    ...list the program.
#include <stdio.h>
#include <signal.h>
int delay;
void childHandler ();
/*********************************************************************/
main (argc, argv)
int argc;
char* argv[];
{
 int pid;
 signal (SIGCHLD, childHandler); /* Install death-of-child handler */
 pid = fork (); /* Duplicate */
 if (pid == 0) /* Child */
   {
     execvp (argv[2], &argv[2]); /* Execute command */
     perror ("limit"); /* Should never execute */
   }
 else /* Parent */
   {
     sscanf (argv[1], "%d", &delay); /* Read delay from command line */
```

---

[1] This means that the child is completely laid to rest and is no longer a zombie.

```
        sleep (delay); /* Sleep for the specified number of seconds */
        printf ("Child %d exceeded limit and is being killed\n", pid);
        kill (pid, SIGINT); /* Kill the child */
    }
}
/******************************************************************/
void childHandler () /* Executed if the child dies before the parent */
{
    int childPid, childStatus;
    childPid = wait (&childStatus); /* Accept child's termination code */
    printf ("Child %d terminated within %d seconds\n", childPid, delay);
    exit (/* EXITSUCCESS */ 0);
}
$ limit 5 ls               ...run the program; command finishes OK.
a.out           alarm           critical        handler         limit
alarm.c         critical.c      handler.c       limit.c
Child 4030 terminated within 5 seconds
$ limit 4 sleep 100        ...run it again; command takes too long.
Child 4032 exceeded limit and is being killed
$ _
```

Suspending and Resuming Processes

The SIGSTOP and SIGCONT signals suspend and resume a process, respectively.
They are used by the UNIX shells (most shells, except for the Bourne shell) that support job control to implement built-in commands such as *stop, fg,* and *bg.*

In the next example, the main program created two children that entered an infinite loop and displayed a message every second. The main program waited for three
seconds and then suspended the first child. The second child continued to execute as
usual. After another three seconds, the parent restarted the first child, waited a little
while longer, and then terminated both children. Here is the code:

```
$ cat pulse.c              ...list the program.
#include <signal.h>
#include <stdio.h>
main ()
{
    int pid1;
    int pid2;
    pid1 = fork ();
    if (pid1 == 0) /* First child */
    {
        while (1) /* Infinite loop */
        {
            printf ("pid1 is alive\n");
            sleep (1);
        }
    }
    pid2 = fork (); /* Second child */
```

```
      if (pid2 == 0)
        {
          while (1) /* Infinite loop */
            {
              printf ("pid2 is alive\n");
              sleep (1);
            }
        }
    sleep (3);
    kill (pid1, SIGSTOP); /* Suspend first child */
    sleep (3);
    kill (pid1, SIGCONT); /* Resume first child */
    sleep (3);
    kill (pid1, SIGINT); /* Kill first child */
    kill (pid2, SIGINT); /* Kill second child */
    }
$ pulse                    ...run the program.
pid1 is alive          ...both run in first three seconds.
pid2 is alive
pid1 is alive
pid2 is alive
pid1 is alive
pid2 is alive
pid2 is alive              ...just the second child runs now.
pid2 is alive
pid2 is alive
pid1 is alive              ...the first child is resumed.
pid2 is alive
pid1 is alive
pid2 is alive
pid1 is alive
pid2 is alive
$ _
```

Process Groups and Control Terminals

When you're in a shell and you execute a program that creates several children, a single *Control*-C from the keyboard will normally terminate the program and its children and then return you to the shell. In order to support this kind of behavior, UNIX introduced a few new concepts:

- In addition to having a unique process ID number, every process is a member of a *process group*. Several processes can be members of the same process group. When a process forks, the child inherits its process group from its parent. A process may change its process group to a new value by using setpgid (). When a process execs, its process group remains the same.
- Every process can have an associated *control terminal*—typically, the terminal where the process was started. When a process forks, the child inherits its control terminal from its parent. When a process execs, its control terminal stays the same.

- Every terminal can be associated with a single *control* process. When a metacharacter such as *Control-C* is detected, the terminal sends the appropriate signal to all of the processes in the process group of its control process.
- If a process attempts to read from its control terminal and is not a member of the same process group as the terminal's control process, the process is sent a SIGTTIN signal, which normally suspends it.

Here's how a shell uses these features:

- When an interactive shell begins, it is the control process of a terminal and has that terminal as its control terminal. How this occurs is beyond the scope of the book.
- When a shell executes a foreground process, the child shell places itself in a different process group before exec'ing the command and takes control of the terminal. Any signals generated from the terminal thus go to the foreground command rather than the original parent shell. When the foreground command terminates, the original parent shell takes back control of the terminal.
- When a shell executes a background process, the child shell places itself in a different process group before exec'ing, but does not take control of the terminal. Any signals generated from the terminal continue to go to the shell. If the background process tries to read from its control terminal, it is suspended by a SIGTTIN signal.

The diagram in Figure 13.49 illustrates a typical setup. Assume that process 145 and process 230 are the process leaders of background jobs, and that process 171 is the process leader of the foreground job. setpgid () changes a process' group and works as shown in Figure 13.50. A process may find out its current process group ID by using getpgid (), which works as shown in Figure 13.51.

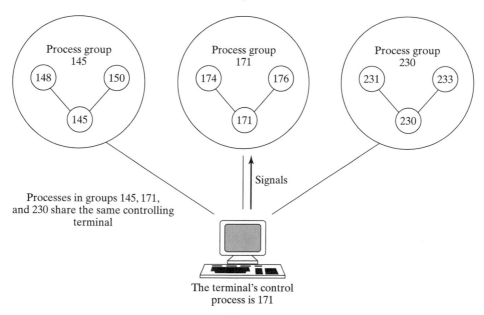

FIGURE 13.49

Control terminals and process groups.

System Call: pid_t **setpgid** (pid_t *pid*, pid_t *pgrpId*)

setpgid () sets the process group ID of the process with PID *pid* to *pgrpId*. If *pid* is zero, the caller's process group ID is set to *pgrpId*. In order for setpgid () to succeed and set the process group ID, at least one of the following conditions must be met:

- The caller and the specified process must have the same owner.

- The caller must be owned by a superuser.

When a process wants to start its own unique process group, it typically passes its own process ID number as the second parameter to setpgid ().
    If setpgid () fails, it returns –1.

FIGURE 13.50

Description of the setpgid () system call.

System Call: pid_t **getpgid** (pid_t *pid*)

getpgid () returns the process group ID of the process with PID *pid*. If *pid* is zero, the process group ID of the caller is returned.

FIGURE 13.51

Description of the getpgid () system call.

The next example illustrates the fact that a terminal distributes signals to all of the processes in its control process' process group. Since the child inherited its process group from its parent, both the parent and child catch the SIGINT signal. The code is as follows:

```
$ cat pgrp1.c                         ...list program.
#include <signal.h>
#include<stdio.h>
void sigintHandler ();
main ()
{
  signal (SIGINT, sigintHandler); /* Handle Control-C */
  if (fork () == 0)
    printf ("Child PID %d PGRP %d waits\n", getpid (),getpgid (0));
  else
      printf ("Parent PID %d PGRP %dwaits\n", getpid (), getpgid (0));
  pause (); /* Wait for asignal */
}
void sigintHandler ()
```

```
{
  printf ("Process %d got a SIGINT\n",getpid ());
}
$ pgrp1                          ...run the program.
Parent PID 24583 PGRP 24583 waits
Child PID 24584 PGRP 24583 waits
^C                         ...press Control-C.
Process 24584 got a SIGINT
Process 24583 got a SIGINT
$ _
```

If a process places itself into a different process group, it is no longer associated with the terminal's control process and does not receive signals from the terminal. In the following example, the child process is not affected by a *Control-C:*

```
$ cat pgrp2.c                       ...list the program.
#include <signal.h>
#include <stdio.h>
void sigintHandler ();
main()
{
 int i;
   signal (SIGINT, sigintHandler); /* Install signal handler */
 if (fork () == 0)
     setpgid (0, getpid ()); /* Place child in its own process group */
 printf ("Process PID %d PGRP %d waits\n", getpid (), getpgid (0));
 for (i = 1; i <= 3; i++) /* Loop three times */
   {
     printf ("Process %d is alive\n", getpid ());
     sleep(1);
   }
}
void sigintHandler ()
{
 printf ("Process %d got a SIGINT\n", getpid ());
 exit (1);
}
$ pgrp2                         ...run the program.
Process PID 24591 PGRP 24591 waits
Process PID 24592 PGRP 24592 waits
^C                              ...Control-C
Process 24591 got a SIGINT      ...parent receives signal.
Process 24592 is alive          ...child carries on.
Process 24592 is alive
Process 24592 is alive
$ _
```

If a process attempts to read from its control terminal after it disassociates itself from the terminal's control process, it is sent a SIGTTIN signal, which suspends the receiver by default. In the following example, I trapped SIGTTIN with my own handler to make the effect a little clearer:

```
$ cat pgrp3.c                          ...list the program.
#include <signal.h>
#include <stdio.h>
#include <sys/termio.h>
#include <fcntl.h>
void sigttinHandler ();
main ()
{
 int status;
 char str [100];
  if (fork () == 0) /* Child */
    {
      signal (SIGTTIN, sigttinHandler); /* Install handler */
      setpgid (0, getpid ()); /* Place myself in a new process group */
      printf ("Enter a string: ");
      scanf ("%s", str); /* Try to read from control terminal */
      printf ("You entered %s\n", str);
    }
  else /* Parent */
    {
      wait (&status); /* Wait for child to terminate */
    }
}
void sigttinHandler ()
{
 printf ("Attempted inappropriate read from control terminal\n");
 exit (1);
}
$ pgrp3                                ...run the program.
Enter a string: Attempted inappropriate read from control terminal
$ _
```

IPC

Interprocess communication (IPC) is the generic term describing how two processes may exchange information with each other. In general, the two processes may be running on the same machine or on different machines, although some IPC mechanisms may support only local usage (e.g., signals and pipes). IPC may be an exchange of data wherein two or more processes are cooperatively processing the data or other synchronization information to help two independent, but related, processes schedule work so that they do not destructively overlap.

Pipes

Pipes are an interprocess communication mechanism that allow two or more processes to send information to each other. They are commonly used from within shells to connect the standard output of one utility to the standard input of another. For example, here's a simple shell command that determines how many users are on a system:

```
$ who | wc -1
```

The **who** utility generates one line of output per user. This output is then "piped" into the **wc** utility, which, when invoked with the **-1** option, outputs the total number of lines in its input. Thus, the pipelined command craftily calculates the total number of users by counting the number of lines that **who** generates. Figure 13.52 shows a diagram of the pipeline.

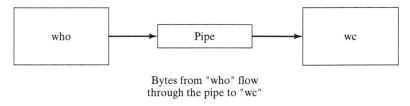

Bytes from "who" flow
through the pipe to "wc"

FIGURE 13.52

A simple pipe.

It's important to realize that both the writer process and the reader process of a pipeline execute concurrently; a pipe automatically buffers the output of the writer and suspends the writer if the pipe gets too full. Similarly, if a pipe empties, the reader is suspended until some more output becomes available.

All versions of UNIX support *unnamed* pipes, which are the kind of pipes that shells use. System V also supports a more powerful kind of pipe called a named pipe. In this section, I'll show you how to construct each kind of pipe, starting with unnamed pipes.

Unnamed pipes: pipe ()

An unnamed pipe is a unidirectional communication link that automatically buffers its input (the maximum size varies with different versions of UNIX, but is approximately 5K) and may be created using the pipe () system call. Each end of a pipe has an associated file descriptor. The "write" end of the pipe may be written to using write (), and the "read" end may be read from using read (). When a process has finished with a pipe's file descriptor, it should close it, using close (). Figure 13.53 shows how pipe () works.

If the code is executed, then the data structures shown in Figure 13.54 will be created. Unnamed pipes are usually used for communication between a parent process and its child, with one process writing and the other process reading. The typical sequence of events is as follows:

```
int fd [2];
pipe (fd);
```

System Call: int **pipe** (int *fd* [2])

pipe () creates an unnamed pipe and returns two file descriptors; the descriptor associated with the "read" end of the pipe is stored in *fd* [0], and the descriptor associated with the "write" end of the pipe is stored in *fd* [1].

The following rules apply to processes that read from a pipe:

- If a process reads from a pipe whose write end has been closed, the read () returns a 0, indicating the end of input.
- If a process reads from an empty pipe whose write end is still open, it sleeps until some input becomes available.
- If a process tries to read more bytes from a pipe than are present, all of the pipe's current contents are returned, and read () returns the number of bytes actually read.

The following rules apply to processes that write to a pipe:

- If a process writes to a pipe whose read end has been closed, the write fails and the writer is sent a SIGPIPE signal. The default action of this signal is to terminate the receiver.
- If a process writes fewer bytes to a pipe than the pipe can hold, the write () is guaranteed to be atomic; that is, the writer process will complete its system call without being preempted by another process. If a process writes more bytes to a pipe than the pipe can hold, no similar guarantees of atomicity apply.

Since access to an unnamed pipe is via the file descriptor mechanism, typically only the process that creates a pipe and its descendants may use the pipe.[2] lseek () has no meaning when applied to a pipe.

If the kernel cannot allocate enough space for a new pipe, pipe () returns –1; otherwise, it returns 0.

FIGURE 13.53

Description of the pipe () system call.

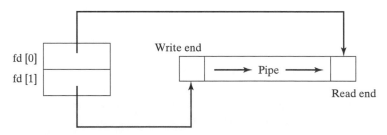

FIGURE 13.54

An unnamed pipe.

---

[2]In advanced situations, it is actually possible to pass file descriptors to unrelated processes via a pipe.

1. The parent process creates an unnamed pipe, using pipe ().
2. The parent process forks.
3. The writer closes its read end of the pipe, and the designated reader closes its write end of the pipe.
4. The processes communicate by using write () and read () calls.
5. Each process closes its active pipe descriptor when it's finished with it.

Bidirectional communication is possible only by using two pipes. Here's a small program that uses a pipe to allow the parent to read a message from its child:

```
$ cat talk.c                            ...list the program.
#include <stdio.h>
#define READ   0       /* The index of the read end of the pipe */
#define WRITE  1       /* The index of the write end of the pipe */
char* phrase = "Stuff this in your pipe and smoke it";
main ()
{
 int fd [2], bytesRead;
 char message [100]; /* Parent process' message buffer */
  pipe (fd); /*Create an unnamed pipe */
 if (fork () == 0) /* Child, writer */
   {
     close(fd[READ]); /* Close unused end */
     write (fd[WRITE],phrase, strlen (phrase) + 1); /* include NULL*/
     close (fd[WRITE]); /* Close used end*/
   }
 else /* Parent, reader*/
   {
     close (fd[WRITE]); /* Close unusedend */
     bytesRead = read (fd[READ], message, 100);
     printf ("Read %d bytes: %s\n", bytesRead, message); /* Send */
     close (fd[READ]); /* Close usedend */
   }
}
$ talk                          ...run the program.
Read 37 bytes: Stuff this in your pipe and smoke it
$ _
```

Notice that the child included the phrase's NULL terminator as part of the message so that the parent could easily display it. When a writer process sends more than one variable-length message into a pipe, it must use a protocol to indicate an end of message to the reader. Methods for doing this include the following:

- sending the length of a message (in bytes) before sending the message itself
- ending a message with a special character, such as a newline or a NULL

UNIX shells use unnamed pipes to build pipelines. To do so, they use a trick similar to the redirection mechanism described in an section to connect the standard output of one process to the standard input of another. To illustrate this approach, consider a program that executes two named programs, connecting the standard output of the first to the standard input of the second. The program doing the connecting assumes that neither program is invoked with options and that the names of the programs are listed on the command line. Here's the code:

```
$ cat connect.c                           ...list the program.
#include <stdio.h>
#define READ    0
#define WRITE   1
main (argc, argv)
int argc;
char* argv [];
{
 int fd [2];
  pipe (fd); /* Create an unamed pipe */
  if (fork () != 0) /* Parent, writer */
    {
      close (fd[READ]); /* Close unused end */
      dup2 (fd[WRITE], 1); /* Duplicate used end to stdout */
      close (fd[WRITE]); /* Close original used end */
      execlp (argv[1], argv[1], NULL); /* Execute writer program */
      perror ("connect");  /* Should never execute */
    }
  else /* Child, reader */
    {
      close (fd[WRITE]); /* Close unused end */
      dup2 (fd[READ], 0); /* Duplicate used end to stdin */
      close (fd[READ]); /* Close original used end */
      execlp (argv[2], argv[2], NULL); /* Execute reader program */
      perror ("connect"); /* Should never execute */
    }
}
$ who                           ...execute "who" by itself.
gglass                  ttyp0        Feb 15 18:45    (xyplex_3)
$ connect who wc                  ...pipe "who" through "wc".
        1       6       57      ...1 line, 6 words, 57 chars.
$ _
```

Later in the chapter, we examine a more sophisticated example of unnamed pipes. Also, the chapter review contains an interesting exercise that involves building a ring of pipes.

Named pipes

Named pipes [often referred to as first-in, first-out queues (FIFOs)] are less restricted than unnamed pipes, and offer the following advantages:

- They have a name that exists in the file system.
- They may be used by unrelated processes.
- They exist until they are explicitly deleted.

Unfortunately, named pipes are supported only by System V. All of the rules that I mentioned in the previous section regarding unnamed pipes apply to named pipes, except that named pipes have a larger buffer capacity—typically, about 40K.

Named pipes exist as special files in the file system and may be created in one of two ways:

- by using the UNIX **mknod** utility
- by using the mknod () system call

To create a named pipe using **mknod**, use the **p** option. (For more information about **mknod**, see Chapter 15.) The mode of the named pipe may be set using **chmod**, allowing others to access the pipe that you create. Here's an example of this procedure, executed from a Korn shell:

```
$ mknod myPipe p              ...create pipe.
$ chmod ug+rw myPipe          ...update permissions.
$ ls -lg myPipe               ...examine attributes.
 prw-rw----   1 glass      cs       0 Feb 27 12:38 myPipe
$ _
```

Note that the type of the named pipe is "p" in the **ls** listing.

To create a named pipe using mknod (), specify S_IFIFO as the file mode. The mode of the pipe can then be changed by using chmod (). Here's a snippet of C code that creates a named pipe with read and write permission for the owner and group:

```
mknod ("myPipe", SIFIFO, 0); /* Create a named pipe */
chmod ("myPipe", 0660); /* Modify its permission flags */
```

Regardless of how you go about creating a named pipe, the end result is the same: A special file is added into the file system. Once a named pipe is opened using open (), write () adds data at the start of the FIFO queue, and read () removes data from the end of the FIFO queue. When a process has finished using a named pipe, it should close it using close (), and when a named pipe is no longer needed, it should be removed from the file system via unlink ().

Like an unnamed pipe, a named pipe is intended only for use as a unidirectional link. Writer processes should open a named pipe for write only, and reader processes should open one for read only. Although a process could open a named pipe for both reading and writing, doing so doesn't have much practical application. Before I show you a sample program that uses named pipes, here are a couple of special rules concerning their use:

- If a process tries to open a named pipe for read only and no process currently has that file open for writing, the reader will wait until a process opens the file for writing, unless O_NONBLOCK/O_NDELAY is set, in which case open () succeeds immediately.
- If a process tries to open a named pipe for write only and no process currently has that file open for reading, the writer will wait until a process opens the file for

reading, unless O_NONBLOCK/O_NDELAY is set, in which case open () fails
immediately.

- Named pipes will not work across a network.

The next example uses two programs—"reader" and "writer"—and works like this:

- A single reader process is executed, creating a named pipe called "aPipe". The
  process then reads and displays NULL-terminated lines from the pipe until the
  pipe is closed by all of the writing processes.
- One or more writer processes are executed, each of which opens the named pipe
  called "aPipe" and sends three messages to it. If the pipe does not exist when a
  writer tries to open it, the writer retries every second until it succeeds. When all of
  a writer's messages are sent, the writer closes the pipe and exits.

Following are the source code for each file and some sample output:

Reader program

```
#include <stdio.h>
#include <sys/types.h>
#include <sys/stat.h>              /* For SIFIFO */
#include <fcntl.h>
/******************************************************************/
main ()
{
 int fd;
 char str[100];
 unlink("aPipe"); /* Remove named pipe if it already exists */
 mknod ("aPipe", S_IFIFO, 0); /* Create named pipe */
 chmod ("aPipe", 0660); /* Change its permissions */
 fd = open ("aPipe", O_RDONLY); /* Open it for reading */
  while (readLine (fd, str)) /* Display received messages */
    printf ("%s\n", str);
  close (fd); /* Close pipe */
}
/******************************************************************/
readLine (fd, str)
int fd;
char* str;
/* Read a single NULL-terminated line into str from fd */
/* Return 0 when the end-of-input is reached and 1 otherwise */
{
 int n;
  do /* Read characters until NULL or end-of-input */
    {
      n = read (fd, str, 1); /* Read one character */
    }
 while (n > 0 && *str++ != NULL);
 return (n > 0); /* Return false if end-of-input */
}
```

Writer program

```
#include <stdio.h>
#include <fcntl.h>
/******************************************************************/
main ()
{
 int fd, messageLen, i;
 char message [100];
  /* Prepare message */
 sprintf (message, "Hello from PID %d", getpid ());
 messageLen = strlen (message) + 1;
  do /* Keep trying to open the file until successful */
    {
      fd = open ("aPipe", O_WRONLY); /* Open named pipe for writing */
      if (fd == -1) sleep (1); /* Try again in 1 second */
    }
  while (fd == -1);
   for (i = 1; i <= 3; i++) /* Send three messages */
    {
      write (fd, message, messageLen); /* Write message down pipe */
      sleep (3); /* Pause a while */
    }
   close (fd); /* Close pipe descriptor */
}
```

Sample output

```
$ reader & writer & writer &    ...start 1 reader, 2 writers.
[1] 4698            ...reader process.
[2] 4699            ...first writer process.
[3] 4700            ...second writer process.
Hello from PID 4699
Hello from PID 4700
Hello from PID 4699
Hello from PID 4700
Hello from PID 4699
Hello from PID 4700
[2]    Done         writer     ...first writer exits.
[3]    Done         writer     ...second writer exits.
[1]    Done         reader     ...reader exits.
$ _
```

Sockets

Sockets are the traditional UNIX interprocess communication mechanism that allows processes to talk to each other, even if they're on different machines. It is this across-network capability that makes sockets so useful. For example, the **rlogin** utility, which allows a user on one machine to log into a remote host, is implemented with sockets.

Other common uses of sockets include the following:

- printing a file on one machine from another machine
- transferring files from one machine to another machine

Process communication via sockets is based on the client–server model. One process, known as a server process, creates a socket whose name is known by other client processes. These client processes can talk to the server process via a connection to its named socket. To do this, a client process first creates an unnamed socket and then requests that it be connected to the server's named socket. A successful connection returns one file descriptor to the client and one to the server, both of which may be used for reading and writing. Note that, unlike pipes, socket connections are bidirectional. Figure 13.55 illustrates the process.

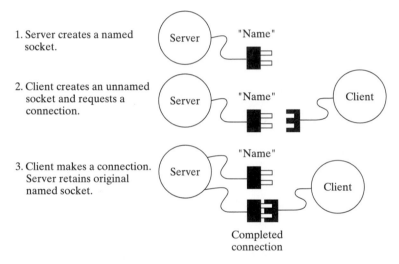

FIGURE 13.55

The socket connection.

Once a socket connection is made, it's quite common for the server process to fork a child process to converse with the client, while the original parent process continues to accept other client connections. A typical example of this is a remote print server: The server process first accepts a client that wishes to send a file for printing and then forks a child to perform the file transfer. The parent process meanwhile waits for more client print requests.

In what follows, we'll take a look at these topics:

- the different kinds of sockets
- how a server creates a named socket and waits for connections
- how a client creates an unnamed socket and requests a connection from a server

- how a server and client communicate after a socket connection is made
- how a socket connection is closed
- how a server can create a child process to converse with a client

The Different Kinds of Sockets

The various kinds of sockets may be classified according to three attributes:

- the *domain*
- the *type*
- the *protocol*

Domains

The domain of a socket indicates where the server and client sockets may reside; the domains that are currently supported include the following:

- AF_UNIX (the clients and server must be in the same machine)
- AF_INET (the clients and server may be anywhere on the Internet)
- AF_NS (the clients and server may be on a XEROX network system)

"AF" stands for "Address Family." There is a similar set of constants that begin with "PF" (e.g., PF_UNIX and PF_INET), which stands for "Protocol Family." Either set may be used, since they are equivalent. This book contains information about AF_UNIX and AF_INET sockets, but not AF_NS sockets.

Types

The type of socket determines the type of communication that can exist between the client and server; the following are the two main types that are currently supported:

- SOCK_STREAM: sequenced, reliable, two-way-connection-based, variable-length streams of bytes
- SOCK_DGRAM: like telegrams—connectionless, unreliable, fixed-length messages

Other types that are either in the planning stages or implemented only in some domains include the following:

- SOCK_SEQPACKET: sequenced, reliable, two-way-connection-based, fixed-length packets of bytes
- SOCK_RAW: provides access to internal network protocols and interfaces

This book contains information only on how to use SOCK_STREAM sockets, which are the most common. SOCK_STREAM sockets are both intuitive and easy to use.

Protocols

The protocol value specifies the low-level means by which the socket type is implemented. System calls that expect a protocol parameter accept 0 as meaning "the correct protocol"; in other words, the protocol value is something that you generally won't have to worry about. Most systems support only protocols other than 0 as an optional extra, so I'll use the default protocol in all the examples.

Writing Socket Programs

Any program that uses sockets must include "/usr/include/sys/types.h" and "/usr/include/sys/socket.h". Additional header files must be included on the basis of the socket domain that you wish to use. The most commonly used domains are shown in Figure 13.56. Other socket domains are defined in socket.h.

Domain	Additional header files
AF_UNIX	/usr/include/sys/un.h
AF_INET	/usr/include/netinet/in.h /usr/include/arpa/inet.h /urs/include/netdb.h

FIGURE 13.56

Common socket domains and corresponding header files.

To illustrate clearly the way in which a program that uses sockets is written, I'll build my description of socket-oriented system calls around a small client–server example that uses AF_UNIX sockets. Once I've done this, I'll show you another example that uses AF_INET sockets. The AF_UNIX example consists of the following two programs:

- "chef," the server, which creates a named socket called "recipe" and writes the recipe to any clients which request it. The recipe is a collection of variable-length NULL-terminated strings.
- "cook," the client, which connects to the named socket called "recipe" and reads the recipe from the server. "Cook" displays the recipe to standard output as it reads it, and then it terminates.

The chef server process runs in the background. Any client cook processes that connect to the server cause it fork a duplicate server to handle the recipe transfer, allowing the original server to accept other incoming connections. Here's some sample output from the chef–cook example:

```
$ chef &                 ...run the server in the background.
[1] 5684
$ cook             ...run a client-display the recipe.
```

```
spam, spam, spam, spam,
spam, and spam.
$ cook              ...run another client-display the recipe.
spam, spam, spam, spam,
spam, and spam.
$ kill %1                        ...kill the server.
[1]     Terminated              chef
$ _
```

Chef–Cook Listing

This section contains the complete listing of the chef and cook programs. I suggest that you skim quickly through the code and then read the sections that follow for details on how the two programs work. In the interests of space, I have purposely left out a great deal of error checking.

Chef Server

```
1   #include <stdio.h>
2   #include <signal.h>
3   #include <sys/types.h>
4   #include <sys/socket.h>
5   #include <sys/un.h>                 /* For AFUNIX sockets */
6
7   #define DEFAULT_PROTOCOL    0
8
9   /*************************************************************/
10
11  main ()
12
13  {
14    int serverFd, clientFd, serverLen, clientLen;
15    struct sockaddr_un serverUNIXAddress;/* Server address */
16    struct sockaddr_un clientUNIXAddress; /* Client address */
17    struct sockaddr* serverSockAddrPtr; /* Ptr to server address */
18    struct sockaddr* clientSockAddrPtr; /* Ptr to client address */
19
20    /* Ignore death-of-child signals to prevent zombies */
21    signal (SIGCHLD, SIG_IGN);
22
23    serverSockAddrPtr = (struct sockaddr*) &serverUNIXAddress;
24    serverLen = sizeof (serverUNIXAddress);
25
26    clientSockAddrPtr = (struct sockaddr*) &clientUNIXAddress;
27    clientLen = sizeof (clientUNIXAddress);
28
29    /* Create a UNIX socket, bidirectional, default protocol */
30    serverFd = socket (AF_UNIX, SOCK_STREAM, DEFAULT_PROTOCOL);
31    serverUNIXAddress.sun_family = AF_UNIX; /* Set domain type */
```

```
32    strcpy (serverUNIXAddress.sun_path, "recipe"); /* Set name */
33    unlink ("recipe"); /* Remove file if it already exists */
34    bind (serverFd, serverSockAddrPtr, serverLen); /* Create file */
35    listen (serverFd, 5); /* Maximum pending connection length */
36
37    while (1) /* Loop forever */
38      {
39        /* Accept a client connection */
40        clientFd = accept (serverFd, clientSockAddrPtr, &clientLen);
41
42        if (fork () == 0) /* Create child to send receipe */
43          {
44            writeRecipe (clientFd); /* Send the recipe */
45            close (clientFd); /* Close the socket */
46            exit (/* EXIT_SUCCESS */ 0); /* Terminate */
47          }
48        else
49          close (clientFd); /* Close the client descriptor */
50      }
51  }
52
53  /*****************************************************************/
54
55  writeRecipe (fd)
56
57  int fd;
58
59  {
60    static char* line1 = "spam, spam, spam, spam,";
61    static char* line2 = "spam, and spam.";
62    write (fd, line1, strlen (line1) + 1); /* Write first line */
63    write (fd, line2, strlen (line2) + 1); /* Write second line */
64  }
```

Cook Client

```
1   #include <stdio.h>
2   #include <signal.h>
3   #include <sys/types.h>
4   #include <sys/socket.h>
5   #include <sys/un.h>                    /* For AFUNIX sockets */
6
7   #define DEFAULT_PROTOCOL    0
8
9   /*****************************************************************/
10
11  main ()
12
13  {
14    int clientFd, serverLen, result;
15    struct sockaddr_un serverUNIXAddress;
```

```
16    struct sockaddr* serverSockAddrPtr;
17
18    serverSockAddrPtr = (struct sockaddr*) &serverUNIXAddress;
19    serverLen = sizeof (serverUNIXAddress);
20
21    /* Create a UNIX socket, bidirectional, default protocol */
22    clientFd = socket (AF_UNIX, SOCK_STREAM, DEFAULT_PROTOCOL);
23    serverUNIXAddress.sun_family = AF_UNIX; /* Server domain */
24    strcpy (serverUNIXAddress.sun_path, "recipe"); /* Server name */
25
26    do /* Loop until a connection is made with the server */
27      {
28        result = connect (clientFd, serverSockAddrPtr, serverLen);
29        if (result == -1) sleep (1); /* Wait and then try again */
30      }
31    while (result == -1);
32
33    readRecipe (clientFd); /* Read the recipe */
34    close (clientFd); /* Close the socket */
35    exit (/* EXIT_SUCCESS */ 0); /* Done */
36  }
37
38  /************************************************************/
39
40  readRecipe (fd)
41
42  int fd;
43
44  {
45    char str[200];
46
47    while (readLine (fd, str)) /* Read lines until end-of-input */
48      printf ("%s\n", str); /* Echo line from socket */
49  }
50
51  /************************************************************/
52
53  readLine (fd, str)
54
55  int fd;
56  char* str;
57
58  /* Read a single NULL-terminated line */
59
60  {
61    int n;
62
63    do /* Read characters until NULL or end-of-input */
64      {
65        n = read (fd,str, 1); /* Read one character */
66      }
```

```
67     while (n > 0 && *str++ != NULL);
68     return (n > 0); /* Return false if end-of-input */
69  }
```

Analyzing the source code

Now that you've glanced at the program, it's time to go back and analyze it. We begin with the server.

The server

A server is the process that's responsible for creating a named socket and accepting connections to it. To accomplish this, the server must use the system calls listed in Figure 13.57, in the order in which they are shown.

Name	Meaning
socket	creates an unnamed socket
bind	gives the socket a name
listen	specifies the maximum number of pending connections
accept	accepts a socket connection from a client

FIGURE 13.57

System calls used by a typical UNIX daemon process.

Creating a Socket: `socket ()`

A process may create a socket by using socket (), which works as shown in Figure 13.58. The chef server creates its unnamed socket on line 30 of the program:

```
30     serverFd = socket (AF_UNIX, SOCK_STREAM, DEFAULT_PROTOCOL);
```

System Call: int **socket** (int *domain*, int *type*, int *protocol*)

socket () creates an unnamed socket of the specified domain, type, and protocol. The valid values of these parameters were described earlier.

If socket () is successful, it returns a file descriptor associated with the newly created socket; otherwise, it returns –1.

FIGURE 13.58

Description of the socket () system call.

Naming a Socket: `bind ()`

Once the server has created an unnamed socket, it must bind it to a name by using bind (), which works as shown in Figure 13.59. The chef server assigns the **sockaddr_un** fields and performs a bind () on lines 31–34:

```
31      serverUNIXAddress.sun_family = AF_UNIX; /* Set domain type */
32      strcpy (serverUNIXAddress.sun_path, "recipe"); /* Set name */
33      unlink ("recipe"); /* Remove file if it already exists */
34      bind (serverFd, serverSockAddrPtr, serverLen); /* Create file */
```

System Call: int **bind** (int *fd*, const struct sockaddr* *address*, size_t *addressLen*)

bind () associates the unnamed socket represented by file descriptor *fd* with the socket address stored in *address*. *addressLen* must contain the length of the address structure. The type and value of the incoming address depend on the socket domain.

If the socket is in the AF_UNIX domain, a pointer to a **sockaddr_un** structure must be cast to a (**sockaddr***) and passed in as *address*. This structure has two fields that should be set as follows:

FIELD	ASSIGN THE VALUE
sun_family	AF_UNIX
sun_path	the full UNIX pathname of the socket (absolute or relative), up to 108 characters long

If the named AF_UNIX socket already exists, an error occurs, so it's a good idea to unlink () a name before attempting to bind to it.

If the socket is in the AF_INET domain, a pointer to a **sockaddr_in** structure must be cast to a (**sockaddr***) and passed in as *address*. This structure has four fields, which should be set as follows:

FIELD	ASSIGN THE VALUE
sin_family	AF_INET
sin_port	the port number of the Internet socket
sin_addr	a structure of type **in_addr** that holds the Internet address
sin_zero	leave empty

(For more information about Internet ports and addresses, see the Internet-specific part of this section.)

If bind () succeeds, it returns a 0; otherwise, it returns –1.

FIGURE 13.59

Description of the bind () system call.

Creating a Socket Queue: `listen ()`

When a server process is servicing a client connection, it's always possible that another client will also attempt a connection. The listen () system call allows a process to specify the number of pending connections that may be queued. It works as shown in Figure 13.60. The chef server listens to its named socket on line 35:

```
35    listen (serverFd, 5); /* Maximum pending connection length */
```

System Call: int **listen** (int *fd*, int *queueLength*)

listen () allows you to specify the maximum number of pending connections on a socket. The maximum queue length is 5. If a client attempts to connect to a socket whose queue is full, it is denied access.

FIGURE 13.60

Description of the listen () system call.

Accepting a Client: `accept ()`

Once a socket has been created and named, and its queue size has been specified, the final step is to accept client connection requests. To do this, the server must use accept (), which works as shown in Figure 13.61. The chef server accepts a connection on line 40:

```
40          clientFd = accept (serverFd, clientSockAddrPtr, &clientLen);
```

System Call: int **accept** (int *fd*, struct sockaddr* *address*, int* *addressLen*)

accept () listens to the named server socket referenced by *fd* and waits until a client connection request is received. When this occurs, accept () creates an unnamed socket with the same attributes as the original named server socket, connects the unnamed socket to the client's socket, and returns a new file descriptor that may be used for communication with the client. The original named server socket may be used to accept more connections.

The *address* structure is filled with the address of the client and is normally used only in conjunction with Internet connections. The *addressLen* field should initially be set to point to an integer containing the size of the structure pointed to by *address*. When a connection is made, the integer that it points to is set to the actual size, in bytes, of the resulting *address*.

If accept () succeeds, it returns a new file descriptor that may be used to talk with the client; otherwise, it returns –1.

FIGURE 13.61

Description of the accept () system call.

Serving a client

When a client connection succeeds, the most common sequence of events is this:

- The server process forks.
- The parent process closes the newly formed client file descriptor and loops back to accept (), ready to service new requests for connection.
- Using read () and write (), the child process talks to the client. When the conversation is complete, the child process closes the client file descriptor and exits.

The chef server process takes this series of actions on lines 37–50:

```
37    while (1) /* Loop forever */
38      {
39        /* Accept a client connection */
40        clientFd = accept (serverFd, clientSockAddrPtr, &clientLen);
41
42        if (fork () == 0) /* Create child to send receipe */
43          {
44            writeRecipe (clientFd); /* Send the recipe */
45            close (clientFd); /* Close the socket */
46            exit (/*EXIT_SUCCESS */ 0); /* Terminate */
47          }
48        else
49          close (clientFd); /* Close the client descriptor */
50      }
```

Note that the server chose to ignore SIGCHLD signals on line 21 so that its children could die immediately without requiring the parent to accept their return codes. If the server had not done this, it would had to have installed a SIGCHLD handler, which would have been more tedious.

The Client

Now that you've seen how a server program is written, let's take a look at the construction of a client program. A client is a process that's responsible for creating an unnamed socket and then attaching it to a named server socket. To accomplish this, it must use the system calls listed in Figure 13.62, in the order shown. The way in which a client uses socket () to create an unnamed socket is the same as the way in which the

Name	Meaning
socket	creates an unnamed socket
connect	attaches an unnamed client socket to a named server socket

FIGURE 13.62

System calls used by a typical UNIX client process.

server uses it. The domain, type, and protocol of the client socket must match those of the targeted server socket. The cook client process creates its unnamed socket on line 22:

```
22    clientFd = socket (AF_UNIX, SOCK_STREAM, DEFAULT_PROTOCOL);
```

Making the Connection: `connect ()`

To connect to a server's socket, a client process must fill a structure with the address of the socket and then use connect (), which works as shown in Figure 13.63. In lines 26–31, the cook client process calls connect () until a successful connection is made:

```
26    do /* Loop until a connection is made with the server */
27      {
28        result = connect (clientFd, serverSockAddrPtr, serverLen);
29        if (result == -1) sleep (1); /* Wait and then try again */
30      }
31    while (result == -1);
```

System Call: int **connect** (int *fd*, struct sockaddr* *address*, int *addressLen*)

connect () attempts to connect to a server socket whose address is contained within a structure pointed to by *address*. If successful, fd may be used to communicate with the server's socket. The type of structure that *address* points to must follow the same rules as those stated in the description of bind ():

- If the socket is in the AF_UNIX domain, a pointer to a **sockaddr_un** structure must be cast to a (**sockaddr***) and passed in as *address*.

- If the socket is in the AF_INET domain, a pointer to a **sockaddr_in** structure must be cast to a (**sockaddr***) and passed in as *address*.

   addressLen must be equal to the size of the address structure. (For examples of Internet clients, see the connect () socket example and the Internet shell program at the end of the chapter.)
   If the connection is made, connect () returns 0. If the server socket doesn't exist or its pending queue is currently filled, connect () returns –1.

FIGURE 13.63

Description of the connect () system call.

Communicating via Sockets

Once the server socket and client socket have connected, their file descriptors may be used by write () and read (). In the sample program, the server uses write () in lines 55–64:

```
55  writeRecipe (fd)
56
57  int fd;
```

```
58
59   {
60     static char* line1 = "spam, spam, spam, spam,";
61     static char* line2 = "spam, and spam.";
62     write (fd, line1, strlen (line1) + 1); /* Write first line */
63     write (fd, line2, strlen (line2) + 1); /* Write second line*/
64   }
```

The client uses read () in lines 53–69:

```
53   readLine (fd, str)
54
55   int fd;
56   char* str;
57
58   /* Read a single NULL-terminated line */
59
60   {
61     int n;
62
63     do /* Read characters until NULL or end-of-input */
64       {
65          n = read (fd, str, 1); /* Read one character */
66       }
67     while (n > 0 &&*str++ != NULL);
68     return (n > 0); /* Return false if end-of-input */
69   }
```

The server and the client should be careful to close their socket file descriptors when they are no longer needed.

Internet Sockets

The AF_UNIX sockets that you've seen so far are fine for learning about sockets, but they aren't where the action is. Most of the useful stuff involves communicating among machines on the Internet, so the rest of this chapter is dedicated to AF_INET sockets. If you haven't already read about networking in Chapter 9, now would be a good time to do so.

An Internet socket is specified by two values: a 32-bit IP address, which specifies a single unique Internet host, and a 16-bit port number, which specifies a particular port on the host. This means that an Internet client must know not only the IP address of the server, but also the server's port number.

As I mentioned in Chapter 9, several standard port numbers are reserved for system use. For example, port 13 is always served by a process that echoes the host's time of day to any client that's interested. The first Internet socket example allows you to connect to port 13 of any Internet host in the world and find out the "remote" time of day. It allows three kinds of Internet address:

- If you enter "s", it automatically means the local host.
- If you enter something that starts with a digit, it's assumed to be an A.B.C.D-format IP address and is converted into a 32-bit IP address by software.

- If you enter a string, it's assumed to be a symbolic host name and is converted into a 32-bit IP address by software.

Here's some sample output from the "Internet time" program. The third address that I entered is the IP address of "ddn.nic.mil," the national Internet database server. Notice the one-hour time difference between my local host's time and the database server host's time.

Sample Output

```
$ inettime                              ...run the program.
Host name (q= quit, s = self): s        ...what's my time?
Self host name is csservr2
Internet Address = 129.110.42.1
The time on the target port is Fri Mar 27 17:03:50 1998
Host name (q = quit, s= self): wotan     ...what's the time on "wotan"?
Internet Address = 129.110.2.1
The time on the target port is Fri Mar 27 17:03:55 1998
Host name (q = quit, s = self): 192.112.36.5    ...try ddn.nic.mil.
The time on the target port is Fri Mar 27 18:02:02 1998
Host name (q = quit, s = self): q        ...quit program.
$ _
```

Internet Time Listing

This section contains the complete listing of the Internet time client program. I suggest that you skim through the code and then read the sections that follow for details on how it works.

```
1   #include <stdio.h>
2   #include <signal.h>
3   #include <ctype.h>
4   #include <sys/types.h>
5   #include <sys/socket.h>
6   #include <netinet/in.h>                    /* For AFINET sockets */
7   #include <arpa/inet.h>
8   #include <netdb.h>
9
10  #define DAYTIME_PORT        13             /* Standard port o */
11  #define DEFAULT_PROTOCOL    0
12
13  unsigned long promptForINETAddress ();
14  unsigned long nameToAddr ();
15
16  /**************************************************************/
17
18  main ()
19
20  {
```

```
21    int clientFd; /* Client socket file descriptor */
22    int serverLen; /* Length of server address structure */
23    int result; /* From connect () call */
24    struct sockaddr_in serverINETAddress; /* Server address */
25    struct sockaddr* serverSockAddrPtr; /* Pointer to address */
26    unsigned long inetAddress; /* 32-bit IP address */
27
28    /* Set the two server variables */
29    serverSockAddrPtr = (struct sockaddr*) &serverINETAddress;
30    serverLen = sizeof (serverINETAddress); /* Length of address */
31
32    while (1) /* Loop until break */
33      {
34        inetAddress = promptForINETAddress (); /* Get 32-bit IP */
35        if (inetAddress == 0) break; /* Done */
36        /* Start by zeroing out the entire address structure */
37        bzero ((char*)&serverINETAddress,sizeof(serverINETAddress));
38        serverINETAddress.sin_family = AF_INET; /* Use Internet */
39        serverINETAddress.sin_addr.s_addr = inetAddress; /* IP */
40        serverINETAddress.sin_port = htons (DAYTIME_PORT);
41        /* Now create the client socket */
42        clientFd = socket (AF_INET, SOCK_STREAM, DEFAULT_PROTOCOL);
43        do /* Loop until a connection is made with the server */
44          {
45            result = connect (clientFd,serverSockAddrPtr,serverLen);
46            if (result == -1) sleep (1); /* Try again in 1 second */
47          }
48        while (result == -1);
49
50        readTime (clientFd); /* Read the time from the server */
51        close (clientFd); /* Close the socket */
52      }
53
54    exit (/* EXIT_SUCCESS */ 0);
55  }
56
57  /***************************************************************/
58
59  unsigned long promptForINETAddress ()
60
61  {
62    char hostName [100]; /* Name from user: numeric or symbolic */
63    unsigned long inetAddress; /* 32-bit IP format */
64
65    /* Loop until quit or a legal name is entered */
66    /* If quit, return 0 else return host's IP address */
67    do
68      {
69        printf ("Host name (q = quit, s = self): ");
70        scanf ("%s", hostName); /* Get name from keyboard */
```

```
 71          if (strcmp (hostName, "q") == 0) return (0); /* Quit */
 72          inetAddress = nameToAddr (hostName); /* Convert to IP */
 73          if (inetAddress == 0) printf ("Host name not found\n");
 74        }
 75     while (inetAddress == 0);
 76     return (inetAddress);
 77   }
 78   /**************************************************************/
 79
 80   unsigned long nameToAddr (name)
 81
 82   char* name;
 83
 84   {
 85     char hostName [100];
 86     struct hostent* hostStruct;
 87     struct in_addr* hostNode;
 88
 89     /* Convert name into a 32-bit IP address */
 90
 91     /* If name begins with a digit, assume it's a valid numeric */
 92     /* Internet address of the form A.B.C.D and convert directly */
 93     if (isdigit (name[0])) return (inet_addr (name));
 94
 95     if (strcmp (name, "s") == 0) /* Get host name from database */
 96       {
 97         gethostname (hostName,100);
 98         printf ("Self host name is %s\n", hostName);
 99       }
100     else /* Assume name is a valid symbolic host name */
101       strcpy (hostName, name);
102
103     /* Now obtain address information from database */
104     hostStruct = gethostbyname (hostName);
105     if (hostStruct == NULL) return (0); /* Not Found */
106     /* Extract the IP Address from the hostent structure */
107     hostNode = (struct in_addr*) hostStruct->h_addr;
108     /* Display a readable version for fun */
109     printf ("Internet Address = %s\n", inet_ntoa (*hostNode));
110     return (hostNode->s_addr); /* Return IP address */
111   }
112
113   /**************************************************************/
114
115   readTime (fd)
116
117   int fd;
118
119   {
120     char str [200]; /* Line buffer */
```

```
121
122     printf ("The time on the target port is ");
123     while (readLine (fd, str)) /* Read lines until end-of-input */
124       printf ("%s\n", str); /* Echo line from server to user */
125   }
126
127   /***************************************************************/
128
129   readLine (fd, str)
130
131   int fd;
132   char* str;
133
134   /* Read a single NEWLINE-terminated line */
135
136   {
137     int n;
138
139     do /* Read characters until NULL or end-of-input */
140       {
141         n = read (fd, str, 1); /* Read one character */
142       }
143     while (n > 0 && *str++ != '\n');
144     return (n > 0); /* Return false if end-of-input */
145   }
```

Analyzing the source code

Now that you've had a brief look through the Internet socket source code, it's time to examine the interesting sections. The program focuses mostly on the client side of an Internet connection, so I'll describe that portion first.

Internet clients

The procedure for creating an Internet client is the same as that for creating an AF_UNIX client, except for the initialization of the socket address. Earlier, I mentioned that an Internet socket address structure is of type **struct sockaddr_in** and has four fields:

- **sin_family**, the domain of the socket, which should be set to AF_INET
- **sin_port**, the port number, which in this case is 13
- **sin_addr**, the 32-bit IP number of the client–server
- **sin_zero**, which is padding and is not set

In creating the client socket, the only tricky part is determining the server's 32-bit IP address. promptForINETAddress () [line 59] gets the host's name from the user and then invokes nameToAddr () [line 80] to convert it into an IP address. If the user enters a string starting with a digit, inet_addr () is invoked to perform the conversion. It works as shown in Figure 13.64. Note that "network-byte" order is a host-neutral ordering of

---

Library Routine: in_addr_t **inet_addr** (const char* *string*)

inet_addr () returns the 32-bit IP address that corresponds to the A.B.C.D-format *string*. The IP address is in network-byte order.

FIGURE 13.64
Description of the inet_addr () library routine.

bytes in the IP address. This ordering is necessary because regular byte ordering can differ from machine to machine, which would make IP addresses nonportable.

If *string* doesn't start with a digit, the next step is to see if the first character is "s," which means the local host. The name of the local host is obtained by gethostname () [line 97], which works as shown in Figure 13.65. Once the symbolic name of the host is determined, the program can look it up in the network host file, "/etc/hosts." This is performed by gethostbyname () [104], which works as shown in Figure 13.66.

System Call: int **gethostname** (char* *name*, int *nameLen*)

gethostname () sets the character array pointed to by *name* of length *nameLen* to a null-terminated string equal to the local host's name.

FIGURE 13.65
Description of the gethostname () system call.

Library Routine: struct hostent* **gethostbyname** (const char* *name*)

gethostbyname () searches the "/etc/hosts" file and returns a pointer to a **hostent** structure that describes the file entry associated with the string *name*.
    If *name* is not found in the "/etc/hosts" file, NULL is returned.

FIGURE 13.66
Description of the gethostbyname () library routine.

The **hostent** structure has several fields, but the only one we're interested in is a field of type (**struct in_addr***) called **h_addr**. This field contains the host's associated IP number in a subfield called **s_addr**. Before returning the IP number, the program displays a string description of the IP address by calling inet_ntoa () [line 109]. inet_ntoa is described in Figure 13.67.

> *Library Routine*: char* **inet_ntoa** (struct in_addr *address*)
>
> inet_ntoa () takes a structure of type *in_addr* as its argument and returns a pointer to a string that describes the address in the format A.B.C.D.

FIGURE 13.67

Description of the inet_ntoa () library routine.

The final 32-bit address is then returned in line 110. Once the IP address **inetAddress** has been determined, the client's socket address fields are filled in lines 37–40:

```
37    bzero ((char*)&serverINETAddress,sizeof(serverINETAddress));
38    serverINETAddress.sin_family = AF_INET; /* Use Internet */
39    serverINETAddress.sin_addr.s_addr = inetAddress; /* IP */
40    serverINETAddress.sin_port = htons (DAYTIME_PORT);
```

bzero (), described in Figure 13.68, clears the socket address structure's contents before its fields are assigned. The bzero () call had its origins in the Berkeley version of UNIX. The System V equivalent is memset (), described in Figure 13.69. Like the IP address, the port number is converted to a network-byte ordering by htons (), which works as shown in Figure 13.70.

> *Library Routine*: void **bzero** (void* *buffer*, size_t *length*)
>
> bzero () fills the array *buffer* of size *length* with zeroes (ASCII NULL).

FIGURE 13.68

Description of the bzero () library routine.

> *Library Routine*: void **memset** (void* *buffer*, int *value*, size_t *length*)
>
> memset () fills the array *buffer* of size *length* with the value of *value*.

FIGURE 13.69

Description of the memset () library routine.

Library Routine: in_addr_t **htonl** (in_addr_t *hostLong*)

in_port_t **htons** (in_port_t *hostShort*)

in_addr_t **ntohl** (in_addr_t *networkLong*)

in_port_t **ntohs** (in_port_t *networkShort*)

Each of these functions performs a conversion between a host-format number and a network-format number. For example, htonl () returns the network-format equivalent of the host-format unsigned long *hostLong*, and ntohs () returns the host-format equivalent of the network-format unsigned short *networkShort*.

FIGURE 13.70

Description of the htonl (), htons (), ntohl (), and ntohs () library routines.

The final step is to create the client socket and attempt the connection. The code for this is almost the same as for AF_UNIX sockets:

```
42      clientFd = socket (AF_INET, SOCK_STREAM, DEFAULT_PROTOCOL);
43      do /* Loop until a connection is made with the server */
44        {
45          result = connect (clientFd,serverSockAddrPtr,serverLen);
46          if (result == -1) sleep (1); /* Try again in 1 second */
47        }
48      while (result == -1);
```

The rest of the program contains nothing new. Now it's time to look at how an Internet server is built.

Internet Servers

Constructing an Internet server is actually pretty easy. The **sin_family**, **sin_port**, and **sin_zero** fields of the socket address structure should be filled in as they were in the client example. The only difference is that the **s_addr** field should be set to the network-byte-ordered value of the constant INADDR_ANY, which means "accept any incoming client requests." The following example of the procedure used to create a server socket address is a slightly modified version of some code taken from the Internet shell program that ends this chapter:

```
int serverFd; /* Server socket
struct sockaddr_in serverINETAddress; /* Server Internet address */
struct sockaddr* serverSockAddrPtr; /* Pointer to server address */
struct sockaddr_in clientINETAddress; /* Client Internet address */
struct sockaddr* clientSockAddrPtr; /* Pointer to client address */
```

```
int port = 13; /* Set to the port that you wish to serve */
int serverLen; /* Length of address structure */
serverFd = socket (AF_INET, SOCK_STREAM, DEFAULT_PROTOCOL); /* Create */
serverLen = sizeof (serverINETAddress); /* Length of structure */
bzero ((char*) &serverINETAddress, serverLen); /* Clear structure */
serverINETAddress.sin_family = AF_INET; /* Internet domain */
serverINETAddress.sin_addr.s_addr = htonl (INADDR_ANY); /* Accept all */
serverINETAddress.sin_port = htons (port); /* Server port number */
```

When the address is created, the socket is bound to the address, and its queue size is specified in the usual way.

```
serverSockAddrPtr = (struct sockaddr*) &serverINETAddress;
bind (serverFd, serverSockAddrPtr, serverLen);
listen (serverFd, 5);
```

The final step is to accept client connections. When a successful connection is made, the client socket address is filled with the client's IP address and a new file descriptor is returned.

```
clientLen = sizeof (clientINETAddress);
clientSockAddrPtr = (struct sockaddr*) clientINETAddress;
clientFd = accept (serverFd, clientSockAddrPtr, &clientLen);
```

As you can see, an Internet server's code is very similar to that of an AF_UNIX server. The final example in this chapter is the Internet shell.

Shared Memory

Sharing a segment of memory is a straightforward and intuitive method of allowing two processes on the same machine to share data. The process that allocates the shared memory segment gets an ID back from the call, assuming that the creation of the shared memory segment succeeds. Other processes can then use that ID to access the shared memory segment.

Accessing a shared memory segment is the fastest form of IPC, since no data have to be copied or sent anywhere else. However, because there is just *one* copy of the data, if more than one process is updating the data, the processes must synchronize their actions to prevent corrupting the data.

The following are some of the common system calls utilized to allocate and use shared memory segments in System V-based versions of UNIX:

- **shmget ()**—allocates a shared memory segment and returns the segment ID
- **shmat ()**—attaches a shared memory segment to the virtual address space of the calling process

- **shmdt ()**—detaches an attached segment from the address space
- **shmctl ()**—allows you to modify attributes (e.g., access permissions) associated with the shared memory segment

After a successful call to shmget (), a shared memory segment exists and can be accessed by means of the ID returned in the call. Note that for any other process to use the same segment, it must also know this ID. The ID can be made available to other processes via another IPC mechanism, or a specific ID can be passed to shmget () to force the use of a specific known ID (with the understanding that the call will fail if that ID has already been used with another shared memory segment).

Once you have obtained a valid ID for a shared memory segment, a call to shmat () will return a pointer to the address in the local process' virtual memory space where the shared memory segment has been attached. You can then use that pointer to index into the block of memory just as you would any other block of memory. (Doing this does presume that you know the format of the data contained in the shared memory segment.) If and when you finish using the shared memory, you can release (detach) it with a call to shmdt () (into which you pass the pointer, not the shared memory segment ID). When the last process to have the shared memory segment attached (which is not necessarily the process that created it) detaches it, the space allocated to the segment is released.

Semaphores

A *semaphore* is not a communication mechanism of the type we've seen with pipes, sockets, and shared memory. No actual data are sent with a semaphore. Rather, a semaphore is a counter that describes the availability of a resource (which could be a shared memory segment).

A semaphore is created and assigned a value that denotes how many concurrent uses of a resource are allowed. Each time a process gets ready to use a certain resource, it checks the semaphore to see whether the resource is available. If the value of the semaphore is greater than zero, then the resource is available. The process allocates "a unit of the resource," and the semaphore is decremented by one. If the value of the semaphore is zero, the process sleeps until the value is greater than zero (until another process has finished its use of the resource).

Semaphores can be used to exclusively lock something by creating a semaphore with a value of one (as soon as one process uses it, the semaphore value be zero). This is known as a *binary semaphore*. Semaphores can also be used to set a maximum number of concurrent uses of a particular resource.

The System V semaphore is a bit more complex than what I've just described. Semaphores are managed as a list or *set* of semaphores rather than individually. This provides a method of defining multiple semaphores for a complex locking mechanism, but requires unnecessary overhead when you only wanted one. Semaphore-related system calls include the following:

- **semget()**—creates a set (an array) of semaphores
- **semop ()**—manipulates a set of semaphores
- **semctl ()**—modifies attributes of a set of semaphores

THE INTERNET SHELL

Have you ever wondered what the inside of a shell looks like? Well, here's a great opportunity to learn how they work and to obtain some source code that could help you to create your own shell. I designed the Internet shell to be a lot like the standard UNIX shells, in the sense that it provides piping and background processing facilities, but I also added some Internet-specific capabilities that the other shells lack.

Restrictions

In order to pack the functionality of the Internet shell into a reasonable size, there are a few restrictions:

- All tokens must be separated by white space (tabs or spaces). This means that instead of writing **ls; date** you must write **ls ; date**. The upshot is that the lexical analyzer is very simple.
- Filename substitution (globbing) is not supported. This means that the standard *, ?, and [] metacharacters are not understood.

These features are nice to have in an everyday shell, but their implementation wouldn't have taught you anything significant about how shells work.

Command Syntax

The syntax of an Internet shell command is similar to that of the standard UNIX shells. We describe it formally using BNF notation (note that the redirection symbols < and > are escaped by a \ to prevent ambiguity; see the appendix for a discussion of BNF):

```
<internetShellcommand> = <sequence> [ & ]
<sequence> = <pipeline> { ; <pipeline> }*
<pipeline> = <simple> { | <simple> }
<simple> = { <token> }* { <redirection>}*
<redirection> = <fileRedirection> | <socketRedirection>
<fileRedirection> = \> <file> | > <file> | \< <file>
<socketRedirection> = <clientRedirection> | <serverRedirection>
<clientRedirection> = @\>c <socket> | @\<c <socket>
<serverDirection> = @\>s <socket> | @\<s <socket>
<token> = a string of characters
<file> = a valid UNIX pathname
<socket> = either a UNIX pathname (UNIX domain socket) or
           an Internet socket name of the form hostname.port#
```

Starting the Internet Shell

I named the Internet shell executable file **ish**. The Internet shell prompt is a question mark.

When **ish** is started, it inherits the $PATH environment variable from the shell that invokes it. The value of $PATH may be changed by using the setenv built-in command that is described shortly.

To exit the Internet shell, press *Control*-D on a line of its own.

Built-in Commands

The Internet shell executes most commands by creating a child shell that execs the specified utility while the parent shell waits for the child. However, some commands are built into the shell and are executed directly. Figure 13.71 lists the built-ins. Built-in commands may be redirected. Before I describe the construction and operation of the Internet shell, let's take a look at a few examples of both regular commands and Internet-specific commands.

Built-in	Function
echo {<token>}*	echoes tokens to the terminal
cd *path*	changes the shell's working directory to *path*
getenv *name*	displays the value of the environment variable *name*
setenv *name value*	sets the value of the environment variable *name* to *value*

FIGURE 13.71

Internet shell built-in commands.

Some Regular Examples

Here are some examples that illustrate the sequencing, redirection, and piping capabilities of the Internet shell:

```
$ ish                                     ...start shell.
Internet Shell.
? ls                                      ...simple command.
ish.c       ish.cs       ish.van          who.socket  who.sort
? ls | wc                                 ...pipe.
      5        5        41
? who | sort > who.sort &                 ...pipe + redirect + background.
[4356]                                    ...PID of background process.
? cat who.sort                            ...show redirection worked.
glass     ttyp2   May 28 18:33 (bridge05.utdalla)
posey     ttyp0   May 22 10:19 (blackfoot.utdall)
posey     ttyp1   May 22 10:19 (blackfoot.utdall)
? date ; whoami                           ...sequence of commands.
Thu Mar 26 18:36:24 CDT 1998
glass
? echo hi there                           ...execute a built-in.
```

```
hi there
? getenv PATH                       ...look at PATH env variable.
::/usr/local/bin:/usr/ucb:/usr/bin:/bin:/usr/etc
? mail glass < who.sort             ...input redirection works too.
? ^D                                ...exit shell.
$ _
```

Some Internet Examples

The Internet shell becomes pretty interesting when you examine its socket features. Here's an example that uses a UNIX domain socket to communicate information:

```
$ ish                       ...start the Internet shell.
Internet Shell.
? who @>s who.sck &         ...server sends output to socket "who.sck".
[2678]
? ls                        ...execute a command for fun.
ish.c       ish.van             who.sock    who.sort
ish.cs      who.sck             who.socket
? sort @<c who.sck          ...client reads input from socket "who.sck".
glass     ttyp2   May 28 18:33 (bridge05.utdalla)
posey     ttyp0   May 22 10:19 (blackfoot.utdall)
posey     ttyp1   May 22 10:19 (blackfoot.utdall)
veerasam ttyp3    May 28 18:39 (129.110.70.139)
? ^D                        ...quit shell.
$ _
```

The really fun stuff happens when you introduce Internet sockets. The first shell in the following example was run on a host called "csservr2," and the second shell was run on a host called "vanguard":

```
$ ish               ...run Internet shell on csservr2.
Internet Shell.
? who @>s 5000 &            ...background server sends output to port 5000.
[7221]
? ^D                        ...quit shell.
$ rlogin vanguard           ...login to vanguard host.
% ish                       ...run Internet shell on vanguard.
Internet Shell.
? sort @<c csservr2.5000 ...client reads input from csservr2.
                            ...port 5000.
IP address = 129.110.42.1...echoed by Internet shell.
glass     ttyp2   May 28 18:42 (bridge05.utdalla)      ...output from
posey     ttyp0   May 22 10:19 (blackfoot.utdall)      ...who on
posey     ttyp1   May 22 10:19 (blackfoot.utdall)      ...csservr2!
veerasam ttyp3    May 28 18:39 (129.110.70.139)
```

```
?  ^D                    ...quit shell.
%  ^D                    ...logout from vanguard.
logout
$ _                      ...back to csservr2
```

Figure 13.72 is an illustration of the socket connection.

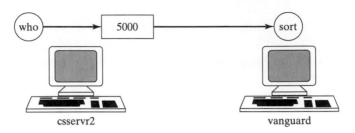

FIGURE 13.72

Internet shell redirection.

The next example is even more interesting. The first shell uses one socket to talk to the second shell, and the second shell uses another socket to talk to the third:

```
$ ish                    ...start shell on csservr2.
Internet Shell.
? who @>s 5001 &         ...background server sends output to port 5001.
[2001]
? ^D                     ...quit shell.
$ rlogin vanguard        ...login to vanguard.
% ish                    ...start shell onvanguard.
Internet Shell.
? sort @<c csservr2.5001 @>s 5002 &    ...background process reads
[3756]                                 ...input from port 5001 on
                                       ...csservr2 and sends it to
                                       ...local port 5002.
IP address = 129.110.42.1              ...echoed by shell.
? ^D                     ...quit shell.
% ^D                     ...logout of vanguard.
logout
$ ish                    ...start another shell on csservr2.
Internet Shell.
? cat @<c vanguard.5002        ...read input from port 5002 on vanguard.
IP address = 129.110.43.128        ...echoed by the shell.
glass    ttyp2   May 28 18:42 (bridge05.utdalla)
posey    ttyp0   May 22 10:19 (blackfoot.utdall)
posey    ttyp1   May 22 10:19 (blackfoot.utdall)
veerasam ttyp3   May 28 18:39 (129.110.70.139)
? ^D                     ...quit shell.
$ _
```

Figure 13.73 is an illustration of the two socket connections.

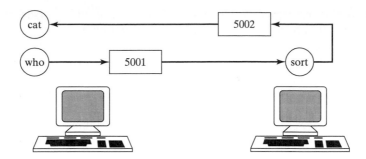

FIGURE 13.73

More Internet shell redirection.

How It Works

The operation of the Internet shell can be broken down into several main sections:

- the main command loop
- parsing
- executing built-in commands
- executing pipelines
- executing sequences
- background processing
- dealing with signals
- performing file redirection
- performing socket redirection

We next describe each operation, together with fragments of code and diagrams when necessary. Before you continue, I suggest that you glance through the source code listing at the end of the chapter to familiarize yourself with its overall layout.

The Main Command Loop

When the shell starts, it initializes a signal handler to catch keyboard interrupts and re-sets an error flag. It then enters commandLoop () [line 167], which prompts the user for a line of input, parses the input, and then executes the command. commandLoop () loops until the user enters *Control*-D, at which point the shell terminates.

Parsing

To check the command line for errors, the line is first broken down into separate tokens by tokenize () [line 321], which is located in the lexical analyzer section of the source code. tokenize () is called by commandLoop () and fills the global **tokens** array with pointers to each individual token. For example, if the input line was "ls -l," **tokens**[0] would point to the string "ls," and **tokens**[1] would point to the string "-l". Once the line is parsed, the global token pointer **tIndex** is set to zero [line 350] in preparation for parsing.

Parsing is performed in a top-down fashion. The main parser, parseSequence () [line 194], is called from the commandLoop () function. parseSequence () parses each pipeline in the sequence by invoking parsePipeline () and records the information that parsePipeline () returns. Finally, it checks to see whether the sequence is to be executed in the background.

Similarly, parsePipeline () [line 222] parses each simple command in the pipeline by calling parseSimple () and records the information that parseSimple () returns. parseSimple () [line 242] records the tokens in the simple command and then processes any trailing metacharacters, such as >, >>, and @>s.

The information that each of these parsing functions gathers is stored in structures for later use by the execution routines. A **struct sequence** [line 75] can hold the details of up to five (MAX_PIPES) pipelines, together with a flag indicating whether or not the sequence is to be executed in the background. Each pipeline is recorded in a **struct pipeline** [line 67], which can record the details of up to five (MAX_SIMPLE) simple commands. Finally, a **struct simple** [line 52] can the hold up to 100 (MAX_TOKENS) tokens, together with several fields that record information related to I/O redirection.

If a command is parsed with no errors, the local variable **sequence** [line 182] is equal to a **struct sequence**, which holds the analyzed version of the command.

Note that although I could have used pointers to return structures more efficiently, I chose to keep the program as simple as I could in order to focus on its UNIX-specific aspects.

Executing a Command Sequence

The main command loop executes a successfully parsed command by invoking executeSequence () [line 444]. This routine does one of two things:

- If the command is to be executed in the background, it creates a child process to execute the pipelines in sequence; the original parent shell does not wait for the child. Before executing the pipeline, the child restores its original interrupt handler and places itself into a new process group to make it immune from hang-ups and other signals. This ensures that a background process will continue to execute even when the shell is terminated and the user logs out.
- If the command is to be executed in the foreground, the parent shell executes the pipelines in sequence.

In both cases, executePipeline () [line 472] is used to execute each pipeline component of the command sequence.

Executing Pipelines

executePipeline ( ) performs one of two actions:

- If the pipeline is a simple built-in command, it executes the simple command directly, without creating a child process. This is very important. For example, the built-in command **cd** executes chdir () to change the shell's current working directory. If a child shell were created to execute this built-in command, the original parent shell's working directory would be unaffected, which would be incorrect.

- If the pipeline is more than a simple built-in command, execute Pipeline () creates a child shell to execute the pipeline; the original parent shell waits for the child to complete its processing. Notice that the parent waits for a specific PID by calling waitForPid () [line 503]. This is because the parent shell might have created some previous children to execute background processes, and it would be incorrect for the parent to resume when one of these background processes terminated. If the pipeline contains only one simple command, then no pipes need to be created, and executeSimple () [line 569] is invoked. Otherwise, executePipes () [line 516] which connects each command with its own pipe, is invoked.

executePipes () is a fairly complicated routine. If the pipeline contains **n** simple commands, then executePipes () creates **n** child processes, one for each command, and **n-1** pipes to connect the children. Each child reconnects its standard input or output channels to the appropriate pipe and then closes all of the original pipe file descriptors. Each child then executes its associated simple command. Meanwhile, the original process that invoked executePipes () waits for all of its children to terminate.

Executing a Simple Command

executeSimple redirects the standard input or output channels as necessary and then executes either executeBuiltIn () [line 635] or executePrimitive () [line 596], depending on the category of the command. builtIn () [line 624] returns *true* if a token is the name of a built-in command. If the command is a built-in, it's possible that it is being executed directly by the shell. To prevent the shell's I/O channels from being altered by redirection, the original standard input and output channels are recorded for later restoration.

executePrimitive () [line 596] simply executes using execvp (). Fortunately (but not coincidentally), **p->token** is already in the form required by execvp (). Built-in functions are executed by executeBuiltIn (), using a simple switch statement.

Redirection

redirect () [line 761] performs all of the preprocessing necessary for both file and socket redirection. The basic technique for redirecting the standard I/O channels is the same as the one I described earlier in the chapter. If file redirection is required, dupFd () [line 806] is invoked to create the file with the appropriate mode and to duplicate the standard file descriptor. If socket redirection is required, either server () [line 950] or client () [line 879] is invoked to create the appropriate type of socket connection. These functions manipulate both UNIX-domain and Internet-domain sockets the same way the earlier socket examples did.

Extensions

I think that it could be a lot of fun and fairly educational to add some new features to the Internet shell. If you're interested, see the "Projects" at the end of the chapter for some suggestions.

Internet Shell Source Code Listing

```
 1  #include <stdio.h>
 2  #include <stdlib.h>
 3  #include <string.h>
 4  #include <signal.h>
 5  #include <ctype.h>
 6  #include <sys/types.h>
 7  #include <fcntl.h>
 8  #include <sys/ioctl.h>
 9  #include <sys/socket.h>
10  #include <sys/un.h>
11  #include <netinet/in.h>
12  #include <arpa/inet.h>
13  #include <netdb.h>
14
15
16  /* Macros */
17  #define MAX_STRING_LENGTH      200
18  #define MAX_TOKENS             100
19  #define MAX_TOKEN_LENGTH       30
20  #define MAX_SIMPLE             5
21  #define MAX_PIPES              5
22  #define NOT_FOUND              -1
23  #define REGULAR                -1
24  #define DEFAULT_PERMISSION     0660
25  #define DEFAULT_PROTOCOL       0
26  #define DEFAULT_QUEUE_LENGTH   5
27  #define SOCKET_SLEEP           1
28
29
30  /* Enumerators */
31  enum { FALSE, TRUE };
32  enum metacharacterEnum
33    {
34      SEMICOLON, BACKGROUND, END_OF_LINE, REDIRECT_OUTPUT,
35      REDIRECT_INPUT, APPEND_OUTPUT, PIPE,
36      REDIRECT_OUTPUT_SERVER, REDIRECT_OUTPUT_CLIENT,
37      REDIRECT_INPUT_SERVER, REDIRECT_INPUT_CLIENT
38    };
39  enum builtInEnum { ECHO_BUILTIN, SETENV, GETENV, CD };
40  enum descriptorEnum { STDIN, STDOUT, STDERR };
41  enum pipeEnum { READ, WRITE };
42  enum IOEnum
43    {
44      NO_REDIRECT, FILE_REDIRECT,
45      SERVER_REDIRECT, CLIENT_REDIRECT
46    };
47  enum socketEnum { CLIENT, SERVER };
```

```
48  enum { INPUT_SOCKET, OUTPUT_SOCKET };
49
50
51  /* Every simple command has one of these associated with it */
52  struct simple
53    {
54      char* token [MAX_TOKENS]; /* The tokens of the command */
55      int count; /* The number of tokens */
56      int outputRedirect; /* Set to an IOEnum */
57      int inputRedirect; /* Set to an IOEnum */
58      int append; /* Set to true for append mode */
59      char *outputFile; /* Name of output file or NULL if none */
60      char *inputFile; /* Name of input file or NULL if none */
61      char *outputSocket; /* Output socket name or NULL if none */
62      char *inputSocket; /* Name of input socket or NULL if none */
63    };
64
65
66  /* Every pipeline has one of these associated with it */
67  struct pipeline
68    {
69      struct simple simple [MAX_SIMPLE]; /* Commands in pipe */
70      int count; /* The number of simple commands */
71    };
72
73
74  /* Every command sequence has one of these associated with it */
75  struct sequence
76    {
77      struct pipeline pipeline [MAX_PIPES]; /* Pipes in sequence */
78      int count; /* The number of pipes */
79      int background; /* True if this is a background sequence */
80    };
81
82
83  /* Prototypes */
84  struct sequence parseSequence ();
85  struct pipeline parsePipeline ();
86  struct simple parseSimple ();
87  char *nextToken ();
88  char *peekToken ();
89  char *lastToken ();
90  char* getToken ();
91
92
93  /* Globals */
94  char* metacharacters [] = { ";", "&", "\n", ">", "<", ">>",
95    "|", "@>s", "@>c", "@<s", "@<c", "" };
96  char* builtIns [] = { "echo", "setenv", "getenv", "cd", "" };
97  char line [MAX_STRING_LENGTH]; /* The current line */
```

```
 98  char tokens [MAX_TOKENS][MAX_TOKEN_LENGTH]; /* Tokens in line */
 99  int tokenCount; /* The number of tokens in the current line */
100  int tIndex; /* Index into line: used by lexical analyzer */
101  int errorFlag; /* Set to true when an error occurs */
102
103
104  /* Some forward declarations */
105  void (*originalQuitHandler) ();
106  void quitHandler ();
107
108
109  /* Externals */
110  char **environ; /* Pointer to the environment */
111
112  /**************************************************************/
113
114  main (argc, argv)
115
116  int argc;
117  char* argv [];
118
119  {
120    initialize (); /* Initialize some globals */
121    commandLoop (); /* Accept and process commands */
122    return (/* EXIT_SUCCESS */ 0);
123  }
124
125  /**************************************************************/
126
127  initialize ()
128
129  {
130    printf ("Internet Shell.\n"); /* Introduction */
131    /* Set the Control-C handler to catch keyboard interrupts */
132    originalQuitHandler = signal (SIGINT, quitHandler);
133  }
134
135  /**************************************************************/
136
137  void quitHandler ()
138
139  {
140    /* Control-C handler */
141    printf ("\n");
142    displayPrompt ();
143  }
144
145  /**************************************************************/
146
147  error (str)
```

```
148
149  char* str;
150
151  {
152    /* Display str as an error to the standard error channel */
153    fprintf (stderr, "%s", str);
154    errorFlag = TRUE; /* Set error flag */
155  }
156
157  /**************************************************************/
158
159  displayPrompt ()
160
161  {
162    printf ("? ");
163  }
164
165  /**************************************************************/
166
167  commandLoop ()
168
169  {
170    struct sequence sequence;
171
172    /* Accept and process commands until a Control-D occurs */
173    while (TRUE)
174      {
175        displayPrompt ();
176        if (gets (line) == NULL) break; /* Get a line of input */
177        tokenize (); /* Break the input line into tokens */
178        errorFlag = FALSE; /* Reset the error flag */
179
180        if (tokenCount > 1) /* Process any non-empty line */
181          {
182            sequence = parseSequence (); /* Parse the line */
183            /* If no errors occurred during the parsing, */
184            /* execute the command */
185            if (!errorFlag) executeSequence (&sequence);
186          }
187      }
188  }
189
190  /**************************************************************/
191  /*                      PARSER ROUTINES                       */
192  /**************************************************************/
193
194  struct sequence parseSequence ()
195
196  {
```

```
197    struct sequence q;
198
199    /* Parse a command sequence and return structure description */
200    q.count = 0; /* Number of pipes in the sequence */
201    q.background = FALSE; /* Default is not in background */
202
203    while (TRUE) /* Loop until no semicolon delimiter is found */
204      {
205        q.pipeline[q.count++] = parsePipeline (); /* Parse */
206        if (peekCode () != SEMICOLON) break;
207        nextToken (); /* Flush semicolon delimiter */
208      }
209
210    if (peekCode () == BACKGROUND) /* Sequence is in background */
211      {
212        q.background = TRUE;
213        nextToken (); /* Flush ampersand */
214      }
215
216    getToken (END_OF_LINE); /* Check end-of-line is reached */
217    return (q);
218  }
219
220  /************************************************************/
221
222  struct pipeline parsePipeline ()
223
224  {
225    struct pipeline p;
226
227    /* Parse a pipeline and return a structure description of it */
228    p.count = 0; /* The number of simple commands in the pipeline */
229
230    while (TRUE) /* Loop until no pipe delimiter is found */
231      {
232        p.simple[p.count++] = parseSimple (); /* Parse command */
233        if (peekCode () != PIPE) break;
234        nextToken (); /* Flush pipe delimiter */
235      }
236
237    return (p);
238  }
239
240  /************************************************************/
241
242  struct simple parseSimple ()
243
244  {
245    struct simple s;
```

```
246    int code;
247    int done;
248
249    /* Parse a simple command and return a structure description */
250    s.count = 0; /* The number of tokens in the simple command */
251    s.outputFile = s.inputFile = NULL;
252    s.inputSocket = s.outputSocket = NULL;
253    s.outputRedirect = s.inputRedirect = NO_REDIRECT; /* Defaults */
254    s.append = FALSE;
255
256    while (peekCode () == REGULAR) /* Store all regular tokens */
257      s.token[s.count++] = nextToken ();
258
259    s.token[s.count] = NULL; /* NULL-terminate token list */
260    done = FALSE;
261
262    /* Parse special metacharacters that follow, like > and > */
263    do
264      {
265        code = peekCode ();/* Peek at next token */
266
267        switch (code)
268          {
269            case REDIRECT_INPUT: /* < */
270              nextToken ();
271              s.inputFile = getToken (REGULAR);
272              s.inputRedirect = FILE_REDIRECT;
273              break;
274
275            case REDIRECT_OUTPUT: /* > */
276            case APPEND_OUTPUT: /* > */
277              nextToken ();
278              s.outputFile = getToken (REGULAR);
279              s.outputRedirect = FILE_REDIRECT;
280              s.append = (code == APPEND_OUTPUT);
281              break;
282
283            case REDIRECT_OUTPUT_SERVER: /* @>s */
284              nextToken ();
285              s.outputSocket = getToken (REGULAR);
286              s.outputRedirect = SERVER_REDIRECT;
287              break;
288
289            case REDIRECT_OUTPUT_CLIENT: /* @>c */
290              nextToken ();
291              s.outputSocket = getToken (REGULAR);
292              s.outputRedirect = CLIENT_REDIRECT;
293              break;
294
```

```
295              case REDIRECT_INPUT_SERVER: /* @<s */
296                nextToken ();
297                s.inputSocket = getToken (REGULAR);
298                s.inputRedirect = SERVER_REDIRECT;
299                break;
300
301              case REDIRECT_INPUT_CLIENT: /* @<c */
302                nextToken ();
303                s.inputSocket = getToken (REGULAR);
304                s.inputRedirect = CLIENT_REDIRECT;
305                break;
306
307          default:
308                done = TRUE;
309                break;
310          }
311      }
312    while (!done);
313
314    return (s);
315  }
316
317  /****************************************************************/
318  /*                  LEXICAL ANALYZER ROUTINES                   */
319  /****************************************************************/
320
321  tokenize ()
322
323  {
324    char* ptr = line; /* Point to the input buffer */
325    char token [MAX_TOKEN_LENGTH]; /* Holds the current token */
326    char* tptr; /* Pointer to current character */
327
328    tIndex = 0; /* Global: points to the current token */
329
330    /* Break the current line of input into tokens */
331    while (TRUE)
332      {
333        tptr = token;
334        while (*ptr == ' ') ++ptr; /* Skip leading spaces */
335        if (*ptr == NULL) break; /* End of line */
336
337        do
338        {
339          *tptr++ = *ptr++;
340          }
341        while (*ptr != ' ' && *ptr != NULL);
342
343        *tptr = NULL;
```

```
344        strcpy (tokens[tIndex++], token); /* Store the token */
345      }
346
347    /* Place an end-of-line token at the end of the token list */
348    strcpy (tokens[tIndex++], "\n");
349    tokenCount = tIndex; /* Remember total token count */
350    tIndex = 0; /* Reset token index to start of token list */
351  }
352
353  /**************************************************************/
354
355  char* nextToken ()
356
357  {
358    return (tokens[tIndex++]); /* Return next token in list */
359  }
360
361  /**************************************************************/
362
363  char *lastToken ()
364
365  {
366    return (tokens[tIndex - 1]); /* Return previous token in list */
367  }
368
369  /**************************************************************/
370
371  peekCode ()
372
373  {
374    /* Return a peek at code of the next token in the list */
375    return (tokenCode (peekToken ()));
376  }
377
378  /**************************************************************/
379
380  char* peekToken ()
381
382  {
383    /* Return a peek at the next token in the list */
384    return (tokens[tIndex]);
385  }
386
387  /**************************************************************/
388
389  char *getToken (code)
390
391  int code;
392
393  {
```

```
394    char str [MAX_STRING_LENGTH];
395
396    /* Generate error if the code of the next token is not code */
397    /* Otherwise return the token */
398    if (peekCode () != code)
399      {
400        sprintf (str, "Expected %s\n", metacharacters[code]);
401        error (str);
402        return (NULL);
403      }
404    else
405      return (nextToken ());
406  }
407
408  /****************************************************************/
409
410  tokenCode (token)
411
412  char* token;
413
414  {
415    /* Return the index of token in the metacharacter array */
416    return (findString (metacharacters, token));
417  }
418
419  /****************************************************************/
420
421  findString (strs, str)
422
423  char* strs [];
424  char* str;
425
426  {
427    int i = 0;
428
429    /* Return the index of str in the string array strs */
430    /* or NOT_FOUND if it isn't there */
431    while (strcmp (strs[i], "") != 0)
432      if (strcmp (strs[i], str) == 0)
433        return (i);
434      else
435        ++i;
436
437    return (NOT_FOUND); /* Not found */
438  }
439
440  /****************************************************************/
441  /*                    COMMAND EXECUTION ROUTINES              */
442  /****************************************************************/
```

```
443
444   executeSequence (p)
445
446   struct sequence* p;
447
448   {
449     int i, result;
450
451     /* Execute a sequence of statments (possibly just one) */
452     if (p->background) /* Execute in background */
453       {
454         if (fork () == 0)
455           {
456             printf ("[%d]\n", getpid ()); /* Display child PID */
457           /* Child process */
458             signal (SIGQUIT, originalQuitHandler); /* Oldhandler */
459             setpgid (0, getpid ()); /* Change process group */
460             for (i = 0; i < p->count; i++) /* Execute pipelines */
461               executePipeline (&p->pipeline[i]);
462             exit (/* EXIT_SUCCESS */ 0);
463           }
464       }
465     else /* Execute in foreground */
466       for (i = 0; i < p->count; i++) /* Execute each pipeline */
467         executePipeline (&p->pipeline[i]);
468   }
469
470   /****************************************************************/
471
472   executePipeline (p)
473
474   struct pipeline *p;
475
476   {
477     int pid, processGroup, result;
478
479     /* Execute every simple command in pipeline (possibly one) */
480     if (p->count == 1 && builtIn (p->simple[0].token[0]))
481       executeSimple (&p->simple[0]); /* Execute it directly */
482     else
483       {
484         if ((pid = fork ()) == 0)
485           {
486             /* Child shell executes the simple commands */
487             if (p->count == 1)
488               executeSimple (&p->simple[0]); /* Execute command */
489             else
490               executePipes (p); /* Execute more than one command */
491             exit ( /* EXIT_SUCCESS */ 0);
492           }
```

```
493        else
494          {
495             /* Parent shell waits for child to complete */
496             waitForPID (pid);
497          }
498      }
499  }
500
501  /***************************************************************/
502
503  waitForPID (pid)
504
505  int pid;
506
507  {
508    int status;
509
510    /* Return when the child process with PID pid terminates */
511    while (wait (&status) != pid);
512  }
513
514  /***************************************************************/
515
516  executePipes (p)
517
518  struct pipeline *p;
519
520  {
521    int pipes, status, i;
522    int pipefd [MAX_PIPES][2];
523
524    /* Execute two or more simple commands connected by pipes */
525    pipes = p->count - 1; /* Number of pipes to build */
526    for (i = 0; i < pipes; i++) /* Build the pipes */
527      pipe (pipefd[i]);
528    for (i = 0; i < p->count; i++) /* Build one process per pipe */
529      {
530        if (fork () != 0) continue;
531        /* Child shell */
532        /* First, connect stdin to pipe if not the first command */
533        if (i != 0) dup2 (pipefd[i-1][READ], STDIN);
534        /* Second, connect stdout to pipe if not the last command */
535        if (i != p->count - 1) dup2 (pipefd[i][WRITE], STDOUT);
536        /* Third, close all of the pipes' file descriptors */
537        closeAllPipes (pipefd, pipes);
538        /* Last, execute the simple command */
539        executeSimple (&p->simple[i]);
540        exit (/* EXIT_SUCCESS */0);
541      }
542
543    /* The parent shell comes here after forking the children */
```

```
544    closeAllPipes (pipefd, pipes);
545    for (i = 0; i < p->count; i++) /* Wait for children to finish */
546      wait (&status);
547 }
548
549 /***************************************************************/
550
551 closeAllPipes (pipefd, pipes)
552
553 int pipefd [][2];
554 int pipes;
555
556 {
557    int i;
558
559    /* Close every pipe's file descriptors */
560    for (i = 0; i < pipes; i++)
561      {
562        close (pipefd[i][READ]);
563        close (pipefd[i][WRITE]);
564      }
565 }
566
567 /***************************************************************/
568
569 executeSimple (p)
570
571 struct simple* p;
572
573 {
574    int copyStdin, copyStdout;
575
576    /* Execute a simple command */
577    if (builtIn (p->token[0])) /* Built-in */
578      {
579        /* The parent shell is executing this, so remember */
580        /* stdin and stdout in case of built-in redirection */
581        copyStdin = dup (STDIN);
582        copyStdout = dup (STDOUT);
583        if (redirect (p)) executeBuiltIn (p); /* Execute built-in */
584        /* Restore stdin and stdout */
585        dup2 (copyStdin, STDIN);
586        dup2 (copyStdout, STDOUT);
587        close (copyStdin);
588        close (copyStdout);
589      }
590    else if (redirect (p)) /* Redirect if necessary */
591      executePrimitive (p); /* Execute primitive command */
592 }
593
594 /***************************************************************/
```

```
595
596  executePrimitive (p)
597
598  struct simple* p;
599
600  {
601    /* Execute a command by exec'ing */
602    if (execvp (p->token[0], p->token) == -1)
603      {
604        perror ("ish");
605        exit (/* EXIT_FAILURE */ 1);
606      }
607  }
608
609  /***************************************************************/
610  /*                    BUILT-IN COMMANDS                      */
611  /***************************************************************/
612
613  builtInCode (token)
614
615  char* token;
616
617  {
618    /* Return the index of token in the builtIns array */
619    return (findString (builtIns, token));
620  }
621
622  /***************************************************************/
623
624  builtIn (token)
625
626  char* token;
627
628  {
629    /* Return true if token is a built-in */
630    return (builtInCode (token) != NOT_FOUND);
631  }
632
633  /***************************************************************/
634
635  executeBuiltIn (p)
636
637  struct simple* p;
638
639  {
640    /* Execute a single built-in command */
641    switch (builtInCode (p->token[0]))
642      {
643        case CD:
644          executeCd (p);
645          break;
```

```
646
647        case ECHO_BUILTIN:
648          executeEcho (p);
649          break;
650
651        case GETENV:
652          executeGetenv (p);
653          break;
654
655        case SETENV:
656          executeSetenv (p);
657          break;
658      }
659  }
660
661  /*************************************************************/
662
663  executeEcho (p)
664
665  struct simple* p;
666
667  {
668    int i;
669
670    /* Echo the tokens in this command */
671    for (i = 1; i < p->count; i++)
672      printf ("%s "> p->token[i]);
673
674    printf ("\n");
675  }
676
677  /*************************************************************/
678
679  executeGetenv (p)
680
681  struct simple* p;
682
683  {
684    char* value;
685
686    /* Echo the value of an environment variable */
687    if (p->count != 2)
688      {
689        error ("Usage: getenv variable\n");
690        return;
691      }
692
693    value = getenv (p->token[1]);
694
695    if (value == NULL)
696      printf ("Environment variable is not currently set\n");
```

```
697    else
698      printf ("%s\n", value);
699  }
700
701  /****************************************************************/
702
703  executeSetenv (p)
704
705  struct simple* p;
706
707  {
708    /* Set the value of an environment variable */
709    if (p->count != 3)
710      error ("Usage: setenv variable value\n");
711    else
712      setenv (p->token[1], p->token[2]);
713  }
714
715  /****************************************************************/
716
717  setenv (envName, newValue)
718
719  char* envName;
720  char* newValue;
721
722  {
723    int i = 0;
724    char newStr [MAX_STRING_LENGTH];
725    int len;
726
727    /* Set the environment variable envName to newValue */
728    sprintf (newStr, "%s=%s", envName, newValue);
729    len = strlen (envName) + 1;
730
731    while (environ[i] != NULL)
732      {
733        if (strncmp (environ[i], newStr, len) == 0) break;
734        ++i;
735      }
736
737    if (environ[i] == NULL) environ[i+1] = NULL;
738
739    environ[i] = (char*) malloc (strlen (newStr) + 1);
740    strcpy (environ[i], newStr);
741  }
742
743  /****************************************************************/
744
745  executeCd (p)
746
747  struct simple* p;
```

```
748
749   {
750     /* Change directory */
751     if (p->count != 2)
752       error ("Usage: cd path\n");
753     else if (chdir (p->token[1]) == -1)
754       perror ("ish");
755   }
756
757   /****************************************************************/
758   /*                        REDIRECTION                          */
759   /****************************************************************/
760
761   redirect (p)
762
763   struct simple *p;
764
765   {
766     int mask;
767
768     /* Perform input redirection */
769     switch (p->inputRedirect)
770       {
771         case FILE_REDIRECT: /* Redirect from a file */
772           if (!dupFd (p->inputFile, O_RDONLY, STDIN)) return(FALSE);
773           break;
774
775         case SERVER_REDIRECT: /* Redirect from a server socket */
776           if (!server (p->inputSocket, INPUT_SOCKET)) return(FALSE);
777           break;
778
779         case CLIENT_REDIRECT: /* Redirect from a client socket */
780           if (!client (p->inputSocket, INPUT_SOCKET)) return(FALSE);
781           break;
782       }
783
784     /* Perform output redirection */
785     switch (p->outputRedirect)
786       {
787         case FILE_REDIRECT: /* Redirect to a file */
788           mask = O_CREAT | O_WRONLY | (p->append?O_APPEND:O_TRUNC);
789           if (!dupFd (p->outputFile, mask, STDOUT)) return (FALSE);
790           break;
791
792         case SERVER_REDIRECT: /* Redirect to a server socket */
793           if (!server(p->outputSocket,OUTPUT_SOCKET)) return(FALSE);
794         break;
795
796         case CLIENT_REDIRECT: /* Redirect to a client socket */
797           if (!client(p->outputSocket,OUTPUT_SOCKET)) return(FALSE);
798           break;
```

```
799        }
800
801     return (TRUE); /* If I got here, then everything went OK */
802   }
803
804   /*****************************************************************/
805
806   dupFd (name, mask, stdFd)
807
808   char* name;
809   int mask, stdFd;
810
811   {
812     int fd;
813
814     /* Duplicate a new file descriptor over stdin/stdout */
815     fd = open (name, mask, DEFAULT_PERMISSION);
816
817     if (fd == -1)
818       {
819         error ("Cannot redirect\n");
820         return (FALSE);
821       }
822
823     dup2 (fd, stdFd); /* Copy over standard file descriptor */
824     close (fd); /* Close other one */
825     return (TRUE);
826   }
827
828   /*****************************************************************/
829   /*                    SOCKET MANAGEMENT                        */
830   /*****************************************************************/
831
832   internetAddress (name)
833
834   char* name;
835
836   {
837     /* If name contains a digit, assume it's an internet address */
838     return (strpbrk (name, "01234567890") != NULL);
839   }
840
841   /*****************************************************************/
842
843   socketRedirect (type)
844
845   int type;
846
847   {
848     return (type == SERVER_REDIRECT || type == CLIENT_REDIRECT);
849   }
```

```
850
851   /***************************************************************/
852
853   getHostAndPort (str, name, port)
854
855   char *str, *name;
856   int* port;
857
858   {
859     char *tok1, *tok2;
860
861     /* Decode name and port number from input string of the form */
862     /* NAME.PORT */
863     tok1 = strtok (str, ".");
864     tok2 = strtok (NULL, ".");
865     if (tok2 == NULL) /* Name missing, so assume local host */
866       {
867         strcpy (name, "");
868         sscanf (tok1, "%d", port);
869       }
870     else
871       {
872         strcpy (name, tok1);
873         sscanf (tok2, "%d", port);
874       }
875   }
876
877   /***************************************************************/
878
879   client (name, type)
880
881   char* name;
882   int type;
883
884   {
885     int clientFd, result, internet, domain, serverLen, port;
886     char hostName [100];
887     struct sockaddr_un serverUNIXAddress;
888     struct sockaddr_in serverINETAddress;
889     struct sockaddr* serverSockAddrPtr;
890     struct hostent* hostStruct;
891     struct in_addr* hostNode;
892
893     /* Open a client socket with specified name and type */
894     internet = internetAddress (name); /* Internet socket? */
895     domain = internet ? AF_INET : AF_UNIX; /* Pick domain */
896     /* Create client socket */
897     clientFd = socket (domain, SOCK_STREAM, DEFAULT_PROTOCOL);
898
899     if (clientFd == -1)
900       {
```

```
901        perror ("ish");
902        return (FALSE);
903      }
904
905   if (internet) /* Internet socket */
906     {
907        getHostAndPort (name, hostName, &port); /* Get name, port */
908        if (hostName[0] == NULL) gethostname (hostName, 100);
909        serverINETAddress.sin_family = AF_INET; /* Internet */
910        hostStruct = gethostbyname (hostName); /* Find host */
911
912        if (hostStruct == NULL)
913          {
914            perror ("ish");
915            return (FALSE);
916          }
917
918        hostNode = (struct in_addr*) hostStruct->h_addr;
919        printf ("IP address = %s\n", inet_ntoa (*hostNode));
920        serverINETAddress.sin_addr = *hostNode; /* Set IP address */
921        serverINETAddress.sin_port = port; /* Set port */
922        serverSockAddrPtr = (struct sockaddr*) &serverINETAddress;
923        serverLen = sizeof (serverINETAddress);
924     }
925   else /* UNIX domain socket */
926     {
927        serverUNIXAddress.sun_family = AF_UNIX; /* Domain */
928        strcpy (serverUNIXAddress.sun_path, name); /* File name */
929        serverSockAddrPtr = (struct sockaddr*) &serverUNIXAddress;
930        serverLen = sizeof (serverUNIXAddress);
931     }
932
933   do /* Connect to server */
934     {
935        result = connect (clientFd, serverSockAddrPtr, serverLen);
936        if (result == -1) sleep (SOCKET_SLEEP); /* Try again soon */
937     }
938   while (result == -1);
939
940   /* Perform redirection */
941   if (type == OUTPUT_SOCKET) dup2 (clientFd, STDOUT);
942   if (type == INPUT_SOCKET) dup2 (clientFd, STDIN);
943   close (clientFd); /* Close original client file descriptor */
944
945   return (TRUE);
946 }
947
948 /***************************************************************/
949
950 server (name, type)
```

```
951
952   char* name;
953   int type;
954
955   {
956     int serverFd, clientFd, serverLen, clientLen;
957     int domain, internet, port;
958     struct sockaddr_un serverUNIXAddress;
959     struct sockaddr_un clientUNIXAddress;
960     struct sockaddr_in serverINETAddress;
961     struct sockaddr_in clientINETAddress;
962     struct sockaddr* serverSockAddrPtr;
963     struct sockaddr* clientSockAddrPtr;
964
965     /* Prepare a server socket */
966     internet = internetAddress (name); /* Internet? */
967     domain = internet ? AF_INET : AF_UNIX; /* Pick domain */
968     /* Create the server socket*/
969     serverFd = socket (domain, SOCK_STREAM, DEFAULT_PROTOCOL);
970
971     if (serverFd == -1)
972       {
973         perror ("ish");
974         return (FALSE);
975       }
976
977     if (internet) /* Internet socket */
978       {
979         sscanf (name, "%d", &port); /* Get port number */
980         /* Fill in server socket address fields */
981         serverLen = sizeof (serverINETAddress);
982         bzero ((char*) &serverINETAddress, serverLen);
983         serverINETAddress.sin_family = AF_INET; /* Domain */
984         serverINETAddress.sin_addr.s_addr = htonl (INADDR_ANY);
985         serverINETAddress.sin_port = htons (port); /* Port */
986         serverSockAddrPtr = (struct sockaddr*) &serverINETAddress;
987       }
988     else /* UNIX domain socket */
989       {
990         serverUNIXAddress.sun_family = AF_UNIX; /* Domain */
991         strcpy (serverUNIXAddress.sun_path,name); /* Filename */
992         serverSockAddrPtr = (struct sockaddr*) &serverUNIXAddress;
993         serverLen = sizeof (serverUNIXAddress);
994         unlink (name); /* Delete socket if it already exists */
995       }
996
997     /* Bind to socket address */
998     if (bind (serverFd, serverSockAddrPtr, serverLen) == -1)
999       {
1000          perror ("ish");
```

```
1001      return (FALSE);
1002    }
1003
1004  /* Set max pending connection queue length */
1005  if (listen (serverFd, DEFAULT_QUEUE_LENGTH) == -1)
1006    {
1007      perror ("ish");
1008      return (FALSE);
1009    }
1010
1011  if (internet) /* Internet socket */
1012    {
1013      clientLen = sizeof (clientINETAddress);
1014      clientSockAddrPtr = (struct sockaddr*) &clientINETAddress;
1015    }
1016  else /* UNIX domain socket */
1017    {
1018      clientLen = sizeof (clientUNIXAddress);
1019      clientSockAddrPtr = (struct sockaddr*) &clientUNIXAddress;
1020    }
1021
1022  /* Accept a connection */
1023  clientFd = accept (serverFd, clientSockAddrPtr, &clientLen);
1024
1025  close (serverFd); /* Close original server socket */
1026
1027  if (clientFd == -1)
1028    {
1029      perror ("ish");
1030      return (FALSE);
1031    }
1032
1033  /* Perform redirection */
1034  if (type == OUTPUT_SOCKET) dup2 (clientFd, STDOUT);
1035  if (type == INPUT_SOCKET) dup2 (clientFd, STDIN);
1036  close (clientFd); /* Close original client socket */
1037
1038  return (TRUE);
1039  }
1040
```

CHAPTER REVIEW

Checklist

In this chapter, I described

- all of the common file management system calls
- the system calls for duplicating, terminating, and differentiating processes

- how a parent may wait for its children
- the terms *orphan* and *zombie*
- threaded processes
- how signals may be trapped and ignored
- the way to kill processes
- how processes may be suspended and resumed
- IPC mechanisms: unnamed pipes, named pipes, shared memory, and semaphores
- the client–server paradigm
- UNIX domain and Internet domain sockets
- the design and operation of an Internet shell

Quiz

1. How can you tell when you've reached the end of a file?
2. What is a file descriptor?
3. What's the quickest way to move to the end of a file?
4. Describe the way that shells implement I/O redirection.
5. What is an orphaned process?
6. How is a task run in two processes different from a task run in two threads?
7. Under what circumstances do zombies accumulate?
8. How can a parent find out how its children died?
9. What's the difference between execv () and execvp ()?
10. Why is the name of the system call kill () a misnomer?
11. How can you protect critical code?
12. What is the purpose of process groups?
13. What happens when a writer tries to overflow a pipe?
14. How can you create a named pipe?
15. Describe the client–server paradigm.
16. Describe the stages that a client and a server go through to establish a connection.

Exercises

13.1 Write a program that catches all signals sent to it and prints out which signal was sent. Then issue a "kill −9" command to the process. How is SIGKILL different from the other signals? [level: *easy*]

13.2 Write a program that takes a single integer argument *n* from the command line and creates a binary tree of processes of depth *n*. When the tree is created, each process should display the phrase "I am process x" and then terminate. The nodes of the process tree should be numbered according to a breadth-first traversal. For example, if the user enters

```
$ tree 4              ...build a tree of depth 4.
```

then the process tree would look like this:

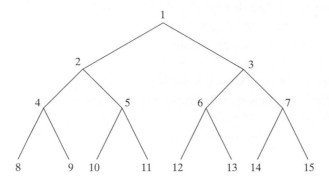

The output would be

```
I am process 1
I am process 2
        .
        .
        .
I am process 15
```

Make sure that the original parent process does not terminate until all of its children have died. This is so that you can terminate the parent and its children from your terminal with *Control*-C. [level: *medium*]

13.3   Write a program that creates a ring of three processes connected by pipes. The first process should prompt the user for a string and then send it to the second process. The second process should reverse the string and send it to the third process. The third process should convert the string to uppercase and send it back to the first process. When the first process gets the processed string, it should display it to the terminal. When this is done, all three processes should terminate. Here's an illustration of the process ring:

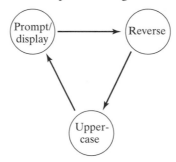

Here's an example of the program in action:

```
$ ring                              ...run the program.
Please enter a string: ole
Processed string is: ELO
$ _
```

[level: *medium*]

13.4 Rewrite the "ghoul" exercise of Chapter 5, using the C language. [level: *medium*]

13.5 Write a program that uses setuid () to allow a user to access a file that he or she would not normally be able to access. [level: *medium*]

Projects

1. Write a suite of programs that run in parallel and interact to play the "Paper, Scissors, Rock" game. In this game, two players secretly choose either paper, scissors, or rock. They then reveal their choice. A referee decides who wins as follows:

- Paper beats rock (by covering it).
- Rock beats scissors (by blunting it).
- Scissors beats paper (by cutting it).
- Matching choices draw.

The winning player gets a point. In a draw, no points are awarded. Your program should simulate such a game, allowing the user to choose how many iterations are performed, observe the game, and see the final score. Here's an example of a game:

```
$ play 3                        ...play three iterations.
Paper, Scissors, Rock: 3 iterations
Player 1: ready
Player 2: ready
Go Players [1]
  Player 1: Scissors
  Player 2: Rock
Player 2 wins
Go Players [2]
  Player 1: Paper
  Player 2: Rock
Player 1 wins
Go Players [3]
  Player 1: Paper
  Player 2: Paper
Players draw.
Final score:
  Player 1: 1
  Player 2: 1
Players Draw
$ _
```

You should write three programs, which operate as follows:

a. One program is the main program, which forks and execs one referee process and two player processes. It then waits until all three terminate. The main program should check that the command-line parameter that specifies the number of turns is valid and should pass the number to the referee process as a parameter to exec ().

b. One program is a referee program, which plays the role of the server. This program should prepare a socket and then listen for both players to send the string "READY", which means that they're ready to make a choice. The referee should then tell each player to make a choice by sending them both the string "GO." Their responses are read, and their scores calculated and updated. This process should be repeated until all of the turns have been taken, at which point the referee should send both players the string "STOP," which causes them to terminate.

c. One program is a player program, which plays the role of the client. This program is executed twice by the main program and should start by connecting to the referee's socket. It should then send the "READY" message. When it receives the "GO" message back from the referee, the player should make a choice and send it as a string to the referee. When the player receives the string "STOP", it should kill itself.

The three programs will almost certainly share some functions. To do a good job, create a makefile that compiles these common functions separately and links them the executable files that use them. Don't avoid sending strings by encoding them as one-byte numbers—that's part of the problem. [level: *medium*]

2. Rewrite Exercise 1, using unnamed pipes instead of sockets. Which program do you think was easier to write? Which is easier to understand? [level: *medium*]

3. Rewrite Exercise 1 to allow the players to reside on different Internet machines. Each component of the game should be able to start separately. [level: *hard*]

```
...execute this command on vanguard.
$ referee 5000            ...use local port 5000.
...execute this command on csservr2.
$ player vanguard.5000    ...player is on a remote port.
...execute this command on wotan.
$ player vanguard.5000    ...player is on a remote port.
```

4. The Internet shell is ripe for enhancements. Here is a list of features that would be challenging to add:

a. The ability to supply an Internet address of the form A.B.C.D. This feature would actually be easy to add, since my first Internet example already has that capability. [level: *easy*]

b. Job control features like fg, bg, and jobs. [level: *medium*]

c. Filename substitution using *, ?, and []. [level: *hard*]

d. A two-way socket feature that connects the standard input and output channels of either the keyboard or a specified process to an Internet socket. This feature would allow you to connect to standard services without the aid of **telnet**. [level: *hard*]

e. A simple built-in programming language. [level: *medium*]

f. The ability to refer to any Internet address symbolically. For example, it would be nice to be able to redirect to "vanguard.utdallas.edu.3000." [level: *medium*]

# CHAPTER 14

UNIX Internals

MOTIVATION

The UNIX operating system was one of the best designed operating systems of its time. Many of the basic underlying operating system concepts embedded in UNIX will continue to be used in some form or fashion for a long time to come. For example, the way that UNIX shares CPUs among competing processes is used in many other operating systems, such as Microsoft Windows. Knowledge of the way in which the system works can aid in designing high-performance UNIX applications. For example, knowledge of the internals of the virtual memory system can help you arrange data structures so that the amount of information transferred between main and secondary memory is minimized. In sum, knowledge of UNIX internals is useful for two purposes: as a source of reusable information that may help you in designing other similar systems and to help you design high-performance UNIX applications.

PREREQUISITES

You should already have read Chapter 13. It also helps to have a good knowledge of data structures, pointers, and linked lists.

OBJECTIVES

In this chapter, I describe the mechanisms that UNIX uses to support processes, memory management, input/output, and the file system. I also explain the main kernel data structures and algorithms.

PRESENTATION

Various portions of the UNIX system are described in their turn.

INTRODUCTION

The UNIX system is a fairly complex thing, and it's getting more complex as time goes by. In order to understand it well, it's necessary to break the system down into manageable portions and tackle each portion in a layered fashion. Accordingly, we discuss the following topics:

- *Kernel basics*: system calls and interrupts.
- *The file system*: how the directory hierarchy, regular files, peripherals, and multiple file systems are managed.
- *Process management*: how processes share the CPU and memory and how signals are implemented.
- *Input/output*: how processes access files, with special attention given to terminal I/O.
- *Interprocess communication* (IPC): the mechanisms that allow processes to communicate with each other, even if they're on different machines.

There are some differences between the ways in which the BSD and System V designers implemented portions of these subsystems. Any major differences in approach are pointed out at the appropriate time.

KERNEL BASICS

The UNIX kernel is the part of the UNIX operating system that contains the code for

- sharing the CPU and RAM between competing processes
- processing all system calls
- handling peripherals

The kernel is a program that is loaded from disk into RAM when the computer is first turned on. It always stays in RAM and runs until the system is turned off or crashes. Although the kernel is written mostly in C, some parts are written in assembly language for efficiency reasons. User programs make use of the kernel via the system call interface.

Kernel Subsystems

The kernel facilities may be divided into the following subsystems:

- memory management
- process management
- interprocess communication (IPC)
- input/output
- file management

These subsystems interact in a fairly hierarchical way. Figure 14.1 illustrates the layering.

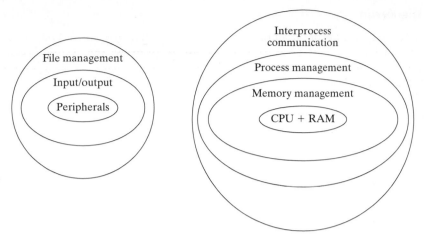

FIGURE 14.1

UNIX subsystems.

Processes and Files

The UNIX kernel supports the concepts of processes and files. Processes are the "life-forms" that live in the computer and make decisions. Files are containers of information that processes read and write. In addition, processes may talk to each other via several different kinds of interprocess communication mechanisms, including signals, pipes, and sockets. Figure 14.2 is an illustration of what I mean.

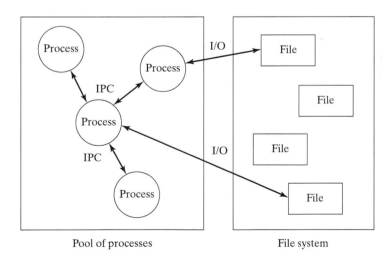

FIGURE 14.2

UNIX supports processes and files.

Talking to the Kernel

Processes access kernel facilities via the system call interface, and peripherals (special files) communicate with the kernel via hardware interrupts. System calls and hardware interrupts are the only ways in which the outside world can talk to the kernel, as illustrated by the diagram in Figure 14.3.

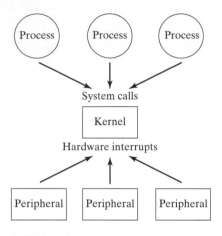

FIGURE 14.3

Talking to the kernel.

Since systems calls and interrupts are obviously very important, I'll begin the discussion of UNIX internals with a description of each mechanism.

System Calls

System calls are the programmer's functional interface to the kernel. They are subroutines that reside inside the UNIX kernel and support basic system functions such as the ones listed in Figure 14.4. System calls may be loosely grouped into three main categories, as illustrated in Figure 14.5.

User Mode and Kernel Mode

The kernel contains several data structures that are essential to the functioning of the system, including the following:

- the *process table*, which contains one entry for every process in the system
- the *open file table*, which contains at least one entry for every open file in the system

These data structures reside in the kernel's memory space, which is protected from user processes by a memory management system that I'll describe to you later. User processes cannot therefore accidentally corrupt these important kernel data structures. System call routines are different from regular functions because they *can* directly manipulate kernel data structures, albeit in a carefully controlled manner.

Function	System call
open a file	open
close a file	close
perform I/O	read/write
send a signal	kill
create a pipe	pipe
create a socket	socket
duplicate a process	fork
overlay a process	exec
terminate a process	exit

FIGURE 14.4

Common UNIX system calls.

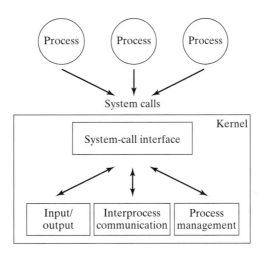

FIGURE 14.5

Major system call subsystems.

When a user process is running, it operates in a special machine mode called *user mode*. This mode prevents a process from executing certain privileged machine instructions, including those which would allow it to access the kernel data structures. The other machine mode is called *kernel mode*. A kernel mode process may execute any machine instruction.

The only way for a user process to enter kernel mode is to execute a system call. Every system call is allocated a code number, starting from 1. For example, the open () system call might be allocated code number 1, and close () might be allocated code number 2. When a process invokes a system call, the C run-time library version of the system call places the system call parameters and the system call code number into some machine registers and then executes a *trap* machine instruction. The trap instruction flips the machine into kernel mode and uses the system call code number as an index into a *system call vector table* located in low kernel memory. The system call vector table is an array of pointers to the kernel code for each system call. The code corresponding to the

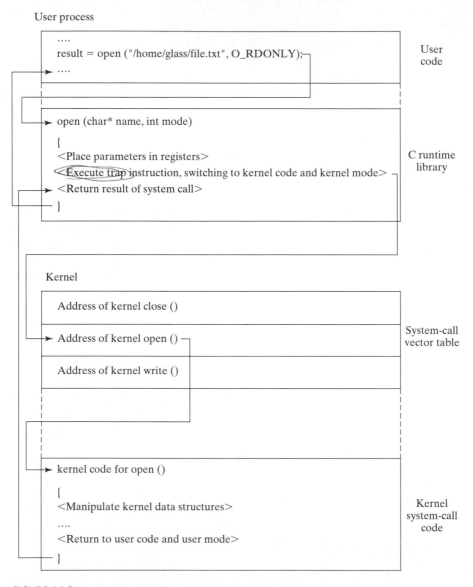

User process

```
....
result = open ("/home/glass/file.txt", O_RDONLY);
....
```
User code

```
open (char* name, int mode)
{
<Place parameters in registers>
<Execute trap instruction, switching to kernel code and kernel mode>
<Return result of system call>
}
```
C runtime library

Kernel

Address of kernel close ()

Address of kernel open ()

Address of kernel write ()

System-call vector table

```
kernel code for open ()
{
<Manipulate kernel data structures>
....
<Return to user code and user mode>
}
```
Kernel system-call code

FIGURE 14.6

User mode and kernel mode.

indexed function executes in kernel mode, modifying kernel data structures as necessary, and then performs a special *return* instruction that flips the machine back into user mode and returns to the user process' code.

When I was first learning about UNIX, I didn't understand why this approach was taken. Why not just use a client–server model with a kernel server process that services system requests from client user processes? That would avoid the need for user processes to execute kernel code directly. The reason is pure and simple: speed. In current architectures, the overhead cost of swapping between processes is too great to make the client–server approach practical. However, it's interesting to note that some of the modern microkernel systems are taking this approach.

From a programmer's standpoint, using a system call is easy: You call the C function with the correct parameters, and the function returns when it finishes processing. If an error occurs, the function returns −1, and the global variable **errno** is set to indicate the cause of the error. Figure 14.6 shows a diagram that illustrates the flow of control during a system call.

Synchronous versus Asynchronous Processing

When a process performs a system call, it cannot usually be preempted. This means that the scheduler will not assign the CPU to another process during the operation of a system call. However, some system calls request I/O operations from a device, and these operations can take a while to complete. To avoid leaving the CPU idle during the wait for I/O to terminate, the kernel puts the waiting process to sleep and wakes it up again only when a hardware interrupt signaling I/O completion is received. The scheduler does not allocate any CPU time to a sleeping process, but rather allocates the CPU to other processes while the hardware device is servicing the I/O request.

An interesting consequence of the way that UNIX handles read () and write () is that user processes experience synchronous execution of system calls, whereas the kernel experiences asynchronous behavior. This disparity is illustrated in Figure 14.7.

Interrupts

Interrupts are the way that hardware devices notify the kernel that they must be attended to. In the same way that processes compete for CPU time, hardware devices compete for interrupt processing. Devices are allocated an interrupt priority based on their relative importance, as shown in Figure 14.8. For example, interrupts from the system clock have a higher priority than those from the keyboard.

When an interrupt occurs, the current process is suspended and the kernel determines the source of the interrupt. It then examines its interrupt vector table, located in low kernel memory, to find the location of the code that processes the interrupt. This "interrupt handler" code is then executed. When the interrupt handler is finished, the current process is resumed. Interrupt processing is illustrated in Figure 14.9.

Interrupting Interrupts

Interrupt processing may itself be interrupted! If an interrupt of a higher priority than the current interrupt arrives, a sequence of events similar to normal interrupt processing

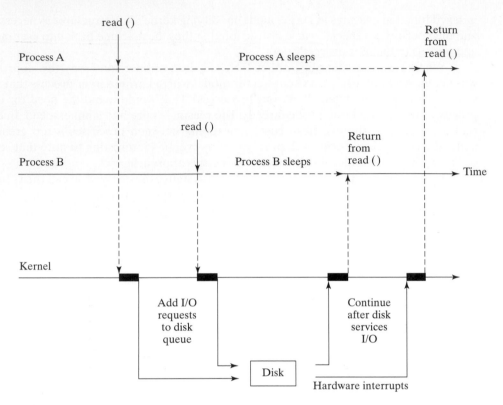

FIGURE 14.7

Synchronous and asynchronous events.

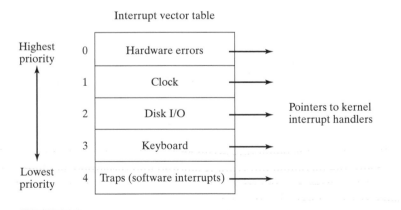

FIGURE 14.8

Interrupts have priorities.

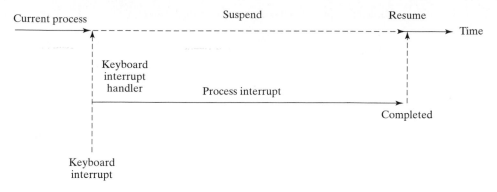

FIGURE 14.9

Interrupt processing.

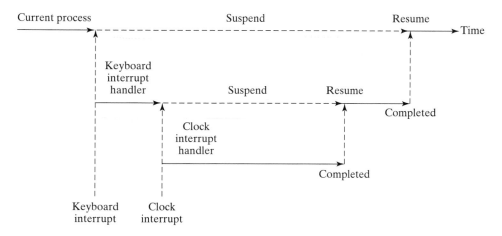

FIGURE 14.10

Interrupts may be interrupted.

occurs, and the lower priority interrupt handler is suspended until the higher priority interrupt is finished. This process is shown in Figure 14.10.

If an interrupt is being processed and another interrupt of an equal or lower priority occurs, the incoming interrupt is ignored and discarded, as shown in Figure 14.11. Interrupt handlers are therefore designed to be very fast, since the quicker they execute, the less likely it is that other interrupts will be lost.

Most machines have instructions that allow a program to ignore all interrupts below a certain priority level. Critical sections of kernel code protect themselves from

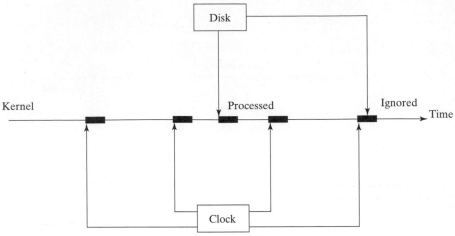

FIGURE 14.11

Interrupts may be ignored.

interrupts by temporarily invoking such instructions. Here's some pseudocode that does just that:

```
            .
            .
            .
  <disable all but highest priority interrupts>
  <enter critical section of code>
            .
            .
            .
  <leave critical section of code>
  <reenable all interrupts>
            .
            .
            .
```

Later in the chapter, we describe the way that peripherals use the kernel interrupt facilities to perform efficient I/O.

THE FILE SYSTEM

UNIX uses files for long-term storage and RAM for short-term storage. Programs, data, and text are all stored in files, which in turn are usually stored on hard disks, but can also be stored on other media, such as tape and floppy disks. UNIX files are organized by a hierarchy of labels, commonly known as a *directory structure*. The files referenced by these labels may be of three kinds:

- *Regular files*, which contain a sequence of bytes that generally corresponds to code or data. Regular files may be referenced via the standard I/O system calls.
- *Directory files*, which are stored on disk in a special format and which form the backbone of the file system. Directory files may be referenced only via directory-specific system calls.

- *Special files,* which correspond to peripherals, such as printers and disks, and interprocess communication mechanisms, such as pipes and sockets. Special files may be referenced via the standard I/O system calls.

Conceptually, a UNIX file is a linear sequence of bytes. The UNIX kernel does not support any higher order of file structure, such as records or fields. This is evident if you consider the lseek () system call, which allows you to position the file pointer only in terms of a byte offset. Older operating systems tended to support record structures, so UNIX was fairly unusual in this regard.

Let's begin our study of the UNIX file system by looking at the hardware architecture of the most common file medium: a disk.

Disk Architecture

Figure 14.12 shows a diagram of typical disk architecture. A disk is split up in two ways: It's sliced up like a pizza into areas called *sectors*, and it's further subdivided into concentric rings called *tracks*. The individual areas bounded by the intersection of sectors and tracks are called *blocks*; they form the basic unit of disk storage. A typical disk block can hold 4K bytes. A single read/write head travels up and down a stationary arm, accessing information as the disk rotates and its surface passes underneath. A special chip called a *disk controller* moves the read/write head in response to instructions from the disk device driver, which is a special piece of software located in the UNIX kernel.

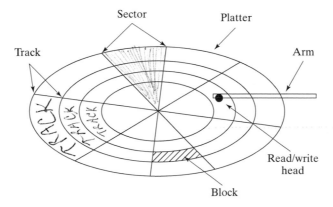

FIGURE 14.12

Disk architecture.

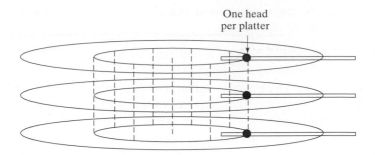

FIGURE 14.13

A multiplatter architecture.

There are several variations of this simple disk architecture. Many disk drives actually contain several platters, stacked one upon the other, as shown in Figure 14.13. In these systems, the collection of tracks with the same index number is called a *cylinder*. In most multiplatter systems, the disk arms are connected to each other so that the read/write heads all move synchronously, rather like a comb moving through hair. The read/write heads of such disk systems therefore move through cylinders of media. Some sophisticated disk drives have separately controllable read/write heads.

Notice that the blocks on the outside track are larger than the blocks on the inside track, due to the way that a disk is partitioned. If a disk always rotates at the same speed, then the density of data on the disk's outer blocks is less than it could be, thus wasting potential storage. Some of the latest disk drive designs attempt to keep the data density constant throughout the surface of the disk by increasing the number of blocks on the outer tracks and then either slowing down the disk's rotation or increasing the data transfer rate as the head moves toward the outside of the disk. Disk storage techniques are shown in Figure 14.14.

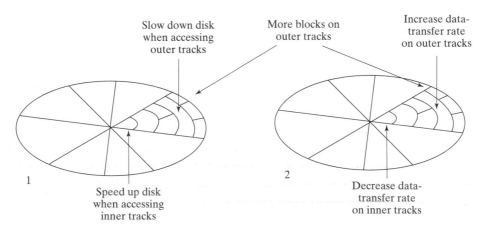

FIGURE 14.14

Disk storage techniques.

Interleaving

When a sequence of contiguously numbered blocks is read, there's a delay between each block due to the overhead of the communication between the disk controller and the device driver. Logically contiguous blocks are therefore spaced apart on the surface of the disk so that by the time the delay is over, the head is positioned over the correct area. The spacing between blocks due to this delay is called the *interleave factor*. Figure 14.15 shows a couple of pictures that illustrate two different interleave factors.

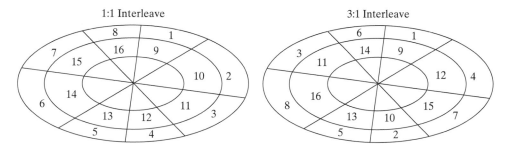

FIGURE 14.15

Disk interleaving.

Storing a File

Assuming a 4K block size, a single 9K UNIX file requires three blocks of storage—one to hold the first 4K, one to hold the next 4K, and the last to hold the remaining 1K.[1] The loss of storage due to the underuse of the last 4K block is called *fragmentation*. A file's blocks are rarely contiguous and tend to be scattered all over a disk, as shown in Figure 14.16.

Block I/O

 I/O is always done in terms of blocks. If you issue a system call to read () the first byte of data from a file, the device driver issues an I/O request to the disk controller to read the first 4K block into a kernel buffer and then copies the first byte from the buffer to your process. (More information about I/O buffering is presented later in the chapter.)

Most disk controllers handle one block I/O request at a time. When a disk controller completes the current block I/O request, it issues a hardware interrupt back to the device driver to signal that it is finished. At this point, the device driver usually makes the next block I/O request. Figure 14.17 is a diagram that illustrates the sequence of events that might occur during a 9K read ().

---

[1]Some file systems remedy this situation by having a disk block contain the last datum in a file. Thus, one disk block can contain fragments from several files.

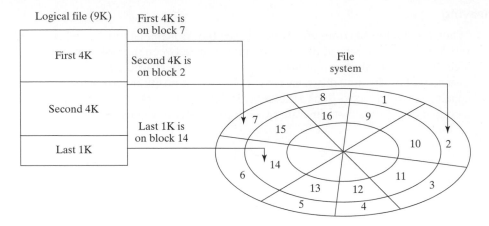

FIGURE 14.16

A file's blocks are scattered.

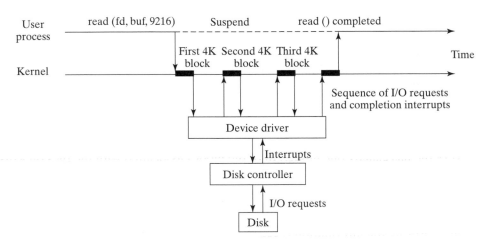

FIGURE 14.17

Block I/O.

Inodes

UNIX uses a structure called an *inode* (**i**ndex **n**ode) to store information about each file. (See Figure 14.18.) The inode of a regular or directory file contains the locations of its disk blocks, and the inode of a special file contains information that allows the peripheral to be identified. An inode also holds other information associated with a file, such as its permission flags, owner, group, and last modification time. An inode has a fixed size and contains pointers to disk blocks, as well as additional indirect pointers (for large files). Every inode in a particular file system is allocated a unique inode number, and

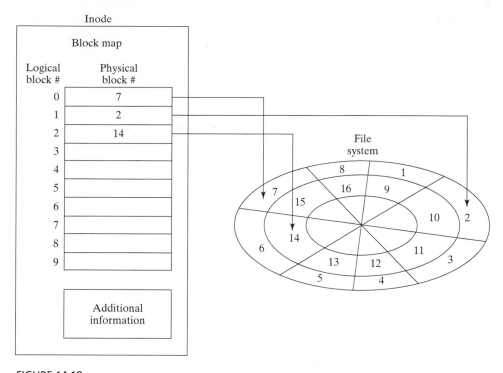

FIGURE 14.18

Every file has an inode.

every file has exactly one inode. All of the inodes associated with the files on a disk are stored in a special area at the start of the disk called the *inode list.*

Inode Contents

The following file information is contained within each inode:

- the type of the file: regular, directory, block special, character special, etc.
- file permissions
- the owner and group IDs
- a hard link count (described later in the chapter)
- the last modification time and last access time
- the location of the blocks if the file is a regular or directory file
- the major and minor device numbers (described later in the chapter) if the file is a special file
- the value of the symbolic link if the file is a symbolic link

In other words, an inode contains all of the information that you see when you perform an "ls -l", except for the filename.

The Block Map

Only the locations of the first 10 blocks of a file are stored directly in the inode. Most UNIX files are less than 40K in size, so this is sufficient in a majority of cases. An indirect access scheme is used for addressing larger files. In this scheme, a single user block is used to hold the location of up to 1024 user blocks. When used in this manner, a block is called an *indirect block*. (See Figure 14.19.) Its location is stored in the inode and is used to address the next 1024 blocks. This approach allows files up to 4 megabytes to be addressed.

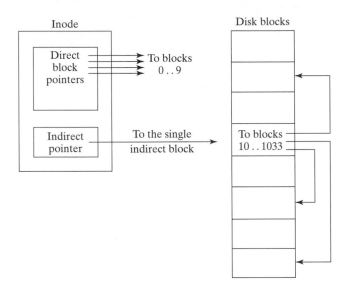

FIGURE 14.19

The single indirect block.

For files greater than 4 megabytes a similar double-indirect scheme is used. A user block is used to hold the locations of up to 1024 other indirect blocks, each of which points to a maximum of 1024 user blocks, as shown in Figure 14.20. The inode holds the location of the double-indirect user block.

Note that as the file gets larger, the amount of indirection required to access a particular block increases. This overhead is minimized by buffering the contents of the inode and commonly referenced indirect blocks in RAM. The buffering mechanism is described later in the chapter.

File System Layout

The first logical block of a disk is termed the *boot block* and contains some executable code that is used when UNIX is first activated. (See Chapter 15 for more information.) The second logical block is known as the *superblock* and contains information concerning the disk itself. Following this is a fixed-size set of blocks called the *inode list* that

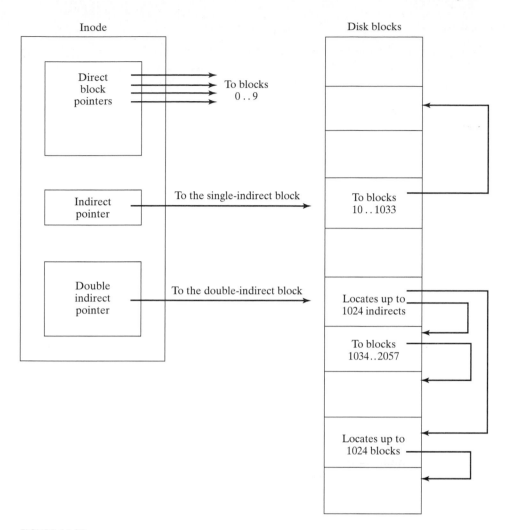

FIGURE 14.20

The double-indirect block.

holds all of the inodes associated with the files on the disk. Each block in the inode list can normally hold about 40 inodes (although this varies with different versions of UNIX). The remaining blocks on the disk are available for storing file blocks and contain both directories and user files. The disk block arrangement is shown in Figure 14.21.

The Superblock

The superblock contains information pertaining to the entire file system. It includes a bitmap of free blocks, as shown in Figure 14.22. The bitmap is a linear sequence of bits, one per disk block. A one indicates that the corresponding block is free, and a zero means it's being used.

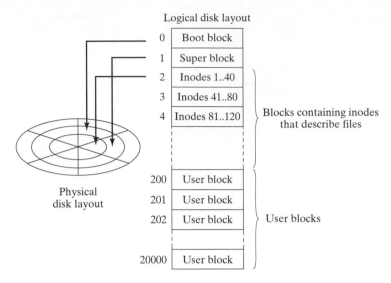

FIGURE 14.21

Usage of disk blocks.

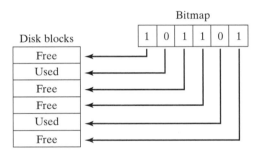

FIGURE 14.22

The free-block bitmap.

The superblock includes the following information:

- the total number of blocks in the file system
- the number of inodes in the inode free list
- the size of a block in bytes
- the number of free blocks
- the number of used blocks

Bad Blocks

A disk always contains several blocks that, for one reason or another, are not fit for use. The utility that creates a new file system, described in Chapter 15, also creates a single "worst-nightmare" file composed of all the bad blocks in the disk and records the locations of all these blocks in inode number 1. This prevents the blocks from being allocated to other files.

Directories

Inode number 2 contains the location(s) of the block(s) possessing the root directory. A UNIX directory contains a list of associations between filenames and inode numbers. When a directory is created, it is automatically allocated entries for ".." (its parent directory) and "." (itself). Since a <filename, inode number> pair effectively links a name to a file, these associations are termed "hard links." Because filenames are stored in the directory blocks, they are not stored in a file's inode. In fact, it wouldn't make any sense to store the name in the inode, as a file may have more than one name. Accordingly, it's more accurate to think of the directory hierarchy as being a hierarchy of *file labels*, rather than a hierarchy of *files*.

All UNIX systems allow a filename to be at least 14 characters, and most support names up to 255 characters in length. Figure 14.23 is an illustration of the root inode corresponding to a simple root directory. The inode numbers associated with each filename are shown as subscripts.

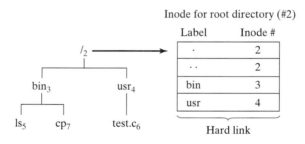

FIGURE 14.23

The root directory is associated with inode 2.

Translating Pathnames into Inode Numbers

System calls such as open () must obtain a file's inode from its pathname. They perform the translation as follows:

1. The inode from which to start the search for the pathname is located. If the pathname is absolute, the search starts from inode 2. If the pathname is relative, the search starts from the inode corresponding to the process' current working directory. (See "Process Management" for more information.)

2. The components of the pathname are then processed from left to right. Every component except the last should correspond to either a directory or a symbolic link. Let's call the inode from which the pathname search is started the *current inode*.

3. If the current inode corresponds to a directory, the current pathname component is looked for in the directory corresponding to the current inode. If it's not found, an error occurs; otherwise, the value of the current inode number becomes the inode number associated with the pathname component that has been located.

4. If the current inode corresponds to a symbolic link, the pathname up to and including the current path component is replaced by the contents of the symbolic link, and the pathname is reprocessed.

5. The inode corresponding to the final pathname component is the inode of the file referenced by the entire pathname.

To illustrate this algorithm, I'll list the steps required to translate the pathname "/usr/test.c" into an inode number. Figure 14.24 contains the disk layout that I assume during the translation process. It indicates the translation path via bold lines and the final destination with a circle.

Sample Pathname-to-Inode Translation

Here's the logic that the kernel uses to translate the pathname "/usr/test.c" into an inode number:

1. The pathname is absolute, so the current inode number is 2.

2. The directory corresponding to inode 2 is searched for the pathname component "usr." The matching entry is found, and the current inode number is set to 4.

3. The directory corresponding to inode 4 is searched for the pathname component "test.c". The matching entry is found, and the current inode number is set to 6.

4. "test.c" is the final pathname component, so the algorithm returns the inode number 6.

As you can see, the translation bounces between inodes and directory blocks until the pathname is fully processed.

Mounting File Systems   *— mount & umount*

When UNIX is started, the directory hierarchy corresponds to the file system located on a single disk called the *root device*. UNIX allows you to create file systems on other devices and attach them to the original directory hierarchy, using a mechanism termed *mounting*. The **mount** utility allows a superuser to splice the root directory of a file system into the existing directory hierarchy. Typically, the hierarchy of a large UNIX system is spread over many devices, each containing a subtree of the total hierarchy. For example, the "/usr" subtree is commonly stored on a device other than the root device. Non-root-file systems are usually mounted automatically at boot time. (See Chapter 15 for more details.) For example, suppose that a file system is stored on a floppy disk in the "/dev/flp" device. To attach it to the "/mnt" subdirectory of the main hierarchy, you'd execute the command

```
$ mount /dev/flp /mnt
```

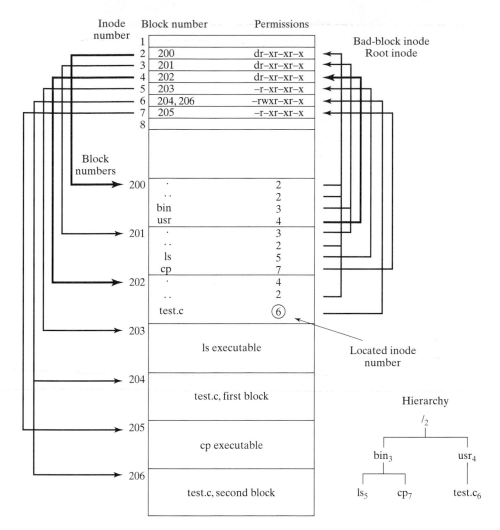

FIGURE 14.24

A sample directory layout.

Figure 14.25 illustrates the effect of this command.

File systems may be detached from the main hierarchy by using the **umount** utility. The command

```
$ umount /dev/flp
```

or

```
$ umount /mnt
```

would detach the file system stored in "/dev/flp".

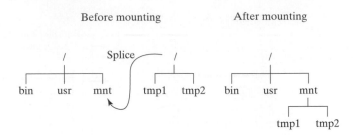

FIGURE 14.25

Mounting directories.

File System I/O

For details about the kernel implementation of file system I/O, see "Input/Output," later in the chapter.

PROCESS MANAGEMENT

In this section, I describe the way that the kernel shares the CPU and RAM among competing processes. The area of the kernel that shares the CPU is called the *scheduler*, and the area of the kernel that shares RAM is called the *memory manager*. The section also contains information about process-oriented system calls, including exec (), fork (), and exit (). For the sake of simplicity, we will not concern ourselves with *kernel threads* (threads that run in kernel mode), since most applications programmers will not have any occasion to use them. However, we should be aware that, just as a user application can run multithreaded tasks, some kernel modules (like device drivers) may also run multithreaded. This introduces most of the same complexities discussed in the previous chapter.

Executable Files

When the source code of a program is compiled, it is stored in a special format on disk. The first few bytes of the file are known as the *magic number* and are used by the kernel to identify the type of the executable file. For example, if the first two bytes of the file are the characters "#!", the kernel identifies the executable file as containing shell text and invokes a shell to execute the text. Another sequence identifies the file as being a regular load image containing machine code and data. This kind of file is divided into several sections containing code or data, with a separate header for each section. The headers are used by the kernel in preparing the memory management system described shortly. Figure 14.26 is an illustration of a typical executable file.

The First Processes

UNIX runs a program by creating a process and then associating it with a named executable file. Surprisingly enough, there's no system call that allows you to say "create a

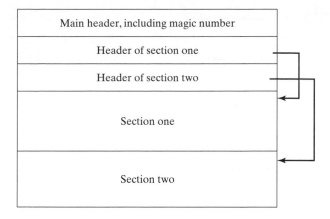

FIGURE 14.26

Layout of an executable file.

new process to run program X"; instead, you must duplicate an existing process and then associate the newly created child process with the executable file "X."

The first process, with process ID (PID) 0, is created by UNIX during boot time. This process immediately fork()s and exec()s twice, creating two processes with PIDs 1 and 2. In System V UNIX, the names of these first few processes are as shown in Figure 14.27. The purpose of these processes is described later in the chapter. All other processes in the system are descendants of the *init* process. (For more information concerning the boot sequence, see Chapter 15.)

PID	Name
0	sched
1	init
2	pageout

— Kernel process
— parent of all user processes
— Kernel process

FIGURE 14.27

The first processes to start on a UNIX system.

Kernel Processes and User Processes

Most processes execute in user mode, except when they make a system call, at which point they flip temporarily into kernel mode. However, the *sched* daemon (PID 0) and *pageout* daemon (PID 2) processes execute permanently in kernel mode due to their importance and are termed *kernel processes*. In contrast to user processes, their code is linked directly into the kernel and does not reside in a separate executable file. In addition, kernel processes are never preempted.

The Process Hierarchy

When a process duplicates by using fork (), the original process is known as the parent of the child process. The *init* process, PID 1, is the process from which all user processes are descended. Parent and child processes are therefore related in a hierarchy, with the *init* process as the root. Figure 14.28 illustrates a process hierarchy involving four processes.

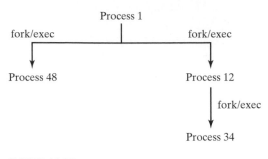

FIGURE 14.28

Process hierarchy.

Process States

Every process in the system can be in one of six states:

- *Running*, which means that the process is currently using the CPU.
- *Runnable*, which means that the process can make use of the CPU as soon as it becomes available.
- *Sleeping*, which means that the process is waiting for an event to occur. For example, if a process executes a read () system call, it sleeps until the I/O request is completed.
- *Suspended*, which means that the process has been "frozen" by a signal such as SIGSTOP. It will resume only when sent a SIGCONT signal. For example, a *Control-Z* from the keyboard suspends all of the processes in the foreground job.
- *Idle*, which means that the process is being created by a fork () system call and is not yet runnable.
- "*Zombified*," which means that the process has terminated, but has not yet returned its exit code to its parent. A process remains a zombie until its parent accepts its return code via the wait () system call.

Figure 14.29 shows a diagram that illustrates the possible state changes that can occur during the lifetime of a process.

Process Composition

Every process is composed of several different pieces:

- a *code area*, which contains the executable (text) portion of the process

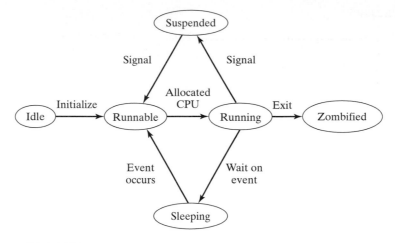

FIGURE 14.29

Process states.

- a *data area*, which is used to contain static data
- a *stack area*, which is used to store temporary data
- a *user area*, which holds housekeeping information about the process
- *page tables*, which are used by the memory management system

The uses of the first three areas should be familiar to you, and I'm going to leave a discussion of page tables until later. The next subsection contains a description of the user area. Process composition is shown in Figure 14.30.

The User Area

Every process in the system has some associated "housekeeping" information that is used by the kernel to manage the process. This information is stored in a data structure called a *user area*. Every process has its own user area, created in the kernel's data region and accessible only by the kernel; user processes may not access their user areas. Fields within a process' user area include the following:

- a record of how the process should react to each kind of signal
- a record of the process' open file descriptors
- a record of how much CPU time the process has used recently

The contents of a user area are described in more detail later in the chapter.

The Process Table

There is a single fixed-size kernel data structure called the *process table* that contains one entry for every process in the system. The process table is created in the kernel's

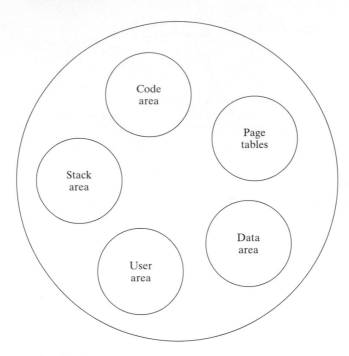

FIGURE 14.30

Process composition.

data region and is accessible only by the kernel. Each entry contains the following information about each process:

- its process ID (PID) and parent process ID (PPID)
- its real and effective user ID (UID) and group ID (GID)
- its state (running, runnable, sleeping, suspended, idle, or zombified)
- the location of its code, data, stack, and user areas
- a list of all pending signals

Figure 14.31 shows the process table that would result from the small process hierarchy that I illustrated earlier in the chapter. It assumes that the process with PID 48 is currently waiting for I/O completion.

The Scheduler

The kernel is responsible for sharing CPU time among competing processes. A section of the kernel code called the *scheduler* performs this duty and maintains a special data structure called a *multilevel priority queue* that allows it to schedule processes efficiently. A priority queue is a linked list of the runnable processes that have similar priorities. The way that the kernel calculates a process' priority is discussed later in the chapter.

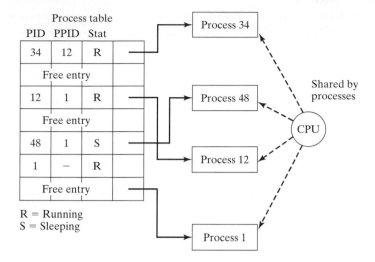

FIGURE 14.31

The process table.

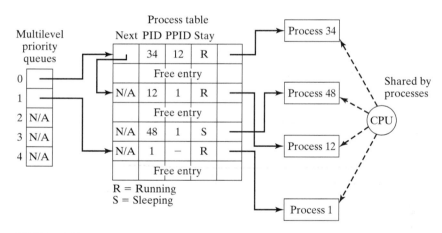

FIGURE 14.32

The process table and priority queues.

Processes are allocated CPU time in proportion to their importance. CPU time is allocated in fixed size units called *time quanta*. On most systems, each time quantum is 1/10 second. Figure 14.32 shows the queues in relation to the process table, based on the small process hierarchy illustrated earlier.

Scheduling Rules

Here are the rules that describe the way the scheduler works:

- Every second, the scheduler calculates the priorities of all the runnable processes in the system and organizes them into several priority queues. The queues are stratified on the basis of the process' priority values.

100ms

- Every 1/10 second, the scheduler selects the highest-priority process in the priority queues and allocates the CPU to it (unless the currently running process is in kernel mode).
- If a process is still runnable at the end of its time quantum, it's placed at the end of its priority queue.
- If a process sleeps on an event during its time quantum, the scheduler immediately selects another process to run and allocates the CPU to it.
- If a process returns from a system call during its time quantum and a higher priority process is ready to run, the lower priority process is preempted by the higher priority process.
- At every hardware clock interrupt (which typically occurs 100 times a second), *10ms* the process' clock tick count is incremented. Every fourth tick, the scheduler recalculates the process' priority value. This tends to reduce a process' priority during its time quantum.

The formula for calculating a process' priority may be stated roughly as follows:

priority = (Recent CPU usage) / constant + (base priority) + (nice setting),

where *base priority* is the threshold priority and *nice setting* is the value set by the nice() system call. This formula ensures that a process' priority diminishes if it uses a lot of CPU time in a particular "window" of time. It also ensures that processes that have a high nice setting will have a lower priority. A consequence of the formula is that interactive processes will tend to have a good response time: As an interactive process waits for a user to press a key, it uses no CPU time, and therefore its priority level rises rapidly.

The act of switching from one process to another is termed a *context switch*. To "freeze" a process, the kernel saves the program counter, stack pointer, and other important details about the process into the process' user area. To "thaw" a process, the kernel reinstates this information from the process' user area.

As a result of these rules, every second the CPU is allocated in a round-robin fashion to processes in the highest nonempty priority queue. At the end of each second, the processes are repositioned in the queues, depending on their new priorities, and the round-robin allocation repeats. Figures 14.33, 14.34, and 14.35 provide some illustrations of the scheduling rules in action.

Run every second

Recalculate all process priorities

FIGURE 14.33

Every second.

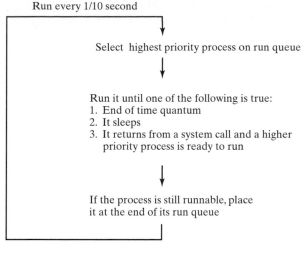

Run every 1/10 second

Select highest priority process on run queue

Run it until one of the following is true:
1. End of time quantum
2. It sleeps
3. It returns from a system call and a higher
   priority process is ready to run

If the process is still runnable, place
it at the end of its run queue

FIGURE 14.34

Every 1/10.

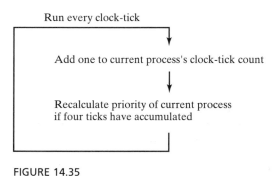

Run every clock-tick

Add one to current process's clock-tick count

Recalculate priority of current process
if four ticks have accumulated

FIGURE 14.35

Every clock tick.

Memory Management

In addition to managing scheduling, the kernel is responsible for sharing RAM among processes in a secure and efficient manner. The next few sections describe the UNIX memory management system.[2]

Memory Pages

The UNIX memory management system allows processes that are bigger than the total RAM capacity of the system to execute. In order to achieve this, it divides RAM, code, data, and stack areas into fixed-size chunks of memory called *pages*, analogously to the

---

[2]Memory management implementations vary among versions of UNIX. The algorithm described here is BSD centric.

way that a disk is divided up into fixed-size blocks. The size of a memory page is typically set to the size of a disk block. The reason for this relationship will soon become evident. Only the pages of a process that are currently being accessed or were recently accessed are stored in RAM pages; the rest are stored on disk.

Page Tables and Regions

The code, data, and stack areas of a process do not have to reside in logically contiguous memory. For example, the compiler might generate a program whose code, data, and stack occupy the logical areas of address space shown in Figure 14.36.

Section	Logical address
code	0K..15K
data	64K..72K
stack	64K..72K

FIGURE 14.36

Sample memory layout.

Each area of contiguous logical address space is termed a *region*; therefore, most processes have three regions. The pages of a region do not have to be stored contiguously in RAM; every region has an associated data structure called a *page table* that records the locations of each of its pages. A process' page tables are created in the kernel's data region and are accessible only by the kernel. The locations of a process' page tables are stored in the process' user area. A page table in the memory management system is analogous to an inode in the file system, as each tracks the location of individual storage units.

Figure 14.37 illustrates the process table, user areas, and page tables.

The RAM Table

The memory manager allocates pages of RAM to a process only when it needs them. A single fixed-size kernel data structure called the *RAM table* records information about each page of RAM, such as whether the page is currently being used and whether it's "locked" into memory. Locked pages are never transferred to disk; for example, all of the pages that contain the UNIX kernel are locked.

Loading an Executable File: exec ()

When a process performs an exec (), the kernel allocates page tables for the process' code, data, and stack regions. At this point, all of the code and initialized data resides on disk in the executable file, so the code and data page table entries are set to contain the locations of their corresponding disk blocks. These locations are extracted from the

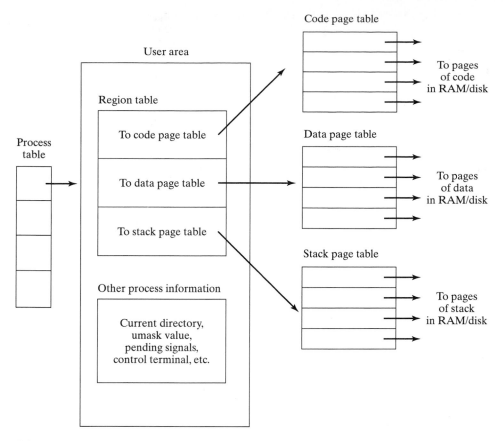

FIGURE 14.37

The user area, regions, and page tables.

executable file's inode and header. When the process accesses one of the pages for the first time, its corresponding block is copied from disk into RAM, and the page table entry is updated with the physical RAM page number.

The stack and uninitialized data regions do not have a corresponding disk location. The kernel therefore marks their corresponding page table entries as *zeroed*. When a zeroed page is accessed for the first time, the kernel allocates a page of RAM and fills it with zeroes *without* loading anything from disk. It then updates the page table entry with the physical RAM page number.

Assuming that the first eight pages of RAM were originally free, Figure 14.38 shows an illustration of a process' memory layout immediately after an exec ().

Address Translation

All of the logical addresses that travel down the hardware address bus from a process must be mapped to a physical address, using the information contained in the process'

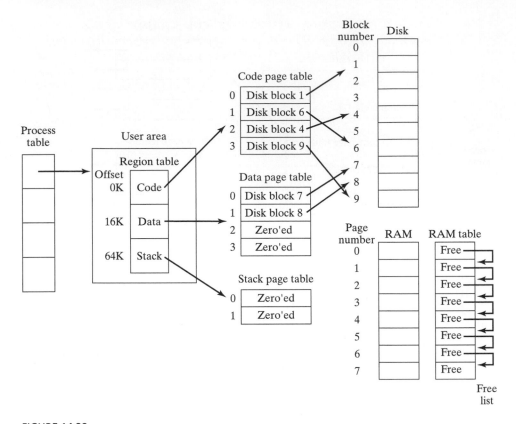

FIGURE 14.38

Memory layout immediately after an exec ().

region and page tables. This translation process is aided by a special piece of hardware called a *memory management unit (MMU)*. Assuming that every page of RAM is 4K and that all addresses are 32-bit values, the memory management unit works as follows:

- When a process is scheduled, several hardware-specific registers in the MMU are set to point to the process' region and page tables. The MMU uses these registers to access those data structures during the address translation process.
- When an address appears on the hardware address bus, the MMU is activated and starts the translation process. I'll call the incoming address **ADDR**.
- The MMU then determines which region the incoming address **ADDR** lies within—either the code, data, or stack region.
- The MMU then subtracts the starting virtual address (**SVA**) of the region from the incoming address **ADDR**. This yields the offset of the incoming address from the start of the region (**OSR**).
- **OSR** is then split into two pieces. The most significant 20 bits correspond to the region page number (**RPN**) of the incoming address, and the least significant 12 bits are equal to the offset within this region page (**ORP**).

- The MMU then consults the region's page table to determine the current location of the logical page **RPN**. If the page is currently in RAM, the incoming logical address is translated into a physical address by replacing the logical page number by the physical RAM number. If the page is not in RAM, the MMU gives up trying to translate the logical address, generates a page validity interrupt, and then processes other incoming logical addresses.
- When UNIX receives a page validity interrupt, it issues an I/O request that loads the page from disk into a free page of RAM. When the page is loaded, the appropriate page table entry is updated with the RAM page number, and the address translation is restarted.

Illustration of MMU Algorithm

Figure 14.39 illustrates the MMU mapping algorithm.

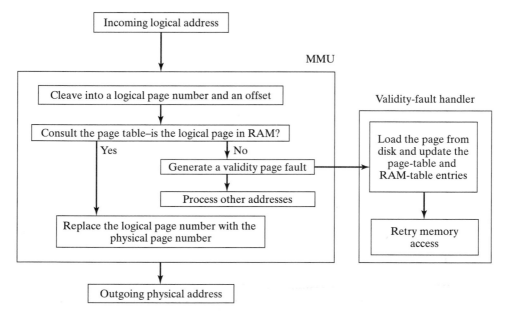

FIGURE 14.39

Memory management algorithm (simplified).

The MMU and the Page Table

Each page table entry contains a number of fields that are used by various facets of the memory management system. Some of these fields are set automatically by the MMU under certain circumstances:

- The *modified bit* is set when a process writes to the page.
- The *referenced bit* is set when a process reads from or writes to the page.

The following additional fields are automatically used by the MMU when translating an incoming logical address:

- If the *valid bit* is set, the MMU replaces the logical page number of the incoming address with the *physical page number* field.
- If the *valid bit* is not set, the MMU generates a page fault.
- If the *copy-on-write bit* is set and a process attempts to modify the page, the MMU generates a page fault, regardless of the state of the *valid bit*.

The Memory Layout after the First Instruction

An exec () causes the first instruction of the executable file to be fetched from memory, which in turn causes the MMU to produce a fault in the first page. The address of the first instruction is stored in the executable's header and tends to be a low memory address. In the diagram shown in Figure 14.40, I assumed that the first instruction was

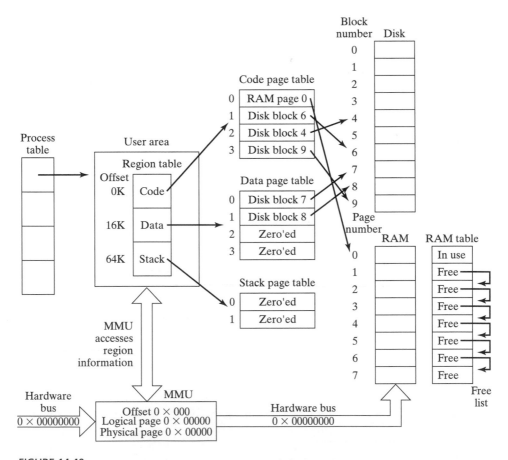

FIGURE 14.40

Memory layout after the first instruction executes.

located at logical address 0 and that page 0 of the code region was paged into physical RAM page 0.

The Memory Layout after Many Instructions

When a process continues to execute after an exec (), it tends to generate faults in more of its code, data, and stack pages. The diagram shown in Figure 14.41 illustrates a situation in which all of the physical pages of RAM have been filled by a single process. This can never happen in a real UNIX system, since the kernel occupies low RAM addresses and several other daemon processes will always occupy portions of high RAM, but it does show how the page tables of a process gradually get filled in with RAM addresses.

The Page Daemon

The diagram in Figure 14.41 illustrates a situation in which all of the physical pages of RAM are filled. If a process produces a fault in another one of its pages, the system

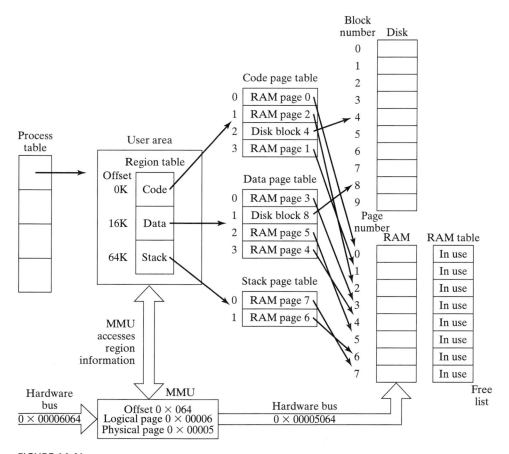

FIGURE 14.41

Memory layout after several instructions.

could save one or more of the RAM pages to disk to make room for the incoming page. In practice, things work out much better if the memory management system always keeps a certain number of RAM pages free for subsequent faults. The minimum number of pages that it tries to keep free is called the *low-water mark*. When the number of free pages drops below this level, the memory management system wakes up a process called the *page daemon* (sometimes called the *page stealer*) to free up some RAM pages. The page daemon uses an algorithm that is described shortly to save pages to a special area of disk called the *swap space* until the number of free pages rises above a *high-water mark*. The page daemon then goes to sleep until it's needed again.

Swap Space

Swap space is a special contiguous area of disk set aside for the efficient transfer of pages to and from RAM. Although it can reside on the root device, swap space is often allocated on a separate disk so that regular file access and paging can occur simultaneously. Swap space is supported by a special kernel data structure called the *swap map* that is used to track the usage of its blocks. The swap map searches for free contiguous chunks of blocks in the swap space and is updated whenever swap space is allocated or deallocated. When two neighboring chunks of swap space become free, the swap map automatically combines them into a single, larger chunk of free space.

The Page Daemon Algorithm

Every page table entry includes three fields called the *modified bit*, the *referenced bit*, and the *age*. Whenever a process accesses a particular page, its referenced bit is set and its age is set to zero. The page daemon uses these two fields in order to free the least recently used pages. The page daemon cycles through every page table in the system, performing the following operation:

- If the referenced bit of a page is set, it resets it and sets the age field to zero; otherwise, it increments the age field.

The age fields of pages that are currently being accessed will hardly increase at all, since they're continually being reset to zero; however, the age fields of pages that are inactive will continue to grow. When the age field reaches a certain system-dependent value, the page daemon attempts to free the page, using the following rules:

- If the page has never been paged out to the swap device, the page is placed on a list of pages to be paged out, and its RAM table entry is marked as "ready to page out."
- If the page has been paged out before and hasn't been modified since, its valid bit is reset and its RAM table entry is immediately marked as "free" and placed on the free-page list.
- If the page has been paged out before and has been modified since, it's placed on the list of pages to be paged out, its RAM table entry is marked as "ready to page out," and its previous swap space area is deallocated.

When the list of pages to page out reaches a certain size, the kernel locates a suitable chunk of swap space by consulting the swap map and then schedules the pages to be written to swap space. When a page is written, its valid bit is reset and its RAM table entry is marked as "free" and placed on the free list.

As a result of this algorithm, the least recently used pages are gradually paged to swap space until the number of free pages rises above the preset high-water mark.

The Memory Layout after Some Page Outs

The diagram shown in Figure 14.42 illustrates the state of the sample process' memory map after code page 1, data page 0, and stack page 1 were paged to swap space.

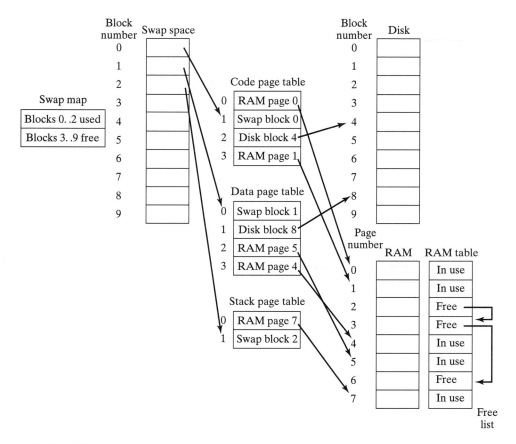

FIGURE 14.42

Memory layout after some page-outs.

Accessing a Page That's Stored in Swap Space

When the MMU attempts to access a page whose valid bit is not set, it generates a page fault. Before requesting that the page be read from disk, the kernel checks to see whether the page is still in RAM, having been freed by the page daemon, but not yet overwritten by another page. It can do this quickly because it maintains a hash table that maps disk block addresses onto RAM page numbers. If the kernel finds that the page is still cached in RAM, it simply updates the page table entry and sets the valid bit. If the page is not found in RAM, one of two cases is possible:

- If the page has never been loaded into RAM, the kernel requests that the page be loaded in from the executable file.
- If the page is stored in swap space, the kernel requests that the page be loaded in from the swap device.

One consequence of this algorithm is that a page is loaded only once from the executable file; from then on, it spends the rest of its lifetime traveling between RAM and swap space. The diagram shown in Figure 14.43 illustrates this behavior.

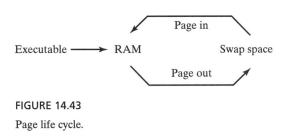

FIGURE 14.43

Page life cycle.

Duplicating a Process: `fork ()`

When a process forks, the child process must be allocated a copy of its parent's code, data, and stack areas. Unfortunately, a process often immediately follows a fork () by an exec (), thereby deallocating its previous memory areas. To avoid any unnecessary and costly copying suggested by these two observations, the kernel processes a fork () in a crafty way:

- It sets the child's code region entry to point to the parent's code page table and increments a reference count associated with the page table to indicate that it's being shared.
- It creates a data page table and a stack page table for the child that are duplicates of the parent's and sets the *copy-on-write* bit for every page table entry of both processes' data and stack tables. If the parent's page table entry points into RAM, the child's page table entry is set to point to the same location, and a reference count associated with the RAM page is incremented to indicate that it's being shared. Similarly, if a parent's page table entry points into swap space, the child's page table entry is set to point to the same location, and a reference count associated with the swap space location is incremented to indicate that it's being shared.

The copy-on-write flag is used by UNIX to process shared RAM and swap pages in a special way, described shortly. Figure 14.44 is an illustration of the parent and child

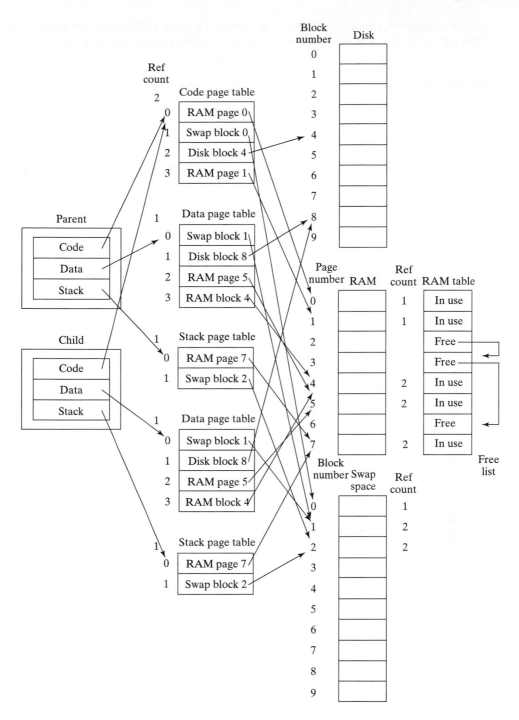

FIGURE 14.44

Layout after fork.

memory maps immediately following a fork (). The small numbers next to the region tables, RAM table, and swap table are reference counts maintained by the kernel.

Processing References to Shared RAM and Swap Pages

UNIX processes shared pages as follows:

- If a process reads a shared RAM page, nothing special happens at all.
- If the page daemon decides to page out a shared RAM page, the page's reference count is decremented and a copy of the page is transferred to swap space. The process whose page was transferred has its page table entry updated to reflect the transfer, but the other processes that share the same page still reference the RAM page. If the RAM page reference count is still nonzero after it's decremented, the RAM page is not added to the free list.
- If a process accesses a shared swap page, it's paged in from swap space, and the process whose page was transferred has its page table entry updated to reflect the page-in. The other processes that share the same swap page still reference the swap space.
- If a process attempts to modify a page whose copy-on-write bit is set, the MMU automatically generates a page fault. The page fault handler checks whether the RAM page's reference count is greater than one; if it is, that means that a process is writing to a shared page. In this situation, the fault handler copies the page into another page of RAM and updates the child's page table entry to point to the new copy. The child's page table entry copy-on-write bit is reset. The fault handler then decrements the original RAM page's reference count and resets its copy-on-write bit if the count dropped to one. If a process attempts to modify a page whose copy-on-write bit is set, and its reference count is equal to one, the fault handler allows the process to use the physical page and resets the copy-on-write flag, but also disassociates the page from its current swap copy. This is because another process related by a fork also may be sharing the same swap copy.

Thrashing and Swapping

If a large number of processes are running at the same time, it's possible that the rate of page faulting causes most of the CPU time to be spent transferring pages to and from swap space. This situation is called *thrashing* and results in poor system performance. When the memory management system detects thrashing, it wakes up the *sched* process, which chooses processes to deactivate and transfer to disk. *sched* selects processes on the basis of their priority and memory usage, marks them as "swapped," and pages all of their RAM pages to swap space. *sched* continues to swap processes to swap space until thrashing stops, at which point it goes back to sleep. Once a predetermined period has elapsed, a swapped process is marked as "ready to run," and its pages are faulted back into RAM in the normal manner.

Terminating a Process: `exit ()`

When a process terminates, the following events occur:

- Its exit code is placed in its process table entry.
- Its file descriptors are closed.
- The reference count of each of its regions is decremented.
- If the reference count of a region drops to zero, the reference counts of all of the process' RAM pages and swap pages (if appropriate) are decremented.
- Any RAM or swap pages that have a zero reference count are deallocated.

The process table entry is deallocated only when the process' parent accepts its termination code via a wait ().

Signals

Signals inform processes of asynchronous events. The data structures that support signals are stored in the process table and the user areas. Every process has three pieces of information associated with signal handling:

- an array of entries called the *signal handler* array in its user area that describes what the process should do when it receives a particular type of signal
- an array of bits in its process table entry called the *pending signal bitmap*, one per type of signal, that records whether a particular type of signal has arrived for processing
- a process group ID, which is used in distributing signals

Figure 14.45 is a diagram of these signal-related kernel data structures. I'll describe the implementation of signals by describing the implementation of the system calls that are related to signals.

`setpgrp ()`

setpgrp () sets the calling process' process group number to its own PID, thereby placing it in its own unique process group. A forked process inherits its parent's process group. setpgrp () works by changing the process group number entry in the systemwide process table. The process group number is used by kill (), as you'll see later.

`signal ()`

signal () sets the way that a process responds to a particular type of signal. There are three options: Ignore the signal, perform the default kernel action, or execute a user-installed signal handler. The entries in the signal handler array are set as follows:

- If the signal is to be ignored, the entry is set to 1.
- If the signal is to cause the default action, the entry is set to 0.
- If the signal is to be processed using a user-installed handler, the entry is set to the address of the handler.

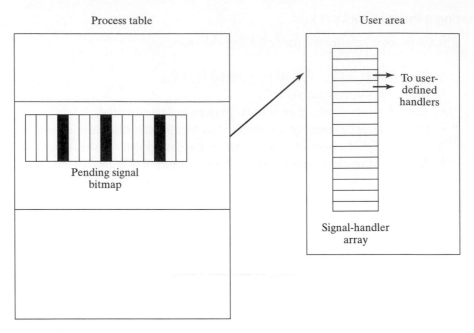

FIGURE 14.45

Signal-related kernel structures.

When a signal is sent to a process, the kernel sets the appropriate bit in the receiving process' signal bitmap. If the receiving process is sleeping at an interruptible priority, it is awakened so that it can process the signal. The kernel checks a process' signal bitmap for pending signals whenever the process returns from kernel mode to user mode (i.e., when it returns from a system call) or when the process enters or leaves a sleep state. Note, therefore, that a signal is hardly ever processed immediately; instead, the receiving process deals with pending signals only when it's scheduled to do so. This makes signals a relatively poor mechanism for real-time applications. Note also that the pending signal bitmap does not keep a *count* of how many of a particular type of signal are pending. This means that if three SIGINT signals arrive in close succession, it's possible that only one of them will be noticed.

Signals After a fork or an exec

A forked process inherits the contents of its parent's signal handler array. When a process executes, the signals that were originally ignored continue to be ignored, and all others are set to their default setting. In other words, all entries equal to 1 are unchanged, and all others are set to 0.

Processing a Signal

When the kernel detects that a process has a pending signal, it either ignores it, performs the default action, or invokes a user-installed handler. To invoke the handler, the kernel appends a new stack frame to the process' stack and modifies the process' program counter to make the receiving process act as if it had called the signal handler from its current program location. When the kernel returns the process to user mode, the process executes the handler and then returns from the function back to the previous program location. The "death of a child" signal (SIGCHLD) is processed slightly differently, as you'll see when I describe the wait () system call.

exit ()

When a process terminates, it leaves its exit code in a field in its process table entry and is marked as a zombie process. The exit code is obtainable by the parent process via the wait () system call. The kernel always informs a parent process that one of its children has died by sending it a "death of child" (SIGCHLD) signal.

wait ()

wait () returns only under one of two conditions: Either the calling process has no children, in which case it returns an error code, or one of the calling process' children has terminated, in which case it returns the child process' PID and exit code. The way that the kernel processes a wait () system call may be split up into a three-step algorithm:

1. If a process calls wait () and doesn't have any children, wait () returns an error code.
2. If a process calls wait () and one or more of its children is already a zombie, the kernel picks a child at random, removes it from the process table, and returns its PID and exit code.
3. If a process calls wait () and none of its children is a zombie, the wait call goes to sleep. It is awakened by the kernel when *any* signals are received, at which point it resumes from step 1.

Although this algorithm would work as it stands, there's one small problem: If a process chose to ignore SIGCHLD signals, all of its children would remain zombies, and that could clog up the process table. To avoid this problem, the kernel treats ignorance of the SIGCHLD signal as a special case. If a SIGCHLD signal is received and the signal is ignored, the kernel immediately removes all the parent's zombie children from the process table and then allows the wait () system call to proceed as normal. When the wait () call resumes, it doesn't find any zombie children, so it goes back to sleep. Eventually, when the last child's death signal is ignored, the wait () system call returns with an error code to signify that the calling process has no child processes.

kill ()

kill () makes use of the real-user ID and process group ID fields in the process table. For example, when this line of code

```
kill (0, SIGINT);
```

is executed, the kernel sets the bit in the pending signal bitmap corresponding to SIGINT in every process table entry whose process group ID matches that of the calling process. UNIX uses this facility to distribute the signals triggered by *Control*-C and *Control*-Z to all of the processes in the control terminal's process group.

INPUT/OUTPUT

In this section, we examine the data structures and algorithms that the UNIX kernel uses to support I/O-related system calls. Specifically, we'll look at the UNIX implementation of these calls in relation to three main categories of files:

- *regular* files
- *directory* files
- *special* files (i.e., peripherals, pipes, and sockets)

I/O Objects

I like to think of files as being special kinds of objects that have I/O capabilities. UNIX I/O objects may be arranged according to the hierarchy shown in Figure 14.46.

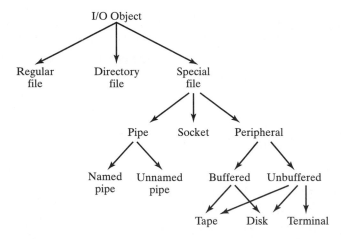

FIGURE 14.46

The I/O object hierarchy.

I/O System Calls

As described in Chapter 13, UNIX I/O system calls may be applied in a uniform way to all I/O objects, with a few exceptions; for example, you can't use lseek () on a pipe or a socket. Here's a list of the system calls that are described in this section:

- sync
- open
- read
- write

- lseek
- close
- dup
- unlink
- ioctl
- mknod/mkdir
- link
- mount
- umount

I/O Buffering

The kernel avoids unnecessary device I/O by buffering most I/O in a fixed-size, systemwide data structure call the *buffer pool*, a collection of buffers that are used for caching file blocks in RAM. When a process reads from a block for the very first time, the block is copied from the file into the buffer pool and then is copied from there into the process' data space. Subsequent reads from the same block are serviced directly from RAM. Similarly, if a process writes to a block that isn't in the buffer pool, the block is copied from the file into the pool and then the buffered copy is modified. If the block is already in the pool, the buffered version is modified without any need for physical I/O. Several hash lists based on the block's device and block number are maintained for the buffers in the pool so that the kernel can quickly locate a buffered block.

When a process accesses a buffer during an I/O system call, the buffer is allocated or locked to prevent other processes from using it. If another process attempts to access an allocated buffer, it is put to sleep by the kernel until the buffer is freed. When UNIX is booted, all buffers in the pool are marked as *free* and placed in the *buffer freelist*.

When the kernel services a process' I/O system call and needs to copy a block from an I/O object into the buffer pool, several steps are required. First, the kernel selects the first buffer in the buffer freelist and marks it as *allocated*. Then it removes the buffer from the buffer freelist and issues an asynchronous read request to the appropriate device driver. Finally, the kernel puts the process to sleep. When the read request has been serviced, the process is awakened and the kernel continues to execute the system call. If the buffer freelist is empty, the process is put to sleep until a free buffer becomes available. If the block is already buffered, the kernel simply allocates the existing buffer. When the system call is finished with the buffer, the buffer is freed and placed on the end of the buffer freelist. This scheme ensures that the least recently used buffer is selected each time a new buffer is required.

It's tempting to think that the kernel copies all of a file's modified buffered blocks back to disk when the file is closed. It doesn't; instead, the kernel sets a "delayed-write" flag in a buffer's header whenever it is modified by a write (). The buffered block is physically written to disk only when another process attempts to remove it from the buffer freelist due to the algorithm described in the previous paragraph. This scheme delays physical I/O until the last possible moment.

Figure 14.47 is an illustration of buffering in action.

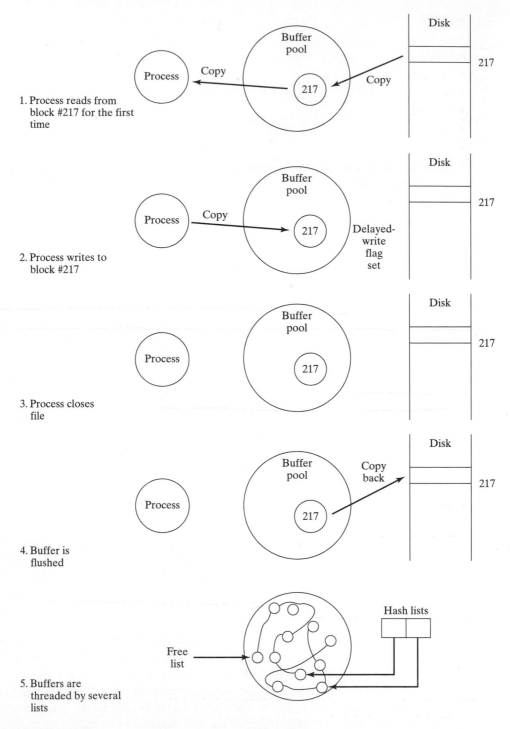

1. Process reads from block #217 for the first time

2. Process writes to block #217

3. Process closes file

4. Buffer is flushed

5. Buffers are threaded by several lists

FIGURE 14.47

Buffering in action.

sync ()

sync () causes the kernel to flush all of the delayed-write buffers to disk. On systems in which the System V daemon **fsflush** is not present, system administrators arrange for the **sync** utility, which invokes sync (), to run regularly. This ensures that the contents of the disk are kept up to date. If **fsflush** runs on the system, it handles the flushing function.

Regular File I/O

open ()

Let's take a look at what happens when a process opens an existing regular file for read-only access. Later, we'll examine the way in which the kernel creates a new file. Suppose that the process is the first one to open the file since the system was last rebooted, and suppose also that it executes the following code:

```
fd = open ("/home/glass/sample.txt", O_RDONLY);
```

The kernel begins by translating the filename into an inode number, using the algorithm described earlier in the chapter. If the inode of the file is not found, an error code is returned. Otherwise, the kernel allocates an entry in a fixed-size, systemwide data structure called the *active inode table* and copies the inode from disk into this entry. The kernel also stores several other values, which are described later, in the entry. The kernel caches active inodes and recently used inodes in the active inode table to avoid unnecessary disk access.

Next, the kernel allocates an entry in another fixed-size, systemwide data structure called the *open file table*. It fills this entry with several useful values, including the following:

- a pointer to the new entry in the active inode table
- the read/write permission flags specified in the open () system call
- the process' current file position, set to 0 by default

Finally, the kernel allocates an entry in the per-process file descriptor array, points this entry to the new entry in the open file table, and returns the index of this file descriptor entry as the return value of open (). Figure 14.48 is an illustration of the process and kernel data structures that result in this example.

If a process opens a nonexistent file and specifies the O_CREAT option, the kernel creates the named file. To do this, it allocates a free inode from the file system's inode list, sets the fields within it to indicate that the file is empty, and then adds a hard link to the appropriate directory file. Recall that a hard link is an entry consisting of a filename and its associated inode number.

Now that you've seen the way in which the kernel handles an open () system call, I'll describe the read (), write (), lseek (), and close () system calls. For simplicity, assume that the sample file is being accessed by just one process; I'll describe the kernel support for multiple users of the same file later in the chapter.

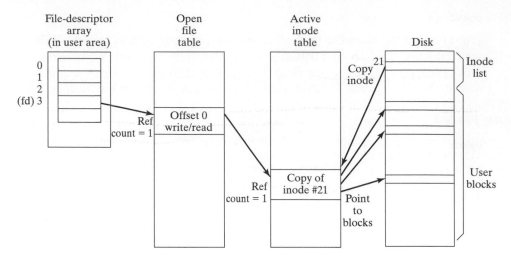

FIGURE 14.48

Kernel file structures.

read ()

Let's see what happens when the sample process executes the following sequence of read () system calls:

```
read (fd, buf1, 100);    /* read 100 bytes into buffer buf1 */
read (fd, buf2, 200);    /* read 200 bytes into buffer buf2 */
read (fd, buf3, 5000);   /* read 5000 bytes into buffer buf3 */
```

Here's the sequence of events that would occur during the execution of these calls:

- The data requested by the first read () resides in the first block of the file. The kernel determines that the block is not in the buffer pool and therefore copies it from disk into a free buffer. It then copies the first hundred bytes from the buffer into **buf1**. Finally, the file position stored in the open file table is updated to its new value of 100.

- The data requested by the second read () also resides in the first block of the file. The kernel finds that the block is already in the buffer pool and therefore copies the next 200 bytes from the buffer into **buf2**. It then updates the file position to 300.

- The data requested by the third read resides partly in the first block of the file and partly in the second block. The kernel transfers the remainder of the first block (3796 bytes) from the buffer pool into **buf3**. It then copies the second block from disk into a free buffer in the pool and copies the remaining data (1204 bytes) from the buffer pool into **buf3**. Finally, it updates the file position to 5300.

Note that a single read may cause more than one block to be copied from disk into the buffer pool. If a process reads from a block that does not have an allocated user block (see Chapter 13 for a discussion of sparse files), then read () doesn't buffer anything, but instead treats the block as if it were filled with ASCII NULL (Ø) characters.

write ()

The sample process now executes the following series of write () system calls:

```
write (fd, buf4, 100);    /* write 100 bytes from buffer buf4 */
write (fd, buf5, 4000);   /* write 4000 bytes from buffer buf5 */
```

Recall that the current value of the file position is 5300, which is situated near the start of the file's second block. Recall also that this block is currently buffered, courtesy of the last read (). Here's the sequence of events that would occur during the execution of our sample process:

- The data to be overwritten by the first write () resides entirely in the second block. This block is already in the buffer pool, so 100 bytes of **buf4** are copied into the appropriate bytes of the buffered second block.
- The data to be overwritten by the second write () reside partly in the second block and partly in the third block. The kernel copies the first 3792 bytes of **buf5** into the remaining 3792 bytes of the buffered second block. Then it copies the third block from the file into a free buffer. Finally, it copies the remaining 208 bytes of **buf5** into the first 208 bytes of the buffered third block.

lseek ()

The implementation of lseek () is trivial: The kernel simply changes the value of the descriptor's associated file position, located in the open file table. Note that no physical I/O is necessary. Figure 14.49 illustrates the result of the following code:

```
lseek (fd, 3000, SEEK_SET);
```

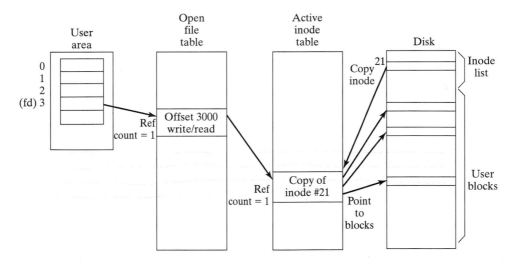

FIGURE 14.49

lseek changes the file offset.

`close ()`

When a file descriptor is closed and it's the only one associated with a particular file, the kernel copies the file's inode back to disk and then marks the corresponding open file table and active inode table entries as *free*. When a process terminates, the kernel automatically closes all of the process' file descriptors.

As I mentioned earlier, the kernel has special mechanisms to support multiple file descriptors associated with the same file. To implement these mechanisms, the kernel keeps a *reference count* field for each open file table entry and each active inode entry. When a file is opened for the first time, both counts are set to one. There are three ways that a file can be shared by several file descriptors:

1. The file is explicitly opened more than once, either by the same process or by different processes.
2. The file descriptor is duplicated by dup (), dup2 (), or fcntl ().
3. A process forks, which causes all of its file descriptor entries to be duplicated.

When a file descriptor is created by the first method, the kernel creates a new open file table entry that points to the same active inode. Then the kernel increments the reference count field in the file's active inode, as shown in Figure 14.50. When a file descriptor is created by either of the latter two methods, the kernel sets the new file descriptor to point to the same open file table entry as the original file descriptor and increments the reference count field in the descriptor's open file table entry, as shown in Figure 14.51.

The algorithm for close () handles the reference count fields as follows: When a file descriptor is closed, the kernel decrements the reference count field in its associated open file table. If the open file table reference count remains greater than zero,

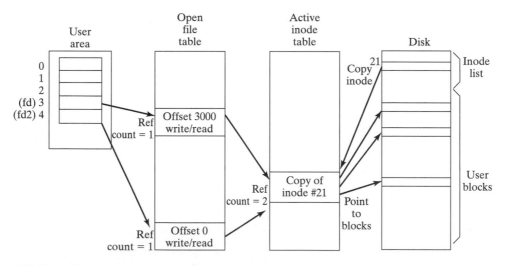

FIGURE 14.50

Open creates a new open file table entry.

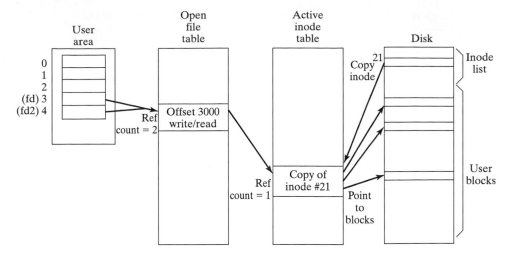

FIGURE 14.51

Duplicating a file descriptor.

nothing else occurs. If the reference count drops to zero, the open file table entry is marked as free and the reference count field in the file's active inode is decremented. If the active inode reference count remains greater than zero, nothing else happens. If the reference count drops to zero, the inode is copied back to disk and the active inode entry is marked as free.

`dup ()`

The implementation of dup () is simple: It copies the specified file descriptor into the next free file descriptor array entry and increments the corresponding open file table reference count.

`unlink ()`

unlink () removes a hard link from a directory and decrements its associated inode's hard link count. If the hard link count drops to zero, the file's inode and user blocks are deallocated when the last process that is using the file exits. Notice that this means that a process may unlink a file and continue to access it until the process exits. The unlink process is shown in Figure 14.52.

Directory File I/O

Directory files are different from regular files in the following ways:

- They may be created only through the use of mknod () or mkdir ().
- They may be read only via getdents ().
- They may be modified only with the use of link ().

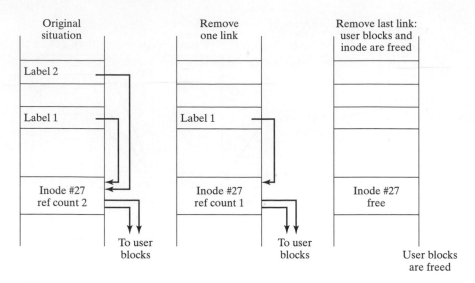

FIGURE 14.52

Unlinking.

These differences ensure the integrity of the directory hierarchy. Directory files may be opened in the same manner as regular files. Let's take a look at the implementation of mknod () and link ().

mknod ()

mknod () creates a directory, a named pipe, or a special file. In every case, the system call starts by allocating a new inode on disk, setting its type field accordingly, and adding it into the directory hierarchy via a hard link. If a directory is being created,[3] a user block is associated with the inode and is filled with the default "." and ".." entries. If a special file is being created, the appropriate major and minor device numbers are stored in the inode (more on this later).

link ()

link () adds a hard link into a directory. Here's an example:

```
link ("/home/glass/file1.c", "/home/glass/file2.c");
```

In this example, the kernel would find the inode number of the source filename "/home/glass/file1.c" and then associate it with the label "file2.c" in the destination directory, "/home/glass." It would then increment the inode's hard link count. Only a superuser may link directories, to prevent unwary users from creating circular directory structures.

---

[3]In many UNIX versions, mkdir () is preferred when one is creating a directory.

Mounting File Systems

The kernel maintains a single fixed-size systemwide data structure called the *mount table* that allows multiple file systems to be accessed via a single directory hierarchy. The mount () and umount () system calls modify this table and are executable only by a superuser.

mount ()

When a file system is mounted using mount (), an entry containing the following fields is added to the mount table:

- the number of the device that contains the newly mounted file system
- a pointer to the root inode of the newly mounted file system
- a pointer to the inode of the mount point
- a pointer to the mount data structure specific to the newly mounted file system

The directory associated with the mount point becomes synonymous with the root node of the newly mounted file system, and its previous contents become inaccessible to processes until the file system is later unmounted. To enable the correct translation of pathnames that cross mount points, the active inode of the mount directory is marked as a *mount point* and is set to point to the associated mount table entry. For example, Figure 14.53 shows the effect of the following system call, which mounts the file system contained on the "/dev/da0" device onto the "/mnt" directory:

```
mount ("/dev/da0", "/mnt", 0);
```

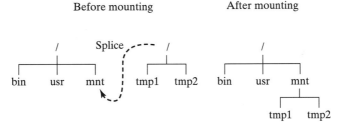

FIGURE 14.53

Direct mounting.

Translation of Filenames

The name translation algorithm uses the contents of the mount table when translating pathnames that cross mount points. This can occur when moving up or down the directory hierarchy. For example, consider the following example:

```
$ cd /mnt/tmp1
$ cd ../../bin
```

The first **cd** command crosses from the root device to the "/dev/da0" device, and the second **cd** command crosses back across to the root device. Here's how the algorithm incorporates mounted file systems into the translation process:

- When an inode that is a mount point is encountered during the translation process, a pointer to the root inode of the mounted file system is returned instead. For example, when the "/mnt" portion of the "/mnt/dir1" is translated, a pointer to the root node of the mounted file system is returned. This pointer is used as the starting point for the rest of the pathname translation.
- When a ".." pathname component is encountered, the kernel checks to see whether a mount point is about to be crossed. If the current inode pointer of the translation process points to a root node and ".." also points to a root node, then a crossing point has been reached. The kernel then replaces the current inode pointer of the translation process with a pointer to the inode of the mount point in the parent file system, which it finds by scanning the mount table for the entry corresponding to the device number of the current inode.

A crossing point is shown in Figure 14.54.

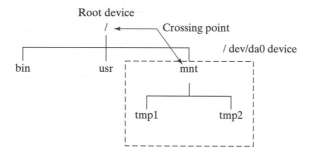

FIGURE 14.54

Crossing point.

`umount ()`

When unmounting a file system, the kernel does several things:

- It checks that there are no open files in the file system that is about to be unmounted. It can do this by scanning the active inode table for entries that contain the file system's device number. If any active inodes are found, the system call fails.
- It flushes the superblock, delayed-write blocks, and buffered inodes back to the file system.
- It removes the mount table entry and removes the "mount point" mark from the mount point directory.

Special File I/O

Most special files correspond to peripherals such as printers, terminals, and disk drives, so for the rest of this section I'll use the terms *special file* and *peripheral* synonymously.

Every peripheral in the system has an associated *device driver*, which is a custom-crafted piece of software that contains all of the peripheral-specific code. For example, a tape drive's device driver contains the code for rewinding and retensioning the tape. A single device driver may control all instances of a particular kind of peripheral; in other words, three tape drives of the same type can share a single device driver. The device drivers for every peripheral in the system must be linked into the kernel when the system administrator configures it. (For more information, see Chapter 15).

Device Interface

A peripheral's device driver supplies the peripheral's *interface*, which can come in the following two flavors:
where block refers to a disk block—pg 673 [handwritten annotation]

- *block oriented*, which means that I/O is buffered and that physical I/O is performed on a block-by-block basis. Disk drives and tape drives have a block-oriented interface.
- *character oriented*, which means that I/O is unbuffered and that physical I/O occurs on a character-by-character basis. A character-oriented interface is sometimes known as a *raw* interface. All peripherals, including disk drives and tape drives, usually have a raw interface.

A peripheral's device driver sometimes contains both kinds of interface. The kind of interface that you choose depends on how you're going to access the device. When performing random access and repeated access to a common set of blocks, it makes good sense to access the peripheral via its block-oriented interface. However, if you're going to access the blocks in a single linear sequence, as you would when making a backup tape, it makes more sense to access the peripheral via its character-oriented interface. This avoids the overhead of the kernel's internal buffering mechanism and sometimes allows the kernel to use the hardware's DMA capabilities.

It's perfectly possible, although not advisable, to access a single device simultaneously via both interfaces. The trouble with this is that the character-oriented interface bypasses the buffering system, possibly leading to confusing I/O results. Here's an example:

- Process A opens a floppy disk, using its block-oriented interface, "/dev/flp." It then writes 1000 bytes to the disk. This output is stored in the buffer pool and marked for delayed writing.
- Process B then opens the same floppy disk, using its character-oriented interface, "/dev/rflp." When it reads 1000 bytes from the disk, the data that were written by process A are ignored, since they're still in the buffer pool.

The solution to this problem is easy: Don't open a device via different interfaces simultaneously!

Major and Minor Numbers

The *major* and *minor* device numbers are used to locate the device driver associated with a particular device. The major device number specifies which device driver that is configured into the kernel will be used to access the device. The minor device number specifies which one of the (possibly many) devices will be used. For example, suppose you have three tape drives in a system and the device driver for a tape drive corresponds to major number 15. If you use the **ls** command to list the block-oriented tape devices, you might see the following output:

```
                              Maj  Min
brw--w--w-  1    root  15,  0 Feb 13 14:27 /dev/mt0
brw--w--w-  1    root  15,  1 Feb 13 14:29 /dev/mt1
brw--w--w-  1    root  15,  2 Feb 13 14:27 /dev/mt2
```

From this, we see that all three tape drives are accessed by the same device driver (signified by the index 15), and each minor number uniquely identifies a specific tape drive. The major and minor numbers are used to index into switch tables to locate the appropriate device driver.

Switch Tables

All UNIX device drivers must follow a predefined format, which includes a set of standard entry points for functions that open, close, and access the peripheral. Block-oriented device drivers also contain an entry point called *strategy* that is used by the kernel for performing block-oriented I/O to the physical device. The entry points of each block-oriented interface and each character-oriented interface are stored in systemwide tables called the *block device switch table* and the *character device switch table*.

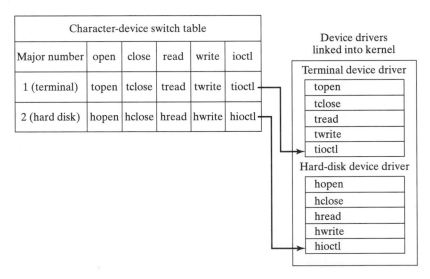

FIGURE 14.55

A small sample switch table.

These tables are stored as arrays of pointers to functions and are created automatically when UNIX is configured. One dimension of the array is indexed by a peripheral's major number, the other by a function code. Figure 14.55 is an illustration of a small sample switch table.

Figure 14.56 illustrates the kernel data structures that might be formed after the following bit of code is executed:

```
fd = open ("/dev/tty2", O_RDWR);
```

lseek (), chmod (), and stat () work the same way for special files as they do for regular files. open (), read (), write (), and close () work in a slightly different way and make use

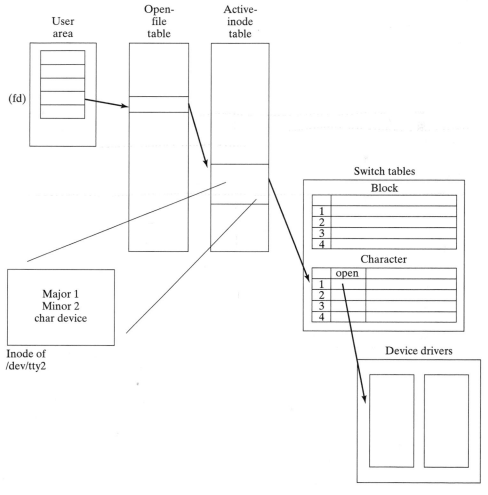

FIGURE 14.56

Special file access.

of the block and character switch tables. In each case, their operation may be split into a peripheral-independent part and a peripheral-dependent part.

open ()

When a process opens a file, the kernel can tell that it's a peripheral by examining the type field of the file's inode. If the field indicates a block-oriented or character-oriented device, it reads the major and minor numbers to determine the class of the device and the instance of the device that is being opened.

When processing open (), the kernel performs peripheral-independent actions followed by peripheral-dependent actions. The peripheral-independent part of open () works just like a regular file open (); The file's inode is cached in the active inode table and an open file table entry is created. The peripheral-dependent part of open () invokes the device driver's open () routine. For example, a tape driver's open () routine usually retensions and rewinds the tape, whereas a terminal driver's open () routine sets the device's baud rate and default terminal settings.

read ()

When reading from a character-oriented device, read () invokes the *read* function in the device driver to perform the physical I/O. When reading from a block-oriented device, read () makes use of the standard I/O buffering mechanism. If a block needs to be physically copied from the device to the buffer pool, the *strategy* function in the device driver is invoked. This function combines both read and write capabilities.

write ()

When writing to a character-oriented device, write () executes the *write* function in the device driver to perform the physical I/O. When writing to a block-oriented device, write () uses the I/O buffering system. When a delayed write eventually takes place, the device's *strategy* function is used to perform the physical I/O.

close ()

The kernel closes a peripheral in the same way that it closes a regular file, except when the process which performs the close () is the last process that was accessing the device. In this special case, the device driver's close () routine is executed, followed by the series of actions for closing a regular file.

The kernel cannot determine that a special file has been closed by its last user simply by examining the active inode's reference count, since a single device may be accessed via more than one inode. Such a situation occurs if one process accesses a device via its block-oriented interface and another accesses the same file via its character-oriented interface. In this case, the active inode list must be searched for other inodes associated with the same physical device.

ioctl ()

ioctl () controls device-specific features via a file descriptor. It simply passes on its arguments to the *ioctl* entry point of the device driver. Examples of device-specific operations include setting a terminal's baud rate, selecting a printer's font, and rewinding a tape drive.

Terminal I/O

Although terminals are a kind of peripheral, terminal device drivers are interesting and different enough that they warrant a separate discussion of their own. The main difference between terminal device drivers and other device drivers is that terminal device drivers must support several different kinds of preprocessing and postprocessing on their input and output, respectively. Each variety of processing is termed a *line discipline*. A terminal's line discipline can be set using ioctl (). Most terminal drivers support the following three common line disciplines:

- *raw mode*, which performs no special processing at all. Characters entered at the keyboard are made available to the reading process based on the ioctl () parameters. Key sequences such as *Control*-C do not generate any kind of special action and are passed as regular ASCII characters. For example, *Control*-C would be read as the character with ASCII value 3. Raw mode is used by applications such as editors, which prefer to do all of their own character processing.
- *cbreak mode*, which processes only some key sequences specially. For example, flow control via *Control*-S and *Control*-Q remains active. Similarly, *Control*-C generates an interrupt signal for every process in the foreground job. As with raw mode, all other characters are available to the reading process, based on the ioctl () parameters.
- *cooked mode* (sometimes known as *canonical mode*), which performs full preprocessing and postprocessing. In this mode, the delete and backspace keys take on their special meanings, together with the less common word-erase and line-erase characters. Input is made available to a reading process only when the *Enter* key is pressed. Similarly, tabs have a special meaning when output, and they are expanded by the line discipline to the correct number of spaces. A newline character is expanded into a carriage return/newline pair.

Terminal Data Structures

The following are the main data structures that the kernel uses to implement line disciplines:

- *clists*, which are linked lists of fixed-size character arrays. The kernel uses these structures to buffer the preprocessed input, the postprocessed input, and the output associated with each terminal.
- *tty structures*, which contain the state of a terminal, including pointers to its clists, the currently selected line discipline, a list of the characters that are to be processed specially, and the options set by ioctl (). There is one tty structure per terminal.

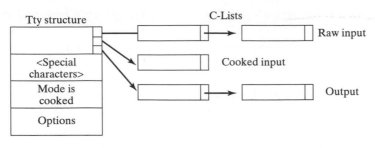

FIGURE 14.57

The tty structure and C-lists.

Figure 14.57 is an illustration of a tty structure and its associated clists.

Reading from a Terminal

When a key is pressed, the keyboard interrupt handler performs the following operations, depending on the mode of the terminal:

- *raw mode*: The character is copied onto the end of the raw clist, and the process waiting on the read is awakened so that it may read from the raw clist. When the process awakens, all characters on the raw clist are moved into the process' address space.

- *cbreak mode*: If the character is a flow control or break character, it is processed specially; otherwise, the character is copied onto the end of the raw clist, and the process waiting on the read is awakened. When the process awakens, all characters on the raw clist are moved into the process' address space.

- *cooked mode*: If the character is a flow control or break character, it is processed specially; otherwise, the character is copied onto the end of the raw clist. If the character is a carriage return, the contents of the raw clist are moved onto the end of the cooked input clist, and the process waiting on the read is awakened. When the process awakens, the special characters, such as backspace and delete, in the cooked input clist are processed, and then the postprocessed contents are copied into the process' address space.

ioctl () allows you to specify conditions that must be satisfied before a reading process is awakened. Among these conditions are the number of characters in the raw clist and an elapsed time since the last read (). If two or more processes try to read from the same terminal, it's up to them to synchronize their operation; otherwise, the input will be shared indiscriminately between the competing processes. Signals generated by special characters in cbreak and cooked modes go to the processes associated with the *control terminal*. (For more information about control terminals, see Chapter 13.)

Writing to a Terminal

When a process writes to a terminal, any special characters it uses are processed according to the currently selected line discipline and are then placed onto the end of the terminal's output clist. The terminal driver invokes hardware interrupts to output the contents of this list to the screen. If the output clist becomes full, the writing process is put to sleep until some of the output drains to the screen.

Streams

When a stream is created with the open () system call, a *stream head* is created. The stream head provides the system call interface to the user application and contains the data structures that represent the stream. It handles subsequent calls to read (), write (), getmsg (), or putmsg () by sending data to, or receiving data from, the first module in the stream.

The stream head, all modules, and the stream driver run in kernel mode. Stream drivers may be inserted into the stream from user mode. This is done by "pushing" the drivers onto the stream. A new module pushed onto a stream goes on top of any existing modules (i.e., it is connected to the stream head). The module list is a LIFO (last in, first out) stack. "Modules are pushed onto streams when …" a driver is installed into the kernel. Like traditional device drivers, modules execute in kernel mode and are linked to the kernel when the kernel is built.

Some newer terminal drivers are implemented with STREAMS rather than the *clist* mechanism just described.

INTERPROCESS COMMUNICATION

The UNIX kernel uses a number of data structures and algorithms to support pipes and sockets.

Pipes

The implementation of pipes differs significantly between System V and BSD, so I'll begin by describing System V pipes.

System V.3 Pipes

There are two kinds of pipes in System V: *named* pipes and *unnamed* pipes. Named pipes are created by pipe (), and unnamed pipes are created by mknod (). Data written to a pipe are stored in the file system, as shown in Figure 14.58. When either kind of pipe is created, the kernel allocates an inode, two open file entries, and two file descriptors.

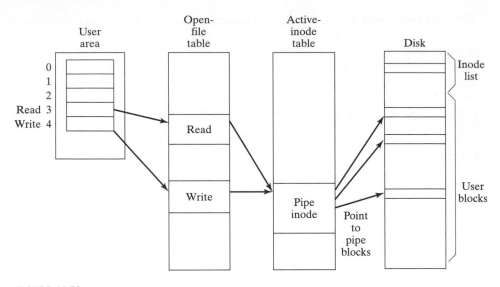

FIGURE 14.58

System V.3 pipes are stored in the file system.

Originally, the inode describes an empty file. If the pipe is named, a hard link is made from the specified directory to the pipe's inode; otherwise, no hard link is created and the pipe remains anonymous.

Pipe Data Structures

The kernel maintains the current write position and current read position of each pipe in its inode, rather than in the open file table entry. This ensures that each byte in the pipe is read by exactly one process. The kernel also keeps track of the number of processes reading from the pipe and writing to the pipe. As you'll soon see, it needs both of these counts to process a close () properly.

Writing to a Pipe

When data are written to a pipe, the kernel allocates disk blocks and increments the current write position as necessary, until the last direct block has been allocated. For reasons of simplicity and efficiency, a pipe is never allocated indirect blocks; this prohibition limits the size of a pipe to about 40K, depending on the file system's block size. If a write to a pipe would overflow its storage capacity, the writing process writes as much as it can to the pipe and then sleeps until some of the data are drained by reader processes. If a writer tries to write past the end of the last direct block, the write position "wraps around" to the beginning of the file, starting at offset 0. Thus, the direct blocks are treated like a circular buffer. Although it might seem that using the file system for implementing pipes would be slow, remember that disk blocks are buffered in the buffer pool, so most pipe I/O is buffered in RAM.

Reading from a Pipe

As data are read from a pipe, the current read position is updated accordingly. The kernel ensures that the read position never overtakes the write position. If a process attempts to read from an empty pipe, it is put to sleep until output becomes available.

Closing a Pipe

When a pipe's file descriptor is closed, the kernel does the following special processing:

- It updates the count of the pipe's reader and writer processes.
- If the writer count drops to zero and there are processes trying to read from the pipe, they return from read () with an error condition.
- If the reader count drops to zero and there are processes trying to write to the pipe, they are sent a signal.
- If the reader and writer counts drop to zero, all of the pipe's blocks are deallocated and the inode's current write and read positions are reset. If the pipe is unnamed, the inode is also deallocated.

System V.4 Pipes

Beginning with System V, Release 4, pipes in UNIX have been implemented using STREAMS.

BSD Pipes

BSD pipes are implemented in terms of sockets. The write and read file descriptors are each connected to an anonymous socket's endpoint within the UNIX system domain.

Sockets

A complete description of the implementation of sockets would be rather lengthy, requiring an explanation of the workings of Internet addressing, routing, and communication. For this reason, I present only a brief overview of the socket system in terms of its memory management and interface to Internet protocols. For a more in-depth discussion of sockets, see Chapter 13 in this book and see also Stevens, (1998).

Memory Management

Data transferred between socket endpoints are buffered by means of a dynamic memory allocation system that uses fixed-size data packets called *mbufs*. Each *mbuf* is 128 bytes long, broken down as follows:

- a 112-byte buffer
- a field that records the size of the data in the buffer
- a field that records the offset of the data in the buffer

Routines that read buffers can strip off protocol headers simply by adjusting the data size and offset fields, rather than having to shift the valid data in memory. The *mbuf* memory manager is relatively efficient, and several other kernel routines use it for non-socket-related purposes.

Sockets and the Open File Table

When a socket is created with the use of socket (), the system in turn creates a socket structure that records all of the information pertaining to the socket, including the following fields:

- the socket domain
- the socket protocol
- a pointer to the socket's *mbuf* lists

In order to tie the file descriptor system to the socket system, the kernel keeps a pointer from the socket's open file table entry to its associated socket structure. This structure is accessed when socket I/O is performed. Figure 14.59 shows a diagram of this arrangement.

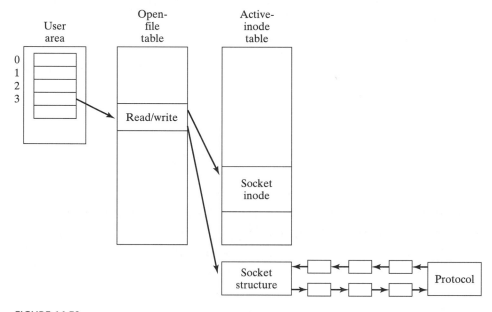

FIGURE 14.59

Berkeley sockets.

Writing to a Socket

Data written to a socket via write () are placed onto the output *mbuf* list for transmission by the protocol module.

Reading from a Socket

Data that arrive at the protocol module are placed onto the input mbuf list for consumption by the process. When the process performs a read (), the data are transferred from the input *mbuf* list into the process' address space.

CHAPTER REVIEW

Checklist

In this chapter, I described

- the layering of kernel subsystems
- the difference between user mode and kernel mode.
- the implementation of system calls and interrupt handlers
- the physical and logical layouts of the file system
- inodes
- the algorithm that the kernel uses for translating pathnames into inode numbers
- the process hierarchy
- the six process states
- how the scheduler decides to allocate the CPU
- memory management and the MMU
- the I/O subsystem, including buffering
- interprocess communication via pipes and sockets

Quiz

1. Why does the kernel maintain multiple priority queues?
2. Why do system calls make use of kernel mode?
3. What happens when an interrupt interrupts another interrupt?
4. How do modern disk designs attempt to increase total storage capacity?
5. Where is the name of a file stored?
6. What information does the superblock contain?
7. How does UNIX avoid using bad blocks?
8. Why is inode 2 special?
9. What is the meaning of the term *magic number?*
10. What is the meaning of the term *context switch?*
11. What information is stored in a process's user area?
12. If a signal is sent to a process that is suspended, where is the signal stored?
13. Describe an overview of the memory mapping that the MMU performs.
14. What does the page daemon do?
15. How does UNIX copy a parent's data to its child?

16. What is the meaning of the term "delayed write"?

17. What is the purpose of the open file table?

18. What is the use of the I/O switch tables?

19. Why does the UNIX terminal driver use clists?

20. What is the main implementation difference between BSD and System V pipes?

Exercises

14.1 Using **ps**, find the process on the system with the lowest process ID (PID). What is the process and why does it have this PID? [level: *easy*]

14.2 The superblock contains a lot of important information. Suggest some ways to minimize disruption to the file system in the case the superblock gets corrupted. [level: *medium*]

14.3 When very small files are created, some disk space is lost due to the minimum allocation unit size. This wasted space is called internal fragmentation. Suggest some ways to minimize internal fragmentation. [level: *medium*]

14.4 Delayed writing normally causes a modified buffer to be flushed when its RAM is needed, not when its file is closed. An alternative method is to flush modified buffers when disk traffic is low, thereby making the best use of the idle time. Critique this strategy. [level: *medium*]

14.5 A low-priority interrupt may be lost if it occurs during the servicing of a higher priority interrupt. How do you think the system's software deals with lost interrupts? [level: *hard*]

Projects

1. Investigate some other operating systems, such as Mach, Plan 9, and Windows NT. How do they compare with UNIX? [level: *medium*]

2. If you know object-oriented techniques, design a basic object-oriented kernel that provides system services by a collection of system objects. How does the design of your kernel differ from that of the UNIX kernel? [level: *hard*]

# CHAPTER 15

System Administration

MOTIVATION

Several administrative duties must be performed on a UNIX system to keep it running smoothly. Without carrying these duties, files may be irrecoverably lost, utilities may become out of date, and the system may run slower than its potential speed. Many UNIX installations are large enough that they warrant a full-time system administrator. Smaller UNIX installations, such as my home system, do not. Regardless of whether you're destined to perform administrative duties, this chapter contains valuable information on how to oversee a UNIX installation.

PREREQUISITES

In order to understand this chapter, you should have read Chapters 1 and 2. It also helps if you've read Chapters 4 and 9.

OBJECTIVES

In this chapter, I describe the main tasks that a system administrator must perform in order to keep a UNIX system running smoothly.

PRESENTATION

The information presented is in the form of several small, self-contained subsections.

UTILITIES

The following utilities, listed in alphabetical order, are examined:

ac	getty	newfs
accton	halt	pac

See pg 669 for a listing of all system calls

config	ifconfig	reboot
cron	last	route
df	mkfs	shutdown
du	mknod	su
fsck	netstat	

INTRODUCTION

The tasks that a system administrator must perform in order to keep a UNIX system running properly, include the following:

- starting and stopping the system
- maintaining and backing up the file system
- maintaining user accounts
- installing operating system and application software
- installing and configuring peripherals
- managing the interface to the network
- automating repetitive tasks
- performing system accounting
- configuring the kernel
- checking system security

Almost all of these tasks require the administrator to be in superuser mode, as they access and modify privileged information. If you don't have access to the superuser password, you'll just have to use your imagination. Even in this case, however, being aware of these functions increases your overall understanding of how UNIX works.

To cover each of these topics in depth would require an entire book, so this chapter simply presents an overview of system administration. (For more detailed information, see Nemeth (2000).

BECOMING A SUPERUSER

The *superuser* has a special user ID (0) with permission to do practically anything on a UNIX system. Because of this, you can see how important it is that not "just anyone" have this access—especially anyone with any malicious intentions. Most administration tasks require that you have superuser powers, and there are two ways to get them:

- Log in as "root," the username of the superuser.
- Use the **su** utility, described in Chapter 3, to create a child shell owned by "root."

Although the first method is direct, there are some dangers associated with it. If you log in as "root," every single command that you execute—even the ones with errors in them—will have superuser privileges. Imagine typing "rm -r*.bak" instead of "rm -r*.bak" while in the "/" directory! Because of this problem, I strongly recommend that you always use the second method. Log into UNIX as a regular user, and become a superuser only when you need to.

Another advantage of the second method is that the **su** command logs who uses it and when. In an environment with more than one system administrator, it is sometimes hard to make sure that the superuser password is given only to those who really need it. Having a log to examine helps you see who is using root privileges.

STARTING UNIX

Depending on the origin of your version of UNIX, there are two ways a UNIX system can run. Berkeley UNIX-based systems usually run in one of two modes:

- *Single-user mode*, which means that a single user may log in from the system console and execute commands from a shell. In this mode, the system runs very few system daemons and is generally used for system maintenance, backups, and kernel reconfiguration only.
- *Multiuser mode*, which means that many users may log in from different terminals. This mode has active system daemons and is the default operational mode for most systems.

System V-based versions of UNIX run at various *run levels*. Run levels describe what runs on the system (much like single-user and multiuser modes in BSD), but provide more granularity in options. Typically, systems have eight run levels: 0–6 and "s" for single-user mode. Each run level can have it's own specific boot scripts and can be configured to suit your local needs. For example, you might configure run level 3 to be everything your system normally runs in operational mode, except your company's product database application. This would permit you to do database maintenance on the database while allowing the rest of the system to be used by the employees.

Some machines allow you to choose the mode by toggling a front panel switch; other machines enter multiuser mode by default, unless the boot sequence is interrupted by *Control*-C. The only way to tell what your own system does is to read the manual.

When you turn on the computer, the following sequence of events occurs:

1. The hardware performs diagnostic self-tests.
2. The UNIX kernel is loaded from the root device.
3. The kernel starts running and initializes itself.
4. The kernel starts *init*, the first user-mode process.

init starts by checking the consistency of the file system, using **fsck**, which is described later in the chapter. If single-user mode was chosen, *init* creates a Bourne shell associated with the system console. If multiuser mode was chosen, *init* performs the following actions:

- It executes the system's *boot scripts*, which perform initialization tasks such as starting the mail daemon and clearing the "/tmp" directory.

- It creates a "getty" process for every terminal in the "/etc/ttytab" file. "/etc/ttytab" contains one line of information for every terminal on the system, including its baud rate and pathname.

The names of the boot scripts vary with different versions of UNIX. BSD-based systems typically run "/etc/rc" to start the standard UNIX daemons and "/etc/rc.local" to start locally maintained services. System V divides the boot files into a more complex set of files, grouping them by subsystem (such as networking, disk, etc.). These files are stored in the "/etc/rc.d" directory. A "getty" process listens for activity on its associated terminal and replaces itself with a "login" process if it detects that someone's trying to log in. The "login" program prompts for a username and a password, checks them against the entries in the "/etc/passwd" file, and replaces itself with the user's start-up program if the password is correct. The start-up program is usually a shell.

rc.a scripts are executed before rc.b scripts, etc.

When a user logs out, *init* receives a SIGCHLD signal from the dying shell. When this happens, *init* removes the user from the "/etc/utmp" file (which contains a list of all the current users) and then appends an entry to the "/var/adm/wtmp" file (which contains a list of all the recent log-ins and log-outs). Finally, *init* creates a new "getty" process for the freed terminal.

init's behavior may be modified by sending it one of the following signals:

- SIGHUP causes *init* to rescan the "/etc/ttytab" file and create "getty" processes for all the terminals in the file that need them. It also kills "getty" processes that don't have an associated terminal. SIGHUP thus allows you to add and remove terminals without rebooting the system.
- SIGTERM causes *init* to take UNIX to single-user mode.
- SIGTSTP tells *init* not to create a new "getty" process when a user logs out. This allows the system to gradually phase out terminals.

init is vital to the functioning of UNIX, as it's responsible for creating and maintaining log-in shells. If *init* dies for any reason, the system reboots automatically.

STOPPING THE SYSTEM

A modern computer fares well if it runs all the time; turning it on and off causes problems. However, there are some circumstances in which it's a good idea to turn the computer off. For example, if a storm is coming, you should disconnect your computer from its power source to avoid high-voltage surges. UNIX should not be shut down directly; instead, you should use one of the **shutdown**, **halt**, or **reboot** utilities.

shutdown, described in Figure 15.1, can be used to either halt UNIX, place it into single-user mode, or place it into multi-user mode. It emits warning messages prior to the shutdown so that users may log out before the system changes state. **halt**, described in Figure 15.2, causes an immediate system shutdown with no warning messages. **reboot**, described in Figure 15.3, may be used to force the system to reboot.

Utility: **shutdown** -hkrn *time* [*message*]

shutdown shuts down the system in a graceful way. The shutdown time may be specified in one of three ways:

- *now*: the system is shut down immediately.
- *+minutes*: the system is shut down in the specified numbers of minutes.
- *hours:minutes*: the system is shut down at the specified time (24-hour format).

The specified warning message (or a default one if none is specified) is displayed periodically as the time of shutdown approaches. Logins are disabled five minutes prior to shutdown.

When the shutdown time arrives, **shutdown** executes **sync** and then sends *init* a SIGTERM signal; this causes *init* to take UNIX to single-user mode. The **-h** option causes **shutdown** to execute **halt** instead of sending the signal. The **-r** option causes **shutdown** to execute **reboot** instead of sending the signal. The **-n** option prevents **shutdown** from performing its default sync. The **-k** option is funny: It causes **shutdown** to behave as if were going to shut down the system, but when the shutdown time arrives, it does nothing. (The "k" stands for "just kidding"!)

FIGURE 15.1

Description of the **shutdown** command.

Utility: **halt**

halt performs a sync and then halts the CPU. It appends a record of the shutdown to the "/var/adm/wtmp" log file.

FIGURE 15.2

Description of the **halt** command.

Utility: **reboot** -q

reboot terminates all user processes, performs a sync, loads the UNIX kernel from disk, initializes the system, and then takes UNIX to multiuser mode. A record of the reboot is appended to the "/var/adm/wtmp" log file. To perform a quick reboot, use the **-q** option. This option instructs reboot not to bother to kill the current processes before rebooting.

FIGURE 15.3

Description of the **reboot** command.

MAINTAINING THE FILE SYSTEM

This section describes the file system–related administrative tasks:

- ensuring the integrity of the file system
- checking disk usage
- assigning quotas
- creating new file systems

File System Integrity

One of the first things that *init* does is to run a utility called **fsck** to check the integrity of the file system. **fsck** works as shown in Figure 15.4. Fortunately, **fsck** is very good at correcting errors. This means that you'll probably never have the joy of patching disk errors by hand, as was done in "the good old days."

Utility: **fsck** -p [*fileSystem*]*

fsck (file system check) scans the specified file systems and checks them for consistency. The kinds of consistency errors that can exist include the following:

- A block is marked as free in the bitmap, but is also referenced from an inode.
- A block is marked as used in the bitmap, but is never referenced from an inode.
- More than one inode refers to the same block.
- A block number is invalid.
- An inode's link count is incorrect.
- A used inode is not referenced from any directory.

For information about inodes, see Chapter 14.

　　If the **-p** option is used, **fsck** automatically corrects any errors that it finds. Without the **-p** option, it prompts the user for confirmation of any corrections that it suggests. If **fsck** finds a block that is used, but is not associated with a named file, it connects the block to a file whose name is equal to the block's inode number in the "/lost+found" directory.

　　If no file systems are specified, **fsck** checks the standard file systems listed in "/etc/fstab."

[Handwritten margin note: There are likely to be hundreds of prompts if you don't use the -p option!]

FIGURE 15.4

Description of the **fsck** command.

Disk Usage

As I just mentioned, disk errors are uncommon and are generally corrected automatically. Disk usage problems, on the other hand, are common. Many users treat the file system as if it's infinitely large and create huge numbers of files without much thought. When I taught UNIX at UT Dallas, the disks would invariably fill up on the last day of the semester, just as all of the students were trying to complete their projects. Students would try to save their work from **vi**, and **vi** would respond with a "disk full" message. When the students quit **vi**, they would find that their file had been deleted.

To avoid running out of disk space, it's wise to run a shell script from **cron** that periodically runs the **df** utility to check the available disk space. **df** works as shown in Figure 15.5. Here's an example of **df** in action:

```
$ df                    ...list information about all file systems.
Filesystem     kbytes     used     avail capacity  Mounted on
/dev/sd3a       16415    10767      4006    73%     /
/dev/sd3g      201631   125513     55954    69%     /usr
/dev/sd3d       60015    34773     19240    64%     /export
$ _
```

Utility: **df** [-k] [-P] [*fileSystem*]*

df displays a table of used and available disk space on the specified mounted file systems. If no file system is specified, all mounted file systems are described.

The output format of **df** differs slightly from one version of UNIX to another. Traditional System V-based versions of **df** display the count of 512-byte blocks, whereas BSD-based and later versions of **df** usually show block counts in terms of 1024-byte (1K) blocks. (The 1K block size makes it easier to compute megabytes: Just divide by 1000.) The layout of the information varies between the versions as well, but nearly all versions have arguments that allow you to select the format and information you want. Use the **–k** option to report block counts in 1024-byte size. Use the **–P** argument to display the output in "POSIX" format (closer to the BSD format). On some systems, when **–k** is used, **-P** is assumed.

FIGURE 15.5

Description of the **df** command.

That same **df** command would produce a different output on a System V-based UNIX system:

```
$ df
/               (/dev/sd3a    ):    21534 blocks     14922 files
/usr            (/dev/sd3g    ):   251026 blocks    108277 files
/export         (/dev/sd3d    ):    69546 blocks     20844 files
$ _
```

Note the absence of headers in the second format. This can be helpful when you are piping the output into another command. (Otherwise you have to remove the header if you intend to treat every line as file system information.) Note also that the number of blocks used is different between the two versions because the block size being counted is different. On this second system, using **df –Pk** would produce output similar to that generated in the first example.

You can also get information about a specific file system by specifying its name or mount point explicitly, as in the following commands:

```
$ df /dev/sd3a          ...list a specific file system.
Filesystem    kbytes    used    avail capacity  Mounted on
/dev/sd3a     16415    10767    4006    73%      /
$ df /                  ...mount point also works.
Filesystem    kbytes    used    avail capacity  Mounted on
/dev/sd3a     16415    10767    4006    73%      /
$ _
```

You can find out how much disk space is left on the device on which your home directory resides just as easily:

```
$ df .
Filesystem    kbytes     used    avail capacity  Mounted on
/dev/sd3d     4194304   4194304     0    100%     /home
$ _
```

If **df** reports that a disk is greater than 95% full, your script could detect this and send you some warning mail. Even better, your script could then run the **du** utility to determine which users are taking up the most disk space and automatically send those users mail suggesting that they remove some files. **du** works as shown in Figure 15.6. In the

---

Utility: **du** [-s] [-k] [*fileName*]*

du displays the number of kilobytes (BSD) or 512-byte blocks (System V) that are allocated to each of the specified filenames. If a filename refers to a directory, its files are described recursively. When used with the **-s** option, **du** displays only the grand total for each file. When used with the **–k** option, space is always reported in kilobytes. If no filenames are specified, the current directory is scanned.

FIGURE 15.6

Description of the **du** command.

following example, I used **du** to find out how many kilobytes my current directory and all its files were using up, after which I obtained a file-by-file breakdown of the disk usage:

```
$ du -s .       ...obtain grand total of current directory.
9291  .
$ du .                    ...obtain file-by-file listing.
91    ./proj/fall.89
158   ./proj/summer.89/proj4
159   ./proj/summer.89
181   ./proj/spring.90/proj2
21    ./proj/spring.90/proj1
204   ./proj/spring.90
```

```
455   ./proj
...                          ...other files were listed here.
38    ./sys5
859   ./sys6
9291  .
$ _
```

Assigning Quotas

Some systems allow a system administrator to set disk quotas for individual users. You may specify the maximum number of files and the maximum number of blocks that a particular user is allowed to create. It's fairly complicated to add quotas, and doing so may involve reconfiguring the kernel, updating the "/etc/rc" file, modifying the "/etc/fstab" file, and creating a quota control file. Quotas are implemented differently in different versions of UNIX, so I suggest you consult your system's documentation to find out more.

Creating New File Systems

If you buy a new disk drive, you must perform the following tasks before your file system can use it:

1. Format the medium.
2. Create a new file system on the medium.
3. Mount the disk into the root hierarchy.

The manufacturer of the device may supply you with a formatting utility. If it does, use the utility to perform step 1. If your version of UNIX has a **format** command, that may also work. The particular means is system specific, so again, you should consult your system documentation about formatting the medium.

Next, create a file system on the medium, using **mkfs** or **newfs**. Figure 15.7 provides a description of **mkfs**. Because it's unlikely that you'll know the correct value of *sectorCount* without looking it up in the manufacturer's handbook, the **newfs** utility (available on most, but not all, versions of UNIX) was designed as a user-friendly front end to **mkfs**. **newfs** is described in Figure 15.8. Note that **newfs** can work only if geometric information about the medium is listed in the "/etc/disktab" file. Once the file system is created, it may be connected to the root file system by using the **mount** utility described in Chapter 3.

Utility: **mkfs** *specialFile* [*sectorCount*]

mkfs creates a new file system on the specified special file. A new file system consists of a superblock, an inode list, a root directory, and a "lost+found" directory. The file system is built to be *sectorCount* sectors in size. Only a superuser can use this command.

FIGURE 15.7

Description of the **mkfs** command.

Utility: **newfs** *specialFile deviceType*

newfs invokes **mkfs** after looking up the *deviceType's* sector count from the "/etc/disktab" file, which contains information about standard device characteristics.

FIGURE 15.8

Description of the **newfs** command.

Backing Up File Systems

Making a backup copy of file system information is the most important, and most frequently overlooked, task a system administrator should do. It's frustrating to spend time doing it, since you believe you'll never need the backup medium. But just like buying insurance on your car, you should do it because if you ever do need it, it will be a big problem if you don't have it. The procedure and utilities for backing up the file system are described in Chapter 3.

MAINTAINING USER ACCOUNTS

One of a system administrator's most common tasks is to add a new user to the system. To do this, you must do the following:

- Add a new entry to the password file.
- Add a new entry to the group file.
- Create a home directory for the user.
- Provide the user with some appropriate start-up files.

The Password File

Every user of the system has an entry in the password file (usually "/etc/passwd"), in the format

```
                    encrypted
username:password:userId:groupId:personal:homedir:startup
                              description
                              of user
```

where each field has the meaning shown in Figure 15.9.

Since the password field is an encrypted value, putting any single character in that field is equivalent to disallowing logins on the account in question. Since there is no string you could type that would encrypt, for example, an asterisk into the text, nothing that could be typed will match anything in such a password field after encryption. Here's a snippet from a real-life password file:

```
$ head -5 /etc/passwd        ...look at first five lines.
root:rcfsmtio:0:0:Operator:/:/bin/csh
daemon:*:1:1::/:
sync:*:1:1::/:/bin/sync
```

leave it empty when creating new; see pg 640

```
sys:*:2:2::/:/bin/csh
bin:*:3:3::/bin:
$ _
```

I used **grep** to find my own entry:

```
$ grep glass /etc/passwd              ...find my line.
glass:dorbnla:496:62:Graham Glass:/home/glass:/bin/ksh
$ _
```

Field	Meaning
username	the user's login name
password	the encrypted version of the user's password
userId	the unique integer allocated to the user
groupId	the unique integer corresponding to the user's group
personal	the description of the user that is displayed by the **finger** utility
homedir	the home directory of the user
startup	the program that is run for the user at login

FIGURE 15.9

Fields in the UNIX password file.

The Group File

To add a new user, you must decide which group the user is in and then search the group file to find the user's associated group ID. As an example, I'll show you how to add a new user called Simon into the "cs4395" group.

Every group in the system has an entry in the group file (usually "/etc/group") in the format

```
groupname:groupPassword:groupId:users
```

where each field is as defined in Figure 15.10. Here's a snippet from a real-life "/etc/group" file:

```
$ head -5 /etc/group       ...look at start of group file.
cs4395:*:91:glass
cs5381:*:92:glass
wheel:*:0:posey,aicklen,shrid,dth,moore,lippke,rsd,garner
daemon:*:1:daemon
sys:*:3:
$ _
```

Field	Meaning
groupname	the name of the group
groupPassword	the encrypted password for the group [not used, and often filled with an asterisk (*)]
groupId	the unique integer corresponding to the group.
users	a list of the users in the group, separated by commas

FIGURE 15.10

Fields in the UNIX group file.

How to create a new User account

As you can see, the "cs4395" group has an associated group ID number of 91. To add Simon as a new user, I allocated the unique user ID number 10 and a group ID of 91 to him and left his password field empty. Here's what his entry looked like:

```
simon::101:91:Simon Pritchard:/home/simon:/bin/ksh
```

Once the entry was added to the password file, I added Simon onto the end of the "cs4395" list in the "/etc/group" file, created his home directory, and gave him some default start-up files, such as ".kshrc" and ".profile". I copied these files from a directory called "/usr/template" that I made to keep the default versions of user start-up files. The relevant commands are as follows:

```
$ mkdir /home/simon                ...create home directory.
$ cp /usr/template/.* /home/simon  ...copy startup files.
$ chown simon /home/simon /home/simon/.*  ... set owner.
$ chgrp cs4395 /home/simon /home/simon/.*   ...set group.
$ _
```

Finally, I logged in as Simon and used **passwd** to change his password to a sensible default value.

To delete a user, simply reverse these actions: delete the user's password entry, group file entry, and home directory.

INSTALLING SOFTWARE

Installing new software or updates to existing software is an important task of a system administrator. However, the details can vary greatly from site to site. If you maintain a large site with many Network File System (NFS) servers, you might install an application on a server so that workstations can access it from a central location. A smaller site or a more expensive piece of software might be installed only on the machines where it is needed.

The longtime tradition in UNIX environments was to install local software in the "/usr/local" directory. That made it obvious that the software did not come with the UNIX distribution. Over time, vendors have modified the name of the "standard" directory they use for application software (e.g., Sun uses "/opt" for optional software, and AIX uses "/usr/lpp" for licensed program products). You may use one or more of these locations, but it is important to maintain some logic to the structure so that you (and others) can find what you're looking for.

Philosophically, there are two ways to install software. One is to create a directory for the software and put *everything* it needs (except, perhaps, system files) under that directory. For example, if I create an application called **pianoman**, I might write installation tools for it which assume that it will be installed in "/opt/pianoman." If the user chooses to install it in "/usr/local/pianoman" instead, he or she should be able to do so. The other philosophy is to put only software in such a central directory and to put any configuration, header, or library files needed in a more centralized location for those types of files. The example here might be that the software required to build the application may live in "/usr/local/pianoman", but when it is installed on the system, the executable file is copied to "/usr/local/bin/pianoman" and the library it uses is copied to "/usr/local/lib/pianolib.a." This method has advantages and disadvantages. The major advantage is that the user community does not have to add another directory to its $PATH definition, since the binary is in a "known" location ("/usr/local/bin") that is already in the path. The major disadvantage is that you have files spread out in many other places besides "/usr/local/pianoman."

How you choose to install software may depend on the default method the developer of the software has chosen. Any good installation tool (script or program) should allow you to change its default location. While it is easier to go with the defaults if they fit into your environment in a reasonable fashion, you are free to configure them to better match your local environment. Any software that hard-codes the installation location is poorly designed.

The **tar** and **cpio** commands are two of the most popular methods of creating an installation image for a UNIX system. The advantage here is that these commands already exist on most versions of UNIX. A shell script that uses **tar** and other standard UNIX commands to install software can be run on most types of UNIX systems without requiring other software. Some UNIX vendors provide their own improved software installation tools (e.g., HP-UX has **swinstall** and AIX has **installp**). While these tools are generally better than generic UNIX commands, their disadvantage is that you lock yourself into one architecture if you use them. Of course, you can write installation instructions for each tool, but that is more work than writing only one installation method for all UNIX platforms your application supports. The best choice of installation method depends greatly on the target customers, their platforms, and their comfort level with UNIX tools.

As the UNIX system administrator, you will encounter just about all possibilities and will need to know how best to integrate the applications into your local environment.

PERIPHERAL DEVICES

Let's assume that you've just bought a new device and you wish to connect it to your system. How do you install it? In addition, if it's a terminal, which terminal-specific files must be updated? This section presents an overview of device installation and a list of the terminal-related files.

Installing a Device

For a system to be able to "talk to" a new device, the hardware must be connected and the software must be installed or activated. Some systems require that new device drivers be loaded into the kernel and the kernel be rebuilt. Others may use dynamically loadable device drivers where sin the driver will be loaded into the kernel when the device is accessed. The basic steps of device installation are as follows:

1. Install the device driver if it isn't currently in the kernel and if loadable device drivers are not used.
2. Determine the device's major and minor numbers.
3. Use **mknod** to associate a filename in "/dev" with the new device.

Once the device driver is installed and the major and minor numbers are known, you must use **mknod**, described in Figure 15.11, to create the special file. In the following example, I installed the 13th instance of a terminal whose major number was 1:

```
                name          type maj min
$ mknod /dev/tty12 c 1 12  ...note the 13th instance is index 12.
$ _
```

The "c" indicated that the terminal was a character-oriented device. In the next example, I installed the first instance of a disk drive whose major number was 2:

```
               name  type Maj minor
$ mknod /dev/dk1 b 2 0      ...note the 1st instance is index 0.
$ _
```

see pg 618

The "b" indicated that the terminal was a block-oriented device.

Major and minor numbers are the fourth and fifth fields, respectively, in an "ls -l" listing. In the following example, I obtained a long listing of the "/dev" directory:

```
$ ls -l /dev    ...get a long listing of the device directory.
crw--w--w-  1       root  1,  0 Feb 13 14:21 /dev/tty0
```

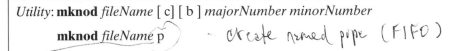

Utility: **mknod** *fileName* [c] [b] *majorNumber minorNumber*

> **mknod** *fileName* p   - create named pipe (FIFO)

mknod creates the special file *fileName* in the file system. The first form of **mknod** allows a superuser to create either a character- or block-oriented special file with the specified major and minor numbers. The major number identifies the class of the device, and the minor number identifies the instance of the device. The second form of **mknod** creates a named pipe and may be used by anyone.

FIGURE 15.11

Description of the **mknod** command.

```
crw--w--w-  1       root  1,  1 Feb 13 14:27 /dev/tty1
brw--w--w-  1       root  2,  0 Feb 13 14:29 /dev/dk0
crw--w--w-  1       root  3,  0 Feb 13 14:27 /dev/rmt0
...
$ _
```

Terminal Files

Several files contain terminal-specific information. Figure 15.12 lists these files and gives a brief description of their function:

Name	Description
/etc/termcap or /etc/terminfo	An encoded list of every standard terminal's capabilities and control codes. The UNIX editors use the value of the environment variable $TERM to index into this file and fetch your terminal's characteristics.
/etc/ttys	A list of every terminal on the system, together with the program that should be associated with it when the system is initialized (usually "getty"). If the terminal's type is constant and known, that information is also included.
/etc/gettytab	A list of baud rate information that is used by "getty" in determining how to listen to a login terminal.

FIGURE 15.12

UNIX system files containing information about terminals.

THE NETWORK INTERFACE

An important aspect of system administration is getting a UNIX machine connected to the local network so that other machines and all users can communicate with it. Some of the basic concepts and tools used to do that were discussed in Chapter 9. Because the details vary so greatly with different versions of UNIX, we'll hit just the high points here. For a detailed view, I strongly recommend reading Nemeth (2000).

Unless you are experimenting with wireless networking, some kind of network cable will have to be connected to your UNIX computer in order for it to talk to the network. Your machine will have to have an IP address and a hostname assigned to it, and the rest of the network will need to be made aware of this name and address (by updating the local host table or DNS database).

Most systems use the **ifconfig** command to configure the network interface. The typical way to activate a network interface is with the code

```
$ ifconfig il0 194.27.1.14 up
```

This causes the interface called "il0" (these are device names somewhere in the "/dev" directory hierarchy) to be assigned the IP address 194.27.1.14 and configured to be up. Other IP attributes can also be configured with **ifconfig**. While you can issue this command by hand at a terminal, it is usually found in boot scripts that initialize all network interfaces. When you add a network interface, you'll have to add the appropriate configuration command to the appropriate boot file.

For your UNIX machine to communicate with any other computer that is not directly connected to the same network cable (segment), routing information on your machine will need to be specified. The **route** command is used to specify routers that provide a path to other networks. Generally, you only have to make sure that a "default" route is established. A packet will be sent to this router when the destination is not on the local network. The packet is sent to the default router with the assumption that upstream routers will know how to get to the destination.

You can look at your current route table with the **netstat** command using the **-r** argument:

```
$ netstat -r
Routing tables
Destination       Gateway         Flags  Refs    Use  If
194.27.1.0        194.27.1.1      U       1     16611  il1
default           194.21.1.1      UG      0    231142  il0
$ _
```

This machine "knows" about two routers, 194.21.1.1 being the default path. Any address not on the local network and not on the 194.27.1 network will be sent to 194.21.1.1 for routing to its destination.

AUTOMATING TASKS

A number of system tasks are fairly simple, but tedious, to perform:

- adding a user account
- deleting a user account
- checking for full disks
- generating reports of log-ins and log-outs
- performing incremental backups
- system accounting
- removing old "core" files
- killing zombie processes

One of the powers of UNIX is its facility to make it easy for the programmer to write simple shell scripts or C programs to automate tasks that you perform by hand. I recommend that you automate as many of these chores as you can. Tasks that must be executed on a periodic basis can be scheduled by the **cron** utility. This utility works in a slightly different way on different versions of UNIX, but in general, it allows you to schedule a program to run anywhere from once every minute to once every year. Any messages generated by the program are sent via e-mail to the user who registered the program to be run.

For example, a simple script to see if any of your file systems are at 95% capacity or greater might be

```
#!/bin/sh
#
df | egrep "9[56789]%|100%"
```

If this script is registered by "root," with **cron** to be run every hour until a file system is at 95% capacity or greater, nothing (visible) happens. The script is run every hour, but no output is generated. When a file system reaches 95%, the search pattern specified to the **egrep** command will be satisfied by the line from **df** about the offending file system, so the script will generate a line of output. This line will be e-mailed to "root", so within one hour of the file system hitting 95%, you'll know about it.

ACCOUNTING

The UNIX accounting facilities allow you to track the activity of UNIX's subsystems. Each subsystem keeps a record of its own history in a special file, as follows:

- *Process management*: A record of the user ID, memory usage, and CPU usage of every process is appended to the "/usr/adm/acct" file. The **sa** utility may be used to report the information in this file. Process accounting is toggled by the **accton** utility.
- *Connections*: A record of the login time, user ID, and logout time of every connection is appended to the "/usr/adm/wtmp" file. The **ac** and **last** utilities may be used to report the information in this file. Connection accounting is enabled by the presence of the "/usr/adm/wtmp" file.
- *Printer usage*: Every printer records information about its jobs in the "/usr/adm" directory. The **pac** utility can generate reports from this information. Printer accounting is toggled by an entry in the "/etc/printcap" file.
- Other subsystems, such as **uucp** and **quota**, also produce log files.

Various subsystems generate files that are converted into reports by utilities and shell scripts. The system administrator is responsible for maintaining accounting records for the target subsystems and for purging and archiving the accounting files periodically.

CONFIGURING THE KERNEL

The UNIX kernel is a program written mostly in C, with a few assembly language sections. When you purchase a UNIX system, the manufacturer includes several pieces of software related to the kernel:

- a generic executable kernel
- a library of object modules that correspond to the parts of the kernel that never change

- a library of C modules that correspond to the parts of the kernel that may be changed
- a configuration file that describes the current kernel setup
- a **config** utility that allows you to recompile the kernel when the configuration file is changed

The kernel configuration files are kept in either the "/usr/conf" (BSD) or the "/usr/src/ uts/cf" (System V) directory. The facets of the kernel that may be changed include the following:

- the device drivers
- the maximum number of open files, clists, quotas, and processes
- the size of the I/O buffer pool and system page tables
- some important networking information
- the physical addresses of devices
- the name of the machine
- the time zone of the machine

To recompile a new kernel, you must follow a multistep process:

1. Edit the configuration file and change the parameters to their new values.
2. Run the **config** utility, which creates some header files, some C source code, and a makefile.
3. Run the **make** utility, passing it the name of the makefile created by **config**. **make** recompiles the newly created source code and links it with the unchanging portion of the kernel to produce a new executable.
4. Rename the old UNIX kernel.
5. Rename the new UNIX kernel to take the place of the old one.
6. Reboot the system.

SECURITY ISSUES

Security is another topic to which it would be possible to devote an entire book for a thorough discussion. For more information, I heartily recommend Garfinkel (1996) and Curry (1992), as well as the security chapter in Nemeth (2000).

As you are no doubt aware, UNIX systems are not 100% secure. No computer connected to any network can be. With the explosion of Internet connectivity, the problems have grown.

UNIX was not originally designed with security in mind. The original UNIX environments were places where everyone trusted each other and there was no need for security. Most UNIX systems are quite secure these days, but this has happened only after years of locating weaknesses and fixing them.

While there are many aspects to UNIX security, the ones with which every user has experience are passwords and file permissions. These mechanisms are tough for a regular user to break, but not so hard for experienced hackers. The best that a system administrator can do is to read about as many of the known security loopholes as possible and adopt strategies to stop them all. To give you an idea of what you're up against, here are a couple of common password-nabbing techniques:

- If you have a regular account and desire a superuser account, you begin by obtaining a copy of the one-way encryption algorithm that is used by the UNIX **passwd** utility. You also buy an electronic dictionary. Next, you copy the "/etc/passwd" file to your home PC and compare the encrypted versions of every word in the dictionary against the encrypted root password. If one of the dictionary entries matches, you've cracked the password! Other common passwords to test for include names and words spelled backward. This brute-force technique is very powerful and may be defended against by asking everyone to pick non-English, nonbackward, nontrivial passwords.

- A scheming individual can use the command overloading technique described earlier to trick a superuser into executing the wrong version of **su**. To use this Trojan horse technique, set $PATH so that the shell looks in your own "bin" directory before the standard "bin" directories. Next, write a shell script called **su** that pretends to offer a superuser login, but really stores the superuser password in a safe place, displays "wrong password", and then erases itself. When this script is prepared, call a superuser and tell him or her that there's a nasty problem with your terminal that requires superuser powers to fix. When the administrator types **su** to enter superuser mode, *your* **su** script executes instead of the standard **su** utility, and the superuser password is captured. The superuser sees the "wrong password" message and tries **su** again. This time, it succeeds, as your Trojan horse script has already erased itself. The superuser password is now yours! The way to defeat this technique is never to execute commands via a relative pathname when you're at an unfamiliar terminal. In other words, execute "/bin/su" instead of just "su".

The best ways to improve your knowledge of cunning schemes is to network with other system administrators and to read specialized system administrator books [Nemeth (2000)].

CHAPTER REVIEW

Checklist

In this chapter, I described

- the main system administration tasks
- how to obtain superuser powers
- how to start and stop UNIX
- the difference between single- and multiuser modes
- some useful disk-utilization utilities
- installing software
- how to create a new file system
- how to add and delete user accounts
- an overview of how a device is installed

- configuring a network interface
- the process of creating a new kernel
- some common security problems

Quiz

1. Under what situations is it appropriate to shut down a UNIX system?
2. Why do most versions of UNIX now use a "shadow" password file in addition to the normal /etc/passwd file?
3. What does a "getty" process do?
4. Why is it better to use **su** to become the superuser than to simply login as "root"?
5. How can you put UNIX into single-user mode?
6. When is the integrity of the file system checked?
7. Which files must be modified when you add a new user?
8. What does the **ifconfig** command do?
9. Which UNIX subsystems generate accounting records?
10. Which kernel parameters may be modified?
11. Describe the "Trojan horse" technique for capturing a superuser password.

Exercises

15.1   Try using **cpio** and **tar** to transfer some files to and from a floppy disk. Which of these utilities do you prefer? Why? [level: *easy*]

15.2   Use **du** to examine your disk usage. Write a script that prints out the full pathnames of your files that are over a specified size. [level: *medium*]

15.3   Obtain a floppy disk, format it, create a file system on it, mount it, and copy some files onto it. You'll almost certainly need a system administrator to help you through this process. [level: *medium*]

15.4   Fill in the functionality of the skeleton script you wrote in Project 1 of Chapter 6 so that it will perform the system administration tasks in your menu-driven interface. Useful tasks to automate include the following:

- automatic deletion of core files
- automatic warnings to those who use a lot of CPU time or disk space
- automatic archiving

[level: *medium*]

Project

Ask your system administrator what he or she believes to be the strengths and weaknesses of UNIX from a system administrator's standpoint. Are these issues being addressed by current UNIX releases or in other operating systems? [level: *medium*]

# CHAPTER 16

The Future

MOTIVATION

Operating systems continue to develop and improve as software and hardware technology expands. Although old, stagnant systems will inevitably hang around for quite a while, systems that incorporate the best concepts and philosophies will eventually replace them. UNIX is over 30 years old and is beginning to show its age in terms of its internal architecture. Knowledge of operating system trends will help you to understand the changes that are bound to occur in UNIX over the next few years, as well as allow you to place the role of UNIX in perspective.

PREREQUISITES

This chapter has no prerequisites, although it may help to have read Chapter 14.

OBJECTIVES

The chapter describes the latest trends in operating system design that are influencing the evolution of UNIX. A quick survey of the major versions in wide use today prepares the reader for further work with UNIX.

PRESENTATION

The first part of the chapter examines topics that are changing the face of UNIX. The second part gives some examples of these influences in the various versions of UNIX and Linux available today.

INTRODUCTION

To set the scene for this chapter, let's look at some of the latest trends in software and hardware:

- object-oriented programming
- Open Source
- distributed and parallel processing
- the move from 32-bit to 64-bit systems and network addressing
- high-bandwidth communication and fault-tolerant systems

These trends represent an exciting and interesting future for UNIX and computing in general. In order to take advantage of them, the software that is UNIX, as well as the hardware platforms upon which it runs, will have to adapt to changing circumstances.

CURRENT AND NEAR-FUTURE INFLUENCES ON UNIX

Many current topics in computer science and improvements in hardware will have a profound effect on the future direction of UNIX systems. Some have already exerted an influence and continue to do so. Others are only now coming into view.

Object-Oriented Programming

Objects have been responsible for much buzz in the computer industry for many years now. The most popular object-oriented languages in use in UNIX environments today are C++ and Java. On the one hand, in many situations, an objected-oriented paradigm can greatly increase the development productivity and manageability of software projects. On the other hand, used simply because they are "cool," objects can actually cause trouble.

Let's take a quick look at object-oriented programming. Obviously, what we have to say will be an extreme oversimplification. Entire volumes have been written on objects and the philosophy behind their use; to hope to do any more than whet your appetite in a few paragraphs would be foolhardy.

What is an object?

An *object* is an abstraction—a way to describe the purpose and use of data. In traditional procedural programming, you defined data structures and then performed operations on those data. Your program had to "know" what data were applicable to what functions and what operations could be performed on the data.

An object is created in accordance with the definition of an *object class*. Think of the class as the blueprint of a house—how you go about building it—and the object as the house itself. From a single blueprint, you can build many houses. In your code, you define the class, or the blueprint, of the object, and then, as you need to work with data, you create, or *instantiate*, as few or as many objects of that class as you need.

The idea behind object-oriented programming is that, rather than simply performing procedural operations on data, you conceptually enclose, or *encapsulate*, the data in an object. Within this object, you define a set of functions, or *methods*, that can operate on the specific data maintained in the object. By invoking a method of the object, you can request that the object execute one of its functions, but you cannot access the data directly. This protects the data from any kind of random modification that might occur because the modifying code thinks it "knows" the format of the data, but there is a bug in the code or the data format has changed.

How objects are used

In addition to any specific methods one defines for any object, two other methods are always defined. Each object must have a way to be created and deleted. In most object-oriented languages, the constructs that perform these tasks are called *constructors* and *destructors*, respectively.[1]

A constructor is the special method that is executed when a new instance of the object is created. In C++ and Java, this occurs when the *new* function is called on the object type. The constructor creates and initializes any data used by the object.

A destructor, as you might guess, does the opposite of a constructor. A destructor is a special method that cleans up when the object is being deleted. Any required terminal processing is performed, and all resources that have been allocated are freed. In C++, this occurs when the *delete* function is called on the object.

So what good is all this?

As a simple example, consider a printer that can be on-line (printing) or off-line (not accepting data to print). The printer might have a byte that defines whether it is on-line or off-line (say, 1 for on-line, 0 for off-line). You might write a program that sets the value to 2 in that byte. What would the printer do? It depends on the printer, but perhaps a 2 means "explode!"

If you wrote a *printer object* in software that encapsulated the printer status byte and defined **printer-on ()** and **printer-off ()** methods, then you couldn't set a 2 in that byte. You could only call **printer-on ()** to set the byte to 1 or **printer-off ()** to set it to 0. How the state is represented in the object is irrelevant outside the object.

Objects, therefore, help you specifically describe what operations can be performed and what data can be affected and prevent changing data in ways that don't make sense.

Inheritance

You can also create new objects based on existing objects. If I had a new printer that had another status variable besides the on-line/off-line variable, I could create a new object class, based on the printer object, that would *inherit* the attributes of the original printer object. I could then add any new methods in my code. I would have an up-to-date, more sophisticated printer object, and I would not have had to rewrite all the same code that they have in common.

If my new printer object required a different mechanism to turn it off and on, I could also *overload* the **printer-on()** and **printer-off()** methods and define my own method that would be used in this object in place of the ones in the parent object. This

---

[1]Java does not provide for destructors, but releases memory used by an object during "garbage collection," when the object is no longer in use.

way, the *subclass* can keep what is useful from the parent object class and implement only the parts that are new and unique to the subclass. Another advantage is that if a change is made to the *base class* (such as fixing a bug or implementing other improvement), the subclass will benefit from the change.

In the art of programming, objects are revolutionary. Used properly, object-oriented programming can decrease development time, foster the reuse of code, and reduce errors.

Open Source Software

The UNIX community has a long tradition of software being available in source code form, either free of charge or for a reasonably small fee, enabling people to learn from the code or improve it to further the state of the art. UNIX itself started out this way, and many components related to (and in most cases now a part of) UNIX share the tradition. So it's no surprise that in a world of otherwise proprietary, shrink-wrapped software, where you buy what's available and conform your requirements to it, those who support the idea of freely available source code have banded together to keep their philosophy alive.

Two major events had a huge impact on the evolution of the idea of Open Source software: the creation of the Free Software Foundation and the appearance of Linux on the UNIX landscape. Fink (2003) is an excellent examination of the phenomenon of Open Source software—why it came about, where it works, and where it does not.

The Free Software Foundation

One of the first proponents of the idea of freely available software was Richard Stallman, founder of the Free Software Foundation (FSF) in the mid-1980s. Stallman believed that everyone should have the right to obtain, use, view, and modify software. He started the GNU[2] Project whose goal was to reproduce popular UNIX tools and, ultimately, an entire UNIX-like operating system, in new code that could be freely distributed because it did not contain any licensed code. Early products included a version of the popular text editor Emacs and the GNU C compiler.

The "free" in the idea of free software does not necessarily mean the software is available at no cost, but rather that it comes with the freedom to use, view, and modify it. In order to retain their ownership and rights to GNU software, but still provide for its use by the widest possible audience, the FSF developed the GNU General Public License, under which GNU software is licensed to the world. The GNU GPL provides for the copying, use, modification, and redistribution of GNU software, provided that the same freedom to use, modify, and distribute it is passed on to anyone who uses your version of the software. Where a *copyright* is used to protect the rights of the owner, the goal here was to protect the rights of the recipient of the software as well. Thus, the FSF coined the term *copyleft* to describe this somewhat inverted meaning.

For more information on the Free Software Foundation, see the Web site

```
http://www.fsf.org
```

---

[2]"GNU" is a recursive acronym standing for "GNU's not UNIX" and pronounced "guh-NEW."

For more information on the GNU Project or the GNU General Public License, visit

```
http://www.gnu.org
```

Linux

The ultimate goal of the GNU Project was to provide a complete UNIX reimplementation, including the kernel. But while GNU applications were numerous and popular, the kernel itself was more challenging. Work is continuing on GNU Hurd, a Mach-based UNIX-like kernel. Meanwhile, in 1991, Linus Torvalds, a student at the University of Helsinki in Finland, wrote his own UNIX kernel to conform to the POSIX standard. He started it as a hobby, but he felt that the world needed an unencumbered version of UNIX which could be distributed freely without having to worry about licensing restrictions. His work wound up complementing the work of the GNU Project almost perfectly.

While in the beginning, Linus and a few friends maintained and modified the source code of Linux, today, developers around the world contribute new code and fixes. The combination of Linux and GNU utilities allows one to create a complete UNIX-like operating system, running on many different hardware platforms, and available in source form so you can make your own bug fixes and enhancements to it.

Parallel, Distributed, and Multiprocessor Systems

Historically, a computer had a single CPU, sat on a desk (or in a computer room), and processed data that were entered into it. As networks proliferate, computers are connected together to share data and cooperate in their processing. As microprocessor technology advances, more than one processor can be put into a single computer.

Parallel Processing

If a problem can be divided into separate and unrelated parts, those parts can be run separately. That way, the problem is solved faster than if each part is run sequentially on a single computer. This approach is known as *parallel processing* (doing more than one task in parallel). Processing can be performed in parallel either by different computers or by different processors inside the same computer, as we will see shortly.

True parallel processing is an extremely difficult goal to achieve. Many tasks have some kind of relationship to one another and cannot easily be separated. Object-oriented programming helps because the processing for a single object can be separated out from that for the others and the object-oriented paradigm has encouraged programmers to think in ways that increase this separation. Multiuser systems also benefit from parallel processors. With 10 users logged on, if each user's shell process can be assigned to a different processor, this is an easy way to provide a lot of processing power to multiple users. But to divide a single application program into semiunrelated pieces that can run independently is a challenging task. An even more challenging task is to write a compiler that can *automatically* determine what parts of a program are unrelated and break up the code during compilation so that the various pieces can be assigned to different processors during execution of the program.

Distributed Systems

One way to execute separated tasks in parallel is to execute them on different computers at the same time. One centralized program can distribute parts to different computers and collect their output as they finish. Some overhead is involved in managing the separation and communication, but if the tasks are reasonably complex, the parallel execution will cause the total elapsed time to be much shorter than it would be if each task were run sequentially on the same computer.

This type of architecture is often referred to as a *shared-nothing* architecture, because each processor does not share any resources with the others. Each system has its own memory, its own disk, and its own data path to the network. While it is possible for processes on different computers to share blocks of memory (just as two processes running on the same computer can), quite a bit of overhead is involved, since the sharing happens over a network.

Multiprocessor Systems

Another way to run separate processes in parallel is to run them on the same computer. If the machine has a single CPU, then it has to split its time across the various processes, which results in no gain (in fact, it results in a loss, with the overhead of multiple processes) over traditional single-process programming. However, if the computer has more than one processor, each separate process can be assigned to its own processor.

Multiple processes running on the same computer do share disk resources. They may also share segments of memory more easily via operating system methods for shared memory access. Therefore, this type of architecture is often called *shared-memory* or *shared-resource* architecture.

Sequent was one of the first UNIX vendors to provide a multiprocessor system specifically designed to allow parallel programs to be written and executed on multiple processors. Today, many UNIX platforms are available in multiprocessor architectures. All the same complexities involved in parallel programming apply here, but the extra complexity of distributing the processes to different computers is avoided.

As CPU speeds continue to increase, the advantage of multiprocessors isn't as obvious for the typical user. However, there will always be applications that need the throughput speed that parallel programming offers.

The Year-2000 "Bug"

Even though December 31, 1999, came and went without much electronic fanfare, this is still a problem worthy of discussion, if for no other reason than that it will likely repeat itself on December 31, 2099, if we didn't learn our lesson this time. I put quotes around the word "bug" because, although the problem was referred to as a bug, it is really poor program design rather than a mistake in coding. Recently, I saw a Volkswagen Beetle with a license plate that read "Y2K BUG," which made me realize that a 2000 model Bug was the only true Y2K bug!

What is it *really*?

The problem is that we—people—insist on specifying years in two digits. We believe that the century will be obvious to anyone, either from context or simply because we're talking about *this* year, in the current century. With a person who can reason, this usually works. However, a computer is different.

Before January 1, 2000, all computer programs were written in the 20th century. Therefore, programmers who dealt with two-digit dates assumed that the other two digits were "19." We fell into a bad habit with this assumption, though, simply because it had never failed us. Obviously, the assumption is not valid.

It would be "the computer's fault" if the system itself could not represent the year 2000, but it can. The problem is the assumption made by the applications programmer.

Two-digit years

Consider the UNIX command **cal**, described in Figure 16.1. For example, to get a calendar for June 1998, we do the following:

```
$ cal 6 1998
```

The result is

```
     June 1998
Su Mo Tu We Th Fr Sa
    1  2  3  4  5  6
 7  8  9 10 11 12 13
14 15 16 17 18 19 20
21 22 23 24 25 26 27
28 29 30
$ _
```

Utility: **cal** [*month year*]

cal prints a calendar for the current month. If *month* and *year* are specified, **cal** prints a calendar for the specified month.

FIGURE 16.1

Description of the **cal** command.

Notice, however, what happens if I assume that I can use a two-digit year:

```
$ cal 6 98
      June    98
Su Mo Tu We Th Fr Sa
             1  2
 3  4  5  6  7  8  9
10 11 12 13 14 15 16
17 18 19 20 21 22 23
24 25 26 27 28 29 30
$ _
```

This calendar doesn't look right, does it? But it is. This is a calendar for June in the year 98 A. D.! Is it the fault of **cal**, or is it my fault? Of course, it's my fault; **cal** did exactly what I asked it to do.

Take another example. Let's say you're looking at an insurance form for a patient, but the patient isn't there. The date of birth on the form reads 06/06/99. Is the patient a child or a senior citizen? Of course, if the patient is sitting in the room with you at the time, you will have enough context to figure it out. But a computer will not be able to apply other information with which to draw a conclusion. There is not enough information available for a computer to do anything but assume that the date is contemporary, so it will assume that the patient is a child. This can be a real problem if the computer's purpose is to dispense a dose of medicine to the patient!

The solution is for software to store and display four-digit dates.[3] Shortcuts that allow two-digit date specifications are fine as long as the user is aware that he or she is using a shortcut and is certain that there is little possibility of ambiguity. Sometimes, though, that assumption made won't work. In those instances, there must be a way to specify the full date.

Years since 1900

The problem also appears with programs and functions that return a value of "years since 1900." For a date in the 20th century, this returns a two-digit value. But in the year 2002, a function that returns a value of years since 1900 will return 102. If your application assumes that it can simply print "19" followed by the value returned, your program will print "19102" for the year (and there are programs in the world doing just that today).

Again, this is a misuse of the function, not really a fault of the system. This one is even easier to fix, since you technically should be adding the return value to 1900 and then printing the result. If you do that, things will work out just fine.

UNIX and the 21st Century

UNIX itself never had a problem with the year 2000. UNIX dates are stored as 32-bit integer values representing the number of seconds past midnight on January 1, 1970 (otherwise known as "the epoch" in the UNIX community). Therefore, the value of 12:00:01 A. M. on January 1, 2000, is simply an integer that is two larger than the value that represented 11:59:59 P. M. on December 31, 1999.

However, this is not to say that UNIX will never have a problem. Astute readers will realize that even a 32-bit value has a limit. In the year 2038, the UNIX date value will roll over to zero (all 32 bits of the value will be 1, and when that value is incremented, all bits will be 0 again). At that point, all UNIX machines will register January 1, 1970, again.

---

[3]If you're *really* thinking ahead, you might use five-digits, but I suppose it would be reasonable to assume that your code won't still be in use 8000 years from now.

The good news is that we have plenty of time to prepare for the event. I feel confident in saying that if what we're using for an operating system in 2038 is even called UNIX, this problem won't be part of it.

Sixty-Four-Bit Systems

The first small computers were 8-bit systems. That is, the *bus* that connected the CPU to the memory had an 8-bit data path. Memory words were 8 bits long. Most memory addressing was 16 bits (since 8 bits can represent only 256 different values). But combining two memory words to make an address reference was complicated to do in hardware.

Later, 16-bit systems were introduced, allowing more data across the bus at one time. A 16-bit value that is all ones (the maximum) is 65,536 or 64K. At the time, people really thought 64K of memory would be enough for anything!

When 32-bit systems finally came about, 4 gigabytes of memory were addressable. Again, more data could be sent across a 32-bit bus. Everyone thought that would be the limit. After all, why wouldn't 4 gigabytes of addressable disk or memory be enough?

Sixty-four-bit processors and systems are common today. A wider bus path allows more data to travel across the bus, so throughput is faster. Addressing is simplified because a 64-bit address can be stored in a single word of memory. This makes it easier to increase the 32-bit limit of 4 gigabytes for memory and disk addresses. If I were now to say that 64-bit architectures would surely be where we'll stop, of course, I'll be wrong later, so I won't say it!

Internet Addressing: IPv6

The current implementation of the Internet Protocol (IP), version 4, implements 32-bit addresses. However, with the growth of the Internet, this is quickly becoming insufficient to support all of the machines that people are connecting to the Internet. Like telephones, we are finding more uses for, and more devices requiring, IP addresses. Many printers also have their own IP addresses, and some laptops have multiple IP addresses for use in different locations.

In the early 1990s, it became clear that a new generation of IP that allowed for many more addresses would be necessary. Work began to define IPng (IP next generation) and a formal proposal for version 6 of IP was released in 1995.

IPv6 specifies addresses to be 128 bits long. Although the two protocols use addresses of different lengths, both protocols can be used on the same network. This is necessary because the Internet is far too large to coordinate a "cut-over" to a new protocol at any moment in time. A smooth transition to a new addressing scheme requires the ability to evolve to it gradually, rather than to require that we all wake up one day using the newer protocol.

IP packets (of both versions) specify a version in the first 4 bits of the packet. Therefore, a computer that "speaks" IPv6 can still recognize and handle an IPv4 packet (if it is configured for both protocols). This allows the two protocols to coexist on the same network. The older machines can be upgraded to IPv6 as implementations become available or as the system administrators have the opportunity to upgrade them without requiring it all to happen simultaneously.

As we discussed in Chapter 9, an IPv4 address is a 32-bit value expressed by four octets, each a decimal number representing an 8-bit value, such as

```
192.127.63.141
```

In IPv6, the 128-bit address would be cumbersome to express the same way. Can you imagine an address like this?

```
192.127.63.141.241.27.88.16.1.77.34.8.191.253.27.61
```

That would drive network administrators into another line of work!

In IPv6, the values are expressed in hexadecimal format, requiring two hex digits for each 8 bits. Instead of being delimited every 8 bits, they are delimited every 16 bits. Another change is that the colon, rather than the period, is used as the delimiter between parts of the address. Thus, the long address in the previous paragraph would be expressed in IPv6 as

```
C07F:3F8D:F11B:5810:014D:2208:BFFD:1B3D
```

True, this isn't drastically shorter, but that is the longest an IPv6 address could possibly be (whereas the decimal example before that could actually have been several digits longer!). In practice, many IP addresses have many 8-bit or even 16-bit values that are zero, and IPv6 also allows for dropping leading zeros as well as eliminating contiguous 16-bit values of zero. So you can actually wind up with much shorter addresses.

In addition to the addressing changes, IPv6 also provides for improvements in routing and automatic configuration. While IPv6 is not currently in wide use, vendors are implementing and testing the new protocol. Over the next few years, IPv6 will be deployed across the Internet. If all goes well, users likely will not even notice. For more information on IPv6, visit the web site at

```
http://www.ipv6.org
```

High-Bandwidth Networks

In the early days of the Ethernet standard, a transmission rate of 1 megabit per second was fast. Today, 100 megabits per second is common in a local network. With fiber optics and other digital media, more data can be pushed through a network than ever before.

Because of the boom in Web browsing over the Internet, larger volumes of data are being sent than ever before. E-mail messages were small compared with images, video, and sound that make up today's web pages. Fortunately, network bandwidth is increasing as fast as disk capacity and CPU speed. As usual, as we find newer, faster, bigger ways to do something, we also find things to do with it. Remember when no one could imagine needing more than 64K of memory?

Fault-Tolerant Systems

As corporations rely more and more on computer systems, downtime becomes a bigger and bigger problem. In certain situations (e.g., routers in the telephone network), almost any downtime is unacceptable.

Traditionally, the solution has been to have *hot backup* systems. These systems run in parallel to the production system, updating the same data and shadowing activity. In the event that the production system crashes, the duplicate system can take over its function almost immediately while engineers fix the first system.

Fault-tolerant systems try to accomplish this within a single system. A system with duplicate CPUs, memory, and devices can use the backup resource if the primary resource fails.

A few companies, of which Tandem (now part of Hewlett-Packard) is the best known, have been active in researching and providing fault-tolerant UNIX systems. Although hardware components are more reliable than they were a decade ago, some applications will always require as close to 100% uptime as is possible to achieve.

SURVEY OF CURRENT POPULAR VERSIONS OF UNIX

Although UNIX had its start in a computer lab in Bell Laboratories, it has had a long and sometimes convoluted evolution since then. An in-depth discussion of how UNIX got to where it is today is beyond the scope of this book, but Salus (1994) gives an excellent view of the rich history of UNIX.

Part of the UNIX lore is the competition between Berkeley UNIX (BSD) and System III (later, System V UNIX, as it began to be called at AT&T). For many years, the UNIX world was divided into these two camps. Most implementations of UNIX were based on one of the two. The differences revolved mainly around the kernel architecture and low-level operating system algorithms (e.g., BSD and System V used radically different memory management algorithms). On the surface, where most users spent their time, the differences were subtle when they were noticeable at all.

When Sun Microsystems and AT&T joined forces to bring the BSD and System V worlds together, System V, Release 4 (SVR4), and Solaris were born. SVR4 blended the best of both worlds.[4] With BSD lovers having most of their favorite capabilities in SVR4-based versions of UNIX, the "UNIX wars" began to subside. Soon, the Open Software Foundation (OSF) was formed by a few companies (most notably, HP and DEC) in order to come up with their own version of UNIX. This was an attempt to prevent AT&T and Sun from completely dominating the perceived ownership, and therefore the future direction, of UNIX. As SVR4-based systems proved to meet customer needs and AT&T and Sun did not completely dominate UNIX as many had feared, this UNIX war, too, subsided, and OSF took its place in history.

Today, while there are still some BSD-centric versions of UNIX, the major differences are related to hardware platforms and performance. Other differences are mainly cosmetic. The basic UNIX system and interfaces are largely the same from one version to another (but just different enough to give you trouble from time to time). Vendors that supply their own distribution of UNIX provide their own "value-added" commands and capabilities that they feel their customers demand. Porting software from one version to another, depending on the depth of operating system function the application might use, is still not trivial, but it usually isn't the huge task that it once was.

---

[4]"Best" being an objective term, of course. You certainly can find people who will argue the point to this day. The *intent* was to merge the best of both versions.

Today, many different versions of UNIX exist. Most are targeted to specific applications (such as real-time computing), specific low-volume hardware, or research based on previous work with UNIX. When you examine the "mainstream" versions of UNIX that are easily available on workstation or small-server hardware, you wind up with a handful of versions of UNIX. The versions discussed in alphabetical order in the subsections that follow do not constitute an exhaustive list, but they are most of the versions you are likely to run into in a typical UNIX environment. All of these versions of UNIX provide facilities (in varying implementations) discussed in previous chapters of this book (i.e., X Window System, TCP/IP networking, most "standard" UNIX commands, etc.).

AIX

AIX (Advanced Interactive eXecutive) is IBM's implementation of UNIX and runs on its RISC System/6000 workstation and server platforms. It is based on System V UNIX with SVR4 and BSD extensions. RS/6000 platforms offer multiprocessor systems as well as 64-bit systems.

If you have used other IBM systems in the past, parts of AIX will seem more familiar than other versions of UNIX. AIX has more verbose error messages than other versions. Most of the messages are indexed with codes to direct you to more information in a manual. While at first this seems cumbersome, especially compared with the terse nature of the original versions of UNIX, it does prove helpful at times.

More information on AIX is available on the web at the following URL:

```
http://www.ibm.com/servers/aix
```

Caldera SCO/Unixware

For many years, the Santa Cruz Operation (SCO) was a leader of software-only UNIX vendors. SCO UNIX ran on low-end hardware such as PCs and was popular with small companies that could not afford higher-priced workstations. During its history, SCO acquired the Unix Systems Laboratories, the UNIX arm of AT&T that produced Unixware, true System V UNIX.

Now Caldera has acquired the UNIX arm of the Santa Cruz Operation, and the company continues to use both names in its commercial UNIX offerings: SCO OpenServer and UnixWare 7.

For more information on Caldera's family of UNIX products, visit

```
http://www.caldera.com/products/unix
```

FreeBSD

FreeBSD, as you might guess, is a free implementation of the Berkeley Standard Distribution version of UNIX. It is one of several Open Source versions of UNIX available today. FreeBSD runs on PC-compatible hardware (386, 486, Pentium CPUs, and most standard PC bus architectures).

Programmers all over the world contribute code to the FreeBSD Project to fix and improve the existing code. The Free BSD web site provides information about the contributors and how to participate.

FreeBSD can be downloaded from the net (but it's big), or it can be obtained on CD-ROM for a small fee. For more information about FreeBSD, visit

```
http://www.freebsd.org
```

HP-UX

The Hewlett-Packard Company's contribution to UNIX is known as HP-UX, and it runs on HP's PA-RISC hardware platform as well as on the new Intel IA-64 Itanium architecture.[5] HP-UX is based on System V with SVR4 and BSD enhancements.

HP-UX is a 64-bit version of UNIX and conforms to all the popular UNIX standards. It is currently the number-one or number-two vendor-supplied version of UNIX, depending on whose statistics you read. For a company that wasn't involved at the beginning of the evolution of UNIX, HP has done a nice job of adopting "the UNIX philosophy" and staying true to it in the company's development of HP-UX.

For more information on HP-UX, go to

```
http://www.hp.com/go/hpux
```

IRIX

Silicon Graphics, Inc., has traditionally set the standard in high-speed, high-resolution graphics hardware. SGI's version of UNIX, known as IRIX, was System V based in the days when most vendors' offerings were BSD based, so compatibility in mixed environments was problematical. You bought an SGI UNIX platform because you wanted an incredible graphics workstation. (When the little girl in *Jurassic Park* walks up to the workstation in the computer room and says, "It's a UNIX box!" it's an SGI box.)

As the world standardized on SVR4, IRIX became more mainstream, having made "the right" choice in the first place. IRIX includes most of the best features of SVR4, as well as BSD UNIX, and is a 64-bit operating system.

For more information on IRIX, visit

```
http://www.sgi.com/developers/technology/irix.html
```

Linux

Linux is easily the most popular of the Open Source versions of UNIX for PC architectures. In addition, it has been ported to the Digital Equipment Corporation (DEC)/Compaq/HP Alpha platform, Sun's SPARC platforms, Intel's Itanium processor, and Motorola's Power PC platforms, to name but a few.

While Linux looks and feels like UNIX to even the most experienced users, it is technically not UNIX, because it shares no common source code with any UNIX distribution. It is a reimplementation of UNIX with all the same interfaces and commands. Because it contains no licensed source code belonging to AT&T, the University

---

[5]The Intel Itanium processor was coinvented by Intel and HP.

of California at Berkeley, or anyone else, Linux can be distributed with the source code. If you want to learn about its internal workings or modify it to suit your own specific purposes, the option is there.

Linux can be modified, redistributed, and even sold, so long as the source code remains available. Several companies have made it their business to sell media, documentation, and support for their own distributions of Linux. The following are just a few of the vendors providing a distribution of Linux (some at a nominal cost, some free of charge):

- Caldera OpenLinux
- Corel Linux
- Debian GNU/Linux
- Mandrake Linux
- RedHat Linux
- Slackware Linux
- SuSE Linux

In addition to these separate Linux distributions, traditional UNIX vendors such as HP, IBM, SGI, and Sun provide Linux on their own hardware platforms.

For more information on the base Linux operating system itself (including information on all of the varied distribution providers), visit

```
http://www.linux.org
```

NetBSD

NetBSD is often confused with FreeBSD. However, they truly are two separate projects, but with similar goals: to provide a free implementation of BSD UNIX.

The NetBSD project is, as are other Open Source projects, a collaborative effort among developers all over the world to maintain and improve the operating system. NetBSD is also called a UNIX-like operating system, but is based on code from 4.4BSD Lite, a subset of the BSD code from Berkeley. Like Linux, NetBSD is distributed with source code.

NetBSD runs on many different platforms, including PCs, DEC Alphas and Vaxes, HP 9000s, Macintoshes, Sun SPARC workstations, and even some handheld devices. For more information about NetBSD, visit the web site at

```
http://www.netbsd.org
```

OpenBSD

OpenBSD is another project intended to provide a free implementation of BSD UNIX, but it is more focused than other implementations on providing tighter security mechanisms. Like other Open Source projects, FreeBSD is a collaborative effort among developers all over the world to maintain and improve the operating system. OpenBSD is based on 4.4 BSD UNIX.

OpenBSD boasts binary emulation for programs from many other UNIX platforms, including FreeBSD, HP-UX, Linux, and SunOS/Solaris. For more information about OpenBSD, visit their website at

```
http://www.openbsd.org
```

Tru64 UNIX

DEC has made several forays into the UNIX world. The company's original UNIX offering, BSD-based Ultrix, never had much more than a cult following. Ultrix ran on DEC's VAX hardware line, and at the time, if you had a VAX and wanted to run BSD UNIX, you simply ran BSD UNIX straight from Berkeley. DEC later adopted a kernel based on OSF/1 and produced Digital UNIX, a 64-bit operating system that runs on the Alpha platform. Digital UNIX was rebranded Tru64 UNIX when Compaq acquired DEC. For more information on Tru64 UNIX, visit

```
http://www.tru64unix.compaq.com
```

At the time of the second edition of this book, Compaq had just acquired DEC. At this writing, HP has merged with Compaq, and the effect that this merger will have on Tru64 UNIX remains to be seen.

Solaris

Sun Microsystems, Inc., is probably credited with starting the modern UNIX revolution. In the early 1980s, most distributions came directly from AT&T or the University of California at Berkeley and ran on whatever hardware you had that those versions supported. A handful of small companies were springing up that took various versions of these basic distributions and tried to make a business out of selling and supporting UNIX systems, most based on the Motorola 68000 CPU.

Early on, SunOS ran on the MC68010 and MC68020. Eventually, Sun decided that it could better serve its customers if it also designed hardware specifically to run UNIX. (Motorola had not designed the 68000 family specifically to run UNIX.) Sun emerged from the pack as the early leader in developing and improving UNIX systems.

Solaris is the current point in the evolution of Sun's UNIX. The original SunOS was based on BSD UNIX, because several of the founders of Sun—most notably, Bill Joy, author of the **vi** editor—came from Berkeley. Sun made a leap from SunOS to Solaris when it entered into a partnership with AT&T to standardize around System V. Solaris, of course, includes all the best BSD and SunOS features to which Sun's customers had become accustomed.

Solaris runs on Sun's SPARC 32-bit and 64-bit platforms, as well as on Intel (PC) platforms. For more information on Solaris, visit

```
http://www.sun.com/software/solaris
```

CHAPTER REVIEW

Checklist

In this chapter, I described

- object-oriented programming
- Open Source
- parallel and distributed systems
- multiprocessing systems
- the year-2000 problem
- 64-bit architectures
- high-bandwidth networking
- fault-tolerant systems
- versions of UNIX that you can use

Quiz

1. Which versions of UNIX are free?
2. How can a company make money selling Open Source software when it's available for free?
3. How is data associated with an object different from traditional data in a computer program?
4. How many bits represent an IP address in IPv6?

Exercise

Download one of the free versions of UNIX from the Internet and install it. [level: *medium*]

Project

Determine the last date and time in the year 2038 that UNIX will be able to represent. [level: *medium*]

Appendix

REGULAR EXPRESSIONS

Regular expressions are character sequences that describe a family of matching strings. They are accepted as arguments to many UNIX utilities, such as **grep, egrep, awk, sed,** and **vi**. Note that the filename substitution wildcards used by the shells are *not* examples of regular expressions, since they use different matching rules.

Regular expressions are formed out of sequences of normal characters and special characters. Figure A.1 list some special characters, sometimes called *metacharacters*,

Metacharacter	Meaning
.	Matches any single character.
[]	Matches any of the single characters enclosed in brackets. A hyphen may be used to represent a range of characters. If the first character after the [is ^, then any character *not* enclosed in brackets is matched. The *, ^, $, and \ metacharacters lose their special meanings when used inside brackets.
*	May follow any character and denotes zero or more occurrences of the character that precedes it.
^	Matches the beginning of a line only.
$	Matches the end of a line only.
\	The meaning of any metacharacter may be inhibited by preceding it with \.

FIGURE A.1

Regular-expression metacharacters.

together with their meanings. A regular expression matches the longest pattern that it can. For example, when the pattern "y.*ba" is searched for in the string "yabad-abadoo", the match occurs against the substring "yabadaba" and not "yaba".

To illustrate the use of metacharacters, consider the following piece of text:

Text

```
Well you know it's your bedtime,
So turn off the light,
Say all your prayers and then,
Oh you sleepy young heads dream of wonderful things,
Beautiful mermaids will swim through the sea,
And you will be swimming there too.
```

Patterns

Figure A.2 shows the lines of text that would match various regular expressions. The portion of each line that satisfies the regular expression is italicized.

Pattern	Lines that match
the	So turn off *the* light,
	Say all your prayers and *the*n,
	Beautiful mermaids will swim through *the* sea,
	And you will be swimming *the*re too.
.nd	Say all your prayers *and* then,
	Oh you sleepy young heads dream of w*ond*erful things,
	And you will be swimming there too.
^.nd	*And* you will be swimming there too.
sw.*ng	And you will be *swimming* there too.
[A-D]	*B*eautiful mermaids will swim through the sea,
	*A*nd you will be swimming there too.
\.	And you will be swimming there too. *(the ".")*
a.	S*ay* all your prayers and then,
	Oh you sleepy young he*ad*s dream of wonderful things,
	Be*au*tiful mermaids will swim through the sea,

FIGURE A.2

Lines matching regular-expression patterns.

a.$	Beautiful mermaids will swim through the se*a*,
[a-m]nd	Say all your prayers *and* then,
[^a-m]nd	Oh you sleepy young heads dream of w*onde*rful things, *And* you will be swimming there too.

FIGURE A.2   (*Continued*)

Extended Regular Expressions

Some utilities, such as **egrep**, support an extended set of metacharacters, described in Figure A.3. Figure A.4 shows some examples of full regular expressions, using the previous text file.

Metacharacter	Meaning
+	Matches one or more occurrences of the single preceding character.
?	Matches zero or one occurrence of the single preceding character.
| (pipe symbol)	If you place a pipe symbol between two regular expressions, a string that matches either expression will be accepted. In other words, | acts like an "or" operator.
()	If you place a regular expression in parentheses, you may use the *, +, or ? metacharacter to operate on the entire expression, rather than on just a single character.

FIGURE A.3

Extended regular-expression metacharacters.

Pattern	Lines that match
s.*w	Oh you *sleepy young heads dream of w*onderful things, Beautiful mermaid*s will sw*im through the sea, And you will be *sw*imming there too.
s.+w	Oh you *sleepy young heads dream of w*onderful things, Beautiful mermaids *will sw*im through the sea,

FIGURE A.4

Lines matching extended regular-expression patterns.

off|will	So turn *off* the light,
	Beautiful mermaids *will* swim through the sea,
	And you *will* be swimming there too.
im*ing	And you will be sw*imming* there too.
im?ing	<no matches>

FIGURE A.4   (*Continued*)

MODIFIED-FOR-UNIX BACKUS—NAUR NOTATION

The syntax of the UNIX utilities and system calls in this book is presented in a modified version of a language known as Backus–Naur Form, or BNF for short. In a BNF description, the sequences shown in Figure A.5 have a special meaning. The last sequence is the UNIX-oriented modification, which allows me to avoid placing large numbers of brackets around command-line options. To indicate [, {, |, or - without its special meaning, I precede it with \.

Some variations of commands depend on which option you choose. I indicate this dependency by supplying a separate syntax description for each variation. For example, take a look at the syntax description of the **at** utility, shown in Figure A.6. The first

Sequence	Meaning
[strings]	Strings may appear zero or one time.
{ strings }*	Strings may appear zero or more times.
{ strings }+	Strings may appear one or more times.
string1|string2	string1 or string2 may appear.
-optionlist	Zero or more options may follow a dash.

FIGURE A.5

BNF notations used in this book.

```
[Utility: at -csm time [ date [, year ]][ +increment][ script]
         at -r { jobId}+
         at -l { jobId}*
```

FIGURE A.6

Example description of the **at** command.

version of the utility is selected by any combination of the command line options **-c, -s,** and **-m.** These must then be followed by a time and an optional date specifier. The optional date specifier may be followed by an optional year specifier. In addition, an increment may be specified, with or without a script name.

The second version of **at** is selected by a **-r** option, and may be followed by one or more job id numbers. The third version of **at** is selected by a **-l** option, and may be followed by zero or more job id numbers.

SYSTEM CALLS: AN ALPHABETICAL CROSS-REFERENCE

Figure A.7 shows a list of references to each system call or library routine in chapter 13. The page number of the call description is in boldface.

Name	Synopsis	Referenced on page(s)
accept	accepts a connection request from a client socket	514, 516, **518**, 519, 529, 558
alarm	sets a process "alarm clock"	**492**, 494
bind	binds a socket to a name	514, 516, **517**, 520, 529, 557
bzero	fills an array with values of zero	523, **527**, 529, 557
chdir	changes a process's current working directory	**481**, 536, 553
chmod	changes a file's permission settings	**464**, 507, 508
chown	changes a file's owner and/or group	462, **463**, 464
close	closes a file	436, 438, 439, 443, 449, **450**, 457, 465, 467, 471, 486, 488, 503, 505, 506, 507, 508, 509, 514, 515, 519, 523, 549, 554, 556, 558
connect	connects to a named server socket	515, 519, **520**, 523, 528, 556
dup	duplicates a file descriptor	463, **465**, 549
dup2	similar to "dup"	463, **465**, 466, 488, 506, 548, 549, 554, 556, 558
execl	replaces the calling process's code, data, and stack from an executable file	**480**, 481

FIGURE A.7

System call and library routine cross-reference.

execlp	similar to "execl"	**480**, 506
execv	similar to "execl"	**480**
execvp	similar to "execl"	**480**, 484, 488, 496, 537, 550
exit	terminates a process	441, 444, 455, 460, 473, 476, **477**, 478, 479, 485, 491, 497, 501, 502, 514, 515, 519, 523, 547, 548, 550
fchmod	similar to "chmod"	463, **464**
fchown	similar to "chown"	462, **463**
fcntl	gives access to miscellaneous file characteristics	436, 437, 463, **466**, 467
fork	duplicates a process	472, 473, **474**, 475, 476, 478, 479, 484, 485, 486, 493, 496, 497, 500, 501, 502, 505, 506, 514, 519, 547, 548
fstat	similar to "stat"	451, **460**, 461
ftruncate	similar to "truncate"	463, **470**
getdents	obtains directory entries	451, 452, 457, **462**, 485
getegid	returns a process's effective group ID number	**483**
geteuid	returns a process's effective user ID number	**483**
getgid	returns a process's real group ID number	**483**
gethostbyname	returns a structure describing a network host	524, **526**, 556
gethostname	returns the name of the host	524, **526**, 556
getpgid	returns a process's process group ID number	449, **500**, 501
getpid	returns a process's ID number	442, 446, 473, **474**, 475, 476, 479 480, 500, 501, 502, 509, 547
getppid	returns a parent process's ID number	473, **474**, 475, 476, 479
getuid	returns a process's real user ID number	**483**

FIGURE A.7 (*Continued*)

htonl	converts a host-format number to a network-format number	**528**, 529, 557
htons	similar to "htonl"	523, 527, **528**, 529, 557
inet_addr	returns a 32-bit value IP address	524, 525, **526**
inet_ntoa	returns a string-format IP address	524, 526, **527**, 556
ioctl	controls a device	463, **467**, 471
kill	sends a signal to a specified process or group of processes	**495**, 497, 498
lchown	similar to "chown"	**463**
link	creates a hard link	463, 467, **468**
listen	sets the maximum number of pending socket connections	514, 516, **518**, 529, 558
lseek	moves to a particular offset in a file	436, 438, 439, 443, **448**, 449, 457, 462, 467, 486, 504
lstat	similar to "stat"	**460**
memset	fills an array with a specific value	**527**
mknod	creates a special file	436, 468, **469**, 507, 508
nice	changes a process's priority	**482**
ntohl	converts a network-format number to a host-format number	**528**
ntohs	similar to "ntohl"	**528**
open	opens or creates a file	434, 435, 436, 437, 438, 439, 442, 444, **445**, 446, 449, 457, 465, 467, 471, 485, 488, 507, 508, 509, 554
pause	suspends the calling process and returns when a signal is received	492, **493**, 494, 500
perror	displays message text from most recent system call error	**434**, 435, 444, 460, 464, 488, 496, 506, 550, 553, 556, 557, 558
pipe	creates an unnamed pipe	503, **504**, 505, 506, 548
read	reads bytes from a file into a buffer	436, 438, 439, 442, 443, 446, **447**, 449, 471, 503, 504, 505, 507, 508, 515, 519, 520, 521, 525

FIGURE A.7   (*Continued*)

setegid	sets a process's effective group ID number	**483**
seteuid	sets a process's effective user ID number	**483**
setgid	sets a process's real and effective group ID number	**483**
setpgid	sets a process's process group ID number	498, 499, **500**, 501, 502, 547
setuid	sets a process's real and effective user ID number	**483**
signal	specifies the action that will be taken when a particular signal arrives	492, **493**, 494, 496, 500, 501, 502 513, 540, 547
socket	creates an unnamed socket	513, 515, **516**, 519, 520, 523, 528, 529, 555, 557
stat	returns status information about a file	451, 452, 456, **460**, 461, 485
sync	schedules all file buffers to be flushed to disk	463, **469**
truncate	truncates a file	463, **470**
unlink	removes a file	438, 443, **450**, 507, 508, 514, 517, 557
wait	waits for a child process	473, 475, 477, 478, **479**, 486, 487, 496, 497, 502, 548, 549
write	writes bytes from a buffer to a file	436, 438, 439, 442, 444, 445, 447, **448**, 449, 465, 466, 467, 471, 503, 504, 505, 507, 509, 514, 519, 520, 521

FIGURE A.7 (*Continued*)

Bibliography

Anderson, Gail, and Paul Anderson. *The UNIX C Shell Field Guide*. Prentice Hall, 1986.

Anderson, Bart (ed.), Bryan Costales, and Harry Henderson. *The Waite Group's UNIX Communications and the Internet*. Sams, 1995.

Andleigh, Prabhat K. *UNIX System Architecture*. Prentice Hall, 1990.

Bach, Maurice J. *The Design of the UNIX Operating System*. Prentice Hall PTR, 1987.

Bolsky, Morris I., and David G. Korn. *The New KornShell Command and Programming Language*, 2d ed. Prentice Hall PTR, 1995.

Cheswick, William R., and Steven M. Bellovin. *Firewalls and Internet Security*. Addison-Wesley, 1994.

Christian, Kaare. *The UNIX Operating System*, 2d ed. Wiley, 1988.

Curry, David A. *UNIX System Security: A Guide for Users and System Administrators*. Addison-Wesley, 1992.

Fink, Martin. *The Business and Economics of Linux and Open Source*. Prentice Hall, 2003.

Fountain, Anthony, Paula Ferguson, and Dan Heller. *Motif Reference Manual*, 2d ed. O'Reilly & Associates, 2000.

Garfinkel, Simson, and Gene Spafford. *Practical UNIX and Internet Security*, 2d ed. O'Reilly & Associates, 1996.

Horspool, R. Nigel. *The Berkeley UNIX Environment*, 2d ed. Prentice Hall, 1992.

Kernighan, Brian, and Rob Pike. *The UNIX Programming Environment*. Prentice Hall, 1992.

Leffler, Samuel J., Marshall Kirk McKusick, Michael J. Karels, and John S. Quarterman. *The Design and Implementation of the 4.3 BSD UNIX Operating System*. Addison-Wesley, 1989.

McNulty Development. *UNIX RefGuide*. Prentice Hall, 1986.

Medinets, David. *Perl 5 by Example*. Que, 1996.

 Nemeth, Evi, Garth Snyder, Scott Seebass, and Trent R. Hein. *UNIX System Administration Handbook*, 3d ed. Prentice Hall PTR, 2000.

Open Software Foundation (OSF). *OSF/Motif User's Guide*. Prentice Hall PTR, 1992.

Quercia, Valerie, and Tim O'Reilly. *X Window System User's Guide—OSF/Motif Edition*, 2d ed. O'Reilly & Associates, 1993.

Roberts, Ralph, Mark Boyd, Stephen G. Kochan, and Patrick H. Wood. *UNIX Desktop Guide to EMACS*. Sams, 1991.

Rochkind, Marc J. *Advanced UNIX Programming*. Prentice Hall PTR, 1986.

Sage, Russell G. *Tricks of the UNIX Masters*. Sams, 1986.

Salus, Peter H. *A Quarter Century of UNIX*. Addison-Wesley, 1994.

Seyer, Martin D., and William J. Mills. *DOS/UNIX—Becoming a Super User*. Prentice Hall, 1986.

Sobell, Mark G. *A Practical Guide to the UNIX System*, 3d ed. Addison-Wesley, 1994.

Stevens, W. Richard. *Advanced Programming in the UNIX Environment*. Addison-Wesley, 1992.

Stevens, W. Richard. *UNIX Network Programming*, 2d ed. Prentice Hall PTR, 1998.

Vahalia, Uresh. *UNIX Internals: The New Frontiers*. Prentice Hall, 1995.

Waite Group and Michael Waite (ed.). *UNIX Papers*. Sams, 1987.

Wall, Larry, Tom Christiansen, Randal L. Schwartz, and Stephen Potter. *Programming Perl*, 2d ed. O'Reilly & Associates, 1996.

Young, Douglas A. *The X Window System: Programming and Applications with XT—OSF/Motif*. Prentice Hall, 1994.

Index

^C + others - 20

HuP, 172

More, 29

netstat, 694

No Hup, 170

TERM environment variable, 53